Context and Contextuality

Towards an Authentic Mission Perspective for the
Churches of the Pacific Coast Slavic Baptist Association

Vyacheslav Tsvirinko

© 2018 by Vyacheslav Tsvirinko

Published 2018 by Langham Monographs
An imprint of Langham Creative Projects

Langham Partnership
PO Box 296, Carlisle, Cumbria CA3 9WZ, UK
www.langham.org

ISBNs:
978-1-78368-396-3 Print
978-1-78368-397-0 ePub
978-1-78368-398-7 Mobi
978-1-78368-399-4 PDF

Vyacheslav Tsvirinko has asserted his right under the Copyright, Designs and Patents Act, 1988 to be identified as the Author of this work.

All rights reserved. No part of this publication may be reproduced, stored in a retrieval system or transmitted, in any form or by any means, electronic, mechanical, photocopying, recording or otherwise, without the prior written permission of the publisher or the Copyright Licensing Agency.

Scripture taken from the New American Standard Bible®, Copyright © 1960, 1962, 1963, 1968, 1971, 1972, 1973, 1975, 1977, 1995 by The Lockman Foundation. Used by permission.

British Library Cataloguing in Publication Data
A catalogue record for this book is available from the British Library

ISBN: 978-1-78368-396-3

Cover & Book Design: projectluz.com

Langham Partnership actively supports theological dialogue and an author's right to publish but does not necessarily endorse the views and opinions set forth here or in works referenced within this publication, nor can we guarantee technical and grammatical correctness. Langham Partnership does not accept any responsibility or liability to persons or property as a consequence of the reading, use or interpretation of its published content.

In the third millennium, missionary work cannot be authentic in the fulfilment of the *missio Dei* if it does not take into account the cultural, social and religious contexts. Dr Tsvirinko's book gives an excellent case study that shows missionary work in the contemporary Slavic diaspora on the Pacific coast of the USA, and also offers concrete ways to improve evangelistic and mission work in immigrant churches. This is a solid theoretical and practical foundation for those who want to study mission in various diasporas and who want to improve the fulfilment of Christ's Great Commission by their congregations.

Dr Sergiy Sannikov
President, Euro-Asian Accrediting Association

In the mission of the church, immigrants have very often played a key role, not only as recipients of the gospel, but also because they, being part of God's mission, are God's vehicle for spreading it. This research work by Vyacheslav Tsvirinko on the mission role of the Slavic Baptists of the Pacific Coast provides a good overview of issues with which immigrants struggle as they find themselves in a different context. He shows their response to the context, how their culture and role as a faith community in the US has changed them, and how their background and culture influences and shapes their views on their role in the mission of God. It is an exemplary research work that also shows how different other immigrant communities have found their role in society and the wider mission. The book points to ways that immigrant Slavic churches can learn from other Christian groups as well as from their own history on how to be a missional and witnessing community. All their experience, if they reflect well, can be seen as formation by God who challenges the Slavic Baptist groups of the US West Coast to authentic and contextually relevant witness in their new homeland as well as in the lands of Eastern Europe they once left behind.

Dr Peter Penner
Director of Advanced Studies, Euro-Asian Accrediting Association

Contents

Abstract xv

Acknowledgments xvii

Introduction 1

Part I: Contextuality: Acquiring the Right Tools for Discernment
of the Task 11

Chapter 1 13
    Authentic Mission in the Theological Context
    1.1. *Missio Dei* 13
        1.1.1. Historical Background for the *Missio Dei* Concept 14
        1.1.2. The Meaning of *Missio Dei* 15
        1.1.3. The Trinitarian Understanding of *Missio Dei* 18
        1.1.4. The Goal (Purpose) of *Missio Dei* 20
        1.1.5. Concerns about Using the *Missio Dei* Concept 22
        1.1.6. Conclusion 28
    1.2. The Kingdom of God, the World, and the Mission
    of the Church 30
        1.2.1. What Is the Kingdom of God? 30
        1.2.2. Relation of the Church to the Kingdom of God 32
        1.2.3. Relation of the Church and the Kingdom of God
        to the *Missio Dei* 33
        1.2.4. A Missiological Model of the Church 35
        1.2.5. Making Disciples – A Key Aspect of Mission 36
        1.2.6. The World Council of Churches (WCC) 39
        1.2.7. The Evangelical/Lausanne Movement 41
        1.2.8. The Anabaptists 43
        1.2.9. The Slavic Baptists 46
        1.2.10. Conclusion 47
    1.3. Conclusion for Chapter 1 47

Chapter 2 49
    Mission of the Church
    2.1. World Council of Churches/Ecumenical Position on Mission 51
        2.1.1. The World Council of Churches (WCC) 51
        2.1.2. The Socio-Political Contexts of the Time When the
        Examined Documents Were Written 53

2.1.3. New Delhi: Integrating Witness, Service,
and Unity (1961) 54
2.1.4. Mexico City: God's Mission and Our Task (1963) 56
2.1.5. Geneva: Church and Society (1966) 58
2.1.6. Uppsala: "Behold, I Make All Things New" (1968) 61
2.1.7. Bangkok: Salvation Today (1973) 64
2.1.8. Summary 67
2.1.9. Nairobi: *Confessing Christ Today* (1975) 68
2.1.10. *Guidelines on Dialogue* (1979) 70
2.1.11. *Christian Witness – Common Witness* (1980) 72
2.1.12. Melbourne: *Your Kingdom Come* (1980) 73
2.1.13. *Ecumenical Affirmation: Mission and Evangelism* (1982) 75
2.1.14. *Witnessing in a Divided World* (1983) 77
2.1.15. *Urban Rural Mission* (1986) 78
2.1.16. *Stuttgart Consultation* (1987) 78
2.1.17. San Antonio: *Mission in Christ's Way: Your Will
Be Done* (1989) 79
2.1.18. *Baar I Statement: Theological Perspectives
on Plurality* (1990) 81
2.1.19. *Justice, Peace, and the Integrity of Creation* (1990) 82
2.1.20. *Come, Holy Spirit* (1991) 82
2.1.21. *Mission and Evangelism in Unity Today* (2000) 83
2.1.22. *Mission as Ministry of Reconciliation* (2005) 83
2.1.23. *Alternative Globalization Addressing Peoples
and Earth (AGAPE)* (2005) 84
2.1.24. *Ecumenical Declaration Presented at the World
People's Conference on Climate Change and the Rights
of Mother Earth* (2010) 84
2.1.25. Summary 85
2.2. Evangelical/Lausanne Movement Position on the Mission
of the Church 86
2.2.1. Lausanne Movement 86
2.2.2. *The Lausanne Covenant* (1974) 89
2.2.3. *The Willowbank Report: Consultation on Gospel
and Culture* (1978) 90
2.2.4. *An Evangelical Commitment to a Simple Lifestyle* (1980) 90
2.2.5. *The Thailand Statement* (1980) 91
2.2.6. *Evangelism and Social Responsibility: An Evangelical
Commitment* (1982) 93
2.2.7. *Transformation: The Church in Response
to Human Need* (1983) 94

2.2.8. *The Manila Manifesto* (1989) 95
  2.2.9. *The Cape Town Commitment* (2010)...............................96
  2.2.10. Summary..99
  2.2.11. WCC vs. Evangelicals: The Great Debate.....................100
 2.3. Anabaptist Position 106
  2.3.1. *Mennonite Confession of Faith* (1963) 106
  2.3.2. *Creation: Called to Care* (1991) 107
  2.3.3. *Confession of Faith in a Mennonite Perspective* (1995)......109
  2.3.4. *Mennonite Creation Care Network Annual Report*...........110
  2.3.5. Summary..111
 2.4. Concluding Summary...111
 2.5. Evangelism and Social Action: The WCC's Use
   of the Term "Witness" and Evangelical Discussions
   of the Issue of Social Justice..115
 2.6. A Contemporary Understanding of Mission from
   a New Testament Perspective..122
  2.6.1. Discipleship...122
  2.6.2. Reconciliation..126
  2.6.3. Bringing Good News to the Poor..................................128
  2.6.4. Conclusion 130
 2.7. Definition of Authentic Mission 130
 2.8. Conclusion for Chapter 2 132

Chapter 3... 135
Challenge of Contextualization in Mission
 3.1. Context..135
  3.1.1. Cultural Context 136
  3.1.2. Language Context..138
  3.1.3. Social Context 139
  3.1.4. Personal Circumstances 140
 3.2. Contextualization 141
  3.2.1. Meaning 141
  3.2.2. Scope..144
  3.2.3. Theological Perspectives and Contextualization..............144
  3.2.4. Concerns 145
  3.2.5. Syncretism...146
 3.3. Homogeneous Unit Model: Contextuality Attempt
   (Strengths and Weaknesses) 146
  3.3.1. Homogeneous Unit Principle (HU): Definition,
    Meaning, Examples...147
  3.3.2. Using the Homogeneous Unit Principle in Mission 149

3.3.3. Critique of the Homogeneous Unit Principle:
Strengths and Weaknesses 150
3.3.4. Concluding Remarks 154
3.4. Conclusion for Chapter 3 155

Part II: Context: Identity Formation – Towards a Conceptualization
of Self-Understanding among Slavic Baptists.................................... 157

Chapter 4 159
Historical Background of Slavic Baptists from the Mission Perspective
4.1. Definition of Terms...159
    Baptists...159
    Evangelical Christians 160
    Evangelical Baptist Movement 160
    Evangelical Christians-Baptists...160
    Evangelicals 161
4.2. Origin of Slavic Baptist Churches: Roots of Slavic Baptists –
Are They Foreign or Indigenous? 161
4.3. Evangelism and Social Action/*Diaconia* in the Life of the
Evangelical Christians-Baptists Churches in Russia and Ukraine
in Historical Perspective 165
    4.3.1. Various Beginnings (1867–1900): Actively Sharing
the New Faith 165
    4.3.2. Attempts to Unite the Streams: Common
Commitment to Mission..174
    4.3.3. Life of Suffering and Growth (1900–1945):
Sharing the Gospel Regardless of Circumstances 177
    4.3.4. Life of Survival after World War II (1945–1985):
Witnessing about Christ under Communist
Government Pressure 185
    4.3.5. Glasnost and Perestroika: New Opportunities for
Evangelism and Service 191
    4.3.6. The Significance of Missiological Writings in Russian
and Their Impact on Russian Baptists 196
4.4. Conclusion for Chapter 4 201

Chapter 5 203
Developing the Slavic Baptist Diaspora in the American Context
5.1. Receiving American Society as the Mission Context.................203
    5.1.1. Ethnicity...204
    5.1.2. Language 206
    5.1.3. Religion 207
    5.1.4. Conclusion 209

5.2. Global Migration as the Mission Context 209
    5.2.1. Impact of Immigration 211
    5.2.2. Concerns Related to the Impact the Migrant
    Churches Are Making 212
5.3. Russian-Speaking Diaspora in America as a Mission Field
in the Historical Prospective 215
    5.3.1. The Impact of the Evolution of the US Immigration
    Policy on Russian Emigration...............................215
    5.3.2. Demographics and Settlement of Russian Immigrants
    in the USA..217
    5.3.3. Acculturation and Assimilation........................219
    5.3.4. Religion..220
    5.3.5. Russian Immigrants' Contributions to
    American Society 221
    5.3.6. Summary 222
5.4. History of the Founding and Organization of the Pacific
Coast Slavic Baptist Association 223
    5.4.1. A Brief Overview of the History of Slavic Baptists
    in the United States.......................................223
    5.4.2. PCSBA: The Humble Beginning Followed by Fruitful
    Ministry (1928–1990) 225
    5.4.3. Years 1990–Present: Time of Significant Membership
    Growth and Expanding Ministries 231
5.5. Conclusion for Chapter 5 235

Part III: Context: Identity Crisis/Transformation – Towards a Paradigm Shift in Self-Understanding among Slavic Baptists in America 239

Chapter 6 241
The Present Mission Work of Slavic Baptist Churches in the US
    6.1. Demographic Studies of Newly Baptized Believers
    in PCSBA Churches..241
    Summary 245
    6.2. Analysis of the Percentage of Mission-Related Spending in the
    Budgets of Selected Churches...............................245
    6.3. Survey of Slavic Pastors and Other Church Leaders Regarding
    Their Views on Church Mission in the Immigrant Context.........246
        Part 1: General Evaluation of Missionary Work in the Local
        Congregation 247
        Part 2: Local Mission Work 250
        Part 3: Overseas Mission 260
        Part 4: Language Barrier and Mission 264

Part 6: In Your Opinion, How Should the Missionary Work
of Your Local Congregation Look in the Future?...................268
6.4. Survey of Youth in PCSBA Churches Regarding Their
View of Immigrant Churches..269
Summary...273
6.5. Survey of the Pacific Coast Slavic Baptist Association
Churches on the Current Situation in Mission..........................275
Summary...276
6.6. Survey of People Who Have Left a Russian-Speaking
Congregation and Joined an English-Speaking Church...............277
6.7. Review of the Methods and Organizational Models
of Missionary Work Used by PCSBA Churches........................278
Summary...285
6.8. Conclusion for Chapter 6 286

Chapter 7 287
*Social Challenges of Immigrant Life for the Slavic Baptist Diaspora
and Their Impact on the Mission of the Church*
7.1. Common Emotional and Psychological Experiences
of Immigrants and Authentic Mission 287
7.2. Cross-Cultural-Encounter Influencing Factors 290
7.2.1. Reciprocal Consequences of Cross-Cultural Encounters...291
7.2.2. Impact of the Homogeneity/Heterogeneity of
the Society on the Immigrant's Experience 292
7.2.3. Impact of the Degree of Difference between Societies....293
7.2.4. Impact of the Visible Characteristics
of Cultural Groups...294
7.3. Diaspora vs. Receiving Society Relations and Mission...............295
7.4. Social and Cultural Specifics of the Current Slavic Diaspora
in America..300
7.5. Challenges Other Immigrant Churches Are Facing in America...300
7.5.1. Korean-Speaking Churches' Experience 302
7.5.2. Chinese-Speaking Churches' Experience.........................304
7.5.3. Spanish-Speaking Churches 306
7.5.4 Conclusion 311
7.6. Conclusion for Chapter 7 313

Chapter 8 315
*Analysis of Mission Challenges and Opportunities for the Slavic Baptist
Diaspora*
8.1. Ethnicity and Mission..315
8.1.1. Ethnicity: Terms and Definitions 316

    8.1.2. Religion and Ethnicity in an Immigrant's Life 317
    8.1.3. Ethnicity and Mission: Bridges and Barriers 320
    8.1.4. Church vs. Ethnic Community in the Russian Baptist
        Diaspora in the Mission Context 322
8.2. Interethnic Relations between Slavic Immigrants and
    Other People Groups 324
8.3. Role of Language in Church Life and Mission 327
    8.3.1. Language as a Vehicle of Spreading the Faith 328
    8.3.2. Language as a Barrier to Spreading the Faith 329
    8.3.3. Role of the Russian Language for Mission Work among
        Russian-Speaking Communities in America and Abroad 331
    8.3.4. Russian Language as an Obstacle for Mission Work
        among the English-Speaking Community 333
    8.3.5. Lack of Spiritual Maturity among the Younger Generation
        as a Result of Using the Russian Language in the Church 335
8.4. Hindrances and Opportunities for Mission 337
    8.4.1. Lack of Financial Support and Inadequate Training
        as Hindrances for Mission 337
    8.4.2. Losing Younger Church Members to English-Speaking
        Congregations as Hindrances for Mission 338
    8.4.3 New Opportunities for Missions as a Result of Political
        Changes in the World 343
8.5. The Multiracial Congregation Model as an Option for the
    Immigrant Churches 343
8.6. The Multiracial Congregation Model in the Early Church 347
    8.6.1. Patterns of Jewish Migration in the Roman Empire 347
    8.6.2. The Social Makeup of First-Century Churches 351
8.7. Conclusion for Chapter 8 356

Part IV: Authentic Mission Perspective: Mission Practices in Light of Context and Contextuality 359

Chapter 9 361

Analysis of the Authenticity and Contextuality of Mission Work of the Pacific Coast Slavic Baptist Association Churches

    9.1. PCSBA Churches: Is Their Mission Work Authentic and
        Contextually Appropriate Today? 361
    9.2. Authenticity and Contextuality of Mission in the Homeland 362
    9.3. Authenticity and Contextuality of Mission in the
        US Immigrant Context 363
        9.3.1. Before the Latest Wave of Immigration (1928–1989) 364
        9.3.2. Church Mission in the Current Period (1989–Present) 365

Summary 371
9.4. Conclusion for Chapter 9 373

Chapter 10 375
Contextualization of Mission Work of Slavic Baptist Churches through Various Models
    10.1. Models of mission work among the
    Russian-Speaking population 375
        10.1.1. Mission Work among the Russian-Speaking
        Diaspora in America 376
        10.1.2. Mission Work among the Russian-Speaking
        Diaspora around the World..379
        10.1.3. Mission Work in the Homeland 380
    10.2. Models of Mission Work among Non-Russian-Speaking
    People 381
        10.2.1. Mission Work among English-Speaking Children
        of Slavic Immigrants 381
        10.2.2. Mission Work among Non-Russian-Speakers
        Living in the Church Neighborhoods................................383
    10.3. Ways of Equipping Contextualized Mission Work 392
        10.3.1. Training of Leaders for Carrying Out Authentic
        and Contextualized Mission 393
        10.3.2. Formation of the Mentality of Slavic Baptist Churches
        Oriented towards an Authentic and Contextualized Mission ..393
        10.3.3. Development of the Appropriate Administrative
        Structure for Implementing Authentic
        and Contextualized Mission Work 395
    10.4. Conclusion for Chapter 10 395
    10.5. Further Research..396

Conclusion.. 399

Appendix for Chapter 4.. 405
Historical Background of Slavic Baptists from the Mission Perspective

Appendix for Chapter 5.. 415
Developing Slavic Baptist Diaspora in the American context
    5.1.A. Global Migration as the Mission Context...........................415
    5.2.A. Brief Overview of History of Russian Immigration
    to America...429
    5.3.A. History of the Founding and Organization of the
    Pacific Coast Slavic Baptist Association 434

Appendix for Chapter 6 437
   The Present Mission Work of Slavic Baptist Churches in the US
      6.2.A. Analysis of the Percentage of Mission-Related Spending
      in the Budget of Selected Churches 437
      6.3.A. Survey of Slavic Pastors and Other Church Leaders Regarding
      Their Views on Church Mission in the Immigrant Context 438
      6.4.A. Survey of Youth in PCSBA Churches Regarding Their
      View of Immigrant Churches 528
      6.5.A. Survey of the Pacific Coast Slavic Baptist Association
      Churches on the Current Situation in Mission 532
      6.6.A. Survey of People Who Left the Russian-Speaking
      Congregations and Joined the English-Speaking Churches 533
      6.7.A. Demographic Data for the Delegates of the
      75th Annual PCSBA Convention, 18–20 October 2012,
      Sacramento, California 541

Appendix for Chapter 7 543
   Social Challenges of Immigrant Life for the Slavic Baptist Diaspora and Their Impact on Mission
      7.1.A. Common Emotional and Psychological Experiences of
      Immigrants and Authentic Mission 543
      7.4.A. Social and Cultural Specifics of the Current Slavic
      Diaspora in America 553

Appendix for Chapter 8 559
   Analysis of Mission Challenges and Opportunities for the Slavic Baptist Diaspora
      8.1.A. Ethnicity and Mission 559
      8.2.A. Interethnic Relations between Slavic Immigrants and
      Other People Groups...561
      8.4.A. Hindrances and Opportunities for Mission 564
         8.4.3.A. New Opportunities for Missions as a Result of
         Political Changes in the World 564

Bibliography 567

Abstract

This study has been undertaken to examine the authenticity and contextuality of the mission work of immigrant churches belonging to the Pacific Coast Slavic Baptist Association (PCSBA) in America. Since 1988, hundreds of thousands of evangelical Christians (Pentecostals and Baptists) have migrated to the United States of America from the former Soviet Union countries. They have formed many Russian-speaking immigrant congregations across the country. Thirty-two of these churches are part of the PCSBA. The goal of this study is to find out how these immigrant churches are fulfilling Christ's Great Commission in their new cultural, social, and religious context.

The study begins with an examination of the modern understanding of the subject of an authentic mission. Through an analysis of the theological context of the discussion on this subject and through studying the positions of the three Christian bodies (WCC, evangelical/Lausanne Movement, and Anabaptists), the definition of an authentic mission has been developed for use in the evaluation of the mission work of the PCSBA churches. Through an analysis of the historical development of Slavic Baptists in their homelands, as well as in America, it has been shown that evangelistic zeal and a desire to provide social actions/*diaconia* have always been present among them. However, in the case of Slavic Baptists in America, their evangelistic efforts and social actions/*diaconia* have been mainly directed toward people of their ethnicity, and not as much toward non-Russian-speakers. Data collected through surveys of church leaders and youth, and through other sources, confirm that the PCSBA churches, which consist predominantly of recent immigrants, are focusing their mission ministry efforts toward the people in the homelands. Limited efforts are being made to reach non-believing Russian-speaking people in America. The non-Russian-speaking population of the receiving American society is being neglected by these churches in terms of evangelistic and social action/*diaconia* efforts. Analysis of the social challenges of immigrant life points to the fact that culture shock, cultural and language barriers, attachment to the homeland, lack of ability to accept people of other ethnicity and color in their midst, suspicious attitudes toward American churches, and other factors provide "natural" obstacles for Slavic immigrant Baptist churches to become involved in mission work among indigenous people who do not speak Russian. The leadership of immigrant churches needs to be aware of these obstacles and has to take the appropriate actions to overcome them. Belonging to the large Russian-speaking diaspora numbering millions of people around the world provides the Slavic immigrant Baptist churches with a great opportunity to witness about Christ to the non-believing majority of this diaspora in America and abroad. At the same time, focusing most of their attention only on their ethnic group, combined with the common tendency of immigrant churches to become ethnic enclaves, keeps Slavic immigrant Baptist churches in America from fulfilling their responsibility to bring the gospel to all people.

The evaluation of the mission work of the PCSBA churches, as an ultimate goal of this study, has demonstrated two results: (1) The mission of Slavic immigrant Baptist churches that are part of the PCSBA is authentic and contextualized when directed abroad, which predominantly includes supporting evangelistic ministry and providing humanitarian aid in their homelands; (2) it is not authentic and not contextualized in its local aspect, which would be concerned about doing mission and conducting social actions among the local non-Russian-speaking people. As the best way of improving the local aspect of their mission, the Slavic immigrant Baptist churches are advised to consider implementing the multiracial model of the church. The existing Slavic immigrant monoracial churches should be transformed into multiracial congregations, and new churches should be planted by Slavic immigrants (most probably by young people) in partnership with believers representing other ethnic groups. Establishing multiracial congregations will provide the PCSBA churches with the possibility to preserve their ecclesiastical culture (at least to some degree) and, at the same time, to be able to create a bridge to the surrounding society in their efforts to do mission work among local native people. This will make the mission work of the PCSBA churches holistic, authentic and contextualized.

Acknowledgments

This book is based on research and data gathered from the Slavic immigrant Christian community in the USA as part of my doctoral studies from 2004 to 2013. Although this project was initiated and conducted by me, I cannot claim it as my own. It exists because of the vital help of others and it would be remiss not to mention those who played an important role in the realization of this project.

First of all, I want to praise God for giving me strength, courage, and the necessary means to complete this challenging and at times painful process of research and writing a dissertation. There are also many people to whom I owe deep gratitude for accomplishing this major project. Without their support, encouragement, guidance, practical help, and kindness, it would never have happened.

A very special thanks to Dr Wendy Wakeman, my direct supervisor at Fresno Pacific University at the time, who back in 2004 believed in my ability to do the doctoral work and encouraged me to take a risk and start this journey. I am very grateful to her.

My original Director of Studies at IBTS, Dr Peter Penner, deserves special appreciation for his guidance, support, and encouragement. His faithful friendship and supportive spirit played an important role in the successful completion of this work. His wife, Katarina Penner, was also helpful as an IBTS librarian with locating the literature resources for me. The person who walked alongside me during all these years providing moral support, giving timely advice, and encouraging me all the time was my supervisor, Dr Sergey Sannikov. I am greatly indebted to him for his guidance and inspiration in the process of study.

My Director of Studies, Dr Parush Parushev, deserves special thanks for his uncompromising encouragement and practical help in reaching my educational goal. His hard work in organizing and leading the annual PhD colloquia in IBTS made them special events that allowed me to meet fellow PhD students from around the world and always served as a source of strong encouragement to continue the research. My appreciation is directed to the IBTS faculty and students for creating a supportive, unique cross-cultural environment. I am very appreciative of my examiners, Dr J. Andrew Kirk and Dr Maurice Dowling, for their careful and critical reading of my thesis and for providing me with helpful feedback that helped to improve my work.

I am grateful to Michael Wurtz and Phil Luna for assisting me with the research process. I appreciate Charles Jensen and Karen Bartlet for their initial proofreading of my text. I am in great debt to Nancy Lively for her heroic work in the final proofreading of my dissertation. Her attention to detail and ability to quickly identify all errors in the paper have been amazing.

My FPU coworkers and especially my supervisor, Cindy Steele, deserve my special thanks for understanding, encouraging, and supporting me on this uneasy journey. I am especially grateful to the co-laborers in Christ, the pastors of PCSBA churches, for their participation in the research process and for sharing with me their joys and struggles of ministering in immigrant churches.

Lastly, I want to express my deep appreciation to my wife, Nina, and our six now-grown sons. Most of the time used for the thesis work was time away from family. With no complaints, they released me to study. Nina gladly took on extra responsibilities to care for me and allow me time to work on the thesis that eventually became this book. The completion of this work is "the reward she has earned" (Prov 31:31).

Introduction

The impact that immigration is making on the economic and social life of America is debated frequently in the mass media. However, its impact on the religious life of the country is not often discussed. Does immigration make any impact on the religious life of America? Do Christian immigrants offer positive contributions to the religious life of Americans, do they minister to their fellow immigrants and the native people with an equal amount of energy, and do they achieve the same success with both people groups? According to Jehu J. Hanciles, the modern "migration movement is essentially a religious movement" and because of this, he claims, "*every Christian migrant is a potential missionary.*"[1] He proclaims that "the new immigrant congregations are performing a vital missionary function by their very presence."[2] Probably because of sharing this conviction with Hanciles, the largest Protestant denomination in America, the Southern Baptist Convention, invests a lot of energy into planting new mono-ethnic congregations among recent immigrants in the US.[3] Another denomination, although not so large as the SBC, the US Mennonite Brethren Conference, makes similar efforts to increase its membership through adopting new

---

1. Jehu J. Hanciles, *Beyond Christendom: Globalization, African Migration, and the Transformation of the West* (Maryknoll, NY: Orbis, 2009), 296. Hanciles is arguing that the "new Christian immigrants and their descendants will clearly have a lasting impact on the American religious landscape."

2. Ibid., 297.

3. According to the SBC North American Mission Board President Kevin Ezell, a strong focus on minority ministry will continue to be maintained by the NAMB in the future. He said, "Since NAMB's formation in 1997, the entity has led Southern Baptists to place an emphasis on ethnic church planting. More than half of all SBC churches planted or affiliated with the SBC since 1997 have been African-American or ethnic . . . NAMB will not take a step back from ethnic church planting." Mike Ebert, "Role to Focus on Increased Ethnic Involvement in SBC," www.namb.net, http://www.namb.net/nambblog1.aspx?id=859011 7418&blogid=8589939695; accessed October 2012.

immigrant ethnic churches into their denominational structure, and is proud to have almost half of their 200 churches across the country worshiping in eleven different languages.[4] Are we approaching a new era of revitalization of Christianity in America and a reversal of its membership decline[5] due to the fact of continued immigration?

This study challenges such rosy expectations. It shows that in the case of churches of the Pacific Coast Slavic Baptist Association (PCSBA),[6] the impact of new Christian immigrants on the religious life of the native English-speaking American population has been minimal, if it has taken place at all. It points to the fact that the immigrant Russian-speaking churches of the PCSBA have a strong tendency to be isolated from the host society and do little to reach local English-speaking people with the gospel. If the attitude of these churches does not change, and they do not transform into multiracial congregations with both immigrants and native people being part of these congregations, they will not be able to make any significant impact on the religious life of American society. Their physical presence in the community, without active contextualized mission work directed toward people living around these churches, is neither producing significant results for God's kingdom nor is it making significant changes in the religious life of America. Without conducting mission work among native people, the

---

4. The official website of the US Mennonite Brethren Conference states, "In the Pacific District alone, there are as many as 80 immigrant churches that are affiliated with our MB family. Slavic, Hispanic and Ethiopian churches make up the bulk of these churches, but there are many other ethnic groups that are a part as well, including Chinese, Japanese, Hmong, Korean and Indian." US Conference of the Mennonite Brethren Churches, "A Diverse Family," www.usmb.org, http://www.usmb.org/a-diverse-family; accessed October 2012. As a former member of the US MB Conference Leadership Board for four years, the author of this study knows that among these eight immigrant churches, about thirty are Slavic congregations that have joined the MB denomination since 1993. All of these Slavic churches use Russian or the Ukrainian language in their services and in church life.

5. Jose B. Fuliga, "Factors Contributing to the De-Christianization of North America," *Asia Journal of Theology* 24, no. 1 (April 2010): 3. The author of this article states that the dominant position of Christianity in the US for two hundred years is changing dramatically in the twenty-first century. According to Fuliga, the "hold of the Christian faith on Americans is rapidly fading. Its churches' pews are almost half empty, only filled with a graying generation. The absence of young faces is noticeable" (3).

6. Pacific Coast Slavic Baptist Association (PCSBA) is the object of this study. It consists of thirty-two churches of recent immigrants from the former Soviet Union. More detailed information about this organization will be provided in chapter 5 of this study.

PCSBA churches are at risk of sharing the fate of other immigrant church groups without a local mission.

Context of the Present Research

Along with religious freedom, one of the unexpected outcomes of perestroika between 1985 and 1990 in the former Soviet Union was the opportunity for evangelical Christians (Pentecostals and Baptists) to leave the country and emigrate to the West, which had been impossible for about seven decades. As a result, hundreds of thousands of evangelical Christians have migrated to the US from 1988 to the present. According to Mark Elliott's estimate, possibly "a half million Evangelicals have emigrated to the West from the former Soviet Union"[7] since 1988. After arriving in the US, they formed many Russian-speaking immigrant churches across the country. Membership in these congregations varies from thirty to fifty to well over a thousand or more.[8] In most cases, worship services and church life in general mirror the way they were conducted in the homeland. From the perspective of an outside observer, it could be concluded that these churches are doing very well. Attendance is strong, members are actively participating in church life, children's ministry and youth ministry are flourishing, and big choirs participating in services bring a special flavor to the church gatherings. However, a more attentive look at the life and service of these churches could raise the following question: Is it really true that they are living a healthy church life in accordance with Christ's expectations and his Great Commission? The careful observer will quickly discover that these vibrant churches are primarily focused on people of their own ethnicity and on establishing their congregational life, and not much energy (if any) is spent on evangelizing and serving the local non-Russian-speaking population. While there is a strong involvement in ministry directed back to the homeland, local ministry in America is neglected. Does such an unbalanced approach to mission (between "foreign" mission to the homeland and "home" mission

---

7. Fuliga, "Factors Contributing to the De-Christianization of North America," 3.

8. The scope of the local church membership is well illustrated by the difference in membership of the churches that are part of the PCSBA. It can be seen in chart 6.1.3 in chapter 6 of this study.

to the immediate surroundings) reflect authentic mission principles? With this question in mind, the author has undertaken this task of finding out if this multitude of Slavic immigrant churches have fulfilled an authentic mission in their new cultural, linguistic, social, and religious context during the last twenty-five years.[9]

Purpose of the Study

Mission in the cross-cultural context has been studied very carefully during the last several decades. In most cases, the studies have been done in the context of foreign missions, where missionaries are sent abroad for short- or long-term stays. In such cases, missionaries are in a new country for a limited period of time and they are supported by their sending agency or the church. It is expected that they will learn the language of the country and will adapt to the new culture in order to be able to reach the local people with the gospel. Also, a good amount of study has been done on the subject of mission work among non-Christian immigrants who arrive in traditionally Christian countries. Their arrival is seen as an opportunity to share the gospel with them.

---

9. Besides an academic interest, the author has a very strong personal motivation for the study. The future of Slavic immigrants and their churches is of great concern to him because he is part of this group. In April 1990, as part of a group of immigrants from the former Soviet Union, he arrived in California with his wife and six sons. Since that time, he has been involved in ministry to and within the community of Slavic immigrants. He served this community soon after arriving in America, working for a mission organization that provided theological educational opportunities for Slavic church leaders. Later, after seminary graduation, he worked as the developer and director of a special educational program for Slavic students at Fresno Pacific University. For ten years he served as senior pastor of a local Slavic Baptist church. At the national level, the author served as a national minister appointed by the US Conference of Mennonite Brethren Churches to serve Slavic immigrant churches associated with this denomination across the United States. For four years, he served the Slavic immigrant community as the elected president of the Pacific Coast Slavic Baptist Association (PCSBA). Currently, he is serving as vice-president for this association.

In God's providence, the author has been placed in a unique position regarding this study. Since his arrival in the United States, he has been involved with the Slavic immigrant community. At the same time, he has been constantly part of the life of the English-speaking community, initially as a student of the Mennonite Brethren Biblical Seminary and later as an employee of Fresno Pacific University. As a result, the author became bilingual and bicultural. Due to these factors, he has the advantage of observing the life of Slavic immigrant churches from two perspectives: from within, as one of its members, and from the outside, as a member of the English-speaking community. This provides additional strength for this study.

However, little research has been accomplished on mission work done by immigrants themselves in their new country,[10] specifically in mission work directed toward local people of the receiving society. This study is intended to contribute to that area of knowledge. The study is done with the following questions in mind: Do immigrant mono-ethnic churches as religious entities adequately communicate with the receiving society? What impact is made by these churches in the religious life of the people of the country in which they now reside? How can an authentic mission be fulfilled by them in their specific immigrant context? Should these churches stay monoracial or should they be transformed into multiracial congregations? Answers to these questions are crucial for the development of a long-term mission strategy for Slavic immigrant churches in the United States. It makes this research important academically and practically. At the end of this study, recommendations are provided on how to apply the principles of authentic mission in the context of Slavic immigrant churches in the USA.

Scope and Method of the Study

Scope of the Research

Hundreds of Slavic immigrant churches of the Baptist and Pentecostal denominations throughout the United States are facing the problem of neglecting mission work among the local indigenous people. All of these churches are going through a similar experience and are in need of a critical analysis of their mission perspective. However, this study is limited only to churches which are part of the PCSBA. This allows for more focused and detailed research. The results of this research could also be applied to other Slavic immigrant churches in the USA.

---

10. Joanne van Dijk, "The Importance of Ethnicity and Religion in the Life Cycle of Immigrant Churches: A Comparison of Coptic and Calvinist Churches," *Canadian Ethnic Studies* 41 (2009): 191–214. The issue of ethnicity and religion plays an important role in the development of immigrants' attitudes toward indigenous people. However, only limited literature is available on this subject. Joanne van Dijk points to three reasons for the lack of study of immigrant religious communities who arrived in the United States after the 1965 Act. "These included a lack of statistical data that would reflect the richness and diversity of the religious experience of immigrant groups; an 'antireligious bias' among researchers; and the limited number of scholars fluent in the languages of these new immigrant communities" (193).

Methodology

The goal of this research is to evaluate the authenticity and contextuality of mission in PCSBA churches. This study uses qualitative research, with an interdisciplinary approach. The steps for the research are as follows: (1) Library research of the historical and theological development of the concept of *missio Dei*; studying the basic statements of three ecclesiological groups (WCC/ecumenical, evangelical/Lausanne Movement, and Anabaptists) regarding their position on the subject of the relationship between the kingdom of God, the world, and the mission of the church; analyzing basic statements on the subject of the church's mission; studying literature on contextualization in mission; analyzing the role of mission for Slavic evangelicals in Tsarist Russia and the Soviet Union through a historical overview of the evangelical movement in Russia and the USSR; exploring the historical development of the Russian-speaking diaspora in America, in general, and Slavic Baptists, in particular, in the context of global migration. This research provides the theological and historical basis for analytical evaluation of the data from the field research. (2) Field research began in 2004 and includes: surveying members of church leadership boards and church youth; examining PCSBA archival material; conducting demographic studies of newly baptized believers in PCSBA churches; analyzing the percentage of mission-related spending in selected church budgets; conducting personal interviews with church leaders; surveying people who have left Slavic immigrant churches and joined English-speaking congregations; and performing an overview of the methods and organizational models of mission work used by PCSBA churches. The valuable information gathered through this research provides empirical data needed for the evaluation of the mission work of PCSBA churches. (3) Study of books and periodical publications addressing issues faced by immigrants in the USA. This study provided the author with a deeper understanding of the personal context of mission work done by immigrants. (4) Integration and analysis of all data obtained through library research, interviews, and other sources. (5) Concluding report on what this study found with a proposal of practical steps on how to address the research question of the thesis and suggestions for further research.

Limitations of This Research

As already mentioned, the field research of this study is limited to churches that are part of the PCSBA, which currently consists of thirty-two churches with a total membership of about 8,000 baptized adults. Analysis of the different issues Slavic immigrants are facing in the US is limited to the perspective of how the mission work of Slavic immigrant churches is affected by these issues. Analysis of social, cultural, and language issues faced by immigrants and how these issues influence their attitude toward mission is focused primarily on the first generation of immigrants. This is because they are currently in leadership positions in Slavic immigrant churches and determine where church mission work should be focused. The experience of youth and their view of church life and mission are explored as well. The extended length of time used for this study (starting in 2004) allowed conducting two sets of surveys of church leaders and youth – five years apart. This enabled the development of the views of church leaders and youth to be seen, which enriched the study. However, since the study deals with the current living and actively functioning immigrant community, some information obtained through the latest surveys could have changed before the completion of the study.

Development of the Argument

The book consists of four parts. Part I is devoted to the task of acquiring the tools needed for evaluation of the mission work of PCSBA churches. In this part, an analysis of an authentic mission and the theological context for its development is provided (chapter 1). Also, the definition of an authentic mission has been developed based on the comparative analysis of the viewpoints on the mission of the church of three different theological church groups: WCC/ecumenical, evangelicals/Lausanne Movement, and Anabaptists (chapter 2). This definition states that the mission of the church is multifaceted and includes evangelism, social action/*diaconia*, overcoming violence and building cultures of peace, justice, care of the environment, worship, dialogue, inculturation, and the ministry of reconciliation. In order to make this study more precisely focused, the evaluation of the mission work of Slavic Baptist churches has been limited to analyzing the evangelism and social action/*diaconia* aspects of this mission. Other aspects of the PCSBA church mission require separate study. Also, in Part I, the important subject of the contextuality of mission is discussed (chapter 3). It is an absolute necessity to contextualize the mission of the church in order to make it authentic. It is imperative for Slavic immigrant Baptist churches to address the challenge of contextualization of their mission in order to be successful in their ministry to local indigenous people.

Part II is devoted to introducing those whose mission this study is evaluating. It consists of materials analyzing the historical background of Slavic Baptists in the homelands and the role of evangelism and social action/*diaconia* in the life of churches during times of persecution and short windows of religious freedom (chapter 4). It is shown that despite the fact that Baptists experienced continuous periods of persecution and oppression in Tsarist Russia and in the USSR, they always shared the gospel with their neighbors and co-workers. Zeal for evangelism was one of the marks of Baptists. Although limited, there is evidence that social action/*diaconia* played an important role in their life as well. Also, in Part II, the development of the Russian-speaking diaspora in America in general, and the development of the Slavic Baptist diaspora in particular, in the context of global migration has been analyzed (chapter 5). The place of mission work in the life of the Slavic immigrant churches has been evaluated. It was found that despite the fact that the membership of the PCSBA churches from 1928 to 1989 was small (less than 400 members), these churches supported different ministries focused on spreading the gospel and cared for the social needs of people. However, almost all of their efforts were directed to Russian-speaking people. The local English-speaking population was left without significant attention.

Part III presents the results of several surveys of Slavic church leaders, youth, and people who have left Slavic immigrant churches and joined English-speaking congregations (chapter 6). This information provides the major empirical data for evaluation of the current situation with mission work in the churches of the Pacific Coast Slavic Baptist Association. Also, an analysis of the social challenges of immigrant life for the Slavic Baptist diaspora and their impact on mission is presented in this part (chapter 7). It shows that facing tremendous pressure from challenging issues that immigrants encounter in a new country intensifies their feelings of ethnic and national identity and isolates them from people of the receiving society. This puts up barriers to local mission engagement by immigrants. Additionally, an analysis of mission challenges and opportunities for the Slavic Baptist diaspora is included in Part III (chapter 8). Knowledge of the Russian language and culture provides Slavic immigrants with wide opportunities to serve Russian-speaking people in America, as well as around the world. At the same time, extensive use of Russian in church life cuts off English-speaking people from joining PCSBA churches.[11] Also, it deepens the intergenerational problems within Slavic immigrant families and churches and undermines the ability of young Slavic believers to be effective witnesses for Christ among English-speaking friends and neighbors. All this raises a question of the authenticity and contextuality of the mission work of the PCSBA churches.

In Part IV, in chapter 9, an analysis of contextuality of the US Slavic Baptist mission is provided. Based on the evaluation of data obtained through personal surveys of church leaders and youth, studying archival materials, and analyzing PCSBA convention reports and individual church annual budgets, a twofold conclusion has been drawn. On the one hand, the mission of Slavic immigrant Baptist churches is authentic and contextualized in its foreign aspect, which includes supporting evangelistic ministry and providing humanitarian aid in their former homelands. On the other hand, it is not authentic and not contextualized in its local aspect, which would be concerned with doing mission and conducting social action among local non-Russian-speaking people. Also, in Part IV, various models for the contextualized mission work of Slavic immigrant Baptist churches is introduced (chapter 10). Models for mission work among both Russian-speaking and

---

11. Using the Russian language and following Russian culture and traditions in church life distinguish Slavic Baptist churches from the rest of society and make them ethnic enclaves. This is not unique to Slavic immigrant churches. Analyzing the life of Korean churches in America, Lee recognizes that while Koreans in diaspora live in the "international communities in an increasingly borderless world, Diaspora churches are busy building bounded communities like those back home in Korea." Gil Pyo Lee, "From Traditional to Missional Church: Describing a Contextual Model of Change for Ingrown Korean Diaspora Church in North America," DMis dissertation, Asbury Theological Seminary, 2010, 6. Although it is beneficial and convenient for immigrants from the social standpoint, at the same time, this "has produced ingrown, inward, self-centered Korean Diaspora churches" (ibid.). A similar situation is taking place among Slavic Baptist churches in America and the description of the Korean immigrant churches could be applied to Slavic immigrant churches.

non-Russian-speaking populations, locally and abroad, are suggested. The most challenging aspect is reaching local non-Russian-speakers in America. The multiracial church model is recommended to Slavic immigrant Baptist churches as the best option to meet this challenge. Also, suggestions for further research are provided.

There are five appendixes accompanying the main text of the book. They consist of empirical data and other additional materials that support the development of the argument.

Part I

Contextuality: Acquiring the Right Tools for Discernment of the Task

This part of the study is the starting point of the work and thus is designed to develop appropriate tools to evaluate the mission work of immigrant churches that are part of the Pacific Coast Slavic Baptist Association (PCSBA). It consists of three chapters in which (1) the theological context of the concept of an authentic mission of the church is discussed; (2) the subject of the mission of the church is analyzed and the definition of mission of the church developed; and (3) the issue of contextualization in mission is examined. The main outcome of this part is the development of a definition of authentic mission of the church. This definition will be used at the end of this study as a measurement tool in evaluating the mission work of PCSBA churches. In order to acquire the desired outcome of Part I, the positions of three Christian ecclesiastical bodies (WCC/ecumenical, evangelical/Lausanne Movement, and Anabaptist communities) are examined in relation to the subjects discussed in this part. The basic statements and other important documents produced by these groups are used as primary sources for understanding their theological positions. These groups were chosen because Slavic Baptist immigrant churches are much more in alignment theologically and ecclesiologically with these particular groups than with other church traditions, such as Catholic or Orthodox. Furthermore, after settling in the USA, if these churches have any relation with indigenous American churches, they usually relate to one of the three theological perspectives presented in this study.

CHAPTER 1

Authentic Mission in the Theological Context

This chapter consists of a brief overview of the theological context for the development of the concept of authentic mission. It introduces the contemporary view of mission as *missio Dei*, and briefly touches on the subject of relations between the mission of the church, the kingdom of God, and the world. This information provides grounds for further discussion of the subject of authentic mission.

1.1. *Missio Dei*

The concept of *missio Dei*, according to J. Andrew Kirk, "has become a popular place to begin an enquiry into the nature of mission."[1] Since the Willingen Conference in 1952, the concept of mission as *missio Dei*, or Mission of God, has been accepted by nearly all branches of Christianity, such as Protestants, Eastern Orthodox, and many evangelical groups.[2] It was also endorsed in Catholic mission theology.[3] "*Missio Dei* has been an ecumenical mantra, possibly the most widely acknowledged metaphor, in missiology."[4] Although it is not always mentioned in the basic statements of these three theological groups, from reading these statements it is clear that

---

1. *What Is Mission? Theological Explorations* (Minneapolis, MN: Fortress, 2000), 25.
2. Mark T. B. Laing, "*Missio Dei*: Some Implications for the Church," *Missiology* 37, no. 1 (Jan 2009): 91.
3. David J. Bosch, *Transforming Mission: Paradigm Shifts in Theology of Mission* (Maryknoll, NY: Orbis, 1991), 391.
4. Edward H. Schroeder, *Deconstructing the Concept of Missio Dei "in the Light of the Gospel,"* IAMS Conference XI materials (Port Dickson, Malaysia, 2004).

13

the concept of *missio Dei* is assumed as a given starting point for any discussion on the subject of mission. That is why it is important to provide a brief overview of the historical development, meaning, Trinitarian understanding, and purpose of *missio Dei*, as well as concerns related to this concept. The section below is devoted to this aim.

1.1.1. Historical Background for the *Missio Dei* Concept

During the long history of Christianity before the twentieth century, mission and its relation to the church has been understood in a variety of different ways.[5] According to David Bosch, "Sometimes it [the mission] was interpreted primarily in soteriological terms: as saving individuals from eternal damnation. Or it was understood in cultural terms: as introducing people from the East and the South to the blessings and privileges of the Christian West. Often it was perceived in ecclesiastical categories: as the expansion of the church (or of a specific denomination)."[6]

In Protestant thinking, the understanding of the relationship between the church and mission was influenced by world missionary conferences. If in Edinburgh (1910) the issue of the relationship between the church and mission was almost not touched, at the Jerusalem Conference of the International Missionary Council (IMC) (1928), this issue was raised in the discussion of the relationship between "older" and "younger" churches.[7] In Tambaram (1938), this discussion continued again, and a significant advance took place over earlier positions. "For the first time the recognition that church and mission belong together indissolubly began to dawn in a way that could no longer be overlooked."[8] The Willingen Conference (1952) took up the same theme. In the first part of the twentieth century, theological conceptualizations on mission were church-centered. "Mission

---

5. Rolf A. Syrday, *To the End of the Earth: Mission Concept in Principle and Practice* (Minneapolis, MN: Augsburg, 1967): the author presents a concise overview of historical development of the understanding of mission from the first century through the middle of the twentieth century; Andrew F. Walls, *The Missionary Movement in Christian History: Studies in the Transmission of Faith* (Maryknoll, NY: Orbis, 2004): this work is one of the more recent fundamental studies of the history of mission.

6. Bosch, *Transforming Mission*, 389.

7. Roger E. Hedlund, *Roots of the Great Debate in Mission* (Madras, India: Evangelical Literature Service, 1981), 50.

8. Bosch, *Transforming Mission*, 370.

was seen as the work of the whole church in the whole world, the work of a church which was now seen as the greatest hope of the world."[9] This church-centered mission concept was loaded with problematic consequences for missionaries because divisions and contradictions in the local churches often led to the same conflicts in the mission field.[10] Before 1952, the shift from an emphasis on a church-centered mission to a mission-centered church took place.[11] During the World Missionary Conference in Willingen in 1952, the new concept of mission, known now as the *missio Dei*, was developed. During the conference, "in a time of major missiological crisis because of the abrupt end of missionary work in China,"[12] it was affirmed that "the missionary movement of which we are a part has its source in the Triune God Himself."[13] At this conference, for the first time, the "mission was so comprehensively anchored in the doctrine of God."[14] The concept of *missio Dei* had first been articulated by Karl Barth at the Brandenburg Mission Conference in 1932, and was coined by Karl Hartenstein in his discussion of the *missio ecclesiae* in 1934.[15] However, only after the Willingen Conference did it become widely used among Christian theologians.

1.1.2. The Meaning of *Missio Dei*[16]

In a critical literary study of the term *missio Dei*, undertaken by Dutch theologian H. H. Rosin, the meaning of the term in Latin is cited. Rosin points out that the Latin term was used far more often in German texts than in English, and that it had been invested with so much new content that the

---

9. Wolfgang Gunther and Guillermo Cook, "World Missionary Conferences," in *Dictionary of Mission: Theology, History, Perspectives* (Maryknoll, NY: Orbis, 1999), 504.

10. Lesslie Newbigin, *The Relevance of Trinitarian Doctrine for Today's Mission*, WCC Commission on World Evangelism (London: Edinburgh House, 1963), 11.

11. Bosch, *Transforming Mission*, 370.

12. Jacques Matthey, "God's Mission Today: Summary and Conclusions," *International Review of Mission* 92, no. 367 (2003): 579.

13. International Missionary Council, *The Missionary Obligation of the Church*, Willingen, Germany, July 5–17, 1952 (Edinburgh House, 1952), 1.

14. Theo Sundermeier, "*Missio Dei* Today: On the Identity of Christian Mission," *International Review of Mission* 92, no. 367 (2003): 560.

15. Steven B. Bevans and Roger P. Schroeder, *Constants in Context: A Theology of Mission for Today* (Maryknoll, NY: Orbis, 2004), 290.

16. *Missio Dei* is a Latin theological term. *Missio* is a Latin translation of the Greek work *apostellew* and means "I send." *Dei* is a Latin translation of the Greek word *Theos* and means "God." Thus *missio Dei* means "God's mission" or "sending of God."

original meaning of the word had been changed by usage.[17] Rosin attributes the first real usage of the Latin term *missio Dei* to Georg Vicedom in his book entitled *Missio Dei*.[18] Vicedom, in turn, attributes the term to the conference in Willingen. But what is interesting is that the term *missio Dei* cannot be found in any articles or documents of that conference.[19] The concept itself emerged during the conference, but the Latin term describing the concept was applied later.[20] The *missio Dei* concept states that "the mission of the Triune God is the starting point for any reflection on missions."[21] It reveals that the source of the missionary movement is not the church but the triune God.[22] The conference provided the following definition: "Mission has its source in the Triune God. Out of the depth of his love to us, the Father has sent forth his own beloved son to reconcile all things to himself that we and all men might through the Holy Spirit be made one in Him with the Father in that perfect love which is the very nature of God."[23]

The Willingen Conference became a watershed event, promoting a conceptual change in thinking about mission. Through introducing the concept of *missio Dei* it was "recognized that the church could be neither the starting point nor the goal of mission. God's salvific work precedes both church and mission. We should not subordinate mission to the church nor the church to mission; both should, rather, be taken up into the *missio Dei*, which now became the overarching concept. The *missio Dei* institutes the *missiones ecclesiae*. The church changes from the sender to being the one sent."[24] Vicedom makes the following general conclusion: "The mission is work that belongs to God. This is the first implication of *missio Dei*. God is the Lord, the One who gives the orders, the Owner, the One who takes care of things. He is

---

17. H. H. Rosin, *"Missio Dei": An Examination of the Origin, Contents and Function of the Term in Protestant Missiological Discussion* (Leiden, Netherlands: Inter-University Institute for Missiological and Ecumenical Research, Department of Missiology, 1972), 3.

18. Ibid., 6.

19. Ibid.

20. Ibid., 8.

21. K. Detlev Schulz, "Revisiting the Missio Dei Concept: Commemorating Willingen, July 5–17, 1952," in *Concordia Theological Quarterly* (July 1952), 365.

22. International Missionary Council, *The Missionary Obligation of the Church*, 1.

23. "A Statement on the Missionary Calling of the Church," *International Review of Missions* 41 (1952): 562.

24. Bosch, *Transforming Mission*, 370.

the Protagonist in the mission. When we ascribe the mission to God in this way, then it is withdrawn from human whims."[25]

Philip L. Wickeri[26] emphasizes the fact that *missio Dei* thinking has very wide implications. It stresses "the radical activity of God in history, and challenges liberal and conservative pietistic and 'good works' ideas of mission."[27] Mission is not one among many activities of the church. Mission is the main activity for which the church exists. This way of thinking "became a way of criticizing the whole missionary enterprise as it was then understood in the churches. God had been working in the world all the time, and in all places, creating and redeeming, liberating and saving, whether the churches in the West realized this or not."[28] In other words, the church shifted from being the ultimate goal for God's salvific work in this world to becoming a vehicle for implementing God's mission in this world.[29] This mission is understood to consist of not just evangelism but also other aspects of God's work in the world. As it is well stated by Paul S. Chung, "Liberating words and healing deeds and actions belong together."[30] The personal observations of the author of this study lead him to believe that Slavic Baptists understand the church as the primary concern for God, as the main reason for Christ's sacrifice, and as the main goal for all missionary efforts. They see mission as being church-centered. The *missio Dei* concept provides a challenge for them and requires making adjustments in their theological views in order to accept this concept which is new to them. They need to learn to see the church as an instrument of God in accomplishing his mission in the world.

---

25. George F. Vicedom, *The Mission of God: An Introduction to a Theology of Mission* (St Louis, MO: Concordia, 1965), 5.

26. Philip Wickeri is Professor of Evangelism and Mission at San Francisco Theological Seminary and the Graduate Theological Union in Berkley, USA. He was formerly the Overseas Coordinator of the Amity Foundation (1985–1998), and worked in Asia for more than twenty years.

27. "Mission from the Margins. The *Missio Dei* in the Crisis of World Christianity," *International Review of Mission* 93, no. 369 (Apr 2004): 187; Nathan C. P. Frambach, "Being Church Today: Living God's Mission Where We Are," *Currents in Theology and Mission* 37, no. 1 (Fall 2010): 8.

28. Ibid., 187

29. Laing, "*Missio Dei*," 92.

30. "Engaging God's Mission and *Diakonia* in Life of Public Spheres: Justification and Economic Justice," *Dialog: Journal of Theology* 49, no. 2 (Summer 2010): 143.

Also, they need to accept the view of the mission of the church as being much broader than only evangelism.

1.1.3. The Trinitarian Understanding of *Missio Dei*

In the idea of *missio Dei*, the concept of mission was introduced as "derived from the very nature of God."[31] Such an approach puts mission work in the context of the doctrine of the Trinity rather than in ecclesiology or soteriology. The classical doctrine of Trinity means God the Father sending the Son, and God the Father and the Son sending the Spirit. The idea of *missio Dei* includes one more sending action: Father, Son, and Holy Spirit are sending the church into the world.[32] This linking of mission with the Trinity is a very important development in missionary thinking as participating in the sending of God. Mission is not primarily an activity of the church, but an attribute of God. God is understood as a missionary God. "It is not the church that has a mission of salvation to fulfill in the world; it is the mission of the Son and the Spirit through the Father that includes the church."[33] In such an understanding, mission becomes a movement from God to the world and the church is an instrument for that mission. "To participate in mission is to participate in the movement of God's love toward people, since God is a fountain of sending love."[34] Lesslie Newbigin emphasizes the importance of referring to the Trinitarian doctrine of God in the conversation about mission. According to Newbigin, "The church-centric view of missions has perhaps been too exclusively founded upon the person and work of Christ and has perhaps done less than justice to the whole trinitarian doctrine of God."[35] Despite the fact that the Trinitarian doctrine played a very important role in the Christian witness to a pagan world in the early church period "during the era of 'Christendom,' the doctrine of the Trinity has not occupied a comparable place in the thought of Christians."[36]

---

31. Bosch, *Transforming Mission*, 390.
32. Ibid.
33. Jürgen Moltmann, *The Church in the Power of the Spirit: A Contribution to Messianic Ecclesiology* (London: SCM, 1977), 64.
34. Bosch, *Transforming Mission*, 390.
35. *Trinitarian Faith and Today's Mission* (Richmond, VA: John Knox Press, 1964), 31.
36. Ibid., 32.

However, in the modern world, the doctrine of the Trinity has again become a starting point of preaching to non-Christians. Referring to the Trinity helps to explain to those who are accustomed to worshipping many gods (such as people in India) who Jesus is and his relation to God the Father.[37] Also, the Holy Spirit participates in the action of witnessing. He helps the evangelist present the gospel in the right way and he enables the listener "to receive the human words of the Evangelist as the Word of God."[38] Newbigin is convinced that "the doctrine of the triune nature of God helps us to understand and fulfill our missionary task in the face of issues which perplex us."[39] Other theologians also emphasize the Trinitarian nature of the *missio Dei*. Kirk insists very strongly, "The trinitarian nature of God's mission is indispensable if one is to understand why God acts in the world."[40] Bevans and Schroeder, pointing to the renewal in Trinitarian theology taking place today, stated that "it is possible to say that the understanding of mission as rooted in the trinitarian mission of God in the world is once again at the forefront of missiological thinking."[41] Robert J. Schreiter emphasizes the explicitly Trinitarian character of mission.[42] Bevans presents a Trinitarian approach to mission, emphasizing the mission of the Holy Spirit and arguing "for a temporal and experiential priority of the Spirit as the Mystery of the Father's love 'inside out' in the world, a presence that is given a concrete 'face' in the ministry, death and resurrection of Jesus."[43]

Wilbert Shenk, linking the renewal of the church to its mission, points to the Trinitarian nature of God's mission, saying: "The character of the mission of God is defined by the ministry of God's messiah, Jesus the servant, whose servanthood was empowered by the Holy Spirit."[44] By this Shenk shows that God's mission is accomplished not only by God the Father, but

---

37. Ibid., 33.
38. Ibid., 34.
39. Ibid., 77
40. J. Andrew Kirk, *What Is Mission? Theological Explorations* (Minneapolis, MN: Fortress, 2000), 27.
41. Bevans and Schroeder, *Constants in Context*, 291.
42. "Mission for the Twenty-First Century: A Catholic Perspective," in *Mission for the Twenty-First Century*, ed. Stephen Bevans and Roger Schroeder (Chicago: CCGM, 2001), 34.
43. Bevans and Schroeder, *Constants in Context*, 293.
44. Wilbert R. Shenk, *Changing Frontiers of Mission* (Maryknoll, NY: Orbis, 1999), 19.

also by God the Son, Jesus, and by God the Holy Spirit. All three persons of the Trinity participate in God's mission.

As cited above, theologians are in agreement that the triune God, God the Father, the Son, and the Holy Spirit, is the source of mission. He has sent the church in this world to serve his purpose and to accomplish his goal. This makes mission to be one of God's attributes, and not one of his actions in the world. A Trinitarian understanding changes the view of God's mission outside the church. Now this mission is viewed as being inclusive towards the world outside the church. Also, the nature of the relationship between God and the church is viewed differently: they are working together in the world.[45] A Trinitarian understanding of the *missio Dei*, according to Darrell Guder, requires more than a theology of the church that sees God's mission as inseparable from the existence and purpose of the church. It calls "for a re-casting of the theological disciplines for the sake of missional formation of church leaders."[46]

1.1.4. The Goal (Purpose) of *Missio Dei*

What does God want to accomplish through his mission? The answer to this question determines the goal of the church's mission. As Vicedom notes, "the meaning and content of [church] work is determined by the *missio Dei*."[47]

---

45. Michael W. Goheen, "The Future of Mission in the World Council of Churches: The Dialogue between Lesslie Newbigin and Konrad Raiser," *Mission Studies: Journal of the International Association for Mission Studies* 21, no. 1 (2004): 97–111. In his article, Goheen points to the fact that, along with producing all these positive results, the Trinitarian understanding of *missio Dei* became a source of disagreement between some theologians. Lesslie Newbigin sees the importance of a Trinitarian approach to mission. At the same time, he sees it as vitally important to keep the centrality and universality of Jesus Christ as a high priority in the ecumenical view of mission. Another ecumenical theologian, Konrad Raiser, also sees the importance of a Trinitarian approach to ecumenism and mission. However, his view of the role of the Holy Spirit is different from Newbigin's view. Raiser keeps the position that "recognizes the universal presence of the Holy Spirit among all peoples and religions, and so would cease to have a Christocentric focus" (ibid., 97). This devalues "the meaning of Jesus Christ and his atoning work on the cross" (ibid.). The difference in these views impacts the understanding of the role of the church in mission and its relation to the world. Also, it affects the basis on which the church engages in dialogue with other religions.

46. Darrell L. Guder, "*Missio Dei*: Integrating Theological Formation for Apostolic Vocation," *Missiology* 37, no. 1 (Jan 2009): 73. Guder makes a strong statement regarding the current status of mission in the church: "I find more and more reasons to insist that the challenge before us is not one merely of renewal, or re-tooling, but of conversion – the conversion of the church to its radically simple missional vocation" (ibid.).

47. Vicedom, *The Mission of God*, 8.

As shown above, the church is not the goal of the *missio Dei*. It is rather "the instrument and the sacrament of God in his dealing with the whole of creation."[48] Vicedom says,

> The mission, and with it the church, is God's very own work. We cannot speak of "the mission of the church," even less of "our mission." Both the church and the mission have their source in the loving will of God. Therefore we can speak of church and mission always only with the understanding that they are not independent entities. Both are only tools of God, instruments through which God carries out *His* mission. The church must first in obedience fulfill His missionary intention. Only then can she speak of her mission, since her mission is then included in the *missio Dei*.[49]

Because of this, the clear understanding of God's goal in the *missio Dei* is the key in keeping church life in alignment with God's will for the church.

Different interpretations for God's actions in creation and human history are provided by theologians. Vicedom says that "the goal of the *missio Dei* is to incorporate mankind in the *baseleia tou Theou* [the kingdom of God], and to convey to mankind the gifts thereof." [50] He also states, "the goal of the mission is the proclamation of the message to all mankind and gathering them into the church . . . However, Scripture is realistic enough not to leave us unaware that only a portion of mankind will accept the message. Since one cannot ascertain who is in this portion, the church has the responsibility for all of humanity."[51]

Johannes Verkuyl said that God "actively engaged in the reestablishment of His liberating dominion over the cosmos and all of humankind."[52]

---

48. *The Church for Others, and the Church for the World: A Quest for Structures for Missionary Congregations. Final report of the Western European Working Group and North American Working Group of the Department on Studies in Evangelism* (Geneva: World Council of Churches, 1967), 38.
49. Vicedom, *The Mission of God*, 6.
50. Ibid., 14.
51. Ibid., 103.
52. Johannes Verkuyl, "The Biblical Notion of Kingdom: Test of Validity for Theology of Religion," in *The Good News of the Kingdom: Mission Theology for the Third Millennium*, ed. Charles Van Engen, Dean S. Gilliland, and Paul Pierson (Maryknoll, NY: Orbis, 1993), 72.

Emilio Castro believes that "the purpose of God is . . . to gather the whole of creation under the Lordship of Christ Jesus in whom, by the power of the Holy Spirit, all are brought into communion with God."[53] According to Shenk, "the redemptive power of God is now being guided by a particular strategy in order to bring the divine purpose to completion by delivering the creation from the powers of decay and death."[54] The goal of God's mission is restoration of a right fellowship between God and human beings, liberation of human beings from sin, and bringing them into God's kingdom. Vicedom puts it in the following words: "The Bible in its totality ascribes only one intention to God: to save mankind."[55] Kirk states that "the mission of God flows directly from the nature of who God is," and the goal of God's mission could be identified as follows: "God's intention for the world is that in every respect it should show forth the way he is – love, community, equality, diversity, mercy, compassion and justice."[56]

As we can see, these different views of the purpose of the *missio Dei* refer to such aspects as bringing people into the kingdom of God, proclamation of the gospel, reestablishing God's liberating dominion, bringing people under the Lordship of Christ in communion with God, delivering the creation, saving mankind, demonstrating God's loving nature to people, and more. In summarizing them, it could be said that the purpose of the *missio Dei* is the establishment of the kingdom of God "as life free from the reign of all those forces which enslave humanity"[57] on earth. This view of the goal of *missio Dei* leads to the conclusion that the mission of the church is much broader than only oral proclamation of the gospel or evangelism. It should include all other aspects of the goal of the *missio Dei*.

1.1.5. Concerns about Using the *Missio Dei* Concept

As mentioned earlier, the *missio Dei* concept has been accepted by nearly all branches of Christianity. However, despite its wide popularity, there are

---

53. Emilio Castro, "Themes in Theology of Mission Arising out of San Antonio and Canberra," in *The Good News of the Kingdom*, 133.
54. *Mission in Bold Humility: David Bosch's Work Considered* (Maryknoll, NY: Orbis, 1996), 84.
55. Vicedom, *The Mission of God*, 4.
56. Kirk, *What Is Mission?*, 28.
57. Ibid., 29.

strong concerns expressed by some theologians about how this concept has been used.⁵⁸ Wilhelm Richebacher's observation is that different theologians "draw different and in part opposing conclusions. It seems that everyone reads into and out of this 'container definition' whatever he or she needs at the time."⁵⁹ Newbigin recognizes that the phrase *missio Dei*

> was sometimes used in such a way as to marginalize the role of the church. If God is indeed the true missionary, it was said, our business is not to promote the mission of the church, but to get out into the world, find out "what God is doing in the world," and join forces with him. And "what God is doing" was generally thought to be in the secular rather than in the religious sectors of human life. The effect, of course, was to look for what seemed to be the rising powers and to identify Christian missionary responsibility with support for a range of political and cultural developments, sometimes bizarre indeed.⁶⁰

---

58. Christopher Duraisingh, "From Church-Shaped Mission to Mission-Shaped Church," *Anglican Theological Review* 92, no. 1 (Winter 2010): 20 (7–28). Duraisingh, exploring "the ecclesiological and theological re-visioning necessary for a move from 'church-shaped' missions to a 'mission-shaped' church" (7), insists that "the new emphasis on the *missio Dei* has its own limitations due to the very different and at times contradicting interpretations of its theological basis, content, and import" (13). His concern is about this concept in itself not being "adequate for the transformation of churches into 'mission-shaped'" (ibid.). He suggests that for this kind of church transformation, the notion of "*concursus Dei*" is more effective than "*missio Dei*". Duraisingh believes "that the term can stand for God's everlasting creative-redemptive activity, God's walking with creation, thus leading creation toward God's own self-surpassing fullness. A reconstruction of the vision of *concursus Dei* will provide us with a pregnant motif for re-framing the shape of the church's responsive mission. It also can broaden our understanding of the nature of the relationship between God and the world and enrich our reformulation of the nature of the church within that relation. For at the base of *concursus Dei* is a vision of God's unceasing accompaniment with creation, calling and evoking its participation in God-movement as God leads it patiently and persuasively, both in judgment and grace, to its future in God's future" (20).

59. Wilhelm Richebacher, "Missio Dei: The Basis of Mission Theology or a Wrong Path?", *International Review of Mission* 92, no. 367 (2003): 589.

60. Lesslie Newbigin, *The Open Secret: An Introduction to the Theology of Mission* (Grand Rapids, MI: Eerdmans 1995), 18.

Jacques Matthey[61] notes that *missio Dei* theology "had contributed to sharpen the conflict between ecumenical and evangelical circles."[62] Matthey points to two major theological trends in reference to the *missio Dei*:

> The first can be summarized as follows: God is in mission through creation, and the sending of the Son and the Spirit to enable the church to witness in the world. This follows the sequence of John 20:21, referring back to 17:18–23. One can call it the "classical" way to refer to the *missio Dei*.
>
> The second trend . . . affirms that God is active in the secular political and social events of the world, through people of good will, whether Christians, people of other religious convictions or atheists. The church's mission is to discern the signs of the times and join God (or Christ) where God is active to transform the world towards shalom.[63]

According to Matthey, in reaction to the second stream of missiology, evangelicals organized themselves on the worldwide level into the Lausanne Movement. In a different paper Matthey, referring to the *missio Dei* underlines the importance of emphasizing "the vertical dimension of a transformative spirituality" in order to avoid "an over-estimation of humanity's capacities"[64] in mission. One evangelical/Lausanne Movement theologian, Arthur F. Glasser, strongly criticizes the WCC theologians for their role in, as he puts it, the "reconceptualization of *missio Dei*."[65] Admitting that a great achievement of the Willingen Conference was producing a Trinitarian approach to the theology of mission, Glasser argues, "In the years that followed, *Missio Dei* became a neologism that blurred God's providential governance

---

61. The Rev Jacques Matthey is executive secretary for ecumenical mission study and coordinator of the Mission and Evangelism team, WCC. He is also the editor of IRM.

62. Jacques Matthey, "Missiology in the World Council of Churches, Update: Presentation, History, Theological Background and Emphases of the Most Recent Mission Statement of the World Council of Churches (WCC)," *International Review of Mission* 90, no. 359 (October 2001): 429.

63. Ibid., 429.

64. Jacques Matthey, "Serving God's Mission Together in Christ's Way: Reflections on the Way to Edinburgh 2010," *International Review of Mission* 99, no. 1 (Apr 2010): 24.

65. "Conciliar Perspectives: The Road to Reconceptualization," in Arthur F. Glasser and Donald A. McGavran, *Contemporary Theologies of Mission* (Grand Rapids, MI: Baker, 1983), 93.

over the nations with the church's mission. Radical formulations came to the fore until *Missio Dei* was so reinterpreted and modified that it came to mean the action of God in carrying out His judgments and His ameliorating work among the nations in the revolutionary movements of our day."[66] He points to the fact that the missionary task of the church was secularized. As a result, the church's approach to the world changed. Churches did not need to confront the world with the call for repentance anymore. There was no significant difference between Christians and non-Christians, and the significant "activity of God was to be found in all movements leading to the humanization of individuals and society."[67] As a consequence of such a change in the interpretation of *missio Dei*, Glasser identifies the fact that the change in theology led to organizational changes. At the Third Assembly of the WCC, in New Delhi in 1961, the International Missionary Council (IMC) was integrated with the WCC. Because the church in its totality was seen now as the real missionary to the world, mission societies were no longer seen as necessary. According to Glasser, because of "the basic changes in the understanding of mission precipitated by the reconceptualization of *missio Dei*, the missionary involvement of churches within the conciliar movement went almost immediately into sharp decline."[68]

Another change that has taken place is how the proclamation of the gospel is now perceived. Based on the new interpretation of the *missio Dei* concept, it was suggested that words such as "evangelization," "witness," and "mission" be replaced by the word "presence." To illustrate this position, Glasser refers to the following definition of "presence," quoted from the World Student Christian Federation (WSCF) document *The Christian Community in the Academic World*. It describes "presence" as "the adventure of being there in the name of Christ, often anonymously, listening before we speak, hoping that men will recognize Jesus for what he is and stay where they are, involved in the fierce fight against all that dehumanizes, ready to act against demonic powers, to identify with the outcast, merciless in ridiculing modern idols and new myths."[69]

---

66. Ibid., 92.
67. Ibid., 93.
68. Ibid., 95.
69. Ibid., 96.

Overall, Glasser's position towards the WCC's understanding of the *missio Dei* could be summarized in the following way: "The reconceptualization of *Missio Dei* and subsequent confusion over the theology of the Christian mission pointed in only one direction: the rapid erosion (within the churches) of biblical conviction about mission."[70] This observation is affirmed by Matthey, who states that due to the fact that *missio Dei* theology in the West was linked to "a theology that gave a mainly positive appreciation of secularization, or even secularism, and favoured a non-religious approach to people and society, and thus criticized the church in an exaggerated way,"[71] evangelism is not on the mission agenda of mainline churches there. Bosch, as a representative of both camps, evangelical and ecumenical, identifies the conflict which arose among some theologians because of the further development of the *missio Dei* concept.

The first theologians to use the term *missio Dei*, Barth and Hartenstein, "had hoped to protect mission against secularization and horizontalization, and to reserve it exclusively for God."[72] However, this did not happen. After the Willingen Conference, the concept of *missio Dei* gradually underwent modification. Strong emphasis has been given to God's concern about the entire world, to all people in all aspects of their existence. Mission has been interpreted as "God's turning to the world in respect of creation, care, redemption and consummation. It takes place in ordinary human history, not exclusively in and through the church."[73]

Theologians and missionaries supporting the wider understanding of the concept "tended to radicalize the view that the *missio Dei* was larger than the mission of the church, even to the point of suggesting that it excluded the church's involvement."[74] Such developments upset theologians who followed in the footsteps of Barth and Hartenstein. According to Bosch, these developments prompted L. A. Hoedemaker to challenge the usefulness of the *missio Dei* concept[75] because this concept "could be used by people

---

70. Ibid., 121.
71. Matthey, "God's Mission Today," 580.
72. Bosch, *Transforming Mission*, 392.
73. Ibid., 390.
74. Ibid., 392.
75. Ibid.

who subscribe to mutually exclusive theological positions."[76] Hoedemaker was correct, to a certain degree. However, as Bosch concludes, "it cannot be denied that the *missio Dei* notion has helped to articulate the conviction that neither the church nor any other human agent can ever be considered the author or bearer of mission. Mission is, primarily and ultimately, the work of the Triune God, Creator, Redeemer, and Sanctifier, for the sake of the world, a ministry in which the church is privileged to participate."[77]

Christopher Ducker points to two important areas in the discussion of the *missio Dei* concept that create a divergence between missiologists. He states,

> Firstly, is the issue of whether the Church has a privileged position and special relationship within the *missio Dei* (as is argued, for example, by Catholic theologian Anekwe Oborji), but which some may regard as trying to introduce the *missio ecclesiae* in, so to speak, via the back door. Secondly, is the issue of whether God's missionary purposes are specifically salvific, or whether His creational (and thereafter sustaining) purposes can be considered part of His *missio*. It is at these two points that theologians tend to diverge.[78]

Tormod Engelsviken points to one of the interpretations of the *missio Dei* which addresses other religions. According to him, for some theologians the *missio Dei* concept allows one to conclude that "the great religious traditions of the world must be seen as legitimate divine revelations and as ways to salvation."[79] Those who keep this theological position argue that what God is doing through the church is not the only way God is working in the world.[80] They state that "God's mission has not [been] and cannot be restricted to one geographical area or one historical or religious context. It has also taken

---

76. Ibid.

77. Ibid.

78. Christopher Ducker, "Explain the Thinking Behind Mission as Missio Dei," http://www.theduckers.org/media/missio%20dei.pdf (accessed May 2012).

79. Tormod Engelsviken, "*Missio Dei*: The Understanding and Misunderstanding of a Theological Concept in European Churches and Missiology," *International Review of Mission* 92, no. 367 (2003): 493.

80. Laing, "*Missio Dei*," 97.

place through other religions. Islam, Hinduism and Buddhism may also be seen as the mission of God."[81] Engelsviken warns that this "pluralistic and inherently relativistic religious understanding of *missio Dei* may form a present and future challenge to a biblically based missiology."[82]

This overview of concerns that theologians are expressing today about the understanding of the concept of *missio Dei* shows that there is a difference between how this concept was understood originally and how it is understood now.[83] Even today, variations exist in its understanding. This concept is like a double-edged sword. It could be used for empowering church participation in the mission of God or it could marginalize the church's role in this mission. A thoughtful approach is necessary in using this concept. It should be properly defined when being used. For Slavic Baptists, such a possibility of dual interpretation of the concept of *missio Dei* provides a serious challenge. They are more accustomed to the "black-or-white" approach to theological questions, and for them to accept a concept that could lead to different conclusions requires courage. It could be a source of controversy among them.

1.1.6. Conclusion

As the result of a long and complicated process of historical development of missiological thought, the concept of *missio Dei* provides theologians and the whole Christian community with a richer understanding of the notion of mission and its source, scope, depth, and nature. It puts God in the right position in relation to mission. He is the source of it. Nobody else can claim ownership of mission except God himself. The Trinitarian nature of God

---

81. Engelsviken, "*Missio Dei*," 493.

82. Ibid., 494.

83. Nico Smith, "From *Missio Dei* to *Missio Hominum*: En Route in Christian Mission and Missiology," *Missionalia* 30, no. 1 (Apr 2002): 21. In his article, Smith describes how his understanding of mission as *missio Dei* has been transformed to *missio hominum*. Starting from mission of God in this world, he eventually came to understand that it is the responsibility of all people to be involved in the process of renovation of this world. According to Smith, "*missio hominum* emphasizes the fact that all people from all religions and even without religion have the responsibility to participate in God's creative dynamic in creation" and "mission will have to be understood as an action of all religions, not trying to propagate their own religions but to transform the world as participation in God's creative transformation of creations, drawing it towards its fulfillment" (ibid.). Obviously, such a position is far away from the original understanding of the concept of *missio Dei* and its practical implications.

provides the framework for mission. This could be correctly understood only in the light of the doctrine of the Trinity.

At the same time, different interpretations of the concept of *missio Dei* and relations between the *missio Dei* and *missio ecclesiae* create divergence among theologians and missiologists and even stimulated a division which took place between the WCC and evangelicals/the Lausanne Movement. Despite this fact, a broad consensus exists among theologians of different Christian traditions that the concept of *missio Dei* is a significant theological development and has important practical implications in the life of the church.

Similar to how Israel was a chosen nation in order to be God's representative among other nations during the Old Testament period, the church is chosen by God to be sent into this world and to witness about Christ during the post-Pentecost time.[84] As Oliver Byar Bowh Si puts it, "only in *missio Dei* does the church have its origin and movement."[85] Ducker states: "The Church's task is specific and divinely mandated. Consequently, the Church cannot be seen as just one of several different arenas where God is at work; its status is more privileged and its responsibility more elevated. That responsibility includes sharing the Gospel of Jesus Christ with people of all nations; but it also includes recognizing where God is at work through 'secular' or non-church forces and discerning where it must participate and encourage."[86]

The concept of *missio Dei* needs to be introduced to Slavic Baptist immigrant church leaders. Taking into consideration the fact that this concept has different interpretations by different theologians, as shown above, this introduction should be done wisely. There is a risk that the Slavic Christian community will reject this concept, seeing it as potentially leading to

---

84. The author of this study has always viewed the mission of the church as being done in obedience to Christ's Great Commission. However, introduction to the view of the *missio Dei* has deepened the author's understanding of the issue of mission. In terms of the relations between the *missio Dei* and the mission of the church, the author keeps the position that although the church is not the ultimate goal of the *missio Dei* and not the only means God is using in the world, it has a special role within the *missio Dei*.

85. Oliver Byar Bowh Si, "Mission as Transformation: An Exploration of the Relationship between Mission and Development," *International Review of Mission* 97, no. 384/385 (Jan–Apr 2008): 95.

86. Ducker, *Explain the Thinking*, 5.

minimizing the role of the church in mission and to promoting collaboration with other religions.

1.2. The Kingdom of God, the World, and the Mission of the Church

Kirk states, "In contemporary mission thinking no one would contemplate trying to grasp the *missio Dei* without a thorough reference to the rule or reign of God."[87] He acknowledges "the complexity of the relationship between kingdom, Church and world in the mission of God" and calls for "some kind of theological integration."[88] Engelsviken points to the fact that the *missio Dei* concept is interpreted differently, depending on one's interpretation of the kingdom of God.[89]

1.2.1. What Is the Kingdom of God?

Bertil Ekstrom, making an observation about the historical development of the concept of the kingdom of God, shows that this understanding went through a long transformation process among Christians. Starting with Augustine, one of the early Fathers, who identified the kingdom of God with the church and believed that "as the church grows, the kingdom grows and is extended in the world,"[90] the definition of the kingdom of God has experienced significant changes. Some Protestant theologians shared the Augustinian view but believed "that the kingdom of God may be identified only with the true church, i.e., the professing church."[91] Some believed "that it is the mission of the Church to win the entire world to Christ and thus transform the world into the kingdom of God."[92] Others held the position that the kingdom of God is "an apocalyptic realm to be inaugurated by a supernatural act of God when a new heavenly order of existence begins."[93]

---

87. Kirk, *What Is Mission?*, 29.
88. Ibid., 35.
89. Engelsviken, "*Missio Dei*," 483.
90. Bertil Ekstrom, "The Kingdom of God and the Church Today," *Evangelical Review of Theology* 27, no. 4 (Oct 2003): 293.
91. Ibid.
92. Ibid.
93. Ibid.

For them this kingdom is "altogether future and supernatural." Followers of Liberation Theology "define the kingdom of God as this world totally and globally transformed in its political, social and economic structures"[94] and criticize the traditional view of God's kingdom "as being a gnostic spiritualized view."[95] According to J. Andrew Kirk, the kingdom of God can be described "as life free from the reign of all those forces which enslave humanity."[96] Referring to the New Testament texts Kirk explains:

> These "powers" are understood as enemies which act against human life here and now – the final enemy being death (1 Cor 15:26). Elsewhere, Paul defines the powers as all those aspects of life which enslave: sin (Rom 7:14), the law (Rom 7:10), vanity and corruption (Rom 8:19–21), this present evil age (Gal 1:4), weak and miserable principles (Gal 4:9), spiritual forces of evil (Eph 6:12). By contrast, the kingdom is life where human beings are no longer subjected to destructive forces.[97]

The kingdom of God is characterized by the control of the Holy Spirit and by the complete and permanent presence of "justice, peace and joy."[98] Craig Ott echoes this view of the kingdom, saying: "The concept of the kingdom of God captures in a single phrase the divine intent to bring all things under his rule, to reconcile all things to himself, to restore that which is fallen and corrupted, and to overthrow all powers in opposition to him and his reign of peace, joy, and righteousness."[99]

Addressing the question of whether the kingdom of God is already present in the world or if it will come in the future, George E. Ladd states that "the redemptive reign of God is dynamically active to establish his rule among men, and that this kingdom, which will appear as an apocalyptic act at the end of the age, has already come into human history in the person and mission of Jesus to overcome evil, to deliver men from its power, and to bring

---

94. Ibid.
95. Ibid., 294.
96. Kirk, *What Is Mission?*, 29.
97. Ibid.
98. Ibid.
99. Craig Ott, *Encountering Theology of Mission: Biblical Foundations, Historical Developments, and Contemporary Issues* (Grand Rapids, MI: Baker Academic, 2010), 86.

them into the blessings of God's reign."[100] Charles Van Engen supports this view, pointing to the consensus taking place among contemporary Christian theologians about the kingdom of God "as both present, inaugurated, and begun, and at the same time eschatological and coming."[101]

1.2.2. Relation of the Church to the Kingdom of God

George Eldon Ladd argues that "the relationship between the Church and the Kingdom of God must be clearly established."[102] He describes these relationships in the following way: "The Kingdom of God is first of all the divine redemptive rule manifested in Christ, and it is secondly the realm of sphere in which the blessings of the divine rule may be experienced."[103] The church is the community governed by Christ, the King, and where "the blessings of the divine rule" are experienced. "The church is constituted by those who are entering and receiving the reign of God. It is where the children of the reign corporately manifest the presence and characteristic features of God's reign."[104] Van Engen insists that we "cannot fully understand the breadth or depth of the congregation's mission unless we see it in relation to the kingdom of God in the world."[105] Describing the role of the church in relation to God's kingdom he states that as "the missionary people of God, local congregations are branch offices of the kingdom, the principal instrument, anticipatory, sign, and primary locus of the coming of the kingdom."[106] Bertil Ekstrom refers to the church as an agent of the kingdom and as "the Body of Christ, the community of the King that makes the kingdom visible, attractive and present in our fallen world."[107] According to Stephanie Spellers, the relationship between the church, mission and the

---

100. George E. Ladd, *A Theology of the New Testament* (Grand Rapids, MI: Eerdmans, 1974), 91.

101. Charles Van Engen, *God's Missionary People: Rethinking the Purpose of the Local Church* (Grand Rapids, MI: Baker, 1991), 108.

102. George E. Ladd, *The Gospel of the Kingdom* (Grand Rapids, MI: Eerdmans, 1971), 114.

103. Ibid.

104. Darrell L. Guder, ed., *Missional Church: A Vision for the Sending of the Church in North America* (Grand Rapids, MI: Eerdmans, 1998), 99.

105. Van Engen, *God's Missionary People*, 101.

106. Ibid.

107. Ekstrom, "The Kingdom of God and the Church Today," *Evangelical Review of Theology* 27, no. 4 (Oct 2003): 301.

kingdom of God could be described this way: "The identity of the church is wrapped up in mission – praying, practicing, and going forth in love to heal, reconcile, and make known the always-breaking-in reign of God."[108] Bertil Ekstrom sees the church as part of the kingdom of God and "not merely an instrument but an agent of transformation of the kingdom, having the responsibility to make the kingdom visible."[109]

It could be concluded that the kingdom of God is not identified with the church. It is larger than the church. However, the church is part of the kingdom and is called to proclaim it, to witness about the kingdom, to make it visible through following kingdom principles in the church's internal life, and to be an agent of the kingdom.[110]

1.2.3. Relation of the Church and the Kingdom of God to the *Missio Dei*

Engelsviken points to fact that the *missio Dei* concept is interpreted differently depending on one's interpretation of the kingdom of God. The kingdom of God could be understood "as the reign or rule of God over the whole of creation (sometimes including redemption), or the present and final salvation that God offers in Christ (sometimes including ethical and social transformation)."[111] Kirk points to the fact that a strong debate took place within the church during the second half of the twentieth century on the subject of the relationship between the *missio Dei*, the church, and the world.[112] He explains that there "have been times in the past when Christians assumed that all God's purposes would be fulfilled exclusively through the

---

108. Stephanie Spellers, "The Church Awake: Becoming the Missional People of God," *Anglican Theological Review* 92, no. 1 (Winter 2010): 33.

109. Ekstrom, "Kingdom of God," 301.

110. On different perspectives of ecclesial appropriation of Christ's vision of the kingdom of God, see Parush R. Parushev, *Christianity in Europe: The Way We Are Now. With a Response by Vija Herefoss*, in the Crowther Centre Monographs Series, Vol. 9 (Oxford: Church Missionary Society, 2009). For the practices of social visibility of the kingdom's realities, see Lina Andronovienė and Parush R. Parushev, "Church, State, and Culture: On the Complexities of Post-Soviet Evangelical Social Involvement," *Theological Reflections: EAAA Journal of Theology* 3 (2004): 174–227 (in English, Russian and Lithuanian); and Parush R. Parushev, "Witness, Worship and Presence: On the Integrity of Mission in Contemporary Europe," *Mission Studies* 24, no. 2 (2007): 305–332.

111. Engelsviken, "*Missio Dei*," 483.

112. Kirk, *What Is Mission?*, 33.

church."[113] As shown above, some theological positions identified the kingdom of God with the church, while others saw it as a pure eschatological event in the future. There are positions that see the role of the church in the *missio Dei* as minimal.

> These see God's direct activity in the world as the clue to his mission. They deny the distinction sometimes drawn between "salvation history," which is focused on the community which God is saving, and "world history," which is focused on the rest of humanity alienated from the ways of God and heading for judgment. In their thinking, the place of salvation is the world, and God works out his purposes through a process of humanization through which the conditions are created, step by step, to make human flourishing possible.[114]

As shown above, in the section of this chapter addressing the issue of the *missio Dei*, the more balanced modern approach to this subject is to see God acting through the church in the world and at the same time acting directly in the world. The church has a special place in the *missio Dei* as a locus and the sign of the kingdom of God. The church as an agent of the kingdom is called to share the good news about an existing possibility to enter God's kingdom through faith in Christ. Kirk states that the church "intentionally bears witness to the meaning and relevance of the kingdom, while not itself being identical with that kingdom."[115] Kirsteen Kim claims that "The church came into being as a result of the purpose of God to bring salvation to the world. The missionary intention of God is the raison d'être of the church, and to fulfill God's missionary purpose is its aim."[116] In the previous part of this chapter (section 1.1.4.) it was shown that the purpose of the *missio Dei* is the establishment of the kingdom of God, "as life free from the reign of all those forces which enslave humanity"[117] on earth.

---

113. Ibid.
114. Ibid.
115. Ibid., 36.
116. Kirsteen Kim, "Mission Theology of the Church," *International Review of Mission* 99, no. 1 (Apr 2010): 42.
117. Ibid., 29.

It could be concluded that the goal of the *missio Dei* is establishing the kingdom of God and that the church is called to participate in this process. Although the kingdom of God is larger than the church, the church is a community of people submitting their lives under the rule of the King, Christ, and living in accordance with the kingdom principles. This kingdom community as shown above is called to participate in the *missio Dei* serving this world.

1.2.4. A Missiological Model of the Church

Because of its role in the *missio Dei* the church has a missional nature. The apostle Peter describes the church's call in the following way: "But you are a chosen race, a royal priesthood, a holy nation, a people for his own possession, that you may proclaim the excellencies of him who called you out of darkness into his marvelous light."[118] This text clearly identifies the church's purpose – to proclaim the gospel. The widely used expression of Emil Brunner, "The Church exists by mission as fire exists by burning,"[119] boldly points to the missional nature of the church. Bertil Ekstrom shares this position, saying: "I believe that we still need to stress the fact that the church has the responsibility for the expansion of the kingdom and a vocation given by God to spread the Good News of salvation to all. The whole church taking the whole gospel to the whole man in the whole world."[120] Darrell L. Guder shares the same conviction, stating that "the church of any place bears a missional calling and responsibility for its own place as well as for distant places . . . 'Mission' is not something the church does, a part of its total program. No, the church's essence is missional, for the calling and sending action of God forms its identity."[121] Arthur Glasser proclaims that "the church is nothing less than the missionary people of the kingdom of God. The church does not establish the kingdom. It is rather the custodian of the good news. It bears witness to the fact that the kingdom has already

---

118. 1 Pet 2:9 (ESV).
119. Quoted in Van Engen, *God's Missionary People*, 27.
120. Ekstrom, "Kingdom of God," 299.
121. Guder, *Missional Church*, 82.

been set up by its King."[122] Bertil Ekstrom sees the church being called to do the following:

> What we need to do is to struggle for the coming of the kingdom, the implantation of the values and the principles of the kingdom, knowing nevertheless that the final establishment of the kingdom of Christ is an eschatological reality. The church must defend and struggle for the issues of restoration of individuals, families and nations. Christians must be paladins of peace and reconciliation, of release from political oppression and freedom from spiritual bondage, of social justice, of equality between races and gender, of concern about the environment and of religious liberty.[123]

All these statements very strongly point to the truth that the church has a missional nature. Without participating in the process of spreading the good news about the kingdom among people who are not yet part of God's kingdom, the church acts against its own nature, cannot fulfill its role in the *missio Dei* and is disobedient to its King, Christ.

1.2.5. Making Disciples – A Key Aspect of Mission

Commissioning his apostles to go into the world to proclaim the gospel, Jesus Christ established a clear goal: "make disciples of all nations."[124] Making disciples is a key aspect of the mission of the church. Van Engen states: "Thus Church, mission, and the kingdom of God are to build one another. They are not identical, yet intimately intertwine in God's mission through God's people in God's world. The Church, therefore, must be understood to be the missionary community of the disciples of the King."[125] The missional calling of the church can be fulfilled only through those who have submitted their lives to Jesus, through his disciples. Kirk points to the truth that the church "is called to the risky task of being the living interpretation

---

122. Arthur F. Glasser with Charles E. Van Engen, Dean S. Gilliland, and Shawn B. Redford, *Announcing the Kingdom: The Story of God's Mission in the Bible* (Grand Rapids, MI: Baker Academic, 2003), 225.
123. Ekstrom, "Kingdom of God," 304.
124. Matt 28:19a.
125. Van Engen, *God's Missionary People*, 108.

of that kingdom; otherwise, the kingdom can be little more than a slogan, ideology or human programme of betterment."[126] To be "the living interpretation of the kingdom" means living in accordance with the kingdom's rules and expectations – in other words, to be the King's disciples. The widely accepted position among Slavic Baptists in America and in the homeland is that for somebody to become a disciple of Christ means to go through the conversion experience. Thus, making disciples means leading people to conversion. Glasser emphasizes that "the church has long understood its mission to involve working for the conversion of non-Christians. Disciples must be made of every people. Not a few biblical texts underscore this obligation."[127] However, this view has been challenged widely, with some arguing "that the conversion of non-Christians is neither necessary nor desirable."[128] Supporters of this view point to such reasons as Christianity being too closely identified with Western colonialism in the past; ethical social values similar to Christian values being present in non-Christian faiths; and "disillusionment with the institutional church."[129] "As a result of this ferment, the religious debate on conversion has shifted in many circles from individual conversion to Christ, followed by incorporation into the church, to speaking of 'conversion' as involvement with a socially concerned community, whether or not its members profess any allegiance to the person of Jesus Christ. Cultural pluralism and religious relativism have diverted many from making Jesus Christ the center of their approach to the subject of conversion."[130]

Such a "secularized" understanding of conversion is foreign to Slavic Baptists. As mentioned above, they believe that without a personal relationship with Christ it is impossible to be his disciple. This position is supported by both Old and New Testaments which clearly call people to conversion in order to bring their relationship with God into right order. Glasser includes conversion in the process of becoming Christ's disciple, saying: "Jesus' call to conversion involved turning around, accepting the

---

126. Kirk, *What Is Mission?*, 36.
127. Glasser et al., *Announcing the Kingdom*, 353.
128. Ibid.
129. Ibid., 353–354.
130. Ibid., 354.

reality of God's rule, and then willingly becoming an expression and extension of that rule in participation with a local congregation of his people."[131] Conversion is a process that takes place in the heart and mind of the person who experiences a personal encounter with Jesus. This internal process has a very visible external expression in the life of the person. Glasser describes it in the following way:

> Viewed externally, conversion involves a process, turning, reviewing, moving forward. More is involved than mere repentance over the past and new resolutions about the future. There is the deliberate disposition of heart and mind to surrender to the will and power of God through encounter with Jesus Christ and then, under his direction, to turn away from the things that are not of God. This reorientation of the whole life and personality is the sine qua non of entrance into the Kingdom of God (John 3:3).[132]

To be a disciple of Jesus means to strive to become Christlike in all aspects of life. Guder states that "the church is challenged to form a people with distinctive habits of the heart. As an alternative social reality, the church is called to teach people how to talk, how to act, how to fight, how to love, how to see the world in a peculiar way – a Christlike way."[133]

It could be concluded that making disciples of Christ is a very important aspect of mission in order for the church to be able to fulfill its missionary call representing and expanding the kingdom of God in the world as part of its role in the *missio Dei*. In chapter 2 of this thesis, it will be shown that the mission of the church is multifaceted and challenging. In order to successfully accomplish it, the church should consist of dedicated disciples who have experienced personal conversion and profess full allegiance to the person of Jesus Christ.

In the following part of the chapter, the author will explore and compare the positions of three ecclesiological groups on this complex issue of the

---

131. Ibid., 355.
132. Ibid., 357.
133. Guder, *Missional Church*, 152.

relationship between kingdom, church and world in the mission of God, as reflected in their basic statements.

1.2.6. The World Council of Churches (WCC)

The WCC position on the issue of the relationship between the kingdom of God, world, church, and mission was expressed at the World Conference on Mission and Evangelism in Melbourne, Australia, in 1980. In its report called "Your Kingdom Come: Mission Perspectives," there is an invitation for churches to pray for God's kingdom to come and a call to work actively together for its coming. As a starting point in their discussion, the authors of the report state that the kingdom of God "brings justice, love, peace and joy, and freedom from the grasp of principalities and powers, those demonic forces which place human lives and institutions in bondage and infiltrate their very textures."[134] Based on this statement, they claim that God is on the side of the poor, and the coming of his kingdom is their hope. At the same time, its arrival means a time of judgment for the rich.[135] The report emphasizes that the church "is commissioned to disciple the nations, so that others may know that the kingdom of God has already drawn near and that its signs and first fruits can be seen in the world around the churches, as well as in their own life. Mission that is conscious of the kingdom will be concerned for liberation, not oppression; justice, not exploitation; fullness, not deprivation; freedom, not slavery; health, not disease; life, not death."[136]

Churches are praised for being active in the realization of the good news in life through witness, the sharing of their goods despite their own poverty (like the base communities in Latin America), redistribution of their wealth (if churches are wealthy) for the benefit of the self-development of the poor, and challenging transnational corporations. The report endorses the fact that through "ecumenical bodies, churches have joined in the search for a new social, political and economic order, and committed themselves to support those organizations, churches and national leaders that share this vision."[137]

---

134. "Your Kingdom Come: Report on the World Conference on Mission and Evangelism, Melbourne, Australia, 1980," in *New Directions in Mission and Evangelization 1*, ed. James A. Scherer and Stephen B. Bevans (Maryknoll, NY: Orbis, 1992), 27.

135. "Your Kingdom Come," 28.

136. Ibid., 29.

137. Ibid.

At the same time, the report condemns churches that are indifferent to the situation of the poor. It condemns churches that, in one way or another, assist the forces of social and economic establishments which exploit the poor, the missionary enterprise of the churches which "has been financed with the fruits of exploitation, conducted in league with oppressive forces, and has failed to join the struggle of the poor and oppressed against injustice."[138] The report provides the following recommendations for churches: (1) become churches in solidarity with the struggles of the poor; (2) join the struggle against the powers of exploitation and impoverishment; (3) establish a new relationship with the poor inside the churches;[139] and (4) pray and work for the kingdom of God.[140]

This brief overview of the report on the issue of the kingdom of God shows that the WCC's position has a strong emphasis on present, physical and social aspects of the kingdom, and not so much on its spiritual characteristics (like a practical acknowledgment of the lordship of Christ in the personal life of believers and their personal relationship with him). Its focus is on the kingdom's present manifestation and not so much its future triumph when Christ will return. The primary role of the church, which is seen as "a sign of the kingdom,"[141] is to be an agent of bringing the new order to the world with justice for all. This strong emphasis on the physical and social aspects of the kingdom is materialized today and sounds similar to the ideas of the social gospel. The author of this study understands that promoting the physical aspect of the kingdom should be in balance with promoting its spiritual realm. Without giving appropriate attention to the spiritual aspect of God's kingdom in its present and future realization, the church could become over-involved in political and social action in society and could undermine its status as a witness to the eternal reality of the kingdom. Slavic Baptists who strongly emphasize the eschatological aspect of the kingdom would be in conflict with the WCC position.

---

138. Ibid., 30.
139. Ibid.
140. Ibid., 31.
141. Ibid.

1.2.7. The Evangelical/Lausanne Movement

The Lausanne Movement's position on this issue is expressed in the World Evangelical Fellowship document "Consultation on the Church in Response to Human Need," Wheaton, 1983.[142] It affirms that "the Kingdom of God is both present and future, both societal and individual, both physical and spiritual."[143] It recognizes that in the past, evangelicals neglected the present, the societal, and the physical aspects of the God's kingdom. Now they are trying to address them as well. They see God's activity in history as being focused on the church. However, they do not see it being limited to the church itself. They state that "the church is called to exist for the sake of its Lord and for the sake of humankind" and that it is called "to infuse the world with hope, for both this age and the next."[144]

Another document that reflects the evangelical position on the issue discussed is the "Iguassu Affirmation."[145] In the "Declarations" section of the document, it is affirmed that the lordship of Christ (read "kingdom of Christ or kingdom of God") must "be proclaimed to the whole world, inviting all to be free from the bondage of sin and the dominion of evil in order to serve the Lord for His glory."[146] The holistic nature of the gospel is emphasized, saying that all the Scriptures "demonstrate God's concern with the whole person in the whole of society." It is further acknowledged "that material blessings come from God, but prosperity should not be equated with godliness."[147] Referring to human governments, it is stated that although they are appointed by God, they are acting out of fallenness, and Christians are called to "pray for those in authority and work for truth and justice."[148]

In the "Commitments" section of the document, the participants committed themselves "to a renewed emphasis on God-centered missiology" and to "a new study of the operation of the Trinity in the redemption of the

---

142. In Scherer and Bevans, *New Directions in Mission and Evangelization 1*, 289.
143. Ibid., 290.
144. Ibid.
145. Richard Tiplady, "Trends in Evangelical Missiology: The Iguassu Affirmation," paper presented to the Standing Committee of the Churches' Commission on Mission, http://www.tiplady.org.uk/pdfs/Iguassu_trends.pdf (accessed May 2012).
146. Ibid.
147. Ibid.
148. Ibid.

human race and the whole of creation, as well as to understand the particular roles of Father, Son and Spirit in mission to this fallen world."[149] The authors of the document affirmed that the "Church in mission is central to God's plan for the world." They committed themselves to strengthening the "ecclesiology in mission, and to encourage the global church to become a truly missionary community in which all Christians are involved in mission."[150] Addressing the issue of growing control in the global economy, the document calls Christians to be aware of the consequences of wealth and poverty. The participants committed themselves "to address the realities of world poverty and oppose policies that serve the powerful rather than the powerless. It is the responsibility of the church in each place to affirm the meaning and value of a people, especially where indigenous cultures face extinction. We call all Christians to commit themselves to reflect God's concern for justice and the welfare of all peoples."[151]

The issue of care for the environment is addressed as well. Proclaiming that the earth belongs to God and that the gospel is good news for all creation, the authors of the document call all Christians to take their part in their God-given responsibility "to all humanity to care for the earth" and to commit "themselves to ecological integrity in practicing responsible stewardship of creation, and we encourage Christians in environmental care and protection initiatives."[152]

Both documents show that evangelicals are trying to demonstrate a balanced approach towards the issue of the kingdom of God, insisting that the church should, on the one hand, call people to true repentance and faith, and, on the other hand, equip its people "to challenge the forces of evil and injustice."[153] Such a balanced approach to the kingdom of God makes the evangelical position different from the WCC position. Also, while the WCC position strongly emphasizes God's work in the world outside of the church, evangelicals put the church in the central role of accomplishing

---

149. Ibid.
150. Ibid.
151. Ibid.
152. Ibid.
153. "Consultation on the Church in Response to Human Need," session 52, 290. https://www.lausanne.org/content/statement/transformation-the-church-in-response-to-human-need.

God's mission in this world. Based on the author's understanding of the Slavic Baptist view on the subject, this position would be more acceptable to Slavic Baptists than the WCC position.

1.2.8. The Anabaptists

The Anabaptist position on the discussed issue is not easy to identify from the basic documents. The Anabaptist world is very diverse and not many of the statements reflect a position common to all participants of the Anabaptist movement. For this study, when possible, the materials of the Mennonite World Conference, as the largest body of Anabaptist churches, will be used. However, these materials lack a well-developed analysis of the issue of the kingdom of God in its relation to the church. For this reason, the work of one of the Anabaptist representatives, John Driver, will be used here.

In the Anabaptist view, according to Driver, the kingdom of God is the presence of the future among people today. The future has been materialized in the coming of Jesus Christ and its presence gives the church hope and determines the mission of the church. In this aspect, the Anabaptist position is similar to the position of other branches of Christianity. Driver underlines that God's kingdom "is not a strictly future reality, nor is it primarily an inner reality limited to the hearts of individuals."[154] The kingdom of God should become visible through the people of God who experience his restorative power, and who live under his salvific rule, reflect its character, and demonstrate God's intention for all humanity.[155] What makes the Anabaptist position unique and different from other positions is its emphasis on the practical application of the Sermon on the Mount in the life of the followers of Jesus.[156] The everyday application of the teachings of Jesus provided in the Sermon is a source of debate among theologians. Craig S. Keener points to

---

154. John Driver, "The Kingdom of God: Goal of Messianic Mission," in *The Transfiguration of Mission: Biblical, Theological and Historical Foundations*, ed. Wilbert R. Shenk (Scottsdale, PA: Herald, 1993), 96.

155. Ibid.

156. Glen H. Stassen and David P. Gushee, *Kingdom Ethics: Following Jesus in Contemporary Context* (Downers Grove, IL: InterVarsity, 2003), 30–31. The authors argue that "the way of discipleship and the commands of Jesus are most explicitly taught" (30) in the Sermon on the Mount and this should be a foundation for Christian ethics. They insist, "We believe that Jesus offered not hard sayings or high ideals but concrete ways to practice God's will and be delivered from the bondage of sin. In other words, he taught his followers how to participate in God's reign" (31).

the existence of at least sixty-five different interpretations.[157] While Harvey King McArthur lists twelve basic positions on this issue,[158] Bert Friesen suggests only five approaches to the interpretation and application of the Sermon on the Mount: the liberal approach, the dispensational approach, the interim ethics approach, the existential approach, and the Anabaptist/Mennonite approach.[159] If the first four approaches are more common to the WCC and evangelical/Lausanne Movement churches, the last is distinctive of the Anabaptists. The Anabaptist/Mennonite approach calls for the literal observation of the Sermon's teaching as much as it is possible in the life of believers. This teaching of Jesus is for Anabaptists not "a utopian program for the future." It is a description of life in the community of those among whom the kingdom of God is present. It offers "a foretaste of the fulfillment to come."[160]

Similar to the position of other groups, as Driver states, Anabaptists see the church as always being challenged in addressing the tension between the "already" and the "not yet" aspects of the kingdom of God in its life and mission. When the church concentrates too much of its attention on the "already" aspect of the kingdom of God, the church itself becomes the center of its own concern and activity and "the Church sees itself as an agent of the kingdom and the dispenser of salvation rather than a sign of the kingdom and a witness to God's amazing grace."[161] On the other hand, over-concentration on the "not yet" aspect puts the church in the position of fleeing the real world "into an unreal and spiritualized sphere"; instead of "offering a message of hope for the present, the church tends to limit its offer of hope to the future."[162] A balance between these two aspects should be sought. Driver states that the church could be referred to as the people of the kingdom or the community of the kingdom. Although the church and the kingdom are closely related, they are not identical. The church

---

157. Crag S. Keener, *The Gospel of Matthew* (Grand Rapids, MI: Eerdmans, 2009), 160.

158. Harvey King McArthur, *Understanding the Sermon on the Mount* (Westport, CT: Greenwood Press, 1978), 37.

159. Bert Friesen, "Approaches to the Interpretation and Application of the Sermon on the Mount," *Direction* 10, no. 2 (Apr 1981): 19–26.

160. Driver, "Kingdom of God," 97.

161. Ibid.

162. Ibid.

is called to teach and preach the gospel of the kingdom and to continue "Jesus' kingdom activity."[163] Its authority is not its own, but is ultimately the authority of the kingdom. The church should submit itself to this kingdom authority and never forget its servant role.[164]

Driver shows that there are two kingdoms engaged in mortal conflict – the kingdom of God and the kingdom of Satan, or the kingdom of this world. The citizens of the kingdom of God are involved in this conflict and will endure persecution and suffering in the same way as Jesus Christ. This cosmic warfare between these two kingdoms creates the context of the mission. Because of this, according to Driver, "to preach the Gospel of the kingdom is to be engaged in battle with the kingdom of this world."[165] This requires God's kingdom citizens to demonstrate "unfailing loyalty, clarity of vision, depth of commitment, and willingness to suffer persecution."[166] As Jesus himself communicated the good news about the arrival of God's kingdom, he also commissioned the church to continue this witness.[167] The church is an instrument in his hands in this process. Driver states that "the church is not the agent or representative of the kingdom . . . the church is servant and messenger of the King."[168]

Comparing the Anabaptist position on this issue, as presented by Driver, with the positions of the other two branches of Christianity shows that there are some commonalities in their positions. Like all other groups, Anabaptists view God's kingdom in both the "already" and the "not yet" aspects. They see the church as a sign of God's kingdom. The kingdom of God is broader than the church, while the latter is part of the kingdom. However, there are some significant differences. Among them are: (1) Strong emphasis on the Sermon on the Mount as a norm for the kingdom community life. As shown above, Anabaptists view this teaching as guidance for the everyday life of believers. Other faith communities do not take it in such a literal way and are more inclined to other approaches of interpretation and application of the Sermon

---

163. Ibid., 98.
164. Ibid., 99.
165. Ibid., 100.
166. Ibid.
167. Ibid.
168. Ibid.

of the Mount. (2) Viewing relationships between the kingdom of God and the world as warfare. None of the other groups present this relationship in such a strong way. In most cases, emphasis is made on God's love towards this world. (3) In the Anabaptist position, much more emphasis is given to the discipleship of believers, to living their communal life by the principles of God's kingdom, and to being a prophetic witnessing community in the world, instead of attempting to improve the present physical, economic and social conditions of the world as part of the church's mission. (4) The main task of the church is to witness in the power of the Holy Spirit about God's kingdom and its king, Christ.

1.2.9. The Slavic Baptists

The Slavic Baptist position on the subject of the kingdom of God is not easy to define. Slavic Baptists do not pay much attention to the doctrine of the kingdom of God in their theological discussions and preaching.[169] At least, this is the case with the immigrant Slavic churches. However, when this topic arises, it is very common for ordinary Slavic Christians to believe that the kingdom of God is identified with the church (of course the "church" in this case means their own version of the church and the presence of other churches is questionable). Because of such theological views and because of a long history of persecution and oppression from secular society, Slavic evangelical Christians are not usually accustomed to being involved in secular or political efforts to change the social order and bring justice to the world. They commonly believe that this world is coming ever closer to its end and God's just judgment is near. Obviously, these views do not encourage Slavic Baptists to become heavily involved in social and political activities in order to improve the lives of people in this world. This is especially true with those who emigrated to America from the former Soviet Union. Often they see their social responsibility limited to providing humanitarian aid to people in their homeland. As the results of the survey of the church leaders show (see table 6.3.7. in chapter 6), PCSBA churches are not very involved in local social action in America.

---

169. This is based on the personal observations of the author of this study which were made through many years of ministry among Slavic Baptists.

Having examined the Slavic Baptist position on this issue, the conclusion could be reached that this position is closer to (although not completely identical with) that of the Anabaptists. The four aspects of the Anabaptist position that are identified above as differentiating points from the position of other theological groups could be identified in the Slavic Baptist position as well.[170]

1.2.10. Conclusion

Comparing the theological positions of the three Christian groups on the issue of the relationship between the kingdom of God, the world, and mission of the church shows that similarities and differences exist between these positions. All three groups recognize the tension between the present and future nature of the kingdom of God. All of them believe that the kingdom of God is larger than the church. However, they differ in their view of how God sees the world and what the church's mission is in the process of implementing God's plans for the world.

Within the Slavic Baptist position, the kingdom of God is often identified with the church. Certain elements in Slavic Baptist beliefs bring their position in line with the Anabaptist position. The challenge for Slavic Baptist churches lies in the necessity to expand their understanding of the kingdom of God through accepting the truth that this kingdom is broader than the church, that God is working in the world and in the church simultaneously, that the kingdom includes other denominations besides their own, and that the church has to address the physical, economic and social needs of society in order to be God's instrument in the fulfillment of his plans for the world. The acceptance of this truth by Slavic Baptist immigrant churches is one of the conditions for making their mission authentic.

1.3. Conclusion for Chapter 1

In this chapter, the theological context of the discussion on authentic mission of the church has been addressed. In the first part of the chapter, the subject of *missio Dei* was analyzed. The historical background of this concept, its

---

170. This conclusion is based on the author's personal observation of the teaching of Slavic Baptist churches.

meaning, the Trinitarian understanding of it, its goal (purpose), and concerns regarding the ways of using the concept of *missio Dei* were examined. This study showed that despite the fact that this concept was, in some instances, used in such a way that the role of the church in the fulfillment of God's plans toward the world was minimized, if not excluded, the concept of *missio Dei* is still a very significant accomplishment of twentieth-century theological thought. It helped to develop a more biblically appropriate Trinitarian view of mission. God himself was identified as the source of mission. The mission of the church was placed in the right position in relation to the mission of God. The scope of the mission of God was defined as widely as the whole creation. As a result, the mission of the church was expanded from primarily focusing on evangelism to being involved in care for the whole person, including physical and social needs. Because God is working in the whole world, the mission of the church should be brought in alignment with his plans for the world. There is no doubt that the development of the concept of *missio Dei* has significantly affected theological and missiological thought in the second part of the twentieth century.

In the second part of this chapter, the complex relationships between the kingdom of God, the world, and the mission of the church were briefly evaluated. The positions of the three ecclesiological groups (WCC, evangelical/Lausanne Movement, and Anabaptists), as well as Slavic Baptists, on this issue were explored and compared. It was shown that there is no full consensus among these groups on the subject discussed. They are in general agreement on certain aspects of this subject, but in disagreement on others. The position of Slavic Baptists to a certain degree (but not completely) is similar to the Anabaptist position.

This brief overview of both the *missio Dei* concept and the relationships between the kingdom of God, the world, and the mission of the church provides an understanding of the theological context for the development of an authentic mission concept and serves as a base for a more detailed discussion on the subject of the mission of the church (*missio ecclesiae*), as provided in chapter 2.

CHAPTER 2

Mission of the Church

After discussing the subjects of *missio Dei* and the relationships between the kingdom of God, the world, and the mission of the church in chapter 1, attention will now be focused on the mission of the church, *missio ecclesiae*. In order to do an appropriate evaluation of the mission work of PCSBA churches, it is important to define what the mission of the church is. What role does the church play in the *missio Dei*? This question is not a new one and has been on the agenda of missiologists and church leaders for years. The answer to this question could be complex. According to J. Andrew Kirk: "In recent years there has been a vigorous debate across the whole spectrum of Christian churches worldwide concerning the extent to which mission is an unchanging task entrusted to Christian communities and the extent to which its implementation is freshly discovered (or rediscovered) in each new generation, acknowledging an always tentative, contingent, and fallible grasp of its nature."[1]

As was shown in the previous chapter, mission is more than a function of the church; it is the reason for the church's existence: "God has called the church into existence for the very purpose of serving his mission."[2] Mission is absolutely essential for church life and wellbeing. Kirsteen Kim describes it in the following way: "Any history of any church begins with mission activity, and continues with mission activity. It is not possible therefore to separate

---

1. J. Andrew Kirk, "Christian Mission and the Epistemological Crisis of the West," in *To Stake a Claim: Mission and the Western Crisis of Knowledge*, ed. J. Andrew Kirk and Kevin J. Vanhoozer (Maryknoll, NY: Orbis, 1999), 157.

2. Craig Ott, Stephen J. Strauss, and Timothy C. Tennent, *Encountering Theology of Mission: Biblical Foundations, Historical Developments, and Contemporary Issues* (Grand Rapids, MI: Baker Academic, 2010), 192.

the church from mission in either theological or historical origin. Nor is it possible to separate church and mission in terms of their purpose."[3] If mission is so important for the church, what does it include? The Edinburgh 2010 Common Call document describing the mission of the church states: "we are called to incarnate and proclaim the good news of salvation, of forgiveness of sin, of life in abundance, and of liberation for all poor and oppressed. We are challenged to witness and evangelise in such a way that we are a living demonstration of the love, righteousness and justice that God intends for the whole world."[4]

David Bosch defines the mission of the church in the following way: "Mission is a multifaceted ministry, in respect of witness, service, justice, healing, reconciliation, liberation, peace, evangelism, fellowship, church planting, contextualization, and much more."[5] According to Bosch, in order to be credible and faithful, mission has to be multidimensional. Kirk shares this view, stating: "The church's inescapable call to evangelism is to be carried out as an integral part of the wider dimensions of mission: serving the needs of the community, helping to resolve conflict, working for justice for the excluded, bringing comfort and healing to those who are suffering."[6]

In order to provide a wider base for developing a definition of mission of the church, the author of this study employed not only views of individual missiologists on this subject but also positions of three major ecclesiological groups – WCC/ecumenical, evangelicals/Lausanne Movement, and Anabaptists. This provided the author with the opportunity to use a solid, more rounded approach to defining how the mission of the church is understood today by missiologists and by the larger church community as well. For this purpose, the positions of the three Christian traditions mentioned above, reflected in their basic statements as primary sources, are examined and compared. The aspects of mission where the convergence of

---

3. Kirsteen Kim, "Mission Theology of the Church," *International Review of Mission* 99, no. 1 (Apr 2010): 42.

4. "Edinburgh 2010," *Mission Studies: Journal of the International Association for Mission Studies* 27, no. 2, (2010): 141.

5. David J. Bosch, *Transforming Mission: Paradigm Shifts in Theology of Mission* (Maryknoll, NY: Orbis, 1991), 512.

6. J. Andrew Kirk, *Mission Under Scrutiny: Confronting Contemporary Challenges* (Minneapolis, MN: Fortress, 2006), 49.

views is identified are considered as part of authentic mission in its modern understanding. This analysis is limited and is not a comprehensive or exhaustive study of the contemporary understanding of mission. The intent is to identify common points in understanding the mission of the church kept by these three ecclesiastical groups in order to prepare a foundation for developing a contemporary definition of mission of the church. The survey is intentionally based on the basic statements of three ecclesiological bodies as primary sources instead of using secondary sources addressing the mission of the church. From the author's perspective, this approach leads to developing a more balanced view of church mission that has been well tested by the world church community.

2.1. World Council of Churches/ Ecumenical Position on Mission

2.1.1. The World Council of Churches (WCC)

The World Council of Churches was founded in 1948 as an inter-church organization. It came into existence in the result of a merger of two movements which originated at the Edinburgh Conference in 1910 – The World Conference of Faith and Order and the Universal Christian Council for Life and Work. These two streams met together in 1937 and from that meeting came a proposal for a World Council of Churches. Due to World War II the merger was delayed until 1948.[7] Currently this organization has member churches in all six continents.[8] The WCC defines itself as

> A fellowship of churches which confess the Lord Jesus Christ as God and Saviour according to the scriptures, and therefore seek to fulfill together their common calling to the glory of the one God, Father, Son and Holy Spirit. It is a community of churches on the way to visible unity in one faith and one eucharistic fellowship, expressed in worship and in common life

---

7. Roger E. Hedlund, *Roots of the Great Debate in Mission* (Madras, India: Evangelical Literature Service, 1981), 46.

8. James A. Scherer and Stephen B. Bevans, eds., *New Directions in Mission and Evangelization 1* (Maryknoll, NY: Orbis, 1992), x.

in Christ. It seeks to advance towards this unity, as Jesus prayed for his followers, "so that the world may believe." (John 17:21)[9]

There are 345 member churches with over 500 million Christians in this fellowship, representing more than 110 countries and territories throughout the world.[10] The governing body of the WCC is a Central Committee elected at the assembly which is the "supreme legislative body" of the WCC and meets once in seven years.[11] The membership of the WCC includes "most of the world's Orthodox churches, scores of Anglican, Baptist, Lutheran, Methodist and Reformed churches, as well as many United and Independent churches."[12] The Roman Catholic Church is not part of the WCC. However, since Vatican II, Roman Catholic observers have participated in CWME conferences and WCC assemblies.[13]

Conciliar ecumenical missiology is expressed in WCC and CWME documents. The authority of these documents over member churches is determined by the fact that "the WCC was constituted in 1948 as the *servant* of its member churches, with power to act only in matters assigned to it by those member churches."[14] These documents "cannot 'dictate' to its member churches; no church is obliged to accept pronouncements of the WCC Central Committee or to endorse statements of WCC units"[15] which are sent to the member churches "for study, guidance, response, and action."[16] There is a significant difference between the authority of documents issued by a Roman Pope within the Catholic Church and the authority of WCC documents within a WCC member church. It is assumed that "ecumenical statements carry only as much authority as they are entitled to have by virtue of their innate wisdom. To have any effect, therefore, they must be essentially

---

9. World Council of Churches, http://www.oikoumene.org/en/about-us (accessed May 2013).

10. Ibid.

11. World Council of Churches, http://www.oikoumene.org/en/about-us/organizational-structure/assembly (accessed May 2013).

12. World Council of Churches, http://www.oikoumene.org/en/about-us (accessed May 2013).

13. Scherer and Bevans, *New Directions in Mission and Evangelization 1*, xi.

14. Ibid.

15. Ibid., xi–xii.

16. Ibid., xii.

self-authenticating in terms of content."¹⁷ This allows the WCC churches a certain freedom in choosing their theological position on the issue of mission. At the same time the absence of any denominational or organizational strict identity of these documents allows them to reach Christian churches and individuals with their message who do not belong to WCC churches. In this way the WCC views on mission have spread among non-conciliar churches as well.

In the following part of the chapter, the documents of ecumenical missionary conferences held from 1961 to 2010 and other specialized reports produced during the same period of time are examined.

2.1.2. The Socio-Political Contexts of the Time When the Examined Documents Were Written

Historians view the year 1945 as a point of transition into the postwar world period in the twentieth century. However, the real change in society and the greater transition from modern time to the postmodern era took place in the decade of the 1960s.¹⁸ It was characterized by a sharp discontinuity with the way of life in the past. "Here were breaks with much of what had been accepted norms of life, belief and behavior which seemed to many to be revolutionary in character. Whether in the focus of a larger historical perspective the decade of the 1960s will be viewed as an aberration or as a period of formative transition to a post-modern age, there can be no denying that it was a time of upheaval, especially in North American and European societies."¹⁹

The wider socio-political context of that time included such extreme events as a culmination in the confrontation between the USA and the USSR that came very close to a nuclear catastrophe during the Cuban conflict in 1962; great advancements in studies in space science leading to the Soviet Union putting a Russian astronaut into space in 1961 and the USA landing an American astronaut on the moon in 1969; the Civil Rights movement in America, led by Dr Martin Luther King, Jr.; the anti-Vietnam war

---

17. Ibid.
18. Timothy Yates, *Christian Mission in the Twentieth Century* (New York: Cambridge University Press, 1994), 163.
19. Ibid.

demonstrations in America; and the assassinations of the US President John F. Kennedy in 1963 and Dr Martin Luther King, Jr. in 1964. The Soviet Union tried to keep under political and ideological control countries that joined the Soviet bloc as a result of World War II. Just as in the 1950s the Soviet Army had suppressed an uprising in Hungary, it continued this attempt at control by violently crushed the "Prague Spring" in Czechoslovakia in 1968. "This new-style imperialism contrasted with the accelerating momentum towards devolution by the old-style imperial governments like Britain."[20] In some parts of Africa, the process of African nations moving to independence from the controlling foreign colonial powers took place.[21] It was a time of turbulence and change. "It was to be expected that the world church, set in such a context, would reflect some of the pressure for change, even revolution."[22] The call for such changes and declaration of them took place at the international missionary conferences. The basic statements of some of these conferences and other documents will be examined below in order to define the mission of the church as influenced by the era of the 1960s.

2.1.3. New Delhi: Integrating Witness, Service, and Unity (1961)

The Third Assembly of the World Council of Churches (WCC) took place in New Delhi in 1961. The assembly "marked an important point in the history of the ecumenical movement."[23] During this meeting, the integration of the International Missionary Council (IMC) and the World Council of Churches took place. The assembly "summarized developments from previous decades and outlined new directions of thought, study and action."[24] The importance of the interrelationship between mission, unity, and service was strongly emphasized.

---

20. Ibid., 164.
21. Ibid., 165.
22. Ibid.
23. Rodger C. Bassham, *Mission Theology 1948–1975: Years of Worldwide Creative Tension – Ecumenical, Evangelical, and Roman Catholic* (Pasadena, CA: William Carey Library, 1979), 61.
24. Ibid.

Mission and service belong to the whole Church. God calls the Church to go out into the world to witness and serve in word and deed to the one Lord Jesus Christ, who loved the world and gave himself for the world. In the fulfillment of our missionary obedience the call to unity is seen to be imperative, the vision of one Church proclaiming one Gospel to the whole world becomes more vivid and the experience and expression of our given unity more real. There is an inescapable relationship between the fulfillment of the Church's missionary obligation and the recovery of her visible unity.[25]

Two questions arose at the assembly: How do the present structures of the church affect mission? and: How should mission shape the structure of the church?[26] The attempt to answer these questions was made in the document called "The Missionary Structure of the Congregation" introduced at the CWME Conference in Mexico City in 1963.

The merger of the IMC with the WCC was the major accomplishment of the Third Assembly of the WCC. The WCC "was declared the legal successor of the International Missionary Council."[27] The IMC became the Commission and Division of World Mission and Evangelism of the WCC. As Hedlund states, "Integration had a noble intent, to take the missionary task into the 'very heart' of the life of the WCC. It was also intended that the mission agencies should see 'their work in an ecumenical perspective and accept whatever new insights God may give through new relationships.'"[28]

Great expectations were held at the time of merger. It was expected that the missionary movement would benefit from stronger support from churches. The churches "would be enriched by the blessings that would come from having the missionary concern at the heart of their life."[29] Due to the merger and establishment of the CWME, evangelism was a very important

---

25. Willem A. Visser't Hooft, ed., *The New Delhi Report* (New York: Association Press, 1962), 121.

26. Bassham, *Mission Theology 1948–1975*, 63.

27. James A. Scherer, *Gospel, Church, and Kingdom: Comparative Studies in World Mission Theology* (Minneapolis, MN: Augsburg, 1987), 105.

28. Hedlund, *Roots of the Great Debate*, 86.

29. Scherer, *Gospel, Church, and Kingdom*, 106.

concern at the assembly. It was affirmed that every member of the church is responsible for witnessing to Christ and "it is a commission given to the whole Church to take the whole gospel to the whole world."[30] Promoting evangelism the assembly at the same time "consistently developed the interrelated nature of evangelism and social action."[31] Also, the issue of the relationship between Christianity and other faiths was addressed through the report *The Word of God and the Living Faiths of Men*.[32]

The WCC Assembly in New Delhi became an important event in the development of ecumenical mission theology. Also, it made an impact on mission work in the world. As a result of the IMC and WCC merger, the mission agencies that were carrying out mission work lost their representations in the newly created CWME. The reason for this is the fact that these organizations were not churches and only churches could obtain membership in the WCC. Thus "the mission societies came to be regarded as an abnormality."[33] It led to a decrease in the number of mission organizations functioning in the world.

2.1.4. Mexico City: God's Mission and Our Task (1963)

The first world conference of the Commission on World Mission and Evangelism (CWME) was held in Mexico City in 1963. The theme of the conference was "God's Mission and Our Task."[34] In four special sessions the following topics were discussed: Christian witnessing to people of other faiths, Christian witnessing to people in the secular world, the witness of the local congregations in their neighborhoods, and the witness of the Christian church across national and confessional boundaries.[35] The conference affirmed that "this missionary movement now involves Christians in all six continents."[36] It was stated that "It must be the common witness of the whole

---

30. Visser't Hooft, *New Delhi Report*, 85.
31. Bassham, *Mission Theology 1948–197*, 64.
32. Ibid.
33. Hedlund, *Roots of the Great Debate*, 86.
34. Bassham, *Mission Theology 1948–1975*, 64.
35. Ibid., 65.
36. Ronald K. Orchard, ed., *Witness in Six Continents: Records of the Meeting of the Commission on World Mission and Evangelism of the World Council of Churches Held in Mexico City, Dec 8–19, 1963* (London: Edinburgh House, 1964), 175.

Church bringing the whole gospel to the whole world."[37] Emphasizing the position that God's mission should be performed in every part of the world, the conference recognized "that the old 'sending and receiving' model of mission was past."[38] A very important contribution of the conference to the WCC missiological position was "a shift away from the preoccupation with the church which had dominated ecumenical mission theology since Madras (1938), to the idea that mission must take place within the world."[39] It was stated that Christians must "discover a shape of Christian obedience being written for them by what God is already actively doing in the structures of the city's life outside the Church."[40] Also, special attention was given to the role of the laity in mission. Recognizing the fact that the laity as the people of God are living and working in the world, the conference encouraged lay Christians to "seek the power of the Holy Spirit to bear witness, by word and by life, to the reality of the living God, in whatever ways are open to them."[41] Addressing the question of dialogue with people of other faiths, the statement declared that "true dialogue with a man of another faith requires a concern both for the gospel and for the other man. Without the first, dialogue becomes a pleasant conversation. Without the second, it becomes irrelevant, unconvincing or arrogant." The issue of dialogue discussed at the conference "was becoming of growing concern in the search for an ecumenical mission theology"[42] and in later years it became a hot issue in debates among missiologists.

The Mexico City conference illustrated that soon after the completion of the act of integration of the IMC into the WCC "the WCC began to reflect an ironic shift away from the post-Willingen view of the church as the agent of God's mission toward a more secular paradigm."[43] The church-centered missionary framework was displaced by "the concept of the world as the locus of God's mission."[44] It was the beginning of the changes in the

---

37. Ibid.
38. Yates, *Christian Mission in the Twentieth Century*, 165.
39. Bassham, *Mission Theology 1948–1975*, 65.
40. Orchard, *Witness in Six Continents*, 175.
41. Ibid.
42. Bassham, *Mission Theology 1948–1975*, 66.
43. Scherer, *Gospel, Church, and Kingdom*, 107.
44. Ibid.

understanding of mission in ecumenical theology which eventually led to a division within world Christianity.

2.1.5. Geneva: Church and Society (1966)

In 1966, the World Conference on Church and Society sponsored by the WCC was held in Geneva.[45] The subtitle of the conference was "Christians in the Technological and Social Revolutions of Our Time." This gathering "is considered the first genuinely world Christian conference on social issues, including equal numbers of representatives from the first, second and third worlds and a large group of observers from the Catholic Church."[46] The programmatic statement of the conference was: "As Christians we are committed to working for the transformation of the world."[47] Lukas Vischer explains the reason for the conference:

> The gathering was called because it had become clear that a far-reaching transformation of society was taking place. Historical developments had already led to new conditions of life and it was clear that further changes were bound to occur. History was rapidly moving ahead . . . The Conference was to formulate a Christian response to the new situation. It had to identify and register the developments which had taken place. But its task was also to show what role the churches had to play in this ongoing process of transformation.[48]

The position on mission expressed in the study project "The Missionary Structure of the Congregation," "which emphasized the work of God in the world as the starting point for mission,"[49] was dominant at the conference.

---

45. Ibid., 110.

46. World Council of Churches, "Geneva 1966: Ethical Challenges Still Relevant Today," 5 September 2006, http://www.oikoumene.org/en/press-centre/news/geneva-1966-ethical-challenges-still-relevant-today (accessed April 2013).

47. M. M. Thomas and Paul Abrecht, *World Conference on Church and Society, Geneva, July 12–26, 1966: The Official Report with a Description of the Conference. Christians in the Technical and Social Revolutions of Our Time* (Geneva: WCC, 1967), 48.

48. Lukas Vischer, "Committed to the Transformation of the World? Where Are We 40 Years after the World Conference on Church and Society in Geneva (1966)?", *Ecumenical Review* 59, no. 1 (Jan 2007): 21.

49. Bassham, *Mission Theology 1948–1975*, 60.

The impact of the Geneva Conference could be observed in the following three areas: (1) it strengthened the thrust of the world as the locus for mission; (2) it provided help in determining the shape and form of the structures needed by the church in order to respond to issues affecting the world; and (3) it attempted "to develop the theological undergirding for mission."[50] Strengthening of the understanding of the world as the arena for mission is evident in the following statement:

> We start with the basic assumption that the triune God is the Lord of his world and at work within it, and that the Church's task is to point to his acts, to respond to his demands, and to call mankind to this faith and obedience. Christians would surely not dispute this . . . In this document, "mission" and "missionary" are used as shorthand for the responsibilities of the Church in the world, and include the prophetic, kerygmatic, and diaconic or serving functions.[51]

At the conference principles were recommended that could be used for determining the structures for mission. The work of laity in secular functions and situations was considered as a basis for mission.[52] Sharing the contemporary view of the progress of science and technology as a potential source of positive changes in the society the participants of the conference had strong confidence in this progress. Because of this they called churches to support it. "The churches should welcome the development of science and technology as an expression of God's creative work. They also should welcome the economic growth and social development which it makes possible, because this helps to free men everywhere from unnecessary work and material insecurity; it also makes it possible for the relatively few richer nations of the world to assist the poorer countries in their enormous task of moving along on the road of self-sustained development."[53]

The participants of the conference believed that a new and more just social order could be established in the world. Due to this, the issue of various

---

50. Ibid., 75.
51. Thomas and Abrecht, *World Conference on Church and Society*, 179–180.
52. Ibid., 180–181.
53. Ibid., 90.

methods of social change was addressed by the participants of the conference. Revolution as one of these methods was discussed and churches were encouraged to promote revolutionary opposition to the political and economic system the Western industrialized countries imposed on the new nations.

> In the past we have usually witnessed through quiet efforts at social renewal, working in and through the established institutions according to their rules. Today, a significant number of those who are dedicated to the service of Christ and their neighbor assume a more radical or revolutionary position. They do not deny the value of tradition nor of social order, but they are searching for a new strategy by which to bring about basic changes in society without too much delay . . . at the present moment it is important for us to recognize that this radical position has a solid foundation in Christian tradition.[54]

Discussions on this subject "produced many new ideas on economic justice, political responsibility, racism, the relation between women and men in community, and the problem of rapid technological change. The conference, however, refused to provide theological endorsement of a specific revolutionary ideology."[55] Bassham, evaluating the contribution made by the conference to the WCC theological development, stated:

> By focusing on the world and identifying the major social issues confronting Christians, the Conference on Church and Society confirmed the direction in which ecumenical theology was moving. It directed attention to the need for Christians to be involved in movements for social change. Prominent in the discussions were issues of revolution and economic development. Christians were challenged to strive for justice and peace. The influence which the conference had on the WCC was significant for "the theological and intellectual ferment thus created very substantially influenced the thinking of the Fourth Assembly of the World Council."[56]

---

54. Ibid., 49.
55. World Council of Churches, "Geneva 1966."
56. Bassham, *Mission Theology 1948–1975*, 78.

This statement clearly shows the significance this conference played in the future development of the WCC position on the mission of God in the world. Thus the WCC reflected in its statements much that was happening in secular society with its movements for such issues as civil rights.

2.1.6. Uppsala: "Behold, I Make All Things New" (1968)

The Fourth Assembly of the WCC met in Uppsala, Sweden, in 1968. This conference was the first full meeting of the WCC following the integration of IMC and WCC in 1961. This was a time of turmoil and big changes in the world and one "of the most notable characteristics of the Assembly was its concern for the world."[57] The study report, *The Church for Others*, and the Geneva Conference on Church and Society documents made a significant impact on the Uppsala Conference.[58] *The Church for Others* points to the world as the arena of God's activity. It states that God is working outside church walls and his goal is the establishment of shalom in the world. The duty of the church, then, "is to be not separate but present in the world in order there to discern signs of God's presence and activity."[59] According to *The Church for Others*, the church was now seen as a segment of the world. "It was proposed that the traditional sequence 'God-Church-World' be revised to read 'God-world-Church.'" It was stated in the document that the focus of God's plan is the world, not the church, and because of this the world provides the agenda for mission.[60] This was a theological foundation of the Uppsala Conference.

There were six sections in the work of the assembly: "The Holy Spirit and the Catholicity of the Church," "Renewal in Mission," "World Economic and Social Development," "Towards Justice and Peace in International Affairs," "Worship," and "Towards New Styles of Living." The position of the assembly on mission was introduced in the document *Renewal in Mission*. This document consists of three parts. A theological introduction is provided

---

57. Ibid., 79.
58. Ibid.
59. Hedlund, *Roots of the Great Debate*, 112. Cf. Parush R. Parushev, "Witness, Worship and Presence: On the Integrity of Mission in Contemporary Europe," *Mission Studies* 24, no. 2 (2007).
60. Hedlund, *Roots of the Great Debate*, 113.

in part 1, "A Mandate for Mission."[61] Part 2, "Opportunities for Mission,"[62] deals with some important situations for mission and outlines some criteria for choosing priorities in mission. The third part, "Freedom for Mission,"[63] points to the necessity for new missionary structures in the church. "A Mandate for Mission" starts with the statement "We belong to a humanity that cries passionately and articulately for a fully human life,"[64] and uses the idea of "a new humanity" in Jesus Christ as its central theological motif. It insists: "There is a burning relevance today in describing the mission of God, in which we participate, as the gift of a new creation which is a radical renewal of the old and the invitation to men to grow up into their full humanity in the new man, Jesus Christ."[65]

"A Mandate for Mission" points to the significance of the life and death of Christ in removing alienation from God. It states that when a person is turning to God this action brings changes in her or his attitudes and relationships. "For there is no turning to God which does not at the same time bring a man face to face with his fellow men in a new way."[66] Obtaining the new life in Christ "frees men for community enabling them to break through racial, national, religious and other barriers that divide the unity of mankind."[67] Christians' part in evangelism is described "as bringing about the occasions for men's response to Jesus Christ" while the Holy Spirit does the work of conversion.[68]

The other two parts of this section of the report address the renewal structure of mission. In these parts, the secular focus of "A Mandate for Mission" statement becomes apparent. Instead of referring to mission as taking place in foreign lands and reaching the unreached, the document brings mission to localities in the secular world "where there is human need, an expanding population, tension, forces in movement, institutional

---

61. "Section II of the Fourth Assembly of the WCC, Uppsala, 1968," in *Ecumenical Review* 21, no. 4 (Oct 1969): 367.
62. Ibid., 368.
63. Ibid., 370.
64. Ibid., 367.
65. Ibid.
66. Ibid.
67. Ibid.
68. Ibid.

rigidities, decision-making about the priorities and uses of power, and even open human conflict."[69] Describing some priority situations for mission the statement refers to the power centers, revolutionary movements, the university in change, urbanization and industrialization, suburbia and rural life, relations between developed and developing countries, and the churches themselves.[70] The statement points to the necessity of evaluation of the missionary activities regarding the appropriateness of their witness to Jesus Christ in contemporary and persuasive terms. The new criteria for determining mission priorities suggest exposing the church to "loss in prestige and finance and detachment from monuments of faithfulness in mission localities of the past."[71] Also, the criteria include the following: "Do they place the church alongside the poor, the defenseless, the abused, the forgotten, the bored?"[72] The churches are called to re-examine their structures at all levels and "the variety of tasks to which the people are called in their ministry to the world."[73] The Mexico City vision of mission in six continents was re-affirmed in the statement.

Giving an overall evaluation of the Uppsala Assembly, Scherer concludes: "For ecumenical missionary thinking, Uppsala's significance lay in the fact that it consolidated the emphasis on mission in the secular world and the focus on the world as the arena for mission, a focus that began shortly after New Delhi."[74] Hedlund gives the following assessment of the assembly: "At Uppsala two basic theologies – two ideologies – were in conflict. It was not a mere question as to the balance between social action and the proclamation of the Gospel. On the one side were the advocates of mission as humanization, on the other side those for whom the primary concern of mission was with the glory of God and the evangelization of the lost. Uppsala did not give priority to discipling the nations."[75] Thus, the WCC position on mission moved even further from its original point reflected in the documents

---

69. Ibid., 368.
70. Ibid., 368–369.
71. Ibid., 370.
72. Ibid.
73. Ibid.
74. Scherer, *Gospel, Church, and Kingdom*, 121.
75. Hedlund, *Roots of the Great Debate*, 118.

of the New Delhi Assembly. It became much more oriented on the secular world. This tendency produced strong opposition from certain theologians and missiologists and led to the great debate about mission of the church in today's world. The arguments of some of the WCC position opponents will be discussed later in this thesis.

2.1.7. Bangkok: Salvation Today (1973)

The Bangkok Assembly of the CWME took place in 1973. There were 330 participants at the conference from sixty-nine countries.[76] The theme of the conference was "Salvation Today." "Bangkok was a direct outgrowth of the 1963 missionary conference in Mexico City. This means that the topic of Bangkok had been under consideration in some form for about ten years."[77] The conference was held in a city in the Global South and more than half of all delegates were from countries in the Global South.[78]

There were three sections at the conference. Section I was on culture and identity, minority groups, subcultures, and how they relate to the experience of salvation.[79] The second section dealt with the subject of salvation and social justice. At this section discussion took place on liberation and humanization. The so-called "theology of Bangkok" came out of this section. "It was this section on salvation and social justice that sounded the notes for which Bangkok was anticipated and for which Bangkok will be chiefly remembered."[80] In this section salvation was defined in four social dimensions: the struggle for economic justice, the struggle for human dignity, the struggle for solidarity against alienation, and the struggle for hope.[81] The third section addressed the subject of the churches renewed in mission and dealt mostly with the mission of the local church.[82] A series of small groups met at the conference "for study and reflection on the meaning of salvation

---

76. Bassham, *Mission Theology 1948–1975*, 92.

77. T. Watson Street, "Salvation Today: Reflections on the Bangkok Conference," *Austin Seminary Bulletin* (Faculty ed.) 89, no. 7 (Apr 1974): 12.

78. Ibid., 14.

79. Ibid., 18.

80. Ibid.

81. Hedlund, *Roots of the Great Debate*, 127.

82. Street, "Salvation Today," 19.

as experienced by the participants."[83] Such an experience-centered approach made it difficult to achieve serious theological reflection on the subject of salvation. This was a deficiency of the conference.[84]

There are at least two different descriptions of salvation presented in the conference report. The first, offered in section II, states that salvation brings wholeness to all life.

> The salvation which Christ brought, and in which we participate, offers a comprehensive wholeness in this divided life. We understand salvation as newness of life – the unfolding of true humanity in the fullness of God (Col. 2:9). It is salvation of the soul and the body, of the individual and society, mankind and "the groaning creation" (Rom. 8:19). As evil works both in personal life and in exploitative social structures which humiliate humankind, so God's justice manifests itself both in the justification of the sinner and in social and political justice.[85]

Salvation was seen as related to liberation movements in the world. It was stated that "we see the struggles for economic justice, political freedom and cultural renewal as elements in the total liberation of the world through the mission of God."[86] The influence of the Geneva Conference on the Bangkok understanding of mission could be seen here.

Another description of salvation was offered in section III. It links salvation with Christ's work of deliverance of people from the bondage of sin. It states: "Salvation is Jesus Christ's liberation of individuals from sin and all its consequences. It is also a task which Jesus Christ accomplishes through His church to free the world from all forms of oppression."[87] This view of salvation puts the church in the position of the primary agent in God's mission in the process of removing oppression. This is quite different from the first description of salvation introduced in section II. Such inconsistency in the Bangkok report could be explained by two different understandings of *missio*

---

83. Bassham, *Mission Theology 1948–1975*, 93.
84. Ibid., 92.
85. *Bangkok Assembly 1973* (New York: WCC, 1973), 88.
86. Ibid., 89.
87. Ibid., 102.

Dei: "Should mission primarily be understood as God's work in the world in which the church participates; or should mission be viewed as something which God accomplishes through the church in the world?" These contrasting views are apparent in sections II and III. On the one hand, in section II, the churches themselves are shown in need of liberation. On the other hand, in section III, the church is described as the bearer of God's mission in the world.[88] An attempt was made at the conference to formulate "an adequate description of salvation in which the personal and social, the individual and corporate dimensions of life each find expression."[89] The report states: "Our concentration upon the social, economic and political implications of the gospel does not in any way deny the personal and eternal dimensions of salvation. Rather, we would emphasize that the personal, social, individual and corporate aspects of salvation are so inter-related that they are inseparable."[90] However, this statement did not match the agenda of the conference. Despite stating that proclamation and service were "inseparable" not much was said at the conference about evangelism, justification by faith, and eternal life. This fact has drawn criticism from conservative evangelicals, at least one Roman Catholic, and part of the Orthodox community.[91]

One of the proposals made at Bangkok was the call for a moratorium "on the sending of funds and personnel to particular churches for a period of time."[92] It suggested re-channeling missionary resources into development projects, "education for mission in the new context, including education for development and justice," neglected areas of mission at home, and "support to those struggling for freedom from unjust and dehumanizing systems."[93] Clearly, a moratorium "was proposed less for the advancement of the Churches and more for the support of liberation movements."[94]

James A. Scherer sees the significance of Bangkok in the fact "that it marked the emergence of the liberation theme as the dominant motif in

---

88. Bassham, *Mission Theology 1948–1975*, 95.
89. Ibid., 96.
90. *Bangkok Assembly 1973*, 87.
91. Bassham, *Mission Theology 1948–1975*, 96.
92. *Bangkok Assembly 1973*, 24–25.
93. Ibid., 87.
94. Hedlund, *Roots of the Great Debate*, 127.

ecumenical mission . . . and the transition from Western mission agency dominance to two-thirds world leadership in the CWME."[95] According to John Corrie the Bangkok Conference "went further than Uppsala in seeing salvation as liberation, and liberation as changing both people and structures in equal measure."[96] Roger E. Hedlund states that "mission at Bangkok came to mean the betterment of human life. Salvation is no longer concerned with a vague future, it must deal with the here-and-now."[97] The Bangkok Conference made its important contribution in the process of moving the subsequent WCC theological thinking into interpreting salvation in a secular and humanistic way.

2.1.8. Summary

The twelve-year period 1961–1973 analyzed above was a pivotal time in the development of WCC theology. The merger between IMC and WCC took place with the hope that mission would become a central task of the church. Instead, ecumenical mission theology was pushed "in the direction of an encounter with the secular world."[98] Scherer describes this process:

> Ecumenical mission theology in this period engaged in radical speculation and innovative thinking about mission which deviated sharply from earlier church-centered missionary thinking in conciliar circles. It assumed that "the world sets the agenda" for the church's mission. This secularizing tendency climaxed at the Uppsala Assembly of the WCC (1968), where "humanization in Christ" (rather than salvation) is taken as the mission aim, and the new "fields" for mission are seen as being the secular world's troubled spots and places of tension.[99]

It could be concluded that the WCC and CWME conferences that took place during this period of time played a decisive role in the historical development of ecumenical theology. Proclamations and recommendations made

---

95. Scherer, *Gospel, Church, and Kingdom*, 124.
96. John Corrie, *Models of Mission in the 20C*, https://www.scribd.com/document/179134545/corrie-models-of-mission-in-20C-pdf (accessed April 2013).
97. Hedlund, *Roots of the Great Debate*, 127.
98. Scherer, *Gospel, Church, and Kingdom*, 39.
99. Ibid., 39.

at these conferences impacted missionary thinking of theologians as well as church leaders' understanding of mission of the church worldwide. This change in the view of mission had very practical implications: the number of missionary sending agencies in the West declined, the number of missionaries sent from the West decreased significantly, funds designed to support evangelistic projects were realigned to support humanitarian projects, a moratorium on sending missionaries and financial support of mission work in countries in the Global South was enacted by some denominations in the West,[100] etc. Also, this new direction in mission theology triggered a serious disunity within world Christianity. The WCC which started in 1948 with the intention to unite all Christians in the world to accomplish the unfinished task of evangelizing the world produced a theology of mission that divided Christians and became the object of a "Great Debate." It could be concluded that dramatic events taking place in the world in the 1960s and 1970s, such as the Vietnam War, the Civil Rights movement, dismantling of the colonial system, etc., impacted the thinking of WCC theologians. They started to teach that the church should be concerned not only about the eternal fate of souls of marginalized people in society but also about their earthly social life conditions. Dramatic societal changes affected the theologians' view of the mission of the church in the world. It is reflected in the documents of the conferences discussed above. Not all theologians shared these new views. A closer look at the critique made of WCC thinking by two representatives of theologians who expressed sharp disagreement with the new direction of the ecumenical theology of mission will be made later in this thesis.

2.1.9. Nairobi: *Confessing Christ Today* (1975)

The document *Confessing Christ Today* came out of the WCC Fifth Assembly which took place in Nairobi, Kenya, in 1975. After divisive debates in Uppsala, this conference was judged to be one of "consolidation and reconciliation" in the ecumenical movement.[101] During this conference efforts

---

100. T. Watson Street states that in response to a call for a moratorium in Bangkok "the United Presbyterian Church USA and the Presbyterian Church US declared a moratorium for at least one year in Mexico . . . The United Methodist Church has declared a moratorium for a period of time in Uruguay and has taken all missionaries out of relationship with a particular church there." "Salvation Today," 19.

101. Scherer, *Gospel, Church, and Kingdom*, 126.

were made "to build bridges toward evangelicals, Romans Catholics, and the Orthodox."[102]

This document points to liturgy and worship as being aspects of the church's mission. According to the WCC position, mission through liturgy and worship infiltrates everything that is done by believers for Christian witness. Everything in life is about confessing Christ. It affects what a person says, does, acts, or thinks. The document affirms that "Our confessing Christ today would deny God's incarnation if it were limited to only some areas of life. It concerns all the wholeness of human life: our words and acts, our personal and communal existence, our worship and responsible service; our particular and ecumenical context."[103] Anything and everything done by Christians should always point to the act of confessing Christ. The life made fuller and richer by proclaiming the Lord, liturgical worship in essence, proclaims the death and resurrection of Christ. As the Lord is proclaimed, people are brought into the body of Christ. According to the document: "Liturgical worship, an action of the Church centered around the Eucharist, in itself thankfully proclaims the death and resurrection of the Lord 'until he comes again' and incorporates people into mystical union with God, because in the act of baptism they have been identified with that death and resurrection."[104]

Another aspect of the mission of the church addressed in *Confessing Christ Today* is evangelism and its relation to social action. The document shows that evangelism is part of mission. However, it states that evangelism coincides with social action. "Through the power of the cross, Christ promises God's righteousness and commands true justice. As a royal priesthood, Christians are therefore called to engage in both evangelism and social action. We are commissioned to proclaim the gospel of Christ to the ends of the earth. Simultaneously, we are commanded to struggle to realize God's will for peace, justice and freedom throughout society."[105]

---

102. Ibid., 129.
103. "Confessing Christ Today," in Scherer and Bevans, *New Directions in Mission and Evangelization 1*, 8.
104. Ibid.
105. Ibid., 4.

Recognizing the gospel proclamation which is evangelism as a responsibility of the church, the document points to social justice as another church responsibility. The two are interrelated. While the church is proclaiming the gospel, additional action should accompany this process. The proclamation should go hand-in-hand with the church's participation in addressing the social problems of society. According to the document *Confessing Christ Today* the responsibility of the church includes the following: "The announcement of God's kingdom and love through Jesus Christ, the offer of grace and forgiveness of sins, the invitation to repentance and faith in him, the summons to fellowship in God's Church, the command to witness to God's saving words and deeds, the responsibility to participate in the struggle for justice and human dignity, the obligation to denounce all that hinders human wholeness, and a commitment to risk life itself."[106] There is an obvious correlation between evangelism and social action. The gospel lifts the person from the position of being in need of salvation. Then it introduces this person to a society which is just and honors humans. The *Confessing Christ Today* document points to the fact that the mission of the church should be carried out through worship and liturgy as well as through evangelism and social action.

2.1.10. *Guidelines on Dialogue* (1979)

This document was adopted at the WCC Central Committee meeting in 1979 in Kingston. It consists of the official stance of the WCC on the controversial issue of Christian communication with people of other faiths. This document discusses and gives guidance regarding such aspects of the church mission as mission through dialogue. The World Council of Churches/ecumenical position understands that dialogue is to be expressed in everyday life for all Christians.[107] While living in a community with people of different faiths, Christians have an opportunity to interact with these people. Because of this, the topic of dialogue and presence should be part of Christians' discussions. Dialogue is not just a statement of faith. It implies on the Christian's side a welcoming attitude and an openness concerning

---

106. Ibid.

107. "Guidelines on Dialogue," in Scherer and Bevans, *New Directions in Mission and Evangelization 1*, 13.

another person's faith. From the WCC prospective, dialogue has its roots in the Ten Commandments and this fact provides a scriptural support for practicing it. "Dialogue can be recognized as a welcome way of obedience to the commandments of the Decalogue: 'You shall not bear false witness against your neighbor.' Dialogue helps us not to disfigure the image of our neighbors of different faiths and ideologies. It has been the experience of many Christians that this dialogue is indeed possible on the basis of a mutual trust and a respect for the integrity of each participant's identity."[108] Due to this, dialogue should be an integral part of the life of Christians in their interaction with the community.

According to the WCC, another reason dialogue is necessary is that Christians live in different religious contexts and are surrounded by people of other faiths and ideologies. The presence of other faiths is not limited to specific regions. Christians are interacting with people of other faiths in their own families and communities. Developing relationships with people of other faiths is imperative for "expressing mutual human care and searching for mutual understanding."[109] In addition to this, dialogue is an effective method for proclaiming Christ in today's world.

> Thus, to the member churches of the WCC we feel able with integrity to commend the way of dialogue as one in which Jesus Christ can be confessed in the world today; at the same time we feel able with integrity to assure our partners in dialogue that we come not as manipulators but as genuine fellow pilgrims, to speak with them of what we believe God to have done in Jesus Christ who has gone before us, but whom we seek to meet anew in dialogue.[110]

Dialogue brings out the aspect of compromise on the issue of religion and faith. From the WCC's perspective, all participants benefit from it. The WCC provides guidelines for churches on how to practice beneficial dialogue with people of other faiths. The first guideline is this: "It is Christian faith in the Triune God – Creator of all humankind, Redeemer in Jesus

---

108. Ibid.
109. Ibid.
110. Ibid.

Christ, revealing and renewing Spirit – which calls us Christians to human relationships with our neighbors."[111] This is "Christian faith which sets us free to be open to the faiths of others, to risk, to trust and to be vulnerable. In dialogue, conviction and openness are held in balance."[112] It is also stated that dialogue "is a style of living in relationships with neighbors. This in no way replaces or limits our Christian obligation to witness, as partners enter into dialogue with their respective commitments."[113] The *Guidelines on Dialogue* document makes it very clear that according to the WCC position dialogue is part of the church's mission today.

2.1.11. *Christian Witness – Common Witness* (1980)

This document was produced by a Joint Working Group which was comprised of the Vatican Secretariat for Christian Unity and the WCC Commission on World Mission and Evangelism. It calls for an ecumenical witness involving local Roman Catholic churches and WCC member churches. According to the WCC, Christ bonds these groups together as he is the foundation and the proclaimer of his good news. The document states:

> The command of Jesus Christ and the power of his grace lead the Church to proclaim the Good News he has brought us; finally this Good News is Christ himself. This gospel message gives Christian communities the common ground for their proclamation. They accept the content of the biblical witness and the Creeds of the early Church. Today they desire to reach beyond what separates them by stressing the essential and returning to the foundation of their faith in Jesus Christ.[114]

The authors then explain that the source of witness is the Father, Jesus Christ, and the Holy Spirit. Several aspects of the mission of the church are mentioned in this important document. The authors of the document call upon churches of different theological traditions to participate in proclamation of the gospel (mission through evangelism), saying:

---

111. Ibid., 16.
112. Ibid.
113. Ibid.
114. Ibid.

> Following the apostles (Acts 2:32) the Church today testifies to these saving acts of God in front of the world and proclaims that Jesus Christ is Saviour and Lord of all mankind and of all creation.[115]
>
> Christ's commission to his Church (Matt. 28:18–20) and the gift of the Spirit to enable this task to be fulfilled impose a missionary obligation upon Christians in every circumstance. It causes them to cross social and geographical boundaries: yet it is present also in their everyday surroundings. It demands obedience even in situations where explicit preaching is impossible and witness has usually to be silent.[116]

Also, in the document's statement can be recognized a call for mission through care for the environment: "Salvation in Jesus Christ has cosmic dimensions. Christian witness is given not only to fulfil a missionary vocation but also to respond to the aspirations of the universe."[117] The call for the church to practice mission through justice is very obvious in the authors' claim that participation in common witness means "involvement in matters of social justice in the name of the poor and the oppressed. We must relearn the patristic lesson that the Church is the mouth and the voice of the oppressed in the presence of the powers that be. Thus Christians witness will mean participation in the struggle for human rights, at all levels, in economic sharing and in liberation from social and political oppression."[118] The brief observation provided above in the WCC document *Christian Witness – Common Witness* shows that mission through evangelism, mission through care for the environment, and mission through justice are considered by the WCC as the components of church mission today.

2.1.12. Melbourne: *Your Kingdom Come* (1980)

This document is associated with the Commission on World Mission and Evangelism (CWME) World Conference on Mission and Evangelism, held

---

115. Ibid., 20.
116. Ibid., 23.
117. Ibid.
118. Ibid.

in Melbourne, Australia, in 1980. This conference is considered "as one of the most important and influential ecumenical missionary conferences for this period."[119] It impacted the future development of the WCC's understanding of the church's mission in its social aspect, specifically in relation to the poor. "Poverty in the Scriptures is affliction, deprivation and oppression. But it can also include abundant joy and overflow in liberality (II Cor. 8.1f). The Gospel which has been given to the Christian Church must express this continuing concern of God for the poor to whom Jesus has granted the blessing of the kingdom."[120]

The document outlines an understanding of social action as it relates to the church's mission by demonstrating that Jesus's blessing for the poor challenges everyone and shows how the kingdom of God is to be received. The poor are "'blessed' because of their longing for justice and their hope for liberation."[121] Because of this the poor can find hope in the coming of the kingdom, while the rich can expect judgment when the kingdom arrives.[122] According to *Your Kingdom Come*, the church "is called to preach Good News to the poor, even as its Lord has in his ministry announced the kingdom of God to them. The churches cannot neglect this evangelistic task."[123] This is a clear call to mission through evangelism. At the same time, the document makes a strong emphasis on the importance for the church to address the social needs of the people who hear its preaching (mission through social actions). Churches are commended by the document for their willingness "to redistribute their wealth for the benefit of the self-development of the poor."[124] The church leaders are applauded for challenging, on behalf of the poor, "the transnational corporations at their business meetings and in their board rooms."[125] Praise is given for times when, "Through ecumenical bodies, churches have joined in the search for a new social, political and

---

119. "Your Kingdom Come: Melbourne, 1980," in Scherer and Bevans, *New Directions in Mission and Evangelization 1*, 27.
120. Ibid., 28.
121. Ibid.
122. Ibid.
123. Ibid.
124. Ibid., 29.
125. Ibid.

economic order, and committed themselves to support those organizations, churches and national leaders that share this vision."[126]

In order to fulfill its Christ-given mission, the churches should enact the following recommendations made in the document:

> a. Become churches in solidarity with the struggle of the poor.
>
> b. Join the struggle against the powers of exploitation and impoverishment.
>
> c. Establish a new relationship with the poor inside the churches.
>
> d. Pray and work for the kingdom of God.[127]

The document makes it very clear that the WCC position is that mission through evangelism and mission through social action are part of the church's mission in the contemporary world, and both of them are equally important. However, the document makes a stronger emphasis on the needs of the poor than on the need to evangelize the non-evangelized.

2.1.13. *Ecumenical Affirmation: Mission and Evangelism* (1982)

This document was written in 1982 by the WCC Central Committee. It declares that "the Church is sent into the world to call people and nations to repentance, to announce forgiveness of sin and a new beginning in relations with God and with neighbors through Jesus Christ."[128] Again, in this document the church's mandate for its mission has been presented as being done through evangelism. Also, the WCC's position on mission through inculturation is expressed clearly in this document. "The planting of the church in different cultures demands a positive attitude towards inculturation of the gospel."[129] The *Ecumenical Affirmation* provides a clear calling to plant a local body of believers, the church, in every human community for the purpose of inculturation of the gospel. "It is at the heart of Christian

---

126. Ibid.
127. Ibid., 30–31.
128. "Ecumenical Affirmation: Mission and Evangelism," in Scherer and Bevans, *New Directions in Mission and Evangelization 1*, 37.
129. Ibid., 4.

mission to foster the multiplication of local congregations in every human community. The planting of the seed of the gospel will bring forward a people gathered around the word and sacraments and called to announce God's revealed purpose."[130]

From the time of the apostles, the WCC sees the church as possessing this goal to be spread to every continent, nation, people group, and village. At present, they are hopeful because they see the labor of faithful disciples who are taking the Great Commission to the ends of the earth. The *Affirmation* puts limits on what inculturation means by clarifying that gathering data does not fulfill the requirements. Rather, participation in the struggle of the less fortunate and identifying with them at their level is the goal. "Inculturation should not be understood merely as intellectual research; it occurs when Christians express their faith in the symbols and images of their respective culture. The best way to stimulate the process of inculturation is to participate in the struggle of the less privileged for their liberation. Solidarity is the best teacher of common cultural values."[131] Thus, inculturation is a way to incarnate, to embody the Word, and to put it into flesh "in a particular individual, community, institution or culture."[132] According to this document, for the WCC, the mission of the church in the world, in addition to the oral proclamation of the gospel (evangelism), includes other components. In the *Ecumenical Affirmation*, it is declared: "Through its internal life of eucharistic worship, thanksgiving, intercessory prayer, through planning for mission and evangelism, through a daily lifestyle of solidarity with the poor, through advocacy even to confrontation with the powers that oppress human beings, the churches are trying to fulfill this evangelistic vocation."[133] According to this document, evangelism, concern for justice, and care for the poor (social action) are part of the church's mission. The importance of care for the poor being provided alongside the oral proclamation of the gospel is underlined again. "A proclamation that does not hold forth the promises of the justice of the kingdom to the poor of the earth is a caricature of the Gospel; but Christian participation in

---

130. Ibid., 18.
131. Ibid., 18–19.
132. Ibid., 18.
133. Ibid., 39.

the struggles for justice which does not point towards the promises of the kingdom also makes a caricature of a Christian understanding of justice."[134] Since many Christians today believe that God pays special attention to the poor, relations with the poor have become "a valid yardstick to apply to our lives as individual Christians, local congregations and as missionary people of God in the world."[135]

Such a sensitive subject as mission and other faiths was addressed in this document as well. It is confirmed that mission should take place in the context of other faiths. "Christians owe the message of God's message in Jesus Christ to every person and to every people."[136] It is affirmed that our salvation is in Christ. Despite the fact that there are still differences among Christians in understanding how salvation in Christ is available for people of other faiths, "all agree that witness should be rendered to all."[137] This witness has to be conducted with the highest respect and love for people of other faiths. "Christians should use every opportunity to join hands with their neighbors, to work together to be communities of freedom, peace and mutual respect."[138]

This document shows that the WCC position on the mission of the church in the world includes such aspects as mission through evangelism, mission through inculturation, mission through justice, mission through social action, and mission through dialogue with people of other faiths.

2.1.14. *Witnessing in a Divided World* (1983)

This document came out when the Sixth Assembly of the WCC met in Vancouver in 1983. The assembly called churches to renew their commitment to mission and evangelism, justice and peace.[139] Along with discussing these aspects of the church's mission, the assembly document discusses the subject of witnessing among people of living faiths. It distinguishes between witness and dialogue. According to *Witnessing in a Divided World*,

---

134. Ibid., 47.
135. Ibid.
136. Ibid., 50.
137. Ibid.
138. Ibid.
139. "Witness in a Divided World," in Scherer and Bevans, *New Directions in Mission and Evangelization 1*, 54.

witness is defined as "those acts and words by which a Christian or community gives testimony to Christ and invites others to make their response to him."[140] Dialogue is presented as an "encounter where people holding different claims about ultimate reality can meet and explore these claims in a context of mutual respect."[141] It is suggested that dialogue with people of other living faiths can help us to better understand God's work in the world and to appreciate the insights and experiences of these people. Through dialogue, the witness for Christ takes place.

This document gives evidence that, for the WCC, the mission of the church includes such aspects as mission through evangelism, mission through social action, mission through justice, and mission through dialogue with people of other living faiths.

2.1.15. *Urban Rural Mission* (1986)

This document provides the theological assumptions and strategic goals of the Urban Rural Mission of the Commission for World Mission and Evangelism (CWME)[142] and is beneficial for understanding the World Council of Churches' position on mission through justice.

2.1.16. *Stuttgart Consultation* (1987)

This document is the result of the meeting of the CWME and other WCC European member churches and agencies that took place in Stuttgart in 1987. The meeting was designed to discuss the place of evangelism in WCC programs. The Stuttgart Consultation document "served as a bridge between conciliar Christians and evangelicals in the period before San Antonio and Lausanne II."[143] It is clear from a study of the *Stuttgart Consultation* that this document affirms strongly both mission through evangelism and mission through social action as part of the mission of the church.

---

140. Ibid., 55.

141. Ibid., 56.

142. "Urban Rural Mission (1986)," in Scherer and Bevans, *New Directions in Mission and Evangelization 1*, 57.

143. "Stuttgart Consultation," in Scherer and Bevans, *New Directions in Mission and Evangelization 1*, 65.

2.1.17. San Antonio: *Mission in Christ's Way: Your Will Be Done* (1989)

This document came out of the fourth WCC-sponsored World Conference on Mission and Evangelism which met in San Antonio, Texas, in 1989. This conference preceded the Lausanne II congress in Manila by a few weeks. These two important events in the worldwide Christian community were linked by a group of "concerned evangelicals" who attended both meetings.[144] The mission agenda of the conference was covered under four sections: (1) "Turning to the Living God," (2) "Participating in Suffering and Struggle," (3) "The Earth is the Lord's," and (4) "Towards Renewed Communities in Mission." According to the message of the conference: "Mission in Christ's Way was understood as a 'creative tension' between spiritual and material needs, prayer and action, evangelism and social responsibility, dialogue and witness, power and vulnerability, the local and the universal."[145]

The WCC position on different aspects of the church mission expressed during the Melbourne Conference (1980), the Stuttgart Consultation (1987), and in the Orthodox Advisory Group (1988) was reaffirmed. It was stated again that the call of the church in this world is to proclaim the kingdom of God,[146] that there is "the inextricable relationship between Christian unity and missionary calling, between ecumenism and evangelization,"[147] that there is a threat to the gospel in the growing secularization of society,[148] and that Christians are under obligation to testify (evangelism) about God's presence in Christ to all people, including those who belong to other faiths, engaging in dialogue with them.[149] During the conference, significant attention was paid to the participation of the church in relieving the suffering and struggles that people are going through in order to build "just" communities. "The followers of Jesus Christ are invited to participate with the people who

---

144. "Mission in Christ's Way: Your Will Be Done," in Scherer and Bevans, *New Directions in Mission and Evangelization 1*, 73.

145. Ibid.

146. Frederick R. Wilson, ed., *The San Antonio Report: Your Will be Done – Mission in Christ's Way* (Geneva: WCC, 1990), 25.

147. Ibid., 27.

148. Ibid., 29.

149. Ibid., 32, 36.

are crushed in their struggle for the transformation of society."[150] Churches are encouraged to support people and organizations that use "creative power" to bring transformation to their communities. The creative power of God for people and for the world is seen in the rising up of the people against injustice. It "overcomes the brutality of death squads, detention centers, pacification programmes, forced relocations, and other means used to break the spirit of the people."[151] The conference extended a very clear call for the churches to take their social responsibility seriously by participating in people's struggles and suffering. "The churches are invited then to recognize the creative power of God at work in the suffering and struggles of people's organizations. They are invited to recognize the energizing power of the Holy Spirit in the awakening, mobilization and resistance of people against the forces that diminish life. And they are invited to participate in these struggles as a missionary task to which they are called."[152]

In addition to exploring the role of the church in bringing justice to people in this world, the stewardship of creation was given major attention at the conference in San Antonio. As a foundational point of the discussion was an affirmation "that the whole creation belongs to the Triune God."[153] If churches would accept this view, it would renew and broaden their mission and their life. According to the conference document, "the responsibility of the church towards the earth is a crucial part of the church's mission."[154] This mission means "to support the struggle for a 'just sharing of land' in concrete actions" such as returning church lands taken in the past from indigenous peoples; to be active "in repealing and opposing the enforcement of colonial and artificial borders and repressive measures," and to participate in many other actions.[155] One of the responses to the fact that the earth is God's property is the church's role as a peacemaker and care provider for the multitudes of refugees and migrants in today's world.[156]

---

150. Ibid., 38.
151. Ibid., 40.
152. Ibid.
153. Ibid., 52.
154. Ibid., 54.
155. Ibid., 58–60.
156. Ibid, 60.

This brief review of *Mission in Christ's Way: Your Will Be Done* shows that according to the WCC's understanding of the mission of the church, this mission includes such aspects as proclamation of the gospel, dialogue with people of other faiths, active participation of the church in social action, the church's participation in the struggle for a just society, and the giving of serious attention by the church to the stewardship of creation.

2.1.18. *Baar I Statement: Theological Perspectives on Plurality* (1990)

This document is a statement of the consultation of delegates from the Orthodox, Protestant, and Catholic traditions which took place in Baar, Switzerland, in January 1990. The focus of the consultation was on the significance of religious plurality, Christology, and the activity of the Spirit in the world.[157] In this document, the more open position of the WCC members toward other religions is represented. It affirms that "God has been present in the seeking and finding"[158] of peoples of different religious traditions and, as a consequence of this, "We find ourselves recognizing a need to move beyond a theology which confines salvation to the explicit personal commitment to Jesus Christ."[159] The document claims that God's "saving mystery" could be expressed in different ways. "It may be available to those outside the fold of Christ (Jn. 10.16) in ways we cannot understand, as they live faithful and truthful lives in their concrete circumstances and in the framework of the religious traditions which guide and inspire them."[160]

At the same time, the *Baar I Statement* emphasizes that the Christ event is "the clearest expression of the salvific will of God in all human history."[161] The recognition of God's salvific work in people of other religions leads to the following recommendation regarding dialogue with these people:

---

157. World Council of Churches, *Baar Statement: Theological Perspectives on Plurality*, 15 January 1990, http://www.oikoumene.org/en/resources/documents/wcc-programmes/interreligious-dialogue-and-cooperation/christian-identity-in-pluralistic-societies/baar-statement-theological-perspectives-on-plurality.html (accessed February 2012).

158. Ibid., part II.

159. Ibid., part III.

160. Ibid.

161. Ibid.

We need to respect their religious convictions, different as these may be from our own, and to admire the things which God has accomplished and continues to accomplish in them through the Spirit. Interreligious dialogue is therefore a "two-way street." Christians must enter into it in a spirit of openness, prepared to receive from others, while on their part, they give witness of their own faith. Authentic dialogue opens both partners to a deeper conversion to the God who speaks to each through the other. Through the witness of others, we Christians can truly discover facets of the divine mystery which we have not yet seen or responded to.[162]

Obviously, this document is very supportive of the dialogue between Christians and people of other religious traditions.

2.1.19. *Justice, Peace, and the Integrity of Creation* (1990)

This document is a product of the Seoul Convocation (5–12 March 1990). This meeting played an important role in the process of enabling the WCC churches to come to a mutual covenant for "Justice, Peace and the Integrity of Creation." The document calls WCC churches to "a greater sense of binding, mutual commitment and solidarity in word and action."[163] Ten affirmations in the document express the position of WCC on justice, peace, and the integrity of creation.

2.1.20. *Come, Holy Spirit* (1991)

This document came out of the Seventh Assembly of the World Council of Churches held in Canberra, Australia, in 1991. The assembly "was devoted to the theology and work of the Holy Spirit – in creation, in the social order, and in the church's calling to mission and unity."[164] Several aspects of the mission of the church are pointed out in this document. It strongly supports mission through dialogue as one of the aspects of the mission of the church. In summary, it could be said that *Come, Holy Spirit* sees mission

---

162. Ibid., part V.

163. "Justice, Peace and the Integrity of Creation," in Scherer and Bevans, *New Directions in Mission and Evangelization 1*, 82.

164. "Come, Holy Spirit," in Scherer and Bevans, *New Directions in Mission and Evangelization 1*, 84.

through building a culture of peace, and mission through dialogue as part of the mission of the church.

2.1.21. *Mission and Evangelism in Unity Today* (2000)

This document was adopted by the WCC Commission on World Mission and Evangelism in March 2000 "as a study document to be used during the preparations for the next world mission conference."[165] In the introduction to this document, it is clarified that *Mission and Evangelism in Unity Today* does not replace the very important document adopted in 1982, *Mission and Evangelism: An Ecumenical Affirmation*, and it does not promote a theology of mission different from the one articulated in that statement. It makes an attempt "to articulate anew the churches' commitment to mission and evangelism in unity within the context of the challenges facing them today."[166] Based on a review of this document, it could be concluded that WCC's position on the mission of the church sees the following aspects being included in this mission: mission through evangelism, *diaconia*, prayer and worship, teaching, inculturation, dialogue with people of other religions, and ministry of reconciliation with God, people, and creation.

2.1.22. *Mission as Ministry of Reconciliation* (2005)

This document was prepared "for reflection and study in preparation for the world mission conference in Athens in May 2005."[167] It offers the ecumenical point of view on the subject of mission as a ministry of reconciliation. Since the San Antonio world mission conference in 1989, "reconciliation has grown in importance both in ecumenical social and political ethics as well as in missiology" and it "became one of the major foci of the programmatic work of the WCC."[168] This document clearly shows that the WCC position on the mission of the church considers the ministry of reconciliation as one of its important aspects.

---

165. *Mission and Evangelism in Unity Today* (Geneva: WCC Commission on World Mission and Evangelism, 2000), http://www.oikoumene.org/index.php?id=795&L=7&type=98 (accessed February 2012).

166. "Mission and Evangelism in Unity Today," in World Council of Churches, *"You Are the Light of the World,"* 63.

167. Ibid., 90.

168. Ibid., 90–91.

2.1.23. *Alternative Globalization Addressing Peoples and Earth (AGAPE)* (2005)

Although the WCC position concerning mission through caring for the environment was mentioned earlier in this chapter, it is important to include the Justice, Peace and Creation Team in this discussion. This team well represents the WCC position on this subject. The Justice, Peace and Creation Team released their background document *Alternative Globalization Addressing Peoples and Earth* in Geneva in 2005. The *AGAPE* document provides clear evidence that mission through care of the environment is an important part of the mission of the church in the WCC understanding.

2.1.24. *Ecumenical Declaration Presented at the World People's Conference on Climate Change and the Rights of Mother Earth* (2010)

A group of representatives of WCC and other organizations gathered together at Cochabamba in April 2010 to discuss "the role of religions and spiritualities in legitimizing systems leading to the collapse of our planet."[169] They expressed their deep concern about the climate change process and its impact on life on earth in general, and especially on the lives of people in poor countries. Their position is that it is the church's duty to care for the environment. They support their view through the reality that humanity lives in the realm of Mother Earth. Because of the impact on the environment made by humanity in the past, the environment today is breaking down and societal problems have developed as a result. Lack of water, food, and daily essentials in undeveloped countries can be traced back to the results of not caring for Mother Earth. "Mother Earth and the whole Creation is groaning and is in pains of childbirth and requires a new holistic and ecological spirituality in order to preserve life."[170] There are a few causes contributing to the suffering of creation which could be mentioned. The first cause is

---

169. World Council of Churches, "Listening to the Cry of Mother Earth," in *Ecumenical Declaration Presented at the World People's Conference on Climate Change and the Rights of Mother Earth, 2010* (Geneva: WCC, 2010), http://www.oikoumene.org/en/resources/documents/wcc-programmes/justice-diakonia-and-responsibility-for-creation/climate-change-water/ecumenical-declaration-at-world-peoples-conference-on-climate-change.html (accessed July 2010).

170. Ibid.

human exploitation. "The desire to increase wealth, the comfort of a luxurious life style, consumerism, indiscriminate exploitation of natural resources and pollution of air, water and soil have brought our planet Earth to the edge of climate breakdown."[171]

According to the *Declaration*, this mentality of dominance over nature is rooted in a wrong interpretation of the traditional Jewish-Christian understanding of humanity's responsibility to care and advocate for creation.[172] In this document, care for the environment becomes parallel with converting people. It states, "We call, together with indigenous peoples and their wisdom, for a deep conversion of the ruling paradigm and of oppressive structures, as well as our mentality, attitudes and way of life, so as to bring our lives into harmony with Nature, the cosmos and the great mystery of life."[173]

The *Declaration* says that the "religions and spiritualities of all peoples and their wisdom" can be brought together and applied to this problem.[174] Churches and religious leaders are called to also join in this endeavor to save the earth for the poorest and for future generations. It is proclaimed: "We thus call on church and religious leaders to make every effort to engage in a wide campaign of awareness-raising and conversion of all believers, in order to contribute to safeguarding life on our planet Earth."[175] Based on this document, it is evident that the World Council of Churches' position on mission through the care of the environment is such that it is obviously a part of the church's mission.

2.1.25. Summary

After analyzing all these WCC documents, it can be concluded that each of them puts a special emphasis on a certain aspect or a few aspects of the church's mission in the world. Although not all aspects of the mission are necessarily mentioned in the same document, those that are not mentioned are not nullified or minimized. Actually, there can be noticed a chronological progression in the development of the WCC understanding of the mission

---

171. Ibid.
172. Ibid.
173. Ibid.
174. Ibid.
175. Ibid.

of the church. It started with evangelism and continued, adding new mission aspects as time progressed and as new perspectives on the mission of the church emerged. In summary, in order to describe the WCC's modern understanding of church mission, it could be stated that it includes all aspects of mission mentioned in the above studied documents. It includes mission through liturgy and worship, mission through evangelism, mission through social action/*diaconia*, mission through overcoming violence and building cultures of peace, mission through justice, mission through care of the environment, mission through the everyday life of Christians, mission through teaching, mission through dialogue with people of other religions, mission through inculturation, and mission through a ministry of reconciliation with God, people, and creation. This is a very comprehensive position. It makes the church responsible for being involved in many aspects of life.

2.2. Evangelical/Lausanne Movement Position on the Mission of the Church

In this part of the chapter, the main documents produced by the evangelical/Lausanne Movement churches from 1974 to 2010 are examined.

2.2.1. Lausanne Movement

The Lausanne Movement had its beginning at the International Congress on World Evangelization, initiated and inspired by Dr Billy Graham, which was held in Lausanne, Switzerland, in July 1974. Around 2,700 people from 150 nations participated in "ten days of discussion, fellowship, worship and prayer."[176] There were several important events that preceded this gathering. The organizers of the congress and leaders of the movement claim that the World Missionary Conference in Edinburgh in 1910 was the "earlier forerunner to Lausanne 1974."[177] Other more recent gatherings of evangelicals preceding and leading to the congress in Lausanne were the Congress on the Church's World-Wide Mission in Wheaton in 1966, sponsored by the Interdenominational Foreign Missions Association (IFMA) and the

---

176. The Lausanne Movement, http://www.lausanne.org/en/about.html (accessed May 2013).

177. The Lausanne Movement, http://www.lausanne.org/docs/101course/A1/player.html, Lesson 1, par. 3 (accessed May 2013).

Evangelical Foreign Missions Association (EFMA),[178] the World Congress on Evangelism in Berlin (1966), sponsored by the Billy Graham Evangelistic Association and *Christianity Today* magazine, the conferences in Singapore (1968), Minneapolis and Bogota (1969), and Australia (1971).[179] All these gatherings prepared the way for the Lausanne Congress in 1974.

The Lausanne Movement came into existence in response to developments that took place in the WCC theology of mission in the 1960s. According to Billy Graham the conciliar ecumenical movement "had departed from its earlier evangelistic vision and commitment after Edinburgh 1910."[180] The Lausanne Congress was called to correct this change in course of mission understanding. In his opening statement to the congress Graham stated that "the common characteristics of earlier great movements for evangelism were that they all took their stand on the basis of the scripture, held a definite view of the need of salvation and the lostness of humans apart from Christ, strongly believed in conversion, and were convinced that evangelism was not an option but an imperative."[181]

Because the WCC was moving away from such a theological position on mission "evangelicals gathered at Lausanne were . . . challenged to take the lead in restoring world evangelization to its rightful place."[182] The main outcome of the congress was the Lausanne Covenant that summarized the evangelical position on mission and "was to become the ongoing basis for evangelical cooperation and a further catalyst to evangelical unity."[183] It is "the most mature and comprehensive statement produced by evangelicals."[184] *The Encyclopedia of Christianity* states: "The Lausanne Movement is an international, transdenominational movement of evangelicals associated with the Lausanne Committee for World Evangelization and dedicated to the

---

178. Hedlund, *Roots of the Great Debate*, 91–95.
179. The Lausanne Movement, http://www.lausanne.org/en/about.html (accessed May 2013).
180. Scherer and Bevans, *New Directions in Mission and Evangelization 1*, xviii.
181. Ibid.
182. Ibid.
183. Ibid.
184. Bassham, *Mission Theology 1948–1975*, 243.

study, promotion, and fulfillment of cooperative evangelism worldwide."[185] To drive the ongoing task of evangelization the Lausanne Committee for World Evangelization (LCWE) was organized in 1976.[186] This is "not a council of churches or religious organizations but rather a loose coalition of individual persons, mission and evangelism agencies, and institutions sharing a common theological position and with a common missionary and evangelistic purpose."[187] The LCWE includes four working groups focused on the following subjects: intercession, strategy, theology, and leadership development.[188] The working groups organize consultations. Reports on these events are published as "Lausanne Occasional Papers." The LCWE organizes world mission and evangelism conferences. Materials on these gatherings are freely available. Through distributing these documents the Lausanne Movement "seeks to resource evangelical leaders around the world with a number of resources related to world evangelization."[189] Since the LCWE is "a loose coalition" of individuals and organizations and does not have a formal membership, all documents produced by Lausanne Movement participants have consultative, suggestive, and recommending status. Churches and individuals have freedom to accept ideas expressed in these materials or reject them. In order to be accepted they should be introduced with clarity and conviction.

Comparing the status of WCC and LCWE documents it could be concluded that both groups of documents share the same status – they are not in any means normative or ruling documents but rather are suggestive and are the subject of discussions in the WCC and Lausanne Movement constituencies.

---

185. "The Lausanne Movement," quoted at The Lausanne Movement, http://www.lausanne.org/docs/101course/A3/player.html, Lesson 3, #9 (accessed May 2013).

186. The Lausanne Movement, http://www.lausanne.org/docs/101course/A3/player.html, Lesson 3, #5 (accessed May 2013).

187. Scherer and Bevans, *New Directions in Mission and Evangelization 1*, xvii.

188. The Lausanne Movement, http://www.lausanne.org/docs/101course/A3/player.html, Lesson 3, #6 (accessed May 2013).

189. The Lausanne Movement, http://www.lausanne.org/en/about/resources.html (accessed May 2013).

2.2.2. *The Lausanne Covenant* (1974)

This document was drafted during the International Congress on World Evangelization (ICOWE) at Lausanne, Switzerland, in 1974. The Lausanne Covenant "has become the ongoing basis for cooperation in mission among evangelicals the world over, and remains the benchmark statement for evangelical mission theology."[190] The covenant affirms the missionary purpose of the triune God, the divine inspiration and authority of the Bible, and the uniqueness of Christ.[191] It outlines its position on mission and evangelism. Mission, according to the covenant, is rooted in the purpose of God for creation. "The one eternal God . . . who governs all things according to the purpose of his will (Eph. 1:11) . . . has been calling out from the world people for himself (Acts 15:14), and sending his people back into the world (Jn. 17:18) to be his servants and his witnesses, for the extension of his kingdom, the building up of Christ's body, and the glory of his name (Eph. 4:12)."[192] This statement affirms the truth that God created everything and gave purpose to everything for his glory. He receives this glory by saving people and sending them as missionaries to the world to preach the good news to other people. This shows that mission is rooted in going forth and proclaiming. Evangelism is the proclamation of the gospel to people who are still under condemnation in their sin. *The Lausanne Covenant* states it this way: "To evangelize is to spread the good news that Jesus Christ died for our sins and was raised from the dead according to the Scriptures (1 Co. 15:3, 4). And that as the reigning Lord he now offers the forgiveness of sins (Acts 2:32–39) and the liberating gift of the Spirit to all who repent and believe (Jn. 20:21)."[193]

Evangelism is the proclamation of a message of the gospel to the world. This is God's design that the lost people of the world would hear this message of hope from people who are already redeemed by him. He gives to those who are redeemed this task to evangelize and to preach the gospel to all who are perishing. This is the mission of the church, to evangelize the lost

---

190. "The Lausanne Covenant," in Scherer and Bevans, *New Directions in Mission and Evangelization 1*, 253.
191. Ibid., 254.
192. Ibid.
193. Ibid., 255.

people in the world. The result of evangelism is his growing church. "The results of evangelism include obedience to Christ, incorporation into His church (Acts 2:40, 47) and responsible service in the world."[194] In addition to emphasizing the importance of evangelism in the mission of the church, the covenant addresses such issues as mission through social action, mission through justice, and mission through inculturation. It is stated that all of these aspects should be included in the mission of the church.

Based on an overview of the *Lausanne Covenant*, the conclusion could be reached that the following aspects of mission are considered by the evangelicals/Lausanne Movement as part of the church's mission: mission through evangelism, mission through social action, mission through justice, and mission through inculturation.

2.2.3. *The Willowbank Report: Consultation on Gospel and Culture* (1978)

Theologians, anthropologists, linguists, and missionaries participated in the consultation on the cross-cultural communication of the gospel that took place 6–13 January 1978 in Willowbank, Bermuda.[195] The *Willowbank Report: Consultation on Gospel and Culture* came as a result of this meeting and it examines different aspects of communicating the gospel cross-culturally. In particular, it addresses the importance of contextualization in the process of sharing the gospel with people of other cultures.

2.2.4. *An Evangelical Commitment to a Simple Lifestyle* (1980)

The international evangelical consultation on simple lifestyle took place 17–21 March 1980 not far from London. Described as "historic and transforming," the commitment deals with "Christian living in relation to evangelism, relief, and justice, against the background of God's Word and the world's need."[196] The commitment was written and endorsed by the consultation.

---

194. Ibid.

195. "Consultation on Gospel and Culture," in Scherer and Bevans, *New Directions in Mission and Evangelization 1*, 263.

196. "Consultation on Simple Life-Style," in Scherer and Bevans, *New Directions in Mission and Evangelization 1*, 268.

The evangelical/Lausanne Movement's position on several aspects of the church's mission can be discovered while studying the commitment.

First of all, it is a position on mission through care for the environment. According to the covenant, care for the environment should be part of the mission of the church. This position is based on the understanding that God is the Creator of all things and because of this Christians are called to be stewards of how God's resources are used. "We worship God as the Creator of all things, and we celebrate the goodness of his creation. In his generosity he has given us everything to enjoy, and we receive it from his hands with humble thanksgiving (1 Tim 4:4, 6:17). God's creation is marked by rich abundance and diversity, and he intends its resources to be husbanded and shared for the benefit of all."[197]

Caring for the environment means to be wise stewards of God's abundance entrusted to mankind. Wasting and exploiting environmental resources should be avoided by all means because not doing so could result in suffering for the poor. "We therefore denounce environmental destruction, wastefulness and hoarding. We deplore the misery of the poor who suffer as a result of these evils."[198]

Other aspects that, according to the covenant, should be part of the mission of the church include mission through justice, mission through social action, and mission through evangelism.

2.2.5. *The Thailand Statement* (1980)

This document is a result of the Consultation on World Evangelization which took place in Pattaya, Thailand, 16–27 June 1980. The purposes of this meeting were "to assess the progress of world evangelization since Lausanne 1974, to develop new strategies for cross-cultural evangelism in specific contexts, and to seek fresh vision and power for the task."[199] Addressing the subject of the Mandate for World Evangelization, the authors insist that Jesus sends his followers into the world "as his witnesses and servants" and "he has commanded us to proclaim his good news in the power of the Holy

---

197. Ibid., 269.
198. Ibid.
199. "Consultation on World Evangelization," in Scherer and Bevans, *New Directions in Mission and Evangelization 1*, 274.

Spirit to every person of every culture and nation, and to summon them to repent, to believe and to follow him."[200] This is a clear call for evangelism. Also, according to the statement, we are called by Christ to imitate him in our service to people in need. The authors admitted: "We confess that we have not sufficiently followed his example of love in identifying with the poor and hungry, the deprived and the oppressed. Yet all God's people should share his concern for justice and reconciliation throughout human society and for the liberation of men from every kind of oppression."[201] This is a call for Christians to be involved in social action. The statement sheds light on the evangelical position on this issue, saying: "Although evangelism and social action are not identical, we gladly reaffirm our commitment to both."[202] Thus, two aspects of the mission of the church were confirmed in this document: mission through evangelism and mission through social action. At the same time the *Thailand Statement* underlines the primacy of evangelism. This is what makes the evangelical position different from the WCC position. The latter is not so clear about the primacy of evangelism. The statement clarifies its position on the issue of the primacy of evangelism, stating: "This is not to deny that evangelism and social action are integrally related, but rather to acknowledge that of all the tragic needs of human beings none is greater than their alienation from their Creator and the terrible reality of eternal death for those who refuse to repent and believe. If therefore we do not commit ourselves with urgency to the task of evangelization, we are guilty of an inexcusable lack of human compassion."[203] Because of this, those Christians who are not evangelizing the world are guilty "of an inexcusable lack of human compassion." However, this clarification created disagreement among participants of the consultation. Almost a third of the participants signed a "Statement of Concern," arguing "against the separation of socio-political involvement from evangelism."[204]

---

200. Consultation on World Evangelization, "The Thailand Statement," in *Consultation on World Evangelism, Pattaya, Thailand, June 16–17, 1980* (Thailand, 1980), http://www.lausanne.org/en/documents/all/pattaya-1980/49-thailand-statement.html (accessed February 2012).

201. Ibid.

202. Ibid.

203. Ibid.

204. Ibid.

The statement explains the role of the local church in the task of evangelism, stating: "We have recognized the local church as the principal agency for evangelism, whose total membership must therefore be mobilized and trained."[205] This assertion provides a serious challenge for the Slavic immigrant churches in America. Being isolated from the surrounding community by language and culture barriers, local Slavic immigrant churches are unprepared to fulfil this task. How could the whole congregation be "mobilized and trained" to do local evangelism if many of its members barely speak English or do not speak it at all? This is a question the author of this study tries to answer through this work.

2.2.6. *Evangelism and Social Responsibility: An Evangelical Commitment* (1982)

This document is the result of intensive work of the Consultation on the Relation of Evangelism and Social Responsibility that took place in Grand Rapids, Michigan, 19–25 June 1982. This consultation was called to provide a clarification of the evangelicals' position on the relationship between evangelism and social responsibility, and "to dissolve the tension between evangelical advocates of social justice and the more traditional evangelical supporters of mission."[206] Summarizing the discussion on the subject of evangelism and social responsibility, the commitment states: "It has been said, therefore, that evangelism, even when it does not have a primarily social intention, nevertheless has a social dimension, while social responsibility, even when it does not have a primarily evangelistic intention, nevertheless has an evangelistic dimension. Thus, evangelism and social responsibility, while distinct from one another, are integrally related in our proclamation of and obedience to the gospel. The partnership is, in reality, a marriage."[207]

According to the document *Evangelism and Social Responsibility: An Evangelical Commitment*, mission through evangelism and mission through social action/*diaconia*, among other aspects of the mission of the church, are strongly affirmed by the evangelical/Lausanne Movement position.

---

205. Ibid.

206. "Consultation on the Relation of Evangelism and Social Responsibility," in Scherer and Bevans, *New Directions in Mission and Evangelization 1*, 276.

207. John Stott, ed., *Making Christ Known: Historic Mission Documents from the Lausanne Movement* (Grand Rapids, MI: Eerdmans, 1996), 182.

2.2.7. *Transformation: The Church in Response to Human Need* (1983)

This document is the result of the Consultation on the Church in Response to Human Need that took place in Wheaton, Illinois, in 1983. Participants from thirty nations gathered together, "seeking to define the biblical relationship among working with the poor, global relief and development, and evangelization."[208] The *Wheaton '83 Statement* they produced became "the landmark evangelical document on the biblical relationship between gospel ministry and the kingdom of God."[209] While addressing such important issues as evangelism, social responsibility, and the stewardship of creation, the statement pays special attention to the role of the local church in bringing transformation to society. It is recognized that historically, local churches "have been the vehicle for the transmission of the gospel of Jesus Christ."[210] They have worshiped and praised Christ, proclaimed in word and deed the gospel, and discipled his new followers. "In this way transformation takes place in the lives of Christians as individuals, families, and communities; through their words and deeds they demonstrate both the need and reality of ethical, moral, and social transformation."[211] At the same time, the local churches are facing situations in which they have to decide whether to speak openly against the evils of society or not to publicly rebuke these evils. The choice should be based on obedience to the Lord. The very important observation is made that "integrity, leadership and information are essential for the transformation of attitudes and lifestyles of members of local churches . . . If church leadership fails to adequately stress the social dimensions of the Gospel, church members may often overlook these issues (1 Tim. 3:1–7; Heb. 13:17)."

This statement is quite relevant to the Slavic Baptist churches in America. In many of these churches, senior pastors speak limited English and are not able to obtain information about the life of the surrounding society because it is provided in English. As a result, they are isolated from society, remain unaware of issues facing people in society, and cannot adequately respond

---

208. "Consultation on the Church in Response to Human Need," 281.
209. Ibid.
210. Ibid., 288.
211. Ibid.

to these issues. Because of this, they are not able to mobilize their congregations for social involvement in the community. This situation is reflected in the results of the survey of Slavic Baptist church leaders that is provided in chapter 6, "The Present Mission Work of the Slavic Baptist Churches in the US." This is one of the challenges Slavic Baptist churches are facing in their attempts to implement an authentic mission in the immigrant context.

Another point made in the statement which is relevant to Slavic immigrant churches is that the local church has "to be understood as being a part of the universal church. There is therefore a genuine need for help and sharing (*diakonia*) built on fellowship (*koinonia*) between churches of different localities and contexts."[212] Because of isolationistic attitudes developed by leaders and congregations as the product of language and culture barriers, Slavic immigrant churches usually are not practicing fellowship with local English-speaking churches. Inter-church relations are almost non-existent between indigenous English-speaking and Russian-speaking immigrant congregations on the local church level. This is disadvantageous for both immigrant churches and English-speaking churches. All these issues will be discussed in more detail in chapter 7, "Social Challenges of Immigrant Life for the Slavic Baptist Diaspora and Their Impact on Mission," and in chapter 8, "Analysis of Mission Challenges and Opportunities for the Slavic Baptist Diaspora."

The overview of the document *Transformation: The Church in Response to Human Need* clearly demonstrates a shift in the position of evangelicals regarding the mission of the church. In summary, it could be said that according to this document, evangelicals see the following aspects of mission as part of the mission of the church: mission through evangelism, mission through social action/*diaconia*, mission through justice, mission through overcoming violence and building cultures of peace, and mission through care for the environment.

2.2.8. *The Manila Manifesto* (1989)

The Second International Congress on World Evangelization (Lausanne II) took place 11–20 July 1989 in Manila. During the congress, the work of smaller evangelical consultations held between 1977 and 1988 was studied

---

212. Ibid.

and affirmed. The *Manila Manifesto* became the official statement of the congress. It is "a public declaration of evangelical convictions, intentions, and motives based on the two Lausanne II Congress themes, 'Proclaim Christ Until He Comes,' and 'Calling the Whole Church to Take the Whole Gospel to the Whole World.'"[213] The *Manila Manifesto* is considered an extension of the *Lausanne Covenant*. In twenty-one affirmations included in the manifesto and in the main text body of the document, the positions of evangelicals are expressed on different aspects of Christian beliefs, life, and ministry. Based on the overview of this document, we could conclude that the manifesto clearly confirms that from the evangelicals' perspective, mission of the church includes evangelism, worship, involvement in social action, addressing injustice in society, overcoming violence, and creating a culture of peace. It should be done in the context of uniting all Christians. It also defines other faiths as the subject of evangelism rather than being alternative ways to God.

2.2.9. *The Cape Town Commitment* (2010)

This document was endorsed by the Third Lausanne Congress on World Evangelization, held in Cape Town from 16 to 25 October 2010. The commitment was designed to serve "as a roadmap for The Lausanne Movement" over the next decade after the congress. As the statement of the congress, it "is framed in the language of love."[214] It has two parts: "Part I. For the Lord We Love: The Cape Town Confession of Faith," and "Part II. For the World We Serve: The Cape Town Call to Action." The opening statement provides a foundation for the whole document: "The mission of God flows from the love of God. The mission of God's people flows from our love for God and for all that God loves. World evangelization is the outflow of God's love to us and through us. We affirm the primacy of God's grace and we then respond to that grace by faith, demonstrated through the obedience of love. We love because God first loved us and sent his Son to be the propitiation

---

213. "The Manila Manifesto," in Scherer and Bevans, *New Directions in Mission and Evangelization 1*, 292.

214. "The Cape Town Commitment: A Confession of Faith and a Call to Action," *International Bulletin of Missionary Research* 35, no. 2 (Apr 2011): 60, http://www.internationalbulletin.org/system/files/2011-02-ibmr.pdf (accessed March 2012).

for our sins."[215] The love of God for the world is expressed through the mission of the church.

There are several aspects of this mission addressed in the second part of the covenant. Section IIA is called "Bearing witness to the truth of Christ in a pluralistic, globalized world" and is devoted to encouraging Christians to be faithful witnesses of the gospel truth in a modern, pluralistic society. They are called to do this at their workplace, where Christians have a unique opportunity to meet non-believers.[216] The truth should be communicated using globalized media, arts, and emerging technologies.[217] The truth should be shared in the public arena. In other words, oral proclamation of Christ's truth, or evangelism, is seen by evangelicals as a vital part of the church's mission in today's world. Section IIB, which is called "Building the peace of Christ in our divided and broken world," points to the fact that "reconciliation to God is inseparable from reconciliation to one another"[218] and calls Christians to reconcile any conflicts of which they are a part. It calls Christians to acknowledge their involvement in "some of the most destructive contexts of ethnic violence and oppression, and the lamentable silence of large parts of the Church when such conflicts take place."[219] It further asks them to become agents of reconciliation and peace builders in the areas of the world where conflict and violence exist today. This could be seen as a call to a ministry of reconciliation. The covenant challenges the church to raise its voice against social evils in today's society, stating: "Let us rise up as the Church worldwide to fight the evil of human trafficking, and to speak and act prophetically to 'set the prisoners free.' This must include addressing the social, economic and political factors that feed the trade."[220]

Christians are called to bring Christ's peace to the poor, the oppressed, and the disabled.[221] Also, Christ's peace should be given to God's suffering creation. We are assigned to be stewards of God's creation and are

---

215. Ibid., 61.
216. Ibid., 68.
217. Ibid., 69.
218. Ibid., 70.
219. Ibid.
220. Ibid.
221. Ibid., 71.

"commanded to care for the earth and all its creatures, because the earth belongs to God, not to us."[222] This could be considered as a call for the church to do mission through overcoming violence and building cultures of peace, through the ministry of reconciliation, and through care for the environment.

Another very important aspect of mission is discussed in the section called "Living the love of Christ among people of other faiths." This is how Christians should relate to people of other faiths. It is stated that people of other faiths should be seen by Christians as their neighbors in a biblical sense, and Christians should be good neighbors to them. In sharing the good news with them, Christians are called "to be sensitive to those of other faiths, and we reject any approach that seeks to force conversion on them."[223] Christians should commit themselves "to be scrupulously ethical in all our evangelism" and their witness should "be marked by 'gentleness and respect, keeping a clear conscience.'"[224] The place of dialogue is described in the following way: "We affirm the proper place for dialogue with people of other faiths, just as Paul engaged in debate with Jews and Gentiles in the Synagogue and public arenas. As a legitimate part of our Christian mission, such dialogue combines confidence in the uniqueness of Christ and in the truth of the gospel with respectful listening to others."[225] In other words, dialogue could be used as an appropriate method of sharing the gospel with people of other faiths.

The covenant addresses the fact that "migration is one of the great global realities of our era"[226] and encourages Christians who are part of indigenous churches to express their love of Christ to newcomers as the Bible commands, "to love the stranger, defend the cause of the foreigner, visit the prisoner, practice hospitality, build friendships, invite into our homes, and provide help and services."[227] Also, it appeals to Christian immigrants themselves, calling them to be active in promoting their faith through words and deeds among people of the new country.

---

222. Ibid.
223. Ibid.
224. Ibid.
225. Ibid., 72.
226. Ibid.
227. Ibid., 73.

> We encourage Christians who are themselves part of diaspora communities to discern the hand of God, even in circumstances they may not have chosen, and to seek whatever opportunities God provides for bearing witness to Christ in their host community and seeking its welfare. Where that host country includes Christian churches, we urge immigrant and indigenous churches together to listen and learn from one another, and to initiate co-operative efforts to reach all sections of their nation with the gospel.[228]

This statement is directly applicable and encouraging to Slavic Baptist immigrant churches. The results of the survey of leaders of these churches (see chapter 6) show that these churches lack "bearing witness to Christ in their host community and seeking its welfare." Their mission efforts are directed mostly to the homeland. Local mission is neglected, creating an unhealthy situation in the church's life and ministry. Also, what is lacking is cooperation in mission with the indigenous English-speaking churches. These issues will be addressed in more detail in chapter 8 ("Analysis of Mission Challenges and Opportunities for the Slavic Baptist Diaspora") of this study.

This overview of the *Cape Town Commitment* illustrates that the evangelical/Lausanne Movement position on the church's mission is such that it includes evangelism, social action, promoting justice, overcoming violence and building cultures of peace, worship, ministry of reconciliation, care for the environment, and dialogue with people of other faiths.

2.2.10. Summary

Based on studying all of these evangelical/Lausanne Movement documents, it can be concluded that different aspects of the mission of the church are emphasized in these documents. The contemporary position of this theological group of churches on the mission of the church can be identified by combining all these different aspects of mission mentioned in the studied documents. Thus, the evangelical/Lausanne Movement position on the mission of the church could be described as an integration of different aspects of mission such as mission through evangelism, mission through *diaconial*

---

228. Ibid.

social action, mission through overcoming violence and building cultures of peace, mission through justice, mission through the ministry of reconciliation, mission through care of the environment, mission through worship, mission through dialogue with people of other faiths, and mission through inculturation. Kirk summarizes it, saying, "The Church fulfills its mission by worshipping, evangelizing and serving."[229]

2.2.11. WCC vs. Evangelicals: The Great Debate

In the discussion of the impact the WCC and CWME conferences made on the WCC understanding of mission provided above, it was shown that after integration of the IMC and the WCC a new direction in the development of ecumenical theology took place. This direction was from the understanding of the church as the agent in the mission of God toward viewing the world as the arena of God's mission. This paradigm shift in ecumenical theology was first introduced at the Conference in Mexico City (1963). It was deepened during the Conference in Geneva (1966) and reached its culmination during the Uppsala (1968) and Bangkok conferences (1973). During these years, there were theologians and missiologists who expressed great concern about the direction in which the WCC was moving in its interpretation of mission. Some of them "saw Bangkok as evidence that the WCC has gone beyond all hope of redemption"[230] and that the time had come to take action to protect the biblical understanding of the mission of the church. Two very prominent theologians spearheaded the opposition movement. They were Donald McGavran (USA) and Peter Beyerhaus (Germany).

When the draft documents for the Uppsala Conference were published prior to its opening, Donald McGavran responded by publishing an article entitled "Will Uppsala Betray the Two Billion?" In this article he expressed great concern that in the materials for the Fourth Assembly of the WCC there was no reference to bringing the gospel to the multitudes – the two billion people in the world who had not yet heard the gospel. By betraying those McGavran stated he meant "planning courses of action whose sure outcome will be that the two billion will remain in their sins and in their

---

229. J. Andrew Kirk, *The Good News of the Kingdom Coming: The Marriage of Evangelism and Social Responsibility* (Downers Grove, IL: InterVarsity, 1983), 119.

230. Hedlund, *Roots of the Great Debate*, 128.

darkness, chained by false and inadequate ideas of God and man."[231] Since the only part of the assembly documents addressing mission issues is Section II, McGavran focused all his attention on critiquing this section. There are several main points in his evaluation of Section II. (1) He reminds readers about the scriptural truth of the necessity of faith in Christ in order to be saved and the need for those who will bring the gospel message to the unsaved. These needs were not reflected in Section II. It "says nothing about the necessity of faith, nothing about the two billion, and nothing about sending messengers."[232] (2) McGavran pointed to the fact that the word "mission" is used very frequently in Section II. However, "its meaning is nowhere that of communicating the Good News of Jesus Christ to unbelieving men in order that they might believe and live." He emphasized that this section "sets forth a sophisticated theory and theology of mission which the vast majority of Christians and biblical scholars will not accept as the clear will of God toward the world of unbelievers."[233] (3) McGavran saw in all critical passages of the document a deliberate purpose of the authors "to divert attention away from men's need to hear about Christ, to confess Him as Savior, to obey Him as Lord, and to proclaim Him as Redeemer and King."[234] From his perspective the "real issue of today is not dialogue with the resistant, but encouragement of the responsive to accept the Lord as their personal Savior and enter at once into abundant and eternal life."[235] (4) McGavran criticized Section II stating that its main concern was not "with mission but with renewing existing churches and getting them involved with all of life in points of tension, revolutionary movements, critical points of society and 'the agenda of the world.'"[236] (5) McGavran made a strong emphasis again on the importance of bringing the good news of Jesus Christ to those who had not heard it yet (two billion). He affirmed that while doing many good deeds to people in its neighborhood the church is obligated to do the most

---

231. Donald McGavran, "Will Uppsala Betray the Two Billion?" in *The Conciliar-Evangelical Debate: The Crucial Documents 1964–1976*, ed. Donald McGavran (Pasadena, CA: William Carey Library, 1977), 233.
232. Ibid., 235.
233. Ibid., 235–236.
234. Ibid., 236.
235. Ibid., 236.
236. Ibid., 236.

important thing – proclaim the gospel to the unsaved. All good deeds related to earthly issues are temporal, but it "makes an eternal difference whether a man believes on Jesus Christ or not, and two billion do not know enough about Him to believe on Him."[237] McGavran boldly accused the authors of Section II of being in a conspiracy against the classical understanding of mission, saying that the preparation of the draft "has fallen into the hands of a small band of men determined to change the course of mission."[238] They do it using the old mission vocabulary but with a new purpose. Doing this "they are launching a radically new system and are directing mission away from the two billion into new channels."[239] This was a very serious accusation and could not be taken lightly by ecumenical theologians.

Alongside McGavran, there were members of the WCC who also were deeply disappointed by this new direction in mission and openly opposed it. Among them were representatives of the Scandinavian and German churches.[240] One of their responses to the situation was the *Frankfurt Declaration on the Fundamental Crisis in Christian Mission* adopted in March 1970[241] "by a group of fifteen German theologians concerned for the theological integrity of mission."[242] One of the architects of the declaration was Peter Beyerhaus. Analyzing reasons for a crisis in mission he identified four reasons. According to Beyerhaus the first was the fact that in spite of its global dimension and goal, "mission has been essentially centered in the western churches and carried on by western missions."[243] The second reason he named was the nationalistic anti-western reaction of non-Christians in the Afro-Asian countries which had led to development of a renaissance of the old religions in these regions. These religions understood mission "as a disguised attempt to prolong the West's spiritual domination of Asia"[244] and "proselytism." Because

---

237. Ibid., 237.
238. Ibid.
239. Ibid.
240. Hedlund, *Roots of the Great Debate*, 118.
241. Peter Beyerhaus, *Shaken Foundation: Theological Foundations for Mission* (Grand Rapids, MI: Zondervan, 1972), 63.
242. Hedlund, *Roots of the Great Debate*, 118.
243. Peter Beyerhaus, *Missions: Which Way? Humanization or Redemption* (Grand Rapids, MI: Zondervan, 1974), 18.
244. Ibid., 19.

of opposition from these religions some Christians "began to dissociate themselves from such 'proselytism'" putting in danger "the decisive goals of true mission."[245] As the third reason for a crisis in mission Beyerhaus saw in the development of Western theology an "inclination toward religious co-existence and syncretism."[246] Instead of confronting people of other religions with the gospel proclamation, Christians were called to dialogue. "According to this view, the aim of the encounter among members of various religions ought not be conversion but rather only a mutually enriching dialogue and a final understanding."[247] The fourth reason was described by Beyerhaus in the following way: "A final crucial undermining of the traditional understanding of mission is the recent, radical supplanting of all basic religious issues by political-social concerns."[248] The Uppsala Conference presents the WCC's attempt to respond to these four reasons for the crisis in mission. As mentioned in this part of the thesis, this attempt was strongly criticized by evangelicals, and as a counter-document to the Uppsala documents the *Frankfurt Declaration* was accepted. The goal of the *Frankfurt Declaration* was "to reaffirm the biblical basis, content, and goal of mission which, in spite of occasional distortions, have provided the deepest motivation for the whole Protestant missionary movement."[249] The declaration identified seven indispensable basic elements of mission.

1. *Authority.* The authors stated that "mission is grounded in the nature of the gospel" and Scripture has full authority in mission-related issues. They stated: "We therefore oppose the current tendency to determine the nature and task of mission by socio-political analyses of our time and from the demands of the non-Christian world."[250]

2. *Goal.* The declaration proclaims: "The first and supreme goal of mission is the glorification of the name of the one God

---

245. Ibid.
246. Ibid., 20.
247. Ibid.
248. Ibid.
249. Beyerhaus, *Shaken Foundation*, 68.
250. McGavran, "The Frankfurt Declaration on Mission," in *Conciliar-Evangelical Debate*, 288.

throughout the entire world and the proclamation of the Lordship of Jesus Christ, His Son . . . *Humanization* is not the primary goal of mission."[251]

3. *Christology.* The authors declare: "Jesus Christ our Savior, true God and true man, as the Bible proclaims Him in His personal mystery and His saving work, is the basis, content, and authority of our mission . . . We therefore oppose the false teaching . . . that Christ Himself is anonymously so evident in world religions, historical changes, and revolutions that man can encounter Him and find salvation in Him without the direct news of the gospel."[252]

4. *Salvation.* The authors recognize: "Mission is the witness and presentation of eternal salvation performed in the name of Jesus Christ by His Church and fully authorized messengers by means of preaching, the sacraments, and service. This salvation is due to the sacrificial crucifixion of Jesus Christ, which occurred once for all and for all mankind."[253]

5. *Church.* The authors insist: "The primary visible task of mission is *to call out the messianic, saved community* from among all people . . . *We therefore oppose* the view that the Church, as the fellowship of Jesus, is simply a part of the world."[254]

6. *Religions.* The authors declare: "The offer of salvation in Christ is directed without exception to all men who are not yet bound to him in conscious faith. The adherents to the non-Christian religions and world views can receive this salvation only through participation in faith . . . We therefore reject the false teaching that the non-Christian religions and world views are also ways of salvation similar to belief in Christ."[255]

7. *Eschatology.* The authors recognize and declare: "The Christian world mission is the decisive, continuous saving activity of

---

251. Ibid., 289.
252. Ibid.
253. Ibid., 290.
254. Ibid., 291.
255. Ibid.

God among men between the time of the Resurrection and the Second Coming of Jesus Christ. Through the proclamation of the gospel, new nations and people will progressively be called to decision for or against Christ."[256]

These seven essential basic elements of mission as presented in the declaration are in clear divergence with the WCC understanding of mission presented in the Uppsala and other documents. McGavran's article "Will Uppsala Betray the Two Billion?" and the *Frankfurt Declaration* alongside other documents produced by evangelicals in response to the WCC's new interpretation of mission openly challenged the ecumenical position on mission.

The significance of the critique made of the WCC position on mission by Donald McGavran and Peter Beyerhaus can be recognized in the following:

1. The bold actions of these two theologians together with others created some barriers on the path of the humanization of the church mission undertaken by the WCC and at least slowed down the process. Open challenges to the WCC view of mission put ecumenical theologians in the position of defending their teaching.
2. The criticism of the WCC missionary thinking encouraged many Christians who did not share the WCC position to arise and unite their efforts to protect the biblical view of mission. As a result, the Lausanne Movement emerged.
3. The Lausanne Movement emerging as the result of the open challenges to the WCC mission thinking by McGavran, Beyerhaus, and other evangelicals preserved the classical view of mission, "that of communicating the good news of Jesus Christ to unbelieving men in order that they might believe and live."[257]
4. The view of mission as "the carrying out of the great commission"[258] through sending missionaries from one country to another is still alive and well due to the open and active opposition of evangelicals to the WCC attempts to change the course of mission and make it focused on local issues.

---

256. Ibid., 292.
257. McGavran, "Will Uppsala Betray the Two Billion?," 234.
258. Ibid.

5. Critique of the WCC position impacted the understanding of mission among evangelicals as well. They realized the necessity of the church's involvement in social action in addition to evangelism as part of its mission, although with evangelism being primary. This is reflected in the *Lausanne Covenant*.

2.3. Anabaptist Position

As pointed out earlier, Anabaptist faith communities are quite diverse and it is a challenge to identify basic documents that reflect the position of all Anabaptist churches worldwide. For the purpose of this study, several documents produced by different Anabaptist church bodies and institutions from 1963 to 2005 will be explored. Even if these documents are not necessarily accepted by every group of churches in the Anabaptist tradition, they provide the author with reasonably accurate information about the position of this theological tradition on the subject of the mission of the church.

2.3.1. *Mennonite Confession of Faith* (1963)

This confession was adopted in 1963 by the Mennonite General Conference, an association of Mennonite congregations in North America. This document affirms that mission is at the heart of the body of Christ, the church: "We believe that Christ has commissioned the church to go into all the world and make disciples of all the nations, baptizing them, and teaching them to observe His commandments. Jesus entrusted to the church the stewardship of the Gospel, and promised the power of the Holy Spirit for the work of evangelism and missions. This ministry of reconciliation is inherent in the very nature of the church."[259] This statement shows that the mission of the church originated in Jesus himself. He commissioned his apostles to go to the world and make disciples in all nations. His command has been fulfilled through the ministry of the Holy Spirit and the church's "stewardship of the Gospel." Stewardship in this case means proclamation of the gospel. It is the church's responsibility to proclaim the gospel throughout the world. The church is called to evangelism. For Anabaptists, bringing people to peace

---

259. Mennonite Church USA, "Article 9: The Mission of the Church in Society," in *Mennonite Confession of Faith, 1963* (Kalona, IA: Historical Committee, 1963), http://www.mcusa-archives.org/library/resolutions/1963confession.html (accessed December 2010).

with God through evangelism and mission is the ministry of reconciliation, which is "inherent in the very nature of the church."[260] According to the *Mennonite Confession*, the function of the church is to share the good news about salvation in Christ with all people and call them to follow him and become his disciples. The confession states: "It is the function of the church to demonstrate to the world the will of God, to witness to all men of the saving power and intention of God in Christ, and to make disciples of all the nations."[261]

This document shows that according to the Anabaptist position, the mission of the church clearly includes evangelism as proclamation of the gospel. While proclamation is at the heart of the church's mission, it does not exclude the need to address the injustices in society as well. The church must care for the social issues in its context in order to be a true witness to God and his kingdom. "The church is interested not only in the spiritual welfare of men but in their total well-being. Jesus Himself fed the hungry, healed the sick, and had compassion on the poor. The church should likewise minister to those who are in physical or social need and to those who are physically or emotionally ill. The church should witness against racial discrimination, economic injustice, and all forms of human slavery and moral degradation."[262]

The *Mennonite Confession of Faith* clearly demonstrates that the Anabaptist position on the mission of the church includes social action and efforts to restore justice in society, as well as evangelism and a ministry of reconciliation.

2.3.2. *Creation: Called to Care* (1991)

This document is a statement adopted by the Annual Conference of the Church of the Brethren, one of the Anabaptist church bodies. It is devoted solely to the subject of the church's relation to creation and could be used as a source for understanding the Anabaptist position on mission through care of the environment. Answering the question, "Why should Christians care about the environment?" the statement insists that according to Genesis, "God has promised to fulfill all of creation, not just humanity, and has made

---

260. Ibid.
261. Ibid.
262. Ibid.

humans the stewards of it."²⁶³ Also, Christ came to the earth to fulfill the promise of God "to save humankind and nature" and the whole creation is "the place where God's will is being done on earth as it is in heaven."²⁶⁴ It is affirmed that God's covenants (old and new) with his people "mean that people of faith are responsible for their part in renewing and sustaining the creation."²⁶⁵ The dangerous situation the creation is in right now is estimated as a global crisis, and it is concluded that "the global environment continues to deteriorate in large part because the lifestyle of an affluent minority puts a tremendous drain on its resources."²⁶⁶ It is underlined that a right relationship with the Creator implies a harmonious relationship with the creation. "The Bible knows nothing of a right relationship with God the Creator that does not include a right relationship with the creation: with land and mountains, oceans and skies, sun and moon, plants and animals, wind and rain. Our vocation is to walk with God in gently tending God's wonderful, strong, fragile, and enduring creation. The meaning of our existence is found in this vocation."²⁶⁷ The roots of the current crisis can be found in the secularization of the view of life and in modern society's understanding the world "apart from any relational reference to God."²⁶⁸ Human sin is the source of this crisis. The statement calls the church to re-evaluate its attitude toward creation and to accept new ways of dealing with it, providing practical care of it.²⁶⁹ The overview of this document shows that from the perspective of this particular Anabaptist group, mission through care of the environment is an integral part of the mission of the church in today's world.

---

263. Church of the Brethren Annual Conference, "Creation: Called to Care," *Church of the Brethren Annual Conference Official Documents*, http://www.brethren.org/ac/statements/1991creationcalledtocare.html (accessed March 2012).

264. Ibid.

265. Ibid.

266. Ibid.

267. Ibid.

268. Ibid.

269. Ibid. The document states, "The church is that part of creation that has received and covenanted itself to embody God's redemption in Christ. As Paul writes in Romans, the whole created universe yearns with eager expectation for the children of God to be revealed. As the body of Christ we are to live out a new and restored relationship to the creation which itself has been won back to God by Christ's redemptive death and resurrection. The church therefore is to live as a visible sign of a restored relationship among humanity, the creation, and God."

The *Creation: Called to Care* document inspired the leadership of the Church of the Brethren denomination to release a *Resolution on Global Warming and Atmospheric Degradation* in 1991, where they set the direction of the Brethren church to care for creation anew, stating "That we are called by God to live in harmony with all of creation, and that our covenantal relationship to care for the creation requires us to be aware of present and impending threats to our environment and to take action to preserve the integrity of creation."[270] This proves that this group of churches is very much concerned about creation and sees care of the environment as their mission.

2.3.3. *Confession of Faith in a Mennonite Perspective* (1995)

This confession is the work of two Mennonite groups in North America: the Mennonite Church (MC) and the General Conference Mennonite Church (GC). It was adopted on 28 July 1995. The position of these Anabaptist groups on the mission of the church can be found through studying different articles of the confession. According to this document, the church is sent by Christ to be his witness in the world. The church is called to proclaim the good news and to make Christ's disciples. "We believe that the church is called to proclaim and to be a sign of the kingdom of God. Christ has commissioned the church to be his witnesses, making disciples of all nations, baptizing them, and teaching them to observe all things he has commanded."[271] It is clear proof that evangelism is part of the church's mission, according to the Anabaptist position. The Anabaptists' social focus is primarily on the church body since they see it as "the spiritual, social, and political body that gives its allegiance to God alone."[272] Even though the church is their primary focus, Christians are still to be subject to the

---

270. Church of Brethren General Board, "Resolution on Global Warming and Atmospheric Degradation," 21 October 1991, http://support.brethren.org/site/DocServer/1991/Global_Warming_and_Atmospheric_Degradation.pdf?docID=922 (accessed August 2010).

271. Mennonite Church USA, "Article 10. The Church in Mission," in *Confession of Faith in a Mennonite Perspective, 1995* (Wichita, KS: Historical Committee, 1995), http://www.mcusa-archives.org/library/resolutions/1995/1995-10.html, (accessed March 2012).

272. Mennonite Church USA, "Article 23. The Church's Relation to Government and Society," in *Confession of Faith in a Mennonite Perspective, 1995* (Wichita, KS: Historical Committee, 1995), http://www.mcusa-archives.org/library/resolutions/1995/1995-23.html (accessed January 2011).

authorities God has ordained and to show compassion to the world in their context. In Article 23, it is stated: "We also witness by being ambassadors for Christ (2 Cor. 5:20), calling the nations (and all persons and institutions) to move toward justice, peace, and compassion for all people. In so doing, we seek the welfare of the city to which God has sent us (Jer. 29:7)."[273] This could be interpreted as an encouragement for churches to take part in social action.

The Anabaptist position concludes that justice is an aspect of the church's witness in word and deed. The church is to give witness to Christ's reign, as well as "proclaiming the reign of God in word and deed."[274] For them, "word explains deed, and deed authenticates word."[275] The further analysis of the *Confession of Faith in a Mennonite Perspective* shows that the Anabaptist position on the mission of the church expressed in this document includes evangelism, social action, and justice, as well as the following aspects: overcoming violence and building a culture of peace, a ministry of reconciliation,[276] and care of the environment.[277]

2.3.4. *Mennonite Creation Care Network Annual Report*

This is a document produced by the Mennonite Creation Care Network (MCCN). This organization is "a network of Mennonite people and agencies actively engaged in the care and restoration of God's creation."[278] It was started in 2005, when the Mennonite Church of Canada and the Mennonite Church of USA appointed their representatives to the MCCN. The vision of the MCCN is as follows: "Christ, who created the world in peace and

---

273. Ibid.
274. Ibid.
275. Ibid.
276. "Article 22. Peace, Justice, and Nonresistance" states, "We believe that peace is the will of God. God created the world in peace, and God's peace is most fully revealed in Jesus Christ, who is our peace and the peace of the whole world. Led by the Holy Spirit, we follow Christ in the way of peace, doing justice, bringing reconciliation, and practicing nonresistance even in the face of violence and warfare."
277. "Article 5. Creation and Divine Providence" proclaims, "All creation ultimately has its source outside itself and belongs to the Creator." By God's design, humanity was given a "special dignity among all the works of creation." Because of this, humanity was created to live at peace with one another and "care for the rest of creation."
278. Mennonite Creation Care Network, "Annual Report 2008," http://blog.goshen.edu/creationcare/2008/12/31/annual-report-2008/ (accessed December 2008).

sustains all things, calls us to be stewards of the earth and to bring rest and renewal to the land and everything that lives on it. In response to this call, we will equip lay people and leaders with tools, resources and models that will educate, encourage, and inspire the church to care for creation, which is an expression of God's love."[279] The MCCN calls the regional grassroots groups, as well as institutional agencies and churches, to promote environmental stewardship activities in order to inspire people "to be agents of change at home and in the global context." Participation of different Mennonite church bodies in the network shows that these churches see care of the environment as part of their mission.

2.3.5. Summary

The overview of the *Confession of Faith* and other documents of the Mennonite churches representing the Anabaptist tradition today shows that the Anabaptist position on the mission of the church includes different aspects of mission. These aspects are mission through evangelism, mission through *diaconia*/social action, mission through overcoming violence and building cultures of peace, mission through justice, mission through the ministry of reconciliation, and mission through care of the environment.

2.4. Concluding Summary

This part of the chapter is devoted to summarizing the findings of the analysis of the basic documents of three church groups (WCC/ecumenical, evangelical/Lausanne Movement, and Anabaptist). The results of studying these basic documents of different groups is presented in the chronological order of their initial publication. This allows for evaluating the progressive development of the theological positions of these groups of churches on the mission of the church.

The WCC position on the mission of the church in the middle of the 1970s included only such aspects of mission as evangelism, social action, and worship and liturgy. Then, as time went by, the new aspects of mission were accepted as part of the church mission by the World Conferences on Mission and Evangelism, the WCC Central Committee, the WCC Commission on

---

279. Ibid.

World Mission and Evangelism, and WCC assemblies. As a result, by 2010, the WCC position on the mission of the church included such aspects as mission through evangelism, mission through social action/*diaconia*, mission through overcoming violence and building cultures of peace, mission through justice, mission through care of the environment, mission through liturgy and worship, mission through the everyday life of Christians, mission through teaching, mission through dialogue with people of other religions, mission through inculturation, and ministry of reconciliation with God, people, and creation. This is an inclusive position! It shows how the WCC has expanded their understanding of the mission of the church.

It is worth mentioning here the historical development of understanding relations between evangelism and the mission of the church from the WCC perspective. This is one of the contemporary issues upon which Christians of different traditions are not always in agreement. The WCC's position on evangelism has gone through various changes with time. Priscilla Pope-Levison explored the chronological development of this position from 1961 to 1991. She has shown that in the beginning of this period, in the documents of the assembly at New Delhi in 1961 and the Commission on World Mission Evangelism (CWME) at Mexico City in 1963, evangelism in its "traditional" form was criticized. According to these documents, "whereas traditional evangelism calls people in conversion to leave the world, a new evangelism should call people in conversion into the world where God is actively at work."[280] During the next several conferences – in Bangkok (1973), Nairobi (1975), Melbourne (1980), Vancouver (1983), San Antonio (1989), and Canberra (1989) – the WCC position on the issue of evangelism went through a series of changes, and as a result, the WCC began to see evangelism in an integral relationship with ecclesiology. Referring to the document *Mission in Christ's Way: Your Will Be Done*, accepted at the World Conference on Mission and Evangelism in San Antonio (1989), Pope-Levison states: "The document unequivocally lifted up the church as the primary evangelist. In addition, the document cited evangelism and the church's nurture through education, worship, prayer, and celebration

---

280. Priscilla Pope-Levison, "Evangelism in the WCC: From New Delhi to Canberra," in James A. Scherer and Stephen B. Bevans, *New Directions in Mission and Evangelization 2* (Maryknoll, NY: Orbis, 1994), 128.

of the sacraments as mutually inspirational activities."[281] This brings the WCC position on evangelism closer to the evangelical/Lausanne Movement position on this issue.

The evangelical/Lausanne Movement position on the mission of the church in the mid-1970s included the following aspects: evangelism, social action, justice, and inculturation. By 2010, their position significantly expanded and now includes evangelism, social action/*diaconia*, overcoming violence and building cultures of peace, justice, care of the environment, worship, presence and dialogue, inculturation, and mission in the context of other faiths. It has become, to some extent, closer to the WCC position since the middle of the 1970s.[282] As Justin Thacker notes, "the vast majority of evangelicals now agree that both evangelism and social action are needed if we are to pursue salvation in the biblical sense."[283]

The Anabaptist position on the mission of the church in the middle of the 1960s focused on evangelism, social action, and justice restoration. By 2005, their position included evangelism, social action/*diaconia*, overcoming violence and building cultures of peace, justice, care of the environment, and worship.

As we can see, the positions of all three ecclesiastical groups on the subject of the mission of the church have gone through a process of transformation during the last few decades. On the one hand, this is the result of the hard work of theologians and missiologists of each ecclesiastical group trying to deepen their understanding of Scripture and what it teaches about the mission of the church. On the other hand, it is the result of a constant search

---

281. Ibid., 128.

282. Richard Yates Hibbert, "The Place of Church Planting in Mission: Towards a Theological Framework," *Evangelical Review of Theology* 33, no. 4 (Oct 2009): 316–331. Hibbert provides a brief overview of how the evangelicals/Lausanne Movement's position on relations between evangelism and social responsibilities has been transformed in the time between the Lausanne Congress in 1974 and Lausanne II Congress in Manila, in 1989. Clearly, it became much closer to the WCC position.

283. "Holistic Gospel in a Developing Society: Some Biblical, Historical and Ethical Considerations," *Evangelical Review of Theology* 33, no. 3 (July 2009): 220. Thacker makes a very important observation, stating that if we are united to Christ, we are taking part in God's mission. And because of this, it is "not *our* compassion that is relevant, but God's compassion flowing through us. It is not *our* evangelism or social action that matters, but God's work in the world exercised through us."

by all these churches for mission strategies that could be more relevant to their social, economic, and political contexts.

It is important to note that not only the number of aspects included in the mission of the church has been changed. The understanding of the role of these aspects in the mission of the church has changed as well. If in the middle of the 1970s the WCC position strongly emphasized the role of social action, and evangelism received not so much emphasis, then in 2010, it sees evangelism to be as important as social action.[284] The two are on an equal basis. If in the middle of the 1970s the evangelical/Lausanne Movement's position strongly emphasized evangelism, and not so much emphasis was placed on social action, then in 2010, it claimed that social action was a very important companion of evangelism. The positions of these two groups of churches were far apart in the mid-1970s. The major point of divergence was the role of evangelism in mission. Today, based on the analysis done in this chapter, it is evident that their positions moved to the point of convergence on most aspects of mission. Significant disagreement still exists between the two groups on the issue of relations with other religions. According to Matthey: "The particular question of a more or less positive theological evaluation of religious convictions and ethical choices of people who do not confess Jesus Christ remains probably the major point of debate between ecumenical and evangelical missiologists."[285]

The existence of these changes in the understanding of mission proves the truth that there is no single agreed definition of the mission of the church in the world. As Bosch states, "there is a constant need for mission itself to

---

284. Jacob Kavunkal provides an interesting comparison of how two terms "mission" and "evangelization" have been used interchangeably in history by Christians of different countries at different times. In certain cases, "mission" meant the verbal proclamation of the gospel, as "evangelization" was used to refer to social justice work, inculturation and dialogue. In other cases, these terms were used in the opposite way. Kavunkal argues that the two terms should have the same meaning and that "Christians have to become the presence of the good news wherever they are, and so make Jesus Christ visible and attractive through their lives. Then their sending in 'mission' will be a living proof that they bear 'Good News' – and so 'mission' will truly be 'evangelization.'" ("Mission or Evangelization?," *Mission Studies: Journal of the International Association for Mission Studies* 21, no. 1 [2004]: 64).

285. Jacques Matthey, "Missiology in the World Council of Churches: Update. Presentation, Theological Background and Emphases of the Most Recent Mission Statement of the World Council of Churches (WCC)," *International Review of Mission* 90, no. 359 (Oct 2001): 429.

be transformed"[286] and the "mission of the church needs constantly to be renewed and re-conceived."[287] Kirk, analyzing challenges the Christian mission is facing in the context of the epistemological crisis of the West, points to the fact that although the mission of the church should constantly go through a "renewal and re-conceive process" and should be "freshly rediscovered in each new generation,"[288] the call of the church is unchangeable. Kirk states: "The task of the church remains, as it always has, the faithful exposition of an unchanging message to individuals. Irrespective of the cultural changes, the fundamental needs of human beings remain unchanged. The church's main responsibility is to offer God's forgiveness and strength in the call for a new style of living following the way of Christ."[289]

Mission is a vibrant, constantly developing function of the church, shaped by the circumstances in which the church finds itself in each particular time in history and in each particular culture. Despite this fact, there is still a need for a definition of mission of the church, at least in its contemporary meaning. This could change in the future, but for making an evaluation of the mission work of the church today, a definition must be established. In order to do so for the purpose of this study, the results of the analysis of the positions of the three ecclesiastical groups will be compared, and aspects of mission where these groups mostly converge will be identified. These aspects will be included in the modern understanding of the mission of the church, which will be used later in this study.

2.5. Evangelism and Social Action: The WCC's Use of the Term "Witness" and Evangelical Discussions of the Issue of Social Justice

The term "evangelism" is often used interchangeably with the term "witness." However, it is important to understand what meaning is included in the term "witness" in each particular case. Jesus Christ himself used this term,

---

286. Bosch, *Transforming Mission*, 511.
287. Ibid., 519.
288. Kirk, "Christian Mission and the Epistemological Crisis of the West," in *To Stake a Claim: Mission and the Western Crisis of Knowledge*, ed. J. Andrew Kirk and Kevin J. Vanhoozer (Maryknoll, NY: Orbis, 1999), 157.
289. Ibid.

saying to his disciples: "You are witnesses of these things"[290] and "you will be my witnesses in Jerusalem and in all Judea and Samaria, and to the end of the earth."[291] The meaning of the word "witness" in these instances refers "to the act of one who has a first-hand experience of an event, can vouch for it, and commends one's account for other people's acceptance."[292] In the New Testament, witness is specifically applied to the life and ministry of Jesus Christ and his identity as Son of God. However, in the WCC documents the term "witnessing" is used in a much broader sense. At the New Delhi Conference (1961) "witness" was defined in the following way: "When we speak of witness, we mean testimony to the whole activity of God in the creation and preservation of the world, but especially in his mighty acts in Israel's history and in the redemption of the world by Jesus Christ."[293] The report of this conference suggests applying the term "witness" to quite a wide variety of aspects of church life: "Witness to the Gospel must therefore be prepared to engage in the struggle for social justice and for peace; it will have to take the form of humble service and of a practical ministry of reconciliation amidst the actual conflict of our times."[294] At the conference in Nairobi (1975), "witness" was presented with a very inclusive meaning:

> "Confessing Christ" or "Christian Witness" describes above all, that continuous act by which a Christian or Christian community proclaims God's acts in history and seeks to manifest Christ as "the Word that was made flesh and dwelt among us" (John 1:14). Our confessing Christ today would deny God's incarnation if it would be limited to only some areas of life. It concerns the wholeness of human life; our words and acts; our personal and communal existence; our worship and responsible service; our particular and ecumenical context.[295]

---

290. Luke 24:48.

291. Acts 1:8.

292. Paulos Mar Gregorios, "The Witness of the Churches: Ecumenical Statements on Mission and Evangelism," *Ecumenical Review* 40, no. 3–4 (July–Oct 1988): 359.

293. Visser't Hooft, *The New Delhi Report*, 79.

294. Ibid., 86.

295. "Confessing Christ Today," in Scherer and Bevans, *New Directions in Mission and Evangelization 1*, 8.

At the Sixth Assembly of the WCC in Vancouver (1983), it was stated regarding witness:

> As the church witnesses to the gospel, it needs to reflect faithfully the totality and universality of God's mission in a world divided into rich and poor, different ideological camps, male and female, young and old, slave and free, able and disabled. In its witness to the poor and the oppressed it can and must be the voice of those who are often rendered voiceless. God's own upholding of the right of the poor, the outcast, the widows and the orphan is a rebuke to complacent Christians and churches, and a summons to repentance and a new commitment to the cause of justice. To claim to witness to the poor and to side with them without working to change the conditions which make for poverty is hypocritical. The churches must struggle to put in place a new international order for a more just world and be willing to change their own structures in response. It must call on those who have power to use their power to make human life more human.[296]

Based on the cited statements of the WCC conferences it could be concluded that the word "witness" in the WCC documents became synonymous with the words "mission" and "evangelism." It includes the church's involvement in movements for social justice and for establishing a more just world. Priscilla Pope-Levison in her study of the presence of the term "evangelism" in the WCC documents states that the terms "mission," "witness," and "evangelism" are used interchangeably in ecumenical literature.[297] Often "both 'witness' and 'mission' are used instead of 'evangelism.'"[298] This is confusing and could be misleading.

The author of this study understands evangelism in the way it is presented in the *Lausanne Covenant*:

---

296. "Issue 1 Report: Witnessing in a Divided World," *International Review of Mission* 72, no 288 (Oct 1983): 656.

297. Priscilla Pope-Levison, "Evangelism in the WCC," in Scherer and Bevans, *New Directions in Mission and Evangelization 2*, 127.

298. Ibid.

> To evangelize is to spread the good news that Jesus Christ died for our sins and was raised from the dead according to the Scripture, and that as the reigning Lord he now offers the forgiveness of sins and the liberating gift of the Spirit to all who repent and believe . . . Evangelism itself is the proclamation of the historical, biblical Christ as Saviour and Lord, with a view to persuading people to come to him personally and so be reconciled to God . . . The results of evangelism include obedience to Christ, incorporation into his Church and responsible service in the world.[299]

Kirk states this truth in a more concise way, saying that "evangelism might be understood . . . as 'spreading the good news that in Jesus Christ God is establishing a new order [a new way of being human] and calling people to renounce all alternatives and embrace this reality.'"[300] Evangelism expects a personal response from those who hear this good news. This response should result in a complete change of life of the person as she/he hands over "the direction of their lives to Jesus Christ"[301] and turns her/his "back on a false way of life."[302] The apostle Paul points to such change, saying about those who responded to his evangelism in Thessalonica that they had "turned to God from idols, to serve a living and true God."[303] This is how the author of this study understands evangelism and its fruit in a person's life.

The subject of the church's response to the contemporary issues of the society it is living in is the source of debate and disagreements. How should the church react to the presence of injustice in society toward the poor and marginalized, inequality in material wealth distribution between people, and discrimination based on race, gender and other factors? Is social action a legitimate part of the church's mission or not? This question has been addressed by evangelicals during different conferences in response to the WCC's move in mission theology towards understanding mission as humanization and liberation. The understanding of this issue by evangelicals

---

299. "The Lausanne Covenant," Paragraph 4, in Hedlund, *Roots of the Great Debate*, 318.
300. Kirk, *What Is Mission?*, 61.
301. Ibid.
302. Ibid., 62.
303. 1 Thess 1:8.

has gone through the process of change and development. During the first part of the twentieth century evangelicals, in reaction to the "social gospel," distanced themselves from social involvement.[304] However, during the second part of the century this situation started to change. Already, at the World Congress on Evangelism in Berlin (1966), it was clearly stated: "Evangelism has social implications, but its primary thrust is the winning of men to a personal relationship to Jesus Christ."[305] At the Congress on the Church's Worldwide Mission in Wheaton (1966) the *Wheaton Declaration* was accepted. In this document, it was recognized that evangelicals "have lost the biblical perspective and limited themselves only to preaching a gospel of individual salvation without sufficient involvement in their social and community responsibilities."[306] The declaration called evangelicals to social action and concern for justice, accompanying such action, where possible, with verbal proclamation of the gospel.[307] In the *Chicago Declaration of Evangelical Social Concern*, evangelism and social transformation are described as indivisible.[308] The *Lausanne Covenant* as the main document of the Lausanne Congress on World Evangelization (1974) addresses the issue of social responsibility and mission, stating: "Although reconciliation with other people is not reconciliation with God, nor is social action evangelism, nor is political liberation salvation, nevertheless we affirm that evangelism and socio-political involvement are both part of our Christian duty . . . When people receive Christ they are born again into his kingdom . . . and must seek not only to exhibit its righteousness ourselves, . . . but also to spread its righteousness in the midst of an unrighteous world."[309]

In the covenant, the WCC definition of mission as social action and presentation of salvation as political liberation are strongly rejected. Both evangelism and social action are presented in the covenant as two distinctive

---

304. "The Grand Rapids Report on Evangelism and Social Responsibility: An Evangelical Commitment," in Stott, *Making Christ Known*, 179.

305. Roger E. Hedlund, "Why the Berlin Congress," in *Roots of the Great Debate*, 249.

306. Roger E. Hedlund, "The Wheaton Declaration," in *Roots of the Great Debate*, 242.

307. Ibid., 243.

308. Craig Ott, Stephen J. Strauss with Timothy C. Tennent, *Encountering Theology of Mission: Biblical Foundations, Historical Developments, and Contemporary Issues* (Grand Rapids, MI: Baker Academic, 2010), 139.

309. "The Lausanne Covenant," in Stott, *Making Christ Known*, 26–27.

parts of a Christian's duty.[310] One of the most significant consultations on the subject was the International Consultation on the Relationship between Evangelism and Social Responsibility held in Grand Rapids, Michigan, in 1982. The report of this consultation, *An Evangelical Commitment*, affirms the importance of both social action and evangelism for the mission of the church and states that there are three ways in which social action could relate to evangelism: (1) social action "is a consequence of evangelism;" (2) social action "can be a bridge to evangelism;" (3) social action "not only follows evangelism as its consequence and aim, and precedes it as its bridge, but also accompanies it as its partner."[311] The report insists: "Evangelism, even when it does not have a primary social intention, nevertheless has a social dimension, while social responsibility, even when it does not have a primary evangelistic intention, nevertheless has an evangelistic dimension. Thus, evangelism and social responsibility, while distinct from one another, are integrally related in our proclamation of and obedience to the Gospel. The partnership is, in reality, a marriage."[312]

Addressing the issue of primacy, the report states that "if we must choose, then we have to say that the supreme and ultimate need of all humankind is the saving grace of Jesus Christ, and that therefore a person's eternal, spiritual salvation is of greater importance than his or her temporal and material well-being."[313] In 1983, at the Consultation on the Church in Response to Human Need held in Wheaton, "evangelicals not only embraced social responsibility but began with greater boldness to speak of holistic mission."[314] There is no consensus among evangelicals regarding the validity of holistic mission. Some of them express concern that "evangelical missiology will develop in the direction of conciliar missiology . . . and that mission may be hijacked by a particular social agenda."[315] At the same time, theologians who come from contexts where poverty and injustice are widely present "view a

---

310. Ibid., 25.
311. "The Grand Rapids Report on Evangelism and Social Responsibility," in Stott, *Making Christ Known*, 181–182.
312. Ibid., 182.
313. Ibid., 183.
314. Ott, Strauss, and Tennent, *Encountering Theology of Mission*, 141.
315. Ibid., 143.

strictly spiritual solution as inadequate."[316] The Third Lausanne Congress on World Evangelism reaffirmed the importance of evangelism saying: "We must *proclaim* the truth. Spoken proclamation of the truth of the gospel remains paramount in our mission. This cannot be separated from living out the truth. Works and words must go together."[317] Also, it calls Christians to active participation in building the peace of Christ in a divided and broken world.[318] This is a clear call for social action.

This brief overview of the development of the evangelicals' position on evangelism and social action shows the importance of the latter for the mission of the church. Although evangelism is primary, the social responsibility of individual Christians is also crucial in the church's mission.

The author of this thesis shares the evangelical position on the issue of social action in the mission of the church. He shares Kirk's view of the church and its responsibility for its neighbors: "The church is a local community. As such it possesses a mission mandate for its own particular situation. It has to identify with the people in whose midst it is set, called to meet their needs and bear their burdens."[319] The author of this thesis believes that the church is called to be "the light and the salt" in society, pointing people when ethical issues need to be addressed to God and his principles. The author also believes that the church is called to take care of the poor, marginalized, and disadvantaged in society. However, all this should be done not in the name of the church, but in Christ's name. The church can make efforts to transform society by calling leaders to more just and ethical decisions. The church can relate to culture and society in different ways depending on particular circumstances. According to Kirk, "Where, for example, it is under pressure to compromise with a particularly distasteful political regime or where it senses the abandonment of ethical norms given by God for human wellbeing, it may have to take a stance against culture. If, however, it is a persecuted minority, such a stance may have to take the form of being

---

316. Ibid.

317. The Lausanne Movement, *The Cape Town Commitment* (2010), http://www.lausanne.org/en/documents/ctcommitment.html#p2-1, section IIA, article 1 (accessed May 2013).

318. Ibid., section IIB, articles 1–6.

319. Kirk, *What Is Mission?*, 94.

above culture. In such circumstances, the only way open to it to maintain its faithfulness may well be withdrawal."[320]

From his personal experience the author knows what it means to belong to a church which is persecuted. In such a position there are not very many options available for the church to make an influence on the government and society in general. The only option is to live a righteous life and extend a caring hand to people around at a personal level since the church as an institution is either not recognized at all or has very limited rights in the society. Of course, this includes sharing the gospel with people where it is possible.

2.6. A Contemporary Understanding of Mission from a New Testament Perspective

On the previous pages of this chapter, positions of three ecclesiastical groups on the subject of mission of the church have been analyzed and compared. Below is a brief theological exploration of this subject based on the New Testament.

2.6.1. Discipleship

The text of Scripture that is widely used in discussions on mission and evangelism is often called the "Great Commission." This is Matthew 28:16–20. There are four different versions of the "great commission," better called the "last commission." There is one in each Gospel (Mark 16:15–18; Luke 24:44–47; John 20:21; cf. 17:18). Mortimer Arias notes that each of these versions "appears in a different context and with a different emphasis."[321] This means that for a right understanding of Matthew's Gospel "we must decipher this 'last commission,' and, conversely, to understand the 'last commission' we must comprehend the totality of Matthew."[322] According to Arias, the method for mission is clearly explained by the Lord in his mandate: "Make disciples of all nations."[323] This means that the call of the church is to make disciples in all nations around the globe. In other words,

---

320. Ibid., 93.
321. Mortimer Arias, "Rethinking the Great Commission," *Theology Today* 47, no. 4 (Jan 1991): 410.
322. Ibid.
323. Ibid., 411.

"mission is discipleship."[324] Based on this assumption Arias emphasizes the importance of a serious approach to discipleship in the church. He points to the following: "Discipleship in the Kingdom, however, is much more than the study of the Scriptures and theoretical teaching and learning. It means the engagement of the whole life in following Jesus on the way of the Kingdom. Jesus' disciples were trained not only in orthodoxy, the right doctrine, but also in orthopraxis, the right way of doing, living, and dying."[325]

The source for discipleship training should be the gospel itself. The Great Commission mandate states very clearly: "Teaching them to obey everything I have commanded you." By the time the "Great Commission" was communicated to the apostles by Jesus they had already learned from him everything that was later included by Matthew in his Gospel. The ethical commands in the Sermon on the Mount are principles for living in the kingdom. In the parable of the two builders Jesus points to the importance of action and deeds (Matt 7). He emphasizes the significance of "producing and showing the fruits of the Kingdom (7:16; 21:43) and the absolute requirement of 'a higher justice,' higher than that of the Pharisees and scribes, in order to enter into the Kingdom (5:20)."[326] Arias states that discipleship "is not merely obeying a commandment but following a person, a commitment to God and the neighbor in Jesus Christ."[327] Jesus calls people to follow him, saying: "If anyone wants to be *my* disciple . . . take up your cross and follow me" (Matt 16:24). Jesus also clarifies that the path to him goes through our neighbor: "Whoever receives a little one in my name receives me," and, "Whatever you have done to one of these . . . you have done it to me" (18:5; 25:40, 45). Arias concludes that "everything we do for our neighbor is not merely activism, social service or social action; it is a service to Christ himself. All our social actions have a Christological meaning. The neighbor becomes 'the sacrament of Christ.'"[328] Kirk points to the truth that the Sermon of the Mount "is a description of the righteousness required by

---

324. Ibid.
325. Ibid., 412.
326. Ibid., 413.
327. Ibid., 414.
328. Ibid.

the kingdom (Matt. 6:33)"[329] and is expected to be observed by disciples. It "defines discipleship and its practice membership in the kingdom (Matt. 5:20; 7:21–23; 25:34ff.)."[330] The result of evangelism as part of the mission of the church "can be viewed from God's point of view as the creation of a whole new life in the image of Jesus Christ (2 Cor. 3:18) – the restoration of the glory lost as a result of sin (Rom. 3:23; Heb. 2:10) – or it can be viewed from the human perspective as a following after Jesus Christ."[331] In other words, the product of evangelism is the transformed lives of people who decide to follow Jesus Christ and are then called "disciples." This proves the truth that the main goal of the Great Commission is making disciples in this world.[332] According to Kirk, "it is safe to conclude, therefore, that central to mission in the way of Christ is the life and witness of a renewed community,"[333] a community of Christ's disciples. The New Testament clearly teaches that the early church observed a distinctive lifestyle in accordance with the teaching of Jesus.[334] The letter to the Ephesians provides a good evidence for this. According to this epistle, "The Christians were exhorted to live 'according to the likeness of God in true righteousness and holiness' (Eph. 4:24), which is the 'way you learned Christ . . . taught in him, as truth is in Jesus' (Eph. 4:20–21). The three fundamental principles that were to guide their life together were *absolute honesty tempered by love* (Eph. 4:1; 4:25–26), *provision for the needy* (Eph. 4:28), and *forgiveness* (Eph. 4:32; 5:2)."[335] This shows that discipleship has very practical implications for people's lives. It affects their relationships with each other. It makes an impact on their attitude toward people outside their Christian community. It calls them to the life of reconciliation.

> The focus of the mission of the church is to make disciples of all nations. This commission from Jesus is recorded in a number of different forms in the Gospels and Acts (Mt. 28:19,20;

---

329. Kirk, *What Is Mission?*, 46.
330. Ibid.
331. Ibid., 69.
332. Ibid.
333. Ibid., 209.
334. Ibid.
335. Ibid., 211.

Lk. 24:46,47; Jn 20:21; Acts 1:8). The message for all time is that "Christ . . . died for sins once for all, the righteous for the unrighteous, that he might bring us to God" (1 Pet. 3:18). This good news is to be proclaimed to all peoples (Jn. 11:51,52; Acts 26:23; Rom. 1:5; 5:15,18,19; 1 Cor. 1:23,24; Eph. 2:16; Heb. 2:9,10).[336]

According to Bosch "the theme of discipleship is central to Matthew's gospel and to Matthew's understanding of the church and mission."[337] Commenting on Matthew 28:19, Bosch affirms that "the followers of the earthly Jesus have to make others into what they themselves are: disciples."[338] John D. Harvey states that "Matthew's gospel has much to say about discipleship" and he points to the truth that according to this gospel "discipleship results in mission: not only will they have a passive role as followers, they will have an active role as 'fishers of men' (4:19)."[339] Harvey identifies three tests of true disciples based on the Sermon on the Mount conclusion: "(1) they enter by the narrow gate (7:13–14), (2) they produce good fruit (7:15–20), (3) they obey the Father's will (7:21–23), and (4) they act on Jesus' words (7:24)."[340] The author notes that the mission task assigned to the disciples of Jesus is to make disciples (Matt 28:19). However, "this task differs considerably from that assigned in the other synoptics, where the emphasis is on the proclamation of the gospel (cf. Mark 16:15; Luke 24:47)."[341] However, there is no contradiction. Proclamation of the gospel and making disciples are inseparable aspects of the mission of the church. In order to become a disciple a person has first to believe in Christ as the Son of God. However, it is impossible to believe without obtaining knowledge about Christ. Here is where proclamation comes in. Through proclamation people learn about the good news in Jesus and those who accept it become Christ's disciples. The apostle Paul states it very clearly: "For everyone who

---

336. Sylvia Wilkey Collinson, "Making Disciples and the Christian Faith," *Evangelical Review of Theology* 29, no. 3 (July 2005): 247.

337. Bosch, *Transforming Mission*, 73.

338. Ibid., 74.

339. John D. Harvey, "Mission in Matthew," in *Mission in the New Testament*, ed. William J. Larkin, and Joel F. Williams (Maryknoll, NY: Orbis, 2002), 130.

340. Ibid., 131.

341. Ibid.

calls on the name of the Lord will be saved. But how are they to call on him in whom they have not believed? And how are they to believe in him of whom they have never heard? And how are they to hear without someone preaching?" (Rom 10:13–14). There is a very obvious connection between preaching (proclamation) and salvation (becoming a disciple). The fruit of preaching is a person following Christ, or a disciple. This is what the mission of the church should seek to produce – disciples.

2.6.2. Reconciliation

Very often the Gospel of Matthew speaks about justice. It shows that justice is "an essential aspect of the 'Great Commission'" and "is the foundation and the fruit of the Kingdom of God: 'Seek you first the Kingdom of God and its justice and all these things will be given to you as well' (6:33)."[342] An important theme in Jesus' teaching is reconciliation: "If you bring your gift at the altar and there remember that your brother has something against you, leave your gift there in front of the altar and first go and be reconciled with your brother" (Matt 5:24). Arias insists: "There is to be no vertical reconciliation without horizontal reconciliation. Again, the vertical and the horizontal come together in the parable of the two debtors and in the Lords' Prayer. There is no forgiveness effective from God unless one gives forgiveness to others (18:21–35; 6:12, 14–15)."[343] In other words, a person's relationship with God is conditioned by her/his relationship with the neighbor. Referring to the apostle Paul's epistles to Ephesians and Colossians, Kirk states that "the Church is placed at the very heart of God's purpose to 'gather up all things in Christ' (Eph. 1:10)"[344] and should be considered "not only to be an instrument of the gospel, but part of the gospel (Eph. 3:6)."[345] He explains this by the truth that "God's reconciling activity in Jesus Christ (2Cor. 5:19) has as its goal not only individuals (Rom. 5:10–11) and the cosmos (Col. 1:20), but human beings with one another."[346] The church is the community of people reconciled with God and with each other. Within a new community,

---

342. Arias, "Rethinking the Great Commission," 413.
343. Ibid., 414.
344. Kirk, *What Is Mission?*, 35.
345. Ibid.
346. Ibid.

the church, "God reconciles the humanly irreconcilable – Jew and non-Jew, 'cultured' and 'non-cultured,' male and female, privileged and exploited, people of every race, culture and class (Rom. 9–11; Eph. 2:13–22; 3:3–7; Col. 3:10–11; Gal. 3:28)."[347] Building conditions of reconciliation and peace should be an aim of Christians in their attempt to follow Jesus Christ, who clearly stated that his disciples are blessed in so far as they are engaged in making peace (Matt 5:9).[348] The gospel challenges those who want to follow Jesus to exceed conventional ethical standards (Matt 5:20; 5:47).[349] "This entails the renunciation of the normal human reaction to intentional injury (Matt. 5:40ff.) and to the concept of enemies (Matt. 5:43ff.). Peacemaking is linked to non-retaliation, to a carefree generosity and to love for the enemy by the promise that those who demonstrate such a lifestyle will show themselves to be genuine children of God (Matt. 5:9; 5:45)."

One of the fruits of mission is reconciliation between a person and God – so-called vertical reconciliation – and reconciliation between people – horizontal reconciliation. Until the late twentieth century, horizontal reconciliation was not considered in any way central to the purpose of mission.[350] However, this reconciliation "has now become increasingly a subject of deep concern in missiology"[351] due to the presence of many different conflicts in the world based on race, religion, nationalism, etc. The apostle Paul describes his missionary work as a ministry of reconciliation, stating: "All this is from God, who through Christ reconciled us to himself and gave us the ministry of reconciliation; that is, in Christ God was reconciling the world to himself, not counting their trespasses against them, and entrusting to us the message of reconciliation. Therefore, we are ambassadors for Christ, God making his appeal through us. We implore you on behalf of Christ, be reconciled to God."[352]

This is vertical reconciliation. This is the first fruit of mission. Only after vertical reconciliation has happened does horizontal reconciliation become

---

347. Ibid., 68.
348. Ibid., 145.
349. Ibid.
350. Ott, Strauss, and Tennent, *Encountering Theology of Mission*, 95.
351. Ibid.
352. 2 Cor 5:18–20 (ESV).

possible.³⁵³ Both of them are based on Christ's work of redemption and are inseparably related.³⁵⁴ One of the examples of horizontal reconciliation is the reconciliation between Jew and Gentile described in Ephesians 2:13–18.³⁵⁵ "The peace with God created by the blood of Christ also creates peace between peoples by creating a new humanity. This new humanity is no longer divided by race, ethnicity, social standing, or gender (Gal. 3:28)."³⁵⁶ Because such great importance is attached to vertical reconciliation it "is more than merely a task of missions; it is central to the overarching purpose and nature of mission . . .The restored relationship with God, and its attendant restored human relations, is central to the message of the gospel."³⁵⁷ The logical conclusion of this is seeing reconciliation with God and people as a very important aspect of mission of the church.

2.6.3. Bringing Good News to the Poor

Kirk states that the New Testament often uses the word "poor" as an inclusive term referring to those who "were excluded from the normal benefits of community existence."³⁵⁸ This category of people included "lepers and other diseased people, 'sinners' who were not sufficiently strict about the law, prostitutes, debtors, collaborators with Rome, bonded labourers."³⁵⁹ They were called "the poor," first, because they did not have sufficient resources to fall back on; second, "because 'normal' society considered them to be deviants in some way."³⁶⁰ Those who were in power in the time of Jesus saw the poor "as useless to society, social misfits, subversives."³⁶¹ By belonging to this category people "had no opportunity to become a full part of civil society, because of discrimination, prejudice and the defense of privilege."³⁶² Because of this "the preaching of the kingdom came to them as good news

---

353. Ott, Strauss, and Tennent, *Encountering Theology of Mission*, 97.
354. Ibid.
355. Ibid.
356. Ibid.
357. Ibid.
358. Kirk, *What Is Mission?*, 48.
359. Ibid.
360. Ibid.
361. Ibid.
362. Ibid.

because it spoke of another kind of system (Luke 6:20)."[363] Talking about solidarity with the poor introduced in the Gospel of Luke, Bosch states that "Luke has a particular interest in the poor and other marginalized groups. Already in the Magnificat (Lk 1:53) we read: '(God) has filled the hungry with good things, and the rich he has sent away empty.'"[364] William J. Larkin Jr., addressing the subject of bringing the good news to the poor presented in the Gospel of Luke, states that "there is the promise of an eschatological reversal of one's present economic fortunes (Luke 1:53–55; 6:20–26 [cf. especially 6:20 and Matt. 5:3]; Luke 16:25)."[365] He notes that because Luke's emphasis is on "the presence of the kingdom in Jesus' ministry and the presence of salvation today (4:21; 11:20; 19:9; 23:43)"[366] the liberation theologians "claim that Jesus intended this eschatological reversal of fortunes to start in his ministry and to continue in the church through its support of struggles for economic justice."[367] Larkin opposes this view, saying that some immediate hope for the poor could be found in economic repentance. The rich "must repent of all behaviors and values that are incompatible with the kingdom. If riches are an idol, they must sell them, give to the poor, and follow Jesus (18:22) . . . They must make involvement with the poor a part of their lifestyle in terms of their social relations (14:13–14)."[368]

According to the Scriptures, God is concerned about the poor and oppressed. It is expected that his people will share that concern as well. One of the texts in the New Testament proving this truth is James 1:27, which states: "Religion that is pure and undefiled before God and the Father is this: to visit orphans and widows in their affliction, and to keep oneself unstained from the world."[369] The teaching of the Scriptures points to the truth that one of the important aspects of the mission of the church is taking care of the poor. This care should be expressed through addressing their physical needs as well as through addressing their spiritual needs. They need to hear

---

363. Ibid.
364. Bosch, *Transforming Mission*, 98.
365. William J. Larkin, Jr., "Mission in Luke," in Larkin and Williams, *Mission in the New Testament*, 161.
366. Ibid.
367. Ibid.
368. Ibid.
369. Jas 1:27 (ESV).

the good news of the kingdom and after accepting it they are expected to live "the life of radical discipleship in devotion to Jesus (9:23–25; 14:33)."

2.6.4. Conclusion

The brief overview provided above of such truths of the Scripture as discipleship, reconciliation, and bringing good news to the poor shows that all of them should be considered as an integral part of the Great Commission given by Jesus to his disciples and, thus, should be considered as part of the church's mission in the world. This conclusion correlates well with the contemporary understanding of mission of the three ecclesiological church bodies whose views on this subject were analyzed in this chapter. Based on this conclusion the definition of authentic mission will be developed in the final part of this chapter.

2.7. Definition of Authentic Mission

This final part of the chapter is devoted to developing a definition of authentic mission based on this evaluation. The table below sets out the mission components included in the positions of the groups studied in this chapter.

WCC/Ecumenical position	Evangelical/ Lausanne Movement position	Anabaptist position
Evangelism	Evangelism	Evangelism
Diaconia/social action	*Diaconia*/social action	*Diaconia*/social action
Overcoming violence and building cultures of peace	Overcoming violence and building cultures of peace	Overcoming violence and building cultures of peace
Justice	Justice	Justice
Care of the environment	Care of the environment	Care of the environment
Liturgy and worship	Worship	
Dialogue with people of other religions	Dialogue with people of other faiths	
Inculturation	Inculturation	
Ministry of reconciliation with God, people, and creation	Ministry of reconciliation	Ministry of reconciliation
Teaching		

Based on the information provided in the table above, it could be concluded that there is a convergence between the three groups in understanding that the mission of the church is complex and includes different aspects. In order to develop a definition of authentic mission for this study, the author has considered those aspects that are the subject of agreement for at least two of the groups studied. Using this approach, the author identified the following nine aspects of mission: evangelism, social action/*diaconia*, overcoming violence and building cultures of peace, justice, care of the environment, worship, dialogue, inculturation, and ministry of reconciliation. These aspects are going to be included in the definition of the authentic mission of the church. This view of mission, being many-sided, is in harmony with the definition of mission of the church suggested by Bosch and Kirk and provided in the beginning of this chapter. It shows that there is agreement between missiologists and the wider Christian church community on the subject of what the mission of the church is. Also, such a view of the mission of the church as being multifaceted correlates with the goal of *missio Dei* described in chapter 1, section 1.1.4, of this study. Thus, the definition of an authentic mission that will be used in this study is as follows: *The authentic mission of the church is multifaceted and includes evangelism, social action/diaconia, overcoming violence and building cultures of peace, justice, care of the environment, worship, dialogue, inculturation, and ministry of reconciliation.*[370] At the same time, as Paul E. Pierson argues, "the center, though not the totality, of mission must always involve calling men and women to faith in Jesus Christ, gathering them into worshipping and witnessing communities."[371]

Taking into consideration the limited space available in this book, the mission work of PCSBA churches will be evaluated only on the aspects of evangelism and social action/*diaconia*. Narrowing down the focus of the study to just these two[372] allows the author to do a more detailed analysis of these two aspects of mission applied to the immigrant churches of the PCSBA. Selecting these two aspects of mission does not minimize the importance of other aspects. After analyzing how these two aspects of mission, evangelism and social action/*diaconia*, are implemented by Slavic Baptist churches in the immigrant context, a new study should be undertaken to analyze the implementation of other aspects of an authentic mission accomplished by this group of churches.

2.8. Conclusion for Chapter 2

In this chapter, the analysis of the key documents of three groups of churches (WCC/ecumenical, evangelical/Lausanne Movement, and Anabaptist) has been accomplished. The purpose of this analysis was to identify the position

---

370. Cf. N. T. Wright, *Surprised By Hope: Rethinking Heaven, Resurrection and the Mission of the Church* (Grand Rapids, MI: Zondervan), 2010. Wright uses a non-traditional approach to defining the mission of the church. He does it in the light of Jesus's bodily resurrection. According to Wright, "the mission of the church is nothing more or less than the outworking, in the power of the Spirit, of Jesus's bodily resurrection and thus the anticipation of the time when God will fill the earth with his glory, transform the old heavens and earth into the new, and raise his children from the dead to populate and rule over the redeemed world he has made" (264).

371. Paul E. Pierson, "Lessons in Mission from the Twentieth Century: Conciliar Missions," in *Between Past and Future: Evangelical Mission Entering the Twenty-First Century*, ed. Jonathan J. Bonk (Pasadena, CA: William Carey Library, 2003), 81.

372. Cf. James L. Bailey, "Church as Embodiment of Jesus' Mission (Matthew 9:36 – 10:39)," *Currents in Theology and Mission* 30, no. 3 (June 2003). Bailey describes the ties these two aspects of mission have in the following way: "The church's mission becomes credible only when the preaching of God's mercy is accompanied by merciful deeds" (192).

of each of these church groups on the mission of the church and, based on this information, to develop a definition of an authentic mission. This definition will be used in the process of evaluating the mission work done by churches of the Pacific Coast Slavic Baptist Association.

This study demonstrates the fact that the views among different ecclesiastical groups on the mission of the church are diverse; thus it is impossible to come to an exhaustive definition of the mission of the church. At the same time, the results of the study show that there is convergence between different ecclesiastical groups on certain aspects of mission included in the mission of the church. This allows use to come up with a combined definition of the mission of the church based on aspects of mission that are commonly present in the positions of all, or at least most, studied groups. The study shows that the mission of the church should be viewed as multifaceted but with the central goal of making Christ known among the people of the world. The position that the mission of the church should have a holistic nature[373] and should include different aspects is widely accepted now.[374] It cannot be narrowed down to only one aspect, such as evangelism or social action/*diaconia*. This holistic, or integral, view of the mission of the church being multifaceted and multidimensional[375] is adopted in this study for use

---

373. Samuel Jayakumar, describing the mission of churches in Asia as holistic mission, insists that the "gospel of Christ has always been *holistic* and has never been un-holistic. The four gospels present a holistic transformation of individuals, families and communities. The command of Jesus was to *preach the gospel, heal the sick and drive out the demons (social evils)*. The early apostles and their followers were committed to *holistic transformation* in the contexts they served" ("The Work of God as Holistic Mission: An Asian Perspective," *Evangelical Review of Theology* 35, no 3 [July 2011]: 228).

374. James Nkansah-Obrempong, addressing the role of evangelism and social responsibility in the church's mission, insists "that there is a consensus on the necessity to integrate the two aspects of our Christian mission without putting a wedge between the two. These two elements of our Christian mission are inseparable and must always be held together. The theological and biblical ground for this position is the very nature of the gospel. The gospel is holistic. It provides answers to human questions and struggles – spiritual, material, mental and physical" ("Holistic Gospel in a Developing Society: Biblical, Theological and Historical Backgrounds," *Evangelical Review of Theology* 33, no. 3 [July 2009]: 196). Because of this, if "the church does not want to become irrelevant to society, a holistic gospel is the answer. A holistic gospel will give credibility to the message and acceptance of the church in society" (212).

375. Inagrace Dietterich underlines that the holistic mission of the church is a work of the Holy Spirit. "The church's mission of proclaiming and embodying the good news of what God has done in Jesus Christ for the salvation of the world is empowered by the Holy

in the following chapters in the process of examining the mission aspect of Slavic Baptist church life in the homeland, in the past, and in America today.

A definition of authentic mission has been developed and adopted for this study. It provides the author with a tool for evaluating the mission work of PCSBA churches. Two aspects of mission will be of primary interest in the evaluation process: evangelism and social action/*diaconia*. However, since PCSBA churches currently live and operate in a different context from their homeland, it is also important to assess their mission in terms of its contextualization. The next chapter provides an analysis of the subject of contextualization in mission and equips the author with information necessary to do an appropriate evaluation of the mission of Slavic immigrant churches.

Spirit" ("A Vision for the Sending of the Church in North America," *Missiology* 38, no. 1 [Jan 2010]: 29).

CHAPTER 3

Challenge of Contextualization in Mission

The important outcome of this study is determining how well the mission work currently done by the PCSBA churches is contextualized. How well the holistic mission of the church, described in the previous chapter, is accomplished by these churches in the immigrant context is the key question of this study. A clear understanding of the concept of contextualization is important for accomplishing this task. This chapter is devoted to exploring this subject.

3.1. Context

A clear understanding of the context is the starting point for accomplishing contextualization.[1] According to Craig Ott and his co-authors, the context "includes everything that shapes a society and each individual person."[2] In discussing the issue of contextualization, Max L. Stackhouse warns the reader to pay very careful attention to determining what the context is. He says, "We are forced to ask what it is that defines the boundaries of a context: regionality, nationality, cultural-linguistic history, ethnicity, political system, economic class, gender identity, social status, or what?"[3] Correctly

---

1. Craig Ott, Stephen J. Strauss, and Timothy C. Tennent, *Encountering Theology of Mission: Biblical Foundations, Historical Developments, and Contemporary Issues* (Grand Rapids, MI: Baker Academic, 2010), 267.

2. Ibid., 268.

3. Max L. Stackhouse, "Contextualization, Contextuality, and Contextualism," in *One Faith, Many Cultures: Inculturation, Indigenization, and Contextualization*, ed. Dean S. Gilliland (Maryknoll, NY: Orbis, 1988), 11.

135

defining the context is essential to finding the correct means of contextualization. The following components could be part of the context: religious or theological heritage, historical era and current events, social, economic, educational group, age, gender, and personal circumstances.[4] It is beyond the scope of this particular study to explore every context listed here. This part of the chapter discusses several contexts which are the most relevant to Slavic Baptist life in America.

3.1.1. Cultural Context

While addressing the concept of context in contextualization, David J. Hesselgrave and Edward Rommen identify two main contexts: culture and language. The definition of culture they use insists that it is "the body of knowledge shared by the members of a group. That knowledge takes the form of rules which govern the way in which individuals relate to and interpret their environment. The utilization of such knowledge leads to culturally specific forms of behavior, patterns of communication (not language per se), sets of values, and types of artifacts."[5]

Understanding the cultural context is absolutely crucial for the process of contextualization. Without a good understanding of the culture, it is impossible to communicate the gospel to the people of that culture in a contextually appropriate way. J. Andrew Kirk, addressing the issue of the most effective means for fulfilling the church's mission in the West today, emphasizes that to "fulfill its evangelistic calling, the Christian community must understand how people are shaped and affected by the culture that surrounds them."[6] George G. Hunter III, discussing the cultural barriers the "outsiders" are facing when they start visiting the church, points to the fact that in order to "reach an undiscipled population, our outreach, ministry, and worship must be indigenous to their culture, because each

---

4. Ott, Strauss, and Tennent, *Encountering Theology of Mission*, 268.

5. David J. Hesselgrave and Edward Rommen, eds., *Contextualization: Meanings, Methods, and Models* (Leicester: Inter-Varsity, 1989), 158.

6. J. Andrew Kirk, "Mission in the West: On the Calling of the Church in a Postmodern Age," in *A Scandalous Prophet: The Way of Mission after Newbigin*, ed. Thomas F. Foust, George R. Hunsberger, J. Andrew Kirk, and Werner Ustorf (Grand Rapids, MI: William B. Eerdmans, 2002), 125.

people's culture is the natural medium of God's revelation to them."[7] He states very clearly that the issue of culture comes up not only when churches are dealing with people of a different ethnicity than their own. He points to the fact that churches have often created their own subculture that "has erected dozens of barriers that separate many people from the possibility of becoming disciples."[8] This is one of the major challenging factors Slavic immigrant churches are facing. The way they run the church, the worship style, music, prayer posture during the service, how people dress going to church, and other aspects of life in Slavic churches are very different from what a "typical" American is accustomed to observing in indigenous churches. Will Slavic immigrant churches be willing to sacrifice their way of "doing church" in order to adjust to the surrounding culture? The answer to this question determines the ability of these churches to contextualize their mission.

An important warning that Hesselgrave and Rommen give points to the danger of overgeneralization in describing a particular culture because it could be misleading (for example, when talking about "African culture," because it is impossible to identify one culture that would be universal for the entire African continent)[9] This danger exists when using the term "American culture" to talk about contextualization of faith in the US. Assuming that there is a universal "American culture" that could be applied to all people living in today's US is an overstatement. As a country of immigrants, America consists of many different cultural groups whose members try to preserve their culture, at least for a certain period of time after arriving in the States. Samuel P. Huntington notes, "America has always had its full share of subcultures."[10] In the past, before the 1960s, the common understanding of American people about their country was that it was a cultural melting pot. It was expected that after coming to their new country, immigrants would abandon their distinctive cultural attributes and eventually assimilate

---

7. George G. Hunter III, "The Case for Culturally Relevant Congregations," in *Global Good News. Mission in a New Context*, ed. Howard A. Snyder (Nashville, TN: Abingdon Press, 2001), 105.

8. George G. Hunter III, *Church for the Unchurched* (Nashville, TN: Abingdon Press, 1996), 64.

9. Hesselgrave and Rommen, *Contextualization*, 165.

10. Samuel P. Huntington, *Who Are We? The Challenges to America's National Identity* (New York: Simon & Schuster Paperbacks, 2004), 59.

with the larger population. However, according to C. Peter Wagner, this was an illusion. He argues that "ethnicity did not disappear in a generation or two, nor will it. The real America is not a melting pot; it never was. The real America is a stewpot. While some prefer using analogies of salad bowl, mosaic, tapestry, or rainbow, I prefer the stewpot. Here each ingredient is changed and flavored by the others."[11] This means that different cultural contexts can be found in different regions of the country and even in different parts of the same city. Therefore, it is important to pay attention to specific cultural contexts when discussing the contextualization of the mission of the church in its global aspect, as well as in its local one. In order for Slavic Baptists currently living in the US to be contextually appropriate in their efforts to reach the community of the area where their church is located, they would have to do a demographic study to find out what predominant ethnic/cultural group(s) live(s) there. The results should determine what approach to use when sharing the gospel with this group. Some Slavic churches are located in predominantly Hispanic, Southeast Asian, or Caucasian communities, with their distinct cultures. Slavic churches should be thoughtful in selecting an appropriate method for reaching these different ethnic/cultural groups. The presence of so many different ethnic groups in American society provides Slavic Christian immigrants with the challenge of overcoming racism in their own hearts. As the results of the church leaders' survey show, there is uneasiness among Slavic immigrants about crossing barriers with other ethnic groups and with accepting other cultures (see chapter 6, tables 6.3.12., 6.3.13., 6.3.14.).

3.1.2. Language Context

The language of the gospel is another important component of context in the process of contextualization. Charles H. Kraft emphasizes that "language is commonly defined as a system of arbitrary vocal 'symbols' employed by the members of a community in socially approved ways for purposes such as communication and expression."[12] It is impossible to overemphasize the

---

11. C. Peter Wagner, "Contextualizing Theology in the American Social Mosaic," in *The Word Among Us*, ed. Dean S. Gilliland (Dallas: Word, 1989), 220.

12. Charles H. Kraft, *Communication Theory for Christian Witness* (Maryknoll, NY: Orbis, 2002), 89.

importance of this aspect of context because language is a powerful tool for communication between people. According to Hesselgrave and Rommen:

> the context of any communicative event is determined by the use of a specific language within the matrix of the culture with which it is associated. Language is a means of expressing and disseminating the content of culture. As such it functions as the key to, and primary vehicle of, the reflective processes which generate the pool of shared knowledge that defines a given culture. Language is also a determining factor in the way in which its users perceive the world. As such it is the interface between individual thought and the "real world."[13]

It is imperative to learn the language of the potential recipients of the gospel. As Kraft emphasizes, "God is receptor-oriented," and because of this, he wants the gospel to be communicated to people in the language they understand. For Slavic Baptist immigrants in America, this means that in order to participate in the contextually appropriate sharing of the gospel with English-speaking people, they have to learn English. Most of them put significant efforts into studying English. They do it in order to be able to work and support their families. However, how many of them are learning English because they want to share the gospel with indigenous Americans? In certain cases, where churches are located in predominantly Spanish-speaking neighborhoods, some Slavic Baptists may be required to learn Spanish in order to do contextually appropriate outreach to their neighbors. A more detailed discussion of the issue of language in the life of PCSBA churches is provided in chapter 8, section 8.3.

3.1.3. Social Context

Social context is very important. It refers to the life of the person in a community and her/his understanding of it. "It implies familiarity, often unconscious, with cultural values and beliefs, institutions and forms, roles and personalities, and the history and ecology of the community. When applied to communicative events and social situations, this knowledge enables the

---

13. Hesselgrave and Rommen, *Contextualization*, 161.

individual to behave in a socially appropriate manner."[14] Based on personal observation, this is exactly what Slavic Baptist immigrants are lacking – a good understanding of the society in which they are currently living. Belonging to the Russian-speaking church/community provides them with enough opportunities for social interactions; thus they do not experience a need for relations with "real" Americans. They often live in ethnic enclaves that are separated from the rest of the society. Therefore, their knowledge of the social context is limited. The results of the survey of people who left Slavic ethnic churches and joined indigenous English-speaking congregations show that for many of these people, lack of understanding of the society and the isolationistic attitude of Slavic churches were among the main reasons for leaving the immigrant church; 56.3 percent of them pointed to the misdirected vision of the church in the new cultural and language context as one of the reasons for leaving. The isolationist attitude among church members towards the society was identified by 38.8 percent of those surveyed as one of the reasons for departure (see appendix for chapter 6, table 6.6.6.). Connecting with the society and understanding it constitute two of the challenges Slavic Baptist churches should meet and overcome in order to conduct contextually appropriate missions among local people.[15]

3.1.4. Personal Circumstances

There is one more component of the context worth considering in studying the contextualization of mission. The process of spreading the gospel includes at least two parties: the one who is sharing the gospel and the one who receives it. The spiritual, emotional, and even physical conditions of the person who shares the gospel play an important role in the ability of this person to witness or to serve others in a contextually appropriate way. A person who is not in a right personal relation with the Lord, or who is

---

14. Ibid., 165.

15. It is important to note that leaders of the evangelical movement in Russia already at its early stage recognized the importance of contextualization in communicating the gospel. Andrey Puzynin points to the fact that Pashkov was very much concerned about illustrations used in the Bible tracts translated from English and designed to be given to Russian children as Sunday school lessons. These illustrations were not adapted to the Russian cultural context and thus did not help children to understand the message of the tracts. (*Traditsiya Evangelskikh Khristian: izuchenie samoidentifikatsii i bogosloviya ot momenta yeye zarozhdeniya do nashikh dney* [Moscow: Izdatel'stvo Bibleysko-Bogoslovskogo Instituta sv. apostola Andreya, 2010], 213).

emotionally stressed or physically ill, will not be very effective in contextualizing his/her evangelistic efforts. These conditions often depend upon the circumstances in which a person finds herself/himself. This is why it is important to consider personal circumstances as another component of the context in mission. Since the main object of this study is the Slavic Baptist immigrant community, it is important to understand what is happening in their hearts and minds in response to the fact that they have found themselves living in a cultural, social, economic, and language environment completely different from their own. A detailed study of immigrant experiences will be provided in chapter 7: "Social Challenges of Immigrant Life for Slavic Baptist Diaspora and Their Impact on Mission." However, at this point, it is important to note that emotional, painful processes are taking place in the immigrant's soul and provide a vulnerable context for the process of contextualization in mission. This should be recognized by the immigrants themselves, as well as by their church.

3.2. Contextualization

3.2.1. Meaning

Stackhouse states "that 'contextualizing the faith' has been a part of the mission of the church from the beginning."[16] He points to the fact that on the day of Pentecost, the apostles, being filled with the Holy Spirit, began to preach in the languages of people of the different ethnic groups who were among their listeners. The crowds heard the apostles speaking in their own native tongues. The New Testament books are written in such a way that they could be understood by the audience to which they were addressed. Not only the language of the audience was taken into consideration, but the social, economic, political, familial, and ideological status of readers were considered as well. "The scriptures are laden with quite specific, concrete references to status groups, leaders and followers, movements, trends, classes, and cultural environments. It is presumed throughout that the gospel, the faith, is pertinent to, and can indeed be contextualized in, each and

---

16. Stackhouse, "Contextualization, Contextuality, and Contextualism," 4.

every context it addresses, and that it will bring change to these settings."[17] Stackhouse states that throughout church history, contextualization of the Christian faith took place in four ways. First, linguistically as the Scriptures were translated into different languages. Second, through many shapes and forms of the church in multiple contexts of the world.[18] Third, while the church has been expanding into different geographical territories, it "has contextualized the faith wherever it went, even if missionaries sometimes resisted indigenization and wanted to preserve the exact forms of confession and practice they brought with them."[19] Fourth, in the contextualization of faith a vision of common humanity has always been present, which "in some measure, overcame the rampant polytheism to which humanity seems to be inclined."[20] What previous generations of faithful followers of Christ did in terms of contextualization of faith in their time should be continued by the contemporary church. Bosch echoes Stackhouse, insisting that "from the very beginning, the missionary message of the Christian church incarnated itself in the life and world of those who had embraced it. It is, however, only fairly recently that this essentially contextual nature of the faith has been recognized."[21] This thought is supported by Kevin Daugherty, who states, "Contextualization is costly; it requires meeting people where they are. So the mission of the church is not only to take a message to a people; it is to live a message among them so as to make God visible again."[22] Or, as Paul De Neui describes it: "partnering with the *missio Dei* requires full incarnation with the culture, identifying with people, speaking their language, allowing the gospel to be understood and to address clearly deep, heartfelt values in ways that make response possible."[23]

---

17. Ibid.
18. Ibid.
19. Ibid., 5.
20. Ibid.
21. David J. Bosch, *Transforming Mission: Paradigm Shifts in Theology of Mission* (Maryknoll, NY: Orbis, 1991), 421.
22. Kevin Daugherty, "*Missio Dei*: The Trinity and Christian Missions," *Evangelical Review of Theology* 31, no. 2 (Apr 2007): 165.
23. Paul De Neui, "Christian Communitas in the *Missio Dei*: Living Faithfully in the Tension between Cultural Osmosis and Alienation," *Ex Auditu* 23, (2007): 98.

Hesselgrave and Rommen point to the fact that by the end of World War II, a significant change took place in churches of the English-speaking world. They insist: "Missiologists, theologians, and other scholars came to appreciate that even though there is but one Bible, one Mediator, and one gospel . . ., nevertheless Christians of various cultures have their own ways of going about the task of understanding and communicating the Christian message."[24] These new views eventually were embodied in the new term, *contextualization*.

The word *contextualization* was introduced for the first time in 1972 by Shoki Coe and Aharon Sapsezian, directors of the Theological Education Fund (TEF).[25] TEF suggested that this new term could replace the familiar term *indigenization*. It was claimed that contextualization "is the capacity to respond meaningfully to the gospel within the framework of one's own situation."[26] Although this term arose from conciliar Protestant circles, it was accepted by conservative evangelicals as well.

Contextualization makes the gospel more relevant to people's lives today, more contemporary, per se.[27] Ott and his co-authors insist: "Contextualization means relating the never-changing truths of scripture to ever-changing human contexts so that those truths are clear and compelling. It is the process of engaging culture in all its varied dimensions with biblical truth. Appropriate contextualization shapes the presentation of the gospel and the release of its transforming power in evangelism, lifestyle, church life, and social change."[28] Contextualization brings life and practical implications to the process of interpreting the Bible.

---

24. Hesselgrave and Rommen, *Contextualization*, 48.

25. Bruce J. Nicholls, *Contextualization: A Theology of Gospel and Culture* (Downers Grove, IL: InterVarsity, 1979), 21.

26. Ibid.

27. David Bosch points to the fact that contextualization is crucial in reflecting the nature of the church as a constantly changing organism. He states, "The Christian church is always in the process of becoming; the church of the present is both the product of the past and the seed of the future. For this reason, theology must not be pursued as an attempt at reconstructing the pristine past and its truths; rather, theology is a reflection on the church's own life and experience" (Bosch, *Transforming Mission*, 422).

28. Ott, Strauss, and Tennent, *Encountering Theology of Mission*, 266.

3.2.2. Scope

The scope of contextualization is very wide. According to Hesselgrave and Rommen: "Contextualization is both verbal and nonverbal and has to do with theologizing; Bible translation, interpretation, and application; incarnational lifestyle; evangelism; Christian instruction; church planting and growth; church organization; worship style – indeed with all of those activities involved in carrying out the Great Commission."[29] Dean Flemming provides the following explanation of the concept of contextualization: "I take contextualization . . . to refer to the dynamic and comprehensive process by which the gospel is incarnated within a concrete historical or cultural situation. This happens in such a way that the gospel both comes to authentic expression in the local context and at the same time prophetically transforms the context. Contextualization seeks to enable the people of God to live out the gospel in obedience to Christ within their own cultures and circumstances."[30]

As these authors show, contextualization should affect every aspect of life and mission of the church. In light of this, for Slavic immigrant churches, it means a complete transformation. If they want to become contextually relevant to the surrounding society, they have to be prepared to make adjustments in many areas of church life. Not only the language used in the church services, but every single aspect of life and ministry of the church should be re-evaluated and brought in compliance with the requirement of contextualization. This process requires strong courage from the church leadership and a highly sacrificial spirit from people in the pews. Taking into consideration the role that the ethnic distinctiveness of their church plays in the life of immigrants (chapter 7 addresses these issues), it seems almost impossible for the immigrant churches to make the necessary changes in order to become contextually appropriate.

3.2.3. Theological Perspectives and Contextualization

It is important to remember that the outcome of contextualization is in direct correlation with the theological perspective of those who try to contextually

---

29. Hesselgrave and Rommen, *Contextualization*, 200.
30. Dean Flemming, *Contextualization in the New Testament: Patterns for Theology and Mission* (Downers Grove, IL: InterVaristy, 2005), 17.

communicate the gospel. The meaning and methods used to implement contextualization are affected by the theological position of the deliverer of the gospel news. Hesselgrave and Rommen advise, "It is essential, therefore, that in analyzing the contextualization attempts of others or in attempting our own we are sensitive to the theological soil which nurtures and sustains them."[31] Different theological positions could bring very different contextualizations.[32]

3.2.4. Concerns

It should be mentioned here that the concept of contextualization has provoked a serious debate among both theologians and missiologists. The concern is where the boundaries for contextualization of the gospel are placed. How can the authenticity of the message be protected when trying to contextualize it? The evangelicals' position on the issue is expressed in the following way: "any understanding of contextualization which is separated from the proclamation of the gospel and the indigenization of the church is unacceptable. Biblical authority, limitarianism, Great Commission mission, world evangelization, the necessity of conversion – such are the points of departure for the church's mission to the world and they must be the foundation for any discussion of contextualization of the gospel."[33]

The existence of these debates illustrates the importance and complexity of the issue of communicating the gospel cross-culturally. As Hesselgrave and Rommen point out, "not all contextualization schemata are valid, that is, not every effort to transculturate revealed truth remains faithful to the original gospel."[34] This is a reminder of the necessity to apply the concept of contextualization very carefully in any given situation in order to protect the message from being damaged. It is very important to be concerned about the authenticity of contextualization, which has to do, according to Hesselgrave and Rommen, "with God's revelation first of all, with faithfulness to the

---

31. Hesselgrave and Rommen, *Contextualization*, 144.
32. Kirsteen Kim, "Missiology as Global Conversation of (Contextual) Theologies," in *Mission Studies: Journal of the International Association for Mission Studies* 21, no. 1 (2004): 43.
33. Hesselgrave and Rommen, *Contextualization*, 52.
34. Ibid., 127.

authority and content of the will of God as revealed in his creation, in man's conscience, and, especially, in his Son and his Holy Spirit-inspired Word."[35]

3.2.5. Syncretism

Syncretism is considered as one of the greatest dangers in the process of contextualization. Gailyn Van Rheenen defines this phenomenon in the following way: "Syncretism . . . is the conscious or unconscious reshaping of Christian plausibility structures, beliefs, and practices through cultural accommodation so that they reflect those of the dominant culture. Or, stated in other terms, syncretism is the blending of Christian beliefs and practices with those of the dominant culture so that Christianity loses its distinctiveness and speaks with a voice reflective of its culture."[36] It is very important for those who participate in the cross-cultural communication of the gospel to pay attention to the possibility of syncretism in their efforts. Awareness of the danger of these interferences in sharing the gospel could help churches preserve their witness from being devalued in the cross-cultural communication of God's message. This is true, not only for mission work taking place overseas, on foreign soil, but also for evangelistic work at home, in America.

3.3. Homogeneous Unit Model: Contextuality Attempt (Strengths and Weaknesses)

This part of the chapter explores one of the attempts to be contextually appropriate in mission – the Homogeneous Unit (HU) principle, used in the Church Growth movement. The HU principle has been chosen for study here because it is relevant to the immigrant churches due to the fact that many of them are based on a certain ethnicity and are homogeneous units. The Church Growth movement is found among evangelical churches and emphasizes the importance of combining missionary work with sociological awareness of the target population. The Church Growth movement is centered on a "discipline which seeks to understand, through biblical, sociological, historical, and behavioral study, why churches grow or decline."[37]

---

35. Ibid., 199.

36. Gailyn Van Rheenen, *Contextualization and Syncretism: Navigating Cultural Currents* (Pasadena, CA: William Carey Library, 2006), 7.

37. Thom S. Rainer, *The Book of Church Growth* (Nashville, TN: Broadman, 1993), 21.

Thom S. Rainer explains, "The Church Growth Movement includes all the resources of people, institutions, and publications dedicated to expounding the concepts and practicing the principles of church growth, beginning with the foundational work of missionary Donald McGavran in 1955."[38] While emphasizing the necessity for the church to strive for fulfillment of the Great Commission of Christ, Church Growth is applying research to attracting new members to their churches. Quantitative methods are used to evaluate the progress in church growth.

The best-known and most controversial aspect of the Church Growth movement is its emphasis on the Homogeneous Unit principle being used in mission work. An analysis of strengths and weaknesses of this principle and its contextual appropriateness to mission is provided below.

3.3.1. Homogeneous Unit Principle (HU): Definition, Meaning, Examples

The basic assumption for the Church Growth movement philosophy is the HU principle. This model seeks to identify common bonds that may exist among individuals that would help in bringing them together for the purpose of mutual spiritual growth. A homogeneous unit is a section of society in which all members share some common characteristics. These common bonds may be "geographical, ethnic, linguistic, social, educational, vocational, or economic, or a combination of several of these and other factors."[39] The common characteristics make people in the group "feel at home with each other and aware of their identity as 'we' in distinction to 'they.'"[40] Sometimes, people within a group cannot even describe why they feel connected with others in the group, but these commonalities are important in making them feel welcome and accepted. This is not a new concept by any means, as subcultures and nationalities have been studied to elicit a greater sense of belonging or bonding with adherents and newcomers. The homogeneous unit model is just another way of defining how people try to

---

38. Ibid., 21–22.

39. Lausanne Committee for World Evangelization and the World Evangelical Fellowship, "LOP 1: The Pasadena Consultation – Homogeneous Unit Principle," *Lausanne Movement* (Lausanne Committee for World Evangelization, 1978), http://www.lausanne.org/en/documents/lops/71-lop-1.html (accessed March 2012).

40. Ibid.

find commonalities from culture that will benefit the church by attracting people of the same group.

The term "Homogeneous Unit principle" was introduced by Donald McGavran, who emphasizes that "men like to become Christians without crossing racial, linguistic, or class barriers."[41] According to McGavran, homogeneous units are to be elastic. By elasticity he means that the concept can be applied to a small, very defined, and very specific grouping of people, or it can be applied to a much larger, more generalized group that is still defined with some commonalities. For example, McGavran writes: "On occasion it indicates one tribe living in one specific territory and speaking its own particular language, as for example the Tzeltal tribe of Indians in Mexico. On occasion, however, it describes a much larger and less limited population. For example, urban middle-class Japanese could be considered a homogeneous unit, especially in contrast to rural Japanese, living in hamlets and cultivating rice."[42] In other words, a homogeneous unit may constitute a single specific group of people with a very narrow set of commonalities that are defined by their language, their geographical location, social or economic status, etc. It may also represent a much broader group of people with fewer commonalities. But the defining factor is that the group has at least one common trait that enables them to identify with each other. It is this factor that makes people feel that they belong. It makes them identify as "us" rather than "them." Some of the boundaries are not very well defined. McGavran cites the example of class boundaries. It is difficult to define where upper class and lower class begin and end. But the reality is that there are different classes. Other boundaries are much easier to define, such as a homogeneous unit (HU) based on language. If one HU could be based on a particular language that is spoken by a group of people, this HU could become much narrower when considered for those that speak a particular dialect of that same language. This HU could be further defined even among genders within that same dialect.

---

41. Donald McGavran, *Understanding Church Growth* (Grand Rapids, MI: Eerdmans, 1990), 223.

42. Donald McGavran, *Church Growth and Christian Mission* (New York, NY: Harper & Row, 1965), 69–70.

So the homogeneous unit can be as broad or as narrow as one chooses to define it. The importance is not in how strictly the homogeneous units are defined but in the reality that they exist and that they affect how people interact and relate to each other. In the case of Russian-speaking immigrants, for example, on the one hand, all of them could be considered as a homogeneous unit because all of them come from the same geographical territory that used to be one country – the former Soviet Union – and speak Russian.[43] On the other hand, there are smaller groups within the Russian-speaking diaspora in America that could be identified as a separate HU by their own native language (Ukrainians, Moldavians, etc.). McGavran points out that "the Church will grow differently, not only in each different culture, but in each of the many homogeneous units that make up most human cultures."[44]

3.3.2. Using the Homogeneous Unit Principle in Mission

For many years missionaries have preached the gospel adding converts to the kingdom one by one. However, often these conversions were multiplied within people groups these converts belonged to, whether those were families, tribes, or from other related associations. It was very natural for the new converts to bring the gospel to those who shared the same culture with them. Out of this reality the homogeneous unit principle came into existence. McGavran stated: "This principle states an undeniable fact. Human beings do build barriers around their own societies. More exactly we may say that the ways in which each society lives and speaks, dresses and works, of necessity set it off from other societies. Mankind is a mosaic and each piece has a separate life of its own which seems strange and often unlovely to men and women of other pieces."[45] Promoting this principle produced controversy among missiologists. Some of them questioned the depth of conversion of people who were part of the homogeneous unit that accepted Christ all together. Although it is difficult to accept, it seems to be true that "it takes no

---

43. See a detailed discussion of the ethnic identity of Slavic Baptists immigrants in the appendix for chapter 8, section 8.1.A. It shows that despite the fact that there are many nationalities represented among Russian-speaking Baptist immigrants, as a group they have many common experiences in their past that have shaped them in such a way that they could be considered for the purpose of this study as one ethnic group. In other words, they can be seen as a homogeneous unit.

44. McGavran, *Church Growth and Christian Mission*, 71.

45. McGavran, *Understanding Church Growth*, 223.

great acumen to see that when marked differences of color, stature, income, cleanliness, and education are present, men understand the Gospel better when expounded by their own kind of people. They prefer to join churches whose members look, talk, and act like themselves."[46]

Both McGavran and C. Peter Wagner understood that the growth of the church and evangelism are the most important things that should be in focus. They believed that although there are concerns associated with the homogeneous unit principle, using this model ultimately could outweigh the potential detriments. The *Pasadena Consultation: Homogeneous Unit Principle* document discusses this issue and notes that "the barriers to the acceptance of the gospel are often more sociological than theological; people reject the gospel not because they think it is false but because it strikes them as alien. They imagine that in order to become Christians they must renounce their own culture, lose their own identity, and betray their own people."[47]

This is why contextualization is so important in communicating the gospel and planting churches cross-culturally. It is not enough to use contextualized ways in reaching people with the gospel in order for them to be able to understand it. What is more important is that "the church into which they are invited must itself belong to their culture sufficiently for them to feel at home in it. It is when these conditions are fulfilled that men and women are won to Jesus Christ, and subsequently that churches grow."[48] This is why it is easier to communicate the gospel and plant churches within cultural lines, and it makes using the HU principle in mission seemingly justifiable. However, there are some problems with this as well. Below is an analysis of strengths and weaknesses of using this principle in mission.

3.3.3. Critique of the Homogeneous Unit Principle: Strengths and Weaknesses

According to Thom S. Rainer, "No single tenet of church growth theology has received so much criticism as the homogeneous unit principle."[49] Since

---

46. Ibid., 227.

47. Lausanne Committee for World Evangelization and the World Evangelical Fellowship, "LOP 1: The Pasadena Consultation – Homogeneous Unit Principle," par. 3.

48. Ibid.

49. Rainer, *The Book of Church Growth*, 254.

the HU principle is so controversial, it certainly makes sense to assume that there are both strengths and weaknesses in the concept.

Strengths: The strength of the homogeneous unit model is in the fact that it allows those who are part of the unit to maintain their original cultural identity. They are not required to change their cultural identity in order to become part of the new group of people. Instead of learning a new culture, people in the homogeneous unit could focus their effort on learning new spiritual doctrines and rituals. Maintaining the indigenous culture provides people with the feeling of being more "at home" and this makes them more open to learning new concepts related to spiritual life. Also, the symbols used in communication are less foreign to people within the homogeneous unit and can be more easily understood. Evangelism within the unit is also easier, as people attempt to bring the gospel message to those who are within their sphere of influence. There are more chances that people will respond positively to the invitation to attend religious meetings if the participants are people of the same cultural background.

Miriam Adeney provides the following five reasons for ethnic churches to exist. They could be considered as strengths of the homogeneous unit principle.

- God is glorified by cultural diversity, which can only find full expression in churches made up of people of a uniform culture;
- Every person has the right to worship in his or her own language;
- If mixed congregations are insisted on, the cultural tradition of the majority will prevail; the cultural minority will feel alienated;
- They are more effective in evangelism within their own ethnic community;
- They are the best way of supporting Christians who are temporary residents overseas.[50]

This reasoning sounds very attractive to Slavic immigrants. It accurately describes their view of their churches' reasons for existence. However, these reasons put aside the question of the necessity to do mission among indigenous people, the question of the ethnic church being a witness to Christ within the surrounding community, which, in most cases, does not share

---

50. Miriam Adeney, *God's Foreign Policy* (Grand Rapids, MI: Eerdmans, 1984), 94.

the same ethnicity as the above-mentioned church. This discrepancy will be discussed later.

The *Pasadena Consultation: Homogeneous Unit Principle* document also emphasizes the importance of preserving everyone's culture, pointing to the fact that cultures have been created by God and demonstrate his creative power. According to the document, "preservation of cultural diversity honors God, respects man, enriches life, and promotes evangelization."[51] All these arguments support the HU principle being used in mission. However, there are serious weaknesses in this approach to mission. They are addressed below.

Weaknesses: The opponents of the idea of using the homogeneous unit principle in mission point to some of the natural weaknesses that exist with the homogeneous model approach. Homogeneous units can potentially promote segregation. Because people who are part of the HU are gathering together based on certain aspects or characteristics of culture, they could have a tendency to separate themselves from people who do not share the same cultural characteristics. Applying the homogeneous unit principle within mission work could lead to the promotion of cultural imperialism. If the missionary is only focusing her/his attention on reaching people within a certain homogeneous unit, there may be hidden or even open pressure on those from the outside of the unit who want to join the group to change certain aspects of their own culture in order to be accepted by people in the HU. People from another cultural group may be open to the missionary's message; however, they experience difficulty in joining the group because of differences in culture. Wagner himself has warned about the risk associated with using the HU model. He said that it is "implicitly placing a seal of approval on segregation, discrimination, racism, the caste system, and apartheid."[52] Rene Padilla, in his argument against using the HU principle in mission, provides five reasons supporting his claim.[53]

---

51. Lausanne Committee for World Evangelization and the World Evangelical Fellowship, "LOP 1: The Pasadena Consultation – Homogeneous Unit Principle," par. 4.

52. C. Peter Wagner, *Church Growth and the Whole Gospel* (San Francisco, CA: Harper & Row, 1981), 169.

53. C. René Padilla, "The Unity of the Church and the Homogeneous Unit Principle," in *Exploring Church Growth*, ed. Wilbert R. Shenk (Grand Rapids, MI: Eerdmans, 1983), 300–301. Padilla states that in the early church (1) "the gospel was proclaimed to all people, whether Jews or Gentiles, slaves or free, rich or poor, without partiality" (300); (2) "The breaking down of the barriers that separate people in the world was regarded as an essential

Although the HU principle is attractive because it offers a seemingly shorter way to growing the congregation, from the biblical perspective, it is not necessarily Christ's way. The *Pasadena Consultation: Homogeneous Unit Principle* shares this view as well. After expressing a strong position on the importance of preserving the diversity of cultures, it expresses a strong commitment to church unity. How can these two commitments, the commitment to cultural diversity and the commitment to church unity, be maintained together, taking into consideration that cultural differences often become the source of division between churches? "More particularly, how can separate HU churches express the unity of the Body of Christ?"[54] Answering this question, the authors of the document declare:

> All of us are agreed that in many situations a homogeneous unit church can be a legitimate and authentic church. Yet we are also agreed that it can never be complete in itself. Indeed, if it remains in isolation, it cannot reflect the universality and diversity of the Body of Christ. Nor can it grow into maturity. Therefore, every HU church must take active steps to broaden its fellowship in order to demonstrate visibly the unity and the variety of Christ's church. This will mean forging with other and different churches creative relationships which express the reality of Christian love, brotherhood, and interdependence.[55]

While acknowledging the legitimacy and authenticity of HU churches in certain situations, the authors point to the obvious deficiencies of such kinds of churches. Indirectly, it also raises questions about the legitimacy of ethnic churches. In most cases, as was mentioned above, they are HU churches. If this statement were applied to these churches, then it could

---

aspect of the gospel, not merely as a result of it" (ibid.); (3) the church "not only grew, but it grew across cultural barriers" (ibid.); (4) the New Testament "clearly shows that the apostles, while rejecting 'assimilationist racism,' never contemplated the possibility of forming homogeneous unit churches that would then express their unity in terms of interchurch relationships" (301); and (5) there "may have been times when the believers were accused of traitorously abandoning their own culture in order to join another culture, but there is no indication that the apostles approved of adjustments made in order to avoid that change" (ibid.).

54. Lausanne Committee for World Evangelization and the World Evangelical Fellowship, "LOP 1: The Pasadena Consultation – Homogeneous Unit Principle," par. 5.

55. Ibid.

be said that the ethnic church "can never be complete in itself" and will remain in isolation as "it cannot reflect the universality and diversity of the Body of Christ. Nor can it grow into maturity." It could be added that these churches cannot fulfill the authentic mission the church is called to in their immediate community. This is a very sober picture of ethnic churches in general and immigrant churches in particular. This is why this particular study is so necessary: to provide the immigrant churches with the challenge to "take active steps to broaden its fellowship in order to demonstrate visibly the unity and the variety of Christ's church," and start "forging with other and different churches creative relationships which express the reality of Christian love, brotherhood, and interdependence."[56]

3.3.4. Concluding Remarks

In conclusion, it could be said that applying the HU principle has great potential for a positive influence on church life, and also has great potential for a negative influence on the life of the church. When evaluating these two possibilities, it could be concluded that the use of the HU principle is not the best example of contextualization in mission. Although there are many attractive aspects in applying this principle, there is also enough evidence that such ethnically, culturally, or linguistically conscious churches will "aid unacceptable ethnic or cultural chauvinism or perpetuate barriers already in existence in society."[57] That is especially true when we are dealing with immigrant churches. As mentioned before, most of them are examples of the homogeneous unit. They consist of people who share the same language, culture, traditions, and so on. Mechanical application of the HU principle to these churches could suggest that these churches will experience rapid growth. In certain cases, this happens. Immigrant churches are growing. However, the health of this growth is questionable. These churches, due to natural reasons such as language and culture barriers, are already separated from the rest of the receiving society. Their growth is based on the fact that people of their ethnicity and language will join them. If this takes place, it happens only in the areas where non-Christian people of the same ethnicity live in close proximity to the ethnic church. Otherwise, if there is not a

---

56. Ibid.
57. Kirk, *What Is Mission?*, 223.

"target population" for ethnic churches that they can reach with the gospel, there is no growth of the church. Obviously, the growth of immigrant churches has limitations. Such churches are able to reach only the first generation of immigrants among their own people. As soon as the second generation of immigrants becomes comfortable with the indigenous language, they usually join local indigenous churches. Very few young people stay with their parents' churches. Also, applying HU principles to immigrant churches deepens the isolation of these churches from people in the receiving society. This undermines their ability to implement an authentic mission among these people and is contrary to Christ's Great Commission and to the gospel teaching that in Christ, there is no difference between nationalities when we are part of his body, called the church.

3.4. Conclusion for Chapter 3

The subject of contextualization in mission has been addressed in this chapter. In order to be able to find appropriate ways of contextualization, it is important to understand the context. The context could be cultural, linguistic, social, personal (spiritual, emotional, etc.), economic, political, etc. In order for Slavic Baptist immigrants in America to carry out a contextually appropriate sharing of the gospel with English-speaking people, they are required to learn English, study the new culture, overcome isolation from the rest of the society, and overcome personal internal struggles caused by the emotional stress common for most immigrants. It is a challenging task.

The scope of contextualization is wide. It is verbal and nonverbal, and addresses such aspects of mission as theologizing; Bible translation, interpretation, and application; incarnational lifestyle; evangelism; Christian instruction; church planting and growth; church organization; and worship style. It is crucial to apply the concept of contextualization very carefully in any given situation in order to protect the message from being damaged. The outcome of the contextualization is in direct correlation with the theological perspective of those who try to communicate the gospel contextually.

One of the attempts to be contextually appropriate in reaching people with the gospel is using the HU principle in the Church Growth movement. It was shown that applying the HU principle has strengths and weaknesses. It has a great potential for both positive and negative influences on church life. Although there are many attractive aspects in applying this principle, there is also enough evidence that such ethnically, culturally, or linguistically conscious churches will assist in the growth of unacceptable ethnic or cultural chauvinism or perpetuate barriers already in existence in society. This is especially true in the case of the immigrant churches. Most of them are homogeneous units. Without their homogeneity being challenged, they will continue to be in isolation from the surrounding society, linguistically, culturally, and socially. This will keep them from being active promoters of the gospel to people in the receiving society; thus they will not be able to accomplish their authentic mission.

The study of the challenge of contextualization in mission provided in this chapter shows the great importance of contextualization. It is an unavoidable necessity to contextualize the gospel message in order to make it understood and accepted by the people to whom this message is directed. In light of this, it is clear that PCSBA churches have to very seriously consider revisiting their relation to the surrounding society, examining the appropriateness of using their native language in church worship, and analyzing their understanding of the culture of the community in which they are living in order to be effective in reaching indigenous people with the gospel. Otherwise, they are in danger of spending their lives without much fruit in winning souls for Christ's kingdom.

The findings of this chapter (as well as the results of chapter 1 and chapter 1) have provided the tools needed to do the task of evaluating the current mission work of the PCSBA churches. Now, the focus of the study will be directed to learning the historical development of these churches from a mission perspective and to exploring the development of the Russian-speaking diaspora in America in the global migration context.

Part II

Context: Identity Formation – Towards a Conceptualization of Self-Understanding among Slavic Baptists

This part of the book is devoted to exploring the presence of evangelism and social action/*diaconia* in the life and ministry of Baptist churches in Russia and the USSR during the time of their identity formation. This historical overview is designed to find the role of these two aspects of mission in the life of these churches since the beginning of the movement. A few serious studies of the history of the evangelical movement in Russia and USSR have now been completed.[58] However, according to the author's knowledge,

---

58. The following scholarly works on the history of the evangelical movement in Russia and the former USSR are mentioned here: All-Union Council of Evangelical Christians-Baptists, *Istoriya Evangel'skikh Khristian-Baptistov v SSSR* (Moscow: AUCECB, 1989); Walter Sawatsky, *Soviet Evangelicals since World War II* (Kitchener, Ontario: Herald, 1981); Sergey N. Savinskiy, *Istoria Evangelskikh Khristian-Baptistov Ukrainy, Rossii, Belorussii (1867–1917)* (St Petersburg: Bible for All, 1999); Sergey N. Savinskiy, *Istoria Evangelskikh Khristian-Baptistov Ukrainy, Rossii, Belorussii (1917–1967)* (St Petersburg: Bible for All, 2001); Yuriy Reshetnikov and Sergey Sannikov, *Obzor Istorii Evangelsko-Baptistskogo Bratstva na Ukraine* (Odessa: Bogomyslie, 2000); Maurice Dowling, "Baptists in the Twentieth-Century Tsarist Empire and the Soviet Union," in *The Gospel in the World: International Baptist Studies*, ed. D. W. Bebbington (Carlisle: Paternoster, 2002), 209–232; Tatyana Nikolskaya, *Russkii protestantizm i gosudarstvennaya vlast v 1905–1991 godakh* (St Petersburg: Izd-vo Evropeiskogo universiteta v Sankt-Peterburge, 2009).

none of them was done with a focus on the role evangelism and social action/*diaconia* played in this movement. That makes this historical overview unique. This information is necessary to provide a historical background of the movement for an appropriate evaluation of the authenticity and contextuality of mission of PCSBA churches whose membership consists mainly of past members of Baptist churches in the former USSR.

Also, the development of global migration, in general, and the Russian-speaking diaspora, in particular, is analyzed in this part of the study in order to gain a better understanding of the potential mission field for PCSBA churches in America and abroad. In addition, the historical overview of the foundation and development of the PCSBA, with a focus on evangelism and social action/*diaconia*, is provided. This information is important for better understanding the role these two aspects of mission played in PCSBA churches in the past and are playing in the present, and provides the necessary data for the evaluation of the mission work of these churches.

CHAPTER 4

Historical Background of Slavic Baptists from the Mission Perspective

The history of the evangelical Baptist movement in Russia is not long but is very rich. It is dramatic, eventful, tragic, and unique. The scope of this study does not allow for an in-depth exploration of this exciting history. Only the main milestone events will be mentioned here in order to help understand the historical background and the role of mission (evangelism and social action/*diaconia* in particular) in the church life of predecessors of those Christians who are now members of churches in the Pacific Coast Slavic Baptist Association.

4.1. Definition of Terms

There is a need to provide a definition of several terms used in this chapter and in the thesis as a whole.

Baptists

As it will be shown in this chapter, there are three major streams that originated the church body known today as Evangelical Christians-Baptists, in the former Soviet Union. One of the streams emerged from the Caucasus region of the Tsarist Russia, in the second part of the nineteen century. This stream has always had a very distinctive Baptist theological and ecclesiological orientation. The Baptist movement started in the Caucasus "grew steadily and in 1884 the Union of Russian Baptists was formed."[1]

---

1. Maurice Dowling, "Baptists in the Twentieth-Century Tsarist Empire and the Soviet Union," in *The Gospel in the World*, ed. David W. Bebbington (Carlisle: Paternoster Press,

Evangelical Christians

The second stream emerged in St Petersburg in the 1870s as a result of evangelistic meetings held by a British nobleman, Lord Radstock, among Russian aristocracy.[2] Numerous prominent persons were converted and Colonel V. A. Pashkov became the leader of the new movement.[3] Later Ivan Prokhanov assumed the leadership role in this movement known as Evangelical Christians. In 1909, the Union of Evangelical Christians was organized.[4] Some differences in dogmatic practice existed in teachings of the Union of Russian Baptists and the Union of Evangelical Christians.[5]

Evangelical Baptist Movement

This term refers to the events that took place in the religious life of Tsarist Russia and Soviet Union marked by turning people from a formal religiosity or open atheism to seeking a personal relationship with God, to experiencing conversion and to living a life of Christian discipleship. The beginning of this movement could be traced to the second half of the nineteenth century.

Evangelical Christians-Baptists

This term is applied to the new denomination that was formed as a merger of two separate, sometimes competing, streams of the evangelical movement in Russia – Baptists and Evangelical Christians. In 1944, the Union of Russian Baptists and the Union of Evangelical Christians merged. Originally, the name of the newly established union was the All-Union Council of Evangelical Christians and Baptists. Later this name was modified and became known as the All-Union Council of Evangelical Christians-Baptists (AUCECB). In 1945, Pentecostals[6] and, in 1966, Mennonites joined the AUCECB.[7] In 1965, the new church body called the Council of Churches of the Evangelical Christians-Baptists (CCECB) was established. After 1944,

---

2002), 212.

2. Walter Sawatsky, *Soviet Evangelicals Since World War II* (Scottdale, PA: Herald, 1981), 34.

3. Ibid.

4. Sergey N. Savinskiy, *An Abridged History of the Russian–Ukrainian Baptist Faith* (Cherkasy, Ukraine: Smirna, 2013), 67.

5. Sawatsky, *Soviet Evangelicals Since World War II*, 44–45.

6. Ibid., 92.

7. Ibid., 281.

members of the Evangelical Christians-Baptists churches were often called simply "Baptists." In this thesis, the terms "Evangelical Christians-Baptists" and "Baptists" are used interchangeably in reference to the after-1944 events in the life of evangelicals in the former Soviet Union.

Evangelicals

This is an inclusive term. In this thesis, the term "evangelicals" when applied to Christians in the former Soviet Union refers to the Christian believers who are part of churches associated with the AUCECB and CCECB, as well as with other Baptist, Pentecostal, and Mennonite churches in the former Soviet Union. Theologically they are very much in alignment with American evangelicals who are described as those "who stress belief in personal conversion and salvation by faith in the atoning death of Christ, and in the Bible as the sole authority in matters of faith: stress is also laid on evangelism."[8]

4.2. Origin of Slavic Baptist Churches: Roots of Slavic Baptists – Are They Foreign or Indigenous?

There are two points of view among historians on the subject of the origin of Evangelical Christians-Baptists churches in Russia, Ukraine, and Belorussia. Many non-evangelical historians hold the position that Baptist ideas were brought to Russia from abroad by German Baptist preachers.[9] The most notable of these preachers was the evangelist, Johanne Oncken, who visited Southern Ukraine in the second half of the nineteenth century and preached very extensively in German colonies. As a result of his preaching, a religious revival took place among colonists, who subsequently were active in spreading the gospel to the indigenous people. Those who accepted this new teaching became the first Baptists in the Russian Empire. This position gained strong support from the Russian Orthodox Church and provided the base for seeing Baptists in Russia, Ukraine, and other republics of the former USSR as a completely foreign religion, without any national roots. Such an explanation of the Baptists' origin in Russia was used to justify the

---

8. John Bowker, ed., *The Oxford Dictionary of World Religions* (New York: Oxford University Press, 1997), 326.

9. N. A. Trofimchuk, *Istoriya Religiy v Rossii* (Moscow: RAGS, 2001), 347.

severe persecutions that ensued initially in the Russian Empire and later in the Soviet Union.

Slavic evangelical historians, on the other hand, firmly argue that Russian Baptists have a unique national origin. They describe it in the following manner:

> The Russian-Ukrainian Evangelical-Baptist movement was a result of revival of people's spirit under the influence of the Spirit of God and His Word. Evangelical revival started with reading of the Word of God by people who were sincerely seeking the truth and the way of salvation. Because they wanted to live a holy life, they compared their life with the Gospel. Similar seeking sentiments were common in the same degree for awakened people from the Orthodox Church, for people from the Molokans, and for Russian Germans. It is impossible to consider this revival as something foreign, something imported from the outside.[10]

Such an interpretation of the beginning of the evangelical movement in Russia was used by participants to prove its indigenous origin, and thus its right to exist on the Russian soil in the same way as the Orthodox Church exists. These views are contradictory and politically charged. However, the truth is somewhere in the middle. The author of this study agrees with Constantine Prokhorov[11] and Albert Wardin,[12] who emphasize that by

---

10. All-Union Council of Evangelical Christians-Baptists (AUCECB), *Istoriya Evangel'skikh Khristian-Baptistov v SSSR* (Moscow: AUCECB Publications, 1989), 52.

11. Prokhorov, "Russian Baptists and Orthodoxy, 1960–1990: A Comparative Study of Theology, Liturgy, and Traditions" (PhD diss., International Baptist Theological Seminary, University of Wales, 2011). Prokhorov is arguing that "there is no doubt that the emergence of evangelical and Baptist life in Russia was indebted to the work of evangelicals and Baptists from outside Russia. However, the Orthodox context in which the growth of these movements took place cannot be neglected if the specific character of the movements is to be understood" (21). He continues, explaining, "Undoubtedly there was foreign influence, but there were also deep preconditions in the national history, not least in the many internal sectarian currents, that caused the streams of the Russian evangelical movement to emerge" (28).

12. Albert Wardin, "How Indigenous Was the Baptist Movement in the Russian Empire?," in *Bogoslovskie Razmishleniya [Theological Reflections]* 10 (2009). Wardin expresses his position on this subject in the following way: "How indigenous are Russian Baptists? There is no easy answer. In origin or development they are simply not an implantation from another nation or culture. On the other hand, Protestant as well as Baptist impulses from abroad have influenced them. As other religious movements, they too may be a hybrid.

God's providence a unique historic situation was designed when the seeds of the gospel were brought from the West by evangelists and were planted in Russian hearts well prepared by the Holy Spirit and produced abundant fruit. This was even recognized by Vasiliy Pavlov, one of the most notable Baptist leaders at the end of the nineteenth and beginning of the twentieth century, who stated that the "push for this great evangelical movement [meaning: Baptist movement] was given by German Baptists."[13] There is much evidence of involvement of Western Christians in establishing the evangelical movement in Russia. For example, Alexey Sinichkin describing the significant role of the Mennonite Brethren minister, Johann Wieler, points to the fact that Wieler organized the first conference (*s'ezd*) in 1884 in Novo-Vasil'evka and was the first chairman of the mission committee designed to coordinate mission work among Ukrainians.[14]

It is important to clarify that Protestantism came to Russia for the first time in the 1520s. Initially, it was peasants and specialists in different vocations who came to Russia from Western Europe to do business there, bringing their new faith with them. They organized their communities and lived in isolation from the rest of Russian society, worshiping God privately in accordance with the Protestant tradition.[15] Later, the Tsar extended invitations to more of these specialists, promising them privileged positions in business. However, they were not allowed to proselytize Orthodox people to their Protestant faith. As a result, Protestantism was present in Russia for three centuries, but there were no Russians among Protestants during all these years. Changes took place in the middle of the nineteenth century, and in the second part of the century the indigenous evangelical movement emerged in several areas of the Tsarist Russia.

How much they incorporate foreign elements and how much they incorporate indigenous elements may simply be in the eye of the beholder" (174).

13. Vasiliy Pavlov, *Baptisty: Tserkov i gosudarstvo* (Moscow: LOGOS Christian Center, 2004), 86.

14. Alexey Sinichkin, *Vsye Dlya Missii* (Erpen, Ukraine: Assotsiatsiya "Dukhovnoye vozrozhdeniye," 2011), 174.

15. Trofimchuk, *Istoriya Religiy v Rossii*, 304.

The Evangelical Baptist movement started simultaneously in different regions of the Russian Empire.[16] This movement had different historical, socio-economic, and religious backgrounds, as well as different shaping forces, different predecessors, and different leaders in each region. Baptist teaching had reached Tsarist Russia through foreigners. However, the souls of many Russian people were prepared to accept this teaching by reading and study they had done in the Scripture printed in the common Russian language and by the work of the Holy Spirit. The religious history of Russia demonstrates clearly that movements similar to that of the evangelicals were common in the Russian lands long before the beginning of the Evangelical Baptist movement of the nineteenth century. From the beginning of the Christian era in Russia, there were people who openly opposed formal, ceremonial Orthodox Christianity. These people had their own interpretation of the Scripture[17] and they wanted to live according to it. Only sixteen years after Christianity was accepted as a state religion in AD 988, the monk Adrian challenged the Orthodox Church and its ceremonial nature.[18] He was imprisoned. Years later, in AD 1125, another man, Dmitr, came forward denying Orthodox Church ordinances.[19] These are examples of two individuals who opposed the Church. The first open movement against the Orthodox Church's rituals and teachings, known as *Strigolniki*, took place in the fourteenth and fifteenth centuries.[20] This movement was marked by public preaching and explanation of the gospel. After the official church and the state destroyed this movement, a new movement called *Nestyazhateli* started among monasteries at the end of the fifteenth century.[21] In the middle of the sixteenth century, the teachings of Bashkin and Kosoy spread widely among different people groups in Russian society. These teachings denied the rituals of the church, the decisions of church councils, and church traditions. Bashkin and Kosoy considered icons to be idols. The elements of the

---

16. Ian M. Randall, *Communities of Conviction: Baptist Beginnings in Europe* (Schwarzenfeld: Neufeld Verlag, 2009), 87.

17. AUCECB, *Istoriya*, 22.

18. Ibid.

19. Ibid.

20. Sergey N. Savinskiy, *Istoria Evangelskikh Khristian-Baptistov Ukrainy, Rossii, Belorussii (1867–1917)* (St Petersburg: Bible for All, 1999), 32.

21. Ibid., 35.

sacrament were understood as merely bread and wine, not as the flesh and blood of Christ. They judged confession before priests not to be valid. The great wealth possessed by the monasteries and the church was seen as inappropriate.[22] At the end of the eighteenth century, the religious movement called *Dukhobors* emerged. The participants of this movement "emphasized that the Holy Spirit lived within all true believers, who were thus able to enjoy immediate contact with God and to receive enlightenment and revelation from God."[23] The teachings of these movements and other similar ones in many aspects resonate with the teaching of the Evangelical Baptist movement of the nineteenth century. This fact illustrates how the Evangelical Baptist movement has its own deep national roots in the historical development of religious thought in Russia. All these different movements prepared the soil of Russian people to accept the living faith that was introduced to them in the middle of 1800s by evangelists from the West. The next part of this chapter describes how this happened.

4.3. Evangelism and Social Action/ *Diaconia* in the Life of the Evangelical Christians-Baptists Churches in Russia and Ukraine in Historical Perspective

4.3.1. Various Beginnings (1867–1900): Actively Sharing the New Faith

The Evangelical Baptist movement in Old Russia emerged almost simultaneously in three different regions of the country: the Caucasus, Southern Ukraine, and St Petersburg.[24]

The Caucasus

The religious context of the Evangelical Baptist movement in the Caucasus area was characterized by a strong presence of Molokans, who are described as follows: "a purely Russian sect which began in the mid-eighteenth century.

---

22. AUCECB, *Istoriya*, 23.
23. Dowling, "Baptists in the Twentieth-Century Tsarist Empire and the Soviet Union," 210.
24. Trofimchuk, *Istoriya Religiy v Rossii*, 348.

One of their leading preachers was Simeon Uklein of Tambov, who emphasized the primacy of Holy Scripture, opposed the sacramentalism of the state church, rejected all militarism, and stressed the equality of all men."[25]

The major difference of the Molokans from Russian Baptists consists in the Molokans' rejection of baptism.[26] As a result of the distribution of the Scriptures by workers of the Russian Bible Society, a revival movement took place among Molokans who lived in the Caucasus region.[27] They were searching for the right understanding of the Scriptures and the proper application of it in daily life. The first member of the Molokan sect to be baptized, and thus to leave his original beliefs, was Nikita Voronin. On 20 August 1867, under the cover of darkness, Voronin was baptized in the Kura River near Tiflis by Martin Kalweit.[28] This date is officially considered as the beginning of the Baptist movement in Russia. After his baptism in 1867, the "first Baptist," Nikita Voronin began to share the gospel with his fellow Molokans. As a result, his close friend, F. A. Arishin, soon was baptized as well, and in 1868, Voronin's wife and several other couples were baptized. Voronin has been described as a person who loved the Lord's ministry and who could not stop talking about Christ's love.[29] Soon, a small Baptist fellowship was organized near Tiflis.[30] Later, the Baptist congregation in Tiflis grew significantly and became a very influential group in the Evangelical Baptist movement, both in the Caucasus region and across Russia. Several prominent leaders came out of this church, including Nikita Voronin, Vasilii Pavlov, Vasilii Ivanov-Klyshnikov, and Ivan Kargel.[31] Vasilii Pavlov is considered by modern Baptists as the "patriarch of Russian baptism."[32] Being a very gifted young Molokan man, he joined a Baptist group in 1871. A few years later, in 1875, the Tiflis congregation sent Pavlov to the Baptist Theological College in Hamburg, where he was ordained in 1876 to the ministry by

---

25. Sawatsky, *Soviet Evangelicals Since World War II*, 32.

26. Ibid., 52.

27. Vyacheslav Tsvirinko, "A Search for Theological Identity among Russian Evangelicals" (MDiv thesis, Mennonite Brethren Biblical Seminary, Fresno, CA, 1995), 48.

28. Sawatsky, *Soviet Evangelicals Since World War II*, 27.

29. AUCECB, *Istoriya*, 74.

30. Tsvirinko, "A Search for Theological Identity among Russian Evangelicals," 49.

31. Ibid., 50.

32. Trofimchuk, *Istoriya Religiy v Rossii*, 347.

Johann Gerhard Oncken.[33] On his return to Russia, Pavlov translated the Hamburg Baptist Confession of Faith written by Oncken, into Russian.[34] It became the ruling document for the Tiflis congregation and a model of church structure for other congregations.[35]

From its beginning, the Tiflis congregation had a vision for spreading the gospel through evangelism, led by several brothers dedicated to this ministry. V. Pavlov, V. Ivanov, and E. Bogdanov were among a few brothers who were committed to ministering in this field.[36] They visited different towns and villages in their region, preaching the gospel mainly to Molokans. Converts were organized into small Baptist congregations for worship and fellowship. V. Pavlov visited the city of Vladikavkaz in Northern Caucasus in 1879, during which seven new believers were baptized. However, even before his visit, E. Bogdanov had organized a group of believers in Vladikavkaz. This was the beginning of the first Baptist congregation in the Northern Caucasus.[37] In April 1879, the Tiflis congregation sent V. Ivanov as a missionary to the Baku region. Through his successful ministry, entire extended families of Molokans in different villages were converted to Baptist teachings. These converts were baptized,[38] and they became the starting nucleus for new Baptist congregations in their places of residence.[39] Through the evangelistic ministry of E. Bogdanov, seventy-eight people accepted Christ and were baptized before 1882. Such a bold evangelistic ministry in the Caucasus region did not initially receive significant resistance from the Tsarist government because the converts to Baptism were primarily from among the Molokans rather than from Orthodox Christians. The law prohibited proselytizing

---

33. Tsvirinko, "A Search for Theological Identity among Russian Evangelicals," 49.

34. AUCECB, *Istoriya*, 77.

35. The fact that Pavlov was educated in Germany and that the Hamburg Baptist Confession of Faith was used as a ruling document in the early Russian Baptist congregation clearly points to a linkage between the new evangelical movement in Russia and Western Baptists.

36. Savinskiy, *Istoria*, 135.

37. Ibid., 136.

38. Marina S. Karetnikova, "The Missionary Movement in Russia: the 19th and 20th Centuries," in *Mission in the Former Soviet Union*, ed. Walter W. Sawatsky and Peter Penner (Schwarzenfeld: Neufeld Verlag, 2005), 66. In the article, Marina S. Karetnikova underlines the role of women in evangelistic efforts at that time, stating, "Baptized people immediately became missionaries and women were the most active among them" (ibid.).

39. Savinskiy, *Istoria*, 137.

among Orthodox Christians; however, proselytizing was permitted among the members of different sects. Since Molokans and Baptists were considered sects, the state did not express great concern in their members switching from one sect to another.[40] As a result of the evangelistic activities of the first Baptist church in Tiflis, a group of Baptist churches was established in the Caucasus region. Clearly, evangelism played a significant role in the early Baptist movement.

There is limited information available about practicing social action/*diaconia* among Baptist congregations in the Caucasus region. Sergey Savinskiy states that at the church business meetings, such issues were discussed as providing material aid to brothers of the Caucasus congregations. Also, such help was provided to brothers living in the Ukraine.[41] Another historical source confirms this information, saying that financial help was provided to brothers in the Caucasus and Ukraine, as well as to those who were in prison.[42] Trofimchuk points to an unusual act of service completed by Baptists in Tiflis. During the Russia–Turkey war (1877–1879), two brothers and two sisters were sent by the congregation to the battle front to help wounded soldiers.[43] Although sources of information on this subject are limited, still it could be suggested that early Baptist churches in this area were practicing social action/*diaconia*.

Southern Ukraine

The second stream of the Evangelical Baptist movement in Russia, independent of the Caucasian movement, issued from the Ukraine. This stream is known as *Stundism*.[44] Most of its participants were ordinary people – agricultural workers. German Mennonite and Lutheran colonists played an important role in starting this movement.[45] As Western colonists, they were not allowed by the Russian government to proselytize among the Russians. However, some of the indigenous people worked for these colonists and

---

40. Ibid., 136.
41. Ibid., 139.
42. AUCECB, *Istoriya*, 79.
43. Trofimchuk, *Istoriy Religiy v Rossii*, 347.
44. AUCECB, *Istoriya*, 50.
45. Dowling, "Baptists in the Twentieth-Century Tsarist Empire and the Soviet Union," 211.

participated in their weekly hours (*Stunde*) of Bible study. As a result, they started their own Bible studies. Under the influence of the Scriptures, some of them were converted and came to understand the necessity of water baptism.[46] In 1869, the Mennonite Brethren leader, Abraham Unger, baptized the first Ukrainian Stundist, Efim Tsymbal.[47] In 1875, Peter Lysenko, who lived in the village of Sofievka, was baptized by a well-known Mennonite minister.[48] Efim Tsymbal, Peter Lysenko, Fedor Onishchenko, Mikhail Ratushnyi, and Ivan Riaboshapka, among other new converts, committed themselves to spreading the good news they learned to their own people. They fearlessly preached the gospel on the streets and markets, shared it in small gatherings or in one-on-one settings. "Women as well as men took part in evangelistic missions."[49] As a result, more and more people followed their way. Initially, *Stundists* attempted to remain within the Orthodox Church. However, the persecution of these sectarians, labeled *Stundists*, intensified, and they were forced to establish their own identity outside of the official church.[50] They held their meetings in private houses, and small congregations were established in different villages. Although they were not as well organized as the Tiflis Baptist congregation, persecution from the Orthodox Church did not stop the new movement. In reality, the persecutions helped the *Stundists* develop a sense of sympathy and support from ordinary villagers.[51] Eventually, *Stundism* spread from the Ukraine to the rest of Russia. The history of the Evangelical Baptist movement (*Stundism*) in the Ukraine during the second half of the nineteenth century shows that evangelism was conducted mainly through the personal witness of those who accepted the new faith and the new way of life. Often, immediately after experiencing conversion, new members of the movement began sharing the gospel with their relatives, neighbors, and friends. For example,

---

46. AUCECB, *Istoriya*, 51.
47. S. I. Golovashchenko, "Pervye shagi evangelskogo dvizheniya na Ukraine: vozniknoveniye, rasprostranenie," in *Istoria evangelsko-baptistskogo dvizheniya v Ukraine: Materily i document*. Source: Istorija Evangel'skogo Dvizhenija v Evrazii, disc 1.0 [*The History of the Evangelical Movement in Eurasia*, disc 1.0] (Odessa: EAAA. 2001), CD.
48. Sawatsky, *Soviet Evangelicals Since World War II*, 34.
49. Randall, *Communities of Conviction*, 89.
50. Sawatsky, *Soviet Evangelicals Since World War II*, 34.
51. AUCECB, *Istoriya*, 68.

Fedor Onishchenko, who is considered to be the first born-again Ukrainian, witnessed to his neighbor and friend, Mikhail Ratushnii, and as a result, Ratushnii was converted in 1860.[52] After his conversion, Mikhail Ratushnii began preaching the gospel in his village Osnovi, in the Odessa region. Soon there were about twenty followers of Ratushnii who gathered together to study the Scripture. In the Ostrikov village, the *Stundist* group emerged among Ukrainians because of the witness of Gerhard Willer,[53] a member of the Mennonite Brethren colony. He handled the Russian language well and explained the New Testament to the Ukrainian people. Dem'yan Wasetstkii became the leader of a group of twenty to thirty people who met on a regular basis to study the Bible. They also visited nearby villages, where they shared their beliefs with the Orthodox community.[54] In the village of Karlovka, among the first people to accept the evangelical truth was Efim Tsymbal in 1866. As mentioned earlier, he became the first baptized Ukrainian. After baptism in 1869 he subsequently baptized Khlistun, Tsarenko, and other individuals. At the end of 1869, due to their active personal witness, the congregation in Karlovka grew to fifty-eight members.[55] Through the active evangelistic ministry of Efim Tsymbal, groups of believers began to meet in eleven different villages in the area.[56] The first *Stundist* in the village of Lubomirka was Ivan Ryaboshapka. Through the witness of Martin Gubner, and through the influence of the Scripture, which he learned to read at the age of thirty, Ryaboshapka experienced a dramatic conversion. Immediately, together with Martin Gubner, he began sharing his new beliefs with his fellow villagers. At that time, he was working in a millhouse, and this was a perfect place for spreading the gospel because people visited the millhouse from all over the area. Very soon, a group of ten families of Ukrainian *Stundists* was having meetings for the study of the Scriptures in the Lubomirka village.[57] Ivan Ryaboshapka became a prominent preacher of the gospel. While a pastor of the Lubomirka congregation, he still traveled a

---

52. Ibid., 58.
53. Ibid., 59.
54. Ibid., 60.
55. Ibid., 63.
56. Ibid., 63.
57. Savinskiy, *Istoria*, 102.

lot, visiting other churches and leading many people to a personal knowledge of Christ through his preaching and through personal witnessing. He also wrote the first Confession of Faith of Ukrainian Baptists in 1881.[58] Contrary to the local government's reaction to the Baptist movement in the Caucasus and in the Ukraine, the reaction of the Orthodox Church and the government to *Stundism* was very negative. Aggressive persecution was directed against the new movement. Because of this oppression, it was impossible to organize systematic evangelistic activities. Mostly, the good news was passed to other people through the personal witness of ordinary believers. Leaders of the new movement received strict attention from the police, and their evangelistic activity was subject to state punishment. They were always at risk of losing freedom and even life itself for their evangelistic actions. Therefore, they often fulfilled their duties secretly. For example, in 1877, Ivan Ryaboshapka baptized fourteen people in the Volyn region at night. In the daytime he was hidden under the threshing-floor, while at night he preached and baptized.[59] Many ministers were exiled. They were brought (sometimes with their families) to remote regions of the Russian Empire. However, they used this opportunity to sow seeds of the gospel even in those remote regions. In some cases, followers of the new faith voluntarily moved to distant areas of the empire in order to avoid persecution.[60] Arriving at these new locations, they started churches, and as a result, many churches in Siberia, Central Asia, and the Caucasus were planted by Ukrainian believers.[61]

Despite the strong opposition from the Orthodox Church and severe persecution from the Tsarist government,[62] the new movement in the Ukraine demonstrated its ability to survive and even to grow substantially. The number of believers had grown from 2,006 in 1884 to 4,670 in 1893.[63]

---

58. Ibid., 128.
59. Ibid., 123.
60. Tat'yna Nikol'skaya, *Russkij protestantizm i gosudarstvennaya vlast' v 1905-1991 godakh* (St Petersburg: Izdatel'stvo Evropeiskogo universiteta v Sankt-Peterburge, 2009), 24.
61. Yuriy Reshetnikov and Sergey Sannikov, *Obzor Istorii Evangelsko-Baptistskogo Bratstva na Ukraine* (Odessa: Bogomyslie, 2000), 121.
62. Dowling, "Baptists in the Twentieth-Century Tsarist Empire and the Soviet Union," 213.
63. Ibid., 114.

Certainly this could be attributed to the total commitment of members of this movement to active evangelism.

St Petersburg

The uniqueness of the third stream of the Evangelical Baptist movement in Russia is that it started among the highest level of Russian society. Its beginning can be traced back to 1813, when the Russian Bible Society was established.[64] Later, in 1874, a revival took place when a British nobleman and member of the Plymouth Brethren, a retired colonel of the British Army, Grenville Waldegrave, known in Russia as Lord Radstock, was invited by a member of the Russian aristocracy, E. I. Chertkovoii, to visit St Petersburg.[65] He was asked to come and share the gospel. He preached in English and French. Only well-educated people were able to listen to him and understand. His simple and clear explanation of the Scriptures impressed many people in the Russian aristocracy, and some of them experienced dramatic changes in their lives as a result. Among them were V. Pashkov (Colonel of the Guards), Count Korff (Master of Ceremonies at the Imperial Court), Count A. Bobrinskii, and Princess Natalia Lieven.[66] They became faithful disciples of Christ and began to implement his teaching in everyday life. They had a great impact on the development of the Evangelical Baptist movement in Russia. V. Pashkov, who was indifferent to religious and spiritual matters before meeting with Lord Radstock, became a zealous activist of the evangelical movement after conversion, which occurred during the meeting with Radstock. He terminated his service in the army and became an active preacher. Later, when Lord Radstock returned home, because of the active role Colonel V. Pashkov played in this new movement, it was named Pashkovism.[67] Using their personal wealth and influence, the Pashkovites were very successful in spreading the gospel in both the rich and poor parts of Russian society. Along with sharing the good news orally, they expressed

---

64. Viktor Zander, *Identity and Marginality among New Australians: Religion and Ethnicity in Victoria's Slavic Baptist Community* (Berlin/New York: Walter de Gruyter, 2004), 269.

65. Savinskiy, *Istoria*, 144.

66. Trofimchuk, *Istoriya Religiy v Rossii*, 348.

67. Sawatsky, *Soviet Evangelicals Since World War II*, 34.

Christ's love to people by deeds.⁶⁸ Social work was conducted among the impoverished, including the distribution of inexpensive food, starting businesses to provide jobs for poor people,⁶⁹ opening schools and orphanages for children, and building shelters for homeless women.⁷⁰ Pashkov and Count Korf visited jails and hospitals with the evangelistic message, tracts and Bible portions were distributed, and Christian literature was published. In 1876, Pashkovists established a Society for Spiritual-Edification Reading Encouragement. This society published Christian books, tracts, and brochures, and it distributed them among noblemen, students, and factory workers. During its eight years in existence, the Society was able to make twelve editions of 200 different books and brochures.⁷¹ The Pashkovists preached not only in St Petersburg, they also went to different distant areas away from the capital of Russia, sharing the good news with poor people by simply reading the gospel to them because few ordinary people in Russia at that time were able to read.⁷² The magazine *Russian Worker* was established with the purpose of bringing good news to the working class of Russian society.⁷³ Due to the influence of the Plymouth Brethren, the Pashkovites did not ordain leaders, baptize, or maintain membership rolls.⁷⁴ They took a looser attitude toward the standardization of doctrine and liturgy than the other two streams of the Evangelical Baptist movement in Russia.⁷⁵ They became the forerunners of the Russian Evangelical Christians, who appeared as a movement in the beginning of the twentieth century. Their new leader, Ivan Prokhanov, continued the work of Pashkov and his co-workers. Prokhanov was a well-educated, gifted, and energetic person. Because of his dedicated work, the Union of Evangelical Christians was organized in 1909.⁷⁶ Later,

---

68. Sofiya Liven, *Dukhovnoe probuzhdeniye v Rossii: Vospominaniya* (Korntal, Germany: Svet na Vostoke, 1990), 46.
69. Ibid., 47–52.
70. Sheril Korrado, *Philosophiya sluzheniya polkovnika Pashkova* (St Petersburg: Bibliya dlya Vsekh, 2005), 114–122.
71. Savinskiy, *Istoria*, 149.
72. Trofimchuk, *Istoriya Religiy v Rossii*, 349.
73. Sawatsky, *Soviet Evangelicals Since World War II*, 148.
74. Ibid., 34.
75. Ibid., 35.
76. Ibid., 35.

this union, along with the Union of Russian Baptists, became one of the two most important and largest bodies of evangelical Christians in Russia. One of the distinctive characteristics of this group of believers from the beginning of the movement was a strong evangelistic zeal. Evangelism often has been accomplished by *diaconia*, as Mary Raber describes it:

> While the evangelicals were guided by simple obedience to the biblical imperative to do good works, their ministries of compassion never existed apart from what they saw as their primary calling of preaching the gospel. To carry out their mission, evangelicals supported a social agenda that would above all allow them freedom to evangelize. For this reason, their charitable activity was carried on as an integral part of preaching the gospel, not as a means of relieving human suffering alone.[77]

Summary

An analysis of the three main streams of the evangelical movement in Russia shows that from the beginning, each was characterized by active involvement in evangelistic efforts. Also, certain social actions were performed, providing material help to believers and taking care of the poor. Despite strong opposition from the Orthodox Church and severe persecution by the Tsarist government, as well as the threat of fines, imprisonment, exile, deprivation of property, and even death, members of the Baptist, Evangelical Christian, and *Stundist* congregations continued to share the good news with their fellow countrymen. Many of them paid a great price for their dedication. This proves that the missionary attitude implemented by local evangelistic efforts was considered, by early believers in Tsarist Russia, to be a natural part of being a Christian.

4.3.2. Attempts to Unite the Streams: Common Commitment to Mission

From the beginning of the Evangelical Baptist movement in Russia, attempts were made to unite the different streams within the movement. In 1879, a conference of representatives of the Caucasus congregations took

---

77. Mary Raber, "Ministries of Compassion among Russian and Ukrainian Evangelicals, 1905-1929" (PhD diss., 2012), chapter 1.

place in Tiflis. The most important issue discussed at this conference was the creation of a Mission Board. Three brothers were elected to the board: N. Voronin, M. Kalweit, and V. Pavlov.[78] In 1882, the united conference of Mennonite Brethren and Baptists took place in the Ryukenau colony under the leadership of I. Willer and P. Friesen. There were nineteen delegates from the Russian and Ukrainian churches at this conference. Among other issues discussed at the conference were (1) how to appoint brothers to be missionaries, (2) financial support of the missionaries, and (3) selecting members for the Mission Board. It needs to be clarified that the term "missionary" at that particular time did not mean somebody going overseas for mission work. It was applied to the evangelists who were working among local indigenous people full time, being supported either by the church or by the mission board. The agenda of the conference in 1882 shows that mission through evangelism was the main focus of those churches' ministry at that time.[79]

In 1884, Pashkov made an official attempt to unite the different streams of Russian evangelicals. More than seventy representatives of the *Stundists*, Baptists, Mennonite Brethren, Pashkovites, Molokans, and Dukhobors met on 1 April 1884 in St Petersburg to discuss the issue of unity.[80] The conference was planned for eight days. Unfortunately, on the sixth day, the authorities interrupted it. Delegates were arrested by the police and were sent back to their homes.[81] However, even the first five days of discussion were enough to show that there were many differences between the ecclesiastical and theological views of the participants.[82] At the same time, all of them were united on the issue of mission. They agreed that evangelists should be supported financially and that the most gifted women should be allowed to preach.[83]

A few weeks later, the unity conference of Russian Baptists took place in the village of Novo-Vasil'evka, in the Ukraine. A total of thirty-three delegates from twelve congregations attended this conference. This conference

---

78. Savinskiy, *Istoria*, 194.
79. Ibid.
80. Ibid., 197. Total number of the participants at this meeting reached 100 people.
81. Ibid., 199.
82. Sawatsky, *Soviet Evangelicals Since World War II*, 44.
83. Savinskiy, *Istoria*, 199.

is officially considered as the beginning of the Russian Baptist Union. The first president of the Baptist Union elected during the conference was Johann Wieler.[84] He was one of the early Mennonite Brethren evangelists.[85] Later he was forced to leave Russia and at the second meeting, in 1886, Dei Mazaev was elected president. The agenda of this conference consisted of twenty-four items; however, the main item was the issue of mission. The Mission Committee was elected. The regions for evangelistic work were designated. Eight missionaries (evangelists) were appointed to do the work.[86]

The main differences in dogmatic practice between the two largest bodies of evangelicals in Russia – Baptists and Evangelical Christians – can be identified in the following ways: "(1) whether the ceremony of laying on of hands on the newly baptized should be performed; (2) whether presbyters and deacons must be ordained; (3) whether only an ordained presbyter was entitled to conduct communion."[87] Evangelical Christians considered all of these practices unnecessary, but they were very important for the Baptists. Also, the evangelicals were divided on organizational issues. Who would be the president of the united evangelical body: I. S. Prokhanov, a prominent Evangelical Christian leader, or A. M. Mazaev, the president of the Baptists? Should the new union have a centralized structure, or a federal structure with greater autonomy for the regional unions?[88] These and other issues kept the main streams of evangelicals from being united. From 27 May to 6 June 1920 a united conference of Baptists and Evangelical Christians took place in Moscow. In the middle of the conference, the chairman of the conference proclaimed that the two unions were officially merged. The news was received with tears of joy. However, during the second part of the conference, while discussing organizational issues of the new union, serious disagreements took place between delegates, and the conference ended fruitlessly – no unity was reached.[89] During the following few years, the distance

---

84. AUCECB, *Istoriya*, 101. This is a clear evidence of the influence the Mennonite Brethren have had on the evangelical movement among Russians and Ukrainians; Savinskiy, *Istoria*, 200.

85. Sawatsky, *Soviet Evangelicals Since World War II*, 34.

86. Savinskiy, *Istoria*, 200.

87. Sawatsky, *Soviet Evangelicals Since World War II*, 44.

88. Ibid., 45.

89. AUCECB, *Istoriya*, 194.

between the two church bodies widened significantly. This circumstance provided great hindrances for evangelistic work. Ordinary people were often confused as to why these two groups of Christians, which were so similar, could not be together. Fortunately, despite the fact that the leadership of the unions did not come to an agreement, from 1919 to 1920 and even later, ordinary lay people and local congregations from both unions were involved in shared ministries and often worshiped together. In some cases, even joint unions were established on the local level (Caucasus region, Crimea).[90]

During the Stalinist persecutions, from 1927 to 1944, when most houses of prayer were closed, believers began attending the meeting houses that were still open, without paying any attention to denominational affiliation. Differences between the two movements were no longer important for the believers.[91] Only in 1944, during World War II, after fruitless attempts to reach unity in the past and after years of unprecedented suffering and great loss of leaders and lay people, did the two main groups of Russian evangelicals join together as part of the All-Union Council of Evangelical Christians-Baptists.[92] It is unfortunate that it took so long for the leadership of both unions to come to an agreement.

Summary

In all attempts to unite the three streams of the evangelical movement in Russia, the central point always was joint evangelistic work. It shows the importance of mission through evangelism for the evangelical believers in Russia in the nineteenth and at the beginning of the twentieth century.

4.3.3. Life of Suffering and Growth (1900–1945): Sharing the Gospel Regardless of Circumstances

The distinctive mark of the Evangelical Baptist movement in Russia is that it was almost constantly under severe persecution. Before 1917, each of the above-mentioned streams of the movement experienced oppression and persecution from the state church – the Orthodox Church. Since the time when Eastern Orthodox Christianity was accepted by the Tsar of Kievan

---

90. Ibid.
91. Sawatsky, *Soviet Evangelicals Since World War II*, 45.
92. AUCECB, *Istoriya*, 232.

Rus (Russia) in AD 988, the Orthodox Church had been the state religion in Russia.[93] Everyone who was born in Russia was considered an Orthodox Christian. The Russian Orthodox Church was so closely linked to the state that criticism of the church or disobedience to church rules was regarded as treason against the state.[94] It is no wonder that from the first day of its existence, the Evangelical Baptist movement in Russia was considered to be a movement of dissidents and experienced persecution from both the Orthodox Church and the state. The intensity of the persecutions varied at different times and within different regions. Although laws were occasionally passed that allowed freedom of conscience, persecution never completely stopped.[95] The history of the Russian evangelical movement in the second half of the nineteenth century and the beginning of the twentieth century is full of horrific stories of families being exiled or torn apart because they were converted to the evangelical understanding of Christianity and joined the new movement. The leaders of the Baptists, *Stundists*, Pashkovites, and other groups were often arrested, imprisoned, and condemned to penal servitude (*katorga*). Many of them died in prison because of ill treatment. One of the Baptist leaders described that time in this way: "This was a time of horrible persecutions. Exiles, arrests, fines, and beatings of believers rained down abundantly upon the audacious followers of the Gospel. Under continual fear of being caught by the police, the brothers nevertheless did not cease their meetings, holding them in basements, across the Dnieper, in the woods, in the cemetery, in ravines, and in the apartments of the more well-to-do brothers."[96]

In 1905, a new law regarding religious tolerance was declared by the Tsarist government. Because of this, many exiled evangelical Christians were able to return home.[97] Although they did not receive complete freedom of

---

93. Ibid., 21. On the emergence of the ethno-centered Russian Orthodox identity, see Parush R. Parushev, "Narrative Paradigms of Emergence of an Ethno-centred Orthodox Theological Identity," *Religion in Eastern Europe* 25, no. 2 (May 2005): 1–39.

94. Tsvirinko, "A Search for Theological Identity among Russian Evangelicals," 57.

95. Ibid., 58.

96. Sawatsky, *Soviet Evangelicals Since World War II*, 35.

97. Nikol'skaya, *Russkij protestantizm i gosudarstvennaya vlast' v 1905–1991 godakh*, 27.

religion, evangelical believers used the new situation to expand their missionary, educational, and charitable activities.[98]

Despite difficult circumstances and the constant threat of being fined, exiled, or even killed, Evangelical Christians and Baptists, as illustrated in previous parts of this chapter, were constantly doing evangelistic work. The result of this sacrificial ministry was significant numerical growth of evangelical believers in Tsarist Russia. According to the official statistics, in January 1912, there were 114,652 Baptists and 30,716 Evangelical Christians in Russia. By 1917, the total number of believers in both groups amounted to from 150,000 to 200,000.[99] Such growth was unprecedented for a movement that was only fifty years old and that was constantly, severely persecuted. This evidence demonstrates that participants of the movement believed in evangelism and were therefore practicing great evangelistic work.

The October Revolution of 1917 brought great relief for Russian evangelicals. One of the first decrees issued by the Bolshevik government proclaimed the separation of church and state. The Orthodox Church was deprived of its privileged position and was reduced to a level of equality with all other religions in the country.[100] In reality, the Orthodox Church became the subject of unprecedented persecution from the new state regime. What the church had inspired in the past towards sectarians (including evangelicals), it was now experiencing itself. Thousands of priests were exiled or killed, church buildings and cathedrals were destroyed, and treasures and land of the church were confiscated.[101] In only two years, "between 1921 and 1923, twenty-seven hundred married priests, thirty-four hundred nuns, and many laymen were killed in the government's confiscation of church valuables for 'famine relief.'"[102] Over all, the Orthodox Church experienced staggering damage. "An estimated forty-two thousand priests lost their lives between 1918 and 1940; most of those perished in the 1930s . . . Massive church closings occurred. By 1933, five hundred of Moscow's six hundred churches

---

98. Ibid., 29.

99. Trofimchuk, *Istoriya Religiy v Rossii*, 353.

100. Ibid., 36.

101. Kent R. Hill, *The Soviet Union on the Brink: An Inside Look at Christianity and Glasnost* (Portland, OR; Multnomah, 1991), 72.

102. Ibid., 74.

had been closed. By 1941, ninety-eight out of every one hundred Orthodox churches were closed down."[103]

At the same time, from 1917 to 1929, sectarians experienced their long-awaited freedom. It was the "golden decade" for them. After the Civil War ended in 1920, Baptists and Evangelical Christians dramatically increased their evangelistic efforts.[104] The 24th Congress of Baptists, in November 1921, proclaimed that evangelism should be considered to be "the most important matter in our spiritual life. All forms of our organization should be considered valuable in such a degree in which they provide support to the successful proclaiming of the gospel."[105] Because of great evangelistic efforts, Baptists and Evangelical Christians experienced unprecedented numerical growth during this time.[106] An unprecedented revival took place in various parts of the country. For example, in Siberia, in May of 1919 alone, a thousand people were baptized.[107] During the seven years after the Bolshevik Revolution in 1917, both Evangelical Christians and Baptists increased their numbers almost fivefold.[108] Sawatsky describes the role of evangelism at that time in the following way:

> One of the primary reasons for this rapid growth was surely the role of the evangelists. The central Baptist and Evangelical Christian unions sent out evangelists to start new churches. The regional unions often maintained a staff of full-time evangelists.

---

103. Ibid., 84.

104. In his article, Maurice Dowling refers to this period, saying that "the first twelve years of Soviet rule were a period of growth for the evangelicals, thanks to the dedicated missionary work which they did and also to the considerable amount of foreign help in the form of literature and money" ("Baptists in the Twentieth-Century Tsarist Empire and the Soviet Union," 219).

105. M. Krapivin, A. Leykin, and A. Dalgatov, *Sud'by Khristianskogo Sektanstva v Sovetskoy Rossii (1917 – konets 1930-kh godov)* (St Petersburg: State University, 2003), 67.

106. Walter W. Sawatsky describes this period of Slavic evangelical history in the following way: "The evangelicals went into a period of growth explosion . . . There was great creativity in ways of doing evangelism and mission – organizing special interest groups for youth, women; establishing Bible schools, publishing centers, seeking to circulate more Bibles; holding special conferences for teaching, engaging the Bolshevik agitators in dialogue and debates on philosophy and Christian faith" ("The Centrality of Mission and Evangelization in the Slavic Evangelical Story," in *Mission in the Former Soviet Union*, ed. Walter W. Sawatsky and Peter Penner [Schwarzenfeld: Neufeld Verlag, , 2005], 48).

107. Sinichkin, *Vsye Dlya Missii* 183.

108. Sawatsky, *Soviet Evangelicals Since World War II*, 39.

By 1927 this evangelization ministry was so well organized in the Ukraine that there were no less than 56 evangelists supported by the Ukraine Baptist Union. At that time there were approximately 1,000 congregations of Baptists and 2,000 congregations or groups of Evangelical Christians in the Ukraine. As early as 1921 the All-Russian Baptist Union had an expense budget of 45 million rubles, most of this for support of evangelists.[109]

In 1926, regional Baptist unions, which were part of the Federal Baptist Union, supported more than 120 full-time evangelists. Besides those, by the end of 1925, there were 3,700 local Baptist preachers (unpaid, lay preachers). In the summer of 1928, their number grew to 5,000.[110] The secretary of the Baptist Union, P. V. Ivanov-Klyshnikov, in his report to the Baptist World Alliance Congress in Toronto in 1928 estimated that there were some 4,000 congregations in Russia.[111] Even more impressive was the mission work done by Evangelical Christians. In the fall of 1919, they supported fifty evangelists. In December 1921, this number doubled. In the summer of 1920, the Union of Evangelical Christians had sent missionaries to China and India – two to each country. Also, a mission organization was formed to reach people of other ethnic and religious groups (Nentsy, Chuvashi, Mordvy, Komi, Votyakov, Kirgiz, Kazakh, Kalmyk, and others).[112] By 1928, this union supported 600 missionaries.[113] The total membership of both Baptists and Evangelical Christians in the USSR in 1928 was close to half a million.[114] Clearly, Russian evangelical believers at that time were mission-minded and their strong evangelistic efforts resulted in significant numerical growth. While placing their primary focus on evangelism, Evangelical Christians and Baptists also responded to the material needs of people. One such example is the Baptists' participation in helping victims of famine in

---

109. Ibid., 39.
110. Krapivin, Leykin, and Dalgatov, *Sud'by Khristianskogo Sektanstva v Sovetskoy Rossii*, 67.
111. Ibid., 42.
112. Ibid., 67.
113. Ibid., 68.
114. Trofimchuk, *Istoriya Religiy v Rossii*, 353.

the Volga River region in 1920. Millions of people suffered from a shortage of food at that time. Many of them died. Churches raised their own funds to help, as well as mobilizing the world Baptist community to send help to suffering people.[115]

Unfortunately, this time of religious freedom for evangelicals in the USSR did not last long. In 1929, a new law regarding religious organizations was accepted by the Soviet government. The law significantly limited the activity of all religious organizations. Any violation of the law was subject to severe punishment.[116] It was the beginning of the "bloody time." The friendly attitude towards sectarians that the Bolshevik government had at the beginning of their term, started to change in the mid-1920s. Unprecedented numerical growth, the successful life of faith-based economic communities over and against those built on the ideology of the Communist party, and the growing sympathy of ordinary people towards evangelicals were all seen as a threat to the new atheistic Soviet ideology.[117] The government's anti-sectarian campaign started with organizing anti-religious societies like *Bezbozhnik*, which actively tried to discredit all religious organizations. An anti-religious campaign in official publications followed. Then, the law on religious cults, mentioned earlier, was approved. "This law introduced detailed regulations for controlling the activities of all religious bodies. But the list of activities forbidden to the religious bodies appears to be a list of the techniques evangelicals had introduced for expanding and strengthening their movement."[118]

Unprecedented persecution of evangelicals followed. The period from 1929 to 1945 was a time of high-scale attack on religion in the USSR.[119] Members of the Evangelical Baptist movement were now considered political enemies of the state. In government controlled periodicals, believers were described as supporters of anti-government activities.[120] Most of the leaders of the Evangelical Christian Union and the Baptist Union were arrested and

---

115. Savinskiy, *Istoria*, 47.
116. Ibid., 116.
117. Ibid., 111.
118. Sawatsky, *Soviet Evangelicals Since World War II*, 46.
119. Nikol'skaya, *Russkij protestantizm i gosudarstvennaya vlast' v 1905–1991 godakh*, 93.
120. Andrey I. Savin, *Sovetskoe gosudarstvo i evangelskie tserkvi Sibiri v 1920 – 1941 gg: Dokumenti i materiali* (Novosibirsk: POSOKH, 2004), 44–61.

imprisoned. Many of them never returned home. In March 1935, the Baptist Union ceased to exist[121] and the activity of the Evangelical Christian Union was limited.[122] Most local congregations were closed, houses of prayer were confiscated by the local governments and converted into places of different public secular activities, and many presbyters and lay leaders were arrested and imprisoned or exiled. By September 1937, in the city of Leningrad, there were only three houses of prayer still functioning (one for Evangelical Christians, one for Baptists, and one for Adventists). Back in 1922, in Leningrad, there had been forty-eight houses of prayer.[123] "Between 1929 and 1935, the number of evangelicals declined dramatically (by about 50%), providing stark evidence of a sharp change in Soviet policy."[124] The pattern of cruel persecution that aimed to completely destroy all evangelical Christians continued until World War II.

During World War II, Stalin changed the policy regarding the church. Instead of trying to destroy it, he began to look for ways of cooperation. First, he established contact with the Orthodox Church. He permitted the Church to hold a council and elect a patriarch, and many Orthodox churches and seminaries were reopened across the country.[125] The second religious group from whom Stalin wanted to gain loyalty was the evangelicals. In 1944, with the permission and "the active encouragement of the authorities"[126] the All-Union Council of Evangelical Christians-Baptists (AUCECB) was formed.[127] Initially this council consisted of only the surviving remnants of the two largest religious bodies of evangelicals in Russia – Evangelical Christians and Baptists. Later, in 1945, the Pentecostals joined the council. In 1947, several other much smaller religious groups joined the AUCECB. Much later, in 1966, the Mennonite Brethren also joined the union.[128] Finally,

---

121. Sawatsky, *Soviet Evangelicals Since World War II*, 47.
122. Trofimchuk, *Istoriya Religiy v Rossii*, 354.
123. Krapivin, Leykin, and Dalgatov, *Sud'by Khristianskogo Sektanstva v Sovetskoy Rossii*, 104.
124. Hill, *Soviet Union on the Brink*, 83.
125. Ibid., 90.
126. Dowling, "Baptists in the Twentieth-Century Tsarist Empire and the Soviet Union," 223.
127. Trofimchuk, *Istoriya Religiy v Rossii*, 354.
128. Ibid., 354.

the major streams of the Evangelical Baptist movement merged. However, the new union did not emerge without its own concerns. "The new union became a point of controversy with its legal validity doubtful and the cooperative role of the state authorities disconcerting. Some joined and later left disappointed; at first primarily Pentecostals, later many Baptists left. Others praised God that a church was open again where God's Word could be preached, and dramatic revivals swept the nation."[129]

The question still remains: How were representatives of both ecclesiological bodies, the Evangelical Christians and the Baptists, selected? Who appointed them to leadership in the AUCECB? Obviously, the Soviet government was actively involved in this process,[130] and it created doubts about the spiritual validity of this new church governing body. Maurice Dowling states that the leadership of the AUCECB was trying to develop a patriotic attitude among believers towards their Soviet homeland as well as to the Communist government. They used their denominational publication, *Bratsky Vestnik*, extensively for this purpose.[131] Also, the international contacts with Baptists abroad became an important part of their activity.[132] Participating at Baptist conferences in different countries, they always promoted Soviet government propaganda, such as calling for establishing peace in the world, expressing protests against the Korean War, or calling for universal and complete disarmament.[133] The main point of their message to the Western world was that Christians in the USSR enjoyed full religion freedom. They did not say anything about government antireligious campaigns that took place in their homeland.[134] Of course, if they would have said anything about this they would never have been allowed to participate in these conferences.

---

129. Sawatsky, *Soviet Evangelicals Since World War II*, 49.

130. Dowling, "Baptists in the Twentieth-Century Tsarist Empire and the Soviet Union," 225.

131. Maurice Dowling, "Russian Baptists and the Cold War," Presentation at the Andrew Fuller Conference: "Baptists and War" (The Southern Baptist Theological Seminary, September 2011), MP3.

132. Nikol'skaya, *Russkij protestantizm i gosudarstvennaya vlast' v 1905–1991 godakh*, 155.

133. Dowling, "Russian Baptists and the Cold War."

134. Ibid.

Summary

This brief overview of forty-five years of the Russian Evangelical Baptist movement's history shows how dramatic life of the participants was during this time. The period of tough persecution initiated by the Orthodox Church (1900–1917) was followed by the period of unprecedented religious freedom for them (1917–1929). After that, the new period of persecution (1929–1944) was followed by the period of weakening of persecution (1944 and later). During all these years, evangelicals were committed to evangelism. When circumstances allowed for freedom, they evangelized openly and actively. Under persecution, they still continued to evangelize, but did so secretly, in more of a direct and personal way. Also, they were involved in social action as circumstances allowed and when it was contextually appropriate. After the new law regarding religious organizations was announced in 1929, not only evangelistic activity was limited but all social actions done by churches were prohibited.

4.3.4. Life of Survival after World War II (1945–1985): Witnessing about Christ under Communist Government Pressure[135]

After World War II, evangelicals experienced a revival. Shaken by the losses of loved ones, the people in the Soviet Union were very sensitive to the gospel, many of them accepted Christ as their personal Savior, and churches were growing. However, in a few years, the clouds of new persecution appeared again. The last five years of Stalin's life, 1948–1953, were difficult for evangelicals because of Stalin's crackdown on religion.[136] Numerous

---

135. The author of this study accepted Christ as his personal Savior during this period of time – in 1974. At that time, he was a graduate student at the prestigious educational institution – Odessa Higher Nautical School of Engineers. After graduating from this school three years earlier with a BS in engineering and teaching for a year in the college, he was in his third (and the last) year in the grad program, finishing his dissertation and preparing to become a professor in that school. Instead, when he became a Christian, he was denied the right to continue his education there, with the explanation given to him by the President of the school that he could not teach Soviet students if he believed in God. Since that time, the author has been barred from obtaining a job in accordance with his education. He was forced to work as a construction worker, refrigerator mechanic, gardener, and in other low-level jobs until immigration in 1989. From his personal experience, he knows very well what it meant to be an evangelical Christian in Soviet society.

136. Hill, *Soviet Union on the Brink*, 93.

restrictive measures were taken against the church. Many church buildings were confiscated from the congregations. Arrests and sentencing of Christian leaders for up to twenty-five years in prison were quite common at that time.[137] After the death of Stalin in 1953, anti-religious propaganda gradually decreased until 1959. During this period of time, Baptist churches experienced considerable growth. According to AUCECB statistics, 12,000 people were baptized in 1954 alone. There were 5,400 congregations, with a total membership of 512,000 individuals, who were all part of the AUCECB at that time.[138] However, in 1959, attacks on the church began again. From 1959 to 1964, Khrushchev's anti-religious campaign took place. The major propaganda assault on religion in general, and on evangelicals in particular, was done through all means of mass information – newspapers, journals, movies, radio, and television.[139] "The Khrushchev antireligious campaign of 1959 to 1964 was second only to the Stalinist persecutions of the 1930s and did major damage to the religious bodies. Many churches were closed; those remaining open had to walk circumspectly."[140]

However, evangelicals were not annihilated as the atheistic government had hoped. Though not as rapidly as in the preceding decade, the movement continued to grow. "Their growth was due to methods of expansion which they had learned during the heavy days of the revival era."[141] Believers placed strong emphasis on the religious education of their children at home. Because of this, most new church members came from the immediate families of believers. The workplace was another important place for witnessing about God. Despite intensive propaganda efforts undertaken by the official government in mass media to paint Christians in a negative manner, they gained popularity as very reliable workers. This provided a good context for witnessing. Workmates were a significant source for gaining converts to evangelical Christianity.[142] During this time of limited freedom to exercise evangelism,

---

137. Ibid.
138. Sawatsky, *Soviet Evangelicals Since World War II*, 67.
139. Nikol'skaya, *Russkij protestantizm i gosudarstvennaya vlast' v 1905–1991 godakh*, 174.
140. Sawatsky, *Soviet Evangelicals Since World War II*, 68.
141. Ibid.
142. Ibid.

evangelicals developed creative techniques to suit the Soviet context. Any legal occasion to gather people together was often used as an opportunity to preach the gospel to non-believers and to encourage believers in their faith. Birthday parties, wedding ceremonies, new house dedications, and funerals were all used to share the gospel with invited, unbelieving guests – relatives, friends, and neighbors.[143] Obviously, during that time, it was impossible to do wide evangelistic work organized by the union or even by the church. Instead, this "grassroots" evangelistic movement became a substitute for a well-organized one coordinated by a central mission organization or mission board. The survival of the evangelical church in the USSR has proven the fact that personal evangelism works as effectively as mass evangelism, if not better.

The leadership of the AUCECB during this time was under great pressure from the Communist government. To avoid confrontation with the secular authorities and to protect the existence of local congregations and the union as a whole, the AUCECB made an attempt to bring their church statutes into conformity with the 1929 law on religious cults.[144] In the summer of 1960, these revised statutes and a "Letter of Instruction" were sent to the senior presbyters. This letter required local congregations to reduce their church life to very limited activities.[145] Such activities as evangelism, mutual aid, baptism of new members younger than eighteen, and work with children and youth were prohibited.[146] The most painful demand was to limit children's attendance of church services. These "instructions" from the leaders of the union were clearly contrary to biblical teaching, and many presbyters of the local churches did not accept them.[147] As a result, a major schism

---

143. Ibid., 71.

144. Michael Nevolin, *Raskol evangel'sko-baptistskogo dvizheniya v SSSR (1959–1963 gody)* (St Petersburg: Shandal, 2005), 46.

145. Sawatsky, *Soviet Evangelicals Since World War II*, 139.

146. Vladimir Vilchinskiy, *Nedarom Prolitiye Slezi* (Brest, 2011), 86–88. In his autobiographical book, Vladimir Vilchinskiy quotes the "Letter of Instruction," showing that this letter had an obvious anti-church nature. It is hard to believe that it was approved by the leaders of the Baptist Union, who themselves suffered imprisonment for their faith in the past.

147. Mikhail Shaptala, *Kak Eto Bilo: Istoriya Vozniknoveniya Nezavisimogo Dvizheniya EXB* (Cherkassy, Ukraine: SMIRNA, 2011), 148–149. Mikhail Shaptala, telling the story of the beginning of the Independent Movement of Evangelical Christian Baptists in the Soviet Union, shares his personal experience of receiving the "Letter of Instruction" in his church. Initially, the Church board rejected the letter. However, later, under the pressure of

took place among members of AUCECB in the beginning of the 1960s. In response to the AUCECB actions, opposition to its "leadership appeared almost at once and was expressed by an Action Group – literally an 'Initiative Group,' hence the label *initsiativniki* – of twelve people headed by Alexei Prokofiev and Gennadiy Kryuchkov."[148] Later this group was reorganized into the "Organizing Committee," with Georgi Vins playing a key role.[149] In September 1965, out of the Organizing Committee, an independent organization called the Council of Churches of the Evangelical Christians-Baptists (CCECB) was established.[150] Leaders of the council, ministers, and members of churches who were part of this organization experienced a harsh onslaught from the angry Communist government. Interruptions of church services by militia, as well as fines, arrests, long sentences, and exile, became part of the life of members of the CCECB churches. Some of their members were placed in psychiatric hospitals and were forcefully treated as mentally ill.[151] Some of them, such as Nikolay Khmara (48),[152] ended their lives in prison as martyrs.[153] There were cases when children were taken away from Christian parents and placed in orphanages or given to non-believing families.[154] Between 1958 and 1988, 2,000 Baptists were sent to labor camps or psychiatric institutions.[155] Suffering was the price that evangelicals paid for the desire to live independently from government control over their church life. Mutual aid among believers played a crucial role in the survival of many Christians during this time. While church leaders and ministry workers were imprisoned, their families were supported by churches and

---

the Senior Presbyter, they changed their minds. As a result, the big group in the church who were not willing to accept the letter were excommunicated from the congregation and went to another city starting a new church, independent from the AUCECB.

148. Dowling, "Baptists in the Twentieth-Century Tsarist Empire and the Soviet Union," 229.

149. Ibid.

150. Hill, *Soviet Union on the Brink*, 99.

151. Savinskiy, *Istoria*, 245.

152. Yuriy Konstantinovich Kruchkov, *140-letnyaya istoriya tserkvi EXB na Rusi v svete bibleyskikh istin* (Sacramento, CA: Brothers Printing, 2010), 274.

153. Ibid., 224.

154. Nikol'skaya, *Russkij protestantizm i gosudarstvennaya vlast' v 1905–1991 godakh*, 191.

155. Hill, *Soviet Union on the Brink*, 251.

individual Christians. It was very common among believers at that time to provide material help for each other.[156]

Since 1961, two church bodies of Baptists, AUCECB and CCECB, have co-existed in the USSR. The mighty atheistic government machine directed its anger against underground CCECB churches. The AUCECB churches enjoyed some relief from government control and oppression. Being in different positions in terms of experiencing unequal degrees of persecution from the government resulted in each of these bodies practicing different approaches towards evangelism. The AUCECB, or so-called "registered" churches, had their own buildings for services (houses of prayer). This provided them with more exposure to the local communities and with better opportunities to invite non-Christians to their places of worship. Many unbelievers were much more willing to attend a worship service at an official place like a church building rather than participate in meetings taking place at a private house or apartment. The CCECB, or underground churches, conducted their worship meetings at their members' houses and apartments or outside of town, in the forests.[157] Of course, not very many ordinary unbelieving citizens were brave enough to join these meetings in such an environment. This is why members of the underground churches witnessed boldly at their workplaces and in their neighborhoods. Only those who became really interested in the good news and the church were brought to the church meetings. "Unregistered" evangelical Christians gave much attention to raising their children in faith. Since families usually had many children, the churches were filled with a natural source of numerical growth. Persecutions of members of underground evangelical churches and even some of the most active officially registered churches continued until mid-December 1988, when the last known evangelical Christian prisoners were released from labor camp or exile.[158]

---

156. Based on his personal experience, the author of this study knows how important it is for families of imprisoned fathers to receive financial and material help, as well as moral support. He has taken part in such actions, helping families and delivering finance to them.

157. One of the many memorable church life experiences that the author of this study had during that time was assisting in conducting a communion service in the forest, during the winter, not far from the city of Riga, Latvia. The snow on the ground was about one foot high. The outside temperature was about minus 10 degrees centigrade. It was cold!

158. Hill, *Soviet Union on the Brink*, 365.

Although the church was deprived by the government of the right to provide material help to people, individual Christians were able to do so. Heinrich Klassen refers to the observations of Baptist evangelistic activities in the Soviet Union made by the communist scientist Belov, who noticed a certain pattern in these activities. In particular, he noticed that one of the successful methods evangelicals used was "assisting people with material or financial problems, or those who have lost a loved one. These activities happen with a purpose to win them for their faith."[159] Klassen points to the fact that believers "helped each other in cases of sickness, accidents and other problems."[160]

The relations between the leaders of the two Baptist unions were always hostile. The CCECB leaders described the leaders of the AUCECB as traitors to the gospel who collaborated with the godless communist government. The AUCECB leaders, in their turn, accused the CCUCB leaders as rebellious radicals who did not want to obey Romans 13:1–7. As Dowling has shown, such a situation was confusing and challenging for Christians in the West.[161] From the AUCECB leaders, as official representatives of Baptists of the USSR, Western Christians were receiving information that in the Soviet Union nobody was persecuted or imprisoned because of their faith. Only those who violated the law of the state regarding religious matters were in trouble.[162] At the same time, the CCECB leaders communicated to the West that the Soviet law was anti-religious, and to comply with it meant to deny the gospel. They pleaded for help. The situation was very complex and not easy for Christians outside the USSR to understand.[163] Unfortunately, the relationships between two unions have not changed even now. The antagonistic attitude towards the AUCECB church members (no longer just towards the AUCECB leaders) is found even among Slavic Baptist

---

159. Heinrich Klassen, "Mission as Bearing Witness: Immigrant Witness in Germany," in *Anabaptism and Mission*, ed. Wilbert R. Shenk and Peter F. Penner (Prague: IBTS, 2007), 169.
160. Ibid.
161. Dowling, "Russian Baptists and the Cold War."
162. Ibid.
163. Ibid.

immigrants in America.¹⁶⁴ The CCECB immigrant churches avoid being officially incorporated, even in the US, and this creates a barrier for them to purchase their own church facilities.

Summary

The brief overview of the four decades after World War II shows that it was a time of survival for evangelical Christians due to the fact of persecution and oppression from the atheistic Soviet government, which committed itself to wiping out the presence of any religion in the USSR, including evangelicals. It is difficult to imagine that any religious group could even survive (not to mention experience growth) while living in such harsh conditions. Surprisingly, evangelicals in the USSR not only survived but also grew in membership during this period of time. The only explanation for this fact is the strong commitment of Russian evangelicals to mission through evangelism. Also, *diaconia* was practiced by Christians at that time, mostly as mutual aid between believers.

4.3.5. Glasnost and Perestroika: New Opportunities for Evangelism and Service

Celebration of the millennium of Christianity in Russia in 1988 became a turning point in the history of religious life in the former Soviet Union. Unexpectedly, because of Gorbachev's policy of "glasnost" and "perestroika," religion was permitted and even welcomed in the predominantly atheistic Soviet society.¹⁶⁵ This freedom of religion came to people of the Soviet Union without warning. Even Christians who had prayed for this for decades were surprised when it happened. Many evangelical Christians responded to the new situation by undertaking unprecedented evangelistic and missionary activities. Since the late 1920s, it had been impossible to hold outdoor evangelistic services and to openly invite nonbelievers to attend these services. However, at the end of 1987, in 1988 and 1989, it became acceptable because of the celebration of the millennium of Christianity in Russia. For example, in Kiev, the capital of Ukraine, in 1988, local authorities permitted

---

164. The author of the study has personal contacts with CCUCB church members and leaders in America and has observed such negative attitudes toward the AUCECB first hand.

165. Nikol'skaya, *Russkij protestantizm i gosudarstvennaya vlast' v 1905–1991 godakh*, 297.

a Baptist church to host an evangelistic service attended by four thousand people. More than one hundred individuals made a public commitment to Christ. Later that same day, other Baptist churches in Kiev held an outdoor evangelistic service along the Dnieper River, which was attended by five thousand people. The next day, Sunday, Kievan evangelical Christians conducted a baptismal service on the river, attended by more than 10,000 individuals, and seventy-five people were baptized.[166] Similar outstanding events took place in other republics and cities of the USSR. Open-air baptismal services and evangelistic meetings took place throughout the Soviet Union. Huge sports complexes and palaces of culture were packed with people when the Millennium Celebration took place in Leningrad, Tallinn, Riga, Kishinev, Brest, and other large cities. Such notable Westerners as American astronauts Jim Irwin and Charles Duke were granted visas by the Soviet government to participate in these events. Irwin and Duke testified openly about their faith. They met with Soviet cosmonauts and scientists, witnessing to them about Christ. Their trip was covered by Soviet television and print media.[167] Earl Poysti, the broadcaster much-loved by Russian Christians and non-Christians, was able to visit his native land, which he had left as a boy in 1927. Since 1946, he had been involved in a radio ministry to the Soviet Union. Victor Hamm, a Russian-speaking evangelist and broadcaster from Canada, participated in several evangelistic crusades from 1988 to 1990, including four music/preaching productions held between 15 and 17 April 1990 in Moscow at the 35,000 seat Olympic Sports Palace, which was rented by Christians for these meetings.[168] These are just a few examples of the many evangelistic activities evangelical Christians organized as part of the celebration of the millennium of Christianity in Russia. They illustrate the magnitude of evangelistic efforts undertaken by believers in the USSR at that time. It was the beginning of a new era in the history of the Evangelical Baptist movement in Russia. The only comparable period would be the "Golden Age" in the history of Russian evangelicals, which took place from 1917 to 1929. Alongside local evangelism in the late 1980s, evangelical Christians began to think very seriously about long-term and

---

166. Hill, *Soviet Union on the Brink*, 302.
167. Ibid., 307.
168. Ibid., 310.

"long-distance" missions. Throughout the Soviet Union, groups within congregations were organized into local outreach or missionary societies. One of the earliest important mission societies to be formed was Light of the Gospel (*Svet Evangeliya*), founded in February 1989 in the city of Rovno, Ukraine.[169] The goal of this organization was to send missionaries to different regions of the former Soviet Union, including Siberia and Central Asia. The founding of many other mission organizations followed. New opportunities, previously unheard of, became available to Christians in the USSR: prison ministry, rehabilitation processes for drug and alcohol addicts, children and youth Christian camps, preaching the gospel to military personnel, providing humanitarian aid to needy people, and sending missionaries to other countries. Just a couple of years beforehand, it was impossible for the church to even dream of such activities being allowed in the Soviet Union. The following fifteen years became years of very busy work for many indigenous Christians in the area of evangelism and missions. Educational institutions to train Christian workers were established throughout the country. It was a time when Western missionaries flooded the former Soviet Union, looking for lost souls, in what they believed to be a godless society, to be converted to their faith.[170]

This unique time in history was not easy for evangelicals to live through. First of all, these opportunities were new for them. No training or experience had been available for the then current generation of believers to be involved in such kinds of ministries. Almost everything needed to be started from scratch. Second, an unexpected challenge was in the form of foreign help. As soon as Western Christian organizations, especially in America,

---

169. Ibid., 303.

170. Walter Sawatsky suggests thinking about missions in the former Soviet Union of the 1990s in three phases or stages: "The first stage that began gathering stream around November of 1987, as celebrations for the Millennium of Christianity in Rus' became certain, lasted till about 1993. It was a period of frantic or even frenetic Evangelism. The second stage can be described as a period of review and retrenchment, from approximately 1994–1996. Thereafter began a new phase of deliberate focus on specific work, of setting realistic priorities. The most striking feature, from my perspective, was the emergence of self-conscious contextualizing of Slavic ministries. Most importantly, the indigenous ministries now were forced to rely on their own resources, on coaching the poverty-stricken churches within the CIS to contribute more resources than they thought they had" ("Return of Mission and Evangelization in the CIS (1980s–Present): An Assessment," in Sawatsky and Penner, *Mission in the Former Soviet Union*, 95).

realized that the iron curtain was down and the Soviet Union was an open mission field, they mobilized great financial and human resources in order to evangelize Russia. Tremendous efforts were made to bring people of the "Empire of Evil" to Christ. In 1996, more than 5,600 missionaries, mostly from the West, entered the former Soviet Union.[171] Unfortunately, these often well-intentioned efforts did not come to fruition in their intended manner. Excited about such a great opportunity to minister in the former Communist land, Western missionaries often were not well prepared for the ministry in this unique area of the world. These missionaries were ignorant of the Russian language, not very sensitive to the culture, used charitable aid to "bribe" people into attending religious gatherings, and displayed religious provincialism, such as US-style "prayer breakfasts," which ignored the particular styles and traditions of Russian Protestantism. These missionaries brought more harm than help. As one knowledgeable American missionary said in the mid-1990s, "It would be better for one-tenth as many foreign missionaries to be in Russia and for them to be ten times better prepared."[172] As a result, serious misunderstandings developed between Evangelical Christians-Baptists in the former Soviet Union and many Western missionaries.[173] The poorly contextualized mission work done by some Western Christians in the former Soviet Union turned their good intentions into producing unwanted bitter feelings and disappointment among indigenous believers in the former USSR. This is especially unfortunate because of the fact that in many cases, Western assistance was very instrumental in developing theological education in Russia, in building greatly needed new church buildings, in training church leaders, and in providing financial support to indigenous

---

171. Peter F. Penner, "Critical Evaluation of Recent Developments in the CIS," in Sawatsky and Penner, *Mission in the Former Soviet Union*, 127.

172. Mark R. Elliot, "Protestant Missions in Russia Today," *East-West Church and Ministry Report* 13, no. 4 (Fall 2005): 2.

173. Walter Sawatsky acknowledges, "Many of the new missions that entered the CIS after 1989 came to bring Christ to Russia for the first time. They came from Christian communities in the West who had learned to think of the Soviet Union as the land of godless communists . . . Many had come to the presupposition that whatever Christian faith had once been present, must have disappeared. All that was left was phony religion in the service of communist propaganda. So they knew no one in the churches, often saw no need to establish relationships" ("The Centrality of Mission and Evangelization in the Slavic Evangelical Story," in Sawatsky and Penner, *Mission in the Former Soviet Union*, 59–60).

missionaries. This proves the need for indigenous churches and mission organizations to take ownership of mission work in the former Soviet Union.

The greatest challenge to mission work in the late 1980s, 1990s and the first decade of the twenty-first century was related to emigration. Dramatic political changes in the former Soviet Union opened the door for evangelical Christians to leave their homeland for the first time since the end of the 1920s. Many evangelical Christians decided to seize this unique opportunity to emigrate. A mass exodus of evangelical Christians (Baptists and Pentecostals) from the former Soviet Union to Austria began to take place, starting in 1988. Initially, this occurred simultaneously with Jews, who were applying for exit visas to go to Israel. However, after arriving in Austria, the evangelicals changed their direction towards the US. Beginning in the fall of 1989, they were applying for US entry visas at the American Embassy in Moscow, and going directly from Moscow to the USA. The number of evangelical immigrants was growing steadily.[174] Many reasons exist as to why believers chose to leave the country. The experience of being discriminated against, oppressed, and persecuted for many years under the Soviet regime was still very fresh in their memory. The current unstable political situation in the former Soviet Union did and does not guarantee that the totalitarian system will not return. Growing opposition from the Orthodox Church towards Protestants does not help convince people that real freedom of religion will soon be granted to the people of Russia. The difficult economic situation, high crime and unemployment rates, political uncertainty, and apocalyptic theology, predicting a terrible fate for Russia, are all factors that contribute to the increase in the number of evangelicals continuing to emigrate to the USA.[175] As a result, evangelical churches in the former USSR are suffering. They are losing leaders and church members. Mature Christians, who endured the times of persecution, are leaving or have already left, and their places are being filled with new converts. Of course, this provides a great challenge for the indigenous churches to be able

---

174. Hill states: "According to World Relief, in fiscal year 1988 (October 1, 1987 to September 30, 1988), 1,000 Evangelicals arrived in the United States; in fiscal year 1989, 8,000; and in 1990, 10,500. This large influx of evangelical émigrés is unprecedented" (Hill, *Soviet Union on the Brink*, 325).

175. Ibid., 329.

to continue extensive mission work throughout the huge territory of the former Soviet Union. At the same time, the encouraging fact is that recent evangelical immigrants in America are providing financial support for mission work in their homelands, and some of them are even going back for short-term mission trips.

Summary

Dramatic political changes in the former Soviet Union have created unprecedented opportunities for evangelism and mission work. Evangelicals have seized upon these opportunities, demonstrating a great zeal for saving the lost souls of their people. Once again, in their history, they have proven the fact that evangelism and missions are central for them when practicing their faith. As evangelism and missions played a crucial role in the life of evangelicals during the time of persecution under the Tsarist and Soviet governments, so in a similar fashion they are the main focus in ministry of evangelical churches in this time of economic hardship and political uncertainty during the post-communist era. Also, social action has become a common part of the church life of Evangelical Christians-Baptists in post-Communist Russia, in Ukraine, and in some other republics of the former Soviet Union. Christians are involved in establishing and running rehabilitation centers for drug and alcohol addicts. Christians are providing support for orphanages. They also provide food to the poor and help to distribute humanitarian aid sent from the West.

4.3.6. The Significance of Missiological Writings in Russian and Their Impact on Russian Baptists

Before the fall of the Soviet Union Baptists had very limited access to theological and missiological literature. While in the western countries Christians enjoyed the privilege of studying books and articles of famous theologians, Christians in the USSR often had no resources for their spiritual growth besides the Bible. Only a very few materials written by native authors were available. These materials usually had been printed before 1927, the year when open persecution of evangelical Christians started. By 1990 they had been out of print and out of date for many decades. Also, there was a very limited amount of resources translated from English or German into Russian. The limited number of copies of these resources which were available were books smuggled to the USSR by Western tourists. Often, these materials were multiplied by Christians inside of the country who retyped their contents using typewriters, making five–six copies of each. It was done secretly, usually at night, in fear of the KGB. Such kinds of activities were considered by the Communist government as anti-government and were illegal. It took many nights to produce these copies as volunteers carefully typed each word of every page.[176] However, these books were considered very valuable because they provided pastors, preachers, and lay people in the church with useful information that helped them to do their ministry. Peter Penner states that in 1995, in the Christian educational institutions that had been established in the Soviet Union after 1990, only a few materials were available in the Russian language which could be used to support the curriculum. He lists the usable teaching materials available at that time as textbooks for studying by correspondence, a Bible concordance, several one volume reference books, and Barkley's *New Testament Commentary*.[177] This was very far from being enough. As well, not very many resources were available on the subject of mission.

Things changed after that time. Many new resources translated from English or German became available in Russian. Books and articles concerning different aspects of church life and ministry began arriving in the former USSR. Currently Christians have a wide variety of materials on Children's ministry, youth ministry, family ministry, pastoral ministry, and on many other subjects. Materials on mission are available as well. Classic fundamental books such as *Transforming Mission* (David Bosch) together with more recent publications on the subject of mission have been translated and are available in Christian bookstores and in the libraries of churches and Christian educational institutions in the former Soviet Union. No doubt this stream of religious literature coming to Russia has made an impact on the theological views of Christians in the former Soviet Union. In order to assess the role missiological writings translated into Russian are playing in

---

176. The wife of the author of this thesis was involved in such a "typewriting" ministry, multiplying materials received from the West or written by indigenous authors. This constantly put her freedom in danger.

177. Peter Penner, *Nauchite Vse Narody: Missiya bogoslovskogo obrazovaniya* (St Petersburg, Russian: Bibliya Dlya Vseh, 1999), 247.

the formation of understanding of mission by Russian Baptists, a survey of four theological schools in the former Soviet Union was conducted. This approach to the acquiring of information about the impact of missiological literature on Russian Baptists was chosen primarily because students of these schools are the most probable audience who would read this literature. In addition, graduates of these schools are going to become leaders in local churches and their views, shaped by Western missiological resources, will be shared with people in these churches. Thus, indirectly, this literature will impact the views of many people in Russian Baptist churches. The schools which were surveyed are located in Minsk (Belorussia), Kiev (Ukraine), Zaporozhie (Ukraine), and Kishinev (Moldova). Leaders of these schools were provided with the list of books on mission translated from English into Russian and were asked to answer two questions: (1) "Do you use this book for teaching the course on Mission/Missiology in your school?" and (2) "If the answer is YES, what kind of impact does his book make on your students? Please share your opinion." The results of the survey are available in table 4.3.6.A. in the appendix for chapter 4.

The analysis of answers shows that there is no great variety in using these books in the mission curricular of the surveyed schools. Out of thirteen books on the list, three books are the most used. *They are Transforming Mission* (David Bosch), *From Jerusalem to Irian Jaya* (Ruth A. Tucker), and *Understanding Church Growth* (Donald A. McGavran). These books are used in all four schools. Because of this the exposure to the subject of mission students receive is limited only to the views of these three authors. This makes the educational experience of students not rich enough. In order to change this situation, each school in its missiology course needs to present multiple viewpoints of multiple authors to the students in order for them to have an opportunity to explore various ideas and come to some good conclusions on what is contextually appropriate for doing mission in their area.

Although the fundamental book on mission, *Transforming Mission* (David Bosch), listed by all respondents as part of their curricular, it is not used as the main textbook. From comments of the respondents it is clear that the content of this book is difficult to comprehend and work with for most students in these schools. Much more preferable to the students is a book on the history of mission – *From Jerusalem to Irian Jaya* (Ruth A. Tucker). This shows that students in these schools are not theologically well prepared to discuss the subject of mission in such a depth as Bosch's book is requiring. They are more comfortable with the book on history of mission that consists of biographical stories of missionaries than with the solid theological analysis of mission provided in *Transforming Mission*. It shows that there is a need for improvement in the ability of students of these schools to be engaged in serious theological analysis of the issue of mission. Indirectly, it also raises an issue of faculty preparedness in these schools. Well-trained, experienced faculty provides good lectures and leads thought-provoking discussions in the classroom that help students in understanding complex materials on the subject of mission. It seems that the mission faculty in the surveyed schools would be benefited from additional training.

The encouraging sign is that a good number of sources on the subject of mission translated into Russian are available now. This allows scholars and church leaders, who have access to these books, to explore views of Western theologians on this very important subject. For many decades Russian Baptists were deprived of the opportunity to develop their own missiology and publish books on this subject. During the same time, Western Christian scholars significantly advanced in developing missiology. It is important for Russian Baptist theologians and church leaders to learn quickly what was developed by Western theologians during all these years when Soviet people lived behind the Iron Curtain and were separated from the rest of the world. This is why it is very important having all these books on mission being translated into Russian and being available to Christians of the former Soviet Union.

However, while studying the works of Western theologians and trying to apply their ideas to their churches, Russian missiologists and church leaders have to contextualize teachings of Western theologians to the social conditions of the former Soviet Union. Mark Elliott, addressing the issue of the necessity of contextualization, refers to one Lutheran pastor who shared his concerns about the incompatibility of teachings of Western theologians with the contemporary reality of post-Soviet Kazakhstan. Elliott writes:

> The impassioned plea of this Lutheran pastor was that pastoral preparation takes into account actual, contemporary social conditions as they exist in Kazakhstan. In other words,

he was urging that the curriculum be contextualized. In the early 1990s, in the first panic to patch programs together post-haste, new Protestant seminaries emerged in the former Soviet Union that took little account of the social and cultural setting. "Western training programs were simply imported and installed." Course texts were mostly translations from English; faculty, of necessity, 139 to start with, were Western, Korean, or Western-trained; course offerings replicated those of schools abroad; and early on, even some seminary libraries held more English than Russian titles. [178]

In other words, in order to make all the good ideas coming from the West on mission and other theological subjects acceptable to Russian believers, they have to be adjusted to the new social, cultural, political, and religious context. These ideas should go through the process of "incarnation." The difference in mentality of people living in Western and Eastern worlds requires contextualization as well. "Too often differences between Western and Slavic mentalities were not sufficiently taken into account,"[179] affirms Elliott. He points to the following interesting fact: "Underscoring the East-West cultural divide, social scientist Geert Hofstede ranked Americans as the most individualistic of some 40 world cultures surveyed, whereas in his study Russians were among the most collectivist, typically deferring to majority preferences and traditions over personal wishes."[180]

Such differences in the mentality of Western and Eastern Christians lead to certain differences in understanding Scripture. In order to develop and maintain equal a partnership in ministry between Christians in the West and East, mutual understanding is very important. One of the ways to achieve it is increasing awareness with each other's literature. This is why making missiological writings available in Russian are so important. They can serve as a means for further improving mutual understanding between

---

178. Mark Elliott, "The Current Crisis in Protestant Theological Education in the Former Soviet Union," *Religion in Eastern Europe* 30, no. 4 (Nov 2010): 19, http://www.georgefox.edu/academics/undergrad/departments/soc-swk/ree/Elliott_The%20Current_Nov%202010.pdf (accessed May 2013).

179. Ibid.

180. Ibid.

Christians in the West and East. At the same time, all these translated materials provide the foundation for Russian Baptist missiologists for their own study of mission. They will not need to repeat the work done by Western missiologists during the last few decades. Russian missiologists could start with a careful study of Western achievements in the area of missiology; adapt them to their own context, and move forward with developing their own, indigenous theology of mission.

4.4. Conclusion for Chapter 4

The brief overview of the history of the Evangelical Christians-Baptists in Russia and the USSR shows that from its beginning in the middle of the nineteenth century, this movement has had a strong emphasis on sharing the gospel with non-Christians. Evangelism is an integral part of the Christian life for individuals and the church as a whole. Throughout most of their history, Baptists in Russia and the USSR have experienced persecution and oppression. Active involvement in evangelism and social actions was limited, if not prohibited. However, despite this fact, believers viewed the sharing of the gospel with non-believers and the helping of others as their Christian duty. It needs to be mentioned that *diaconia* in the form of helping each other was a common feature of Evangelical Christians-Baptists throughout their history. Without mutual help, they would not have survived under severe persecution. At the same time, participation in social action in the society was usually not widely practiced. The only exception was during the twelve years after the Revolution in 1917, when it was allowed. The rest of the time in their history, such kinds of church practice were strictly prohibited by the Communist government, which declared that its responsibility was to take care of all social needs of their citizens. This is why Evangelical Christians-Baptists did not have much experience in this aspect of mission by the time perestroika began. However, as soon as the opportunity became available, they started to be involved in social ministry. When the opportunity arrived after glasnost and perestroika, Evangelical Christians-Baptists undertook unprecedented evangelistic campaigns, reaching millions of people in their country with the gospel. At the same time, they became involved in many social actions. It shows that these two aspects of authentic mission, evangelism and social action/*diaconia*, are considered by Evangelical

Christians-Baptists as important parts of the mission of the church. A good number of members of this movement immigrated to the States with such attitudes towards these two aspects of the church mission. How and if they apply this attitude in the new immigrant context is the question this study is trying to answer. The data about current mission work of the Pacific Coast Slavic Baptist Association churches is presented in chapter 6 and provides empirical data for a critical evaluation of this work done in chapter 9 of the book. Also, in the current chapter, it is shown that significant number of books on the subject of missiology have been translated from English or German into Russian during the last twenty years. These sources are used in the courses of Christian educational institutions in the former Soviet Union and are making an impact on students' understanding of mission.

The following chapter is devoted (1) to studying the context in which the mission work of Slavic Baptist churches is occurring currently and (2) to analyzing the role evangelism and social action/*diaconia* played in life of the PCSBA churches during the historical development of this church body.

CHAPTER 5

Developing the Slavic Baptist Diaspora in the American Context

In order to complete an evaluation of the contextuality of the mission work of the Pacific Coast Slavic Baptist Association (PCSBA) churches, a good understanding of the mission context these churches are dealing with in America and abroad is required. Also, an understanding of the historical development of the PCSBA is needed in order to come to the right conclusion about its present position in regard to evangelism and social action/*diaconia*. This chapter is designed to provide information in these two areas. It is accomplished through exploring (1) American society as a mission context, (2) the development of global migration as a contemporary worldwide mission context, (3) the historical development of the Russian-speaking diaspora as a mission context in America, and (4) the history of the founding and organization of the PCSBA as an agent for carrying out missions among Russian-speaking immigrants in the US and abroad. This is not an extended history of Russian immigration and Russian Baptists in America, or an exhaustive history of the PCSBA. This study is limited to a scope wide enough to provide a general understanding of the historical development of both the Russian-speaking diaspora and Russian-speaking Baptist communities in the context of global migration. In studying the historical development of the PCSBA as an organization, the author's goal is to identify the position of evangelism and social action/*diaconia* in the life of churches belonging to the PCSBA.

5.1. Receiving American Society as the Mission Context

American society provides a unique and challenging general context for the local mission work of Slavic immigrant Baptist churches. As a nation America is the product of a continuing immigration process. Every American, except Native Americans, "is an immigrant or descended from immigrants. Immigration is integral to American society and lies at the heart of its multicultural and multiracial identity."[181] Upon arrival in America, immigrants bring their language and culture with them. By year after year absorbing immigrants from different continents and countries, America has become a multiethnic and multilingual country. Since the influx of new immigrants never stops, American society is going through the process of transformation all the time. For instance, the size of the foreign-born population changed dramatically during the twenty-five years from 1980–2005. In 1980, it was 14.1 million (6.2% of total national population); by 1990, the foreign-born population had grown to 19.8 million (7.9%); by 2000, it reached 31.1 million (11.1% of the total population);[182] and by 2009, it reached the mark of 38.5 million (12.5%).[183] It is growing by more than a million annually. As a result, American society has become very diverse. It is diverse ethnically, culturally, religiously. According to Hanciles, "the racial composition and cultural diversity of present immigration represents a radical development" in the history of this country.

5.1.1. Ethnicity

It is difficult to find a country in the world as ethnically diverse as the USA. The United States Census Bureau provides the latest information about the ethnicity of people who are part of American society today. In the 2009 table below, information is presented about the US population by selected ancestry group.[184]

---

181. Jehu J. Hanciles, *Beyond Christendom: Globalization, African Migration, and the Transformation of the West* (Maryknoll, NY: Orbis, 2008), 230.

182. Alejandro Portes and Ruben G. Rumbaut, *Immigrant America: A Portrait* (Berkeley and Los Angeles, CA: University of California Press, 2006), xvi.

183. United States Census Bureau, "Native and Foreign-Born Population by Place of Birth and State," Table 38 in *Statistical Abstract of the United States: 2012*, https://www2.census.gov/library/publications/2011/compendia/statab/131ed/2012-statab.pdf (accessed June 2013).

184. United States Census Bureau, "Population by Selected Ancestry Group and Region: 2009," Table 52 in *Statistical Abstract of the United States: 2012*.

Ancestry group	Number (in millions)	Ancestry group	Number (in millions)
American	18,7	Italian	18,08
Arab	1,68	Mexican*	31,55
British	1,17	Norwegian	4,64
Central, South American*[185]	7,58	Polish	10,09
Czech	1,61	Portuguese	1,48
Cuban*	1,65	Puerto Rican*	4,22
Danish	1,48	Russian	3,16
Dutch	5,02	Scotch-Irish	3,57
English	27,66	Scottish	5,85
European	3,2	African	2,85
French	9,4	Swedish	4,35
Canadian	2,15	Swiss	1,02
German	50,7	Welsh	1,98
Greek	1,39	West Indian	2,54
Hungarian	1,55	Ukrainian	0,98
Irish	36,9	Jamaican	0,95

There are other ethnic groups, with less than 1 million people, who are represented among the American population but not included in the table above. Among them are Afghan, Albanian, Armenian, Australian, Austrian, Belgian, Brazilian, Bulgarian, Croatian, Finnish, Iranian, Romanian, Slovak, Haitian, Yugoslavian, and others. This mosaic of ethnicities which makes up the American society provides churches, including Slavic Baptist immigrant churches, with the challenge in reaching people of these different ethnicities with the gospel. All these people represent different nationalities, ethnicities, and races with distinctive cultures and languages. In order to communicate the good news to them a cross-cultural approach should be used. Despite the fact that all these people live in America today, they still have their own

---

185. United States Census Bureau, "Social and Economic Characteristics of the Hispanic Population: 2009," Table 37 in *Statistical Abstract of the United States: 2012*. With * are marked the groups that are included in the total Hispanic population of 47,485,000.

distinctive cultural characteristics different from the common American culture of the past that have to be taken into consideration in the process of sharing the gospel with these people. In other words, the gospel message has to be contextualized in accordance with the culture of the people to whom it is communicated. The challenge is in the significant numbers of all these different ethnic groups. In order to be successful in their work among all these groups, churches should be very careful in choosing their way of approaching these groups with the mission among them.

5.1.2. Language

The linguistic diversity of American society is illustrated by the fact that English is not the only language spoken in American homes. The results of the latest census show that only 80 percent of the people in the country use English at home as a primary language. The rest of the population use other languages. For instance, Spanish is spoken at home by 12.4 percent of the American population. The table below consists of information about what languages are spoken in American homes and by how many people.[186] Those five years old and over were surveyed for this aspect of life of Americans. The total population in this category was 285,797,000 at the time of the last census.

Language	Number (in millions)	Language	Number (in millions)
English only	228,7	Arabic	0,845
Spanish	35,5	Other Asian languages	0,783
Chinese	2,6	African languages	0,777
Vietnamese	1,251	Italian	0,753
Tagalog	1,513	Portuguese	0,731
French	1,3	French Creole	0,659
German	1,1	Polish	0,593
Korean	1,039	Hindi	0,560
Russian	0,881	Japanese	0,445

---

186. United States Census Bureau, "Language Spoken at Home: 2009," Table 53 in *Statistical Abstract of the United States: 2012.*

Other languages spoken at home in the American population by fewer than 0.5 million people are Yiddish, Scandinavian languages, Greek, Serbo-Croatian, Armenian, Persian, Gujarathi, Urdu, Mon-Khmer, Cambodian, Hmong, Thai, Laotian, other Pacific Island languages, Navajo, other Native American Languages, Hungarian, Hebrew, others.[187] At home, people, if they have a choice, usually use the language that they are the most comfortable with. In most cases, it is the language of their heart. This is the language that should be used in the process of sharing the gospel with people who speak this language. This large number of different languages spoken by American families provides a challenge to English-speaking churches in their efforts to reach these families with sharing the gospel with them as well as with demonstrating Christian love in deeds toward them. The language barrier is a serious obstacle in mission work not only in overseas work but also at home, in America. This situation provides the immigrant churches belonging to each of these ethnic groups respectively with the chance and privilege to serve their countrymen using their common language.

5.1.3. Religion

According to the Census Bureau, the US is a predominantly Christian country. The number of people identified themselves as Christians in 2008 was 173,402,000.[188] This is 78 percent of the total number of people surveyed. The total number of Christians increased by 22 million from 1990 to 2008.[189] The increase is about 14.5 percent. American Christianity is represented by a very wide spectrum of different denominations. The largest church body in America is the Roman Catholic Church with 57,199,000 parishioners in 2008.[190] Next are different Baptist groups with a total membership of 36,148,000.[191] The largest Baptist convention or group is the Southern Baptist Convention with 16 million members.[192] Among the mainline

---

187. Ibid.
188. United States Census Bureau, "Self-Described Religious Identification of Adult Population: 1990, 2001, and 2008," Table 75 in *Statistical Abstract of the United States: 2012*.
189. Ibid.
190. Ibid.
191. Ibid.
192. "Fast Facts about American Religion," *Hartford Institute for Religion Research*, http://hirr.hartsem.edu/research/fastfacts/fast_facts.html#multiracial (accessed June 2013).

Protestant denominations the largest are Methodist/Wesleyan and Lutheran with 11,366,000 and 8,674,000 members respectively. Membership of other Christian denominations fluctuates from 67,000 (Full Gospel) to 5,416,000 (Pentecostal/Charismatic).[193] The list of Christian denominations in addition to those already mentioned is long. It includes Presbyterian, Episcopalian/Anglican, Churches of Christ, Seventh-Day Adventists, Assemblies of God, Church of the Nazarene, Orthodox, Mennonite, Church of the Brethren, Foursquare gospel, Amish and others.[194]

The number of people associated with other than Christianity religions in 2008 was 8,796,000. In 1990, this number had been only 5,853,000. The increase is about 50 percent. Among these "other religions" are Jewish, Muslim, Buddhist, Unitarian/Universalist, Hindu, Native American, Sikh, Wiccan, Pagan, Spiritualist, and others.

Among people who did not specify any religion were Atheists (1,621,000), Agnostics (1,985,000), Humanists (90,000), and people who answered the census question about religion saying "No religion" (30,427,000). In 1990, the total number of people in this category was 14,331,000. In 2008, it was 34,169,000. The increase is 138.4 percent. Such a significant increase of this category of the American population should motivate churches to intensify their efforts in sharing their faith with these people who are not associated with any religion.

According to Hartford Institute for Religion Research, there are about 350,000 religious congregations in the United States. About 314,000 of them "are Protestant and other Christian churches, and 24,000 are Catholic and Orthodox churches. Non-Christian religious congregations are estimated at about 12,000."[195] About 20 percent of Americans attend church services every weekend.[196] Most Christian churches are mono-racial and "eleven o'clock Sunday morning continues to be the most segregated hour in America."[197] However, notable changes are taking place. If in 1990, only

---

193. United States Census Bureau, "Self-Described Religious Identification of Adult Population: 1990, 2001, and 2008."
194. Ibid.
195. "Fast Facts about American Religion."
196. Ibid.
197. Ibid.

7–8 percent of US congregations were multiracial (with 20% of members being racially different from the dominant race of the congregation), in 2010 this number increased and reached 12.5 percent among Protestant churches and 27 percent among other Christian churches.[198]

5.1.4. Conclusion

The facts provided above clearly demonstrate how diverse American society is in such aspects as ethnicity, language, culture, and religion. This diversity is not static. It is a continuous process. More and more immigrants are coming to the "country of opportunity." This fact raises concern among some scholars in sociological studies. They are afraid that the national identity will be eroded by assimilating such a significant number of new immigrants, primarily Hispanics.[199] For Christian churches the fact of such a great diversity of the society provides a challenge to revisit the view of their mission and develop a new strategy striving to transform these churches into multiethnic congregations. This is a call to overcome the segregation so common today among churches in America, and start working on developing congregations that reflect by their membership the society these churches are part of.

5.2. Global Migration as the Mission Context

One of the marks of modern times is an increasing number of migrants in the world. Although migration is not a new phenomenon, it has expanded dramatically in recent decades. Different reasons motivate people to leave their homeland.[200] Among them is a fear of invasion, an attempt to escape political or religious persecution, a search for better pasture, and the creation

---

198. Ibid.
199. Samuel P. Huntington, *"Who Are We?" The Challenges to American's National Identity* (New York: Simon & Schuster, 2004), 17–20.
200. The report provided by the WCC Consultation, held at Utrecht in the Netherlands on 16–21 November 2010, identifies two categories of migrants: those who leave their countries by choice and those who are forced to leave. "Those who are forced to migrate, research has shown, are those who leave their homes and countries because of war, environmental degradation, religious and/or political conflicts and persecution, corrupt political regimes, repression and poverty further accelerated by the impact of neo-liberal market economies" ("World Council of Churches (WCC) Consultation on Mission and Ecclesiology of the Migrant Churches," *International Review of Mission* 100, no. 1 [Apr 2011]): 104).

of new commercial links.²⁰¹ "In recent times, however, migration is capturing people's imagination and fascination primarily due to its explosion. Spurred by globalization's marginalization of third-world economies and sophisticated developments in communication and transport technology, more and more people today move from place to place at an increasingly faster pace."²⁰² This fact creates a new context for church missions and provides it with new challenges.²⁰³ Since studying global migration is not the main goal of this work but still important to understanding the general worldwide mission context, a detailed survey of mission-related issues of global migration is provided in the appendix to chapter 5. In the appendix, migration statistics are provided, a history of migration at a glance is included, attempts to explain the migration phenomenon are discussed, types of immigrants to the US are introduced, challenges of contemporary migration to mission are discussed, reimagining mission in the context of contemporary migration is suggested, the impact of migration on the countries of origin is analyzed, and the role of immigrant congregations in American religious life is explored.

---

201. Gemma Tulud Cruz, "Expanding the Boundaries, Turning Border into Spaces: Mission in the Context of Contemporary Migration," in *Mission After Christendom: Emergent Themes in Contemporary Mission*, ed. Obgu U. Kalu, Peter Vethanayagamony, and Edmund Kee-Fook Chia (Louisville, KY: Westminster John Knox, 2010), 71.

202. Ibid.

203. J. A. B. Jongeneel indicates that there are about 18 million legal and 2.6 million undocumented migrants in Western Europe. By his estimate, about one million of these migrants are Christians. When they arrive in the new place of settlement, Christian migrants often start their own congregations. Usually they are Protestant because "Christian migrants, who are members of episcopal churches, cannot establish new congregations and churches apart from an existing ecclesiastical structure. In the latter case, the bishops will take the initiative to extend the existing congregations in one way or another to migrants" ("The Mission of Migrant Churches in Europe," *Missiology* 31, no. 1 [Jan 2003]: 30). According to Jongeneel, Christian migrants usually "are more mission-minded than the members of established congregations and churches in Europe" (31). There are three categories of missionary and evangelistic activities that the Christian migrants could participate in: (1) Internal mission – they witness to people of "their own ethnic, national, and linguistic communities"; (2) Reverse mission – they preach the gospel to secular Europeans in the same way as in the past European missionaries preached to their ancestors in their homeland; and (3) Common mission – they participate in mission work in cooperation with established congregations and churches of indigenous people (32).

5.2.1. Impact of Immigration

Migration is a complex process and it is not easy to find a theory that explains it completely.[204] The difference in the direction of migration streams today from previous waves of immigration is that in the past, migrants were moving from economically advanced countries to economically poor countries. Today, it is the opposite. People from poor counties in the Global South are migrating to rich countries in Europe and North America. Modern global migration provides church missions with challenges and opportunities.[205] Global migration affects the social, economic, and religious life of the country of origin, as well as the country of destination.[206] To ad-

---

204. Hanciles, *Beyond Christendom*, 183. For example, several reasons explain the mass Slavic evangelical migration from the former Soviet Union to the States. Among them are vast experiences of persecution for their faith in the past and concern about how permanent the new freedom of religion announced in their homeland is; concern about the physical wellbeing of their children; economic instability in their country; the relationship factor ("Since many relatives and friends have emigrated, I have to do it as well in order to be with them"); the US government regulations of the immigration process opening the door for religious refugees from the Soviet block to enter the US under refugee status; political changes in the USSR that made it possible to emigrate from that country; and faith/eschatological factors (it is common among Pentecostal churches to have prophecies about God's wrath coming on their homeland and that believers should leave that place). This one particular group is a good illustration of the complexity of the reasons for migration.

205. Jehu Hanciles, exploring the modern migration phenomenon, argues that Christian immigrants will challenge the spiritual condition of Christianity of countries to which they have immigrated. He insists, "In both North America and Europe, these new emigrant Christian groups embody a fresh and vital spirituality that is likely to have an impact far beyond their immediate sphere of witness and influence" ("Migration and Mission: Some Implications for the Twenty-First-Century Church," *International Bulletin of Missionary Research* 27, no. 4 [2003]: 151).

206. Hanciles, *Beyond Christendom*, 194–206. There is no doubt that migration has had an impact on the life of the church in the country of origin. In the situation where Slavic evangelicals have emigrated during the last two decades, it could be stated that in many cases, their exodus from the former Soviet Union negatively affected their local congregations. The migration of believers left many churches with fewer members today and fewer potential members in the future, since children were taken along with their parents. Often, people who emigrate are active in church life. This means that with their departure, fewer church workers remain in the congregations. With the migration of many believers, the witnessing ability of some congregations is decreasing. The migration of church members demoralizes the rest of the congregation. This is the most significant impact congregations experience when church leaders leave. It is often a very painful and dramatic process. Of course, due to the conversion of new people, the church will eventually accept new members, and new leaders will eventually arise. This provides an opportunity for "new blood" to be injected into the life of the local congregation. However, the mass departure of believers that took place in the former Soviet Union in a relatively short period of time has affected the ability of more mature, experienced believers, who lived through the time of persecution, to pass their experience on to the new converts joining the church in a completely different social

dress complex migration issues, a broad range of interdisciplinary research (economics, sociology, psychology, demography, etc.) is involved. However, theology is usually missing from this list. Daniel G. Groody argues that since "migration touches so many aspects of life and society," it should be a subject of theological study.[207] Migration has transformed America into the most culturally diverse nation in the world, and it has changed the face of American Christianity. Since many migrants are Christians, this migration movement is considered by some authors as a missionary movement. It potentially could bring about a revival of the religious life in the countries in which immigrants are arriving.[208] Immigrant congregations are a means of reaching people of their own ethnic background in the new land as well as in the homeland. However, these congregations have limitations in their local missionary efforts since they are usually ethnically focused and this is what deters people of other ethnicities from joining them.

5.2.2. Concerns Related to the Impact the Migrant Churches Are Making

As was mentioned in the introduction to this book, Jehu J. Hanciles has a very high view of immigrant congregations regarding their role in global mission and their impact on the religious life of the receiving society. He views them as "centers of change and transition."[209] With the prospect of continuous immigration to the US in the foreseeable future, immigrant congregations, according to Hanciles, are potentially going to be urban-based and "will continue to inhabit the most strategic intersections of mobility,

---

and political situation. Remittances (sending funds to the homeland) definitely take place among Slavic evangelical immigrants. They are actively supporting their relatives and gospel ministries back in their homeland. This is a positive result of the migration of believers.

207. Daniel G. Groody, "Crossing the Divide: Foundations of a Theology of Migration and Refugees," *Theological Studies* 70, no. 3 (Sept. 2009): 664. According to Groody's position, a "theology of migration not only dialogues with other disciplines but integrates their findings into the overall task of faith seeking understanding in the modern world. Moreover, social science and theology need each other in this difficult debate. Social science without theology does not give us a perspective wide enough to account for the deeper relational and spiritual dimensions of human life that shape, define, and sustain human existence – a fact that becomes more evident especially amid crisis and trial. Theology without social science leaves us less equipped to read the signs of the times, engage contemporary issues, or speak to the pressing questions that affect large portions of the world."

208. Hanciles, *Beyond Christendom*, 278.

209. Ibid., 299.

dynamism, and change within American society. As veritable centers of transmigration or transnationalism, immigrant congregations have great potential to play a critical role in global Christian missions."[210]

Alongside such high expectations from these congregations in regard to their missionary role, certain notes of caution should be expressed. First, although it is true that the immigrant congregations provide a good opportunity for reaching people in their homelands, as well as their ethnic groups in America, they are not as effective at reaching English-speaking people and representatives of other ethnic groups. Hanciles says: "Immigrant congregations continue to flourish not only because they function as sites of religious conversion and religious renewal but precisely because they help to preserve ethnic identity."[211] By this statement, he affirms the truth that immigrant congregations are intended for people with a certain ethnic identity. This is the most sobering fact about these churches. People of different ethnicities do not fit well into these churches. It limits their ability to execute mission work locally with people of the surrounding society who do not share the ethnicity of the immigrant churches. This fact alone makes it questionable to put so much weight on these churches in global mission, at least in the local capacity.

Another of Hanciles' statements that raises the same concern is: "the ethnic factor and language barrier not only confine the ministry and outreach of most immigrant congregations to specific national groups, but they also help to explain the high conversion rate these congregations enjoy. Yet, even by evangelizing other immigrants – many of whom are far more open to religious conversion than they were before they migrated and would not otherwise be won to the Christian faith – these congregations represent a cutting edge of Christian growth in America."[212] How could immigrant congregations represent "a cutting edge of Christian growth in America" if they will only be reaching their own people? The percentage of recent immigrants, when compared with the total US population, is still very low. If the immigrant churches only do their mission work among people of their ethnicity, then only a limited part of the general population will be affected.

---

210. Ibid.
211. Ibid., 288.
212. Ibid., 297.

Another troubling statement Hanciles has made is that "the new immigrant congregations are performing a vital missionary function by their very presence."²¹³ The presence of immigrant congregations is beneficial and could be viewed as doing a missionary function only for the people of the same ethnicity. For others, its presence could be meaningless or even undesirable. When ethnicity dominates church life and ministry, a church could be considered "absent" for the rest of the society. However, the church "must be 'in' the world, in order to speak intelligibly to the world."²¹⁴ When addressing the issue of the possible disappearance of the missionary function of new Christian immigrant congregations after the first generation, Hanciles rightly points to the fact that "immigrant churches are typically sites of intergenerational conflict and cultural tension. While the new immigrants and their descendants are nurtured by the spirituality and cultural values brought from their homelands, they also experience the pull of cultural adaptation – more intensely so among the younger members or generation."²¹⁵ Recognizing the fact that some immigrants will deny their cultural tradition in favor of full assimilation into the new culture, Hanciles insists that the number of those will not be significant. He explains it by saying that even assimilated immigrants still experience "xenophobic intolerance or racial rejection." He believes that because the immigrant congregations "almost by definition function as cultural centers where immigrants nurture ethnic connections, intentionally preserve aspects of their cultural values, and socialize the next generation,"²¹⁶ there is no danger of these congregations experiencing significant departure of the younger generation. It contradicts his other statement: "Second-generation Korean Americans have abandoned the churches of their parents (in a 'silent exodus') to form English-language congregations in which Koreanness is downplayed and contemporary forms of worship are preferred."²¹⁷ This statement reflects the well-proven reality that preserving ethnic culture and language in a church puts the children

---

213. Ibid.
214. Alex Araujo, "Globalization and World Evangelism," in *Global Missiology for the 21st Century*, ed. William D. Taylor (Grand Rapids, MI: Baker Academic, 2000), 62.
215. Hanciles, *Beyond Christendom*, 300.
216. Ibid., 300.
217. Ibid., 287.

and youth of this church in awkward positions relative to the life of the congregation, and eventually pushes them away from the church. This process is currently taking place in Slavic immigrant churches. They are losing their young people, especially those who have been educated in the States, to English-language churches. A survey of those who have left Slavic churches, provided in chapter 6 of this thesis, shows that the main reason for their departure is a search for deeper sermons delivered during the church services. These believers are more concerned, not about the cultural traditions of their parents, but about the nurturing of their souls.

The concerns expressed above are providing a serious challenge to the view that the immigrant churches, if they will stay mono-ethnic, will make a significant impact on the religious life of American society. The findings of this study point to quite the opposite conclusion, at least in the situation with PCSBA churches.

Now, after drawing a larger picture of global migration, the smaller representative of this big movement, migration of Russians to the US, must be discussed. It will be viewed as the mission context for Slavic Baptist churches in the States.

5.3. Russian-Speaking Diaspora in America as a Mission Field in the Historical Prospective

One of the main reasons justifying the existence of ethnic churches often referred to by their advocates is evangelizing people of their nationality. It is expected that Russian-speaking churches in America will be reaching their own people with the gospel. This is why it is important to evaluate the situation with the Russian-speaking diaspora in America and determine if it is truly a mission field for Slavic Baptist immigrant churches.

The brief overview of the historical development of the Russian-speaking diaspora in America is provided in the appendix to chapter 5, section 5.2.A.

5.3.1. The Impact of the Evolution of the US Immigration Policy on Russian Emigration

In response to Soviet Jewish emigration, the US immigration policy passed through three distinct phases. This changed the way in which entrance eligibility had been established, what number of applicants received permission to enter the United States, and which way newcomers to the US were going to travel to reach the US (from Russia to Austria to Italy to the US, or directly from Russia to the US).

First phase: 1980–August 1988. During this phase, the US government attempted to accept all Soviet citizens seeking resettlement in the United States as refugees. Refugee status was decided after an interview by the INS in Rome. Very few applicants were denied this status.

Second phase: August 1988–September 1989. Most Soviet Jewish and Pentecostal applicants seeking resettlement in the US during this time continued to pass through Rome. For others, in-country processing began in Moscow.

Third phase: October 1989–present. People of the former Soviet Union seeking resettlement in the US were and are currently required to register their interests with the US Embassy in Moscow. Not all registrants are interviewed. Interviewing priority is given to those with close relatives or other links in the US. Those without such links are denied entrance to the United States. Those interviewed could be either allowed to enter the US or denied entrance. If they obtain permission to enter they could either receive a refugee status (if they are eligible) or are offered parole into the United States.[218]

The number of immigrants coming from Europe in general and from the former Soviet Union in particular has been declining lately. For example, the following numbers of refugees were allocated for different regions during the Fiscal Year 2011:

Africa	15,000
East Asia	19,000
Europe and Central Asia	2,000
Latin America/Caribbean	5,500
Near East/South Asia	35,500
Unallocated Reserve	3,000[219]

---

218. Gregg A. Beyer, "The Evolving United States Response to Soviet Jewish Emigration," *Journal of Palestine Studies* 21, no. 1 (Autumn 1991): 141.

219. "President Issues FY 2011 Refugee Admissions Numbers and Authorizations," *Immigration.com*, 7 December 2010, http://www.immigration.com/news/refugee-and-

Out of 80,000 immigrants allowed to be admitted to the USA under refugee status, only 2,000 come from Europe, including the former Soviet Union republics. This is a very low number compared with how many were admitted to the States from that region in the past. This will slow growth of the Russian-speaking population in the US, decreasing the potential Russian-speaking mission field for Slavic Baptist churches.

5.3.2. Demographics and Settlement of Russian Immigrants in the USA

Demographics

Different sources provide different information about the size of the Russian-speaking population currently living in the US. According to some sources, the Russian-American population is estimated at between 4 and 5.5 million people.[220] The American Association for Russian Language, Culture and Education suggests that there are 5.1 million Russian-Americans in the US, which is about 2.04 percent of the US population.[221] In the 2000 census, 2,652,214 people in the US claimed Russian ancestry. Some 81 percent of the Russian-speakers are not US-born.[222] Fifty-five percent of American Russian-speaking families have an annual income of about $55,000. About 70 percent of Russian-speaking individuals are employed in management, sales, medicine, and education. Many have careers in the high-tech and computer industries. Fifty-seven percent of Russian-speaking families buy their own house within one to three years after arriving in the US. Fifty-two percent of Russian-speakers have a bachelor's degree or higher.[223]

Settlement

In 1990, 44 percent of nearly three million Americans of Russian descent lived in the Northeast. Russian Jews went to New York City, Philadelphia,

---

political-asylum/president-issues-fy-2011-refugee-admissions-numbers-and-authorizat (accessed April 2012).

220. "Russian-American Communities in USA," *RusUSA.com*, http://www.rususa.com/immigration/russian-american-residence.asp (accessed April 2012).

221. American Association for Russian Language, Culture and Education, "Russian Population and Statistics," http://www.aarce.org/index.php/en/russian-culture-in-us/statistics (accessed April 2012).

222. Ibid.
223. Ibid.

Boston, and other large cities. Non-Jewish Russians settled in the same large cities, as well as Chicago, Cleveland, Pittsburgh, Baltimore, Miami, Atlanta, Detroit, Denver, Seattle, San Diego, and others.[224] Those who left the Russian Far East and Chinese Manchuria at the beginning of the twentieth century settled in California, particularly in San Francisco and Los Angeles.[225] Nearly 5,000 members of the Russian Christian religious group known as the Molokans settled in California during the first decade of the twentieth century. They formed the nucleus of what has become a 20,000-member Russian Molokan community that is concentrated today in San Francisco and Los Angeles.[226] Although not very many members of this community are associated with the Molokan church today, they still consider themselves Russians. A good number of them also live in Kerman, a small city near Fresno, California.

Nearly 90 percent of the Russian-speaking population in the US live in and around major urban centers, with large concentrations in New York City and the surrounding tri-state area, as well as Boston, Philadelphia, Baltimore, Miami, Atlanta, Cleveland, Chicago, Detroit, Denver, Houston, Los Angeles, San Diego, San Francisco, and Seattle.[227] The percentage distribution of Russian Americans throughout the country is as follows: DC and Maryland 3%, Florida 7%, Massachusetts 8%, Pennsylvania 10%, Illinois 16%, California 16%, and the New York tri-state area 24%.[228] The two states with the largest Russian-speaking populations in the States are New York and California. The American Association for Russian Language, Culture and Education (AARCE) provides the following information:

> **New York Population**. New York leads the nation in the number of Russian Americans. About 1.6 Million reside in New York Tri-State area. About 600,000 reside in the City of New York representing 8% of the population. Numbers exceed those of other leading ethnic groups like Chinese (760,000) and Dominican (620,000).

---

224. Ibid.
225. Ibid.
226. Ibid.
227. "Russian-American Communities in USA."
228. Ibid.

California Population. There are an estimated 600,000 Russian-speaking people in Southern California. Major resident areas are: Hidden Hills, Calabasas, Los Angeles, Westlake Village, Agoura Hills and Simi Valley, in declining order of affluence. Median household incomes range from $80,000 for Simi Valley to $200,000 for Hidden Hills. Bachelor Degree holders range from 40% for Simi Valley to 75% for Calabasas.[229]

This shows that the majority of Russian-speaking populations are concentrated in several metropolitan areas of the country. The information cited above points to the Russian-speaking Diaspora in general. However, the Russian-speaking evangelical population is distributed around the US differently. Large groups of them are concentrated in the following areas: Sacramento, CA; Portland, OR; Seattle, WA; Minneapolis, MN; and New England. In these areas live many thousands of Russian-speaking evangelicals (Baptists and Pentecostals) who have recently arrived in the States. Many small groups are scattered alongside the East Coast and throughout the country. Because of this disproportion in the settlement locations, reaching the non-believing Russian-speakers with the gospel by Slavic Baptists is difficult. It will require a relocation of Christians to the areas where their non-Christian countrymen are living.

5.3.3. Acculturation and Assimilation

For the most part, Russian immigrants and their descendants have succeeded in assimilating into mainstream American life. The exceptions are small groups of traditionalists, such as the Orthodox Christian Old Believers and the non-Orthodox Molokan Christian sect. The use of the Russian language at home and in the church and the distinct dress and religious-based lifestyle continue to keep them at a social distance from other Americans and distinguish them from the rest of the community.[230] But the majority of Russian immigrants have tried hard to assimilate into American life and society. However, this has not always been easy to accomplish. During the past seventy years, American society has had a negative opinion of the Soviet Union.

---

229. "Russian Population and Statistics."
230. Paul Robert Magocsi, "Russian Americans," *Countries and Their Cultures*, http://www.everyculture.com/multi/Pa-Sp/Russian-Americans.html (accessed April 2012).

As a result, Russian-Americans experienced negative attitudes towards their community from other Americans. They have frequently been suspected of being potential Communist spies or socialists and anarchists.[231] After World War II, the United States was once more struck by the Red Scare. Again, Russians and all things Russian were associated with Communism, so Russian-Americans were forced to maintain a low profile, and some even renounced their heritage. Most recently, Russians in the United States have been linked to organized crime. In today's mainstream American media, it is common to find references to the dangers of the Russian mafia and, through implication, of all Russians.[232] Obviously, all of these factors did not help the process of assimilation for Russian immigrants in the US. However, despite this difficulty, immigrants from the former Soviet Union are going through the process of acculturation and assimilation very well. Because they are predominantly white, they do not experience such a strong racist bias against themselves as other ethnic groups sometimes do.

5.3.4. Religion

Based on religious criteria, Russian-Americans can be classified as Orthodox Christians, Protestants, Jews, or nominal Jews. The large pre-World War I arrival of Jews from the Russian Empire consisted mainly of those who used to faithfully observe the Jewish law and traditions back in Russia. They attended synagogue regularly, observed the Sabbath, and respected the rabbi as their community leader. Coming to the New World, Jewish people at that time maintained their religious traditions within the confines of the home and synagogue.[233] Russian Jews, who arrived in the United States after the early 1970s, stand in absolute contrast to their pre-World War I predecessors. Living in the officially atheistic Soviet Union, many Jews found it very convenient, both politically and socially, to forget or to even deny their Jewish heritage. The majority of Soviet Jews had no knowledge of Yiddish or Hebrew and had never attended a synagogue.[234] "These Russian-speaking nominal Jews found it difficult to relate to English-speaking religious Jews

---

231. Ibid.
232. Ibid.
233. Ibid.
234. Ibid.

when they arrived in the United States. While a small percentage of the newcomers learned and accepted the Jewish faith while in the United States, most follow no particular religion and have remained simply Russians or Russian Americans who are Jews in name only."[235]

The idea of being Russian in America is often associated with the Orthodox Christian faith. During the history of Russian immigration to the US, the Russian Orthodox Church ministered to many immigrants from Russia. It also served as a missionary church, attracting new adherents. The church converted over 12,000 Aleutians and some Eskimos to Orthodoxy before Alaska was purchased by the United States. The Orthodox Russian Bishop Innokentii Veniaminov (1797–1879) codified a written Aleut language for which he published a dictionary, grammar guide, Bible, and prayerbooks.[236] Around 50,000 converts joined the Russian Orthodox Church during the 1890s and during the first decade of the twentieth century in America. During the rest of the twentieth century, the Russian Orthodox Church helped immigrants from Russia meet their spiritual needs. There are three factions within Russian Orthodoxy in America. One faction consists of the original Russian Orthodox Church that started in Alaska before moving to California and New York. Today, it is known as the Orthodox Church of America. The second faction consists of the post-World War I "White" Russian émigrés, whose numbers included some clergy and lay members. The third faction consists of individual parishes that remained directly under the jurisdiction of the patriarch in Moscow. The Orthodox Church of America is the largest among the three Orthodox churches in the US. Since 1970, this church has conducted all its services in English.[237]

5.3.5. Russian Immigrants' Contributions to American Society

This information is provided in the appendix for chapter 5, section 5.2.3.A.

---

235. Ibid.
236. Ibid.
237. Ibid.

5.3.6. Summary

Russians are no strangers to American soil. They have been coming here for more than two centuries. They emigrated mostly because of the hardships they experienced in their homeland, which has had a turbulent and violent history. Despite prejudice from American society, Russian immigrants are going through the painful process of acculturation and assimilation very well. Some of them have made significant contributions to the development of this nation.

As a mission field, the Russian-speaking population in America has both potential and challenges. On the one hand, because of the significant number of them living in the United States, Russian-speaking immigrants make up an important potential mission field for Slavic Baptist churches in America.[238] On the other hand, there are a few challenges in targeting this particular part of the American population. Economically, Russians usually do well in this country and are satisfied with life. As such, they are usually difficult to reach with the gospel. They are not necessarily seeking God to be part of their lives. Decades of atheistic propaganda in the former USSR implanted an indifference to God in the hearts of many Russians. Also, as illustrated above, the majority of Russian-speaking immigrants are of Jewish descent. Most of them do not have strong, if any, religious roots. They could be considered atheists or agnostics. This fact underlines the importance of focusing evangelistic efforts of American Slavic Baptist churches towards this group of people. At the same time, it is important to remember that Jews are not an easy mission field with whom to work. Working with them requires the use of a special approach and the possession of appropriate skills. Few members of Slavic Baptist churches have these skills. In order to be able to reach this group, churches need to learn how to evangelize Jewish people. The challenge is also in the fact that the largest populations of Russian-speaking

---

238. This fact motivates the Southern Baptist Convention to invest in planting Russian-speaking congregations in America. The California Southern Baptist Convention (CSBC) Church Starting Group department created the church planting catalyst position in January 2007. The primary area of responsibility of this person is "the planting of churches for California's Slavic speakers, which includes those speaking Belarusian, Moldavian, Romanian, Russian, Ukrainian, and other Indo-European languages," *CSBC.com*, http://www.csbc.com/article190612.htm?title=1&img=1&imgsize=medium&imgalign=right&wraptext=1&links=1&body=1 (accessed December 2012).

Baptists are not settled in the same areas where the largest populations of Russian-speaking non-believers are living.

5.4. History of the Founding and Organization of the Pacific Coast Slavic Baptist Association

The main subject of this study is the church body called the Pacific Coast Slavic Baptist Association (PCSBA). It is important to understand its historical development in order to be able to make an evaluation of its current mission ministry at the end of this study. The brief overview of PCSBA history provided below is focused on the role of evangelism and social action/*diaconia* in the life of churches associated with this organization. This overview is preceded by a brief historical sketch of Slavic Baptist life in the US.in general.

5.4.1. A Brief Overview of the History of Slavic Baptists in the United States

In the context of the large-scale Russian immigration that took place during the twentieth century, a much smaller but very important process took place among recent Christian immigrants to America. It was the process of planting Baptist churches among Russian-speaking immigrants and gathering these churches together into one union or association.

Some of the Russian immigrants who arrived in the States during the last two centuries were Baptists or Evangelical Christians before they left their homeland. Others were converted to this faith either on the way to or after their arrival in the United States. Once settled in the new land, they began to look for people with similar beliefs, and when they found them, they started churches. The first known Baptists to emigrate from Russia to the US were Hariton Sabarovich and his family. They arrived in the US in 1889 and settled in Louisville, Kentucky.[239] They encouraged others to take the risk and follow them. However, those who accepted Sabarovich's invitation and came to America faced tremendous difficulties trying to survive, and eventually, some of them returned to Russia. In May 1899, seven Baptist

---

239. George Boltniew, "A Functional Analysis of Ethnic/Bilingual Baptist Churches Ministering to Russian-Speaking Immigrants in the USA" (DMin diss., Eastern Baptist Theological Seminary, Philadelphia, 1986), 252.

families from the Ukraine arrived in Harvey, North Dakota, where they established the first colony, called Liberty.[240] Through the spring of 1900, Baptists from Russia continued to flow to North Dakota. The first Russian-speaking Baptist congregation in the US was organized in North Dakota, at the Liberty colony, on 4 April 1901, and the first Russian Baptist church building was built there in 1902.[241] In 1903, there were five places of worship in that colony. "The greatest growth of the colony occurred in the years 1910 to 1925 when there were as many as 30,000 immigrants from Russia living in North Dakota."[242] Liberty was later renamed Kief because most of the settlers were from the Kiev region in the Ukraine. At one time, there were about sixteen Russian-speaking Baptist churches in North Dakota. However, by 1985, only the congregation in the city of Max was functioning, and today, its worship services are conducted in English, not Russian.[243]

The early 1900s were marked by the growing emergence of Russian-speaking Baptist congregations in New England and the Midwest. New Russian-speaking Baptist churches were planted in places such as New York, NY (1903); Scranton, PA (1903); San Francisco, CA (1905); Los Angeles, CA (1908); Detroit, MI (1910); Pittsburgh, PA (1910); Buffalo, NY (1911); and Philadelphia, PA (1912).[244] This spiritual awakening was not the result of organized efforts made by any existing religious body in America. It was the result of lay witnessing by Russian-speaking immigrants. Those who heard the gospel simply shared it with other immigrants.[245] Newly established churches were looking for cooperation and mutual support. The first efforts to organize immigrant churches into one union were made in 1915 and 1917 by a Latvian Baptist pastor Rev. Wilhelm A. Fetler, who came to the US in 1915 after he was exiled from Russia. Eventually, his desire to unite Slavic immigrant Baptist churches in one union was fulfilled by organizing the Russian-Ukrainian Evangelical Baptist Union (RUEBU) in

---

240. Ibid., 253.
241. Ibid., 254.
242. Ibid.
243. Ibid., 255.
244. Ibid., 257.
245. Ibid., 390.

April 1919.[246] The RUEBU consisted of twenty-one churches in the USA and three churches in Canada at its inception. By 1923, RUEBU churches had a total of 651 members, as compared to 354 members in 1920.[247] Often, established English-speaking American churches, concerned about ministry among recent immigrants, provided help to Russian-speaking churches. In July 1901, for example, Alexander Nicolaus was commissioned by the Home Mission Society of the Northern Baptist Convention as its first missionary among the Russian-speaking immigrants in America.[248] Financial assistance was provided to ethnic pastors, missionaries working among immigrants were supported, and church facilities were offered for worship purposes to Russian-speaking groups throughout America.[249] The Convention continued its support of the Russian-speaking ministry in North Dakota until 1952. The Russian-Ukrainian Evangelical Baptist Union received substantial help from the Northern Baptist Convention, known today as the American Baptist Churches of the USA, from the early 1900s to 1952. The Southern Baptist Convention was partially involved in the ministry of Russian-speaking churches in California.[250]

The following pages are devoted to creating a brief historical overview of the PCSBA. The history of the PCSBA can be divided into two very distinctive periods. The first period is from 1928 to 1990. The second period is from 1990 to the present. The separation point between these two periods was the arrival of thousands of Evangelical Christians-Baptists emigrants from the former USSR to America starting in 1988–1989. Their arrival created a paradigm shift in the life and ministry of PCSBA churches.

5.4.2. PCSBA: The Humble Beginning Followed by Fruitful Ministry (1928–1990)

5.4.2.1. The Beginning
While New England and the Midwest experienced rapid growth in the number of Russian-speaking Baptist churches, such was not the case on the West

---

246. Ibid., 259.
247. Ibid., 393.
248. Ibid., 254.
249. Ibid., 258.
250. Ibid., 353.

Coast. The first Russian-speaking Baptist congregations on the West Coast were started in San Francisco, CA (1905) and in Los Angeles, CA (1908). Later, in 1917, churches were started in Fresno, CA, and Kerman, CA. In 1918, a Slavic Baptist church was started in Seattle, WA. Initially, PCSBA was organized as the Western Association of Russian Evangelical-Baptists.[251] Its official beginning took place at the First Convention, which was held on 12–14 October 1928 in the small city of Kerman in Central California. The first president of the association, elected during the convention, was Nikita Rodionov.[252] The purpose of the association was, as stated during the convention, to organize united efforts of Slavic churches for evangelistic work among many Russian-speaking immigrants in California.[253] However, during the first eleven years after the official beginning of the association, not much work was done. The Second Convention took place only in 1939. It was held in Los Angeles, CA on 22–26 November. During this convention, Jacob Prigodich was elected as the President of the Association.[254] Participants of this event experienced a high level of spiritual excitement and went home with great enthusiasm to work for the Lord.[255] During this convention, it was decided that annual membership dues from each member of all the churches in the association should be collected. The purpose of this was to raise funds to support evangelistic work in California and to cover other expenses. The dues were $3 per year.[256] Starting from this time, annual conventions have been held on a regular basis without interruption until the present time.

5.4.2.2. Evangelistic Work in Focus

The Third Convention with sixty-seven delegates, held in San Francisco on November 1940, was marked by strong evangelistic sentiments. A resolution to begin wide evangelistic work along the whole Pacific Coast, from

---

251. Ibid., 399.

252. Adolf Pichaj, "70-tiletniy Yubiley Ob'edineniya Slavyanskikh Baptistov Tikhookeanskogo Poberezh'ya," *Vestnik Obyedineniya* 3 (Dec 1998): 1.

253. Ibid.

254. "Minutes of the 2nd PCSBA Convention (1939)," PCSBA Archive, Sacramento, CA, 1.

255. "Letter of the Secretary of the Association, N. Pavlyuk, to Churches, 12.06.1939," PCSBA Archive, Sacramento, CA.

256. "Minutes of the 2nd PCSBA Convention (1939)," PCSBA Archive, Sacramento, CA, 2.

Historical Background of Slavic Baptists from the Mission Perspective

the Mexican border up to the Canadian border, was unanimously accepted. In order to start such an ambitious project, it was decided that a gifted evangelist from Western Europe, Brother G. K. Urban, should be invited. Financial support for his ministry would come from the association and the Russian Evangelical Mission, directed by M. M. Billester.[257] A year later, in November 1941, a Fourth Convention took place in Los Angeles. The president of the conference was Ivan Kmeta. With great sadness, the delegates learned that Brother G. K. Urban was not able to come to America because of the war in Europe. In order to continue evangelistic efforts on the Pacific Coast, it was decided that a radio evangelistic ministry should be supported with $50 per year. During this convention, a women's ministry was mentioned for the first time in the churches of San Francisco and Los Angeles.[258] The next two conventions were not marked by any significant decisions. However, during the Seventh Convention, the necessity of evangelism was underlined again and churches were called to evangelize people in their area. Also, it was recommended for the women's ministry department to emphasize the development of a mission-oriented attitude among women of the Slavic churches. In addition, the issue of organizing a youth ministry was addressed.[259]

The following several years were marked by activities directed toward self-organization of the association. A decision was made to incorporate the organization, and bylaws were developed and approved by the Tenth Convention in November 1947 in San Francisco. It was also decided that a farm would be purchased in the Kerman area in order to build small houses for elderly people from Slavic Baptist churches. It was clearly a socially oriented project, with the good intention of taking care of elderly sisters and brothers in Christ. However, this project became "a thorn in the flesh" for the leadership of the association for several years. After purchasing the farm and paying off the debt, the issue arose of how to finance the building of houses on the farm. Those who lived on the farm believed that the

---

257. "Minutes of the 3rd PCSBA Convention (1940)," PCSBA Archive, Sacramento, CA, 2.

258. "Minutes of the 4th PCSBA Convention (1941)," PCSBA Archive, Sacramento, CA, 2.

259. "Minutes of the 7th PCSBA Convention (1944)," PCSBA Archive, Sacramento, CA, 3.

financing of this project should be the main priority of the association. However, the leadership of the association considered evangelistic ministry as its main priority. Because of this, some tensions arose.[260] Unfortunately, two important aspects of the mission of the church, evangelism and social action/*diaconia*, were placed in opposition with each other in this case. In the end, the project never was completed and the land was later sold. Another socially oriented project, the support of orphanages in Latin America, was much more successful.[261]

A major decision was made during the Fourteenth Convention, held in November 1951 in Bryte, California. It was decided that a full-time position of an evangelist, who would travel along the Pacific Coast visiting churches and conducting evangelistic meetings, would be created. One half of this position was funded by the association and the other half by the Russian Evangelical Mission.[262] The association remained mission-focused. Life of the PCSBA churches in 1950s is well described by George Boltniew:

> The Russian-speaking Baptist churches in California, in the meantime, were benefiting from the immigration of Russian-speaking Baptists who in 1950 came to America from Shanghai by way of the Philippines. They were the remnants and descendants of the first Russian emigration that fled from Russia to China following the October Revolution. They came to America within the time frame of the second Russian emigration. Their arrival revived the bilingual ministry of Russian-speaking Baptist congregations in California. Gradually some of the DPs [DP = displaced people] who settled on the East Coast moved to the West Coast, strengthening the ministry of Russian-speaking Baptist churches in California, Oregon and Washington. Among them were a number of ministers.[263]

---

260. "History of Slavic Baptists of California," in the "Official Attachment to the Minutes of the PCSBA Board Meeting on February 16, 1952," Brite, CA (PCSBA Archive, Sacramento, CA), 5–6.

261. Pichaj, "70-tiletniy Yubiley," 1.

262. "History of Slavic Baptists of California," 5.

263. Boltniew, " Functional Analysis," 399.

Boltniew describes the life of PCSBA churches after 1960s in the following way: "These churches are well-organized, with active women's and young people's branches, radio ministries in Los Angeles, Portland and San Francisco, and a Russian Christian newspaper *Our Days*. From 1976 to 1981 the Slavic Baptist Church of Hollywood had a weekly Russian religious TV program, the first of its kind in America."[264] During annual conventions, delegates reported about evangelistic work being done by local churches. For example, during the Thirty-First Convention in November 1968, Pastor Chehovich of Bethany Church in Los Angeles reported a revival movement among Molokans in that city. Some of them had already been baptized and joined the church while others were preparing to be baptized as well.[265]

5.4.2.3. Different Means to Spread the Word

In order to share the good news, Slavic Baptist churches at that time used different means. Among them were publishing Christian literature, publishing the newspaper *Our Days*, and a radio ministry. Obviously, everything was done in the Russian language.

1. Publication of Christian literature. The association was actively involved in the publication of Christian literature. During the Seventeenth Convention, held in November 1954 in San Francisco, CA, it was decided that an apologetic book regarding the teaching of Adventists should be published. Delegates of the Eighteenth Convention, held on November 1955 in Bryte, CA, passed a resolution to publish another apologetic book about Jehovah's Witnesses.[266] Since that time, at almost every convention, questions have been discussed and decisions have been made regarding the publication of different kinds of Christian literature in Russian, such as apologetic, evangelistic, theological, historical books, poems, and novels. This literature is distributed among Russian-speaking people in the States and was also smuggled into the USSR. Among the church members of the association were very gifted writers who have written excellent books that have influenced the life of many Russian-speaking people in the US and

---

264. Ibid., 413.

265. "Minutes of the 31st PCSBA Convention (1968)," PCSBA Archive, Sacramento, CA, 2.

266. Pichaj, "70-tiletniy Yubiley," 3.

abroad. Among these famous authors were Pavel Rogozin, Rodion Berezov, Nikolay Wodnevskiy, Vera Kushnir, and John Mark.

2. Newspaper Our Days. The major, long-lasting publication project of the association is the newspaper *Our Days*, which was started in 1966.[267] Since its inception, this newspaper has been designated as an evangelistic tool to reach Russian-speaking people around the world. Nikolay Wodnevskiy was its first editor. His personal enthusiasm, tremendous sacrifice, vision, unique giftedness as a writer and editor, and deep commitment to God inspired those who were involved in this project at the beginning and through all the years of its ministry. Three years after it began, the newspaper had 1,165 subscribers and a circulation of 1,600 per week.[268] In 1971, *Our Days* was sent out on a weekly basis to thirty-two countries.[269] In 2006, it celebrated its fortieth anniversary. The newspaper is published in Russian. It has also been published in the Ukrainian language for some time. It is currently still sent to thirty-two countries every week. In forty years, 1,978 issues have been published. This newspaper has touched the lives of multitudes around the world during the more than four decades of its ministry, and continues to be an effective evangelistic tool, owned and supported by the PCSBA.

3. Radio ministry. The association also has used a radio ministry as another way to do evangelistic work. As mentioned above, at the Fourth Convention in 1941, a decision was made to support a radio ministry. Later on, it became a very important tool to bring the good news to the lands of the former Soviet Union. For many years, the only way to bring the gospel to this area was through broadcasting on shortwave radio. The members of the association took a significant part in this ministry. In 1972, the new missionary organization Word to Russia was started.[270] Its purpose was to broadcast radio programs in the Russian language to Russia and around the world. Programs were prepared with the help of preachers and choirs from Slavic Baptist churches in California. The following broadcasters became well known in Russia and in many other countries: Nikolay Wodnevskiy, Michael Loktev, Alexander Efimov, Adolf Pichaj, Platon Kharchlaa, Vera

---

267. Ibid., 4.
268. Ibid., 5.
269. Ibid., 6.
270. Ibid.

Kushnir, and others. Through this ministry, non-believers heard the good news and some of them accepted Christ as their personal Savior. For many Christians behind the Iron Curtain, among whom was the author of this study, this ministry provided encouragement and spiritual support in a time of persecution. Becoming a Christian in 1974, the author of this study experienced persecution from the atheistic Communist government. Listening to Christian radio programs from abroad helped him keep the faith and grow in understanding of the Scripture.

Summary

The first period of PCSBA history was characterized by the evangelistic enthusiasm of believers. Although churches were small and the membership of the entire association was only around 300–400 people, they were able to carry the significant financial burden of supporting the evangelistic projects described above. Also, churches expressed social concerns, trying to help their elderly members as well as taking care of orphans in Latin America. All evangelistic efforts were focused on Russian-speaking people in America and overseas. Nothing is mentioned in the archive materials about evangelistic efforts specifically focused on English-speaking people. At the same time, some churches included sermons in English in their services. For example, the Bethany Baptist Church of Los Angeles conducted services in both languages, Russian and English, during the 1960s. American speakers were invited to preach in English.[271] The important motivation for doing this was the fact that children of believers were more comfortable with English than with Russian. It is important to note that English-speaking Baptist churches helped in starting and developing an evangelistic ministry among Russian-speaking immigrants during that time.

5.4.3. Years 1990–Present: Time of Significant Membership Growth and Expanding Ministries

At the end of the 1980s, the Soviet government opened the door for the emigration of evangelical Christians (Pentecostals and Baptists). Thousands of evangelicals used this window of opportunity to leave the land where

---

271. Adolf Pichaj, "Brief History of the Bethany Baptist Church," in *100th Jubilee* (Los Angeles: Bethany Baptist Church of Los Angeles, 2010), 61.

they had suffered so much due to past persecution for their faith. Most of them arrived in the USA. The vast majority of them did not know any English, so they obviously looked for Russian-speaking churches. Because of this, the existence of Russian-speaking congregations was a great benefit for newly arrived immigrants. The new stream of believers who joined the Russian-speaking churches brought new energy to the life and ministry of these churches and marked the beginning of a new period in the history of the PCSBA.

5.4.3.1. Membership Growth

Transition from one period to another was reflected in the membership of the association, which had not changed much during the first period of its history from its beginning until 1990. It stayed at about 300–400 members the entire time. However, starting in 1990, membership began to grow. The reason for this was the latest wave of immigration, which started in 1989. Before this year, very few immigrants came to the US from the former Soviet Union. After 1989, however, thousands of them began arriving in the States. Many of them were Evangelical Christians-Baptists. Immediately after arrival, they began looking for Russian-speaking churches in the area and soon after finding them, they usually joined. As a result, the membership of Slavic Baptist churches and the Association as a whole began to grow rapidly. Table 5.3.2.A. and chart 5.3.3.A. in the appendix to chapter 5, section 5.3.2.A., illustrate the growth dynamic of the PCSBA.

Membership growth affected the life of local churches and the association as a whole. The dynamic of life had been changed. From a small group of people in which almost everyone knew each other, the association became a relatively large organization with a well-developed organizational structure. It became impossible for all members to know each other. Newcomers found their predecessors, the so-called "old immigrants," to differ from them in their understanding of worship style, church practice, and theology. At certain points, it became a source of tension between these two groups within the association. It was an encounter of two groups of Christians who spoke the same language, Russian, but came from very different backgrounds. One group, the recent immigrants, came from a USSR that had been shaped by persecution, the Soviet government system, and society. The other group, the "old immigrants," consisted of people who either left

Russia a very long time ago or who had accepted Christ in the USA or Latin America and did not know how Christian life was in the USSR. Two different church cultures clashed within the local churches as well as within the association as a whole. It was a painful process. However, the two groups were eventually able to find common ground and continue to serve God together while being part of the same churches. As can be seen in the PCSBA membership table 5.3.2.A and membership growth chart 5.3.3.A in the appendix for chapter 5, church membership grew dramatically during the last twenty years. It grew fifteen times its previous size. The number of churches during the same period of time did not increase as much; it only tripled. This meant that membership of local churches grew significantly. For some churches, this growth was phenomenal. For example, the church in West Sacramento, California, on Solano Street, had about seventy-five members in 1990. In 2011, its membership was around 2,000. Such dramatic growth was a source of joy for immigrant churches. Churches continue accepting new members, many of whom are very gifted in different areas of ministry. Many talented singers and choir directors have joined these churches. This allowed immigrant churches to organize and to maintain a high quality of music ministry. Choir and music ministry have become a very important focus of life in immigrant churches. A significant portion of the Sunday service is usually given to choir singing and other musical performances. Many ordained ministers, presbyters, and deacons arrived from the homeland and joined immigrant churches, as well. All of this growth was at the expense of the Baptist churches in the homeland, which lost all of these active church members and leaders.

5.4.3.2. The Organizational Structure of the PCSBA

The Annual Convention of church delegates possesses the highest authority in making decisions for the association. Each church that is a member of the association is autonomous in its life but has to obey the bylaws and support the convention's decisions. The ruling body of the association is the Leadership Board, elected for two-year terms by the Annual Convention. Until 2006, the board consisted of nine members. But at the Sixty-Ninth Convention, in October 2006, the number of board members was increased to eleven people. Different ministries are managed by different departments. The heads of departments are appointed by the board. In 2004, at the

Sixty-Eighth Convention, a Spiritual Care Committee was formed. Four members of the committee are experienced ministers who have spent many years in pastoral ministry. They are called upon to provide assistance to the pastors of local congregations with their duties. However, the committee members are not above pastors or churches; rather, they stand next to them, ready to help. Under the current organizational structure, the president of the association plays an important role in determining in which direction the association, as an organization, is going. The president is also the Chairman of the Leadership Board. In most cases, the president works hard, combining a secular job, ministry in the local church, and service in the association. Names of brothers who have served as the PCSBA president are provided in the table 5.3.4.A. in the appendix to chapter 5, section 5.3.2.A. In 1996, during the Fifty-Ninth Annual Convention, Nikolay Martinchuk, who belonged to the "new immigrants," was elected as president of the association. Since that time, the leadership role in the PCSBA has belonged to those who have come to America recently, after 1990.

5.4.3.3 Ministry Expansion and Church Life

Different aspects of ministry are addressed by PCSBA churches. In order to carry on these ministries, appropriate departments have been established. At the Seventy-Fourth Annual Convention of the PCSBA, in October 2011, reports of nineteen different departments were submitted to the delegates. These departments represent the following ministries: mission ministry, youth ministry, teenage ministry, children's ministry, the newspaper *Our Days*, music ministry, education, prison ministry, Awana Club, Internet ministry, humanitarian aid, radio ministry, women's ministry, mothers in prayer ministry, care for orphans and widows, *God's Vineyard* magazine, video ministry, property management, and the financial office.[272] This shows how wide the spectrum of ministries that the PCSBA churches are trying to cover is. They are in danger of spreading themselves too thin. However, what allows them to maintain such a high number of ministries is the fact that more than half of the almost 8,000 members of the association reside in one area, the city of Sacramento, California. This closeness in geographical proximity provides them with an opportunity to communicate with each

---

272. *Almanac for the PCSBA 74th Convention* (Sacramento, CA: PCSBA, 2011), 11.

other easily and to meet with each other in person often. At the same time, it puts churches located in other cities in a disadvantaged position. In most cases, these churches do not have a large membership and do not have many gifted and experienced church members. Because of this, they cannot afford to carry out all these different ministries, putting these churches in an unequal position with churches located in Sacramento.

One of the important developments in the life of PCSBA churches during the last two decades has been building or purchasing new church facilities. Although most of the Russian-speaking churches of the "old immigrants" owned their own church buildings, these facilities were not able to accommodate significant membership growth. Because of this, several churches undertook expensive projects for the construction or purchase of their own church buildings. It put these congregations under long-term financial obligations. At the same time, it has provided them with the opportunity to conduct their services and other activities at times that were convenient to them. It was a big accomplishment for these churches, which consisted mostly of recent immigrants who were not at all wealthy.

A more detailed review of the mission-related aspects of life of PCSBA churches will be provided in chapter 6.

Summary

The second period in the history of the PCSBA is marked by a membership growth explosion, expansion of existing and development of new ministries, establishment of the worship order and church life, and the building or purchasing of new church facilities. This success has been due to the hard work of immigrants of the previous wave, the "old immigrants." They laid down a foundation for the recent immigrants on which to build their churches and ministries. The significant membership growth, due to the last wave of immigration, provided the association with new opportunities to be involved in mission work in the homeland, as well as local evangelism.

5.5. Conclusion for Chapter 5

American society as a product of continuing immigration process has become a multiethnic, multicultural, and multilingual society. This diversity provides

American churches with the challenge requiring them to pay very serious attention to the issue of contextualization of their mission.

Global migration provides the church with new challenges and opportunities. It brings significant changes in the social, economic, and religious life of both the countries of origin and the countries of destination. It requires new approaches to be used in church mission. As part of the global migration process that took place in the twentieth century, a Russian-speaking diaspora came to exist in America. The majority of people in this diaspora are not evangelical Christians. A relatively small part of it is Russian-speaking Baptists. The great majority of these Baptists immigrated to America during the last twenty-plus years. For them, the rest of the Russian-speaking diaspora is a potential mission field. However, this field is not an easy one in which to work and provides serious challenges for the Baptists' efforts to spread the gospel among the people belonging to this field. This rough overview of the history of Russian-speaking Baptists in America shows that they have been around for at least a century. However, their churches have struggled to survive and have not always done so with success. Fraternal help provided to them by indigenous English-speaking churches was very important for their continuing existence.

The history of the Pacific Coast Slavic Baptist Association has two distinctive periods. The first period, from 1928 to 1990, was marked by the hard work of a small group of churches, who had a total membership of about 300–400. At their annual conventions, they always emphasized the importance of spreading the gospel among Russian-speaking non-believers. By using radio, literature, and newspaper publications, they were able to make significant accomplishments in the evangelistic efforts to reach the Russian-speaking world with the gospel. At the same time, they were able to reach Russian-speaking non-believers locally and to connect them with Christ. As a result, new baptisms took place and churches, if not growing rapidly, at least survived. Also, social concern was expressed through support of orphanages in Latin America. It could be said that two aspects of authentic mission, evangelism and social action/*diaconia*, examined in this study, were present in the PCSBA churches that existed during the "first historical period" of this organization. However, it needs to be noted that there were no visible signs of active evangelistic efforts directed towards

Historical Background of Slavic Baptists from the Mission Perspective   237

the English-speaking population and no readiness of churches to switch into English in their services, although bilingual services did take place in some churches.

The second period of PCSBA history has been marked by remarkable membership growth, transition in leadership in local churches and the association, the building and purchasing of church facilities, the establishment of a certain order in services and church life, and the organizing of different departments in the association, in addition to the existing ones, to carry out many different ministries. Using the old organizational structure of the association, new immigrants have filled the organization with new energy and enthusiasm. More detailed information about current mission work of the PCSBA churches is provided below, in chapter 6. This information is critical for making an evaluation of the authenticity and contextuality of the mission work of this group of churches.

Part III

Context: Identity Crisis/Transformation – Towards a Paradigm Shift in Self-Understanding among Slavic Baptists in America

This part of the book is focused on the current life and ministry of PCSBA churches. After living in the US for more than twenty years, the representatives of "new immigrants" in Slavic Baptist churches have established their congregational life well. However, due to the fact that the second generation of immigrants in some of these churches is starting to drift away from ethnic immigrant churches, PCSBA churches are approaching a point in their history when they have to go through a paradigm shift in their self-understanding. Are they going to continue to stay as mono-ethnic immigrant Russian-speaking churches or are they going to broaden their "base" and open doors for English-speaking people? This part of the study provides some light on this question and consists of (1) empirical data about the ministry of PCSBA churches, (2) analysis of the challenges of immigrant life based on sociological conclusions about the immigrant experience, and (3) exploration of the mission challenges and opportunities with which PCSBA churches are concerned. All this information is needed to do a realistic evaluation of the mission work of these churches provided in chapter 9.

CHAPTER 6

The Present Mission Work of Slavic Baptist Churches in the US

This chapter provides factual materials about the mission ministry of Pacific Coast Slavic Baptist Association (PSSBA) churches. These materials are needed to answer an important question: Is the present mission work of PCSBA churches contextually appropriate and in alignment with authentic mission? In order to answer this question, the following studies have been made: a demographic study of newly baptized believers in PCSBA churches, an analysis of the percentage of mission-related spending in selected church budgets, a survey of Slavic pastors and other church leaders regarding their views on church mission in the immigrant context, a survey of the youth in PCSBA churches regarding their views of immigrant churches, a survey of the current church mission situation, a survey of former members of Slavic churches who have switched to English-language churches, and a review of the methods and organizational models of missionary work currently used by PCSBA churches.

6.1. Demographic Studies of Newly Baptized Believers in PCSBA Churches

To discover the effectiveness of PCSBA churches in reaching out to those in the Russian-speaking community in America who are not affiliated with the church, a demographic study of newly baptized believers was conducted. Information regarding newly baptized people from 2003 through 2005 was gathered for all PCSBA churches. In order to make an objective comparison on the effectiveness of churches in this area, the following three

measurements were calculated based on the total church membership and the number of individuals baptized:
a) The percentage of all baptized people in the church.
b) The percentage of baptized people who came from non-Christian families.
c) The percentage of baptized people who came from Christian families.

It is presumed that the effectiveness of the congregation's work with unchurched people can be measured by the number of people joining the church from non-Christian families. The higher the percentage of baptized people coming from non-Christian families, the higher is the effectiveness of church work with unchurched people.

The three charts below compare the percentage of baptized people from within the church membership with the percentage of baptized people who came from non-Christian families; organized by year from 2003 to 2005.

Chart 6.1.1.

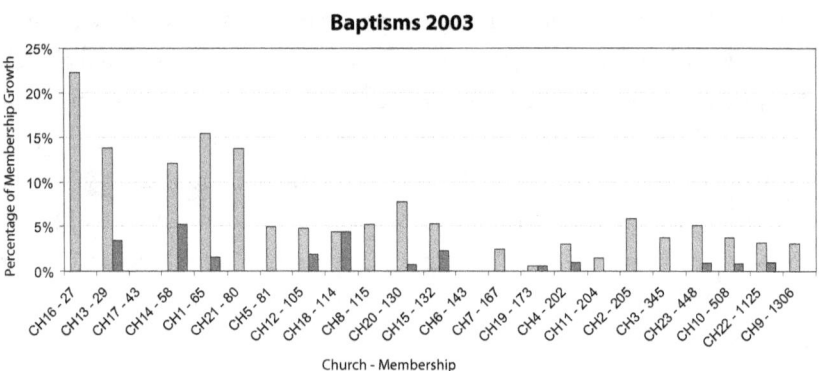

Chart 6.1.2.

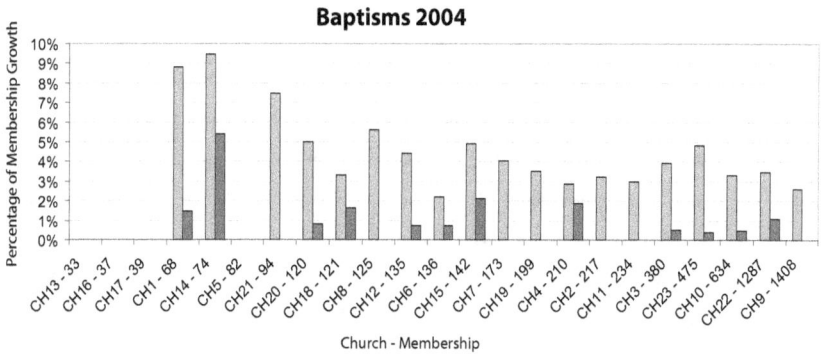

Chart 6.1.3.

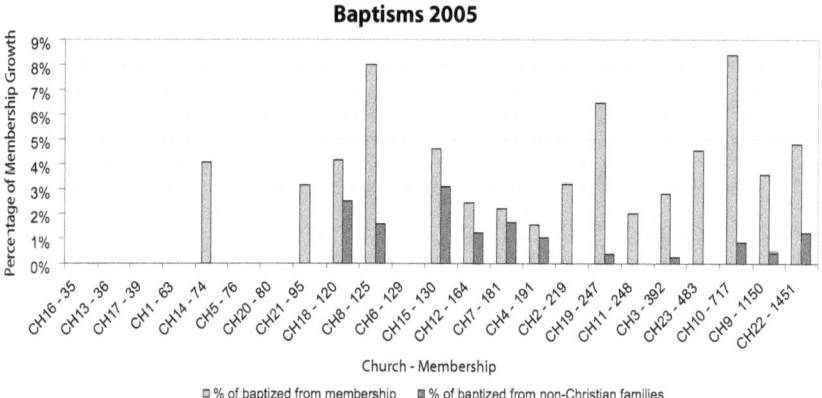

An analysis of the results from the demographic study leads to the following conclusions:

1. The majority of newly baptized people in the surveyed PCSBA churches came from Christian families. Only about 17 percent of all baptized people in PCSBA churches during the examined three-year period were converted to Christianity from a completely non-Christian background. The rest of those who were baptized during this period of time were children of believers.

2. The growth of membership in the association due to the baptism of those who had come from non-Christian homes remained a consistent 1 percent.

3. In every PCSBA church, the number of baptized people coming from non-Christian families was significantly lower than the number of baptized people who came from Christian homes. Almost half of the churches did not have anyone from non-Christian families among their newly baptized believers. Each year, ten–eleven churches out of twenty-three (about 43–48%) did not baptize even a single person coming from a non-Christian home.

4. In PCSBA churches, the size of church membership did not correlate with the church's effectiveness in evangelism. The percentage of baptized people in relation to the total church membership is significantly higher in churches with lower membership. The larger churches were not necessarily more effective at evangelism. Smaller churches were more effective in their witness to people and in leading them towards baptism.

5. In PCSBA churches, the percentage of baptized people coming from non-Christian families was higher in churches with lower membership. This means that smaller churches were more effective than larger churches in reaching people in the Russian-speaking community with the gospel, bringing them to Christ, and leading them to baptism.

6. All of these facts show that even though baptismal services are taking place in most Slavic churches on a regular basis, not many people are converted from outside of the church body. The reason for this could be that churches are not actively working among non-believing, Russian-speaking people in the American society.

When it comes to the issue of baptizing people from non-Christian homes, it is clear that there are several churches in the association that are more effective in doing this than other churches. These more "productive" churches are relatively small and they are located in areas with a very high percentage of Russian-speaking, non-Christian population, such as San Diego, Los Angeles, and San Francisco. In Sacramento, California, there is a very large Russian-speaking community; however, most of these people are already part of the church or are related to people who do belong to the church. This could be one of the reasons why the percentage of baptized people coming from non-Christian families in Sacramento is lower than in San Diego, Los Angeles, or San Francisco.

Summary

Information obtained through a demographic study of newly baptized believers in the PCSBA churches shows that an overwhelming majority of the baptized are children of believers. Essentially no English-speaking people are being baptized in Slavic churches. This raises a question of the contextuality of the evangelistic efforts of these churches. It seems as though they are focused mainly on children of their own members. This does not correlate with the definition of authentic mission of the church developed in chapter 2 of this study. The church exists to proclaim the gospel and to serve those outside of the church. According to the results of these demographic studies, this is not happening in PCSBA churches.

Another conclusion that can be made, based on the results of the demographic studies of new believers, is that in order to be effective in reaching people from non-Christian families, the Slavic immigrant church does not need to have a large membership. In smaller churches, newcomers from the "outside" world receive more personal attention from believers than in larger churches, and because of this, they continue attendance at the smaller churches more often. This means that large churches should consider separating part of their membership and using them as a nucleus to start new church plants. The location of the church, in terms of the presence of a Russian-speaking, non-Christian population in town, could affect the percentage of baptized people from non-Christian families. This means that new church plants should be considered in the cities with a large Russian-speaking population.

6.2. Analysis of the Percentage of Mission-Related Spending in the Budgets of Selected Churches

One of the best reflections of a church's ministry priorities is its annual budget. In order to find out how valuable mission work is in PCSBA churches, a survey of their budgets was done. The results are available in table 6.2.1.A. in the appendix to chapter 6, section 6.2.A. The survey showed that the percentage of mission spending varies. It could be as low as 0 percent or

3 percent, and as high as 62 percent. For most churches, it did not change much from year to year. However, the amount of financial support that was sent to ministries overseas (usually back to the homeland) was growing in many Slavic immigrant churches. Even if the percentage of mission spending in the budget is unchanged, the annual amount was growing because the budget in almost every church was growing significantly.

6.3. Survey of Slavic Pastors and Other Church Leaders Regarding Their Views on Church Mission in the Immigrant Context

The church structure of most Slavic Baptist immigrant churches is congregational[1] and reflects the long-time tradition of Baptist churches in the former Soviet Union. According to this tradition, the ruling body of the church is the Board of Elders ("*Bratsky Sovet*"), elected by the congregation at a business meeting. Nearly all issues of the congregational life are addressed by this board. This body has strong influence on the development of the philosophy of ministry in the local church. It also reflects the views of the common people in the church, because it consists not only of ordained ministers but also of ordinary members of the church. In order to understand how Slavic churches view mission work and what is actually done in this area, it is crucial to find out the opinions of the members of each board of elders in each of these churches on this issue. An extensive questionnaire was developed with the purpose of surveying members of the boards of elders of Slavic churches. This survey was conducted in 2005. The board of elders in each of the twenty-two churches participated in the survey. Each of the 184 respondents answered thirty-seven questions in the questionnaire.

The same questions were used to conduct a survey of four other groups of PCSBA church leaders: youth leaders, Sunday school teachers, leadership board, and department directors. Using the same set of questions for conducting surveys among these different groups of PCSBA leaders provided an opportunity for comparative analysis of the views of different subgroups of church leaders, and allowed a broader and more accurate picture of mission

---

1. Paul R. Jackson, *Doctrini i ustroy'stvo baptistskikh tserkvey'* (Schaumburg, IL: Regular Baptist Press, 1980), 31.

work in churches. Although the results of the surveys of all five groups of leaders will be considered in the study, the main focus will be in analyzing the results of the church board survey, as this group is the determining body for the course that the local churches will take in all aspects of its ministry, including missions.

Five years later, in 2009, the same questionnaire was used to conduct a survey of the church boards of selected PCSBA churches. A total of fifty-two leaders from ten churches took part in this survey. The purpose of this second survey was to find out if mission work in churches has changed since the first survey and if the PCSBA church leaders' position on mission has changed during this period of time, as well.

Due to the limited space of the book, not all results of the leadership board surveys and their analysis will be provided in this chapter. Although all of them are important and provide very valuable information, only the results that will be directly referred to in the following chapters are included in this chapter. The remaining results of the church board surveys, as well as the results of the surveys of the other groups of the church leaders mentioned above, are available in the appendix for chapter 6, section 6.3.A.

Part 1: General Evaluation of Missionary Work in the Local Congregation

Question 1. What is the main focus of missionary work in your church?

Table 6.3.1.

	Year	2005	2009
	Number of participants in the survey	184	52
Answer codes	Answers		
A	A) Supporting missionaries in Russia	35.7%	29.4%
AB	A) Supporting missionaries in Russian; B) Short-term mission trips	22.0%	37.3%
ABC	A) Supporting missionaries in Russian; B) Short-term mission trips; C) Witnessing to Russian-speaking people in the US	2.7.%	3.9%

	Year	2005	2009
	Number of participants in the survey	184	52
Answer codes	Answers		
ABCD	A) Supporting missionaries in Russian; B) Short-term mission trips; C) Witnessing to Russian-speaking people in the US; D) Work among English-speaking people in the US	1.6%	5.9%
ABD	A) Supporting missionaries in Russian; B) Short term mission trips; D) Work among English-speaking people in the US	1.1%	3.9%
AC	A) Supporting missionaries in Russian; C) Witnessing to Russian-speaking people in the US	8.8%	0.0%
B	B) Short-term mission trips	9.3%	11.8%
BC	B) Short-term mission trips; C) Witnessing to Russian-speaking people in the US	1.1%	0.0%
C	C) Witnessing to Russian-speaking people in the US	8.2%	0.0%
CD	C) Witnessing to Russian-speaking people in the US; D) Work among English-speaking people in the US	1.6%	0.0%
D	D) Work among English-speaking people in the US	0.5%	0.0%
NA	No answer	7.1%	7.8%

The results of this part of the survey clearly show that the main focus of Slavic church mission efforts is directed toward people in their homeland, the former Soviet Union. This is not a surprise. It is natural for the first generation of immigrants to support ministries in their country of origin. However, this has special significance at the current time. In the context of switching attention of American Christian organizations from the former Soviet Union as a primary mission field to other geographical areas, such as China and Africa, financial support of Christian work in Russia and other former Soviet Republics by Slavic churches in America has become crucial. Because of this fact, the strong concentration of mission efforts towards the former Soviet Union is a positive thing. At the same time, limited attention towards local evangelistic efforts among non-believing Russian-speaking people and low interest towards English-speaking non-believers makes the authenticity and contextuality of the mission work done by PCSBA churches questionable. Even right now, it looks as if the immigrant churches are fulfilling Christ's Great Commission by supporting mission work in their homeland, but it is only a partial fulfillment of the commission. According to Christ's sequence of actions in the process of fulfilling His commission, it should be done in the following order: "you will be my witnesses in Jerusalem and in all Judea and Samaria, and to the end of the Earth" (Acts 1:8, ESV). For immigrants, "Jerusalem" is the place where they live now – it is America. Changing the order in an effort to evangelize the world causes the development of an unhealthy attitude among church members when they do not see the importance of local evangelism. This leads to the transformation of immigrant churches into closed ethnic communities. It is a very threatening perspective. Also, it undermines the future growth and survival of the Slavic immigrant churches. If the younger generation does not participate in witnessing to non-believers and has no evangelistic experience, they will grow up unprepared to share the gospel and to lead people to Christ. As a result of this, it is only a matter of time before the immigrant churches begin to suffer a decline in their membership.

Part 2: Local Mission Work

Question 7. How often does the church participate in the needs of the city and the country (USA) in general?

Table 6.3.7.

	Year	2005	2009
	Number of participants in the survey	184	52
Answer codes	Answers		
A	A) Every time a need is made known	31.5%	52.9%
AB	A) Every time a need is made known; B) Every time when the need involves Russian-speaking people	0.5%	2.0%
B	B) Every time when the need involves Russian-speaking people	11.4%	9.8%
C	C) Very rarely	32.6%	25.5%
D	D) Never	15.8%	9.8%
NA	No answer	7.6%	2.0%

A close look at the results of the survey done in 2005 among five different groups of Slavic church leaders (see results in the appendix for chapter 6, table 6.7.3.A.) showed that all five surveyed groups almost unanimously stated that their churches participated in the needs of the city and the country very rarely (from 27.8% to 34.8%). However, answers were much more diverse when it came to more specific questions. Almost half of the youth leaders surveyed (44.4% – see appendix for chapter 6) saw such participation as being ethnically influenced. Contrarily, church leaders did not see it this way. Only 10.3%–11.4% of them believed that churches were responding to the needs of the larger society when these needs were related to the Russian-speaking people. Similar polarization was shown in choosing the answer option "Every time a need is made known." The youth leaders' percentage of answering in this way was the lowest, at 16.7%. On the other hand, the percentage of the church boards and other church leaders who chose this option was the highest: 31.5%–48.3%. Such a difference in opinions between the youth leaders and church leaders could be explained by the fact that the youth often have higher views of church involvement in meeting social needs of people in the world and have higher expectations in this area of church mission than the older generation. This is especially true for the immigrant church community. Young people learn English quickly and become aware of the needs in the society around them much faster than their parents. As a result, the youth understand the social needs in the world and expect the church to address these needs more actively than it actually happens. At the same time, church leaders who usually are part of the older generation often do not know English well enough, and because of this, do not understand what is happening in the society in which they now live and how their church could be involved in addressing the needs of this society.

Another aspect related to the issue of church involvement in addressing the needs of the city and the country and which needs to be mentioned here is the fact that for decades evangelical Christians involved in the church and living in the former Soviet Union were unwelcome to participate in the social life of the surrounding society. The government intentionally tried to exclude evangelical churches from social life as much as possible. As was shown in chapter 4, the church was deprived of rights to take care of needy people and to take part in meeting other social needs. The government kept this right for itself. This developed within evangelical churches a sense of indifference to what was happening in the "world," or what was understood as the surrounding society. "Separation from the world" was equated to isolation from society. In coming to a new country, Slavic Baptists brought with them their old attitude towards the "world." Isolationism towards society among Slavic immigrants grew even stronger here because of the cultural differences and the language barrier. It was not surprising, then, that 48.4% (lines C and D) of the church board members surveyed in 2005 stated that their churches either never or very rarely participated in the needs of the city and the country. At the same time, a relatively high number, 31.5% (line A), stated that their churches participated when information was communicated to them. This shows that there is progress in shifting from isolationism toward understanding that the churches are part of the society, and their influence on it, including local mission, depends on their participation in addressing society's needs. As is shown above, by comparing results of surveys from 2005 and 2009, Slavic churches are becoming more open to responding to the needs of the surrounding society. This means that there is an improvement in one of the aspects of authentic mission – social action/*diaconia* – taking place among the PCSBA churches.

Question 8. How many people from the surrounding community come to worship services?

Table 6.3.8.

	Year	2005	2009
	Number of participants in the survey	184	52
Answer codes	Answers		
A	Many	4.3%	3.8%
B	Some	29.3%	19.2%
C	Few	18.5%	21.2%
D	Very few	34.8%	38.5%
NA	No answer	13.0%	17.3%

It is obvious that culture and language barriers are playing a significant role in the process of integrating Slavic immigrants into American society. In the same way, Americans experience difficulty in joining this new social group. While it is true in general, this phenomenon is especially prevalent in the church scene. Based on the answers to this question, it is obvious that not very many or, better to say, only a few or very few people from the surrounding community attend worship services in Slavic churches in America. Even if they come, in most cases, this is just because they want to learn more about the Russian culture or language, but not because they want to hear the gospel . This indicates that so far, the trend in Slavic churches has not changed. They are still very much isolated from the surrounding community. Comparing results from two surveys conducted in 2005 and 2009 revealed a sad truth that there are no signs of a decrease in this isolation. Slavic immigrant churches exist as ethnic and cultural enclaves within the larger American society, and it is contradictory to the understanding of authentic mission, as presented in chapter two.

Question 9. How many Russian-speaking non-believers come to worship services?

Table 6.3.9.

	Year	2005	2009
	Number of participants in the survey	184	52
Answer codes	Answers		
A	Many	2.7%	0.0%
B	Some	54.8%	33.3%
C	Few	15.8%	13.7%
D	Very few	35.3%	43.1%
NA	No answer	10.3%	9.8%

The main argument often used to support the existence of ethnic churches (including Russian-speaking churches) is that these churches should share the gospel with people of their ethnic group and should bring them to fellowship with believers. Someone could expect that a large (or even a small), well-organized, predominantly Russian-speaking church community would be a strong drawing factor for other Russian-speaking immigrants in the surrounding community, even if they were not Christians. However, this is not happening in most cases for PCSBA churches. A significant number (51.1%–82.4%, depending on the group surveyed) of surveyed leaders said that only a "few" or "very few" Russian-speaking non-believers come to worship services in these churches. A much lower number (11.8%–34.8%) of leaders stated that "some" Russian-speaking non-Christians come to church services. It is very disappointing information. It seems the situation is not getting better over time. It could be interpreted as the fact that Slavic immigrant churches are not practicing an authentic and contextual mission. It should be mentioned that Russian-speaking immigrants who are non-believers do not come to church easily. If they came from the former Soviet Union, they bring with them prejudices towards the church, and especially towards Baptists. It seems that personal evangelism is the best way to reach these people in the US. Before being invited to a church service, Russian-speaking non-believers should be introduced, in an informal environment, to a family or small group of Russian-speaking Christians. Personal acquaintance with Christians helps non-believers overcome prejudices they have towards believers.

Question 10. How many English-speaking non-believers come to worship services?

Table 6.3.10.

	Year	2005	2009
	Number of participants in the survey	184	52
Answer codes	Answers		
A	Many	0.0%	0.0%
B	Some	3.8%	3.8%
C	Few	9.8%	7.7%
D	Very few	61.4%	61.5
NA	No answer	25.0%	25.0%

Answers to this question clearly demonstrate that English-speaking people who do not believe in Christ are not frequent attendees of Slavic Baptist churches. Out of all respondents, 61.4% to 82.6% stated that very few English-speaking non-believers were coming to their worship services. The reason is obvious. The language used in the worship service in most Slavic churches (Russian or Ukrainian) is not familiar to English-speakers. It creates a strong communication barrier between English-speaking visitors and Russian/Ukrainian-speaking hosts (church members). On the other hand, it blocks the message of the gospel from being understood and from being accepted by the non-believing attendees. As a result, a very important part of the mission of the church – witnessing to unbelievers – is not fulfilled by Slavic churches in terms of witnessing to the surrounding English-speaking community. This is a clear warning signal about the mission of the PCSBA churches not being authentic and contextual.

Question 11. Number of activities organized by the church for non-believers in the community (in 2004)?

Table 6.3.11.

	Year	2005	2009
	Number of participants in the survey	184	52
Answer codes	Answers		
A	Once a week	2.2%	1.9%
B	Once a month	3.3%	3.8%
C	Several times a year	49.5%	48.1%
D	No activities have been organized	29.3%	25.0%
NA	No answer	14.7%	21.2%

Analyzing answers to the question above, the conclusion could be reached that not very many activities for non-believers have been organized by the PCSBA churches during this particular year. Very few of the respondents (2.2%–4.3%) stated that such activities took place once a week. The range for the answer "once a month" was quite wide – from 3.3 % to 22.2%. Such inconsistency could be explained by the fact that the highest percentage – 22.2% – belonged to youth leaders (see appendix for chapter 6). Usually, the youth are more active in holding different activities, including activities for non-believers. Answering this question, they probably included activities that the church leaders are not even aware of, activities organized and conducted by the church youth themselves. The average for this answer was 8.4%. The percentage for the answer "Several times a year" also had a wide range: 39.1%–58.6%. The average for this answer was 48.9%. The range for the answer "No activities have been organized" was 23.5%–43.5%. The average for this answer was 30.3%. On average, almost half of the respondents (48.9%) stated that only occasionally, several times a year, activities for non-believers took place in their churches. A total of 30.3% stated that such kinds of activities did not take place at all. This was not a very encouraging picture. It shows that reaching non-believers in the community is not a very high priority for PCSBA churches. Such situations show that one of the very important aspects of an authentic mission – evangelism among non-Christians – is not a priority among Slavic immigrant churches. A comparison of answers of two surveys of the church boards conducted in 2005 and 2009 shows that no significant change in this aspect of church ministry took place during this period of time. A positive sign could be found in the fact that the percentage of those who answered, "No activities have been organized" had dropped from 29.3% in 2005 to 25.0% in 2009. Although the decline is not big, it still provides some hope for future positive changes in the churches' focus on non-believers in the community.

Question 12. Do you have activities organized in collaboration with representatives of other ethnic groups (evaluate the year 2004)?

Table 6.3.12.

	Year	2005	2009
	Number of participants in the survey	184	52
Answer codes	**Answers**		
A	Once a week	0.5%	0.0%
B	Once a month	1.1%	0.0%
C	Several times a year	27.2%	23/1%
D	No activities have been organized	58.7%	61.5%
NA	No answer	12.5%	15.4%

The vast majority (55.2%–70.6%) in all five groups surveyed (see appendix for chapter 6) confirmed the discouraging fact that no activities had been organized by their churches with representatives from other ethnic groups. It shows that distance exists between the PCSBA churches and other ethnic groups living in their area.[2] The situation has not improved with the passing of time. It could be considered as one of the obstacles in the realization

---

2. Daniel Shinjong Baeq, Myunghee Lee, Sokpyo Hong, and Jonathan Ro, "Mission from Migrant Church to Ethnic Minorities: A Brief Assessment of the Korean American Church in Mission," *Missiology* 39, no. 1 (Jan 2011): 31. It is worth mentioning that Slavic immigrants are not unique in their negative attitude towards other ethnic groups they encounter in America. Korean-Americans display similar feelings in relation to non-Koreans. The study of the Korean American Church concludes that in order for these churches to be successful in mission work in the multiethnic American society, they have "to overcome a great obstacle: the negative attitude toward other ethnic groups."

of authentic mission by these churches. At the same time, an encouraging sign was that at least some respondents (11.8%–27.6%) indicated that their churches were practicing activities with other ethnic groups at least several times a year.

Question 13. Is your church planning evangelistic activities targeting other ethnic groups during the year 2005?

Table 6.3.13.

	Year	2005	2009
	Number of participants in the survey	184	52
Answer codes	Answers		
A	YES	20.1%	21.2%
B	NO	44.0%	38.5%
E	Unable to say	32.6%	40.4%
NA	No answer	2.7%	0.0%

It seems that some Slavic Baptist churches are planning evangelistic activities targeting other ethnic groups. The number of respondents in all five groups surveyed indicated the presence of such plans in their churches. However, the percentage of those was not high – the average is about 27%. The average percentage of those who said "no" is about 35%. This is equal to the percentage (35%) of those who were not able to say if such plans were under consideration in their churches. Basically, about 70% of those surveyed either had not seen plans or did not have information about them. This is an indication that other ethnic groups are not the focus of mission activities of PCSBA churches. The situation did not change much in the next four years. This continues to prove that Slavic churches concentrate their outreach efforts mostly on their own people.

Question 14. How do the church members respond to interracial marriages?

Table 6.3.14.

	Year	2005	2009
	Number of participants in the survey	184	52
Answer codes	Answers		
A	Positively	2.2%	0.0%
B	Understandingly	27.7%	30.8%
BC	B) Understandingly; C) Negatively	0.5%	0.0%
C	Negatively	29.3%	23.1%
D	Unable to say	37.0%	44.2%
NA	No answer	3.3%	1.9%

Interracial marriage is always a sensitive issue. This is especially true for immigrant communities. According to the survey results, on average, 33% of the respondents saw their churches reacting to this issue with an understanding as to what it could mean with tolerance, but not enthusiastically. At the same time, an average of 22% saw their churches responding negatively. About 35% did not have an opinion on the church position regarding this issue. It is obvious that interracial marriage is not a desirable thing among Slavic Baptist churches. At the same time, it is not as intolerable as it is among other ethnic immigrant groups, such as the Molokans, who expel from their midst those members who have married somebody from the outside of their community. Comparative surveys have shown that the attitude of Slavic churches towards interracial marriages did not change during the four years.

Question 15. Is your church planning to be and is it actively involved in planting new churches in the US?

Table 6.3.15.

	Year	2005	2009
	Number of participants in the survey	184	52
Answer codes	Answers		
A	YES	16.3%	15.4%
B	NO	58.2%	36.5%
E	Unable to say	21.2%	48.1%
NA	No answer	3.8%	0.0%

More than half of the surveyed in all five leadership groups, 55.2%–64.7% (line B), answered that their churches are not involved and are not planning to be involved in the organizing of new churches in the US. This reflects the tendency of many Slavic immigrant churches, in general, and PCSBA churches in particular, to stay together as a congregation and an unwillingness to let some members leave and start a new church. This happens even when the church lacks the necessary space in their building for all of the attendees and it is obvious that another church should be planted. The fear of leaders experiencing membership decline and the unwillingness of members to leave their comfort zone of an established congregation are among the key factors preventing voluntary divisions of Slavic churches with the purpose of organizing new ones. The positive sign was (although a very small one) that 11.1%–17.2% (line A) of the surveyed leaders in five groups testify that their churches are involved or plan to be involved in the church planting process. Comparing the results of the two surveys of the church board members conducted in 2005 and 2009 shows that the situation of planning and active involvement in organizing new churches in the US did not improve. In 2005, a positive answer was given by 16.3% versus 15.4%, in 2009. This was down 0.9%. The idea of spreading the gospel through planting new churches is not very attractive for PCSBA churches. This fact could be seen as an undermining factor in the ability of these churches to do authentic mission. As shown in the first part of this chapter, churches with smaller memberships often are more effective in reaching unchurched people with the gospel.

Part 3: Overseas Mission

Question 17. Where do the missionaries supported by your church work, predominantly?

Table 6.3.17.

	Year	2005	2009
	Number of participants in the survey	184	52
Answer codes	Answers		
A	A) In Russia or Ukraine	47.8%	32.7%
AB	A) In Russia or Ukraine; B) In other countries of the former USSR	12.0%	30.6%
ABC	A) In Russia or Ukraine; B) In other countries of the former USSR; C) In non-Russian-speaking countries	0.5%	4.1%
AC	A) In Russia or Ukraine; C) In non-Russian-speaking countries	2.7%	2.0%
B	In other countries of the former USSR	20.7%	22.4%
BC	B) In other countries of the former USSR; C) In non-Russian-speaking countries	0.5%	0.0%
C	In non-Russian-speaking countries	3.8%	0.0%
D	Unable to say	2.7%	0.0%
NA	No answer	9.2%	8.2%

Analysis of the responses shows that the vast majority of respondents in each of these five surveyed groups – 84.2%–94.5% – stated that the predominant areas where missionaries supported by their churches were serving were Russia, Ukraine, and other republics of the former Soviet Union. It is a clear indication that PCSBA churches are very much attached to their former homelands in their vision for mission work. That is understandable. As shown in the previous chapter, it is common for immigrants to experience a strong psychological attachment to their homeland. Such a strong focus on their country of origin is beneficial for expanding mission work there. At the same time, it undermines an extension of mission efforts of immigrant churches in the non-Russian-speaking world. For the first generation of immigrants, this could be seen as not a big problem. However, for the youth it is a disadvantage because it creates a language barrier for them since they are becoming less comfortable with the Russian language and more proficient in English. Because they are more proficient in English, the youth are often more easily accepted in the non-Russian-speaking world than in Russia. Since they are viewed by people in Russia as Russians, it is expected that they should speak Russian well. Maybe it is not accidental that in the answers to this particular question the highest percentage – 22.2% – of those who indicated that their church missionaries are serving in non-Russian-speaking countries, in addition to Russian-speaking areas, are youth leaders (see appendix for chapter 6). Such a discrepancy in the answers of the church boar members (4.8%) and youth (22.2%) could mean that the church leadership is not necessarily aware of their youth's mission involvement. Sometimes young people are involved in mission activities in non-Russian-speaking countries going there with churches different from their own, often with English-speaking churches or mission organizations.

A comparison of the results of 2005 and 2009 surveys shows that the situation with the predominant area of mission involvement did not improve much. Actually, in 2009, a higher percentage of the church board members (91.8% in 2009 versus 84.2% in 2005) stated that the predominant area of their missionary ministry was in Russia, in Ukraine, or in other countries of the former USSR. This indicates that the leadership of PCSBA churches is maintaining a trend of being involved primarily in mission work in their homelands.

Question 20. Do short-term missions take place in your church?

Table 6.3.20.

	Year	2005	2009
	Number of participants in the survey	184	52
Answer codes	Answers		
A	YES	63.0%	86.5%
B	NO	22.3%	1.9%
E	Unable to say	9.8%	11.5%
NA	No answer	4.9%	0.0%

According to the answers of those surveyed, five different groups of church leaders, most PCSBA churches are involved in short-term missions. A total of 63.0% – 82.8% (line A) of the respondents stated that short-term mission trips were taking place in their churches. A comparative survey of the church board members done in 2009 showed that short term mission activity had increased and almost all PCSBA churches are involved in it. In 2005, 63.0% of the surveyed church board members answered positively and 22.3% negatively on the question of whether their churches participated in sending out short-term mission groups. In 2009, these percentages were very different – 86.5% and 1.9%, respectively. It shows that such types of mission activities are gaining in popularity in PCSBA churches. Through this, most churches continue to keep contact with their former homelands. Every summer (sometimes even in winter), hundreds of young people from the Slavic immigrant churches in America go back to the former Soviet Union. For one or two months (some of them stay longer), they participate in different evangelistic events, help organize and run Christian children's and youth camps, visit orphanages, and distribute humanitarian aid. When coming back to the States, these young people bring exciting stories about God's blessings that they have experienced there, enthusiasm for ministry, and a strong desire to serve others, especially in their homelands. This helps people in Slavic churches keep memories about their homeland refreshed and delays the time for full assimilation into American society.

Question 21. Are there plans to send out missionaries for long-term assignments?

Table 6.3.21.

	Year	2005	2009
	Number of participants in the survey	184	52
Answer codes	Answers		
A	YES	19.0%	21.2%
B	NO	51.6%	61.5%
E	Unable to say	26.6%	17.3%
NA	No answer	2.7%	0.0%

Not many of the PCSBA churches have plans for sending long-term missionaries. Only 17.2%–30.4% (line A) of the respondents in five groups of leaders surveyed answered that their churches had plans to send long term missionaries. At the same time, 27.8%–55.2% (line B) said that there were such plans in their churches and 24.1%–39.1% (line C) were unable to answer this question. This situation has not changed much with time.

A comparative survey of the church board members has shown that the percentage of positive responses increased a little – from 19.0% in 2005 to 21.2% in 2009 (line A). At the same time, the percentage of negative responses increased significantly – from 51.6% in 2005 to 61.5% in 2009 (line B). Several reasons for a limited interest in this important method of mission ministry could be mentioned. The main reason is a lack of finances. It is much more expensive to send a missionary from the States to the former Soviet Union than to provide support to the indigenous worker who already lives there. Most PCSBA churches are not yet strong enough financially to make such commitments.

Part 4: Language Barrier and Mission

Question 25. How often are sermons in English preached during worship services in your church?

Table 6.3.25.

	Year	2005	2009
	Number of participants in the survey	184	52
Answer codes	Answers		
A	Once a week	13.0%	20.5%
B	More than once a week	1.1%	9.1%
C	Once a month	17.9%	36.4%
D	Several times a year	44.0%	29.5%
E	Unable to say	17.9%	0.0%
NA	No answer	6.0%	2.3%

The answers for this question by the five groups of leaders clearly indicate that sermons in English are not heard often during worship services in PCSBA churches. A relatively small number – 13.0%–27.6% (line A) – of the respondents said that a sermon in English was preached in their churches "once a week." 17.2%–35.3% (line C) of the surveyed stated that this happened "once a month." 44.0%–50.0% (line D) responded saying that sermons in English were preached only "several times a year." A comparative survey completed by members of church boards indicated some progress with this aspect of the immigrant church life. If in 2005, 13.0% of respondents in this category said that a sermon in English was preached "once a week" in their churches, in 2009 this percentage increased to 20.5%. If in 2005, 17.9% stated that they heard a sermon in English in their church "once a month," in 2009, the percentage of those who answered this way grew to 36.4%. Obviously, this is a positive trend. English language use in the church is a very hot issue. Different churches use different approaches to solving this issue. Some churches have announced a taboo on using the English language in church. Other churches give the "cold shoulder" to the language of the country in which they live. Very few churches welcome the use of English by the younger generation in the church. The author's personal observation is that churches with larger memberships provide less support for using English in their church. Also, a larger surrounding Russian-speaking community correlates with the lesser use of English in the church. The limited practice of English in Slavic immigrant churches could mean a low level of contextualization of their mission efforts towards the surrounding English-speaking community.

Question 26. Do you see a need for sermons in English being preached in Slavic churches?

Table 6.3.26.

	Year	2005	2009
	Number of participants in the survey	184	52
Answer codes	Answers		
A	YES	64.1%	56.9%
B	NO	23.9%	35.3%
C	Don't have an opinion	8.7%	7.8%
NA	No answer	3.3%	0.0%

Answers to this question given back in 2005 were encouraging. An overwhelming majority – 64.1% to 95.7% (line A) – of all five groups of leaders surveyed saw a clear need for sermons in English in their churches. This allowed believing that a significant part of the church leadership had a positive attitude toward using English in their churches. This left room for hope that the younger generation, who is more comfortable with English than with Russian, would feel welcome in Slavic churches. At the same time, 11.1% to 23.9% of the respondents answered that they did not see such a need. A comparative survey of the church boards in 2009 showed a negative change in the opinion of board members on the subject of a sermon in English in Slavic churches. In 2005, 64.1% had a positive view versus 56.9% in 2009, a 7.2% decline. In 2005, 23.9% said that there was no need for a sermon in English in their churches. In 2009, this percentage grew to 35.3%, an 11.4% increase. This is an alarming sign. The people in leadership (even according to the survey results they are in a minority) could create opposition to using

English in church services. Taking into consideration the fact that members in the church who represent the first-generation immigrants usually lean towards using primarily Russian in services could lead to the conclusion that English will not soon take an important place in worship services of Russian-speaking churches. The results of this could be twofold. Those among the younger generation who are more comfortable with English will look for a solid spiritual source in English and will eventually leave the Slavic church for an English-speaking church. Others from the younger generation, who are also more comfortable with English than with Russian but still decide to stay in a Russian-speaking church for various reasons (parents' requests, attachment to friends, etc.), will not receive solid spiritual nurturing and will not produce good spiritual growth. Both options are unhealthy for Slavic immigrant churches. Of course, departure of spiritually advanced English-speaking youth will undermine the ability of Slavic immigrant churches to implement authentic mission among people of the surrounding community who speak English.[3]

---

3. Despite this not very encouraging prospect, some positive changes have been observed lately among leaders of the PCSBA churches in their view of the place of English in the church service. During the 75th PCSBA Annual Convention, 18–20 October 2012, 300 delegates and guests were surveyed (see appendix for chapter 6, section 6.7). They were asked a question: Do you think your church needs a sermon in English? 83.6% of the participants answered positively, 16.4% said "No." Also, they were asked: Do you think your church needs to have a separate service in English? It is a bold question since a separate service in English could eventually lead to a separate congregation. This is what people of the older generation in immigrant churches are most afraid of. Surprisingly, 60% of the respondents said "Yes," while 40% answered "No." This is a significant positive shift in the position of the church leaders on such a sensitive issue as using English in the predominantly Russian-speaking immigrant churches. This gives room for hope that eventually English will find its appropriate place in Sunday services of the PCSBA churches. It would be a very important step towards making the local mission work of these immigrant churches contextualized.

Question 27. How do you see your church in 20–30 years?

Table 6.3.27.

	Year	2005	2009
	Number of participants in the survey	184	52
Answer codes	Answers		
A	Russian-speaking	16.3%	11.8%
B	Russian- and English-speaking	52.7%	49.0%
C	Completely English-speaking	3.3%	5.9%
D	Unable to say	23.4%	29.4%
NA	No answer	3.8%	3.9%

The overwhelming majority, 52.7%–89.7% (line B), of those surveyed in all five groups of leaders foresaw a bilingual (Russian and English) church in the future. At the same time, 5.6%–16.3% of the respondents believed that their church will be an only Russian-speaking congregation. Almost the same percentage of the respondents, 3.3%–13.0%, foresaw their church becoming a completely English-speaking congregation in twenty–thirty years. A comparative survey of the church board members indicates that there were no significant changes in the opinion of this very influential group of the church leaders. Very few of them foresaw the future of their churches as being solely English-speaking. Half of them saw their churches becoming bilingual in twenty–thirty years. However, in order to become only English-speaking or bilingual in the future, current PCSBA churches should make the appropriate decisions now, before many young people leave Slavic churches, as has happened in the past with churches of the previous generation of Russian-speaking immigrants.[4]

---

4. Part 5 is available in the appendix for chapter 6, section 6.3.A.

Part 6: In Your Opinion, How Should the Missionary Work of Your Local Congregation Look in the Future?

Question 34. What should be the primary focus in mission?

Table 6.3.34.

	Year	2005	2009
	Number of participants in the survey	184	52
Answer codes	Answers		
A	Evangelism of our children	21.2%	28.8%
AB	A) Evangelism of our children; B) Evangelism of the society around us	13.6%	11.5%
ABC	A) Evangelism of our children; B) Evangelism of the society around us; C) Evangelism in Russia	15.2%	11.5%
AC	A) Evangelism of our children; C) Evangelism in Russia	3.3%	0.0%
B	Evangelism of the society around us	17.9%	19.2%
BC	B) Evangelism of the society around us; C) Evangelism in Russia	2.2%	3.8%
C	Evangelism in Russia	8.2%	5.8%
D	Unable to say	5.4%	7.7%
NA	No answer	13.0%	11.5%

Obviously, Slavic Baptist immigrants are concerned about the spiritual wellbeing of their children. This is reflected in the answers of the church board members to the question above. The results show that from 21.2% to 28.8% of them claimed that evangelism of their children should be the main focus of their church mission. This is a very narrow understanding of the mission call of the church. If churches follow only this philosophy, they will eventually become socio-ethnic clubs. Fortunately, not all board members in PCSBA churches think this way. A significant percentage of the respondents included evangelism of the society around them as one of the main components of church mission. In 2005, 48.9% and in 2009, 46% of the church board members expressed the necessity of reaching people in the society. Although the question asked above does not specify who in the society they believe should be reached (Russian-speaking or English-speaking people), it is nevertheless encouraging to see that almost half of the leadership of Slavic churches surveyed understands the importance of reaching people in the community. The previously discussed results of this survey show that currently Slavic immigrant churches do not make many efforts to reach the society in which they are now living (see answers to Question #11). This understanding, by their leaders, of the importance of such kinds of efforts produces hope that in the future, these immigrant churches will become more active in sharing the gospel with their non-believing neighbors, both Russian-speaking and English-speaking.

This concludes the section of this chapter with the results of the surveys conducted among leaders of the PCSBA churches.

6.4. Survey of Youth in PCSBA Churches Regarding Their View of Immigrant Churches

The future existence of Slavic Baptist immigrant churches in general and their effectiveness in mission ministry in particular depends very much on how young people perceive themselves in Slavic churches today, what their perspective of the church is, and what quality of "spiritual food" they receive which helps them to grow to spiritual maturity. In 2004, the director of the Youth Ministry Department, under the supervision of the author of the current study, conducted an extensive survey of the youth in PCSBA churches. The goal of the survey was to gather basic demographic information and to find the opinion of the youth on such important issues as worship service, structure, preferred style of music in worship, the need for sermons in English during services at Slavic churches, and other things. This information was designed to help pastors of local congregations better understand their youth's needs and challenges. The youth of twenty different churches were surveyed, and a total of 859 people took part in the survey. The results of this survey were presented at the 67th Annual PCSBA Convention in October 2004. Six years later, the same survey was conducted among youth of the Pacific Coast Slavic Baptist Association churches. This time, 182 young people participated in the survey. The selected results of the surveys and a brief analysis of each are presented below. The remaining results of the survey are available in the appendix for chapter 6.

Question 1. How long have you lived in the United States?

Table 6.4.1.

		2004	2010	Difference
	Number of participants	859	182	
A	0–1 year	9%	5%	-4%
B	1–3 years	14%	2%	-12%
C	3–5 years	21%	11%	-10%
D	6 and longer	55%	82%	28%

More than half (55%) of the youth in Slavic churches had lived in America for more than six years in 2004. In 2010, the percentage of young people living in America more than six years increased significantly – up to 82%. Six years living in the new country is a significant period of time for young people. It is long enough for them to learn the language and to adapt to the culture. At the same time, six years is not long enough for older people to become fluent in the new language and to become comfortable with the new culture. This creates a challenging, sometimes even conflicting, situation between older and younger people in the church.

Questions 2. Are you a member of a church? If yes, which one?

Table 6.4.2.

		2004	2010	Difference
	Number of participants	859	182	
A	YES	60%	76%	16%
B	NO	37%	24%	-13%

More than half of the youth (60%) responded in 2004 that they were baptized members of the church. They had confessed Jesus Christ as their Lord and committed their lives to him. At the same time, about 40% of young people in PCSBA churches were not yet baptized. Since churches, according to the results of the survey discussed in the previous section of this chapter, are not working actively in the surrounding society to reach people with the good news, the young people in the church are the main target group for the churches' evangelistic efforts. In 2010, a higher percentage of young people answered that they were baptized. A total of 76% of them were members of the church, and 24% were not. This means that the group of people the Slavic churches are trying to reach with the gospel is getting smaller and smaller. The day will come when churches will not have people to baptize and their membership will start to decline.

Question 3. Your age?

Table 6.4.3.

		2004	2010	Difference
	Number of participants	859	182	
A	13–15	16%	18%	1%
B	16–18	35%	21%	-14%
C	19–21	22%	26%	4%
D	21 and older	25%	36%	11%

The largest age group (35%) among Slavic youth in 2004 was sixteen to eighteen years old. This is the age during which people often make important life decisions, including decisions regarding their relationship with God. This age group should receive special attention from church leaders in order to keep them in the church and to help them establish a close personal relationship with Christ. In 2010, the largest age group (36%) among youth, according to the survey, was twenty-one and older.

Questions 4–7 and their answers are available in the appendix for chapter 6.

Question 8. Should there be a sermon in English in Slavic churches?

Table 6.4.8.

		2004	2010	Difference
	Number of participants	859	182	
A	YES	59%	89%	30%
B	NO	35%	11%	-24%

The issue of a sermon in English being included in the Sunday service at Slavic churches is a hot one. Older generations in the Slavic churches painfully observe the fact that young people are becoming ever more comfortable with English than they are with Russian. Having sermons in English during Sunday services is taken by some older people as a clear sign of capitulation towards the American way of religious life. This, in their view, is unacceptable. The results of the survey show that many young people have a different view. In 2004, 59% of the respondents preferred a sermon in English to be included in the Sunday service of the Slavic church. At the same time, a significant number (31%) of the young people did not think this way. This shows that the process of acculturation is not taking place equally fast for different people, even among the youth. In 2010, the situation changed dramatically. The number of young people who saw the necessity of a sermon in English during Sunday services grew by 30% and reached 89%! Only 11% of the respondents in 2010 were not interested in a sermon in English at the Slavic church service. This correlates well with the length of stay in America of those who responded. According to the answers to Question #1, 5% had lived in America less than a year. A total of 2% had lived here for one to three years. And 11% had lived in the States three to five years. With a high degree of probability, it could be said that those who do not like to have a sermon in English are part of this group of young people who have lived in America less than five years.

The interesting fact is that in 2005, a significant number of members of the church boards in the PCSBA churches – 63.2% (see Question #26 in the previous part of the chapter) – saw the need of a sermon in English being preached during the Sunday services in Slavic churches. A total of 23.8% of church leaders had an opposite opinion at that time. However, five years later, in 2009, a lower number, 56.9%, of surveyed church board members believed in the necessity of a sermon in English, and 35.5% opposed this idea.

Question 9 and its answer are available in the appendix for chapter 6.

Question 10. Do you have any English-only-speaking friends that you would like to invite to your church?

Table 6.4.10.

		2004	2010	Difference
	Number of participants	859	182	
A	YES	55%	77%	22%
B	NO	41%	23%	-18%

More than half, 55%, in 2004 and 77% in 2010, of the surveyed young people have friends among the English-speaking youth whom they would want to invite to their church. This is where the great potential for local evangelism in Slavic immigrant churches lies. However, the Russian language used in the services creates a barrier for this to happen. At the same time, a very significant number, 41% in 2004, did not have any English-speaking friends to invite to the church. This is an indication that almost half of the Slavic youth lived in a certain isolation (at least they did not have close friends to invite to the church) from the rest of the American society at that time. This is a troubling sign. If a significant percentage of young people in the PCSBA churches are not communicating well with people outside of the Slavic community and do not share the gospel with them, then it is difficult to expect that these churches will fulfill the Great Commandment given to them by Jesus. It seems that the situation has changed during the next five years. Only 23% of surveyed young people answered that they do not have English-only speaking friends in 2010. This is still a significant number, but it is an improvement from how it was back in 2004. It is a positive development. This requires the church leadership to make important decisions regarding the place of the English language in the church service and church life.

Question 11 and its answer are available in the appendix for chapter 6.

Summary

According to the results of the survey, the majority of young people in churches of the PCSBA are between sixteen and twenty-one years of age.

More than half of them have been living in America for more than six years. Many of them are baptized believers. Most of them are students in junior high and high schools or are in college and university. Most of the time, young people are satisfied with the spiritual food they receive in Slavic churches. More than half of them prefer to have one or two sermons during the service. Many of them believe that the senior pastor should preach at least three times a month during the Sunday service. The majority want a sermon to be preached in English during the Sunday worship service. The majority would want to see a choir and a worship team participating in the Sunday service at the Slavic church. Many of them have English-speaking friends who they would want to invite to church. Only half are satisfied with the amount of time church leaders spend with them currently. Youth are still an integral part of Slavic immigrant churches. However, they are experiencing a strong influence from American society in general and from American churches in particular. This influence could be noticed in their perception of the church worship – how many times per week the senior pastor should preach, what kinds of music should be practiced in the church, and how many sermons should be preached during one Sunday service. These individuals are the main force for local evangelism to be carried out by Slavic immigrant churches. The fact that more than half of them have English-speaking friends and want to invite them to the church shows that these young people have a strong potential for participation in evangelistic work. However, an evangelistic vision, understanding of the context, guidance and support are required from leaders of Slavic immigrant churches in order to use this very valuable force – youth – fruitfully. The results of the surveys of church leaders provided in the previous part of this chapter indicate that few leaders have an evangelistic vision for the place where their churches are located, and not many of them understand well the immigrant context in terms of reaching local indigenous people with the gospel . This has created a challenging situation for churches. If the biblically based desire of young people is not matched by an evangelistic vision from the church leaders, then their support in the youth's efforts to bring people to the church will result in one of two scenarios: (1) when young people realize that the church is not interested in saving the souls of their friends and neighbors, they will leave the Slavic church and join an English-speaking church that is practicing evangelism; or (2) after realizing that the church does not want to make the effort to save their English-speaking friends and neighbors, the youth may abandon their evangelistic zeal and adjust their spiritual life to the regular attendance of church services, similar to the older generation in their church.

6.5. Survey of the Pacific Coast Slavic Baptist Association Churches on the Current Situation in Mission

This survey was conducted by the Mission Department, under supervision of the author of the current study, in October 2010. Sixteen PCSBA churches participated in the survey.

Question 1. How many missionaries have been supported by the surveyed churches in 2010?

Table 6.5.1.

	Geographical area	Number of missionaries	Percentage
A	In the former Soviet Union?	71	90%
B	In other countries of the world?	8	10%
C	Total	79	100%

Question 2. What is the approximate percentage of the total local church budget that is spent on its missionary ministry and how is it distributed?

Table 6.5.2.

A	Percentage of a total church budget spent on mission	19%
B	Supporting mission work overseas	80%
C	Local evangelistic ministry in America	20%

Question 3. How many people were baptized in the surveyed churches in the previous year (2009)?

Table 6.5.3.

A	Total number baptized people in surveyed churches	115	100%
B	Baptized Russian-speaking people coming from a non-church background (from the "world")	6	5%
C	Baptized non-Russian-speaking people	0	0%

Summary

This survey clearly indicates that the mission ministry priorities for Slavic immigrant churches are still focused on the former Soviet Union. As the survey shows, 90% of all missionaries from Slavic churches were supported in their former homeland. Only 10% are located in other countries. The survey also shows that churches were seeing mission work as an important ministry, investing in it a significant part of their budget – approximately 19%. At the same time, distribution of this money was not equally balanced. A total of 80% of the mission money is going back to the former Soviet Union republics to support missionaries there. Only 20% stayed in the States to support local evangelism. The results of such an unequal financial investment were reflected in the baptisms conducted by churches in 2009. Only 5% of the baptized came from Russian-speaking non-believing families (from the "world") and none of the baptized came from the English-speaking community. The vast majority of the baptized are children of the church members. Mainly "biologically" based growth is not healthy and cannot sustain the necessary quantitative and qualitative increase in church membership required in order for the congregation to maintain its membership size and to be healthy spiritually. Focusing primarily on evangelizing their own children is common for many immigrant churches and is not in accord with the way an authentic mission is supposed to be implemented. Although it is very important to bring our own children to Christ, the main focus of a church that tries to practice an authentic mission should be the world outside of the church. This is what leaders of Slavic immigrant churches have to recognize and teach to their constituency.

6.6. Survey of People Who Have Left a Russian-Speaking Congregation and Joined an English-Speaking Church

The mission work of Slavic immigrant churches could be undermined if church members start leaving these churches in order to attend English-speaking congregations. According to the report presented by the author of this study to the 74th Annual PCSBA Convention in October 2011, the total membership of the Association reached its peak in 2009 and began to slightly decline in 2010 and 2011. Two main reasons could be given for this fact. On the one hand, lately the number of immigrants arriving from the republics of the former USSR has dropped significantly. On the other hand, the number of people leaving Slavic churches and joining English-speaking churches is growing. This trend of switching membership from Slavic churches to English-speaking congregations could be especially damaging for the life and mission work of Slavic churches because it is usually young people who are leaving Slavic churches in order to join "the real American" churches. In order to understand this process better, to find the reasons that make people leave the church, and to learn how to prevent this, a survey was conducted from July to December of 2011. This was done among people who had already left Russian-speaking congregations and had established their membership in English-speaking churches. Eighty people responded to the invitation to participate in this survey. Most of them represent different churches and live in different cities. A total of 46% of the participants are male and 54% are female. Below is a table with answers to the question: What was/were the reason(s) for leaving the Slavic church?

Table 6.6.6.

1	The quality of sermons was not high enough	78.6%
2	Misdirected vision for the church in the new cultural and language context	56.3%
3	Sunday service experience was not satisfying enough	52.3%
4	Doctrinal position of the church was not clear	50.0%
5	Doctrinal position of the church did not fit my understanding of the Bible	42.5%
6	Lack/absence of evangelistic efforts toward the surrounding community	41.3%
7	Isolationism attitude among church members	38.8%
8	Lack of practical service opportunities for church members among local people (e.g. feeding the homeless, helping the poor, etc.)	32.5%
9	Isolationism attitude among church leadership	26.3%
10	Conflict with the leadership of the church	26.3%
11	Long Sunday services	16.3%
12	My personal limitation in understanding the Russian/Ukrainian language compared to English	11.3%
13	Other	1.3%

The answers to other questions of the survey are provided in the appendix for chapter 6, section 6.6. The results of this survey will be used in the analysis of hindrances to mission work provided in chapter 8.

6.7. Review of the Methods and Organizational Models of Missionary Work Used by PCSBA Churches

In order to review the current methods and organizational models of missionary work used by PCSBA churches, the annual conference reports were used. These reports are good, primary sources for information about overall activities that PCSBA churches support. Based on the 73rd Annual Convention (21–23 October 2010) report, currently nineteen different departments are part of the association. Among them the following PCSBA departments could be identified as those that are called to implement an authentic mission directly through their ministry.

1. Mission Department. Delegates of the 60th Annual Convention established a Missionary Fund in November 1997 in order to provide financial support to Christian workers in the former Soviet Union.[5] When candidates were selected for such support, special emphasis was given to "white" areas of the former USSR – territories where no or very few Christians live. Over several years, the number of native missionaries supported through this fund has risen to ten long-term missionaries in the field.

In 2003, the Missionary Fund was reorganized into the Missions Department. The Leadership Board of the association created a part-time paid position for the director of this department. The mission of this department is creating a mission-focused culture in PCSBA churches, building a vision and developing a strategy for short-term and long-term mission ministry, maintaining awareness in churches about needs on the mission field and progress in mission projects, developing partnership relations with other mission organizations, and providing care for the long-term missionaries supported by the PCSBA.[6]

2. Power in Truth. This is a youth mission organization. It is part of the Mission Department. Its focus is on promoting, organizing, and coordinating short-term mission trips. Although these trips are predominantly directed towards republics of the former USSR, some teams have gone to such countries as Mexico, Israel, Portugal, Italy, Greece, Spain, and Haiti. Participants of these mission trips are mostly young people from seventeen to twenty-two years of age. They raise funds for the trip during the year by themselves, working extra hours at jobs they hold, doing car-washes and collecting donations, making and selling cookies at churches, or whatever they can do to generate funds. Usually, short-term trips take place during the summer and winter, when colleges and universities release their students for breaks. According to the report given by Power in Truth to the 73rd Convention, nine teams went on mission trips in the winter of 2009–2010 and twenty-two teams during the summer of 2010. These teams of young

---

5. "Minutes of the 60th PCSBA Convention (1997)," PCSBA Archive, Sacramento, CA.
6. *Almanac for the PCSBA 75th Convention* (Sacramento, CA: PCSBA, 2012), 12.

people, in the places of their short-term ministry, are participating in children and youth camps, visiting orphanages and distributing humanitarian aid, participating and assisting in evangelistic crusades, and other various missionary activities.

3. *Youth Ministry Department.* According to the archival documents, the leaders of the association have always paid special attention to the youth in their churches. Young people have been encouraged to take an active part in church life and evangelism. During the 33rd Convention in November 1970 in Sacramento, California, the leader of Youth Ministry of the association reported to the delegates that 100 young people are involved in this ministry. They live in harmony with the older leaders of the churches and participate in church ministry. The youth choir "Bethany" has recorded songs to be used in radio programs.[7] After 1990, the Youth Ministry began to grow rapidly. In 2004, more than 2,000 youth attended churches of the association. The Youth Ministry department organizes conferences for the youth, youth camps, and recreational activities, and young people are actively involved in mission.[8] Short-term mission trips to the homeland have become a very important part of youth life. During the summer of 2005 alone, the youth of the association participated in more than forty camps in the former Soviet Union. More than 2,500 children and young people were served. Youth are also concerned with local evangelism in the USA and try to take the first steps in making it happen.

4. *Women's Ministry Department.* Historically, the Women's Ministry of the association has been active in supporting mission work and in sending humanitarian aid abroad. As a department, this ministry was organized during the 33rd Convention in November 1970. Helping orphanages in Latin America is one of the long-lasting projects of the association in which women in PCSBA churches have been actively involved. Different churches have sent their support to this region. One of the examples is a church in Fresno which has supported an orphanage in Argentina.[9] As a result of

---

7. Adolf Pichaj, "70-tiletniy Yubiley Ob'edineniya Slavyanskikh Baptistov Tikhookeanskogo Poberezh'ya" ["Seventieth Jubilee of The Pacific Coast Slavic Baptist Association"], *Vestnik Obyedineniya* 3 (Dec 1998): 5.

8. *Almanac for the PCSBA 75th Convention*, 26.

9. Pichaj, "70-tiletniy Yubiley," 6.

the new immigrants arriving since 1990, women's ministry has expanded significantly. Almost every church of the association has an active women's ministry committee. The Women's Ministry department organizes regional conferences for women, encourages women in churches to support their husbands in ministry, makes arrangements for sending humanitarian aid to needy people in the homeland, and raises funds to support missionaries.[10]

5. *Newspaper Our Days.* Already published for forty-six years, this weekly newspaper is designed to be evangelistic in nature. The goal is to share the gospel with Russian-speaking people around the globe. Some 10,000 copies are sent to forty countries every week. There are around 4,600 subscribers of this newsletter in the USA.[11] Often, believers in America are paying for subscriptions for their friends, relatives, or churches in their homeland. A copy of *Our Days* is sent to them directly. It is an effective evangelistic tool, reaching people around the world with articles and other printed materials on spiritual subjects. Many people testify that this newspaper became a leading source for their knowledge of Christ and Christianity and influenced their decision to accept Christ as their personal Savior.

6. *Radio Ministry.* The PCSBA provides financial support to a radio ministry based in Sacramento at the First Slavic Baptist Church. Programs developed at the Sacramento radio studio are broadcast in Sacramento and in the former Soviet Union, as well. According to the annual report of this ministry, 113 programs, each thirty minutes long, were prepared and broadcast during the year.[12] This ministry is an effective method for bringing the good news to people in different areas of the world. Many letters come to the studio, expressing appreciation for the ministry and testifying about the life-changing experience people have had because of the PCSBA radio ministry.

7. *Prison Ministry.* This ministry has existed for only a few years and is financed by PCSBA churches. According to the report for 2012, eighty-six prison visits were conducted by participants in this ministry during the reported year.[13] When visiting prisons, Slavic believers try to find

---

10. *Almanac for the PCSBA 75th Convention*, 13.
11. Ibid., 25.
12. Ibid., 19.
13. Ibid., 24.

Russian-speaking inmates first and minister to them by witnessing about Christ. However, they do not limit themselves to only Russian-speaking inmates. They preach the gospel to other people there with translations from Russian into English. Heartbreaking testimonies are shared with churches by those who are involved in this ministry.

8. Department of Mercy. This department was established to provide timely material help to people in need. The PCSBA Board constantly receives requests for financial and humanitarian help. The Department of Mercy is responsible for investigating the need and providing appropriate help based on funds available.[14] Also, this department is called to encourage churches to be involved in providing humanitarian and financial help to people who are struggling because of natural disasters, catastrophes, wars, or other reasons. This department organizes relief efforts in response to such gigantic catastrophes as earthquakes in China and Japan, and for personal tragedies such as losing a house because of fire. In most cases, such relief help is directed to the former Soviet Union. Clearly, such help is provided in the name of Christ as part of the implementation of this aspect of authentic mission as social action/*diaconia*.

9. Department of Ministry to Widows, Orphans and the Lonely. This department was established a few years ago. Its ministry is focused on a very specific group of people – widows, orphans, and lonely people.[15] Often, people going through the tragedy of losing a loved one find themselves on the brink of losing faith and trust in God. Often, timely loving counsel and support can prevent a person from making a wrong step, can help children to stay on the right way in their life, and can encourage a lonely person to trust the Lord and find personal comfort in serving others. Clearly, this ministry is a social action/*diaconia* aspect of authentic mission.

10. Social Aspects of Mission in the PCSBA. The results of surveys of Slavic immigrant Baptist church leaders show that social actions conducted locally among English-speaking people are not very common among Slavic Baptist immigrant churches. At the same time, this does not mean that such kinds of actions are not taking place at all. Examples of such kinds of actions

---

14. Ibid., 21.
15. Ibid., 17.

practiced by the Russian-speaking Baptist churches in America listed below show that these churches see these actions as very important.

People of the Slavic Baptist diaspora in the US are very sensitive to needs of people in their homeland. Shortly after arriving in the USA, Slavic Baptists started sending financial support and humanitarian aid to the former Soviet Union. The remittances from the Russian-speaking Christians in the US flow steadily to their former homeland.[16] They go to individuals and families, as well as to organizations such as orphanages, hospitals, rehabilitation centers for alcohol and drug addicts, senior centers, care centers for disabled people and other institutions. This help is provided either on a personal level by individuals or as centralized actions organized by the local immigrant congregations. Funds are raised through designated love offerings in churches or through preparing and selling food to their members after services. Clothes, imperishable food, and different supplies are donated by members of Slavic churches and shipped to the former Soviet Union in cargo containers. Inside the republics of the former USSR, the process of receiving and distribution of humanitarian and financial aid usually is coordinated not by government agencies but by the local churches. Because of this it reaches the neediest people there.

Slavic Baptist immigrants in America are extending a helping hand not only to the poor at their homeland but to other countries as well. During the last several years a new mission field has been explored by the Russian-speaking immigrant churches. This field is Mexico. The close proximity of Mexico to the USA makes it convenient for believers from Slavic churches in California to travel to this country and see how great the need is there. PCSBA churches are providing humanitarian aid to poor people in this country. Financial help is provided in building church facilities in Mexico.[17] Also, teams of Russian-speaking volunteers are traveling to Mexico to participate in construction of houses of prayer as well as houses for people who currently live in slums. Another non-Russian-speaking country where Slavic

---

16. This statement is based on the author's personal observation during many years of ministry among Russian-speaking churches in the US and in conversations with Slavic church leaders on both sides in America and the former Soviet Union. The church leaders in the former USSR are very grateful for financial and humanitarian aid.

17. *Annual Report of the PCSBA Leadership Board for 2007–2008* (Sacramento, CA: PCSBA, 2008), 19.

immigrant churches are involved is Haiti. After the earthquake there, PCSBA churches collected funds to provide humanitarian aid for the victims of this tragic event. A group of PCSBA leaders together with several nurses from Slavic immigrant churches traveled to Haiti and stayed there for a week distributing humanitarian aid and providing medical help to poor people.[18]

In America, the Slavic Baptist churches are practicing social actions among Russian-speaking people. As it was stated earlier, the Department of Mercy and the Department of Women's ministry of the PCSBA organize actions designed to provide moral, spiritual and material support to widows and orphans within the Slavic community. Also, occasionally financial aid is provided to people in the immigrant churches who find themselves in challenging financial situations because of illness, loss of loved ones, unemployment, auto accidents, and other unfortunate circumstances. Funds for such help may be raised by one local congregation or by the joint efforts of a few congregations or even through participation of many Slavic immigrant churches across the country. It depends on how great the need is and how well the need is announced within the Slavic immigrant community nationwide.

In addition to providing financial help to each other, Slavic Baptist immigrant churches are making efforts to address one of the social problems common to the American society today which is alcohol and drug addiction. Slavic Baptist immigrant churches in Sacramento have organized a rehabilitation center, Redemption House, for drug addicts. Unfortunately, quite a few Russian-speaking people in America, mostly the youth, became victims of drug addiction. In order to help them to get out of this dependency, Redemption House was organized in 2006.[19] This ministry is financially supported by PCSBA churches. Volunteers serving at the center also come mostly from these churches. This ministry is one of the ways for the PSCBA churches to be involved in social action.

These examples of social actions show clear evidence of the strong desire among Slavic Baptist immigrant churches to provide help to the poor and disadvantaged in their former homeland, as well as in other countries

---

18. *Almanac for the PCSBA 74th Convention*, 10.
19. *Annual Report of the PCSBA Leadership Board for 2007–2008*, 32.

including their new homeland – America. It shows that these churches see the mission of the church not only as evangelism, but also in addressing physical needs of people. It could be concluded that these churches are open to a holistic view of the mission of the church. Of course, they see helping people to reconcile with God as a primary task of the church. However, next to this task is helping the poor, marginalized, and disadvantaged. Examples of such actions listed above show that the Slavic Baptist immigrant churches are trying to practice the holistic mission as much as they can in their circumstances. Of course, the holistic mission as it was shown in chapter 2 of this thesis includes other aspects in addition to evangelism and social action/*diaconia*. These other aspects should be a subject of a different study. However, information provided above allows the author to make a conclusion that the holistic mission view is acceptable to PCSBA churches. The only concern is that this mission is not yet widely practiced by these churches among English-speaking people in America.

Summary

The review of the different mission-related ministries conducted by PCSBA churches shows that these ministries cover a wide spectrum of mission needs, from evangelism to social services. However, most of these ministries are focused on Russian-speaking people either in America or in other countries around the world, or back in the homeland, Russia. What is lacking is evangelism and social service/*diaconia* provided to non-Russian-speaking people in America where PCSBA churches are now located. This situation reflects the natural attitude of the older generation of immigrants towards their homeland – positive – and towards people of the country in which they now live – indifferent or even negative. This is an unhealthy situation for churches. By ignoring their responsibility to reach people in their new "Jerusalem," which is America, churches are not fulfilling this important part of the Great Commission given to them by Christ. In addition, focusing mission efforts only on Russian-speaking people discourages English-speaking people from joining Slavic churches, which could eventually lead to significant membership decline.

6.8. Conclusion for Chapter 6

In this chapter, the results of the following surveys and other studies were represented and discussed: a demographic study of newly baptized believers in PCSBA churches; an analysis of the percentage of mission-related spending in selected church budgets; a survey of Slavic pastors and other church leaders regarding their views on church mission in the immigrant context; a survey of the youth in PCSBA churches regarding their views of immigrant churches; a survey of the current church mission situation; and a review of the methods and organizational models of missionary work currently used by PCSBA churches. The purpose of collecting this data was to provide needed information for evaluating the authenticity and contextuality of mission work currently done by Slavic Baptist immigrant churches and for developing practical recommendations for further improving of mission work in these churches. This evaluation is done in chapter 9 and recommendations are provided in chapter 10.

In order to do a reasonable evaluation of the situation with the mission work in PCSBA churches, in addition to obtaining empirical data about their mission work, it is important to understand the psychological and emotional feelings the members of these churches have experienced as the result of the social challenges they are facing as recent immigrants. The following chapter explores these challenges and feelings immigrants experience and how they impact the immigrants' mission work.

CHAPTER 7

Social Challenges of Immigrant Life for the Slavic Baptist Diaspora and Their Impact on the Mission of the Church

In chapter 3 of this study, it was shown that it is very important to understand the context in which the mission work of the church is conducted in order to make it contextually appropriate. One of the contexts is the personal circumstances of the person who shares the gospel with others. In order to make a well-rounded evaluation of the mission work of PCSBA churches, it is important to understand this component of their mission context. What members of these churches experience as new immigrants impacts their deep emotions and attitudes towards the surrounding community and eventually their mission work among this community. This chapter consists of an analysis of social challenges that immigrants are facing, and how these challenges affect the willingness of recent Christian immigrants to share their faith with and to serve the people in the receiving society. Also, other factors of immigrant life that impact the mission work of Christian immigrants are explored. In this chapter, author argues that there are natural forces of a psychological and sociological nature that keep immigrants from active participation in mission work among the native people of their new country.

7.1. Common Emotional and Psychological Experiences of Immigrants and Authentic Mission

Despite the fact that immigrants belong to different ethnic groups and come from different countries, most immigrants share certain common emotional and psychological experiences when they settle in a new country.[1] Of course, certain experiences are unique to specific groups. Also, it is important to note that the experience of first-generation immigrants is different from the second generation's experience. Because the vast majority of immigrants in PCSBA churches currently belong to the first generation, and in most cases they hold key leadership roles in these churches, this part of the chapter will refer mainly to the experiences of first-generation immigrants. The views of this group of first-generation immigrants determine, to a high degree, the direction of PCSBA church development and how authentic is the mission implemented by these churches. The views of these church leaders are particularly affected by the psychological and emotional experiences they have gone through and are now going through as immigrants.

Oscar Handlin, in his classic study of immigration, points to the fact that emigration is the central experience of many people, and includes "broken homes, interruptions of a familiar life, separation from known surroundings, the becoming a foreigner and ceasing to belong. These are the aspects of alienation; and seen from the perspective of the individual received rather than of the receiving society, the history of immigration is a history of alienation and its consequences."[2] Thomas C. Wheeler describes the immigrant experience in the following way: "For the America of freedom has been an America of sacrifice, and the cost of becoming American has been high. For every freedom won, a tradition lost. For every second generation assimilated, a first generation in one way or another spurned. For the gains of goods and services, the identity lost, and uncertainty found."[3]

---

1. Brian M. Howell provides the following concise description of the new immigrants' experience as a mission context in the US: "Immigrant groups to North America arrive with particular traditions, world views, practices, and family norms of their homeland – the classic stuff of culture. Upon arriving, however, they find themselves in new relations of economic and racial inequality, changing generational norms, and shifting family dynamics. Younger generations seeking assimilation, along with women and men of the first generation dealing with role loss, changing gender expectations and norms, and unfamiliar racial and ethnic hierarchies, find themselves practicing some familiar customs, but with radically new meanings" ("Multiculturalism, Immigration and the North American Church: Rethinking Contextualization," *Missiology* 39, no. 1 [Jan 2011], 81).

2. Oscar Handlin, *The Uprooted* (Boston,: Little, Brown, 1951), 4.

3. Thomas C. Wheeler, ed., *The Immigrant Experience: The Anguish of Becoming American* (Baltimore, MD: Pelican, 1972), 1.

Zalman I. Levin, in his systematic and socio-cultural analysis of immigrant groups, states that life in diaspora is a unique experience. Immigrants came to a foreign, often hostile world, with its different lifestyle, traditions, understandings of what is good and what is evil, and unique views on the ways of solving life's problems. Usually immigrants, with some small exceptions, feel themselves lost and uprooted in the new world. They have lost the environment that they were accustomed to and the norms of relationships between people. They have to accept the change in their social status, as well as the unavoidable limitations in food, social contacts, and conducting of religious rituals.[4]

Susan Wiley Hardwick, addressing difficulties in the adjustment process experienced by immigrants, states, "There can be no doubt that the experience of leaving one's homeland and adjusting to a new place can be extremely stressful. Feelings of uprootedness and vulnerability, a sudden disconnection with homeland, friends, and family, and the difficulties of adjusting to a new place are only a few of the problems faced by refugees."[5] Hardwick also points to the language barrier, along with economic and cultural differences, as the major challenges in the adjustment process.[6] This is a universal experience for immigrants of all ethnic groups.[7]

Adrian Furnham and Stephen Bochner, in their comprehensive study of the psychological consequences of exposure to unfamiliar cultural environments, point to two opposite assumptions related to this subject. One assumption supports experiencing a second culture as beneficial because "such exposure is said to broaden one's perspective, promote personality growth and provide insight into the culture of origin through a contrast

---

4. Zalman I. Levin, *Mentality of Diaspora: Systematic and Socio-cultural Analysis* (Moscow: Kraft, 2001), 8.

5. Susan Wiley Hardwick, *Russian Refuge: Religion, Migration, and Settlement on the North American Pacific Rim* (Chicago: University of Chicago Press, 1993), 156.

6. Ibid., 158.

7. Miguel A. Palomino, addressing Latino immigration in Europe, describes the immigrants' experience in the following way: "These men and women suffer a traumatic uprooting experience in leaving their homeland, with all its social and affective bonds. They must enter a foreign culture, where they will have to adapt themselves to a new language, another legal identity, and new ways of relationship, as well as new food, music, transportation, finance, and lots more" ("Latino Immigration in Europe: Challenge and Opportunity for Mission," *The International Bulletin of Missionary Research* 28, no. 2 [Apr 2004], 56).

with other world-views."⁸ The opposing point of view is that "exposure to an unfamiliar culture may be, and often is, stressful and hence potentially harmful. Rather than expanding the mind and providing a satisfying and interesting personal experience, the hypothesis states that unfamiliar environments create anxiety, confusion and depression in individuals so exposed. In extreme cases, physical illness may be a direct consequence. Rather than creating better mutual understanding, culture contact often leads to hostility and poor interpersonal relations among those involved in the interchange."⁹

The list of opinions among different authors on the subject of the immigrants' experience could continue. However, the views already presented in this part of the chapter show that there is almost a consensus among those who are studying the subject of cross-cultural encounters and immigration issues on the subject of the immigrants' experience: almost all agree that this experience is usually difficult and challenging. The most common aspects of the immigrant experience are culture shock, language barrier, attachment to homeland, separation from known surroundings, becoming a foreigner, ceasing to belong, uprootedness, vulnerability, and confrontation with American religious pluralism. Analysis of these aspects of immigrant experience is provided in the appendix for chapter 7. All these negative experiences of immigrants are powerful natural forces pushing immigrants into isolation from the surrounding society and effectively blocking Christian immigrants (at least, representatives of the first generation) from enthusiastic implementation of such aspects of authentic mission as evangelism and social action/*diaconia* directed towards the native local people.

7.2. Cross-Cultural-Encounter Influencing Factors

Several observations made by A. Furnham, S. Bochner, M. Winkelman, and other researchers in the field of cross-cultural experience are applicable to this study and are discussed below.

---

8. Adrian Furnham and Stephen Bochner, *Culture Shock: Psychological Reactions to Unfamiliar Environments* (New York: Methuen, 1986), 3.

9. Ibid., 4.

7.2.1. Reciprocal Consequences of Cross-Cultural Encounters

Furnham and Bochner, in their study of cross-cultural encounters, emphasize "that all contacts have two-way reciprocal consequences, although the extent to which each party is affected by the interaction depends on a variety of factors."[10] This shows that immigrants have a role in shaping the society in which they are now a part. Even without intentional efforts to do such shaping, they make an impact on the receiving society by their everyday presence within this society.[11] It could be positive or negative, or both. If Christian immigrants had the courage to take responsibility for the kind of influence they are making on the rest of society, and became more intentional and strategic in doing this, they could make a considerable difference in the lives of the people around them. This is what Jehu J. Hanciles is hoping for.[12] Unfortunately, as was illustrated by the results of the surveys of church leaders presented in chapter 6 of this study, what is common today for PCSBA churches is indifference to the spiritual, economic, and social conditions of the people around them. Of course, this is contrary to understanding authentic mission. Authentic mission would encourage Slavic immigrant churches to become involved in local ministry, addressing the needs of poor and marginalized people in their area. Unfortunately, new Slavic evangelical Christian immigrants are often preoccupied with their own needs, thinking that their economic situation is the worst in comparison to that of other people. However, in reality, many indigenous people live in much worse conditions. As was mentioned in chapter 5, most Slavic immigrant believers are eligible for public financial assistance because they entered the country with refugee status. Many immigrants of other ethnic groups are not eligible for such kinds of assistance. Some of them are in this country illegally and are experiencing great struggles. By not paying attention to their needs and by not helping them, PCSBA churches are missing an opportunity to make

---

10. Ibid., 11.

11. For similar line of thought, see Lina Andronovienė and Parush R. Parushev, "Church, State, and Culture: On the Complexities of Post-Soviet Evangelical Social Involvement," *Theological Reflections: EAAA Journal of Theology* 3 (2004): 208–209.

12. Jehu J. Hanciles, *Beyond Christendom: Globalization, African Migration, and the Transformation of the West* (Maryknoll, NY: Orbis, 2008), 297.

a positive impact on the receiving American society, and as a result, they are not implementing authentic mission locally.

7.2.2. Impact of the Homogeneity/Heterogeneity of the Society on the Immigrant's Experience

Furnham and Bochner state that the outcome of a cross-cultural encounter for the newcomer could depend on the homogeneity/heterogeneity of the society she/he is entering. They believe that "it would be reasonable to predict that in highly heterogeneous societies ethnic identity is regarded as trivial, since being different is not unusual and hence is unremarkable. On the other hand, it could also be argued that in such societies people develop a high degree of sensitivity to their own and the others' cultural membership."[13] This observation is very important. Most churches of the Pacific Coast Slavic Baptist Association are located in California. Since California is the most ethnically diverse state in the US, it is correct to assume, based on the statement above, that people in California are much more accustomed to sharing life with different ethnic groups, and, because of this, they are more receptive and more sensitive to other cultures. It leads to the conclusion that the new Slavic immigrants in California are in a more favorable position compared with those in other states in the US or in other countries in terms of how they are treated by native people and what kind of experiences they have as a result of the cross-cultural encounter. Such favorable conditions make the lives of the new Slavic immigrants in California easier than in other states. At the same time, these less challenging conditions play a negative role in the process of the adaptation of immigrants here because they do not force immigrants to work hard in order to overcome, as much as possible, the cultural differences they have with people in the receiving society. This keeps them separated from the rest of the local people, and negatively influences their ability to address the spiritual and other needs of these people. It slows down the process of preparing them to do authentic mission in the new immigrant context.

---

13. Furnham and Bochner, *Culture Shock*, 20.

7.2.3. Impact of the Degree of Difference between Societies

Furnham and Bochner, as well as Winkelman, argue that the degree of difference between the society the person is coming from and the society that the person is entering also affects the cross-cultural experience of this person. The difference could be in climate, geography, economic resources, and socio-cultural patterns. The authors refer to their prior study of the experiences of foreign students attending English universities. The results of this study show "that as the distance between the culture of origin and the host society increased, so did the social difficulty of the students."[14] Applying this observation to Slavic evangelical immigrants, it could be suggested that they are coming from a culture (or, more accurately, cultures, since the former USSR was culturally a very diverse country) that is different from American culture in many ways. Of course, these differences are not as strong as for people coming from some other countries, such as Asian cultures (Hmong, Khmu, and others). Still, the differences exist and they create difficulties in the cross-cultural encounter for immigrants from the former USSR. In addition to general differences between Soviet and American cultures, it is important to remember that political and social life is very different in these two countries. Coming from a mostly authoritarian political system to a free democratic society provides Slavic immigrants with an additional challenge in adaptation. The challenge is not only to learn how the political aspect of American life functions, but also how the church fits into society in general, and to the political life in particular. Coming from an environment where the church was not officially recognized in public life, and where the evangelical expression of Christianity was historically almost always oppressed or persecuted, Slavic evangelical Christians in America have a long way to go if they are to understand their new role as a church in the American context. This is also true when attempting to understand how they can practically fulfill an authentic mission in the new political context. Inherited from many years of oppression and severe persecution, political and social indifference has characterized Soviet evangelical Christians in the past. This indifference has been carried on to the new country. It has become even stronger here because of the natural feelings of alienation that immigrants experience in

---

14. Ibid., 20.

the new land. Hard work to overcome this indifference towards political and social life, in addition to overcoming the cultural differences, is required from evangelical immigrants from the former USSR in order to be able to implement an authentic mission in America.

7.2.4. Impact of the Visible Characteristics of Cultural Groups

Furnham and Bochner point to the fact that the visible characteristics that distinguish different cultural groups, such as race, skin color, language, accent, and religion, all bring to the minds of people in the receiving society and newcomers "a categorization of the participants into an 'us' versus 'them' classification, which in turn colours any interaction between persons so categorized. Usually, once the categorization has been made, it leads to some form of discriminatory behavior in favour of those people classified as belonging to the in-group."[15] When it comes to the Slavic immigrants in America, the most distinctive characteristic that makes them different from people in the receiving society is clearly the language. The vast majority of the newcomers do not know much English. This is especially true for the evangelical Christians.[16] It puts them immediately into the "them" category. Later, when time passes, they learn English. However, it does not matter how good their English becomes, as they usually still have an accent. Of course, this does not apply to children who grow up in America. The accent keeps the first generation of adult immigrants in the "them" category for almost all of their lives. It affects their experience in cross-cultural encounters. It does not necessarily provoke hostile relations towards them from other people in the receiving society, although in certain situations this could be the case. What is more common is the distancing of relationships between immigrants and native people because of the "them" versus "us" factor. Often, friendly relationships do not mean really close relations between Slavic immigrants and American native people.

---

15. Ibid., 23.

16. During the Soviet times, evangelicals in the USSR were not permitted to travel abroad. They were denied visas. Because of this fact evangelicals did not have an opportunity to practice English or other foreign language even they studied it in school as part of their curriculum. Also, evangelicals were denied admission to the universities. This prevented them from an advanced studying of English.

Race and skin color are other visible characteristics that distinguish different cultural groups. Slavic immigrants are predominantly Caucasians. A significant part of the American population is Caucasian as well. Because of this, Slavic immigrants are not the subject of prejudice based on their skin color or race. Further, they have a similar religious faith to many people in the United States. Slavic evangelical immigrants fit well (at least by the name of their denomination, not necessarily by their theology and ecclesiology) into the mainstream evangelical Christianity of America. These last characteristics (skin color, race, and religion) do not create barriers between Slavic evangelical newcomers and native people. This provides them with a favorable environment for practicing an authentic mission among people in the receiving society. At the same time, the language barrier is a challenge they face from the time they arrive in America, and for some of them, through their whole lives.

7.3. Diaspora vs. Receiving Society Relations and Mission

The impact of immigrants on the receiving society is a subject of endless discussions among politicians, sociologists, government officials, businessmen, and others, in all countries that attract immigrants, both legal and illegal. George M. Szabad[17] and Gary E. Rubin,[18] addressing this issue, state, "Immigrants have a widespread impact on the entire society. They affect the economy, social life, intergroup relations, and values of their new homeland. That is why immigration specialists are increasingly turning to the study of the acculturation, the process by which newcomers adapt to – and help shape – American society. In this process, the immigrant's culture and the American culture come into contact and influence each other, with neither disappearing in the encounter."[19] It is assumed that immigrants are shaping the religious life of the receiving society as well. This current study is

---

17. George M. Szabad is the Chairman of the American Jewish Committee's Task Force on the acculturation of immigrants to American life.

18. Gary E. Rubin is the Director of National Affairs for the American Jewish Committee.

19. George M. Szabad and Gary E. Rubin, *The Newest Americans: Report of the American Jewish Committee's Task Force on the Acculturation of Immigrants to American Life in Immigration and Ethnicity* (Westport, CN: Greenwood Press, 1992), 281.

an attempt to find out what impact the particular immigrant group Slavic Baptists are making on American society through implementing such aspects of an authentic mission as evangelism and social action/*diaconia*. It can be assumed that the willingness and the ability of immigrants to implement authentic mission among the people of the new homeland depend, to a high degree, on their level of adaptation in the new society and their acculturation to American life.[20] According to Levin, the adaptation of an immigrant is not an isolated process in which only the individual person participates. This process takes place in the context of the immigrant community, and depends very much on the way this community is developing and on its adaptation to the new life conditions. Levin insists that the influence of the immigrant community (diaspora) on an individual who is part of this community, in terms of his adaptation in the new country, is very significant. Even more so, an immigrant is a product of the diaspora's influence. The immigrant's adaptation is not the result of the direct impact of the receiving society on him or her. The receiving society influences the individual immigrant through influencing the diaspora's mentality, and then the diaspora's mentality shapes the process of the adaptation of the individual.[21] When this issue is addressed in the church community context, it can be said that the influence of the church on the process of personal adaptation of its members is very strong. This means that understanding the relationship between the immigrant community (diaspora) and the receiving society is very important for developing a correct understanding of the process of personal adaptation

---

20. Stephanie Kotin refers to the views of many researchers that the term "segmented assimilation" is a more appropriate model for immigration today. In this model, immigrants preserve their own values and keep connected with the homeland and, at the same time, practice selected assimilation to the American culture. According to Kotin, "Under this model, religion has multiple social roles, and they are not contradictory in an era of global connectedness . . . , since the mid-1960s, churches, temples, mosques, synagogues and other faith-based organizations, as well as community-based organizations that build on the religious affiliations of their members, have expanded their roles for many immigrants and their children as they become instruments to mediate between the country of origin and the country of residence, serving as one of the most important points of reference for individuals as they create multicultural identities" ("Immigration and Integration: Religious and Political Activism for/with Immigrants in Los Angeles," *Progress in Development Studies* 11, no. 4 [July 2011]: 268).

21. Levin, *Mentality of Diaspora*, 80.

of immigrants in general, and Christian immigrants in particular. This helps in understanding their ability to implement authentic mission.

As Levin states, an immigrant community as an ethno-social group is a foreign object for the receiving society.[22] Consciously or unconsciously, the receiving society tries to push the immigrant community out of its midst or, at least, it tries to isolate it, and usually makes the immigrant community serve the interests of the receiving society. It forces "aliens" to act in a certain way.[23] A clash takes place between an immigrant community and the receiving society. It is important to notice that the perception of immigrants by the general public is not founded on an understanding of the historical relations between the US and the countries of origin, nor on the knowledge of the economic and social forces driving the immigration process. According to Portes and Rumbaut, "The public view is guided instead by surface impressions. When foreign accents and faces are few, they are ignored. However, when they grow in number and concentrate in visible spaces, they trigger increasing apprehension. Natives are put on the defensive, fearing that their way of life and their control of the levers of political and economic power will be lost to the newcomers."[24] Because of this, it can be concluded that the size of the diaspora affects how natives respond to its presence among them. If the number of immigrants is significant, it creates unpleasant feelings towards them from the native people. On the other hand, if the number is small, the indigenous people may be indifferent or even sympathetic towards immigrants. This is what is observed in the case of Slavic immigrants from the former Soviet Union. They are not always welcomed by the local people in areas where a significant number of them are settled. They certainly feel suspicion and unkind attitudes directed toward them. At the same time, in cities where only a handful of them reside, Slavic people are usually treated well and considered as a very special people who represent the former and now defeated Soviet empire.[25]

---

22. Ibid., 24.

23. Ibid.

24. Alejandro Portes and Ruben G. Rumbaut, *Immigrant America: A Portrait* (Berkeley and Los Angeles, CA: University of California Press, 2006), 346.

25. For many years the author of this study has observed this situation, visiting different Slavic immigrant churches located in different cities of the US. For example, the local native people of Sacramento, CA, are not very appreciative of the fact that there are very many

According to Levin, the decisive factor for the survival of a diaspora is the social environment in which it finds itself. This environment can be favorable or unfavorable.[26] If the receiving society is welcoming to the individual immigrant and encourages her/his adaptation, the social environment is unfavorable for the diaspora. It undermines the unity of the immigrant community and creates conditions for quick dissolution of the diaspora because individual immigrants assimilate with the receiving society easily. The opposite situation arises when the receiving society is not very open to accepting the individual immigrant, and does not help her/him in the process of adaptation. In response, an immigrant tries to find support and comfort from the diaspora. The more difficult the life experiences, the more important connections with the diaspora are for the immigrant.[27] As a result,

> The unity of the community is growing, the ghetto syndrome, isolation of the Diaspora is growing. The specific ethno-racial elements of this group are preserving in the Diaspora mentality. The stronger discrimination and prejudices, the more united the community becomes, the less process of adaptation is advanced: in the Diaspora, the protection mechanism in the immigrant's fight for survival is activating, the process of the community erosion is slowing down, as well as decreasing the cultural distance between an immigrant and his social environment. The immigrant's sense of belonging to the community life is growing.[28]

Based on this, it could be suggested that the Slavic evangelical diaspora is more stable and long lasting in cities where its population is higher. In cities with a small number of Slavic people, the diaspora does not last long. This conclusion is supported by what is observed among Slavic Baptist churches in the US today. In cities with a large number of Russian/Ukrainian-speaking Christians, Slavic churches are able to keep their membership high. At the

---

immigrants from the former Soviet Union – more than 100,000. At the same time, in Fresno, a city 170 miles south of Sacramento, where only a few hundred recent Slavic immigrants live, they are welcomed and appreciated.

26. Levin, *Mentality of Diaspora*, 28.
27. Ibid.
28. Ibid.

same time, in cities with a small number of Slavic evangelicals, the membership of Slavic churches is declining. The unfortunate fact, in relation to the local mission work of PCSBA churches, is that with the disappearance of smaller churches, the effectiveness of local mission is declining significantly due to the fact that PCSBA churches with a smaller membership are more effective in local mission work than churches with a large membership. This was demonstrated in chapter 6, section 6.1.[29]

In the case of the Slavic Baptist diaspora in America today, it can be concluded that the receiving society is, in general, welcoming to the individual Russian immigrant. Russians are Caucasians, educated at least to high-school level, and learn quickly how to survive in the new environment. They usually have not experienced significant discrimination in the US, especially since the end of the Cold War. The high number of them in certain areas could create some negative attitudes towards them among the native people. However, this is offset by the positive attitude towards them in areas with small numbers. This means that American society is unfavorable to the diaspora as a separate entity. Welcoming individual Russians to its midst undermines the Russian diaspora in general, and Russian-speaking church congregations in particular. Of course, church congregations are stronger than the diaspora because their members have much more in common with each other; that is what keeps them together, rather than members of the diaspora in general. Despite this, churches also are experiencing the destructive influence of the receiving society. At a certain point of their adaptation, some individual members of the Russian-speaking congregations, especially representatives of the younger generation, start leaning towards indigenous American churches more than to their own ethnic church. Eventually, some of them leave the Russian-speaking church and join "regular" American

---

29. Susan Wiley Hardwick points to several general processes that are part of the experience of all migrations, "of all people in all places that impact adaptation of immigrants in the new country" (*Russian Refuge: Religion, Migration, and Settlement on the North American Pacific Rim* [Chicago: University of Chicago Press, 1993], 189). She insists that they are true for immigrants from the Soviet Union as well. These processes are: "1. Long-distance travel and lack of communication with their homeland increases the groups' sense of isolation in their new environment. 2. Larger immigrant groups tend to need outsiders less; thus the size of the incoming group affects the acculturation process. 3. Groups that settle in tightly focused enclaves remain more attached to their original culture than do groups that settle in a more dispersed pattern. 4. Groups that cling to antecedent religious affiliations adjust more slowly to life within mainstream culture than do groups that abandon original spiritual connections."

churches. Usually this happens with younger, better-educated people. This triggers negative feelings among remaining members of the immigrant churches toward their American counterparts and toward American people in general. It affects their willingness to practice authentic mission among the latter. The fact that members of the Russian-speaking congregations start attending English-speaking churches and later switch their membership causes mounting hostility among Russian believers towards American churches. It creates, among Russian-speaking Christians, an attitude of antagonism towards American Christians and creates a barrier in developing a partnership between these two groups of Christians in fulfillment of an authentic mission among the people with whom they now live. The problems described above, and the processes experienced by immigrants in general, as applied to the Slavic Christian diaspora, lead to the isolation of churches from the rest of society and create an unhealthy environment for the implementation of an authentic mission.

7.4. Social and Cultural Specifics of the Current Slavic Diaspora in America

The analysis of social and cultural specifics of the current Slavic diaspora in America is provided in the appendix for chapter 7, section 7.4.A. It shows that common to the immigrants from the former Soviet Union are specific characteristics such as stress caused by the intensity and superficiality of American life, unrealistic expectations, sense of entitlement, loss of sense of security, loss of status, overdependency, manipulative behavior, and difficulty in establishing trusting relationships. These specific characteristics provide additional obstacles for the Slavic Baptists in America to be engaged in mission efforts directed towards indigenous people.

7.5. Challenges Other Immigrant Churches Are Facing in America

The main focus of this study is Russian-speaking immigrant Baptist churches in America. Comparing their immigrant experiences with challenges other immigrant ethnic churches are facing in the US helps to better understand similarities and differences that exist in the life of immigrant churches of different ethnicities. As a result, it will be possible to see which ethnic churches are facing greater challenges in their ministry to their fellow citizens as well as to the native people of the US. Each ethnic church represents its own immigrant community. Understanding a particular ethnic immigrant community in general helps to understand challenges the church belonging to this community is facing.

If before 1965 most immigrants arriving in the US were Western Europeans, the "post-1965 immigration has been marked by an increase in immigration from Latin America, Asia, the Caribbean, and Africa, alongside a decrease in Western European immigration."[30] In contrast to European immigrants, the last wave of post-1965 immigrants "are extraordinarily diverse with respect to national origins, religion, race, and ethnicity, language, social class, and education."[31] The social status of these newcomers varies greatly. Some of them are "well-to-do professionals who enter the United States with sterling educational credentials."[32] Others are "low-wage laborers who may have only finished fourth grade in their countries of origin."[33] Among immigrants who entered the US during the last fifty years, some "are captains of corporations and owners of small businesses, but others are illegal immigrant workers who are often highly in debt from the journey."[34] Obviously, such great diversity among the newly arrived immigrants leads to the creation of very diverse immigrant communities in the United States. Ethnic churches associated with these communities face challenges that are common for all immigrant churches as well as unique challenges determined by the uniqueness of each particular immigrant group(s). In this part of the thesis, we will explore challenges faced by Korean-speaking, Chinese-speaking and Spanish-speaking churches in America.

---

30. Fabienne Doucet, "Divergent Realities: The Home and School lives of Haitian Immigrant Youth," *Journal of Youth Ministry* 3, no. 2 (Spring 2005): 37.

31. Pierrette Hondagneu-Sotelo, "Religion and a Standpoint Theory of Immigrant Social Justice," *Religion and Social Justice for Immigrants* (New Brunswick, NJ: Rutgers University Press, 2006), 9.

32. Ibid.

33. Ibid.

34. Ibid.

7.5.1. Korean-Speaking Churches' Experience

The number of Korean-speaking immigrants in the US has grown rapidly since 1970 and is now above one million, making them one of the largest immigrant groups in America. Almost all of them come from South Korea.[35] Around 27 percent of them entered the US in 2000 or later. The majority of Korean immigrants have become naturalized citizens.[36] More than half of the Korean adults entering the USA had a bachelor's or higher degree. Fifty-seven percent of Korean immigrants have limited proficiency in English. About 40 percent of employed Korean-born men are working "in management, business, finance, and sales."[37] The number of unauthorized Korean immigrants in America is estimated at 230,000.[38]

The first Korean immigrant church was founded in 1902, in San Francisco.[39] In 2001, there were 3,375 Korean immigrant churches in America,[40] with 1,108 of them in California.[41] According to a recent study, "70 percent of the Koreans in America are affiliated with Korean ethnic churches. In these churches, the majority of the members are women, although men hold the positions of leadership." The first Korean Baptist church in America was founded in 1956. It was affiliated with the Southern Baptist Church denomination. Since that time, many more Baptist churches have been planted. Starting in the 1970s, Korean Baptist churches multiplied quickly and by 2001 "Korean Baptists . . . have had the largest number of local churches of all the Korean denominations in the United States."[42] Despite this remarkable growth which Korean Baptist churches experienced in the past, they are now facing a crisis. The multiplication of churches is slowing down or has stopped completely. Churches are experiencing controversy

---

35. Aaron Terrazas and Cristina Batog, "Korean Immigrants in the United States," *Migration Policy Institute*, 24 August 2010, http://migrationinformation.org/USfocus/display.cfm?id=716 (accessed May 2013).

36. Ibid.

37. Ibid.

38. Ibid.

39. Chul Tim Chang, "A History of the Korean Immigrant Baptist Church Movement in the United States," *Baptist History and Heritage* 40, no. 1 (Winter 2005): 58 (58–64).

40. Ibid., 59.

41. Ibid.

42. Ibid., 60.

within the membership that often leads to splits. Because of this "at least one-half of the new churches were the result of splits."[43] Such experiences lead to weakening of the congregational life. Many congregations are small (twenty–thirty members) and are struggling financially and spiritually. There is a lack of ordained ministers.[44]

There are various functions the Korean ethnic church fulfills in relation to immigrants. The church "(1) functions as a social center and a means of cultural identification (specifically for language and traditional values); (2) serves an educational function by teaching American-born Koreans the Korean language, history and culture; and (3) keeps Korean nationalism alive."[45] There are also "the nonreligious, secular functions of the Korean immigrant church: The church functions as 'a pseudo-extended family' and as 'a broker between its congregation and the bureaucratic institutions of the larger society.'"[46] The church also provides "emotional support and a helping hand to those individual members who are psychologically distressed or experiencing other personal crises in their new environment." The Korean ethnic church provides "focal points of social belonging, recognition, emotional comfort, and recreation, and maintains a vital link to the old country via ethnic fellowship and solidarity."[47] Korean churches are facing the same issues that all immigrant churches are dealing with. Among them are overcoming language and culture barriers, fighting the tendency of their congregations to be self-centered, ingrown and inward-looking,[48] resolving intergenerational conflict within the church,[49] and trying to keep the young people from leaving their ethnically focused church.[50]

---

43. Ibid., 62.
44. Ibid.
45. Won Moo Hurh and Kwang Chung Kim, "Religious Participation of Korean Immigrants in the United States," *Journal for the Scientific Study of Religion* 29, no. 1 (March 1990): 21 (19–34).
46. Ibid.
47. Ibid., 32.
48. Gil Pyo Lee, "From Traditional to Missional Church: Describing a Contextual Model of Change for an Ingrown Korean Diaspora Church in North America" (DMis diss., Asbury Theological Seminary, 2010), 6.
49. Daniel Shinjong Baeq, Myunghee Lee, Sokpyo Hong, and Jonathan Ro, "Mission from Migrant Church to Ethnic Minorities: A Brief Assessment of the Korean American Church in Mission," *Missiology* 39, no. 1 (Jan 2011): 31
50. Ibid.

There are also specific issues common mostly to Korean churches. One of them is racial prejudice. Young Koreans, despite the fact that they speak English very well, experience difficulty in being accepted by indigenous predominantly white English-speaking congregations. The reason is their race. At the same time, when young Korean believers conduct separate services in English and try to bring white Americans to these services, their guests feel uncomfortable being among mostly Korean worshipers. The issue of race is very real for Korean churches in America. Also, underemployment of their members is one of the issues Korean churches are facing. As shown above, most Korean immigrants are educated people. While many of them held either professional or technical occupations in their homeland, in America not very many of them have been able to obtain similar positions. This puts extra stress on them.[51]

7.5.2. Chinese-Speaking Churches' Experience

In 1980, Chinese were the tenth-largest immigrant group in the United States. By 2006, they became the third-largest immigrant group in the US, with about 1.6 million foreign-born people from China.[52] They made up more than 4 percent of all immigrants in the United States. Over 50 percent of them were naturalized citizens of the US in 2006 and two-thirds of them have limited English proficiency.[53] About 40 percent of immigrants coming from China have a bachelor's or higher degree. About one-quarter of Chinese-born immigrant men "were employed in management, business, finance, and information technology occupations."[54] Two percent of all unauthorized immigrants in the US, in 2006, were from China.[55] Chinese immigrants come from Hong Kong, Taiwan, Vietnam, and from the People's Republic of China.[56]

---

51. Hurh and Kim, "Religious Participation of Korean Immigrants in the United States," 31.

52. "Chinese Immigrants in the United States," *US in Focus*, http://www.migrationinformation.org/USfocus/display.cfm?id=685#5 (accessed May 2013).

53. Ibid.

54. Ibid.

55. Ibid.

56. Ezer Kang, John J. Chin, and Elan Behar, "Faith-Based HIV Care and Prevention in Chinese Immigrant Communities: Rhetoric or Reality?," *Journal of Psychology & Theology* 39, no. 3 (Fall 2011): 271.

Ninety percent of Chinese churches in the US "have been established by post-1965 immigrants, well-educated from China and Southeast Asia . . . Socioeconomic class, diasporic history, education, language, and theological positioning of the church significantly influence the sinicization of Christianity or the rendering of Christianity to reflect the traditions and practices of the Chinese culture."[57] Among important values supported "by many conservative Chinese churches were family harmony and the moral upbringing of children."[58] Parents are very much concerned about "the extent to which their children were influenced by a sexually permissive culture – namely one that permits premarital sexual activity, teenage pregnancy, and homosexuality . . . As such separation between the church and the outside world was considered essential in maintaining social-ethical values upheld by Christianity and Chinese cultures."[59] The majority of Chinese Protestant churches in the US are nondenominational and evangelical in theology. The membership of these churches comprises ethnic Chinese from different countries.[60] In these churches, there are "constant tensions between maintaining . . . Chinese character and striving for universalism beyond ethnic boundaries."[61] There are Cantonese-speaking churches as well as Mandarin-speaking churches.[62] Although some of these churches extend their mission to non-Chinese and invite them to their services, the number of non-Chinese in these churches "is still small and many of these are interethnic couples."[63] The Chinese churches in America "have become some of the most well-structured social groups among the Chinese community. Many new immigrants naturally turn to the church for help. The common language, cultural, and social background are key factors in their sense of identification."[64]

---

57. Ibid.
58. Ibid., 274.
59. Ibid.
60. Helen Rose Ebaugh and Janet Saltzman Chafetz, *Religion and the New Immigrants* (Walnut Creek, CA: AltaMira, 2000), 180.
61. Ibid.
62. Ibid.
63. Ibid., 188.
64. T. K. Chuang, "The Chinese Church in Greater Boston," *Emmanuel Gospel Center*, http://www.egc.org/chinese (accessed May 2013).

Like Korean immigrant churches, the Chinese churches are facing issues common to almost all immigrants. The major challenges for members of the Chinese churches "include identity problems, language barriers, relationship problems, and lack of economic and social resources . . . With respect to social resources, the Chinese Christian church plays an important role in coping, acculturation, and assimilation processes for many Chinese immigrant families."[65] Also, the intergenerational problem is present in these churches and tensions "between the American-born or American-raised Chinese and adult immigrants have been clearly present since the early 1970s."[66] The most significant weakness in the Chinese church is limited interaction with people who are not Chinese. Church members "have minimal contact, if any, with the non-Chinese community."[67] Another problem is the relatively small membership of these churches and the resultant financial struggles. Their personnel are limited, the pool of volunteers is small, and programs for youth and children are poor.[68] The potential threat for a church split "always looms overhead."[69] Similar to Korean immigrants, Chinese believers experience difficulty in being accepted by the predominantly white English-speaking churches because of their race. It is also difficult for whites to become part of the Chinese church for to the same reason – Chinese people dominate the congregation.

7.5.3. Spanish-Speaking Churches

Latinos in the United States "are a heterogeneous group comprising all those who trace their ancestry to the Spanish-speaking world, the Caribbean and Latin America."[70] The terms Hispanic and Latino are used "interchangeably to refer to all individuals of Latin American ancestry or with ties to

---

65. Yaxin Lu, Loren Marks, and Loredana Apavaloaie, "Chinese Immigrant Families and Christian Faith Community: A Qualitative Study," *Family and Consumer Sciences Research Journal* 41, no. 2 (Dec 2012): 118–130.

66. Fenggang Yang, "Gender and Generation in the Chinese American Church," Conference Papers, American Sociological Association, 2003 Annual Meeting, Atlanta, GA, 1 (1–15).

67. Chuang, "The Chinese Church in Greater Boston."

68. Ibid.

69. Ibid.

70. Daniel A. Rodriguez, *A Future for the Latino Church: Models for Multilingual, Multigenerational Hispanic Congregations* (Downers Grove, IL: IVP Academic, 2011), 38.

the Spanish-speaking world who reside either legally or illegally within the borders of the United States of America."[71] This group of people is identified by language not by race. It is important to note "that the term Hispanic is a term developed and used uniquely in the United States."[72] Among Latinos in the US are Mexicans (65.5%), Puerto Ricans (9.1%), Cubans (3.5%), Dominicans (2.8%), Central Americans (8.7%), and South Americans (5.9%).[73] According to the Census Bureau, in 2010, the Hispanic population in America "reached 50.5 million, representing more than 16.3 percent of the US population."[74] It is the largest minority group in the US today. According to the recent Pew Hispanic Center survey, 62 percent of all Latinos in America were born in the US, and 61 percent of those who are native-born are English-dominant, 35 percent are bilingual, and only 4 percent are Spanish-dominant.[75] Sixty-eight percent of Latinos are Roman Catholics, 15 percent "identify themselves as evangelical or 'born-again,'" and 5 percent belong to mainline Protestant churches.[76] Mexican immigrants are the largest group among Latinos in America. They are the largest single group arriving in the US annually. Thirty percent of the foreign-born population of the US consists of Mexicans.[77] In 2011, around 11.7 million Mexican immigrants lived in the United States.[78] This immigrant group in 2006 made up "the majority of undocumented immigrants in the United States, and about 80 percent of current Mexican migration to the United States is undocumented."[79] In 2011, this percentage dropped to 59 percent. In 2011 only 5 percent of Mexican-born adults older than twenty-five living in America had a bachelor's degree or higher. This is a very low percentage

---

71. Ibid., 25.
72. Ibid.
73. Ibid., 39.
74. Ibid., 38.
75. Ibid., 19.
76. Ibid., 58.
77. Hondagneu-Sotelo, "Religion and a Standpoint Theory of Immigrant Social Justice," 10.
78. Jie Zong, and Jeanne Batalova, "Mexican Immigrants in the United States," in *US in Focus*, http://www.migrationinformation.org/USFocus/display.cfm?ID=935 (accessed May 2013).
79. Hondagneu-Sotelo, "Religion and a Standpoint Theory of Immigrant Social Justice," 10.

compared with the 27 percent of all immigrant adults in America.[80] Also, "59 percent of Mexican-born adults had no high school or GED diploma."[81] Only 26 percent of immigrants from Mexico speak English very well. This means that "about 71 percent of Mexican immigrants were Limited English Proficient (LEP)."[82] This is in great contrast to "51 percent of all immigrants [who] reported limited English proficiency in 2011."[83] Mexican migration to America has never ended, unlike other migrations such as the mass Italian and Polish migrations in the past. Mexican migration has continued for over a century.[84] Because of Mexico being the neighboring country to the USA, "not only could migrants return home with relative ease, but those who stayed were constantly receiving fresh arrivals who nourished and reinforced their religious traditions."[85]

Most immigrants coming from Mexico are Catholics. However, some of them "have left the church [Catholic Church] to embrace various Protestant denominations."[86] Immigrant Spanish-speaking churches provide different ministerial services to immigrants from Latin America. "They provide support through social networks, helping with basic needs (food, shelter, transportation and money), pastoral guidance and fellowship, empathy and advocacy, among other things. They also are a healing place for all the suffering caused by civil wars and extreme poverty."[87] Salvadoran immigrants testify that evangelical pastors "often served as counselors, spiritual guides and confidantes. They dealt with concerns on a case-by-case basis and took an active stance to guide their members. Oftentimes the pastors acted as father figures and advised and scolded their followers."[88] Because of this the church has remained crucial for Spanish-speaking immigrants. It is

---

80. Ibid.
81. Ibid.
82. Ibid.
83. Ibid.
84. Portes and Rumbaut, *Immigrant America*, 333.
85. Ibid.
86. Ibid., 335.
87. Kretcha Roldan-Rodriguez, "Finding a Home in the Immigrant Church," *Family and Community Ministries* 23, no. 1 (Spring 2009): 41.
88. Cecilia Menjivar, "Religion and Immigration in Comparative Perspective: Catholic and Evangelical Salvadorans in San Francisco, Washington, D.C., and Phoenix," *Sociology of Religion* 64, no. 1 (Spring 2003): 36.

important to note that the role of the church on the behalf of Salvadoran immigrants differs from that for other Latino immigrants.

> In a comparative study of Guatemalans, Salvadorans and Cubans in Phoenix, Salvadorans (and Guatemalans) had received more types of assistance from the church and thus deemed the place of the church as vital in their lives, whereas Cubans saw the church mainly as a source of spiritual comfort . . . Therefore, regardless of particular community dynamics in specific locations, the church (and its activities) is a key in these immigrants' lives; it is an effective antidote to forces that may undermine these immigrants' emotional, spiritual, material strength and resilience.[89]

As for all other immigrant churches, Spanish-speaking churches deal with such issues as language and cultural barriers, limited economic resources available to them, language used in the church services, racism, and other issues. The study of this ethnic group shows that "a growing number of US-born Latinos are not only English dominant, but they do not speak Spanish at all!"[90] At the same time the primary focus of the Spanish-speaking ministry is directed to foreign-born Latinos and is "unintentionally designed to preserve the language and cultural preferences"[91] of this group. As a result, the native-born group which represents 60 percent of all Latinos in America and is mostly English-dominant has been "largely ignored by denominational and local church leaders who uncritically equate 'Hispanic ministry' with 'Spanish-language ministry.'"[92] This leads to the departure of some of English-dominant people from the Latino churches. Often those who leave are potential leaders. Manuel Ortiz acknowledges: "We are all [Latino, Korean and Chinese churches] losing many of our emerging leaders to other congregations because too often we are unwilling to make cultural transitions."[93] Daniel A. Rodriguez names as one of the

---

89. Ibid., 41.
90. Rodriguez, *A Future for the Latino Church*, 16.
91. Ibid., 20.
92. Ibid.
93. Manuel Ortiz, "Foreword," in Rodriguez, *A Future for the Latino Church*, 10.

challenges Hispanic churches are facing the resistance to change demonstrated by many Hispanic church leaders. He points to several reasons for this. Among them is a strong intention to sustain cultural values, language and practices. Because of this, "for some churches dominated by foreign-born Latinos, incorporating English-language programs and ministries to accommodate native-born Latinos undermines their efforts to sustain and reinforce the values, language and practices of the immigrant generation."[94] Another reason for the resistance to change is a theological one. Referring to the apostle Paul's call for Christians to be holy in their conduct and be separated from the world (1 Pet 1:14–16), the first generation of Latino Christian immigrants sees "their cherished traditions and prohibitions . . . not . . . as 'cultural preferences,' but rather as reflecting the value of personal and communal holiness."[95] Contrary to this, to many native-born Hispanic Christians "some of the traditions and corresponding prohibitions appear legalistic and nonsensical." Many young believers, frustrated by this situation in the church, leave the church.[96] One more reason for resisting change is "a sense of cultural superiority prevalent among many first-generation Hispanic evangelicals" toward those Latinos who do not speak Spanish. References to Spanish as the language spoken in heaven "betray 'a racist and ethnocentric attitude' that unnecessarily alienates and offends English-dominant native-born Latinos."[97] Many native-born English-speaking young people "feel discriminated against by first-generation *Boricua* based on their inability to speak Spanish well or at all"[98] and leave the church.

Among the challenges the Spanish-speaking churches are facing is the issue of undocumented immigrants. Although Korean and Chinese immigrant communities have undocumented immigrants among them as well, Spanish-speaking churches face this issue more often. The close proximity of Mexico to the US makes this country the main sending country of illegal immigrants to the USA. Also, migrants from other Latin American countries are entering the US by illegally crossing the Mexico–USA boarder. Despite the fact that

---

94. Rodriguez, *A Future for the Latino Church*, 151.
95. Ibid., 153.
96. Ibid., 154.
97. Ibid., 156.
98. Ibid.

in recent years, the US government has taken "unprecedented steps to restrict the entry of unauthorized migrants by beefing up police activities along the border,"[99] the number of illegal immigrants arriving in the US from Mexico is still significant. It is a well-known fact that "immigrants and refugees have met with a deeply ambivalent and often mean-spirited public reception in the United States."[100] This is especially true in the case of illegal immigrants. Such an attitude toward undocumented immigrants can be observed "in institutions across society, in the media, in workplaces, in the legislature, and in the campaign platforms of politicians at election time." These illegal immigrants attending Spanish-speaking churches in the US put these churches in a delicate situation in relation to the law. On the one hand, churches are called by Scripture to provide help to strangers in the land and take care of the poor. On the other hand, undocumented immigrants are in the country illegally and thus they violate the immigration law of the US. By helping them, churches put themselves in a situation where they can be accused of helping people who are in conflict with the law of the land. Currently, it is not officially illegal to provide help to undocumented immigrants (except, of course, hiring them as employees – this is illegal). However, there are efforts being made among legislators to prohibit such help. In 2006, one bill pending in Congress proposed "to make it a federal crime to offer assistance or services to undocumented immigrants."[101] Congress's acceptance of this legislation would place churches at risk of criminal prosecution simply for providing humanitarian aid and social services to illegal immigrants.[102] In spite of this dangerous prospective, churches are "providing humanitarian services for journeying migrants."[103]

7.5.4 Conclusion

The brief overview of experiences of these three ethnic immigrant groups and their churches shows that there are similarities and differences in the

---

99. Jacqueline Maria Hagan, "The Church vs. the State," *Religion and Social Justice for Immigrants* (New Brunswick, NJ: Rutgers University Press, 2006), 93.

100. Hondagneu-Sotelo, "Religion and a Standpoint Theory of Immigrant Social Justice," 3.

101. Ibid., 6.

102. Ibid.

103. Hagan, "The Church vs. the State," 94.

challenges these churches are facing. The similarities are in such aspects of immigrant life as language and culture barriers, intergenerational tensions and conflict, material resources limitations, the language used in the church services, and losing the young generation of believers who are leaving the ethnic church. Slavic Baptist immigrant churches could identify with all these challenges mentioned above. The differences in the challenges these ethnic churches are experiencing are based on different factors. The difference in education and socio-economic status of their members is one of them. The more educated church members of immigrant churches usually keep better-paid jobs and are able to provide better financial support to their churches. Because of this, Korean and Chinese churches are in better financial positions than Hispanic churches due to the fact that most Korean and Chinese immigrants come to America, as shown above, with good educations. This is not the case with Latino immigrants who are significantly less educated than the other two groups. Slavic Baptist immigrants are in a privileged position compared with the Latino immigrants since the vast majority of them have completed high school in their country of origin. However, they do not have as many people in their midst with bachelor's and higher degrees as do the Asian immigrant churches because evangelical Christians were not permitted by the Communist government to be accepted at the universities. Another factor is race. All three groups which are being compared with the Russian-speaking group face this challenge. Even those among them who speak English very well cannot hide the fact that they belong to their particular ethnic group. Because of this they are exposed to racism and prejudice. People in Slavic Baptist churches in America are in a different situation. They seldom experience racism expressed toward them by the indigenous people. Since they are Caucasians, it is only their accent when they use the English language that identifies them as foreigners. Because of this they are in a privileged position compared with Korean, Chinese and Hispanic churches as far as racism goes.

Immigrant status makes a big difference for ethnic churches. As was shown above, all three immigrant groups in this comparison have undocumented immigrants in their midst. These people are in a special category. They are the most vulnerable and disadvantaged people in American society. The churches of all three ethnic groups discussed above are facing the challenge of dealing with the needs of these people. This is especially true for the Spanish-speaking churches. The Slavic immigrant churches do not face this issue since in their midst there are very few people from the former Soviet Union who are illegally in the US. In fact, most Slavic Baptists entered the USA with refugee status, which provides them with such privileges as eligibility for public financial assistance and medical assistance. This is a huge help for those who start life in this new country. It can be concluded that Slavic Baptist churches face fewer economic challenges than those faced by other ethnic groups. In fact, in some aspects of their lives, these challenges are actually lighter than those faced by others.

7.6. Conclusion for Chapter 7

The purpose of this chapter was to use the results of sociological studies to analyze how the social challenges of immigrant life affect the ability of PCSBA churches in America to do evangelism and to practice social action/*diaconia* directed towards the indigenous people. The analysis provided in this chapter concludes that sociological studies of immigrants show very clearly that such experiences as culture shock, language barriers, attachment to homeland, separation from known surroundings, becoming a foreigner, ceasing to belong, and uprootedness cause immigrants to go through deep emotional and psychological pain. The author of this study sees these very personal ("internal") experiences as powerful forces that could keep Christian immigrants from active participation in mission work among the native people. Other influencing factors of the cross-cultural encounter that have to be considered during evaluation of the mission work of the PCSBA churches are (1) reciprocal consequences of cross-cultural encounters; (2) impact of the homogeneity/heterogeneity of the society on the immigrant's experience; (3) impact of the degree of difference between societies; and (4) impact of the visible characteristics of cultural groups. These factors, together with the relationship between the diaspora and the receiving society, create a group of "external" forces that impact negatively the churches' willingness and ability to practice evangelism and social action/*diaconia* among local native people. All this information points to the conclusion that there are many natural forces that push immigrants to isolationism from the receiving society and that it is beyond a reasonable expectation to require recent immigrants, including the PCSBA churches, to be voluntarily involved in mission towards native people. Strong encouragement from leaders who are filled with the vision to do such mission, and a sacrificial willingness of the church members to leave their cultural and linguistic comfort zones are necessary for making these churches become actively involved in this mission. Also, the challenges facing by Korean-speaking, Chinese-speaking and Spanish-speaking churches were explored in this chapter. Churches of different ethnic groups are encountering similar challenges as well as more specific ones. The Russian-speaking churches are in a privileged position since their members are mostly Caucasians and do not experience racial discrimination to the same degree as representatives of other groups. Also, most members of Slavic churches are legally in the US having entered this country with refugee status. This provides them with great economic benefits.

Within this chapter, the PCSBA churches' local mission challenges were examined based on the available results of sociological studies; the next chapter will continue discussing the challenges, as well as the opportunities, in mission for the PCSBA churches, focusing attention on more specific issues such as the role of ethnicity, language, interethnic relations, and other aspects in mission. Gathering this information is necessary for completion of the evaluation of mission work in which the PCSBA churches are currently involved.

CHAPTER 8

Analysis of Mission Challenges and Opportunities for the Slavic Baptist Diaspora

This chapter is devoted to analyzing both the challenges and the opportunities that Slavic Baptist believers are facing when sharing the gospel with and providing social action/*diaconia* for the surrounding American society. Issues such as the role of ethnicity in mission work, the role of language in the life and mission of the church, the status of interethnic relations between Slavic immigrants and other people groups, and contemporary hindrances and opportunities for mission in the Slavic Baptist diaspora context are discussed. All of this information is needed for accomplishing the task of this study – evaluation of the authenticity and contextuality of the mission work of PCSBA churches.

8.1. Ethnicity and Mission

Ethnicity plays an important role in many aspects of a person's life, including religion. The ways that people express their faith and relate to each other in the faith community are often significantly shaped by their ethnicity. No less important is ethnicity's role in mission. This part of the study will explore this role in relation to the Slavic Baptist immigrants and their mission in America.

8.1.1. Ethnicity: Terms and Definitions

The term "ethnicity" is not always used in the same way. According to John H. Redekop, it "may have several shades of meaning."[1] Talcott Parsons states that an ethnic group has a "distinctive identity which is rooted in some kind of a distinctive sense of its history."[2] Donald Kraybill states, "Ethnic identity is the symbolic process by which a group answers the question, 'Who are we?' Distinctive symbols, belief systems, and cultural practices are the collective answer to the identity question: 'we are the people who . . .' Ethnic traditions and identities fused with experience over the centuries have an amazing resilience to change when legitimated and empowered by religious symbols."[3] Alan Anderson and James S. Frideres point to four key ethnic identification factors: ethnic origin, the mother tongue, ethnic-oriented religion, and folkways, i.e., the practices of certain customs unique to the group.[4] Max Weber has the view that an ethnic group is based on the shared conviction(s) of its members, which came about from their common descent. The following statement helps one to understand the dynamic of ethnic group formation: "ethnic membership does not constitute a group; it only facilitates group formation of any kind, particularly in the political sphere. On the other hand, it is primarily the political community, no matter how artificially organized, that inspires the belief of common ethnicity."[5] Marietta Stepaniants, professor of the Institute of Philosophy at the Russian Academy of Sciences, gives the following definition of ethnicity: "The term 'ethnicity' is usually used to define a group of persons sharing a common cultural heritage. The latter is made by common history, environment,

---

1. John H. Redekop, *A People Apart: Ethnicity and the Mennonite Brethren* (Winnipeg, MB: Kindred Press, 1987), 5.
2. Talcott Parsons, "Some Theoretical Considerations on the Nature and Trends of Change of Ethnicity," in *Ethnicity, Theory, Experience*, ed. N. Glazer and D. Moynihan (Cambridge, MA: Harvard University Press, 1975), 56–57.
3. Donald Kraybill, "Modernity and Identity: The Transformation of Mennonite Ethnicity," a paper read at Conrad Grebel College, May 1986, 7–9.
4. Alan Anderson and James S. Frideres, *Ethnicity in Canada: Theoretical Perspectives* (Toronto: Butterworths, 1981), 36.
5. G. Roth and C. Wittich, *Economy and Society* (Berkeley, CA: University of California Press, 1978), 389.

territory, language, customs, habits, beliefs, in short, by a common way of life. Undoubtedly, religion is an important component of any cultural heritage."[6]

The positions listed above by different authors on the issue of ethnicity illustrate the fact that there is a wide variety of opinions and definitions on the subject of ethnicity. This study will adopt Stepaniants' definition of ethnicity as the most comprehensive and concise. Discussion of the issue of ethnicity applied to the Slavic Baptist diaspora is provided in the appendix for chapter 8, section 8.1.1.A.

8.1.2. Religion and Ethnicity in an Immigrant's Life

Joanne Van Dijk states that the "link between religion and ethnicity continues to be a complex"[7] one and "that religious identity, intertwined with ethnic identity, makes a stronger bond than ethnic identity alone."[8] Philip Gleason insists that "ethnicity and religion must both be taken into account and that the interaction between them is not only complex but also shifting and situational – that is, shaped by generational transition and a multitude of contingent historical factors."[9] In their discussion on the religion and ethnicity of immigrants, Helen Rose Ebaugh and Janet Saltzman Chafetz argue that "religious and ethnic identities are so intertwined that it is often difficult to separate them." The authors affirm that "the religious factor in ethnic identity is strengthened by the migration experience. The process of uprooting, migration, and resettlement produce intensification of religious commitment on the part of immigrants."[10] It is not an understatement to say that religion plays an extremely important role in the life of immigrants. In his overview of the issues related to immigration and its relationship

---

6. Marietta Stepaniants, "Ethnicity and Religion," Institute of Philosophy, Russian Academy of Sciences, http://www.dartmouth.edu/~crn/crn_papers/Stepaniants2.pdf (accessed February 2011).

7. Joanne Van Dijk, "The Importance of Ethnicity and Religion in the Life Cycle of Immigrant Churches: A Comparison of Coptic and Calvinist Churches," *Canadian Ethnic Studies* 41, no. 1–2 (2009): 193.

8. Ibid., 209.

9. Philip Gleason, *Speaking of Diversity: Language and Ethnicity in Twentieth-Century America* (Baltimore, MD: Johns Hopkins University Press, 1992), 272.

10. Helen Rose Ebaugh and Janet Saltzman Chafetz, *Religion and the New Immigrants: Continuities and Adaptations in Immigrant Congregations* (Walnut Creek, CA: AltaMira, 2000), 94.

to religion, Alex Stepick notes, "Numerous recent and historical studies have documented the important role religion holds in the lives of many immigrants."[11] He supports this statement by referring to Karen Richman, who said the following about Haitian immigrants: "For the Pentecostal congregants . . . the church is the center of life outside of their (service) jobs. They spend long hours in church, including most evenings after work, part of Saturday, and most of Sunday. Those with young children take them along into the pews."[12] This importance of religion to immigrants is reflected in the fact that immigrants usually attend church more frequently than Americans who were born in the US.[13] Nora E. Thompson and Andrea G. Gurney, through exploring the role of religion in the lives of immigrant youth, came to a similar conclusion: "This study reveals the perceived importance of religion in the lives of immigrant youth. In response to two simple questions regarding religion and belief in God, they spoke of real, rich, and powerful personal experiences. The intensity and richness of their responses suggest that religion is perceived to be helpful and meaningful in their lives."[14] This position is supported by a study completed by Ilana Redstone Akresh, who argues that religion is important to immigrants not only in the beginning of their stay in the US.[15]

According to Stepick, "the emerging research emphasizes that immigrant religion maintains and reinforces immigrants' national or ethnic identity with their home country."[16] He is referring to Robert W. Schrauf's argu-

---

11. Alex Stepick, "God Is Apparently Not Dead: The Obvious, the Emergent, and the Still Unknown in Immigration and Religion," in *Immigrant Faiths*, ed. Karen I. Leonard, Alex Stepick, Manuel A. Vasquez, and Jennifer Holdaway (Lanham, MD: AltaMira, 2006), 13.

12. Alex Stepick, "The Protestant Ethic and the Dis-Spirit of Vodou," in Leonard et al., *Immigrant Faiths*, 169.

13. Stepick, "God Is Apparently Not Dead," 13.

14. Nora E. Thompson and Andrea G. Gurney, "He Is Everything: Religion's Role in the Lives of Immigrant Youth," *New Directions for Youth Development* 100 (Winter 2003): 87.

15. According to Akresh, religion continues to play a significant role in the life of immigrants after being in this country for a long time. It is reflected in their religious attendance. According to the results of Akresh's study, "there is a tendency towards greater religious attendance with increased time in the US and no evidence of a decline, consistent with the role of religion in the maintenance of social capital and with the 'new' paradigm of increased religious participation and religious pluralism" (Ilana Redstone Akresh, "Immigrants' Religious Participation in the United States," *Ethnic & Racial Studies* 34, no. 4 [Apr 2011[: 657).

16. Stepick, "God Is Apparently Not Dead," 13.

ment "that religious practice is one of the few factors that preserves native language among immigrants and their offspring."[17]

Pyong Gap Min states that the study of different immigrant groups arriving in the US after 1965 supports "the hypothesis that there is a relationship between participation in an ethnic congregation and the preservation of ethnicity."[18] He is quoting the conclusion of Carl Bankston and Min Zhou, based on a survey of Vietnamese high school students, which states that "religious participation consistently makes a greater contribution to ethnic identification than any of the family or individual characteristics examined."[19] Alan Anderson and James S. Frideres state, "Many of the functions of religion are oriented toward the preservation of ethnic identity . . . it promotes social integration; it attempts to validate people's customs and values; it inculcates values through socialization; it affirms the dignity of the ethnic group members . . . ; it tends to be a pillar of conservatism; and it often encourages social isolation from outsiders."[20]

G. W. Allport makes an important observation in saying that among ethnic groups, religion "usually stands for more than faith – it is the pivot of the cultural tradition of a group . . . The clergy . . . may, often do, become defenders of a culture."[21] In her description of the multiethnic church, Kathleen Garces-Foley notes, "There is little doubt that ethnic churches are effective spaces for reproducing ethnicity. Immigrants to the United States have always formed ethnic churches to meet both religious and social needs."[22] Ebaugh and Chafetz state, "Immigrant religious institutions provide the physical and social spaces in which those who share the same traditions, customs, and languages can reproduce many aspects of their native cultures for themselves and attempt to pass them on to their children."[23]

---

17. Ibid.
18. Pyong Gap Min, "Religion and the Maintenance of Ethnicity among Immigrants," in Leonard et al., *Immigrant Faiths*, 99.
19. Ibid., 100.
20. Anderson and Frideres, *Ethnicity in Canada: Theoretical Perspectives* (Toronto: Butterworths, 1981), 41.
21. G. W. Allport, *The Nature of Prejudice* (Garden City, NY: Anchor/Doubleday, 1954), 415–416.
22. Kathleen Garces-Foley, *Crossing the Ethnic Divide* (New York: Oxford University Press, 2007), 116.
23. Ebaugh and Chafetz, *Religion and the New Immigrants*, 80.

All of these authors point to the same truth: ethnicity and religion are interrelated in the immigrant context, and their influence on each other is much greater in the land that they emigrated to than it was in the homeland.[24] Religion helps preserve the ethnic characteristics of the immigrant group. In addition, ethnicity pulls people from the same people group together and provides an additional bond to the religious group of immigrants. Because of this, the religious organizations of immigrants fulfill more functions than their religious nature requires. They often play the roles of social centers and protectors of the language and culture of the particular immigrant group. This truth is very well proven in the life of the immigrant congregations of the PCSBA. For many members of these churches, especially for the representatives of the older generation, church involvement is the primary arena of social life. Most, if not all, relationships are developed within the congregation. What happens within the congregation is almost the only source of their joys or sorrows. Such an attitude keeps people in the church, as well as maintains their desire to satisfy religious needs. This could be seen as a positive fact because it helps build strong congregations. At the same time, it contains a danger for the church to become not so much a spiritual organism anymore, but an ethnic enclave that has a purpose and function different from those of the church. Such confusion between the two could affect the ability of the immigrant church to fulfill its authentic mission.

8.1.3. Ethnicity and Mission: Bridges and Barriers

When discussion takes place about the issue of the evangelistic efforts of immigrants, it is usually assumed that ethnic churches in the immigrant context will be successful in their attempts to share the gospel with people who have the same ethnic and cultural background and are now living in America. It is true that people of the same ethnic group could be reached

---

24. Dewi Hughes points to the phenomenon of contemporary explosion of ethnic consciousness. He claims that it is due to several factors. First, it is because of "the extreme individualism and relativism of post-modernist culture, which says that there is no religious, political or any other creed that can make universal claims" ("Following Jesus as His Community in the Broken World of Ethnic Identity," *Evangelical Review of Theology* 31, no. 4 [Oct 2007]: 333). The second factor is "the spiritual-ecological manifestation of post-modernist culture, which has strong links with New Age religion" (ibid.). The third factor is globalization and revolution in communications. There are no signs that the issue of ethnic identity will go away.

more easily by representatives of the same ethnicity who speak their language than by native-born Americans who do not speak the same language. At the same time, if the evangelistic efforts of immigrant churches are limited only to their fellow countrymen, they will not be able reach English-speaking Americans with the gospel. This is how Ebaugh and Chafetz address this situation: "Immigrant congregations are attractive to their members precisely because they reproduce the language and customs of the old country and thus create a comfort zone for their uprooted congregants. This allows them to successfully attract and often convert fellow ethnics. However, these same attributes are off-putting and alienating to most native-born Americans, who can readily choose congregations where they will not constitute a conspicuous minority of outsiders."[25]

On the one hand, being an ethnic church provides a bridge towards unchurched people from the same ethnic group. On the other hand, it is an obstacle when attempting to reach native-born Americans. Somebody would probably assume that this is not a big problem because the native-born Americans speak English and have a wide variety of English-speaking churches to choose from, if they wanted to attend church. However, the problem lies in the fact that an ethnic church, which concentrates its efforts only on people of its own ethnicity, is in danger of becoming an enclosed society. It is very unhealthy for church life, much in the same way as for a physical organism, to be isolated from the outside world. It betrays the fulfillment of the Lord's Great Commission, which requires the spreading of the gospel "starting from Jerusalem" (that is, where the church is located at the present time). Andrew Kirk addresses this issue by referring to Eddie Gibbs' critique of the homogeneous unit principle of church growth movement, saying, "The Church is bad news if the ethnic identity of some is justified as a reason for not working for the overthrow of racial, cultural and class barriers: 'A church which identifies itself exclusively with one group may live a self-centered, impoverished life . . . which may result in the exclusion of the majority of the surrounding population.'"[26]

---

25. Ebaugh and Chafetz, *Religion and the New Immigrants*, 36.
26. J. Andrew Kirk, *What Is Mission? Theological Explorations* (Minneapolis, MN: Fortress, 2000), 222.

Canadian pastor James Nikkel warns about the potential for an ethnic problem in church ministries: "Churches with an ethnic or cultural history are particularly vulnerable to growth barriers. If our roots and heritage do not help us to be faithful to the Scripture, they will become a barrier to fulfilling the great commission."[27] John H. Redekop echoes Nikkel, saying, "In discussing ethnicity we must be careful to distinguish between two uses of ethnicity. Christianity is always transmitted through a language and a culture but Christians were specifically enjoined by the Founder of their faith from wedding that faith to any one race or ethnic group."[28] He also suggests that "only where a particular church, for very specific language reasons, ministers to one ethnic group, can it justify, usually only for a transitional period, a narrowly ethnic designation."[29] It can be concluded that ethnic churches are pulled in two opposite directions. On the one hand, they feel a call to serve their own compatriots, who want and deserve to hear the gospel and worship in their native language. On the other hand, they are required by the Great Commission to put efforts into reaching the surrounding population, not just their "fellow ethnics." How can this dilemma be solved? Kirk suggests the following solution: "In the light of the overwhelming evidence from the New Testament that ethnically separate churches would have been perceived as a denial of the Gospel, it is incumbent on those who would defend ethnically centered evangelism (and the grounds for *beginning* there are strong) to say how it would result in multi-ethnic, multicultural churches."[30] Following this suggestion, the solution for ethnic churches is to develop a plan to eventually become multiethnic churches.

8.1.4. Church vs. Ethnic Community in the Russian Baptist Diaspora in the Mission Context

Personal observations, from this study's author, of the life of Slavic Baptist churches throughout many years of ministry among them have led him to the conclusion that the issue of church versus ethnic community exists within the Russian-speaking Baptist diaspora in America. This is reflected in

---

27. Quoted in Katie Funk Wiebe, *Who Are The Mennonite Brethren?* (Winnipeg, MA: Kindred Press, 1984), 6–7.
28. Redekop, *A People Apart*, 6.
29. Ibid., 134.
30. Kirk, *What Is Mission?*, 223.

the results of the surveys conducted among the leaders of PCSBA churches. Slavic Baptist churches are not communities of believers in Christ which are built solely on the fulfillment of the religious needs of their members. Rather, these communities are built on the fact that their members share the same ethnicity. The ethnic nature of the church, not necessarily its theological orientation, is what attracts Russian-speaking believers. These churches have become distinctive ethnic communities. There are certain positive aspects to this, including the ability of Russian-speaking immigrants to serve their people around the world. How this is currently done by PCSBA churches is listed in chapter six, section 6.7, "Review of the Methods and Organizational Models of Missionary Work Used by PCSBA Churches,' and in the appendix to chapter 8, section 8.4.3.A., "New Opportunities for Missions as a Result of Political Changes in the World." In addition, it could be mentioned that Slavic churches are providing material, informational, and emotional support services to one another, and especially to newly arrived immigrants. All of these are potential or actual mission-focused works that are positive outcomes of the existence of ethnic Slavic churches in America.

However, there are also certain aspects of these churches that raise concern. (1) An isolationistic attitude towards American society in general, and the Christian community in particular, keeps church members at a distance from the "real Americans." This slows down the processes of acculturation in and adaptation to the new country. Slavic churches are becoming ethnically closed enclaves, and such a situation is unhealthy for immigrant congregations. (2) The strongly demonstrated ethnic nature of the church and use of foreign languages in services keeps native-born Americans away from Slavic immigrant churches. This limits the churches' ability to do evangelistic outreach among these people, and as a result, English-speaking people are denied an opportunity to join these congregations. Therefore, churches are not fulfilling Christ's Great Commission locally. As a result, they are putting themselves in serious danger of experiencing a decline in membership and eventually disappearing. The membership of immigrant churches continues to grow due to the fact that emigration from the homeland is still taking place and those who are believers are joining ethnic immigrant churches. However, as soon as this stream of newcomers stops, ethnic churches will lose their main source of growth. The biological source of growth, that is, the children of the immigrants becoming members of the ethnic churches, is not and will not be able to sustain the current level of membership. It will lead to a situation where membership will begin to shrink and churches will not be able to support the mission projects that they are now carrying. (3) The lack of communication between Slavic churches and other local English-speaking churches creates a ground for suspicious attitudes among the immigrant believers towards native-born American Christians. It is weakening the body of Christ, which is his church. It also puts immigrant churches in a position of disconnect with the reality of religious life in their new country. They are not fully aware of the contemporary issues that Christians are facing in this society and, because of this, are not prepared to react to them in the appropriate manner. (4) Although developing a subculture within the congregation is common for most churches, it becomes a very serious issue and barrier to evangelism when dealing with immigrant ethnic churches. The subculture in these churches is based on keeping outdated traditions and maintaining very close-knit relationships between the members of the church. Church members have known each other for a long time and they know each other very well. Many of them have become relatives because of marriage between their children. It is very difficult for a Russian-speaking unchurched person, who does not have a previous history of attending church in the homeland, to visit a church, to find room for herself/himself in the network of relationships that exist within the congregation, and to develop a sense of belonging to the church body. This could be one reason that Slavic Baptist churches have so few new converts from the outside world among their members, as demonstrated through the survey of newly baptized members that was shown in chapter 6, section 6.1.

8.2. Interethnic Relations between Slavic Immigrants and Other People Groups

The nature of relations between immigrants and people in the receiving society is interethnic because, in most cases, immigrants belong to a different ethnic group than the people in the new country. These relations affect the immigrants' willingness and ability to do mission work among people of a different ethnicity. The development of interethnic relations is shaped by both of the ethnic groups involved in these relations. In this part of the chapter, relations between immigrants and people in the receiving society are discussed.

In reality, the "receiving" society very seldom plays the role of a true receiving society. For indigenous people, immigrants will always be aliens, and their presence often annoys local people. Even when immigrants do not create competition in the job market and there is no discrimination policy against immigrants on the official level, indigenous people still have unfriendly feelings towards them. They see them as the source of all problems and have an instinctive mistrust towards them.[31] Such attitudes among people in the receiving society do not help in creating good relations between them and the newcomers, and often lead to racism.[32] Immigrants, on the other hand, have their own reasons for distancing themselves from the indigenous people. When an individual finds himself in a foreign country with a different language and culture, his ethnic consciousness awakens.[33] An immigrant constantly feels his estrangement in the new land and often acknowledges his difference from the new society. This is especially true when he is experiencing difficulties in his social surroundings and when he is reminded by people around him that he is not like them.[34] Oppression, discrimination, and humiliation of immigrants, based on ethnicity, help the diaspora become united and feed its hostility towards the indigenous people. Sometimes it leads to the diaspora's self-isolation and creates social tensions.[35] All researchers point to the fact that it is difficult to establish friendly neighborhood relations between the immigrants and indigenous people in areas that are populated predominantly by immigrants.[36]

---

31. Zalman I. Levin, *Mentality of Diaspora: Systematic and Socio-cultural Analysis* (Moscow: Kraft, 2001), 33.

32. Trying to avoid facing racism in the society, immigrants are looking for a safe place in churches of their ethnicity. Nancy Abelmann notes, "ethnic churches offer a safe haven from racism" ("Christian Universalism and U.S. Multiculturalism: An 'Asian American' Campus Church," *Amerasia Journal* 34, no. 1 [2008]: 65).

33. Levin., *Mentality of Diaspora*, 29.

34. Ibid., 37.

35. Ibid., 29.

36. Ibid., 35.

A uniqueness of US society is that it is a mixture of many different ethnic groups who live together. This means that discussion about the relations between Slavic immigrants and the receiving society refers to those between ethnic Russians or Ukrainians and other different ethnic groups (Hispanic, Asian, African-American, etc.). This provides Slavic immigrants with the challenge of seeing these different ethnic groups as equal to them. One of the indicators of the immigrant churches' good attitude towards people in the receiving society, which, in the American context, means different ethnic groups, would be their willingness to collaborate and work with them as a congregation on a regular basis. As clearly seen in table 6.3.12. in chapter 6, not very many of these activities are conducted by Slavic churches. Almost 60 percent of the leaders of these churches that were surveyed stated that their churches did not organize any activities in collaboration with representatives from other ethnic groups. A total of 27 percent stated that these types of activities take place only several times per year. This is an indication that relations between these churches and other ethnic groups in the receiving society are not very strong. Another indicator of how good these relations are would be the immigrants' efforts to reach people from the receiving society with the gospel through different evangelistic efforts. Table 6.3.13. in chapter 6 shows that few churches were planning evangelistic activities for reaching other ethnic groups (see comments on Question 13 of the PCSBA church leaders survey in chapter 6). One of the strongest indicators of the quality of the relations between immigrants and other ethnic groups is each side's acceptance of interracial marriage. The stronger these relations are, the more often interethnic marriages take place and the less often they are accepted with criticism and animosity. Table 6.3.14. in chapter 6 presents the answers to the question, "How do the church members respond to interracial marriages?" that was asked in a survey of the leaders of the PCSBA churches. It shows that only 2.2 percent of the respondents answered this question by saying that their church looks at interracial marriage positively. This shows that there is still a distance between Slavic Baptist newcomers to America and indigenous ethnic people who already live here. All of these indicators point to the fact that no strong relations between Slavic immigrants and other ethnic groups currently exist. This means that Slavic immigrant churches in America are not very open to evangelizing and providing social help to people of different ethnicities as part of an authentic mission.

It is appropriate to point to the fact that there is a paradigm shift taking place in American education and society regarding their understanding of the nature and character of interethnic relationships. Much more ethnic diversity and culture tolerance than with the previous paradigms is encouraged.[37] Newly arrived immigrants are not forced to assimilate quickly. This will keep them isolated from other language and cultural groups. For the Slavic Baptists, this could hinder implementation of an authentic mission outside of their own Russian/Ukrainian ethnic group and could become a barrier in conducting cross-ethnic evangelism and social action/*diaconia*. A more detailed discussion of the paradigm shift taking place in America and in society regarding their understanding of the nature and character of interethnic relationships is provided in the appendix for chapter 8, section 8.3.A.

8.3. Role of Language in Church Life and Mission

In chapter 3, section 3.1.2., a brief discussion on the subject of language as a mission context was presented. In this chapter, the subject of language is explored from the perspective of its use in immigrant church life and mission. As one of the main communication tools for people, language is crucial for people's lives in general, and for their church life in particular. According to Ebaugh and Chafetz, "language usage in new immigrant religious institutions is simultaneously contested terrain and a bedrock for member unity and institutional commitment."[38] The use of a language that is different from English in the life of the congregation distinguishes the ethnic church from the local native church. The language of the church is the first and often the main characteristic of the church that makes it unique and different from others in the area. Ebaugh and Chafetz say, "The use of the native language in immigrant religious institutions serves two primary purposes: to allow the laity to understand their religious rituals and doctrine and to make them feel

---

37. Rod Janzen, "Five Paradigms of Ethnic Relations," *Social Education* 58, no. 6 (1994): 349.
38. Ebaugh and Chafetz, *Religion and the New Immigrants*, 100.

comfortable within, and therefore more committed to their congregation."[39] This part of the chapter will address the language usage issue in immigrant church life and how it relates to the mission work of immigrant churches.

8.3.1. Language as a Vehicle of Spreading the Faith

In his essay "Why Does Semantics Matter?" Hans H. Penner makes the following statement: "Language is a necessary condition for the existence of religion."[40] In his discussion of the issue of religious language, Peter Donovan strongly emphasizes the meaning of language for religions, saying that the "language of religious traditions is the chief means by which people can interpret what they take to be religiously meaningful phenomena."[41] Both of these authors make it clear that language is crucial for religion's existence.[42] It is the primary means for describing and interpreting religious doctrines, rituals, and rules. It is the main vehicle in passing religion on from person to person and from generation to generation. It is the main instrument in spreading the gospel among people. In his foreword to the book *Globalizing Theology*, Wilbert R. Shenk says, "Our interaction with the gospel relies on human language, worldview, and cultural context . . . We are utterly dependent on human language to speak about the gospel. The gospel engages the full range and all facets of human experience through the narratives of countless people, each speaking in their own vernacular and from within

---

39. Ibid., 107.

40. Hans H. Penner, "Why Does Semantics Matter?," in *Language, Truth, and Religious Belief*, ed. Nancy K. Frankenberry and Hans H. Penner (Atlanta, GA: Scholars Press, 1999), 497.

41. Peter Donovan, *Religious Language* (New York: Hawthorn Books, 1976), 100. Donovan insists, "Religions are systems of belief and behavior by which meaning are found in a very wide range of things encountered and experienced in human life . . . Not all interpreting is in words. People may interpret by their reactions, rituals, and other forms of behavior with which they respond to and express the meaning they find in things. But verbal interpretation is generally more important than any other kind, especially in the universal religions which depend very much on language for expressing and transmitting themselves."

42. An important observation about relations between language and religion is made by William Safran in his study of language, ethnicity and religion relations. He states, "Language and religion are related; both have deep structures and both are regarded as constitutive aspects of 'primordialism' in the sense that individuals are born into one, the other, or (in most instances) both. The relationships between religion and language have varied with time and place, and the causal direction between the two has been complex. Religion and language may be clearly associated and feed upon each other; language may be a substitute for religion; or religion may trump language" ("Language, Ethnicity and Religion: A Complex and Persistent Linkage," *Nations & Nationalism* 14, no. 1 [2008]: 171).

their worldview."⁴³ However, describing language as a vehicle in spreading the gospel is only true when the language used is the language that people understand. The native languages of people should be used in order to successfully bring the gospel to them. Ebaugh and Chafetz believe that the use of the immigrants' native languages in congregational life is beneficial for current church members and helps bring new converts to the congregation. They describe it in the following way: "The use of native vernaculars enables clergy to better instruct the laity in the meaning of their religious beliefs and practices, permits immigrants to understand religious services, and creates a sense of comfort and familiarity for newcomers who often feel estranged and bewildered in their new community. In turn, comfort and familiarity contribute to institutional commitment by members and, in many cases, to the religious conversion of fellow language-speakers."⁴⁴

Clearly, a common language opens the door for the non-believers to the church. As was illustrated in chapter 6, section 6.7., knowledge of the Russian language allows members of PCSBA churches to reach their own people with the gospel around the world.

8.3.2. Language as a Barrier to Spreading the Faith

Unfortunately, the language described above as the main vehicle in passing on religion from generation to generation could, in certain situations, become a barrier to spreading the faith. This happens when people try to share their faith using a language that the potential "receiver" of the faith does not understand well. Such situations take place within immigrant communities when the older generation of immigrants uses their native language in religious matters, including church services, assuming that their children understand their native language well. In most situations, it is not the case. The younger generation usually learns the language of the new country quickly and becomes very comfortable with it.⁴⁵ Nelly Elias in her analysis

---

43. Wilbert R. Shenk, "Foreword" in *Globalizing Theology*, ed. Craig Ott and Harold A. Netland (Grand Rapids, MI: Baker Academic, 2006), 9.

44. Ebaugh and Chafetz, *Religion and the New Immigrants*, 110.

45. Referring to the presence of the generational gap within the immigrant communities, Stephen R. Warner points to the fact that "despite cultural flows from the home county, the American-raised and American-born second generation of most new immigrant groups are for the most part acculturating very rapidly, becoming English-dominant and losing fluency in their parents' native tongues. At a minimum, they often find immigrant religious activities

of trends in Russian-language media consumption in Israel points to the following fact: "the children who arrived at a very young age or who were born in Israel refrain from using media in Russian and . . . the two generations of the immigrant family end up living in separate media worlds."[46] This is often true not only for the "media worlds" but for the "church worlds" as well.

Ebaugh and Chafetz, in their study of immigrant issues, point to the fact that, "Although most immigrant parents want their children to be fluent in English . . . they also want them to remain attached to their ethnic and religious heritages, which are themselves typically closely intertwined. The obvious strategy to retain second-generation members within the ethnic congregation is to create English language services geared in style and format, as well as language, to their offsprings' tastes."[47] "The obvious strategy" that the authors are referring to is not always obvious for the leaders and for members of immigrant churches. They try to insist on keeping their native language as the main language of church life and try to impose it on the younger generation, usually with limited success. This creates misunderstanding and tension between the representatives of the older and younger generations in the church.[48] Eventually, it usually results in the youth leaving the church. When describing the issue of generational differences, Stepick states that it seems universal among the children of immigrants to have conflict or stress between them and their parents.[49] While immigrant parents attempt "to protect their children from what they view as the dangers of American culture," the youth "seek to enjoy what they view as the freedoms

---

incomprehensible and boring, and many first generation leaders are worried that their children will leave the fold" ("Religion and New (Post-1965) Immigrants: Some Principles Drawn from Field Research" *American Studies* 41, no. 2/3 [Summer/Fall 2000]: 280).

46. Nelly Elias, "Russian-Speaking Immigrants and Their Media: Still Together?," *Israel Affairs* 17, no. 1 (Jan 2011): 85.

47. Ebaugh and Chafetz, *Religion and the New Immigrants*, 104.

48. In his article, Michael Kisskalt said that if we will analyze the cultural challenges of the second generation of immigrants who are living between two cultures, "we might understand that tensions in which they must find their way – torn between the values and behavioral patterns of their parents, which are also the guidelines in the monoethnic churches, and the norms and social patterns in the new home country" ("Cross-Cultural Learning: Issues of the Second Generation of Immigrant Churches," in *Ethnic Churches in Europe: A Baptist Response*, ed. Peter Penner [Schwarzenfeld: Neufeld Verlag, 2006], 146).

49. Stepick, "God Is Apparently Not Dead," 19.

Analysis of Mission Challenges and Opportunities for the Slavic Baptist Diaspora   331

of American society."⁵⁰ Stepick confirms, "In this struggle, youth frequently have an advantage over their parents as they usually speak better English and are more familiar with American ways."⁵¹ When referring to the struggle of the youth with the religion of their parents, Alex Stepick states, "Second-generation immigrant youth usually prefer services in English, consider religious leaders as much out of touch with American culture as their parents, and view religion as an effort to limit their freedom and control them . . . In response, immigrant youth are more likely than their parents to shift religious affiliation or even reject religion all together."⁵²

A problem of language use, such as the use of the language of the former homeland versus English in the immigrant church life and service, is one example of language becoming a barrier in spreading the gospel.⁵³ In this case, parents are trying to evangelize their children with the hopes of passing their faith onto them, using a language children do not understand well enough. Another example of a problem of language use is the inability of non-English-speaking immigrants to share their faith with their neighbors and other people whom they encounter in the new country. The difference in the languages that people speak creates a wall of separation between native-born Americans and newcomers to the States.

8.3.3. Role of the Russian Language for Mission Work among Russian-Speaking Communities in America and Abroad

The fact that Russian is used by PCSBA churches as the main language in their life and worship provides them with the unique opportunity to reach

---

50. Ibid.
51. Ibid.
52. Ibid.
53. It is important to note that language used during the worship is not the only issue in the intergenerational relations the immigrant churches are facing. Wendy Cadge points to the results of the study that "shows how members of the second generation remain distinct from their parents' generation while still worshipping in an ethnic-specific context" ("Immigration and Religion," *Annual Review of Sociology* 33, no. 1 [2007]: 369). Another piece of research, according to Cadge, "shows that members of the second generation sometimes have different ideas about the content of their religion, with the first generation viewing Christianity according to ascribed religious and ethnic criteria and the second generation viewing Christianity according to the more achieved and individualistic criteria they perceive as evangelical" (ibid.). This illustrates the complexity of the process of passing on the faith of the first generation immigrants to their children.

their fellow immigrants from the former USSR with the gospel. As it was mentioned in chapter 5, section 5.3.2., about five million Russian-speaking people currently live in the US. If most of them are not Christians (which is very probable), they make up a great mission field on which Slavic immigrant churches could focus their evangelistic attention. According to the results of a survey of Slavic Baptist church leaders that was conducted in 2005, this is what the churches are trying to do. About 20 percent of respondents stated that witnessing to Russian-speaking people in the US is part of the main mission focus of their churches. Of course, it is not a very high percentage, but it still shows that Slavic churches are paying attention to this part of the population of the United States. The Russian language serves as a connecting point, as a bridge, between Russian-speaking believers and Russian-speaking unbelievers. In the context of the predominantly English-speaking society of America, meeting somebody who speaks their native language is usually a touching experience for immigrants, especially for new arrivals. This person becomes very dear and it is usually easy to start a friendship with him/her. In these cases, the Russian language plays a very important role in connecting people and creating an opportunity to share the gospel with Russian-speaking non-Christians. The challenge for Slavic churches in America, when reaching their fellow ethnics, is that Russian-speaking unbelievers do not necessarily live in the same city or area of the country where these churches are located. As shown in chapter 5, section 5.2.4., the settlement pattern for non-Christians from the USSR in America differs from that of the Baptists from the USSR. The largest groups of Russian-speaking people in the US are living in Los Angeles, CA and its vicinity, and in New York City. Most of these people are of Jewish descent. Statistical information shows that there are hundreds of thousands of them living in these two locations. At the same time, there are very few Russian-speaking Baptist churches located in these areas. These churches are relatively small and have limited resources for carrying out a strong evangelistic campaign that would allow them to reach this multitude of non-Christians from their homeland. The PCSBA is currently attempting to plant new churches in areas that contain large populations of non-Christian Russian-speaking people.

Keeping the Russian language functional in immigrant church life is also beneficial for developing mission work abroad. Millions of Russian-speaking people live outside of their homeland, around the world. Most of them have left republics of the former Soviet Union relatively recently, after the collapse of the USSR, looking for a better life or for a job to support their families at home. They still speak Russian well and are interested in radio and Internet programs in Russian or in meeting somebody in person who speaks their native language. This worldwide Russian-speaking diaspora is also a mission field. It could be reached through radio broadcasting in Russian with the support of PCSBA churches. Regularly broadcast Sunday services of immigrant churches in America, which are conducted in Russian, is one of the ways of reaching Russian-speaking people around the world. These means of communication are used by PCSBA churches in order to bring the good news to Russian-speaking people living in different countries. In addition to the efforts to reach Russian-speaking people abroad through the radio and Internet, PCSBA churches in America are also trying to reach them through personal contact. For this purpose, they send short-term mission teams to areas of the world where Russian-speaking people reside. One of these areas is Western Europe.

These few examples of the use of the Russian language in spreading the gospel illustrate the importance of preserving this language by Slavic immigrants in America in order to conduct mission work among Russian-speaking people around the world.

8.3.4. Russian Language as an Obstacle for Mission Work among the English-Speaking Community

As it was pointed to in the previous part of the chapter, the gospel has to be proclaimed in the language that people understand in order to be accepted by them. This is why missionaries starting their work in a new country among new people first learn the language of those people. A similar approach should be used by immigrants if they want to reach the non-believers among people in the receiving society with the gospel. Using their own language in religious matters separates immigrants from their new neighbors, and disables them in such an important aspect of Christian life as being personal witnesses to people about salvation in Christ. On one hand, one of the greatest needs of immigrants is to be able to worship God and to be instructed in religious doctrines in their native language. On the other hand, the people around them need to hear the gospel in the language of the country in which immigrants have arrived. This is a dilemma that Slavic Baptist immigrants are struggling with in America. The problem exists not only in the fact that immigrants have a limited ability to communicate the content of the gospel to people who only speak English. The problem is broader. Even if immigrants were able to share the gospel with their English-speaking neighbors, witnessing without appropriate follow-up and without bringing a person to the church family is not fruitful. In chapter 1, section 1.2.5., it was shown that the important aspect of mission is making disciples and this should be done in the context of church community. Because of this productive witnessing should be accompanied by an invitation to non-Christians to a small-group Bible study first and then eventually to the church. Unfortunately, it is impossible for Slavic Baptist immigrants to do so because of the language barrier. It puts people, especially the youth who want to witness and bring people to the church, in a difficult position. They want to be obedient to the Lord in fulfilling his Great Commission but, at the same time, they do not have the church's support to do so. Surveys of the young people at PCSBA churches that were conducted in 2004 and 2010 show that many of the youth (55% of the respondents in 2004 and 77% in 2010) have English-speaking friends whom they would like to invite to their church (chapter 6, table 6.4.10.). However, they cannot do so because the church services use only the Russian language. This is a very serious obstacle when trying to do evangelistic work among native-born Americans. It is especially problematic because it discourages the young people in the church from doing personal evangelism among English-speakers. As a result, some of the young people in Slavic churches lose their zeal to do this and reduce their religious life to participation in church activities done within the church and designed only for church members who speak Russian. Those who cannot accept this situation leave the Slavic church and join an English-speaking congregation. Because of this, the Slavic immigrant churches are losing the most enthusiastic and mission-oriented young people. This issue will be discussed in more detail in section 8.4.2. of this chapter.

8.3.5. Lack of Spiritual Maturity among the Younger Generation as a Result of Using the Russian Language in the Church

Due to the fact that church services are conducted in Russian which children don't understand well when it comes to the subject of teaching the Bible, the children of Christian parents, while physically growing in the church, do not produce a noticeable growth in their personal faith. This leads to a lack of spiritual maturity among a segment of the second generation of Slavic immigrant churches. As such, certain percentages of the young people in Slavic churches become nominal Christians, attending church only to meet and socialize with their friends. Spiritual matters are not a great concern for them. Some of them are baptized and become members of the church. However, they do not bear spiritual fruit in their lives. Others are leading a double life. When they are in the church, they act as believers. When they are outside of the church community, they act in accordance with the life style of the non-Christian community around them.

Another percentage of the Slavic youth is striving for a better understanding of the Bible and its doctrines, and for progress in personal spiritual growth. These young people are searching for sources to satisfy their hunger for better theological knowledge, and they are looking for guidance in the complex contemporary religious issues of the world around them. Because they are not always able to receive adequate help from their church leaders, they turn their attention to the resources available in English. There are plenty of them available in America today. Books, radio programs, CDs, DVDs, and websites are full of different kinds of materials that were developed with the purpose of teaching people about religious matters. The Slavic youth are using them widely. They attend different conferences in English that address spiritual issues. Without the knowledge of their parents and Slavic church leaders, the youth are going through the process of spiritual formation under the strong influence of preachers and speakers from English-speaking churches. Doctrinally, they often stand on different theological ground than the Slavic Baptist leaders. The Slavic youth absorb the views and doctrinal positions of the English-speaking leaders to whom they listen. Usually, by the time that the Slavic church leaders discover this, it is already too late. Their youth already have accepted positions of the

English-speaking preachers. When discussion takes place between representatives from the older and younger generations in Slavic churches about disputed theological issues, the older people have difficulty convincing their youth to keep positions that have been traditionally kept by Slavic Baptists for decades. It often ends with the young people leaving the church.

The exodus of young people from the church, especially those with leadership potential, puts the future of the church in question. As Tom W. Sine, Jr. rightly said, "If the western church is to have a future we must give our fullest support to this new generation of leaders and invite them to help reinvent the church for the twenty-first century."[54] This is true for the Western church in general. It is even truer for the Western immigrant churches. In a survey of Slavic people who left Russian-speaking congregations (table 6.6.6.), 50.0 percent of the respondents said that one reason why they left the Slavic church was because the doctrinal position of the church was not clear; 42.5 percent of the respondents declared that one of the reasons why they left was the fact that the doctrinal position of the church did not fit their personal understanding of the Bible. There is a high chance that this "personal understanding of the Bible" had been developed by the preaching and teaching of English-speaking Christian leaders. The issue of younger generation leaving Slavic immigrant churches will be discussed in more detail in section 8.4.2. of this chapter.

In conclusion, it could be said that using the Russian language in church creates a twofold situation. On the one hand, some young people demonstrate a lack of spiritual maturity because they do not receive the appropriate teaching in the language they understand, which is English. On the other hand, some of the youth find themselves in a different theological camp from their parents and the Slavic church leaders because, in search of spiritual growth, they turned their attention to the English-speaking preachers and teachers instead. As a result, a division on theological grounds takes place in Slavic churches between the older and younger generations.

---

54. Tom W. Sine, Jr., "Globalization, Creation of Global Culture of Consumption and the Impact on the Church and its Mission," *Evangelical Review of Theology* 27, no. 4 (Oct 2003): 369.

8.4. Hindrances and Opportunities for Mission

8.4.1. Lack of Financial Support and Inadequate Training as Hindrances for Mission

In the discussion of hindrances for mission among Slavic churches, some of them can be identified which are common for most organizations involved in mission, both ethnic and native. Among them are the lack of financial support and inadequate training of potential missionaries. In a survey of PCSBA church leaders, the results of which are provided in chapter 6 of this study, the following question was asked: "What hinders missionary work in our circumstances?" One of the most common answers was, "Lack of firm financial grounding for mission." Although Russian immigrants are known for their generosity, the funds available in churches are still very limited when it comes to the question of supporting mission. Despite the fact that some church members have prospered in America, own businesses, and have well-paid jobs, the majority in the church are still struggling financially and do not have much to give to mission. This is an ongoing problem.

Another problem is the inadequate training of those who want to participate in mission projects. In a Slavic church leadership survey conducted in 2005, the following question was asked: "If you are not satisfied with the mission work in your church, then what is unsatisfactory?" (The answers to this question are available in the appendix for chapter 6.) The following answers were among those stated the most often:

- Those participating in mission trips themselves need to hear about God.
- Lack of spiritual training.
- Those going on mission trips are young and ignorant of the Scriptures.
- Only trained and committed brothers and sisters should be sent on missions.

It is obvious that church leaders see the need for more training for those who plan to participate in mission work. This is the challenge that the PCSBA churches are trying to meet by providing training seminars and workshops for the members of short-term mission teams before they leave for the mission field.

These two hindrances to mission work are not unique to Slavic immigrant churches. Probably all churches, in one way or another, are facing either one or both of these problems. However, the PCSBA churches are facing something that is common only to the ethnic immigrant churches: As was already mentioned above, some of the younger church members are switching their membership to English-speaking churches. This issue deserves special attention and is discussed below.

8.4.2. Losing Younger Church Members to English-Speaking Congregations as Hindrances for Mission

On 14 April 2010, in personal correspondence with the author of this study, Boltniew wrote: "I'm convinced that ethnic churches are extremely important because they minister to both the young and the old. They also provide American churches with faithful members and, thus, contribute to the spiritual vitality of America . . . Eventually bilingual, or ethnic churches, provide American churches with faithful and active members. In this way we contribute to the spiritual strength of America."[55] Boltniew sees it as beneficial for "the spiritual strength of America" when former members of ethnic churches join American (read: "English-speaking") churches. This is true in general. However, at the same time, it is disadvantageous for the particular ethnic church to lose its members, especially if they are "faithful and active members." Gerardo Marti, referring to the mono-ethnic immigrant churches in Los Angeles as "an ethnic haven for recent immigrants," points to the important reality: "The children of these immigrants are now finding their way into a more broadly Americanized setting. Their schools and their workplaces are diverse, but their churches are not. Mosaic[56] provides a haven for second- and third-generation ethnics escaping from mono-ethnic home churches and the ethnic enclaves of their parents and grandparents."[57]

---

55. George Boltniew, Interview by author, 14 April 2010, e-mail.

56. "Mosaic" in Southern California is one of the largest multiethnic congregations in America.

57. Gerardo Marti, *A Mosaic of Believers: Diversity and Innovation in a Multiethnic Church* (Bloomington, IN: Indiana University Press, 2005), 156.

Unfortunately, it seems unavoidable for ethnic churches to go through this experience sooner or later.[58] It looks like PCSBA churches are approaching this point. As was shown in chapter 6, section 6.6., despite an increase in the number of churches that are a part of the association, its total membership during the last couple of years not only did not increase, but actually decreased slightly. One of the contributing factors to this is clearly losing members to English-speaking churches. Although by doing so, the Slavic Baptist churches "contribute to the spiritual vitality of America," a decrease in membership affects their strength in different aspects of their life, including the ability to do mission work in America and abroad. Because of this, losing members to English-speaking churches could be seen as a serious hindrance to mission among PCSBA churches.[59]

How can this process be stopped or at least slowed down? In order to obtain the necessary information to find an answer to this vital question, a survey was conducted among those who have left Russian-speaking congregations and who have joined English-speaking churches. This survey is unique in its nature and provided the author with helpful information. The results of the survey and its analysis are provided in the appendix for chapter 6, tables 6.6.1. to 6.6.16. Very interesting answers were received in reply to the question, "What were the reasons causing people to leave the church?"

---

58. In her reference to the transnational practices among the second generation of immigrants, Peggy Levitt insists that "the children of immigrants born in the U.S., or who spend most of their formative years in this country, would feel their strongest sense of attachment to their family's adopted, rather than ancestral, home" ("Between God, Ethnicity, and Country: An Approach to the Study of Transnational Religion" [paper presented at workshop on "Transnational Migration: Comparative Perspectives," Princeton University, 30 June–1 July 2001], 26).

59. Losing the younger generation from the immigrant churches means more than decreased membership. This means losing very valuable workers for mission ministry. The study of Korean-American churches indicates that "if the second generation could be properly equipped, motivated, and directed to join in mission, their contribution would be phenomenal. The second generation has a bi-cultural identity that uniquely equips them, so that while they possess all the great qualities of the North American missionaries, they also know how to thrive as a minority in a foreign land. They not only speak English fluently, but their bi-cultural qualities will connect them to the global mission community as well. With the added spiritual heritage of a fervently praying spirit, handed down from the first generation, they have the potential to thrive in missional settings" (Daniel Shinjong Baeq, Myunghee Lee, Sokpyo Hong, and Jonathan Ro, "Mission from Migrant Church to Ethnic Minorities: A Brief Assessment of the Korean American Church in Mission," *Missiology* 39, no. 1 [Jan 2011]: 31).

(see chapter 6, table 6.6.6.). The top reason, as named by 78.6 percent of the respondents, is the low quality of sermons in the Russian-speaking church. It shows that there are high expectations for the sermon quality of Slavic churches. If these expectations are not met, some people would leave the church. The second top reason (56.3%) is a misdirected vision for the church in the new cultural and language context. People are looking for a clear and relevant vision for the church among their church leaders. They feel that immigrant churches need contextualization of the church's life and ministry. When people lose the hope of seeing it in their churches, they leave and join English-speaking congregations. Slightly more than half of the respondents (52.3%) stated that the Sunday service experience in Slavic churches was not satisfying enough for them. This shows that keeping the old worship style in the church is not wise. Although the older generation in the church wants to preserve it, the younger generation is looking for a style that could be similar to those of the English-speaking churches. Contextualization is required in this aspect of the church life as well.[60]

As mentioned in the previous part of this chapter, exactly half of the respondents (50.0%) stated that the unclear nature of the doctrinal position of the church was one of the reasons why they abandoned their membership in the Slavic church. Historically, because of the persecutions that evangelical Christians experienced in the former Soviet Union for a long time, they did not have many opportunities to develop and systematize their theological views. They tried to survive, and paid more attention to the practical application of their faith in the hostile Soviet environment than to the development of their theological doctrines. While living in America, Slavic churches are not as much concerned about their doctrinal position as they

---

60. It seems that most of the first generation of immigrants in Slavic churches do not understand the cultural difference that exists between them and youth in their churches. It causes rising expectations towards youth that are unrealistic and simply inappropriate. Similar experiences take place in other ethic churches. The study of Korean-American churches states that "the second generation KAs [KA – Korean-Americans], including those who already attend KACs [KAC – Korean-American Churches], need to be regarded as ethnic minority communities that need, if not greater, at least similar support from the first generation KACs: the first generation KACs should not view them as younger versions of themselves that can be controlled by them, but rather as a different people group with a different culture. By regarding them as another ethnic minority, the first generation KAs will be able to lay aside set expectations and let the second generation KAs run a style of church that best accommodates their interests and needs" (ibid.).

are about day-to-day church life practical issues. Of course, the American, English-speaking churches have a much better articulation of their doctrinal position. When it comes to discussion about controversial theological issues, their leaders are much better prepared to address these issues and to defend their position than the leaders of the immigrant churches.[61] The younger generation of Slavic immigrants has been exposed to different controversial theological issues through the means of mass communication. They often take the side of the American leaders in theological discussions. As a result, divisions occur between the younger and older people of Slavic churches. Because of this, some young people leave.

Three are other reasons directly related to the mission of the church in the world are named as causes of departure from the Slavic church by some people. The lack of evangelistic efforts directed by the church towards English-speaking people is one of the most important reasons why they left the Russian-speaking congregation; 41.3 percent of respondents in the survey stated that one of the reasons they left their ethnic immigrant church was the lack or absence of evangelistic efforts towards the surrounding community. The lack or absence of these efforts could be explained mainly by the language barrier. 38.8 percent pointed to the isolationist attitude among church members as one of the reasons why they departed the church. A large degree of the isolationist attitude among immigrants is the product of language and culture differences between them and the people around them. 32.5 percent said that the lack of practical service opportunities for church members among local people (e.g. feeding the homeless, helping the poor, etc.) prompted them to make a decision to leave. The inattentiveness

---

61. Michael O. Emerson and Christian Smith, studying inter-racial relations, claim that religion in America is a marketplace where people have a choice as to where and with whom to worship. As in other marketplaces, there is competition in the religion marketplace as well. "Because survival of religious organizations in the United States depends primarily on the religious consumer, not on state support, and a vast number of religious and nonreligious alternatives exist, religious groups compete for adherents" (*Divided By Faith: Evangelical Religion and the Problem of Race in America* [New York: Oxford University Press, 2000], 140). Young Slavic immigrant believers are subject to this competition. Slavic immigrant churches are in a disadvantaged situation while they try to compete for their youth with established English-speaking churches. Reasons for this are reflected in the answers to the question "What attracted you to the English-speaking church?" of the survey of people who left the Russian-speaking churches. The results of this survey are available in the appendix to chapter 6. See the table 6.6.7.

of Slavic churches to the needs of the people around them is not due to a lack of compassion among their members. They are usually a very compassionate people. It mainly takes place because of the limited communication between them and the people in the community, which is created by this very language barrier.

It is obvious that there are those in the Slavic immigrant churches who are not satisfied with the "self-centeredness" of these churches. They see the mission of the church as serving others, starting with their immediate surroundings. The oral proclamation of the gospel to non-Christians and social action/*diaconia* through serving people in the community with their practical needs are viewed by these people as the foundational activities of every congregation. When they do not see it happening, and there is no sign that it will start happening in the near future, they switch to English-speaking churches. It is a great loss for Slavic immigrant churches when mission-minded people are leaving. When the number of these people who are a part of the congregation decreases, the lower the chance is for the church to reorient itself and become "outward-centered" and local mission focused. Other factors, such as conflict with the leadership of the church (26.3%) and long Sunday services (16.3%), are also listed among reasons for leaving Slavic immigrant churches. The most surprising result of this survey is that only 11.3 percent of the respondents included their personal limitation in understanding the Russian/Ukrainian language, when compared to English, as one of the reasons for leaving the Slavic church. The common belief is that the younger generation is leaving the immigrant churches because of the difficulty in understanding the language used in the church services. However, according to this survey, this reason is the least used. The issue of younger people leaving Slavic immigrant churches is much more complex and cannot be reduced to the limitations of understanding the language. It should be addressed in its full complexity in order to make a difference in the efforts of PCSBA churches to keep their youth with them as their main resource to practice authentic local mission in the immigrant context.

The analysis of the results of the survey of the former members of Slavic churches clearly shows that the reasons people leave these churches vary. The problem with limitations in understanding the native language of their parents and the language used in the church service is not the only reason for departure. It is not even the main reason. It is actually the reason that is referred to least. In order to keep the younger generation in Slavic churches, and by doing so, protect the ability of the church to do mission in this world, the leadership, together with the whole church body, should be prepared and willing to go through the process of contextualization of their church life. They should be prepared to sacrifice many of their habitual church practices in order to make necessary adjustments in the church life and to bring it into alignment with the life of the English-speaking American churches. This is a challenge that Slavic Baptist churches are facing in America today.

8.4.3 New Opportunities for Missions as a Result of Political Changes in the World

New mission opportunities for Slavic Baptist immigrant churches have developed because of the political changes that have recently taken place in the world. Discussion of these opportunities is provided in the appendix for chapter 8, section 8.4.3.A.

8.5. The Multiracial Congregation Model as an Option for the Immigrant Churches

When addressing the issue of the racial segregation that is widely present in American congregations today, Curtiss Paul DeYoung and three coauthors suggest that the solution for this problem is multiracial congregations.[62] They strongly insist that "Christian congregations, when possible, should be multiracial."[63] To support this claim, they point to the New Testament story of Jesus, which states "that Jesus' inclusive table fellowship and vision of a house of prayer that was for all the nations was a precursor to what we call multiracial congregations."[64] Multiracial congregations are better equipped

---

62. The Biblical foundation for the multiethnic churches is well developed by Mark Deymaz in his book *Building a Healthy Multi-Ethnic Church* (San Francisco: Wiley Imprint, 2007).

63. Curtiss Paul DeYoung, Michael O. Emerson, George Yancey, and Karen Chai Kim, *United by Faith: The Multiracial Congregation as an Answer to the Problem of Race* (New York: Oxford University Press, 2003), 2.

64. Ibid, 20.

to fulfill the Great Commission.[65] DeYoung and his coauthors recognize the reasons for the existence of uniethnic congregations in America. Among them are: the unique history and culture of ethnic groups, their unique symbols of faith, their unique theology, and preservation of the ethnic culture and language in a new land. Although they recognize all of these reasons as being important and valuable, DeYoung and his team defend their vision for multiracial congregations by providing their response to the arguments based on the reasons mentioned above. They believe that despite the fact that "racial separation may be sociologically comfortable," it is not necessarily what God wants. Since God originally created only one race, "Jesus and the first-century church believed they were commissioned to create congregations that more accurately reflected God's original intention for the human family. The day of Pentecost birthed a multicultural church that served as a re-creation of God's original intention."[66]

Therefore, multiracial churches today better reflect God's design for humanity than racially segregated congregations.[67] Although they recognize the fact that it could be difficult for newly arrived immigrants to establish or to maintain multiracial congregations and, in certain cases, the temporary existence of ethnic immigrant communities as a transitional phenomenon could be justified, DeYoung and his coauthors emphasize that "as the technical possibilities for simultaneous translation become more affordable, this exception is less compelling."[68] For the second generation of immigrants, establishment of multiracial congregations should not be a problem. Also, in regard to the effectiveness of mission by this type of congregation, the authors "have argued that in the twenty-first century, multiracial congregations can be effective in evangelizing the highly diverse United States."[69] Multiracial congregations could become a place where people of different

---

65. Mark Deymaz and Harry Li, *Ethnic Blends: Mixing Diversity into Your Local Church* (Grand Rapids, MI: Zondervan, 2010), 37.

66. DeYoung et al., *United by Faith*, 131.

67. According to the WCC Consultation on Mission "the church was intentionally started as a multiracial, multinational and multicultural community of faith (Acts 2, with Is. 66:18)" ("Report of the World Council of Churches (WCC) Consultation on Mission and Ecclesiology of the Migrant Churches," *International Review of Mission* 100, no. 1 [Apr 2011]: 105).

68. DeYoung et al., *United by Faith*, 132.

69. Ibid.

cultural, ethnic, and racial backgrounds meet. They worship God together as his children. This would help overcome the mutual prejudices that exist widely in society today. In these congregations, "people of color cross the divide of race and learn to interact with one another amid cultural differences. Multiracial congregations are places to live out God's call to unity. For future race relations to be healthy, there must be a mutual accountability to each other and no group can have a dominant position over another group."[70]

These congregations could be a place of reconciliation between ethnic groups that have had a history of interracial struggles. These multiracial congregations should raise their voices against the racial and social injustices in society, and the "multiracial witness can further strengthen the possibility for reform in society."[71] One of the main reasons that is often referred to for the existence of racially separate congregations is their role in embracing and nurturing ethnic culture. DeYoung and his coauthors point to the fact that such attempts are illusory because all cultures are undergoing the process of continual change. There is no way to prevent these changes, especially in such a culturally diverse society as that of America. Cultures shape each other.[72] The only question is if these changes are positive or negative. "To this end, a multiracial congregation with egalitarian relationships between the races offers the best opportunity to learn about other cultures. It also encourages us to learn to accept the cultural changes that are best for our own culture while rejecting the potential changes that may be harmful."[73]

Being in church with people of many different cultures provides believers with valuable benefits, such as "it pushes us to understand others; we put ourselves in another's shoes; and we are forced to get out of our own cocoon." Living and worshiping together as a multiracial church will change the cultural portrait of the church. "Over time, a new culture is developed,

---

70. Ibid., 134.

71. Ibid., 136.

72. Robert Schreiter points to the fact that in our time, because of globalization, cultures are impacted by many forces and are experiencing constant change. He states that through the "processes of migration and urbanization, cultures tend to lose their erstwhile rural integrity and become more porous, plural, and undefined. The processes of globalization only exaggerates these phenomena" ("Christian Mission in a 'New Modernity' and Trajectories in Intercultural Theology," in *From World Mission to Inter-Religious Witness*, ed. Linda Hogan, Solange Lefebvre, Norbert Hintersteiner, and Felix Wilfred [London: SCM, 2011], 32).

73. DeYoung et al., *United by Faith*, 138.

one that did not exist before. People will move beyond simply representing their separate groups. They will forge a new, common identity, even as they maintain their uniqueness."[74] Integration, not assimilation, is the goal of this process.[75] One of the models used in the multiracial church is the "Church within a Church" model, in which the overall membership is multiracial. "However, there can be special fellowship groups within the larger congregation that exist to meet the specific need of particular populations."[76] This model could be used for first-generation immigrants. "Language-specific worship services could be offered while at the same time the broader social networks of the entire congregation are available to meet the transition and networking needs of immigrant families."[77]

This model could help new immigrants overcome culture and language barriers more rapidly than could be done in a uniethnic congregation. Overall, the multiracial[78] congregation model is a good option for immigrant

---

74. Ibid., 139.

75. Gerardo Marti points to the fact that race and ethnicity are not static, as many people believe. According to Marti, "A more fluid understanding of ethnic and racial identity" ("Fluid Ethnicity and Ethnic Transcendence in Multiracial Churches," *Journal for the Scientific Study of Religion* 47, no. 1 [March 2008]: 15) should be adopted. He shows that one of the important results accomplished by multiracial congregations is producing an inclusive religious identity that prevails over divisive aspects of ethnic identity. He states, "I found that coming to terms with the fluidity of ethnic and racial identity provided a heuristic that encourages greater openness to appreciating the inherent – and often unexpected – richness of social processes in multiracial settings" (ibid.). In another article, Gerardo Marti states, "Evidence from Mosaic and Oasis suggests that the experience of becoming a member of a multiethnic/multiracial congregation reorients personal identity such that people of various ethnic and racial heritages subdue their ethnoracial distinctions in favor of a common religious identity that forms the basis for affiliation with their congregation and structures these cross-ethnic interactions as nondisruptive" ("Affinity, Identity, and Transcendence: The Experience of Religious Racial Integration in Diverse Congregations," *Journal for the Scientific Study of Religion* 48, no. 1 [March 2009]: 63). Marti identifies three "moments" or phases in the experience of multiracial church members as they are going through the process of developing new relationships. These phases are affinity with the congregation, identity reorientation, and ethnic transcendence (ibid. 57).

76. DeYoung et al., *United by Faith*, 140.

77. Ibid., 142.

78. While Paul DeYoung and his co-authors are using the term "multiracial" extensively, there are others who use the term "multiethnic." Gerardo Marti deliberately uses the term "multiethnic" in reference to the "Mosaic" – the congregation he is serving as Senior Pastor, in Los Angeles. In his book, Gerardo Marti argues that the term "multiracial" is often perceived as describing white/black relationships. According to Marti, "multiracial most often means biracial, a congregation with significant proportions of both whites and blacks" (*A Mosaic of Believers*, 29). This is an important concern. In relation to the immigrant churches that

churches to consider. Of course, it is very challenging to start this kind of congregation with first-generation immigrants being the majority in the church and in its leadership. It requires a willingness to leave the comfort zone of being surrounded by people of the same ethnicity and language in the church and a readiness to accept those who are different, both culturally and linguistically, into the fellowship and church friendship.

The argument DeYoung and others are making for multiracial Christian congregations has its support in the history of the early church. Because of the fact that many different countries were conquered by Romans and became part of the empire the Roman society was very diverse ethnically, culturally and linguistically. Voluntary and forced (due to persecution) migration of Christians during the first century brought them to encounters with many different people groups. In the next part of this chapter, the impact of migration on the social makeup of the early church is discussed. The results of this brief analysis provide support to the idea of establishing multiracial Christian congregations in the US.

8.6. The Multiracial Congregation Model in the Early Church

8.6.1. Patterns of Jewish Migration in the Roman Empire

Migration is a part of the history of the people of God. Migration was a part of life for Jews in Old Testament times. It has also been a part of the life of Christianity since its beginning. The Bible contains many stories of migration of God's chosen people. Jehu J. Hanciles claims that "the biblical story and message would be meaningless without migration and mobility."[79] There is a link between the mission of God (*missio Dei*) and migrant movements. Since the missionary nature of God is demonstrated through the fact that he "makes himself known to human beings through ordinary, culturally conditioned experiences,"[80] migration as one these experiences has been

---

will try to incorporate other ethnic groups in their midst, the term "multiethnic" could be more acceptable than "multiracial."

79. Jehu J. Hanciles, *Beyond Christendom: Globalization, African Migration, and the Transformation of the West* (Maryknoll, NY: Orbis, 2008), 140.

80. Ibid.

used by God to bring truth about him to people of different countries. The patriarchs of Israel and their families were often migrants (Gen 12:1–4, 10–16; 26:3; 28:10–15; 26:1).[81] Among the examples are Abraham, Joseph, Ruth, and others. The long history of Israel as a nation demonstrates that the "Jews were familiar with exile, persecution, and captivity . . . Such captivities included those under the Assyrians . . . , the Babylonians . . . , and the Egyptians."[82] Jews were expelled from their homeland and were sent to foreign lands. As a result the Jewish diaspora emerged. Ekkehard W. and Wolfgang Stegemann explain: "The term Diaspora designates the Jewry living outside the land of Israel. It was already common in ancient times (2 Macc 1:27; cf. also John 7:35) and actually means 'scattering.' Within the Roman empire in New Testament times there were Jewish Diaspora communities in Syria, Asia Minor, Greece, on Crete and Cyprus, in Egypt and Cyrenaica, and finally also in Italy. The most important were in Syrian Antioch, Alexandria, and Rome."[83]

Theissen states that in time of Jesus "there were Jews all over the then-known world," and that "there were more Jews in the Diaspora than in Palestine."[84] He points to four reasons for emigration of Jews. Some of them emigrated as mercenaries; others were enslaved prisoners of war; others escaped abroad as political refugees; others "were attracted by the prospect of better conditions" and moved to a new land.[85] When migrating to new territories, Jews carried their faith with them. "In exile, religious faith (or covenant relationship with Yahweh) had to be more deliberately explored and explicitly expressed because the visible structures and symbols of that faith were no longer available."[86] Practicing their faith in the foreign lands Jews witnessed about the living God Yahweh. Hanciles states: "enforced mobility and exile necessitated missionary encounters (cf. Dan 2:26–30;

---

81. Ibid., 143.

82. Wesley Rose, "Jewish versus Christian Diaspora," http://www.academia.edu/414495/Jewish_versus_Christian_Diaspora (accessed May 2013).

83. Ekkehard W. Stegemann and Wolfgang Stegemann, *The Jesus Movement: A Social History of Its First Century* (Minneapolis, MN: Fortress, 1999), 255.

84. Gerd Theissen, *Social Reality and the Early Christians: Theology, Ethics, and the World of the New Testament* (Minneapolis, MN: Fortress, 1992), 67.

85. Ibid., 68.

86. Hanciles, *Beyond Christendom*, 145.

Esth 2:5–11; 8:11–17)."[87] During time of Jesus some Jewish religious groups like the Pharisees made active efforts to convert Gentiles to Judaism. Their "missionary activity was encouraged and furthered by the large number of Jews already living abroad in the diaspora."[88] Jesus himself as a child experienced the life of a refugee when his parents fled to Egypt from Bethlehem escaping persecution from Herod the king (Matt 2:14–15). Most of his life Jesus lived in Galilee which "was populated by migrants and the dispossessed and 'an abundance of orphans, widows, poor, and unemployed,'" and where very many Gentiles lived.[89] Hanciles suggests "that Jesus' life and ministry embodied the interconnection of mission, boundary-crossing movement, and the alienation of exile and migration."[90] The Christian church that came into existence as the result of Jesus' life, death, and resurrection shared a fate similar to its Founder's destiny. Very soon it found itself on the move, as "God's pilgrim people among the nations."[91] Although in the beginning the early Jewish Christians were reluctant "to move beyond Jerusalem or outside the Jewish orbit"[92] the plan of the *missio Dei* took them from the comfort zone of their homeland and native language and culture and sent them preach the gospel "to the end of the earth." Acts 7 and 8 describe how after Stephen's death vigorous persecution of the early church erupted and "produced dispersion and migration."[93] Although there is no doubt that this dispersion radiated in different directions, "the biblical record focuses on the migrant movement to the north and west: to Phoenicia, Cyprus, and Antioch (Acts 11:19)."[94] Christian migrants who relocated to the new regions of the Roman Empire because of persecution in Jerusalem established "new Christian congregations in various towns throughout the regions of Judea, Galilee, and Samaria (Acts 8; 9:31; 10:1–48)."[95] This unexpected and

---

87. Ibid., 146.
88. Donald Senior and Carroll Stuhlmueller, *The Biblical Foundations for Mission* (Maryknoll, NY: Orbis, 1989), 30.
89. Hanciles, *Beyond Christendom*, 149.
90. Ibid., 150.
91. Ibid.
92. Ibid., 151.
93. Ibid.
94. Ibid.
95. Ibid.

unplanned migration of Christians "produced momentous developments that radically altered the life of the church and decided the future of the faith."[96] Originally, Christianity was part of Judaism. "The Christians of the first generation were all Jews – diverse, perhaps, in background and outlook, Hebraist and Hellenist, conservative and liberal – but without the slightest idea that they had 'changed their religion by recognizing Jesus as Messiah.'"[97] The new Christian congregations met in synagogues and were very much a Jewish phenomenon. The situation changed because of migration. Jewish Christians in Antioch "made a point of preaching the gospel to Hellenists or Greeks who joined the new congregation in Antioch (Acts 11:19–21). The act of migration unleashed missionary purpose and galvanized cross-cultural expansion."[98] As a result, translation and adaptation of the faith became necessary. If until this point "the message of the gospel had been proclaimed in exclusively Jewish concepts" presenting Jesus as the Messiah, the Savior of Israel, with the migration of Christians to Gentile territory the contextualization of this message to this new context became necessary. This prompted a serious debate among Jewish church leaders in Jerusalem about the conditions under which Gentiles could join the church (cf. Acts 9:1–2; 22:5). As the result the decision was made "that Gentile converts need not conform to the strict laws of Judaism in order to be accepted as followers of Christ (Acts 15:22–29)."[99] This is a good example of what the church should do when it finds itself in the new socio-cultural environment – the church should be prepared to contextualize its message in order to allow indigenous people to join its fellowship.

Summary

The Jewish diaspora in the Roman Empire prepared the ground for the early Christianity to be spread across the ancient world. Initially Jewish Christians shared the gospel only with their fellow Jews who were part of the diaspora. This shows that migration of God's people is used by God to accomplish his mission in the world. The examples of Israel in the Old Testament and the

---

96. Ibid.

97. Andrew F. Walls, *The Missionary Movement in Christian History: Studies in the Transmission of Faith* (Maryknoll, NY: Orbis, 2004), 16.

98. Hanciles, *Beyond Christendom*, 152.

99. Ibid.

early church in the New Testament point to the fact that God's people, when relocated voluntarily or forcefully to a new place, are called to be God's witnesses to people of the new country. Their message should be contextualized according to the new cultural and language context. This makes immigrant churches responsible for reaching not only their countrymen with the gospel in the new country but indigenous people as well.

8.6.2. The Social Makeup of First-Century Churches

Ekkehard W. Stegemann and Wolfgang Stegemann state that Christianity, after starting in Palestine, spread through the Roman Empire establishing Christ-confessing communities in urban regions of the empire.[100] "They were composed of Jews and (in the majority) Gentiles and enjoyed more or less unrestricted religious and social interaction between their Jewish and non-Jewish members."[101] Such composition of the early Christian communities created a problem in Jewish–Gentile relations. The important issue was whether non-Jewish Christians had to accept Judaism first "in order to be able to participate in the messianic salvation of Israel."[102] The Apostolic Council in Jerusalem (Acts 15) concluded "that believers in Christ no longer had to fulfill the central Jewish mark of identity, circumcision, as a condition for participation in the future redemption."[103] This fundamental decision of the early church lifted a significant barrier for non-Jewish people in joining the church. Christian converts of different ethnicities and races received an opportunity to join the church freely, avoiding the hindrance of becoming a Jew first. Obviously, this decision was one of the reasons for the first church becoming multiethnic.

The important source for learning about the social makeup of the first century church is the New Testament, in particular the book of Acts and the epistles. Thorsten Prill argues that the churches in the early times of Christianity were multicultural and multiethnic. He proves this point of view by analyzing the book of Acts.

---

100. Stegemann and Stegemann, *The Jesus Movement*, 266.
101. Ibid., 264.
102. Ibid., 267.
103. Ibid.

The Jerusalem Church

During the first century, "Jerusalem was a multi-lingual and multi-cultural city" with the major languages spoken being Aramaic and Greek.[104] At the beginning, the church in Jerusalem consisted of only Jewish Christians. In Acts 2:5 Luke points to the fact that "there were devout Jews from every nation under heaven." No Gentiles are mentioned as being present at the event of Pentecost, except Jewish proselytes (2:10), who "were filled with the Holy Spirit and to speak in other languages" (2:4).[105] The apostle Peter directs his speeches, presented in Luke 2–3, to a Jewish audience and addresses listeners as "men of Judea" (2:14), "Israelites" (2:22, 29; 3:12), and "brothers" (2:37). Although, according to the book of Acts, the first Jerusalem church consisted of mostly Jews, Luke also shows that it was not a completely homogeneous group.[106] Describing a dispute in the Jerusalem church over the food distribution (6:1–7) he mentions Hellenists and Hebrews as participants in this dispute. Prill insists that although being part of the same church these "Hellenists and Hebrews had their own social meetings."[107] According to him, "Luke presents the early Christian church in Jerusalem as a diverse mono-ethnic community. The church consisted of an Aramaic-speaking majority and a Greek-speaking minority."[108]

Paul Barnett makes the point that the original founding group of the Jerusalem church, one hundred and twenty Galilean "brothers" who attended the meeting in the upper room (Acts 1:13–14), consisted of Aramaic-speaking people with some familiarity with Greek.[109] However, on the day of Pentecost (Acts 2:41), "three thousand were added to the community, the majority of whom were Jews from the diaspora, whose common language was Greek."[110] Both these groups, Aramaic-speaking and Greek-speaking, "met together in the temple precincts, worshiping together (in Aramaic?)

---

104. Thorsten Prill, "Migration, Mission, and the Multi-ethnic Church," *Evangelical Review of Theology* 33, no. 4 (Oct 2009), 333.
105. Ibid.
106. Ibid., 334.
107. Ibid.
108. Ibid., 335.
109. Paul Barnett, *Jesus and the Rise of Early Christianity: A History of New Testament Times* (Downers Grove, IL: InterVarsity, 1999), 207.
110. Ibid.

and being instructed (in Aramaic?) by the apostles."[111] They also had separate meetings as well.[112]

The Church in Antioch

Antioch was the capital of the Roman province of Syria. It was a free city, the third-largest city of the Roman Empire, attracting people of many different languages and cultures from around the world.[113] Prill argues that "in the Book of Acts, Luke emphasizes that the multi-ethnic character of the city of Antioch was reflected both in the composition of its first Christian church and in the church's leadership."[114] In Acts 11:19–21, the author describes how the church in Antioch was started by Christians who fled persecutions in Jerusalem. Initially, they were evangelizing only Jews (11:19).[115] However, later they "began to preach the gospel to members of the Hellenist population also (11:20)."[116] As a result, a multiethnic congregation was established. Prill concludes that Luke "indicates that the multi-cultural church of Antioch became not only the sponsoring church for their missionary activities but also the church model that the two missionaries sought to replicate in other cities of the Roman Empire."[117]

The Philippian Church

The Macedonian city of Philippi at the time of Paul and Silas's visit of it in AD 49 was populated mainly by Romans and the Greek-speaking Thracians. Latin was the official language in Philippi. However, "it was Greek that dominated both business and everyday life."[118] Prill refers to Acts 16, stating that in this chapter Luke tells the readers "how the first church on the European continent was founded by Paul and Silas, and again Luke points to the social and ethnic diversity of the Christian church."[119] Luke does this

---

111. Ibid., 208.
112. Ibid.
113. Prill, "Migration, Mission, and the Multi-ethnic Church," 336.
114. Ibid.
115. Stegemann and Stegemann, *The Jesus Movement*, 253.
116. Prill, "Migration, Mission, and the Multi-ethnic Church," 336.
117. Ibid., 337.
118. Ibid., 338.
119. Ibid.

by describing in detail "the conversions of a woman named Lydia and her household (16:13–15), as well as those of a jailer and his family (16:23–24)."[120] Lydia being an immigrant from Thyatira (16:14) was a "worshipper of God" (16:14). In other words, she was "a Gentile attracted to the Jewish religion."[121] Being "a dealer in purple cloth" (16:14), which was a luxury trade at that time, shows she probably was a wealthy woman. The social and national status of the jailor "is in contrast to Lydia and is representative of a completely different subgroup of Philippian society."[122] Because of his position he was part of the Roman administration and it is very possible that he was a Roman citizen. Both these people belonging to very different parts of the contemporary society were part of the first church in Philippi. Taking this fact into consideration Prill concludes that "the core group of the church in Philippi is portrayed by Luke as a very diverse community. Luke stresses that they had not only been brought up in different cultures but also belonged to different social classes."[123]

Other churches planted by Paul and Silas in Thessalonica, Beroea, and Corinth represented "a similar ethnic, cultural and social mix."[124] In Acts 17:4, Luke describes the first church in Thessalonica as being "composed of Jews, a great number of God-fearing Gentiles and a considerable number of leading Macedonian women."[125] According to Acts 17:12, "the new Christian church in Beroea included a large group of Jews and some Greek women and men."[126]

Social Diversity of Early Christianity

Rooney Stark points to the change that has taken place lately in viewing early Christianity as "a movement of the dispossessed – a haven for Rome's slaves and impoverished masses."[127] The view has been kept by the historians and

---

120. Ibid.
121. Ibid.
122. Ibid.
123. Ibid., 339.
124. Ibid.
125. Ibid.
126. Ibid.
127. Rooney Stark, *The Rise of Christianity: A Sociologist Reconsiders History* (Princeton, NJ: Princeton University Press, 1996), 29.

sociologists for a long time. One of the key texts in the New Testament from which to draw the conclusion that early Christianity was represented mostly by the poor masses is 1 Corinthians 1:26–28. In this text, Paul addressing the church in Corinth states: "not many of you were wise according to worldly standards, not many were powerful, not many were of noble birth" (1 Cor 1:26b). This text has been over-interpreted and has been read by historians with the understanding that Paul was saying that none of the members of the Corinth church were wise, mighty, or noble. However, when Paul is saying "not many" he means that there were at least some who were wise, mighty, or noble. Many scholars today believe, based on Romans 16:23 and 2 Timothy 4:20, that Erastus, "the city treasurer," was a member of the church at Corinth.[128] Referring to these facts, Stark claims that "a consensus has developed among New Testament historians that Christianity was based in the middle and upper classes."[129] Of course this does not exclude lower-class people from being part of the early Christian churches. It proves that Christianity was socially a very diverse movement from the beginning. Ekkehard W. and Wolfgang Stegemann support this position, saying that in recent research "the predominant opinion seems to be that men and women from all strata of the population became believers"[130] and joined the early church with the urban elite playing a dominant role. Slaves, freed men, women, local aristocracy, and "perhaps even the senatorial nobility" were part of the early church communities.[131] This position is in opposition to the politically motivated "proletarianization" of early Christianity that took place in the past and even now is supported by some historians.[132] Ekkehard W. and Wolfgang Stegemann argue that, based on general socio-historical data, the upper-stratum membership was "extremely rare among Christ-confessing women"[133] in the early church and "lower-stratum membership, however, was absolutely predominant among Christ-confessing women."[134]

---

128. Ibid., 30–31.
129. Ibid., 31.
130. Stegemann and Stegemann, *The Jesus Movement*, 288.
131. Ibid., 290.
132. Ibid.
133. Ibid., 292.
134. Ibid., 293.

Summary

This brief analysis of various New Testament churches shows that early Christian churches were multicultural, multiethnic, and socially very diverse in nature. This was a result of the intentional church-planting ministry of the apostles and migration of Christians. Their cross-cultural mission work described in the books of Acts provides the reader "with guidelines or principles that can help us to develop strategies for the integration of migrants into local indigenous churches."[135] The fact that congregations of the early church were multiethnic suggests that contemporary Slavic immigrant churches in America should strive to become multiethnic as well. For PCSBA churches, making this happen would mean denying themselves, to a certain degree, which is not an easy step to take. However, it could be one of the most viable options to consider if these churches are seriously interested in being obedient to Christ's Great Commission and making disciples in all nations. Further discussion on this subject is provided in chapter 10.

8.7. Conclusion for Chapter 8

Ethnicity and religion both play an important role in the life of immigrants and are two aspects of life that are important to their hearts. Ethnicity can be a bridge in the process of sharing the gospel with people of the same ethnicity. However, it can also be a barrier when there is an opportunity to witness to somebody from a different ethnic group. The existence of Slavic ethnic churches is beneficial to people of a Slavic background. But at the same time, ethnicity isolates these churches from the rest of American society. Relations between immigrants and people in the receiving society have the form of interethnic relations because in most cases, immigrants belong to an ethnic group different from that of the people in the new country. This is especially true in America because of its ethnic diversity. These relations affect the immigrants' willingness and ability to do mission work among people of different ethnicities. Results of the surveys of PCSBA church leaders show that no strong relations between Slavic immigrants and other ethnic groups currently exist. This means that Slavic immigrant churches in America are not very open to evangelizing and providing social help as

---

135. Prill, "Migration, Mission, and the Multi-ethnic Church," 343.

part of an authentic mission among people of different ethnicities, and this provides a hindrance to mission.

One of the expressions of ethnicity is the language that people speak. It plays a dual role in a mission context. It is a vehicle in spreading the faith when it takes place among people who use the same language, and it is a barrier when the potential recipient of the good news does not understand the language of the messenger. Slavic Baptist churches in America are familiar with both experiences. The use of the Russian language in church life provides these churches with the ability to reach Russian-speaking people with the gospel in America, as well as abroad. However, using Russian in the church service builds a wall of separation between the church and the surrounding community, which speaks English. It also discourages the younger generation of the church from reading and studying the Bible in English, which is their primary language. This results in a lack of spiritual maturity among the younger generation and deprives them of an important tool for sharing the gospel with their English-speaking friends: knowledge of biblical English.

There are hindrances and opportunities for mission work for PCSBA churches. Among the most serious of these hindrances is the process of losing younger church members to English-speaking congregations. It weakens the Slavic churches and threatens to decrease their ability to conduct mission work in the same quantity and quality as it is currently done. There are also new opportunities for missions as a result of political changes in the world. Today, Slavic churches in the States have the possibility to do outreach ministry in the US, in the republics of the former Soviet Union, and among Russian-speaking immigrants in Western Europe. They can also be involved in evangelistic and humanitarian ministry in other countries, such as Haiti and Mexico, by using English which young people in Slavic churches speak fluently as an international language in their communication with local people.

The multiracial congregation model could be considered as a valuable option for these immigrant churches. This model would help new immigrants in overcoming culture and language barriers and would help them to do the mission work among indigenous people. This model was used by the congregations of the early church which originally emerged in a very diverse Roman society.

In conclusion, it could be said that Slavic Baptist churches face unique challenges and opportunities in mission. The ability of these churches to find the appropriate way to meet these challenges and to use these opportunities determines their ability to implement evangelism and social action/*diaconia* in the local immigrant context as part of an authentic mission. In the following chapter, an evaluation of the authenticity and contextuality of the mission work of the PCSBA churches is provided.

Part IV

Authentic Mission Perspective: Mission Practices in Light of Context and Contextuality

This final part of the book is designed to bring together all materials presented so far in this study and to make an evaluation of the mission work of Slavic Baptist immigrant churches. Based on the results of the evaluation, recommendations are made on how the mission work of these churches could be improved in order to be authentic and contextualized.

CHAPTER 9

Analysis of the Authenticity and Contextuality of Mission Work of the Pacific Coast Slavic Baptist Association Churches

This chapter consists of the analysis of the authenticity and contextuality of the mission work conducted by churches of PCSBA today. The analysis is based on all materials provided in previous chapters of the book. Based on this analysis, recommendations for the further development of the mission work of PCSBA churches in America will be developed and introduced in chapter 10.

9.1. PCSBA Churches: Is Their Mission Work Authentic and Contextually Appropriate Today?

This study has been launched with the goal of finding out if Slavic immigrant churches associated with the PCSBA are fulfilling Christ's Great Commission in their new cultural, social, and religious context, and how an authentic mission can be fulfilled by them in their specific immigrant context. In order to reach this goal, a considerable amount of space in the study was devoted, first, to exploring what authentic mission is, what contextualization in mission is, and what provides a challenge in contextualization of mission. It was shown that the source of mission is God himself and the *missio Dei* concept is the framework for discussion of mission in this study. The church is an instrument of God in implementing the *missio Dei* in the world. The mission of the church, it was concluded, is multifaceted. Out of the list of facets included in the definition of authentic mission, two aspects – evangelism and social action/*diaconia* – were chosen to be evaluated in the mission work of PCSBA churches. The next step made in this study was analyzing the attitude of Baptists in Tsarist Russia and the USSR towards these two aspects of the church's mission from the historical perspective, and exploring the contemporary mission context in the USA. It was shown that evangelism and social action/*diaconia* have always been part of the identity of Slavic Baptists in the homeland. The third step towards accomplishing the goal of this study was analysis of the different challenges PCSBA church members are facing as immigrants, and how these challenges impact the churches' ability to implement authentic and contextualized mission in their new cultural, linguistic, social and religious context. Now it is time to take a final step – to make an evaluation of the mission work of PCSBA churches, using the acquired tools and all the information gathered so far. The evaluation of both the mission work done by PCSBA churches in countries considered by them to be "the homeland" and the mission work accomplished locally, in the USA, is completed below.

9.2. Authenticity and Contextuality of Mission in the Homeland

The brief overview of the history of the Evangelical Christians-Baptists in Russia and the USSR provided in chapter 4 shows that from its beginning, this movement has had a strong emphasis on evangelism. Despite persecution, threats of imprisonment, and even murders, Christians in the pre-Communist past, as well as during the Soviet era, shared the gospel with non-believers. They have continued doing this in the post-Soviet period, as well. Based on these facts, it can be concluded that evangelism, as one of the aspects of an authentic mission, has had in the past and still has today its central presence in mission work of Baptist evangelical churches of the former Soviet Union.

The historical overview of the mission work of evangelicals in the former Soviet Union provided in chapter 4 points to the fact that practicing social action/*diaconia* by Baptist churches was outlawed by the government during most of the time that this movement was in existence. Due to this fact, few examples remain of how the church as an institution provided service to the community as part of its mission during the pre-perestroika period. At the same time, at the individual level, *diaconia* in the form of Christians helping each other, as well as their neighbors, was very common for Baptists throughout their history. Without helping each other, they would not have survived under severe persecutions. As was shown in chapter 4, when serving the community in the name of Christ was allowed, evangelical Christians used these opportunities and provided care for people outside of the church. The last two decades are a good example of this. Since perestroika, Baptists have been involved in many social actions. Of course, it only takes place in those republics of the former Soviet Union where it is allowed by the government. In some former Soviet republics, where Islam is a dominant religion, it is still impossible. However, where it is possible, Baptist churches, as well as Baptists as individuals, are practicing *diaconia*.

Based on this information, a conclusion can be made that the mission of Baptist churches in the homeland was in the past, and is currently, authentic and contextualized in regard to such aspects as evangelism and social action/ *diaconia*. This is a part of the Baptist church's self-understanding.

9.3. Authenticity and Contextuality of Mission in the US Immigrant Context

It is logical to expect that when Christians with such "self-understanding" come to another country, they will demonstrate the same enthusiasm towards evangelism and social action/*diaconia* to the community in the new country. Information provided in chapter 5 shows that the emigration of people from the former Soviet Union to the US, as part of a global migration phenomenon, created a significant (about 5 million) diaspora of Russian-speaking people in this country. Most of them are non-Christians. Slavic Baptist churches, as part of this diaspora, are a natural vehicle for bringing the gospel to them. One could assume that since evangelism is part of their self-understanding, these immigrant churches would try to reach their countrymen first, as well as their new neighbors, the indigenous people, with the good news. In order to find out if these expectations have been and are being materialized through the life and ministry of PCSBA churches in America, the data gathered in this study is analyzed below.

9.3.1. Before the Latest Wave of Immigration (1928–1989)

The overview of the history of the Pacific Coast Slavic Baptist Association provided in chapter 4 shows that during the period of time before the current immigration wave from the former USSR, churches of PCSBA expressed a strong enthusiasm for evangelism. Although their membership was quite small at that time, these churches supported ministries with an evangelistic focus such as radio, newspaper, literature publications, and television. They baptized some new believers who came from outside of the Christian community. Also, churches expressed social concerns and tried to help people among them in need, as well as supporting orphanages in South America.

All their evangelistic efforts and social actions were directed towards Russian-speaking people, either abroad or in America. Although some churches included a sermon in English in their services, it was not widespread for all churches. This information allows the conclusion to be made that PCSBA churches, during this period of time, practiced such elements of authentic mission as evangelism and social action/*diaconia*. However, taking into consideration that the primary focus was given to Russian-speaking people and not much attention was paid to evangelism among the English-speaking population, their mission was not appropriately contextual. In order to follow the Christ-given order in spreading the gospel in the world, every church should start from "Jerusalem" or, in other words, from the church's location. Since the immigrant churches are located in English-speaking cities, alongside with caring for people of their ethnic group, churches should be concerned with English-speaking people, as well. There are good historical illustrations of what is happening with churches focused primarily on their own ethnic group. A strong attachment to the Russian language in church life and church ministry could be pointed to as one of the main reasons why PCSBA churches at that period of time did not grow significantly in membership. From 1963 to 1988, the total membership of the association increased from 350 members to 418 (see table 5.3.2.A. and chart 5.3.3.A. in the appendix for chapter 5) – a sixty-eight-member increase in twenty-five years. When the current wave of immigration started in 1989, the first Slavic Baptist immigrants arriving in the States found the local churches of "old Slavic immigrants" consisted mostly of older people. Most of the youth had left their churches by then and had joined English-speaking congregations. In personal conversations with representatives of the "old immigrants" in Slavic Baptist churches, the author of this study heard their sobering stories about the fact that young people left their churches because the English language was not widely (if at all) used in churches. As a result, the average age of the church membership was rising continuously, but the church membership itself did not grow much.

9.3.2. Church Mission in the Current Period (1989–Present)

The second period of PCSBA history (starting in 1989) has been marked by a rapid membership growth due to mass emigration of Christians from the former Soviet Union and by both reestablishing existing congregations and planting new local congregations, as well as strengthening the association as an organization. This period is the main focus of this study. The role of evangelism and social action/*diaconia* in Slavic churches during this period were the focus of surveys conducted among leaders of PCSBA churches. Information obtained through these surveys (available in chapter 6) has been used for the analysis of the current mission work of PCSBA churches.

The detailed analysis of the data obtained through surveys clearly demonstrates that PCSBA churches analyzed in this study are considering aspects of an authentic mission as very important parts of the church mission. The following facts point to this conclusion:

1. A significant amount of their finances (on average 20% of the annual church budget) is devoted to supporting mission work (table 6.2.1.).
2. Supporting indigenous missionaries and church workers in the homeland is common for most PCSBA churches (table 6.3.1.).
3. Short-term mission trips have become the norm of church life for many congregations (table 6.3.20.).
4. The Mission Department of the PCSBA actively promotes missionary thinking among churches, mobilizes teams of youth and adults to go to other countries, and participates in evangelistic and service ministries (chapter 6, sections 6.7.1. and 6.7.2.).

5. Such evangelistic ministries as radio and the newspaper *Our Days* reach thousands of Russian-speaking people around the world with the good news because of the financial support provided by PCSBA churches (chapter 6, sections 6.7.5. and 6.7.6.).
6. The newly established Prison Ministry brings the gospel to many Russian-speaking and other inmates in the California prison system (chapter 6, section 6.7.7.).
7. Material help is provided to people in need by the Department of Mercy (chapter 6, section 6.7.8.).

All of these facts about ministry in PCSBA churches could lead the outside observer to the conclusion that these churches are implementing such aspects of an authentic mission as evangelism and social action/*diaconia*, and since it is done in the Russian language and with an understanding of Russian culture, this implementation is contextually appropriate.

However, there are other facts that deserve the observer's attention. They are listed below.

1. In most cases, the major attention of the PCSBA churches is given to evangelism and service taking place in the homeland (table 6.3.17). Most of the mission budget (80%) was spent on supporting missionary ministry overseas and very little was spent locally, in America (table 6.5.2.).
2. A demographic study of newly baptized believers during 2003–2005 (chapter 6, section 6.1) has shown that the majority of newly baptized church members come from Christian families. Usually, they are children of Christian immigrants. Very few came from the non-believing population. All of the newly baptized are Russian-speaking people. The results of a more recent survey conducted in 2010 (table 6.5.3.) show that nothing has changed in the demographics of newly baptized believers. Only 5 percent of those baptized in 2010 came from a non-church background. None of the baptized came from the English-speaking part of society. This is an indication that churches are neither very active in their efforts to reach non-believers among the Russian-speaking community nor among the English-speaking neighbors.

3. The lack of attention to non-believers has been revealed by the results of a survey conducted among church board members. These results demonstrate that (1) very few people from the surrounding community come to Slavic church worship services (table 6.3.8) in general; (2) not very many (some) Russian-speaking non-believers attend Slavic church worship services (table 6.3.9); (3) almost none (very few) English-speaking non-believers attend these services (table 6.3.10); (4) only a handful of times a year do churches organize activities for non-believers in the community (table 6.3.11). With such minimal attention to non-believers in the community, it is difficult to expect to have a significant percentage of their representatives among newly baptized church members. It shows that local evangelistic efforts directed towards the surrounding population are not strong enough and it raises a question about the authenticity of missions conducted by Slavic Baptist immigrant churches in America.

4. The survey of church leaders shows that most Slavic immigrant churches are not actively involved in church planting in America at the current time and do not have plans to do so in the future (table 6.3.15.). Planting new churches is usually considered as one of the most effective ways of bringing people to Christ. This view correlates well with one of the results of this study, which reveals that small Russian-speaking immigrant churches baptize more converts from the non-Christian community than the large congregations (chapter 6, section 6.1., charts 6.1.1., 6.1.2, and 6.1.3.). The common tendency among immigrants to build congregations with as large a membership as possible and the lack of desire to let people leave the church and do church planting is an obstacle in the way of practicing fruitful evangelism.[1]

---

1. This leads to a situation when all the people coming to the church service are Christians. As a result, when evangelistic sermons are preached in the service (which happens quite often in Slavic immigrant churches) there are no non-believers to hear them and respond to the call to accept Christ. Charles Van Engen rightly states "that it makes no sense for evangelistic proclamation to be made by Christ's disciples only to Christ's disciples within the confines of the local church. The proclamation is only kerygmatic when it is intentionally addressed to those who have not accepted Jesus as Lord" (*God's Missionary People: Rethinking the Purpose of the Local Church* [Grand Rapids, MI: Baker, 1999], 94).

5. The main focus of the mission of Slavic immigrant churches today is evangelism and social actions in their homeland (table 6.3.1.). Although these are right things for churches to do in the immigrant context, it is not satisfactory to only do this back in the former homeland. Without being involved in local evangelism and social actions directed towards the English-speaking community, the mission of the church becomes one-sided and incomplete. It cannot be considered contextually appropriate. Fortunately, according to table 6.3.34., about half of the surveyed church board members see the need in the future to evangelize the society around them. It is a positive sign. However, it is not currently happening
6. The growing number of youth in Russian-speaking churches have English-speaking friends whom they want to invite to their church (table 6.4.10.). However, because Russian is the primary language used in the church, they cannot bring friends from the local community to the church. This creates a barrier for the youth in Slavic churches to evangelize their classmates and the youth in their neighborhoods and to practice a follow-up step, which is bringing them to the church.
7. Slavic immigrant churches very rarely participate in the needs of the city and the country they live in as a whole (table 6.3.7.). Although certain positive changes could be noticed during the time between the two surveys of the church leaders, this participation is very limited. It points to the fact that local social actions are not very common among Slavic Baptist immigrant churches. This undermines the authenticity and contextualization of their mission.
8. Most Slavic Baptist immigrant churches do not practice activities organized in collaboration with the representatives of other ethnic groups (table 6.3.12.). It shows that a distance exists between Slavic immigrant churches and other ethnic groups living in their area. Such a situation could be considered one of the obstacles in the realization of an authentic mission by these churches. In such an ethnically diverse country as the United

States, it is crucial to work in collaboration with other ethnic groups. This is part of the process of contextualization of mission in the American context.

9. Only a limited number of surveyed leaders stated that their churches are planning evangelistic activities designed to reach other ethnic groups with the gospel (table 6.3.13.). This is additional proof that Slavic immigrant churches are mostly focusing their mission efforts on their own people, not on other ethnic groups. This makes their mission not contextually appropriate.

10. According to the survey results, most Slavic churches are not enthusiastically endorsing interracial marriages (table 6.3.14.). Some express an understanding of it, but others see it negatively. Such a division in opinions points to the presence of a struggle on issues of cross-ethnic relations among Slavic Baptist believers. In order for their mission to be contextually appropriate, participants in the mission and their churches should have their ethnic prejudices completely removed.

11. The Russian language is used predominantly in the life and ministry of Slavic Baptist immigrant churches. Sermons are very rarely preached in English (table 6.3.25.). While this allows the Russian-speakers to enjoy the comfort of using their native tongue in church, it also cuts off other people, who do not speak this language from participation in the life of the church. It creates a serious obstacle in reaching the surrounding English-speaking community with the gospel and makes the mission of PCSBA churches not contextualized in relation to the indigenous population.

12. According to the survey results, a majority of the church board members (57% in 2009) see the need for sermons in English to be preached in Slavic churches (table 6.3.26.). This is an encouraging fact; however, there are still a significant number of those in the leadership (35% in 2009) who oppose preaching sermons in English in their churches. This is a troubling sign. If there is no unity among leaders on this issue, it will be very

difficult to find support among ordinary church members to include sermons in English in church services. Without such sermons, the mission of the immigrant church in the American context will not be contextually appropriate.

13. The vast majority of respondents among the youth (89% in 2010) believe that it is necessary for a sermon in English to be preached in the Russian-speaking church (table 6.4.8.). The percentage of youth holding this view is significantly higher than the percentage of the church board members (89% vs. 57%). This is not surprising. It points to the fact that there is a disconnect between the younger and older generations in their position on such a critical issue as using English in the church service. If this disconnect is not eliminated soon, it will cost immigrant churches a high price, as many of their youth will leave Russian-speaking churches due to the fact that the language they understand better, English, is not used in the church life often enough.

14. The survey shows that half of the church board members and the majority of other leaders see their churches as being bilingual (Russian and English-speaking) in twenty–thirty years (table 6.3.27.). This fact could be interpreted as a positive sign since it shows that there is recognition among some church leaders of the reality that they live in an English-speaking society, and the willingness to accept this reality exists. However, the percentage of those among the church board members is not high enough. This is a negative sign. In order to become a church that is bilingual in all aspects of its life in twenty–thirty years, congregations have to start preparations for this transition process now. But this is impossible without full support of the church leadership.

15. The results of the survey of the former members of Slavic immigrant Baptist churches who switched their membership to English-speaking churches reveal that although the lack of understanding Russian is one of the reasons for leaving Slavic churches, it is not the main reason. The respondents included the

following among the most important causes: dissatisfaction with the quality of sermons and with the Sunday service experience, misdirected vision for the church in the new cultural and language context, lack/absence of evangelistic efforts toward the surrounding community, and a lack of practical service (e.g. feeding the homeless, helping the poor, etc.) directed towards locals (table 6.6.6.). In other words, people who left the churches have observed limited contextualization of the church mission in the new immigrant context and a lack of evangelism and social action/*diaconia* practiced by these churches among the local community. This raises a very serious question about the authenticity and contextualization of the missions of Slavic immigrant Baptist churches.

These fifteen facts point to the conclusion that the mission of the PCSBA churches in relation to the local English-speaking community is not contextualized and is not authentic.

Summary

The data gathered through different surveys of church leaders, youth and other members of Slavic immigrant Baptist churches shows that the missions of these churches have a very strong focus on the former homelands of church members. These churches are very much preoccupied with financially supporting evangelistic activities in the former Soviet Union. They try to participate in these activities through short-term mission trips. Also, social action/*diaconia* is practiced mostly in the homeland or within the local Slavic immigrant churches. The local non-Russian-speaking community currently is out of the mission focus of the PCSBA churches. No significant evangelistic activity is observed towards Russian-speaking non-believers living in the area where churches are located. As well, no actions are taken towards reaching English-speaking non-believers in the local community. It seems as if, from the local perspective, the life of these churches is self-centered and inward-focused. This is incompatible with the authentic mission of the church. Although the common view is that "mission always takes place somewhere where the church is not already established," it is the church's responsibility to spread the gospel locally as well.[2] Charles E. Van Engen addresses an issue of the relationship between the local and global responsibilities of the church: "A healthy congregation of disciples of Jesus lives out its catholicity by intentionally and actively participating in Christ's mission in a glocal fashion. It is active simultaneously in global and local mission, dynamically fostering the glocal interaction between the global and local."[3] Applying this view to immigrant churches leads to the conclusion that the mission of these churches is only authentic when it simultaneously includes evangelism and social action/*diaconia* being provided by these churches locally, as well as in other regions of the world, including their homeland. This is what the mission work of Slavic immigrant Baptist churches is lacking currently. The combination of steps in the process of spreading the gospel that Jesus Christ has revealed (Acts 1:8) has still to be practiced today. As Van Engen explains it, "These glocal believers – no matter where they are in the world – are therefore commissioned to be 'witnesses in Jerusalem, *and* in all Judea *and* Samaria, *and* to the ends of the earth' (Acts 1:8) simultaneously. Thus, a healthy glocal group of believers in this new century must be involved, at the same time, in God's mission locally *and* globally, that is, glocally."[4]

Based on this, the conclusion can be made that the mission of the PCSBA churches is only partially authentic. It is authentic and contextualized only concerning those living abroad, mainly in the homeland but not in its local aspect in the USA. The mission of PCSBA churches should go through the process of significant transformation in its local aspect.[5] Suggestions regard-

---

2. J. Andrew Kirk, *The Mission of Theology and Theology of Mission* (Valley Forge, PA: Trinity Press International, 1997), 30.

3. Charles E. Van Engen, "The Glocal Church: Locality and Catholicity in a Globalizing World," in *Globaliazing Theology: Belief and Practice in an Era of World Christianity*, ed. Craig Ott and Harold A. Netland (Grand Rapids, MI: Baker Academic, 2006), 178.

4. Ibid., 179.

5. Wonsuk Ma, describing the development of a very successful, strongly mission-minded Korean-American immigrant church, Grace Korean Church (GKC) in Los Angeles, points to a very serious threat this congregation faces. Despite the fact that in thirty years (1982–2012) this congregation grew from a few families into a membership of 6,500 and developed a very effective mission ministry worldwide (including the republics of the former Soviet Union), this congregation, which based its work mainly on first generation immigrants, could inherit the fate of many other immigrant churches in the past. Ma provides a warning, saying, "The very elements that made GKC's mission an incredible success can also cause

ing what needs to be done in order to make the mission of these churches fully authentic and contextual are provided in chapter 10.

9.4. Conclusion for Chapter 9

The evaluation of mission work of Slavic Baptist churches in the homeland, as well as in the US, has been completed in this chapter. It was shown that despite the almost uninterrupted persecutions of the past, the mission of Baptist churches in Russia and the USSR was authentic and contextualized. This is currently true in the republics of the former Soviet Union, where freedom of religion is granted. The detailed analysis of the mission work of PCSBA churches based on the obtained data has revealed that the mission work conducted by these churches abroad usually is authentic and contextualized. However, the local aspect of the mission work of these churches is weak and is not authentic or contextualized. The PCSBA churches are paying most of their attention towards supporting ministries in the homeland and are neglecting their responsibility of reaching their neighbors with the message of salvation and with Christ's love in action. A logical question comes to mind: Why is such an unbalanced approach to mission between "foreign" mission to the homeland and "home" mission to people in the USA taking place in PCSBA churches? An explanation could be found in chapter 7 of this study. The analysis provided in that chapter leads to the conclusion that common to all immigrants, painful experiences such as culture shock, language barrier, attachment to homeland, separation from known surroundings, and others, cause immigrants to go through deep emotional and psychological pain. This pain, combined with not always pleasant experiences of the cross-cultural encounters between the diaspora and the receiving society, builds in the immigrants' hearts an attitude of alienation towards the surrounding society and negatively impacts the willingness and

---

its downfall. The resolute first-generation determination cannot continue indefinitely. After two decades of its missionary enterprise, the operation remains strictly first-generation led. Unless the new generation, most of whom were born in the United States, successfully inherits the church's mission conviction and vision, the future will hardly be as bright. A proper training mechanism, evaluation process, and structure are necessary to ensure transparency and accountability" ("Grace Korean Church, Fullerton, California: Mission from the Margins," *International Bulletin of Missionary Research* 36, no. 2 [Apr 2012]: 71). This warning could be equally addressed to the Slavic Baptist immigrant churches in America.

ability of Christian immigrants to practice evangelism and social action/ *diaconia* among local native people. Chapter 8 provides additional light on this situation, addressing such issues in immigrants' lives as ethnicity and mission, interethnic relations, use of language in church, and mission work. It is shown that while the same ethnicity and common language serve as bridges in mission work, at the same time, differences in ethnicity and language create a barrier between people and impact the ability and willingness of immigrant Christians to practice authentic and contextualized mission among people in the receiving society. In other words, these experiences, common to most immigrants, both psychological and sociological, block Christian immigrants from implementing authentic and contextualized mission among native people of their new country. This means that in order to bring their mission in balance and to start serving the locals, the PCSBA churches have to realize the existence of these blocks and be willing and able to overcome them. It is the greatest challenge they are now facing. The local aspect of mission work of the PCSBA churches needs significant improvements in order for their mission to become authentic and contextualized. The following (and final) chapter of this study consists of suggestions on how these improvements could be accomplished by the PCSBA churches.

CHAPTER 10

Contextualization of Mission Work of Slavic Baptist Churches through Various Models

This final chapter is devoted to a discussion of several possible models for mission work that could be used by Slavic immigrant Baptist churches for improvement of their mission in such a way that it could become fully authentic and contextualized.

10.1. Models of mission work among the Russian-Speaking population

Ethnicity and language provide Russian-speaking churches with a logical starting framework for mission. This includes Russian-speaking people in America, around the world, and in the homeland. Although there is a common language for these three groups, they differ in the context of their environment and in some socio-ethnic characteristics. These differences should be taken into consideration in choosing models appropriate for mission work among representatives of each group. It needs to be clarified that the mission work of the Russian-speaking immigrant churches should not be limited to only Russian-speaking people. It should be just a starting point. However, eventually, this mission, in order to be authentic and contextual, should include indigenous people of the country in which these churches are located, the United States.

10.1.1. Mission Work among the Russian-Speaking Diaspora in America

As was demonstrated in chapter 5, a Russian-speaking diaspora has existed in America since the eighteenth century. Currently, around 5 million Russian-speaking people reside in the States. Several models could be recommended for reaching this ethnic group with the gospel by PCSBA churches.

Radio ministry. PCSBA churches have supported radio ministry for many years. However, the radio programs were always developed specifically for people living behind the Iron Curtain. The broadcasting has been directed towards that geographical territory. In order to reach non-believing Russian-speaking people in the US, the content of the radio programs has to be adjusted to the American immigrant context. They should be evangelistic and apologetic in nature. Also, these programs have to be broadcast through radio stations that reach an American audience.

TV ministry. TV is a powerful communication tool that provides access to almost every household in the US. today. TV evangelistic ministry is common for English-speaking Christianity in America. Some non-Baptist Slavic denominations in America use it as well. PCSBA churches have to develop this ministry. It is very costly to run. However, it is a very effective way of reaching people for Christ.

Internet ministry. Another modern, powerful communication tool is the Internet. Using it for evangelistic purposes is an appropriate and effective method of reaching people with the gospel. Large PCSBA churches currently broadcast their Sunday services online, allowing many Russian-speaking people throughout the country and around the world to watch their services. This is the first step in using this communication tool for mission purposes. Broadcasting live services does not require additional time for preparation and video recording in advance. It is relatively simple to operate. Of course, for believers who cannot attend the service personally for any reason, it is beneficial and encouraging to be able to watch the church service via Internet.

However, such a direct broadcast of Sunday church services has certain limitations in the aspect of reaching non-believers. Unchurched people probably will not be interested in watching a church service via the Internet. They most likely would visit websites with information about the Christian faith and Scriptures, with testimonies, and Q&As. An Internet ministry has a great potential for reaching Russian-speaking people not only in the States but also around the world. The challenge is to direct people who, in response to visiting the PCSBA website, would be interested in visiting a Russian-speaking church in their area. Such churches are not available everywhere so helping these people to find a local congregation and join it would be challenging.

Newspaper Our Days. As was mentioned in chapter 6, this weekly publication has been in operation since 1966. From its inception, this newspaper was planned to be evangelistic in nature. It has accomplished this goal during all these years. This newspaper should continue to be published and should continue to be an evangelistic tool.

Church planting. More Russian-speaking people live in some areas of the country than in other areas. In regions with high populations of this ethnic group, planting new Russian-speaking churches seems to be an appropriate method of doing mission. This requires creating teams of church planters and relocating them to these regions. If funds are available, church planters could be in this ministry full time. Otherwise, they could move to the new church plant area and find employment in order to be self-supporting. The first option would be more effective since with this model, the church planters have more time to create outreach efforts. The church-planting teams should be formed from members of PCSBA churches. Many experienced ministers are now part of these churches. While in the homeland they were very active in church ministry, in the States, the gifts and experience of many of them are not used to the full because opportunities in the immigrant churches are not available to all of them. Participating in planting new churches would provide these ministers with the opportunity to practice their ministry skills through reaching non-believers for Christ. In order to make the mission of these new church plants authentic and contextualized, the new churches from the beginning should have a vision for reaching people beyond their ethnic group. The multiracial church model is described in the final part of this chapter (section 10.2.2.), where mission work among the non-Russian-speakers in the church neighborhoods is discussed. If starting a multiracial church from the beginning is not feasible, the new Russian-speaking church should not be viewed as an independent local entity but should be assigned to one of the local English-speaking congregations in a mother/sister-church relationship. The Russian-speaking participants of the newly planted church should be either members of the English-speaking mother/sister-congregation and be part of the Russian-speaking ministry of this church, or be very close partners in ministry with the congregation. This approach is not in alignment with common practices used when ethnic churches are planted in America today. Usually, in such cases, the ethnic churches are encouraged to be independent. However, the independence of the ethnic church is often an obstacle, limiting adaptation for its members in the new society and making it easy for the ethnic church to enter an isolationist mode and to become an ethnic enclave. This is exactly what is observed in many Russian-speaking congregations and has to be avoided as much as possible with new church plants.

Reaching Russian-speaking Jewish people. Many of the Russian-speaking immigrants are Jewish people. As was mentioned in chapter 5, section 5.2.6., the most recent arrivals of Jewish people from the former Soviet Union do not observe their traditional religion, Judaism. Many of them are agnostics or atheists. In most cases, when attempting to reach them with the gospel, they should be considered as people without faith in God. At the same time, often their Jewish traditions, as well as the historic denial of Jesus as their Messiah, provide additional barriers for them to accept Christ as the Savior. Because of this, it is important to understand how to deal with all these issues while making evangelistic efforts towards Jews in America.[1] It is important to understand that mass events such as evangelistic crusades are not an appropriate way to reach Jews with the truth about Christ as their

---

1. Parush R. Parushev argues that in order to start dialogue with Jewish people, Christians have to admit their misdeeds towards Jews in the historical past. It requires repentance, condemning anti-Semitism, "educating itself [church] and the society around it of another way of living together and witnessing together" ("Walking in the Dawn of the Light: On the Salvation Ethics of the Ecclesial Communities in the Orthodox Tradition from a Radical Reformation Perspective" [PhD diss., School of Theology, Fuller Theological Seminary, 2006], 342); also, "there should be readiness for the pastoral embrace and caring for those abused because of their race, ethnicity, of faith" (ibid.). See also his "Emergence of Russian Orthodox Antisemitism," in *Anatomy of Hatred: Essays on Anti-Semitism*, ed. Věra Tydlitátová and Alean Hanzová (Plzeň, Czech Republic: Fakulta Filozofická Západočeské Univerzity v Plzni, 2009), 5–10; and "Embodied Visions: On Antisemitism and the Resilience of Goodness," in Zbyněk Tarant, Věra Tydlitátová et al., *Faces of Hatred: Contemporary Antisemitism in Its Historical Context* (Plzeň, Czech Republic: Fakulta Filozofická Západočeské Univerzity v Plzní, 2012), 7–44.

Messiah.[2] The best practice is working individually with these people, building trust and credibility among them. The most effective way to develop relationships with them is done by living among them. It would be very beneficial for Slavic immigrant Baptist churches to engage in these efforts in partnership with the American organizations that have a rich experience of working with this ethnic group. One such organization is Friends of Israel. This group is working with local churches trying to share the gospel with the Jewish people.

10.1.2. Mission Work among the Russian-Speaking Diaspora around the World

After the fall of the USSR, millions of Russian-speaking people left their homelands and went abroad looking for jobs, and, if possible, permanent homes. They are present today on different continents and in many countries. Most of them are non-believers. The struggles they are going through as immigrants have made their hearts much more open to the gospel than if they had stayed at home. This is a mission field "prepared for harvest." There are several ways in which PCSBA churches could participate in this "harvest." Some of these ways have already been mentioned above. They are TV ministry, Internet ministry, and the newspaper *Our Days*. These ministries are able to cross country boarders. Besides these media-based methods of reaching Russian-speaking immigrants around the world, there are opportunities to share the gospel with them in person. One of these current opportunities exists in Western Europe. According to different sources, more than 7 million immigrants from the former Soviet Union are currently living in Western Europe. They moved there looking for a job. Some of them are there legally. Others are not. An attempt to reach these people with the gospel has been undertaken by the PCSBA Mission Department recently. This is a great opportunity for Slavic Baptists in America to serve their countrymen in Western Europe, who are going through a similar immigrant experience.

---

2. Parush R. Parushev, "Jews and Christians after the *Shoah*: Christian Teological Perspectives on the Future of the Jewish-–Christian Relationship,"' in *Reflections on Anti-Semitism: Anti-Semitism in Historical and Anthropological Perspectives*, ed. Věrá Tydlitátová and Alena Hanzová (Plzeň, Czech Republic: Fakulta Filozofická Západočeské Univerzity v Plzni, 2008), 35–44; and his "Baptists and Jews and Judaism," in *A Dictionary of European Baptist Life and Thought*, ed. John H. Y. Briggs, Studies in Baptist History and Thought, vol. 33 (Milton Keynes: Paternoster, 2009), 275–278.

10.1.3. Mission Work in the Homeland

Supporting evangelistic work and providing humanitarian aid back to the homeland are natural components of mission work done by PCSBA churches. These are very much underway right now and should continue in the form of supporting indigenous evangelists, church planters, and church workers. Also, short-term mission trips should continue taking place.[3] They are beneficial for both those who are hosting them in the homeland as well as those who are part of the teams coming from America. Of course, the training of these teams should be improved in order to make their ministry more fruitful. The cross-cultural aspect of the training should be emphasized. The fact that young people coming from America speak Russian does not mean that they are Russians culturally. They are more American than Russian, and have to be equipped with the cross-cultural skills in order to be useful in ministry in their parents' homeland.[4]

---

3. A. Scott Moreau, Gary R. Corwin, and Gary B. McGee, in their book *Introducing World Missions*, point to the fact that a very common way of doing mission today is short-term missions. There are positive and negative sides of it. According to the authors, one of the negative sides is that "career missionaries can be sidetracked by having to watch over a loud, brash group of young people who are insensitive to the host culture and unaware of the images they project" (*Introducing World Missions* [Grand Rapids, MI: Baker Academic, 2004], 279). As a positive side of the short-term missions, the fact could be noted that "short-term projects not only can be a healthy vehicle for people to consider long-term service, but also, in the best of cases, they can assist long-term missionaries or nationals in completing significant projects for God's kingdom that would not otherwise ever be done" (ibid.). During the last ten–fifteen years, as short-term mission trips became part of life for Slavic Baptist churches in America, both these things were observed. It is reflected in the answers of the church leaders who participated in the survey (see appendix for chapter 6: Table 6.3.30 – effectiveness; table 6.3.31. – usefulness; table 6.3.32 – preparedness of the short-term missions). Only about 2/3 of the participants gave "high" or "medium" approval to these missions. It is crucial to assign the short-term mission teams to the appropriate project in ministry. Many years of sending short-term mission teams by PCSBA churches has shown that one of the best areas for Slavic young people going back to the homeland and other countries is participating in organizing and conducting children/youth Christian camps.

4. Karla Ann Koll, analyzing the recent phenomenon in short-term mission trips, underlines the importance for those who go on short-term mission to be open to learn from people they are planning to serve. Ability to listen is crucial for the short-term missionaries. Koll warns: "I suspect that as long as mission is defined by the act of going, the task undertaken, or the target population, it will be impossible for the groups who travel to understand listening as a vital part of what they are called to do in that new place" ("Taking Wolves Among Lambs: Some Thoughts on Training for Short-Term Mission Facilitation," *International Bulletin of Missionary Research* 34, no. 2 [Apr 2010]: 96). However, it is absolutely essential for a successful mission trip to develop this ability. "The sisters and brothers we encounter on a short-term mission trip can help break our conformity to this age, that we might experience

10.2. Models of Mission Work among Non-Russian-Speaking People

10.2.1. Mission Work among English-Speaking Children of Slavic Immigrants

According to the results of the surveys of church leaders provided in chapter 6, the spiritual wellbeing of their children is the major concern for immigrant believers. For many of them, the main reason for immigration was a desire to ensure a better future for their children, as opposed to what they would have experienced in their homeland, including enjoying freedom of religion. Of course, leading children to Christ is the greatest goal for many Christian immigrants. How could immigrant churches help parents in reaching this goal in the new linguistic and cultural context?

Conducting Sunday school in English. Sunday school for children plays a supplemental role in educating them in religious matters. In the immigrant context, it could play the role of a bridge for children between the Russian-speaking church community and English-speaking society. The vast majority of first-generation Slavic immigrant parents are teaching their children the Bible in their native language. However, school-age children are living most of the time in an English-speaking environment. This is why it is important for them to know the Bible stories and Bible terminology in English. Because of this, Sunday school classes should be conducted in English. A detailed discussion of the role of language used in the church for spiritual growth of the younger generation has been provided in chapter 8, section 8.3.5. Sunday school teachers should know English well. Also, it is important for teachers to be trained in how to lead children to Christ.

Providing the youth with opportunities to attend conferences in English. In the American religious context, there is no shortage of different conferences, workshops, and seminars available for Christian youth. These are designed to help them with their spiritual growth and to equip young people for ministry in the contemporary cultural context. Often, the leaders of Slavic immigrant churches, due to a lack of understanding of English, are not aware of such

---

the renewal of our minds and live together with them toward God's new creation (Rom. 12:2). But only if we are able to listen to them" (ibid.).

kinds of events and do not inform parents and youth about these opportunities. Also, sometimes, when they know about such events, they discourage their youth from attending them because they are concerned about the youth being exposed to the American version of Christianity and its teaching. However, in order to equip their young people to do authentic and contextualized mission locally, the Slavic immigrant church leaders have to encourage their youth to be involved in different inter-church events taking place in America. For young people in Slavic immigrant churches, America is their homeland and they should be connected to the English-speaking Christian community here in order to be effective witnesses for Christ in this country. This is why it is important for church leaders to overcome their own prejudice against indigenous American Christians and let their youth collaborate in ministry with their counterparts in English-speaking churches.

Providing children and young people with the opportunity to worship in English. In chapter 8 of this work (sections 8.3.4., 8.3.5., and 8.3.6.), a detailed analysis of the impact of using the Russian language in the church for spiritual growth of young people has been provided. It is clear that young people are pulled in two directions in terms of the language used in the church. One of the challenges that the church leaders should overcome is convincing their congregations that because they live in an English-speaking society, their youth are now more comfortable with English than Russian. Because of this, they have the right to worship God in English. Of course, this creates a conflict situation because of the similar rights of people who are more comfortable with Russian than English. They want to worship in Russian. It requires a lot of effort and wisdom for the leadership to prepare older people in the pews to accept the fact that, for their children and grandchildren, English is the primary language. A culture of tolerance and mutual understanding between older and younger generations should be created and nurtured within the immigrant congregations. The youth should be allowed to sing in English during the Sunday service. Sermons in English should be delivered addressing issues that children and the youth are dealing with today. A summary of the content of the songs and sermons should be provided in Russian to those who do not understand English well. Of course, an "infusion" of English into the service brings certain challenges into the flow of the event. However, it is worth tolerating because it provides young people with the opportunity to worship God together with their parents and grandparents. Also, opportunities should be created in which the entire worship service is conducted in English. This could be a youth meeting or a separate service. Sensitivity on the part of the church leadership and the older believers in the congregation is required towards the issue of the youth worshiping in English in order to help them to better understand the Scriptures and God. This will also help keep young people in the Slavic immigrant churches.

10.2.2. Mission Work among Non-Russian-Speakers Living in the Church Neighborhoods

In chapter 9, it was shown that the mission work of PCSBA churches is not authentically appropriate and is not contextualized in the aspect of reaching non-Russian-speaking unbelievers with the gospel and with social action/ *diaconia* in the surrounding society. This is the most challenging task for immigrant churches in general, and for the Slavic immigrant Baptists in particular. In order to be able to do this, they have to overcome the "internal" and "external" forces pulling them away from doing authentic and contextualized mission, as mentioned in the conclusion to chapter 9. The most important barriers to overcome are language and culture. How could this be done practically? One of the most effective ways to do this is organizing the multiracial congregations.

10.2.2.1. The Multiracial Church Model: A Way of Making the Church Mission Authentic and Contextualized

Including English in the church services is usually the first step that immigrant churches do in order to become more contextualized in the new environment. Some of them eventually become fully bilingual. In most cases, these churches are making this step not because they are trying to bring more English-speaking people to their congregations, but in order to accommodate their children, who over a short period of time become more comfortable with English than with the language of their parents. Bringing a congregation into the bilingual stage is a step in the right direction. However, taking this step is not sufficient to make the congregation able to do mission work among people in the surrounding community. George Boltniew notes, "The period of bilingual ministry is not something permanent, but transitional . . . Still it is absolutely essential. During the transition period, from a church which serves only immigrant families to a church which services the entire community, it is extremely important that the pastor be bilingual and bicultural."[5] In other words, during the transitional time, the immigrant congregation continues serving primarily its own members (both Russian-speaking and English-speaking) while not trying to reach people in the community and bring them to the church. Obviously, if the congregation is bilingual and English is used in the service, English-speakers could visit these services and be able to understand what is going on there. However, joining the congregation as a member is still difficult, unless they find elements of their culture present in the life of the church. This transitional time could continue for many years until the older generation that needs Russian to be spoken in the church passes away. It is an unacceptable waste of time from the mission perspective. It makes life in the church during this period almost fruitless. Hopefully, some children of believers will come to faith during this time, which is an important element for the kingdom. However, in order to be authentic, the mission of the church should be focused not only on the children of Christians, but also directed outward, to people in the world. The only way to make an immigrant church effective in local mission work is to make it go through the process of overcoming both language and culture barriers simultaneously. Switching to English is only a partial solution for the issue of contextuality of the church mission. As a practical way of making the mission of Slavic immigrant Baptist churches in the US contextualized and authentic, this study suggests considering the multiracial church model.[6] In chapter 8, section 8.1.4., the benefits of using this model for reaching people with the gospel in the multiracial American society were

---

5. George Boltniew, ""A Functional Analysis of Ethnic/Bilingual Baptist Churches Ministering to Russian-Speaking Immigrants in the USA,"" (DMin diss., Eastern Baptist Theological Seminary, 1986), 280.

6. Thorsten Prill challenges the position of the Church of England and the North American Mission Board of the Southern Baptist Convention on the issue that planting ethnic churches should be the way of working with immigrants today and that it has proof in the example of the New Testament churches. Through the detailed studies of churches in the New Testament, Prill shows that Luke's descriptions of churches in the book of Acts "clearly contradict the view that the early church had a strategy of planting ethnic churches. On the contrary, they provide us with guidelines or principles that can help us to develop strategies for the integration of migrants into local indigenous churches" ("Migration, Mission and the Multi-ethnic Church," *Evangelical Review of Theology* 33, no. 4 [Oct 2009], 343).

introduced. After studying this model more carefully, the author is convinced that it reflects the biblical view of the church and is the appropriate model, from the missiological perspective in the American immigrant context, for both existing indigenous English-speaking congregations and immigrant churches. Becoming a multiracial congregation, the local church crosses both language and cultural barriers. This is what is needed in order for immigrant congregations to start working with local English-speakers. Due to the fact that the first generation of immigrants still is not comfortable enough with English and the American culture, it is the second generation (children of immigrants), with the support of the first generation of immigrants, who should initiate and lead the process of transformation of uniracial churches to multiracial ones.[7] The remaining part of this chapter is focused on this model as the most appropriate for adoption by PCSBA churches.

10.2.2.2. Types of Multiracial Congregations

There are several categories of multiracial congregations and types of congregational cultures. They are listed in the table below.

---

7. The experience of second-generation Korean American churches should be taken into consideration when an ethnic church starts the process of transformation from a uniracial to a multiracial congregation or before starting a new multiracial church. Sharon Kim provides useful insights on the issues that twenty-two new Korean American churches in Los Angeles are facing in their attempts to overcome ethnic boundaries and become relevant to the American society in general, and still be culturally sensitive to their own people. ("Shifting Boundaries within Second-Generation Korean American Churches," *Sociology of Religion* 71, no. 1 [Spring 2010], 98–122).

Table 10.2.2. Characteristics of Multiracial Congregation Models[8]

	Assimilated multiracial congregation	Pluralist multiracial congregation	Integrated multiracial congregation
Organizational culture	Reflects one dominant racial culture	Contains separate and distinct elements of all racial cultures represented in the congregation	Maintains aspects of separate cultures and also creates a new culture from the cultures in the congregation
Race of leadership (lay or clergy)	Dominant race	Representative of the different races in the congregation	Representative of the different races in the congregation
Degree of social interaction across races	Can be high or low	Low	High

Assimilated model. In this model, one racial group is the dominant group within the congregation and this is reflected in the worship services, in church life, and in leadership. Members of the congregation "who do not belong to that dominant racial group simply 'assimilate' into the existing culture."[9] Usually, assimilated multiracial congregations are the result of the transformation of uniracial congregations. However, in certain situations, they could start as a multiracial congregation with an assimilated model from the beginning "if there is one racial group whose power and racial culture is imposed on church culture."[10]

Pluralist model. In this model, members of different racial groups have decided to gather in the same church and participate in the same worship service. They are part of the same church membership. "Although this physical integration is notable, members do not move beyond coexistence to real

---

8. Curtiss Paul DeYoung, Michael O. Emerson, George Yancey, and Karen Chai Kim, *United by Faith: The Multiracial Congregation as an Answer to the Problem of Race* (New York: Oxford University Press, 2003), 165.
9. Ibid.
10. Ibid., 166.

integration of social networks. While official committees may be multiracial, the informal social networks still remain segregated by race."[11]

In this model, elements of the different racial cultures represented in the congregation could be included in the life of the church. The degree to which elements of all racial cultures are reflected in church life and the amount of informal interaction between church members belonging to different racial groups determine if the congregation is assimilated or pluralist.[12] One of the options for this model which could be considered is the so-called "congregation within a congregation," suggested by Thorsten Prill.[13] Obviously, this option does not provide close interactions between members of different ethnic groups in the church, but it could be considered as a first step in the direction of being fully integrated eventually.

Integrated model. The congregation with this model "has developed a hybrid of the distinct cultures that have joined together in one church," and this new hybrid culture "is an expression of the congregation's unified collective identity."[14] In the congregation with this model, relationships among church members representing different racial groups are strictly egalitarian. Although no equal representation of different racial groups is required for the multiracial congregation to be considered as an integral model, no one racial culture is dominant in such congregations, regardless of the percentage of its representatives in the membership. Further, "congregation members develop a new way of doing things that is particular to their own church."[15] This could be illustrated by comparing this congregation to a choir: "As a

---

11. Ibid., 167.
12. Ibid.
13. Thorsten Prill believes that based on the example of the Jerusalem church in the New Testament, "it might be necessary for a minority ethno-cultural group within a local church to have not only its own meetings but also its own ministers (cf. Acts 6:1–7). Where language barriers make it difficult for an ethno-cultural minority to take part fully in the church life of the majority group, a church needs to offer separate language meetings and select, if possible, ministers from the different groups to serve these groups. For a local church that has one or more groups of immigrants, this means that it might need to develop a *congregation within a congregation* structure. In such a structure, immigrants have a worship service, house group or Bible study meeting in their own language. However, this does not mean that they form a separate church; they remain part of the local church. As one local church, all its congregations accept one overall church leadership, make important decisions together, and share resources with each other" ("Migration, Mission and the Multi-ethnic Church," 343).

14. DeYoung et al., *United by Faith*, 168.
15. Ibid., 169.

choir with sopranos, altos, tenors, and basses produces a richer sound than can any single voice range alone, so it is with an integrated multiracial congregation."[16] The result of such a harmonious life of the congregation will be the spiritual growth of its members.[17]

Barriers to the integral model.[18] The integral model is the theological ideal. However, it is the most difficult to implement. There are a few barriers to implementing this model that could be mentioned here.

1. Multiracial churches have to work against sociologically natural leanings. There are "a number of sociological factors – such as the need for symbolic boundaries and social solidarity, similarity principles, and the status quo bias – which constantly drive religious congregations to be racially homogeneous."[19]
2. Lack of leadership. Leaders should be convinced that it is God's design for the church to be multiracial and they have to be passionate about it. Leaders have to have a history of multiracial life. They "cannot lead a congregation in becoming multiracial if they, themselves, are living segregated lives."[20]
3. Trying to establish a multiracial congregation "solely with human power rather than with God's power."[21]
4. Interracial dating of the youth.[22] It is unavoidable to have youth dating across racial lines within congregations. Not all parents are prepared to accept it.

---

16. Ibid.

17. Kevin Gushiken, analyzing the spiritual formation of multiethnic congregations, states, "Spiritual integration has relevancy to minorities as they oftentimes preserve two or more separate worlds, one with their ethnic group and another with those outside of it . . . Therefore, in multiethnic congregations, it is critical to disciple towards a unified biblical worldview that connects culture and personality to the redemptive work of Christ. In doing so, individuals begin to cultivate a spiritual framework to understand and experience all of life. On the other hand, ethnic expression should be preserved by providing space for cultural elements within the church creating a richness that accommodates individual ethnicity rather than suppress it" ("Spiritual Formation and Multiethnic Congregations," *Journal of Spiritual Formation and Soul Care* 4, no. 2 [Fall 2011]: 202).

18. David A. Anderson provides practical guidance for running a successful multicultural ministry in his book *Multicultural Ministry* (Grand Rapids, MI: Zondervan, 2004).

19. DeYoung et al., *United by Faith*, 170.

20. Ibid.

21. Ibid.

22. Ibid., 171.

5. Cultural racism.[23] Some believers are overly passionate about their own culture. When they notice that certain elements of their culture are fading away in the church, they react negatively.
6. The exercise of power by the dominant racial group.[24]
7. Overemphasizing unity and assimilation and neglecting to acknowledge the uniqueness of each culture represented within the congregation.[25]
8. Inattention of the majority group to the opinions and views of the non-majority groups in the church in addressing church life issues.[26]

This list of barriers in the process of transforming an existing uniracial congregation into a multiracial congregation or while planting a new church as a multiracial congregation shows how challenging is this process. Only a clear understanding that it is God's will for the church to be multiracial, and a willingness to be obedient to this will, can help the local immigrant congregation to start this process.

10.2.2.3. Ways of Moving from a Uniracial to Multiracial Congregation

The following ways of starting the process of moving from uniracial to multiracial congregation could be identified.

1. The group of uniracial church members leaves their congregation and joins the uniracial congregation of a different race with an agreement with the leadership of this congregation to start the process of developing the multiracial church.
2. Two (or more) uniracial congregations merge together with the intention to start a joint multiracial church.
3. Planting a new church with the goal of making it eventually multiracial through reaching non-believing people of different races in the community.[27]

---

23. Ibid.
24. Ibid.
25. Ibid., 172.
26. Ibid., 174.
27. Ibid., 175.

It should be clarified that the church service in a multiracial congregation is to be translated simultaneously into languages of the ethnic groups represented in the church. Also, it needs to be mentioned that it is beyond this study to provide detailed instructions on how to go through the process of church model transformation. Appropriate materials are available on this subject.[28]

10.2.2.4. Issues to be Concerned About

There are a few issues to be addressed by the uniracial congregation while it is becoming multiracial.

1. Culturally diverse worship. It should include "the cultural elements of more than one racial group. The worship style of most integrated multiracial congregations tends to be a mixture of several different racial worship styles."[29] It is important to have it this way because the culturally diverse worship symbolizes to visitors acceptance of other races. "An inclusive worship style communicates to visitors of different races that they, and their cultures, are respected."[30] Kevin D. Dougherty and Kimberly R. Huyser argue that the form of worship makes a difference in how diverse the congregation could be. According to them, "Congregations that emphasize experiential, charismatic worship will have more racially diverse memberships than will congregations with less charismatic forms of worship."[31]

2. Racially diverse leadership. It is very important for multiracial congregations that their leadership reflect the diversity of the membership. "Multiracial leadership is important because members of different racial groups need to feel represented."[32]

---

28. George Yancey's *One Body, One Spirit: Principles of Successful Multiracial Churches* (Downers Grove, IL: InterVarsity, 2003) is one of the sources that consist of practical advice on the subject and could be recommended for Slavic churches.

29. DeYoung et al., *United by Faith*, 176.

30. Ibid.

31. Kevin D. Dougherty and Kimberly R. Huyser, "Racially Diverse Congregations: Organizational Identity and the Accommodation of Differences," *Journal for the Scientific Study of Religion* 47, no. 1 (March 2008): 28.

32. DeYoung et al., *United by Faith*, 177. When there is a possibility to make a choice between pastors representing different ethnic groups in the congregation, it is better to give the leadership position to one who represents a minority in the church. Dougherty and Huyser advise: "Congregations led by clergy from a cultural background not dominant in the congregation (e.g., a black pastor in a predominantly white church, or a white Hindu

3. Intentionality. Creating a multiethnic congregation is a task facing many obstacles. It is very important to be intentional in all aspects of the process of accomplishing this task. "Intentionality is important because the social tendencies in the United States lean toward racial separation instead of integration."[33] One of the aspects of intentionality "is the creation of structures in the church that allow people of different races to meet together and get to know one another across racial groups."[34]

4. Adaptability. This is one of the requirements for the multiracial congregations in order to be successful in their ministry. Since, in such congregations, people of several different cultures are meeting together, "members of multiracial churches need to have flexibility and readiness to handle new problems"[35] in order to keep these people together. Dougherty and Huyser point to the fact that adaptability "grows from the relational ties among participants. Strong relational ties permit congregations to recognize and to respond to internal cultural challenges."[36]

10.2.2.5. Challenging But Promising Perspectives

Based on the brief overview of barriers and challenges that could be faced by those who try to implement a multiracial church, it could be concluded that it is a very difficult path to travel. It requires vision, "time, energy, and focus that could be used elsewhere."[37] However, the final goal makes this road worth traveling. The goal is not the multiracial congregation itself, but the goal is reaching people of different races for Christ and living a Christian life that reflects Christ's teaching about how people should relate to each other. The goal is to be a church of today, and "being church today, means living God's mission *where we are.*"[38] Based on the study undertaken by DeYoung, Yancey, Deymaz, Marti and other leaders of the multiracial church-planting

---

priest in a temple populated primarily by Asians) will display greater membership diversity than congregations in which leaders and the majority of members share the same cultural background" ("Racially Diverse Congregations," 28).

33. DeYoung et al., *United by Faith*, 178.
34. Ibid.
35. Ibid., 179.
36. Dougherty and Huyser, "Racially Diverse Congregations," 28
37. DeYoung et al., *United by Faith*, 180.
38. Nathan C. P. Frambach, "Being Church Today: Living God's Mission Where We Are," *Currents in Theology and Mission* 37, no. 1 (Fall 2010)" 11.

movement in America, multiracial congregations are the most appropriate church model in which to implement an authentic and contextualized mission in the ethnically diverse American society. This model could be used not only by the indigenous churches but by the immigrant congregations as well. Adopting this model and using it as a church-planting model by Slavic immigrant Baptist churches would help them to free themselves from their ethnic enclaves and start reaching their neighbors of different races with the gospel. At the same time, they will still be able to preserve some elements of their Russian culture while it is integrated with other cultures within multiracial congregations. Implementing this model by the immigrant churches will give them an opportunity to become instrumental in the work of Christ today in their local multiracial American context. It will give them an opportunity to pass on their beliefs to their children and to people of other races. It will make the mission of their churches authentic and contextualized.

10.3. Ways of Equipping Contextualized Mission Work

George Yancey notes that since "multiracial churches do not naturally spring up, it will take a significant amount of effort to create and sustain them."[39] The experience of churches that are serving second-generation Korean Americans and are trying to become multiracial shows that it is a very challenging task.[40] In this part of the chapter, several key aspects of making contextualized mission work among Slavic immigrant Baptist churches possible are discussed.

10.3.1. Training of Leaders for Carrying Out Authentic and Contextualized Mission

As mentioned above, the role of the leadership is crucial in the process of establishing multiracial congregations. Because of this, equipping leaders for such work is important. Currently, the Pacific Coast Slavic Baptist

---

39. Yancey, *One Body One Spirit*, 29.
40. Pawan Dhingra, "We're Not a Korean American Church Any More: Dilemmas in Constructing a Multi-Racial Church Identity," *Social Compass* 51, no. 3 (Sept. 2004): 374.

Association has an Educational Department, which is called to provide leadership training to church workers of different church ministries. In light of this enormous task of switching into a multiracial church model, this department has to develop a special training program for church planters, with a strong cross-cultural emphasis. This program would be useful for training both those who will be involved in multiracial church planting and those who will participate in missionary work abroad. This training program should be developed in collaboration with local English-speaking churches that are already practicing a strong cross-cultural ministry or multiracial model of the church.

10.3.2. Formation of the Mentality of Slavic Baptist Churches Oriented towards an Authentic and Contextualized Mission

One of the serious tasks Slavic church leaders have to accomplish in order to prepare the ground for transforming the mission work of their churches to be authentic and contextualized is developing support for the idea of a multiracial church among church members. The results of the surveys of church leaders provided in chapter 6 and analyzed in chapter 9 (section 9.3.2.) clearly illustrate that separation exists between Slavic Baptist immigrants and other ethnic groups in terms of collaborating with Christians of these ethnicities and reaching non-believers for Christ. If this separation remains, and the attitude of Slavic immigrants towards other ethnic groups does not change, it will be very difficult, if not impossible, to convince them to accept people of other ethnicities and races into their churches.[41] Leaders should work very hard to teach their constituencies about God's view of ethnicity and race, about reconciliation with people of other races, about the practical application of Galatians 3:28 in church life, and about the reality of racism in our hearts and its danger for our personal spiritual life. This is

---

41. Concluding his PhD dissertation Vladimir Ubeivolc insists: "To rethink *missio Dei* among Evangelicals in an Orthodox context means to be open to new insights, collaboration, partnership and much more – to be open to change" ("Rethinking *Missio Dei* among Evangelical Churches in an Eastern European Orthodox Context," [Carlisle, UK: Langham Monographs, 2016], 298). This is exactly how the situation with Slavic Baptist immigrant churches in America could be described. In order to be faithful to the *missio Dei*, they have to be ready for the most difficult thing – change. The main change should be in their attitudes toward society in general, and toward other ethnic groups and cultures in particular.

a tremendous task. Another equally important task is to develop a willingness among Slavic immigrant believers to leave their linguistic and cultural comfort zone. They need to allow English to be used in their churches on a regular basis. They have to be ready for change. Also, leaders have to develop a correct understanding of the role of the church. From seeing the church as existing solely for believers as a place of refuge, comfort, and belonging, Slavic believers have to learn to see the church as God's means of bringing the good news to the world. They have to start viewing the church as being called to serve others above itself.[42] Personal visitation and speeches in churches done by leaders who are committed to the idea of the multiracial church, as well as conferences, seminars, and meetings with individual believers, will be needed in order to make a shift in the mentality of the Slavic Baptist diaspora towards a more inclusive attitude regarding other ethnic groups and more evangelistic and service-oriented views of church mission. This is a tremendous task and it will take time to be accomplished. This task should be accomplished before any attempts are made to convert existing Russian-speaking immigrant congregations into multiracial congregations. However, Slavic believers do not have to wait as long to plant new multiracial congregations. Many young people in PCSBA churches currently are open

---

42. One of the findings Alexander Popov has introduced in his dissertation is that for "many ECB authors, such as *BV*'s [*BV – Bratsky Vestknik*, the official publication of the AUCECB] last chief editor, V. Kulikov, being biblical meant being set apart from the reality of the world around: biblical interpretation created a world view that was in some sense an escape from the great difficulties of existence in the hostile atmosphere of a totalitarian regime" ("The Evangelical Christians-Baptists in the Soviet Union as a Hermeneutical Community: Examining the Identity of the All-Union Council of the ECB (AUCECB) Through the Way the Bible was Used in its Publications" [PhD diss., International Baptist Theological Seminary, University of Wales, 2011], 295). This could be one of the reasons why Slavic Baptists in America, in most cases, are not involved in the life of the society they are living in now. They avoid such kinds of involvement not only because of the immigrant social challenges they are facing in America (as it was shown in chapter 7 of this study), but also because of many years of teaching they were exposed to through reading the official publication of the AUCECB, the magazine *Bratsky Vestnik*. Another observation made by Alexander Popov related to this subject is the impact of persecution on formation of the mentality of Russian Baptists in relation to the mainstream society. According to Popov, as the result of persecutions in the early stage of their history, Baptists in Russia developed a more sectarian, isolationist worldview against the society than their counterparts of that time, Evangelical Christians, who came to existence later than the Baptists did not experience as much persecution as Baptists in the beginning of their movement (ibid., 290). Taking into consideration Popov's assumption, and the fact that persecutions were part of life of evangelicals in Russia through almost their entire history, it is not surprising that Slavic Baptists in America demonstrate indifference towards American society.

to the idea of planting new churches. With the support of the association leadership, and after appropriate training, groups of young people who speak both Russian and English could be commissioned for the process of planting new multiracial churches together with the representatives of other ethnic groups. Existing Slavic churches could join this process later.

10.3.3. Development of the Appropriate Administrative Structure for Implementing Authentic and Contextualized Mission Work

In order to promote the idea of planting multiracial congregations among PCSBA churches and to organize the process of implementing this idea, a new Department of Inter-racial Relations should be established within the structure of the PCSBA. It could be part of the existing Mission Department or a separate entity.

10.4. Conclusion for Chapter 10

It was determined in chapter 9 that the current mission of Slavic Baptist churches is not fully authentic and contextualized because it does not include in its focus indigenous non-Russian-speaking people. While continuing ministry to Russian-speaking people in America and around the world, as well as in their homeland through different means of communication (radio, TV, Internet, newspaper *Our Days*) and financial help, PCSBA churches have to put significant efforts into finding new methods for reaching the non-Russian-speaking people in their neighborhoods with the gospel and to practice Christ's love (social action/*diaconia*). The multiracial church model should be adopted by PCSBA churches as a way of breaking through linguistic and cultural barriers and opening the door for cross-cultural, cross-ethnic, and cross-racial missions among the non-Russian-speaking people of American society. Although there are multiple barriers to the successful implementation of the multiracial church idea and a few serious issues to consider, efforts to start new multiracial churches, as well as attempts to transform the existing uniracial Slavic Baptist congregations into multiracial congregations, are worth undertaking. The successful results of this process will make the mission of PCSBA churches authentic and contextualized. Only through establishing multiracial congregations will Christian immigrants make a significant impact on the religious life of American society. It is the only way for the realization of Hanciles' presumption that "the new immigrant congregations are performing a vital missionary function by their very presence."[43] In order to ensure the success of this process, serious leadership training, with a strong emphasis on cross-cultural ministry, should be implemented. PCSBA churches should develop among their members an understanding of the mission of the church as a serving community, a willingness to leave the comfort zone of the uniracial church, and a readiness to accept people of other ethnic groups in their midst. Meanwhile, groups of young Slavic believers could consider starting multiracial churches in partnership with believers from other ethnic groups. Finally, a department called to promote, organize, and maintain the process of transformation from uniracial to multiracial churches should be established within the PCSBA structure.

10.5. Further Research

This study has revealed a few areas where further research is desirable.

1. Since this study has addressed only two aspects of authentic mission – evangelism and social action/*diaconia* – the implication of other aspects of authentic mission, such as overcoming violence and building cultures of peace, justice, care of the environment, worship, dialogue, inculturation, and ministry of reconciliation by the Slavic Baptist immigrant churches, needs to be analyzed.

2. Because the strong recommendation of this thesis is a close cooperation between Slavic immigrant churches and native English-speaking churches, a comparative analysis of theology, as well as ecclesiology, of these two church groups should be conducted. Such a study would help to identify the most compatible combinations of PCSBA churches and indigenous churches for sister-church relationships.

3. Studying the Eastern versus Western mentality encountered in the context of intergenerational relations within Slavic Baptist immigrant churches, and the impact of these mentalities on the ability of these churches to

---

43. Jehu J. Hanciles, *Beyond Christendom: Globalization, African Migration, and the Transformation of the West* (Maryknoll, NY: Orbis, 2008), 297.

become multiracial, is highly desirable. This study would provide valuable information for those who will try to start multiracial churches.

Conclusion

This study has been undertaken with the intention of answering the following research question: In light of the specific immigrant context, what does an authentic mission imply for the immigrant Slavic Baptist churches in America? This question has been raised in light of the fact that hundreds of thousands of evangelical Christians have immigrated to the United States from the republics of the former Soviet Union during the last twenty-five years. They left their homeland at a time when religious freedom had arrived there; when many opportunities to carry out an authentic mission among their countrymen became available. They left the land where they shared the same language and culture with the rest of the society, the land where their mission was contextual and greatly needed. Now, living in a new country, with a new linguistic and cultural context, how fruitful are they in fulfillment of Christ's Great Commission? Are their efforts to do mission work in America producing equal results to what they could do if they lived in their homeland? Is it beneficial for God's kingdom that such a massive move of evangelical Christians took place from one continent to another? If the answer is "no," what needs to be done in order to change the situation? In the attempt to answer the research question, the following steps were made.

First of all, in Part I of the study, the tool to evaluate the current mission work of Slavic immigrant Baptist churches was acquired. In order to be able to make an appropriate evaluation of the mission work of immigrant churches, the contemporary meaning of the term "authentic mission" was defined. For this purpose, the theological context of the development of this concept was introduced and discussed. This context includes the *missio Dei* as a framework for the mission of the church and the kingdom of God as the goal of this mission. Then, in order to provide a foundation for defining an authentic mission, the positions of three different theological groups within Christianity (WCC, evangelicals/Lausanne Movement, and Anabaptists) on the subject of mission were reviewed and compared. Based on this analysis, an authentic mission was defined as a multifaceted task that includes such aspects as evangelism, social action/*diaconia*, overcoming violence and building cultures of peace, justice, care of the environment, worship, dialogue, inculturation, and ministry of reconciliation. Finally, in Part I, the importance of contextuality in mission and its challenges were discussed as well.

The second step (Part II) was a discussion of the identity formation of Slavic Baptists through the historical perspective, both in the homeland and in America. For this purpose, the historical background of Slavic Baptists in their homeland has been evaluated from the perspective of evangelism and social action/*diaconia*. Also, the development of the general Russian-speaking diaspora in America as a potential mission field and the development of the Russian-speaking Baptist diaspora in America as the bearer of mission in the context of the global migration have been analyzed. There are about 5 million Russians living in America. Most of them are non-believers. Potentially, this is a mission field for Slavic Baptists in America. The history of the founding and organization of the Pacific Coast Slavic Baptist Association was reviewed as well.

The third step (Part III) included the analysis of the paradigm shift in self-understanding by Slavic Baptists in America and the identity crisis/transformation they are going through from the mission perspective. It was done through analysis of data concerning their mission work and collected through surveys of the church leaders, youth, and other sources. This data provided the basis for the evaluation process of the mission work of PCSBA churches. Also, the social challenges of immigrant life and their possible impact on the local mission of Slavic Baptists in America were analyzed. It was shown that common to all immigrants, social challenges serve dual roles. On the one hand, they motivate believing immigrants to lean toward the local immigrant church much more strongly than they probably did in their homeland. On the other hand, these challenges create barriers for them to carry on the mission work among indigenous people. Also, the mission challenges and opportunities for Slavic Baptists in America were analyzed. Among the challenges are ethnicity and the language barrier that separate

Slavic Christians from the rest of the society, creating a barrier for them to implement mission work among indigenous people. At the same time, their ethnicity and ability to speak Russian provide the Slavic believers with the opportunity to serve the Russian-speaking non-believers in America and around the world.

The final step (Part IV) in the accomplishment of the goal of the study was designed to provide an authentic mission perspective on the mission work of PCSBA churches, and to point to the best mission practices for them in light of the context and contextuality. The evaluation of the mission work of the Pacific Coast Slavic Baptist Association churches has been done in this part based on the data provided in chapter 6. The conclusion of the evaluation is as follows: (1) the mission of Slavic immigrant Baptist churches is authentic and contextualized in its foreign aspect, which includes supporting evangelistic ministry and providing humanitarian aid in the homeland; and (2) it is not authentic and not contextualized in its local aspect, and so is not concerned with doing evangelism and conducting social actions among the non-Russian speaking people locally. This second part of the conclusion strongly challenges Jehu J. Hanciles' argument that the immigrant congregations "represent a cutting edge of Christian growth in America."[1] In the case of PCSBA churches, there is no growth occurring based on conversion of people out of the non-Slavic world, and there is a very limited growth based on conversion of people from a non-churched Slavic diaspora. As a way of improving the local aspect of their mission, PCSBA churches are advised to consider implementing the multiracial model of the church. Either existing Slavic immigrant mono-racial churches could be transformed into multiracial congregations or new churches could be planted by Slavic immigrants (most probably by young people) in cooperation with the representatives of other ethnic groups. Establishing multiracial congregations will provide the Slavic immigrant churches with the possibility to preserve some of their cultural characteristics and the core of their theological principles and, at the same time, to be able to create a bridge toward the surrounding society in their efforts to do mission work among local native people. From the perspective of this study, it is an answer to the research question of this study.

---

1. Ibid.

It is understood that a multitude of challenges limit the implementation of this recommendation. However, it is clear that there is no alternative option for the Slavic immigrant churches to make their mission authentic in both aspects, abroad and locally.[2]

After making this recommendation, the author of this study wants to challenge the current approach that the established American Christian denominations are using towards Christian immigrants. The common philosophy today is to help immigrants to establish their own congregations and, if possible, to help them to obtain their own church facilities, and then leave them alone. It is assumed that these churches will become self-governed, self-supported, and self-propagating.[3] However, in doing this, the indigenous Christians allow their brothers and sisters in immigrant churches to become isolated from society in general, and from the indigenous Christian community in particular. By this, native Christians are doing a disservice to the immigrant churches. Certainly, the local immigrant congregations from their inception should be under caring, supportive supervision from the local indigenous congregations.[4] Strong sister-church relationships should be established and carefully and intentionally maintained, with the purpose of providing support and guidance to the immigrant congregation in the process of its transformation from a uniracial/monoethnic congregation serving only the particular ethnic group in the society to a multiracial

---

2. What could be an encouragement for Slavic immigrant churches for starting this uneasy process is to know that it has been done by other ethnic groups and "through these minority groups, the Spirit is working by drawing attention to the viability of the gospel of Jesus Christ in former Christian contexts that have jettisoned Christian values in favour of moral relativism and secularization" (J. Kwabena Asamoah-Gyadu, "Unwanted Sectarians: Spirit, Migration and Mission in an African-Led Mega-Size Church in Eastern Europe," *Evangelical Review of Theology* 34, no. 1 [Jan 2010]: 78).

3. Paul E. Pierson, "Lessons in Mission from the Twentieth Century: Conciliar Missions," in *Between Past and Future: Evangelical Mission Entering the Twenty-First Century*, ed. Jonathan J. Bonk (Pasadena, CA: William Carey Library, 2003), 73.

4. Brian M. Howell recommends that the wider North American churches in their response to an increasing number of immigrants in the country should "emphasize biblical values of hospitality, justice, compassion, and proclamation" ("Multiculturalism, Immigration and the North American Church: Rethinking Contextualization," *Missiology* 39, no. 1 [Jan 2011], 83). Eventually, it will lead to formation of multicultural churches: "as second and third generation immigrants cross the bridges being built by North Americans of various ethnicities, Christians will cross in both directions and the image of the multicultural Kingdom can begin to appear" (84).

church serving the whole society.⁵ The clear conclusion of this study is that the most desirable model of relationship between Christian immigrants and indigenous Christians is the establishment of new multiracial churches. Of course, to do this is challenging for both immigrants as well as indigenous Christians. However, this road is worth traveling because it helps the immigrant churches, as well as indigenous churches, to practice an authentic and contextualized mission and to eventually be more effective in fulfilling the Great Commission.

---

5. Michael Kisskalt states that "the immigrants coming into our countries have the right to establish their own, monoethnic churches. They cannot integrate in a few weeks, months or even years into our German churches. It is important that there be bridges so that they do not live in cultural isolation. The challenge is that our native churches help them to live their identity but also help them to open themselves up to the new context" ("Cross-Cultural Learning: Issues of the Second Generation of Immigrant Churches," in *Ethnic Churches in Europe: A Baptist Response*, ed. Peter Penner [Schwarzenfeld: Neufeld Verlag, 2006], 147). It is true in Germany; it is also true in America. Unfortunately, not many native churches meet this challenge of providing the immigrant churches with guidance on how to integrate in the new context. It is also true that very few immigrant churches are open to such guidance.

APPENDIX FOR CHAPTER 4
Historical Background of Slavic Baptists from the Mission Perspective

4.3.6. The Significance of Missiological Writings in Russian and Their Impact on Russian Baptists

Results of the survey of the Baptist theological schools in the former USSR on the subject of the impact missiological books translated from English into Russian are making on students are provided in table 4.3.6.A. below.

Table 4.3.6.A.

	Name of the book	Author	Do you use this book for teaching the course on mission/missiology in your school?	If the answer is YES, what kind of impact does this book make on your students? Please share your opinion.	School surveyed
1	*Transforming Mission*	David Bosch	YES. This book is recommended for reading (certain parts of it)	No answer (N/A)	Zaporozhskiy Bible College and Seminary.
			YES	This is a fundamental book that broadens a biblical (New Testament) and historic understanding of mission. However, the theological understanding of mission common to our context has not come to appreciate the importance of this textbook. I believe Russian-speaking students will come to this appreciation in the future. Currently, this book is the most significant book on mission available in Russian.	Ukrainian Evangelical Theological Seminary
			YES	This book is difficult for students on the baccalaureate program. However, it is very helpful in broadening students' understanding of the subject.	Kishinev Theological College
			YES	The majority of our students are enrolled in the diploma programs. This book is too global in order to make a specific impact on them. It is considered as a good source for introduction to the philosophy of ministry.	Minsk Theological Seminary

	Name of the book	Author	Do you use this book for teaching the course on mission/missiology in your school?	If the answer is YES, what kind of impact does this book make on your students? Please share your opinion.	School surveyed
2	God's Missionary People: Rethinking the Purpose of the Local Church	Charles Van Engen	YES. This book is recommended as elective/additional reading.	N/A	Zaporozhskiy Bible College and Seminary
			NO	N/A	Ukrainian Evangelical Theological Seminary
			NO	N/A	Kishinev Theological College
			N/A	N/A	Minsk Theological Seminary
3	Soviet Evangelicals Since World War II	Walter Sawatsky	YES. This book is recommended for elective/additional reading.	N/A	Zaporozhskiy Bible College and Seminary
			NO	N/A	Ukrainian Evangelical Theological Seminary
			YES. Elective reading.	Don't have an answer.	Kishinev Theological College
			N/A	N/A	Minsk Theological Seminary

Name of the book	Author	Do you use this book for teaching the course on mission/missiology in your school?	If the answer is YES, what kind of impact does this book make on your students? Please share your opinion.	School surveyed
4 *From Jerusalem to Irian Jaya*	Ruth A. Tucker	YES. Required reading.	Biographical stories (personal experiences of missionaries) make a very meaningful impact on the personal commitment of students and help them in discerning their future ministry.	Zaporozhskiy Bible College and Seminary
		YES.	This book is making a positive impact on students because it introduces the history of mission in a concise way, especially in regard to the Protestant mission. Actually, it is almost the only source we have on the subject of history of missions.	Ukrainian Evangelical Theological Seminary
		YES. Elective reading.	Don't have an answer.	Kishinev Theological College
		YES.	This book is preferable to the book *Transforming Mission* (Bosch) for many students (and for the instructor as well). The book is encouraging for the readers. It introduces a realistic picture of ministry.	Minsk Theological Seminary

Appendix for Chapter 4

	Name of the book	Author	Do you use this book for teaching the course on mission/missiology in your school?	If the answer is YES, what kind of impact does this book make on your students? Please share your opinion.	School surveyed
5	Missionary Methods: St Paul's or Ours	Roland Allen	NO. We don't have this book.	N/A	Zaporozhskiy Bible College and Seminary
			YES.	This is a very important book which introduces the mission philosophy and strategy of the apostle Paul. Unfortunately, this is the only book that studies the mission work of Paul from the missiological perspective.	Ukrainian Evangelical Theological Seminary
			YES.	This book helps students to understand the reason for a change of the missionary paradigm.	Kishinev Theological College
			N/A	N/A	Minsk Theological Seminary
6	Missions in the Plan of the Ages	William Owen Carver	YES. This book is recommended as elective/additional reading.	N/A	Zaporozhskiy Bible College and Seminary
			NO	N/A	Ukrainian Evangelical Theological Seminary
			YES. Elective reading.	Don't have an answer.	Kishinev Theological College
			N/A	N/A	Minsk Theological Seminary

	Name of the book	Author	Do you use this book for teaching the course on mission/missiology in your school?	If the answer is YES, what kind of impact does this book make on your students? Please share your opinion.	School surveyed
7	*Understanding Church Growth*	Donald A. McGavran	YES. This book is recommended as elective/additional reading.	N/A	Zaporozhskiy Bible College and Seminary
			YES.	Currently, this book has relative importance, for different reasons. It is useful to students since it helps them to understand the conditions and principles of church growth, national movement development, the importance of social structures, etc.	Ukrainian Evangelical Theological Seminary
			YES.	This book often creates perplexity in the reader's mind.	Kishinev Theological College
			YES.	The same comments could be shared about this book as were said about Bosch's book.	Minsk Theological Seminary
8	*The Mission of the Church in the World*	Roger E. Hedlund	YES.	N/A	Zaporozhskiy Bible College and Seminary
			N/A	N/A	Ukrainian Evangelical Theological Seminary
			N/A	N/A	Kishinev Theological College
			N/A	N/A	Minsk Theological Seminary

Appendix for Chapter 4

	Name of the book	Author	Do you use this book for teaching the course on mission/missiology in your school?	If the answer is YES, what kind of impact does this book make on your students? Please share your opinion.	School surveyed
9	*Let the Nations Be Glad*	John Piper	YES.	N/A	Zaporozhskiy Bible College and Seminary
			NO.	N/A	Ukrainian Evangelical Theological Seminary
			N/A	N/A	Kishinev Theological College
			N/A	N/A	Minsk Theological Seminary
10	*An Open Secret*	Lesslie Newbigin	N/A	N/A	Zaporozhskiy Bible College and Seminary
			YES	This is a very good book, especially in terms of theological and philosophical comprehension of mission. The book helps in developing the theological understanding of mission as mission of the Trinity.	Ukrainian Evangelical Theological Seminary
			N/A	N/A	Kishinev Theological College
			N/A	N/A	Minsk Theological Seminary

	Name of the book	Author	Do you use this book for teaching the course on mission/missiology in your school?	If the answer is YES, what kind of impact does this book make on your students? Please share your opinion.	School surveyed
11	*The Expansion of Christianity in The First Three Centuries* (1904)	Adolf von Harnack	N/A	N/A	Zaporozhskiy Bible College and Seminary
			YES.	This is an excellent source for history of mission during the first three centuries. It opens up well the holistic nature of the early church's mission.	Ukrainian Evangelical Theological Seminary
			N/A	N/A	Kishinev Theological College
			N/A	N/A	Minsk Theological Seminary
12	*Missions in the Age of the Spirit*	John York	N/A	N/A	Zaporozhskiy Bible College and Seminary
			YES.	This book is one of the few that touch on the subject of *missio Dei* and suggest a missiological reading of the Bible.	Ukrainian Evangelical Theological Seminary
			N/A	N/A	Kishinev Theological College
			N/A	N/A	Minsk Theological Seminary

	Name of the book	Author	Do you use this book for teaching the course on mission/missiology in your school?	If the answer is YES, what kind of impact does this book make on your students? Please share your opinion.	School surveyed
13	*Natural Church Development: A Guide to Eight Essential Qualities of Healthy Churches*	Christian Schwarz	N/A	N/A	Zaporozhskiy Bible College and Seminary
			N/A	N/A	Ukrainian Evangelical Theological Seminary
			N/A	N/A	Kishinev Theological College
			YES.	Some pastors are trying to build their ministry in accordance with the suggestions provided by Schwartz (or they try to evaluate their church based on his criteria).	Minsk Theological Seminary

APPENDIX FOR CHAPTER 5

Developing Slavic Baptist Diaspora in the American context

5.1.A. Global Migration as the Mission Context

5.1.1.A. Some Migration Statistics

In 2005, the number of people living outside their country of origin (the technical definition of a migrant) increased from 120 million in 1990 to more than 191 million in 2005. One in 35 persons in the world today is a migrant. In 2005, 2.9 percent of the world population were migrants, and 48.6 percent of all migrants are women.[1] The West is not the main destination for all migrants, as people often assume. In 2005, the intake of migrants by continent was as follows: Europe 34%, North America 23%, Asia 28%, Africa 9%, Latin America 3%, and Oceania 3%. As shown by these statistics, Asia receives more migrants than North America.[2] The number of migrants in the world keeps growing. Statistics show that "the global stock of migrants has more than doubled in the past four decades and that the number of migrants in the world today, both legal and illegal, is thought to total perhaps 200 million."[3] From 2002 to 2006, the United States has accepted about one million legal immigrants, which is more than all other

---

1. Gemma Tulud Cruz, "Expanding the Boundaries, Turning Border into Spaces: Mission in the Context of Contemporary Migration," in *Mission after Christendom: Emergent Themes in Contemporary Mission*, ed. Obgu U. Kalu, Peter Vethanayagamony, and Edmund Kee-Fook Chia (Louisville, KY: Westminster John Knox, 2010), 71.
2. Ibid., 72.
3. Ibid.

nations combined.⁴ Because the origins of modern immigrants often differ from those of the past, "the number of minorities in the United States reached the 100 million mark for the first time in 2006, making them now a third of the U.S. population."⁵

5.1.2.A. History of Migration at a Glance

The beginning of the new era of European exploration and colonial expansion at the end of the fifteenth and beginning of the sixteenth century led to massive migration. "Maritime technology and ocean travel allowed commercial activity, movements of peoples, and interaction of cultures on a scale and diversity without precedence in human history."⁶ This period of international migration, from AD 1500 to the present, is usually divided into following phases: (1) mercantile, 1500–1800; (2) industrial, 1800–1925; (3) limited migration, 1925–1960; and (4) postindustrial, after 1960. Such classifications of migration history are Eurocentric and "reflects a wholly economic understanding of international migration." However, it does not reflect political dimensions and other forces that have shaped the emerging world order. Jehu J. Hanciles suggests a different way for the periodization of migration history:

- 1500 to 1850: European expansion and the Atlantic slave trade
- 1800 to 1960: high imperialism and industrial growth
- From the 1960s: global migrations⁷

Through the European expansion (1500–1850), the world changed dramatically. From the beginning, "European overseas exploration was linked to conquest and settlement." As a result, significant portions of the Americas, Africa, Asia, and Oceania were appropriated and occupied.⁸ During this period, "religious impulses and Christian missionary initiatives were intimately intertwined with these processes of European colonial expansion."⁹

---

4. Ibid.
5. Ibid.
6. Jehu J. Hanciles, *Beyond Christendom: Globalization, African Migration, and the Transformation of the West* (Maryknoll, NY: Orbis, 2008), 158.
7. Ibid., 159.
8. Ibid.
9. Ibid., 160.

The second phase of international migration (1800–1960) "was also defined by European movement, political expansion, and economic needs." Hanciles links migration at that time with imperial expansion and colonial acquisitions, saying, "The escalation of European migration and resettlement went hand in hand with an explosion of imperial expansion and colonial acquisitions through which Europeans extended or intensified their economic and political domination of non-European peoples and renewed their efforts to impose key aspects of European culture around the world."[10]

There was undeniable collusion between Christian missions and the Western empire during that period. At times, it was complex and tension-ridden. There were common interests between parties, missions, and the empire, such as the spreading of education, which helped to overcome conflicting purposes. Ultimately, "serious-minded Protestants were convinced that the timing and gains of imperial ventures reflected 'divine providence,' even 'manifest destiny.' The doctrine of 'divine providence' was prominent among nineteenth-century Protestants."[11] Hanciles makes the point that the fact that Britain was the world's economic superpower at that time "had a lot to do with its status as the world's premier missionary-sending nation."[12] After the outbreak of World War I, European migration began to decline.

Although four centuries of European colonial expansion stimulated an unparalleled rise in international migrations, decolonization and the end of an empire brought an even greater intensification to migration flow. "From the 1960s, international migrations have escalated in volume, velocity, and complexity and transformed into a truly global phenomenon no longer dominated by European needs and initiatives."[13] The direction of the migration movement has changed, as well. Instead of going from economically developed regions of the world, as was the case before 1960, after the 1960s "migrant movement has been predominantly from areas with weak economic and political systems to the centers of global dominance and advanced industrial growth."[14] The present direction of global migration

---

10. Ibid., 162.
11. Ibid., 164.
12. Ibid., 166.
13. Ibid., 172.
14. Ibid.

flow is largely determined by political and economic structures associated with Western empire building.[15] The limited space of this work does not allow more details about the different political and economic reasons that influence current migration flows.

5.1.3.A. Attempts to Explain the Migration Phenomenon

The unprecedented nature of current trends of international migration has stimulated fresh analysis of the migration phenomenon. Different theories try to explain the structural forces that promote emigration from developing countries: the structural forces that attract immigrants into developed countries; the motivations, goals, and aspirations of people who respond to these structural forces; and the social and economic structures that arise to connect areas of out- and in-migration.[16] A few of these theories are the following. The *neoclassical economic* perspective "explains international migration in terms of the supply and demand for labor."[17] The *historical-structural* theory "focuses on the unequal distribution of economic and political power" and "explains international migration mainly in terms of capitalist expansion and initiatives from the 'core' states."[18] The *social-capital* theory "draws attention to the significance of intangible resources within family, communities, and networks for international migration."[19] Relationships between people make an impact on the migration process. The *cumulative-causation* theory insists "that over time international migration becomes self-sustaining or self-perpetuating."[20] The most recent theory is *migration systems*. This theory "seeks to examine both ends of the migration flow and study all the linkages between the places concerned, whether within specific regions or between different regions."[21] The migration-system theory is more holistic because it recognizes the role of the state in the migration process, as well as the role of the family in the decision-making process regarding immigration. This theory addresses "the deficiencies in the other models while incorporating

---

15. Ibid., 173.
16. Ibid., 183.
17. Ibid.
18. Ibid., 184.
19. Ibid.
20. Ibid., 185.
21. Ibid.

their main arguments."[22] The existence of so many different theories indicates the complexity of the issue of contemporary international migration; it is often impossible to provide a single explanation.

5.1.4.A. Types of Immigrants in the US

Immigrants can be classified by their ethnicity or their country of origin. A national group of immigrants may include individuals representing different types of immigrants. These types "are distinguished by a series of common characteristics of socioeconomic origin and motives for departure that tend to be associated with different courses of adaptation in the United States."[23] There are two main dimensions that define the category to which an immigrant belongs. The first dimension is the immigrant's personal resources, in terms of material and human capital. It refers to "foreigners who arrive with investment capital or are endowed with high educational credentials," as well as to "those who have only their labor to sell."[24] The second dimension defines the immigrants' official status and refers to "migrants who arrive legally and receive government resettlement assistance," as well as to those who are in the country illegally. For immigrants arriving in a new country without significant material capital, receiving financial assistance is extremely important, especially at the beginning. In the US, "only persons granted refugee status or admitted as legal asylees have received any form of official resettlement assistance."[25] The great majority of Slavic evangelicals who emigrated to the US from the former USSR have been granted refugee status because they were coming from a former Communist country. This status made them eligible for resettlement assistance. "Being granted asylum has significant advantages over other immigration channels. The central difference is that while refugees have legal status and the right to work, and they can avail themselves of the welfare provisions of the 1980 act, those denied asylum have none of these privileges and, if they stay, are classified as illegal aliens."[26] This resettlement assistance and access to welfare provisions has

---

22. Ibid., 186.
23. Alejandro Portes and Ruben G. Rumbaut, *Immigrant America: A Portrait* (Berkeley and Los Angeles, CA: University of California Press, 2006), 20.
24. Ibid.
25. Ibid.
26. Ibid., 31.

made the recent immigrant experience of Slavic evangelicals very different from the experience of other immigrant groups who entered America with a different status or illegally. Slavic evangelicals have avoided many financial struggles, which are so common to other immigrant groups, by obtaining refugee status.

5.1.5.A. Contemporary Migration's Challenges to Mission

The relocation of a great number of people from one part of the world to another in a short period of time provides new challenges to mission work.

A question of justice. Since many migrants are coming from poor countries, they "become contemporary globalization's flexible, expendable, and disposable capital"[27] in the receiving countries and may be exploited and abused. This is especially true for undocumented immigrants. They are the lowest-paid, "the first to be victimized in times of economic slow-down," and are "targets of problematic stereotypes."[28] Immigrants are accused of taking away local jobs, driving wages down, and committing crimes. The challenge for the church is to reach these people with the gospel and to be an advocate for justice for them.

Strong connection to the homeland and vibrant local ethnic communities. Migrants also play an important role in providing "some form of economic salvation, not just for migrants and receiving countries, but also for the sending countries." This latter is done by sending their hard-earned money back to their homelands. In 2005, the money sent by migrants worldwide was estimated at $232 billion (compared with $167 billion of development aid given to the poor countries).[29] They not only help their relatives back home but also "help build and maintain vital infrastructures like schools, wells, and health centers (even churches); put up funds for scholarships; or raise money for calamity victims."[30] The difference between today's immigrants and those in the past is that they have higher profiles and "are more likely to demand stronger legal rights and formal recognition than previous

---

27. Cruz, "Expanding the Boundaries," 73.
28. Ibid.
29. Ibid., 74.
30. Ibid.

waves of migration."[31] Some of them can even vote in their home country's elections. It is clear that "migrants today are also more organized as well as more open, insistent, and defensive about their religious and cultural identity."[32] Their keeping a strong connection with their land of origin and creating ethnic communities in their land of destination make it more difficult for the church to reach immigrants with the gospel. The building of social, economic, and religious bridges between these ethnic enclaves and the Christian communities is required.

The challenge of diversity. When immigrants come to a new country, they bring with them their cultures and religions. As a result, social diversification comes with migration. "Migration has also drastically changed not just the cultural landscape, but also the religious demographics of many cities and countries around the world."[33] There are many religions in America today that were not present just a few decades ago, and as a result, spiritual diversity in the United States is on the rise.[34] Hinduism, Buddhism, Islam, and other religions are becoming ever more common on American soil. Christian immigrants also bring diversity within American Christianity because "new immigrant Christian groups embody a fresh spirituality, particularly since they reproduce or exhibit the same dynamic, creative, and celebratory character of religious rituals in their homeland,"[35] as well as evangelistic zeal. The challenge that indigenous American churches are facing is their (in)ability to "fully accept or embrace their (immigrant) sisters and brothers in faith who exhibit differences in terms of culturally based religious beliefs and practices."[36] Although immigrant congregations are often using local English-speaking church facilities for their worship services, this does not necessarily mean integration between the two congregations. Often, they are very much separated from each other. In these cases, the indigenous American congregations are missing an opportunity to express their Christianity by providing biblical hospitality to the "strangers" in their

---

31. Ibid., 75.
32. Ibid.
33. Ibid., 77.
34. Ibid.
35. Ibid.
36. Ibid.

land by establishing closer, personal relationships with the newcomers and helping them with adaptation to the new society.

5.1.6.A. Reimagining Mission in the Context of Contemporary Migration

How should a Christian mission respond to the issues raised by global migration? How can it minister to the increasing number of immigrants? Two possible missionary responses could be suggested as a way of answering these questions. Gemma Tulud Cruz argues "that mission in the context of contemporary migration, first, has to be contextually liberative . . . mission needs to be done with primary consideration of the context and from the perspective of liberation."[37] It is right to provide pastoral care and counseling to immigrants in the new country. However, that is not enough. The issues in the immigrants' home countries that are causing migration should be addressed as well. Transformation of the conscience and conversion of the government leaders in those countries should take place. Strong actions should be taken "against unscrupulous traffickers, employers, transnational companies, and financial institutions that prey on immigrants."[38] In order to combat the roots and sources of oppression, Christians should respond to it on the local and global levels. Cruz states, "There not only has to be critical and continuous international collaboration between and across religions or religious denominations; religious groups and institutions should also actively seek and fight for the transformation of the very structures that contribute to the oppression and migration of migrants themselves."[39] Thus, the first response to the issue of migration is the contextuality of liberating the mission of the church. The second response is that mission work should be intercultural. Migrants need to be prepared to live in societies with cultural and religious pluralism. "The church is needed not only in helping migrants to deal with their experiences of injustice, but also in showing them how to witness to and celebrate their faith amid different cultures and religions."[40]

---

37. Ibid., 79.
38. Ibid.
39. Ibid.
40. Ibid., 81.

Immigrants experience cultural alienation not only in the new country but sometimes even within their religious communities as well.

On the other hand, "Christian mission is also challenged to creatively draw from the richness that comes from this migration-induced cultural and religious pluralism."[41] Migrants often demonstrate a tendency to participate in deep and steadfast witness and become missionaries. Churches become sites where the immigrants' identity and community is expressed and celebrated. "Immigrant churches themselves are often veritable centers and sources of socioeconomic needs for immigrants, making migration a potent source of missionary activity today."[42] Various social services are organized by many immigrant churches. They may include language classes, charities, scholarship funds, special crisis funds, advertisement boards for jobs and used cars for sale, food donations, help with applying for job training, classes on getting insurance, and so forth. Some immigrant churches develop an evangelistic ministry, support missionary work back in their home country, and send missionaries to other parts of the world.[43] Immigrants "bring diversity and breathe new life into the faith communities of their host countries."[44]

Cruz states that the call of the church is "to engage in a mission that brings about contextual and borderless liberation." She concludes, "Moreover, mission in the face of contemporary migration should not only be a mission beyond inculturation, but also a mission of interculturation: a mission that more deeply respects, embraces, and transcends differences and enables people to live in harmony with diversity. Only when mission is both contextually liberational and interculturally dialogical can mission truly respond to the cry of today's stranger par excellence: the migrant."[45] In order to meet the challenges of doing mission work in the complex context of migration, an appropriate reimagining of mission has to be made. As shown above, the different facets of a Christian mission should be included in order to execute

---

41. Ibid., 82.
42. Ibid.
43. Ibid.
44. Ibid.
45. Ibid., 83.

it properly. In particular, the mission, in addition to being inculturated, should be liberational and intercultural.[46]

5.1.7.A. The Impact of Migration on the Countries of Origin

The departure of significant numbers of citizens makes a certain mark on the countries in which they used to live. One of the results of migration is called "brain drain." This term is applied to "the increasing international flows of highly skilled and educated migrants from the developing countries of the South to the industrial wealthy countries of the North."[47] In 1990, the United States had more than 2.5 million highly educated immigrants.[48] In 2000, highly skilled workers constituted only 6 percent of the entire Asian population in Asian countries. At the same time, they made up 43.5 percent of Asian emigrants.[49] Undeniably, the statistical evidence points "to a tremendous flow of skilled migration from developing to developed countries." The impact of this process on those who left behind could be described as follows:

> a. First and foremost, skilled migration represents a heavy loss of costly investments in subsidized education and training.
>
> b. Skilled migration diminishes the pool of taxpayers and potential leaders.
>
> c. By reducing the human capital stock . . . skilled migration severely curtails the country's productivity and growth prospects.
>
> d. The depletion of professional skills contributes directly to the decline of essential services in health and education.
>
> e. High levels of out-migration can have tremendous inimical impact on social structures in the area of origin, by depriving families and communities of critical leadership or imposing enormous strains on marriages.

---

46. Solange Lefebvre and Luiz Carlos Susin, eds., *Migration in a Global World* (London: SCM, 2008), 57.
47. Hanciles, *Beyond Christendom*, 194.
48. Ibid., 195.
49. Ibid., 196.

f. Migrant remittances (which arguably offset the negative effect of brain drain) decline over time.[50]

The following three aspects could be mentioned among the positive benefits of skilled migration: (1) When the highly educated cannot find a job in their home country, immigration helps them avoid unemployment;[51] (2) skilled migration could lead to the establishment of diaspora networks among emigrants and non-migrants, "which facilitate the feedback or circulation of knowledge and technology and promote integration into the global economy;"[52] and (3) migrants are sending a portion of their earnings (remittances) back to their countries of origin, providing an important source of revenue for developing countries. The amount of remittances sent through formal channels was $93 billion in 2003 and $167 billion in 2005.[53] An important impact on the country of origin takes place because of the transnational nature of modern migration. Migrants are still connected with the homeland, sending back not only money but also information about their day-to-day life in America. Peggy Levitt describes this aspect of migration in the following way:

> For one, sometimes migration is as much about the people who stay behind as it is about people who move. In some cases, the ties between migrants and nonmigrants are so strong and widespread that migration also radically transforms the lives of individuals who stay home. They don't have to move to participate across borders. People, money, and what I have called social remittances – the ideas, practices, social capital, and identities that migrants send back into their communities of origin – permeate their daily lives, changing how they act as well as challenging their ideas about gender, right and wrong, and what states should and should not do.[54]

---

50. Ibid., 197.
51. Ibid.
52. Ibid., 198.
53. Ibid.
54. Peggy Levitt, *God Needs No Passport: Immigrants and the Changing American Religious Landscape* (New York: New Press, 2007), 23.

As shown, migration has a significant impact on the society and economy of the immigrant's homeland.

5.1.8.A. Immigrant Congregations and American Religious Life

As mentioned above, the current streams of migration are flowing from the non-white world. With regard to this fact, Hanciles states, "that contemporary nonwhite immigration will arguably have an impact on the American religious landscape that surpasses all but that of the original European migrants who laid the foundation of America's religious culture."[55] He argues that "migrant movement from the new heartlands of Christianity (in southern continents) to the old centers where the faith is experiencing dramatic erosion and marginalization constitutes a missionary movement; and that this development, in turn, implicates the West as a new frontier of global Christian expansion."[56] As a result of this "missionary movement," new congregations of immigrant believers are established in different parts of the country. They play a very important role in the life of their members. "Religious assembly and affiliation constitute the most powerful means available to immigrants in their search for self-identity, communal acceptance, and social integration. Religious congregations serve to facilitate the immigrants' assimilation into American life while simultaneously allowing them 'to nurture their ethnic ties even as they ease their adjustment into their new country.'"[57]

Hanciles argues that immigrant congregations potentially have a missionary function because these churches "model religious commitment, apply the message of the gospel directly to daily exigencies, and comprise communities that interact on a daily basis with other marginalized segments of society."[58] Throughout history, the missionary function of immigrant/ethnic congregations has altered the religious landscape of America. For example, the establishment of a high number of new black congregations and the significant membership growth they experienced completely changed the face of

---

55. Hanciles, *Beyond Christendom*, 277.
56. Ibid.
57. Ibid., 278.
58. Ibid.

Christianity in America. In 1860, about 931 black congregations existed in America. By 1900, this number grew to 212,200 congregations, consisting of 17 percent of all the nation's local churches.[59] The predominantly White Anglo-Saxon Protestant (WASP) American Christianity became a mixture of white, black and other ethnic churches. Historically rooted in the painful experience of African slaves transported to America against their will, black congregations are very proactive in establishing and observing civil rights. They transformed "the nation's identity, conscience, and moral obligation to practice fairness and mercy toward its most disfranchised citizens."[60] Perhaps the highest achievement of the public mission of black churches is the civil rights movement, which emerged from these churches.

New immigrant congregations are often located in the areas of cities abandoned by native churches that have moved to the suburbs. Immigrants often congregate in areas where disadvantaged and marginalized populations live. "Often they represent the main forms of evangelical ministry and outreach within the areas and sections of the American population least impacted by the dominant culture."[61] This kind of missionary commitment is described as "incarnational" and "emphasizes effective presence and participation as the basis for proclamation."[62] This enables immigrant Christians to reach their own people, as well as natives.

Another example is the impact immigrant congregations had on the theological landscape of American religious life. The earliest immigrants to America were predominantly Protestants, as Roman Catholics were not welcome here at that time. Over the years, this situation changed dramatically. Due to waves of Catholic immigrants coming from different parts of the world, the number of Catholics increased tremendously, and today, the Roman Catholic Church is the largest church body in the US.[63] These historical examples show "that immigration and immigrant churches have played a significant role in shaping American religious life."[64]

---

59. Ibid., 280.
60. Ibid., 281.
61. Ibid., 298.
62. Ibid.
63. Ibid., 282.
64. Ibid., 283.

However, according to Hanciles, even stronger than the influence of the missionary function that the immigrant congregations made within American society is their impact on overseas or foreign missionary movements in America. From its beginning, "the black church movement stimulated African American missionary consciousness and initiatives"[65] and was instrumental in sending many black missionaries back to Africa to preach the gospel to their people. Missionary activity increased not only among the black churches but also among other immigrant/ethnic groups and resulted in a significant increase in mission agencies and missionaries.[66]

Summary. The brief overview of the subject of global migration shows that although migration has been a part of the human experience for centuries, it has apparently become a global phenomenon only within the last few decades. Different reasons cause people to leave their homeland and to take the risk of becoming immigrants. Migration is a complex process, and it is not easy to find a theory that completely explains it. The difference in the direction of migration streams today from previous waves of immigration is that in the past, migrants were moving from economically advanced countries to economically poor countries. Today, it is the opposite. People from poor counties in the Global South are migrating to rich countries in Europe and North America. Modern global migration provides the church mission with challenges and opportunities. In order to be effective in reaching today's migrants, the church's mission should not only be inculturated but it should also be liberational and intercultural. Global migration affects the social, economic, and religious life of the country of origin, as well as the country of destination. It has transformed America into the most culturally diverse nation in the world, and it has changed the face of American Christianity. Since many migrants are Christian, this migration movement could, to some degree, be considered as a missionary movement. It brings about a revival of religious life in the countries in which the immigrants are arriving. Immigrant congregations are a means of reaching their ethnic people in the new land, as well as in the homeland. These congregations

---

65. Ibid.
66. Ibid., 285.

have limitations in their missionary efforts since they are usually ethnically focused and therefore inhibit people of other ethnicities from joining them.

5.2.A. Brief Overview of History of Russian Immigration to America

5.2.1.A. Russian Colony of Alaska

Russian-speaking people are no strangers to the "Land of Opportunities." For the past three centuries, they have been coming to America in steady waves. The first Russian settlers in America were fur traders. They began to cross the Bering Strait into Alaska in 1747 to secure land for fur trading. Alaska soon became a colony of Russia, a frontier society with explorers searching for fur and gold. Eventually, Russia's possessions extended far into the Pacific coast, reaching all the way to Ross, California, a mere 100 miles north of San Francisco.[67] Not only did fur traders cross the strait to reach Alaska but persecuted religious groups did so as well in order to escape government oppression in Russia. They converted many Eskimos to their religions. Orthodox Church missionaries also reached Alaska. In 1867, Alaska, a landmass which is larger than Texas, California, and Montana combined, was purchased by the United States for $7.2 million (about two cents per acre), which equals $120 million today.[68] Because of this, most Russians living in that area returned home. However, the Russian influence in Alaska persisted in the form of the Orthodox Church. About 12,000 of the native Inuit and Aleut people were converted to Orthodox Christianity at that time.[69]

5.2.2.A. Four Waves

Large-scale Russian emigration to the United States began in the late nineteenth century. Since that time, four waves of immigration can be identified: 1880s–1914, 1920–1939, 1945–1955, and 1970–present. The reasons for

---

67. Paul Robert Magocsi, "Russian Americans," *Countries and Their Cultures*, http://www.everyculture.com/multi/Pa-Sp/Russian-Americans.html (accessed April 2012).
68. "Alaska Purchase," http://www.loc.gov/rr/program/bib/ourdocs/Alaska.html (accessed June 2012).
69. Magocsi, "Russian Americans."

emigration from Russia include economic hardship, political repression, religious discrimination, or a combination of some or all of those factors.[70]

The first wave, 1880–1914. From 1880 to 1914, over 3.2 million immigrants came from the Russian Empire to America.[71] Around 60 percent of the arriving immigrants were Jews. The rest were Poles, ethnic Russians, Ukrainians, Belarussians, Lithuanians, and German Mennonites.[72] Ethnic Russians made a very small percentage of the group because the imperial Russian government barred them from leaving the country. The primary motive for immigration during this wave of immigration was to improve economic status. Some of these Russian immigrants were circular immigrants – they planned to stay only long enough to save some money and then return home to Russia.[73] However, many of the more than 1.6 million Jews left Russia because they feared *pogroms* – attacks on Jewish property and persons that occurred sporadically in the Russian Empire.[74] This was a result of the policy that the Russian Tsarist government implemented in 1870 in an attempt to stamp out different ethnic groups within the country. Many people, including Jews, were deprived of their basic rights and were forced to move to settlements in the western region of Russia and eastern Poland. Life in these settlements was very difficult. Violent *pogroms* caused many deaths among Jews. Because of this, many Jewish people emigrated to America.[75] A tough economic crisis in agriculture also contributed to the increase of emigration from Russia and Ukraine at the beginning of the twentieth century.

The second wave, 1920–1939. This wave of immigration was directly related to the political upheaval in the former Russian Empire: the Bolshevik Revolution and the Civil War. Over two million people fled Russia between 1920 and 1922. They were against the new Bolshevik/Communist regime in their homeland and were known as "Whites" because they were opposed

---

70. Ibid.
71. Ibid.
72. David Livinson and Melvin Ember, *American Immigrant Cultures: Builders of a Nation* (New York: Simon & Schuster Macmillan, 1997), 750.
73. Magocsi, "Russian Americans."
74. Ibid.
75. Ibid.

to the communists, who were called "Reds." As many as 30,000 of the "Whites" settled in the United States during that time.[76] Among them were military men, aristocrats, professionals, business persons, artists, intellectuals, peasants, engineers, scientists, actors, Orthodox clergy, and representatives of the Russian nobility.[77] This wave of Russian immigration is often called "Aristocratic." "White" Russian refugees were stripped of their citizenship *in absentia* and could never legally return home. In the late 1930s, approximately 14,000 more Russian immigrants arrived in the United States, fleeing the advance of Nazi Germany and Japan's invasion of Manchuria.[78]

The third wave, 1945–1955. This wave was a direct outcome of World War II. During the war, hundreds of thousands of Russians were captured or deported to work in Germany. After the war, due to the so-called "Yalta agreement," many of them were forced to return home.

> According to the 1945 Yalta agreement, "displaced persons" (prisoners of War, laborers, and refugees) from the Soviet Union who were left out in territories occupied by Allies had to be returned to the USSR regardless of their desires. This resulted in forced repatriations, with violation of human rights and suicides. Displaced persons of other nationalities had the option to return to their native lands or to resettle to other countries. Eleanor Roosevelt interceded at the United Nations on behalf of displaced persons from the USSR. As a result, they were granted safety and freedom in the United States. Russians from Manchuria and the rest of China became refugees in 1949–1950s due to the Communist takeover and immigrated in great numbers to the United States and Canada.[79]

Not very many of the displaced persons (DPs) of Russian origin managed to emigrate to the United States. During this period, approximately 20,000 Russian DPs arrived in the US.[80] The DPs, like "White" Russians,

---

76. Ibid.
77. Ibid.
78. Ibid.
79. Livinson and Ember, *American Immigrant Cultures*, 750.
80. Magocsi, "Russian Americans."

were stripped of their citizenship and were never allowed legally to return home. They were viewed as Nazi collaborators and traitors to their country.

The fourth wave, 1970s–present. Both the Tsarist Russian and Soviet governments had placed restrictions on emigration. In 1885, the Imperial Russian government passed a decree prohibiting all emigration, except of Poles and Jews. By the early 1920s, the Soviet government implemented further controls that effectively banned all emigration.[81] During the Communist era in Russia and the Cold War, there was no legal way for citizens of the USSR to emigrate. The enactment of the Jackson-Vanik Amendment in the 1974 Trade Act targeted Soviet restrictions on Jewish emigration from the Soviet Union. This resulted in the Soviet government's issuance of exit visas to Jewish residents of the Soviet Union. This applied only to Jews and to no other ethnic group.[82] This was the beginning of the fourth wave of Russian immigration. It lasted until the end of the 1980s and is often called the "Jewish immigration wave." Although Jews leaving the Soviet Union were granted permission only to go to Israel, many of them had the United States as their true goal. Nearly 300,000 of them reached the United States by 1985.[83] After 1985, the more liberal policy of the Soviet government, under Mikhail Gorbachev, allowed more people to leave the Soviet Union. Thousands more Jewish and non-Jewish Russians emigrated to the United States. During the last decade of the twentieth century, Russian emigration had slowed because Russia became an independent country with a democratically elected government. Because of this, people who wanted to emigrate to the US could not justify their claim to do so based on political or religious persecution.[84]

5.2.3.A. Russian Immigrants' Contributions to American Society

During the long history of their presence in America, some Russians have made important contributions to American life. Below are the names of such contributors.

---

81. Ibid.
82. Livinson and Ember, *American Immigrant Cultures*, 750.
83. Magocsi, "Russian Americans."
84. Ibid.

Sergey Brin (1973–) is a co-founder of Google, Inc. He provided users with the technology for searching the online world, and a number of other important features. Sergey emigrated to the US from Moscow when he was six. He earned a PhD from Stanford University. In 2009, he was ranked the twenty-sixth richest person in the world by Forbes.[85]

John Basil Turchin (1822–1901) served in the Union Army during the Civil War and was promoted to the rank of US Brigadier General – the first Russian American to be elevated to such a high position.[86]

George Kistiakovsky (1900–1982) was a research chemist who emigrated to the US in 1925. He was a research fellow at Princeton University and a faculty member at Harvard University. He wrote more than 200 articles on different areas of chemistry.[87]

Igor Sikorsky (1889–1972) was an aeronautical engineer who emigrated to the US and formed the Sikorsky Air Engineering Company in 1923. The S-29, the first twin-engine plane made in the USA, was built by this company. Sikorsky is credited with designing the first helicopter (VS-300) in 1939 and the first large American four-engine clipper (S-40), built in 1931.[88]

George Vernadsky (1897–1972) was a historian at Yale University and author of a five-volume history of Russia.[89]

Michael Yarymovich (1933–) served as chief scientist of the US Air Force and assistant director to the Apollo Flight System in the 1960s. In 1975, he was appointed Assistant Administrator for the Laboratory and Field Coordination of the Energy Research and Development Administration.[90]

Vladimir Ipatieff (1867–1952) was a prominent research chemist and author of seventy American patents for refining petroleum, which helped America and the Allies win World War II.[91]

---

85. "Famous Russian-Americans," *The Russian American Cultural Heritage Center*, http://www.rach-c.org/pages/russianamericans.htm (accessed November 2012).

86. Ibid.

87. "George Kistiakowsky (1900–1982)," *Atomicarchive.com*, http://www.atomicarchive.com/Bios/Kistiakowsky.shtml (accessed November 2012).

88. "Famous Russian-Americans."

89. "Vernadsky, George," *Infoplease*, http://www.infoplease.com/encyclopedia/people/vernadsky-george.html (accessed November 2012).

90. "Ukrainian Americans," *Countries and Their Cultures*, http://www.everyculture.com/multi/Sr-Z/Ukrainian-Americans.html (accessed November 2012).

91. "Famous Russian-Americans."

Vladimir Zworykin (1889–1982) was a physicist and electronics engineer, who is known as the father of television.[92]

Wassily Liontieff (1905–1999) was a Nobel Prize-winning economist who formulated the influential input–output system of economic analysis.[93]

Vladimir Nabokov (1899–1977) was a great Russian novelist who lived in America from 1940.[94]

Many other immigrants from Russia have made significant contributions to American art, literature, military, music, science, and technology.

5.3.A. History of the Founding and Organization of the Pacific Coast Slavic Baptist Association

5.3.2.A. PCSBA: The Humble Beginning, Followed by a Fruitful Ministry (1928–1990)

Table 5.3.2.A. PCSBA Membership 1963–2012

Year	1963	1964	1965	1966	1967	1970	1988	1994
PCSBA membership	350	364	389	387	387	414	418	2,051
Number of churches	8	8	8	8	9	9	10	11
Year	1995	1996	1998	2000	2001	2002	2003	2004
PCSBA membership	2,353	2,537	3,500	4,453	4,622	5,127	5,510	6,405
Number of churches	11	12	14	16	17	20	20	21

---

92. Ibid.
93. Ibid.
94. "Vladimir Nabokov," *Encyclopaedia Britannica*, http://www.britannica.com/EBchecked/topic/401299/Vladimir-Nabokov (accessed November 2012).

Year	2005	2006	2007	2008	2009	2010	2011	2012
PCSBA membership	6,467	7,023	7,270	7,699	7,722	7,605	7,669	7,411
Number of churches	23	24	29	31	32	32	32	32

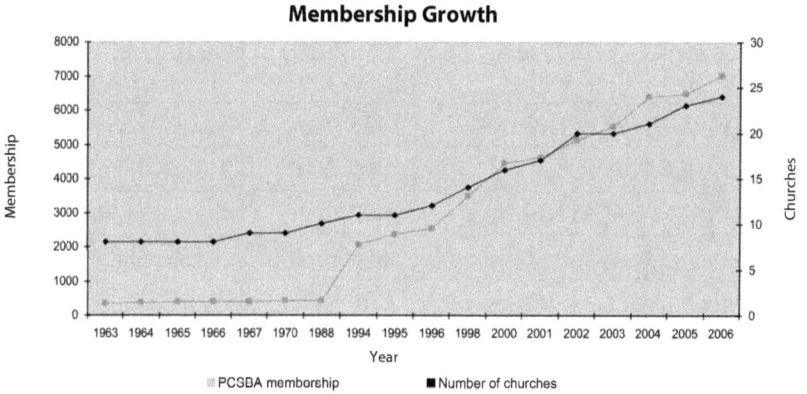

Chart 5.3.3.A. Membership Growth

Table 5.3.4.A. Presidents of the Pacific Coast Slavic Baptist Association

Year	Name	Year	Name
1928–unknown	Nikita Rodionov	1968–1973	Alexandr Efimov
Unknown–1939	A. Nikolaus	1973–1983	Theodor Karpets
1939–1940	Jacob Prigodich	1983–1984	Ivan Vlasyuk
1940–1947	Ivan Khmeta	1984–1987	Theodor Karpets
1947–1949	Peter Potlov	1987–1990	Alexandr Kuzichev
1949–1950	Peter Pawluk	1990–1992	Theodor Karpets
1950–1953	Josef Parfenov	1992–1996	Alexandr Efimov
1953–1959	Peter Potlov	1996–2002	Nikolay Martinchuk
1959–1962	Vladimir Gusaruk	2002–2006	Vyacheslav Tsvirinko
1962–1964	Peter Potlov	2006–present	Nikolay Bugriev
1964–1968	Alexandr Kuzichev		

APPENDIX FOR CHAPTER 6

The Present Mission Work of Slavic Baptist Churches in the US

6.2.A. Analysis of the Percentage of Mission-Related Spending in the Budget of Selected Churches

Table 6.2.1.A. Percentage of the Annual Budget Used for Mission

Church	Percentage of the annual budget used for mission		
	2003	2004	2005
CH1	23	23	23
CH2	27.9	24.8	45.3
CH3	20	20	40.8
CH4	10	10	10
CH5	0	0	0
CH6	23	23	23
CH7	10	10	10
CH8	12	12	8
CH9	18	23	25
CH10	15	15	15
CH11	10	20	24
CH12	15	15	15
CH13	28	20	15

CH14	0	20	24
CH15	30	30	30
CH16	60	62	54
CH17	N/A	N/A	N/A
CH18	25	25	25
CH19	13	2.5	19
CH20	25	25	25
CH21	5.8	8.1	20.3
CH22	3	3	3
CH23	10	10	10

6.3.A. Survey of Slavic Pastors and Other Church Leaders Regarding Their Views on Church Mission in the Immigrant Context

Part 1: General Evaluation of Missionary Work in the Local Congregation

Question 1. What is the main focus of the missionary work in your church? The answers to this question, given by five different groups of Slavic Baptist church leaders, are provided in table 6.3.1.A.

Table 6.3.1.A. What Is the Main Focus of the Missionary Work in Your Church?
(CB=Church board, PEC=Pastors exec. committee, PLR=Participants of leadership retreat, PSSR=Participants of Sunday school retreat, PYLR=Participants of youth leadership retreat)

	Surveyed	CB	PEC	PLR	PSSR	PYLR
	Number of participants in the survey	184	27	23	17	18
Answer codes	Answers	%	%	%	%	%
A	A) Supporting missionaries in Russia	35.7%	13.8%	0.0%	23.5%	33.3%

The Present Mission Work of Slavic Baptist Churches in the US 439

	Surveyed	CB	PEC	PLR	PSSR	PYLR
AB	A) Supporting missionaries in Russia; B) Short-term mission trips	22.0%	44.8%	52.2%	41.2%	11.1%
ABC	A) Supporting missionaries in Russia; B) Short-term mission trips; C) Witnessing to Russian-speaking people in the US	2.7.%	3.4%	0.0%	5.9%	22.2%
ABCD	A) Supporting missionaries in Russia; B) Short-term mission trips; C) Witnessing to Russian-speaking people in the US; D) Work among English-speaking people in the US	1.6%	10.3%	0.0%	0.0%	0.0%
ABD	A) Supporting missionaries in Russia; B) Short-term mission trips; D) Work among English-speaking people in the US	1.1%	3.4.%	4.3%	16.9%	16.7%
AC	A) Supporting missionaries in Russia; C) Witnessing to Russian-speaking people in the US	8.8%	10.3%	4.3%	23.5%	0.0%
B	B) Short-term mission trips	9.3%	0.0%	17.4%	5.9%	11.1%

	Surveyed	CB	PEC	PLR	PSSR	PYLR
BC	B) Short-term mission trips; C) Witnessing to Russian-speaking people in the US	1.1%	0.0%	0.0%	0.0%	0.0%
BCD	B) Short-term mission trips; C) Witnessing to Russian-speaking people in the US; D) Work among English-speaking people in the US	0.0%	0.0%	0.0%	0.0%	0.0%
BD	B) Short-term mission trips; D) Work among English-speaking people in the US	0.0%	0.0%	0.0%	0.0%	0.0%
C	C) Witnessing to Russian-speaking people in the US	8.2%	8.2%	13.0%	0.0%	5.6%
CD	C) Witnessing to Russian-speaking people in the US; D) Work among English-speaking people in the US	1.6%	1.6%	0.0%	0.0%	0.0%
D	D) Work among English-speaking people in the US	0.5%	0.5%	4.3%	0.0%	0.0%
E	E) Unable to say	0.0%	0.0%	0.0%	0.0%	0.0%
NA	No answer	7.1%	7.1%	4.3%	0.0%	0.0%

Church board members. The majority of church board members – 70.8% (lines: A – 35.7%, AB – 22.0%, ABC – 2.7%, ABCD – 1.6%, and AC – 8.8%) stated that an important part of the missionary work in their church is supporting missionaries in Russia. The short-term mission trips were named as part of the main mission focus by 37.8% of the respondents (lines: AB – 22.0%, ABC – 2.7%, ABCD – 1.6%, ABD – 1.1%, B – 9.3%, and BC – 1.1%). 19.7% of the church board members included witnessing to Russian-speaking people in the US as the main mission focus of their church (line ABC – 2.7%, line AC – 8.8% and line C – 8.2%). Work among English-speaking people in the US is mentioned as part of the main mission focus by 4.8% of the church board members (line ABCD – 1.6%, line ABD – 1.1%, line CD – 1.6% and line D – 0.5%). According to these answers, the main focus of their Slavic church mission is financially supporting missionaries in the homeland (70.8%). The second focus of mission is short-term mission trips (37.8%). Witnessing to the Russian-speaking people in the US is the third focus of the mission activities of Slavic churches (19.7%). Work among English-speaking people in the US is the lowest priority in the mission of Slavic churches, and is practiced by a limited number of churches (4.8%).

Leadership board, pastors, and department directors meeting. The majority of respondents, 82.6%, said that supporting missionaries in Russia is part of the main focus of mission in their church (lines: A – 13.8%, AB – 44.8%, ABC – 3.4%, ABCD – 10.3%, and AC – 10.3%). Short-term mission trips are part of the main focus of mission in the churches of *61.9%* of respondents (lines: AB – 44.8%, ABC – 3.4%, ABCD – 10.3%, ABD – 3.4%, B – 0%, and BC – 0%). 17.1% of the respondents included witnessing to Russian-speaking people in the US as the main mission focus of their church (line ABC – 3.4%, line AC – 10.3% and line C – 3.4%). Work among English-speaking people in the US is mentioned as part of the main mission focus by 13.7% of respondents (line ABCD – 10.3%, line ABD – 3.4%, line CD – 0% and line D – 0%). The priority order in mission activities of their church, according to this group of respondents, is the same as in the first group: (1) Supporting missionaries in the homeland (82.6%); (2) short-term missions (61.9%); (3) witnessing to the Russian-speaking people in the US (17.1%); and (4) work among English-speaking people (13.7%).

Leadership retreat. The majority of respondents in this group, 73.9%, believe that short-term mission trips are an important part of the main focus of mission in their church (lines: AB – 52.2%, ABC – 0%, ABCD – 0%, ABD – 4.3%, B – 17.4%, and BC – 0%). A significant number of respondents, 62.4%, said that supporting missionaries in Russia is part of the main focus of mission in their church (lines: A – 0%, AB – 52.2%, ABC – 5.9%, ABCD – 0%, and AC – 4.3%). 17.3% of the respondents mentioned witnessing to Russian-speaking people in the US as part of the main mission focus of their church (line ABC – 0%, line AC – 4.3% and line C – 13.0%). Work among English-speaking people in the US is mentioned as part of the main mission focus of their church by 8.6% of this group of respondents (line ABCD – 0%, line ABD – 4.3%, line CD – 0% and line D – 4.3%). The priority order in mission given by this group of respondents is a little bit different from the first group order: Short-term missions is the first priority (73.9%); supporting missionaries in the homeland is the second priority (62.4%); witnessing to the Russian-speaking people in the US is the third priority (17.3%); and work among English-speaking people is the last priority (8.6%).

Sunday school teacher retreat. The majority of respondents, 94.1%, said that supporting missionaries in Russia is part of the main focus of mission in their church (lines: A – 23.5%, AB – 41.2%, ABC – 5.9%, ABCD – 0%, and AC – 23.5%). The short-term mission trips are part of the main focus of mission in the churches of 53.0% of the respondents (lines: AB – 41.2%, ABC – 5.9%, ABCD – 0%, ABD – 0%, B – 5.9%, and BC – 0%). 29.4% of the respondents included witnessing to Russian-speaking people in the US as the main mission focus of their church (line ABC – 5.9%, line AC – 23.5% and line C – 0%). Work among English-speaking people in the US is mentioned as part of the main mission focus by 0% of this group of respondents (line ABCD – 0%, line ABD – 0%, line CD – 0%, and line D – 0%). The priority in mission among churches of this group of respondents is given in the same way as in the first group: (1) Supporting missionaries in the homeland (94.1%); (2) short-term missions (53.0%); (3) witnessing to the Russian-speaking people in the US (29.4%); and (4) work among English-speaking people is not done at all (0%).

Youth leadership retreat. The majority of the respondents, 66.6%, said that supporting missionaries in Russia is part of the main focus of mission in their church (lines: A – 33.3%, AB – 11.1%, ABC – 22.2%, ABCD – 0%, and AC – 0%). Short-term mission trips are a part of the main focus of mission in the churches of 61.1% of the respondents (lines: AB – 11.1%, ABC – 22.2%, ABCD – 0%, ABD – 16.7%, B – 11.1%, and BC – 0%). 27.8% of the respondents included witnessing to Russian-speaking people in the US as the main mission focus of their church (line ABC – 22.2%, line AC – 0% and line C – 5.6%). Work among English-speaking people in the US is mentioned as part of the main mission focus by 16.7% of the surveyed youth (line ABCD – 0%, line ABD – 16.7%, line CD – 0% and line D – 0%). The priority order in mission among churches of this group of respondents is the same as in the first group: (1) Supporting missionaries at the homeland (66.6%); (2) short-term missions (61.1%); (3) witnessing to the Russian-speaking people in the US (27.8%); and (4) work among English-speaking people (16.7%).

Question 2. Who is involved in the work of missions?

Table 6.3.2.A. Who Is Involved in the Work of Missions?
(CB=Church board, PEC=Pastors exec. committee, PLR=Participants of leadership retreat, PSSR=Participants of Sunday school retreat, PYLR=Participants of youth leadership retreat)

	Surveyed	CB	PEC	PLR	PSSR	PYLR
	Number of participants in the survey	184	27	23	17	18
Answer codes	Answers	%	%	%	%	%
A	A) Youth	22.8%	27.6%	65.2%	29.4%	33.3%
AB	A) Youth; B) Older adults	2.2%	3.4%	0.0%	5.9%	0.0%
ABC	A) Youth; B) Older adults; C) Youth and older adults	2.7%	0.0%	0.0%	0.0%	0.0%
AC	A) Youth; C) Youth and older adults	2.7%	13.8%	13.0%	5.9%	22.2%
B	B) Older adults	5.4%	3.4%	0.0%	5.9%	0.0%
C	C) Youth and older adults	54.3%	51.7%	21.7%	52.9%	38.9%
D	D) Unable to say	4.9%	0.0%	0.0%	0.0%	5.6%
NA	No answer	4.3%	0.0%	0.0%	0.0%	0.0%

There is a need to clarify that in the current Slavic church immigrant context, the term "missions" is often understood as a definition of the short-term mission trips made overseas, mostly to the former homeland. It is important to remember this while interpreting the results of the survey shown in table 6.3.2.A.

Church board members. The majority of church board members, 61.9% (the sum of the lines: AB – 2.2%, ABC – 2.7%, AC – 2.7%, C – 54.3%), observe the joint efforts being directed towards missions by youth and older adults in their church. Only 22.8% (line A) stated that only youth are involved in mission work.

Leadership board, pastors, and department directors (executive committee) meeting. The majority of respondents, 68.9% (the sum of the lines: AB – 3.4%, ABC – 0%, AC – 13.8%, C – 51.7%), state that youth and older adults are involved in mission. 27.6% (line A) of the respondents see only youth being involved in mission in their churches.

Leadership retreat. Most of the respondents, 65.2% (line A), see mission work being done by youth only. 34.7% (the sum of the lines: AB – 0%, ABC – 0%, AC – 13.0%, C – 21.7%) state that youth and older adults are involved in mission work in their churches.

Sunday school teacher retreat. Most of the respondents, 64.7% (the sum of the lines: AB – 5.9%, ABC – 0%, AC – 5.9%, C – 52.9%), state that youth and older adults are doing mission work together. 29.4% (line A) see only youth being involved in mission.

Youth leadership retreat. Most of the youth leaders, 61.1% (the sum of the lines: AB – 0%, ABC – 0%, AC – 22.2%, C – 38.9%), state that the mission work in their church is done by the joint efforts of youth and older adults. 33.3% (line A) of them see only youth being involved in mission work at their church.

Comparison of the church board survey results:

Table 6.3.2.A.B. Who is Involved in the Work of Missions?

	Year	2005	2009
	Number of participants in the survey	184	52
Answer codes	Answers		
A	A) Youth	22.8%	30.8%
AB	A) Youth; B) Older adults	2.2%	7.7%
ABC	A) Youth; B) Older adults; C) Youth and older adults	2.7%	1.9%
AC	A) Youth; C) Youth and older adults	2.7%	7.7%
B	B) Older adults	5.4%	0.0%
C	C) Youth and older adults	54.3%	51.9%
D	D) Unable to say	4.9%	0.0%
NA	No answer	4.3%	0.0%

In 2005, the majority of church board members, 61.9% (combined results of lines: AB, ABC, AC, and C), saw missions as being done by the joint efforts of the youth and older adults in their churches. Only 22.8% (line A) stated that only youth are to be involved in mission work. In 2009, 69.2% (combined results of lines: AB, ABC, AC, and C) of the church board members believed that most of the mission work should be done by youth and older adults working together. There was an increase in percentage of those who answered the question this way in comparison to the 2005 results (61.9% in 2005 vs. 69.2% in 2009). Also, there was an increase in 2009 among those who believed that the mission work in their church was work solely completed by the youth (22.8% in 2005 vs. 30.8% in 2009). This increase in both categories at the same time looks contradictory. However, it could be explained by the fact that in the results of 2009 survey, there were no answers in the following boxes: "Older adults," "Unable to say," and "NA." In the 2005 survey, there were small percentages listed in these boxes. In general, it looks like the situation with the church leaders' perceptions of the involvement of only youth versus youth and older adults has not changed significantly between 2005 and 2009.

Summary

A vast majority of the respondents to the question "Who is involved in the work of mission?" stated that the mission work is a product of the joint efforts of youth and older adults. Only participants of the leadership retreat saw a different picture in their church. Most of them stated that only youth were involved in mission work. In reality, it is often true that only young people are going overseas on the short-term mission trips. However, they are able to do it only because of the moral, prayer, and financial support of the "older adults" – their parents, relatives, and friends in the church.

The participation of youth in mission work is encouraging. According to the author's personal observation, those who are involved in missions usually become more dedicated to Christ and his church as a result of being part of mission trips. In many cases, they become leaders in different areas of church ministry. However, not every young woman or man in the local congregation is able to go overseas on a missions trip. Only a small percentage of young people are involved in actual mission work in their parents' homeland. This means that the majority of young people in immigrant churches do not have an important evangelistic experience. They grow up without training to do this important work for the kingdom. Even though they speak English, they are not prepared to go to the English-speaking world to preach the good news. They have not seen their parents doing this, and have not gone on mission trips to do it. As a result of this, the next generation of immigrants is in danger of becoming fruitless for God's kingdom. This should be a serious concern for the Slavic immigrant church leaders.

Question 3. What percentage of the church is involved in missions?

Table 6.3.3.A. What Percentage of the Church Is Involved in Missions?
(CB=Church board, PEC=Pastors exec. committee, PLR=Participants of leadership retreat, PSSR=Participants of Sunday school retreat, PYLR=Participants of youth leadership retreat)

	Surveyed	CB	PEC	PLR	PSSR	PYLR
	Number of participants in the survey	184	27	23	17	18
Answer codes	Answers	%	%	%	%	%
A	5–15%	49.5%	34.5%	78.3%	35.3%	55.6%
B	15–25%	12.5%	34.5%	17.4%	35.3%	5.6%
C	25–35%	10.3%	10.3%	4.3%	17.6%	38.9%
D	35–45%	12.5%	13.8%	0.0%	0.0%	0.0%
E	Unable to say	0.5%	0.0%	0.0%	0.0%	0.0%
NA	No answer	14.7%	3.4%	0.0%	11.8%	0.0%

Church board members. According to almost half of the respondents, 49.2% (line A), only 5–15% of the members of their church are involved in missions. Another 12.4% (line B) of surveyed church leaders believe that 15–25% of people in their churches are involved in missions.

Leadership board, pastors, and department directors meeting. Out of all respondents in this group, 34.5% believe that 5–15% of their congregations are involved in mission work. Another 34.5% think that 15–25% are participating in mission. Some (10.3%) believe that 25–35% of the congregation is involved. Others (13.8%) believe that this percentage is even higher – 35–45%.

Leadership retreat. The majority, 78.3%, of respondents in this group are convinced that 5–15% of their congregations are taking part in mission work. 17.4% of this group believe that 15–25% of their church membership is involved in mission work.

Sunday school teacher retreat. According to 35.3% of respondents in this group, 5–15% of their congregations are involved in mission. Another 35.3% believe that 15–25% of their church bodies are participating in mission work. 17.6% of this group responded saying that 17.6% of the congregations are doing mission.

Youth leadership retreat. 55.6% of the youth leaders believe that 5–15% of their local congregations are involved in mission work. Another 38.9% believe that 25–35% of the congregation is part of the mission work.

Comparison of the church board survey results:

Table 6.3.3.A.B. What Percentage of the Church Is Involved in Missions?

	Year	2005	2009
	Number of participants in the survey	184	52
Answer codes	Answers		
A	5–15%	49.5%	50.0%
B	15–25%	12.5%	21.2%
C	25–35%	10.3%	13.5%
D	35–45%	12.5%	3.8%
E	Unable to say	0.5%	0.0%
NA	No answer	14.7%	11.5%

According to almost half of the respondents who participated in the 2005 survey, 49.2% (line A), only 5–15% of the members of their church are involved in missions. Another 12.4% (line B) of surveyed church leaders believe that 15–25% of people in their church are involved in missions. Four years later, 50.0% (vs. 49.5% in 2005) of the church board members surveyed stated that in their church, 5–15% of the congregation participate in mission work. A total of 21.2% (vs. 12.5% in 2005) of them believed that 15–25% are participating. A total of 13.5% (vs. 10.3% in 2005) of the respondents saw 25–35% of the congregation participating in mission work. According to the results of the surveys, the percentage of church board members seeing 15–25% of the church participating in mission increased from 12.5% to 21.2%. This indicates that mission activity has increased in churches during the four years between the surveys.

Summary

Surveys of different groups of Slavic church leadership show that significant percentages of the church leaders stated that only 5–15% of their congregations are participating in mission work. If only 15% (or 25%) of the church membership participate in mission, then the rest of the congregation, 85% (or 75%), are not involved in such a vital part of church life. It is an alarming picture of the situation in Slavic immigrant churches. On the one hand, most of the believers are not involved in mission work overseas, in their homeland, and, on the other hand, they are not involved in evangelistic work with English-speaking people in the States. If this situation does not change soon, Slavic churches that are part of PCSBA are in danger of becoming more like socio-religious clubs than the real church of Jesus Christ that is marked by a strong zeal for missions. This certainly does not fit with the description of the authentic mission of the church as provided in chapter 2. However, the encouraging sign is that, according to the 2009 survey, the percentage of the church body involved in mission grew slightly.

Question 4. Are you satisfied with the current status of missions work in your church?

Table 6.3.4.A. Are You Satisfied with the Current Status of Missions Work in Your Church?
(CB=Church board, PEC=Pastors exec. committee, PLR=Participants of leadership retreat, PSSR=Participants of Sunday school retreat, PYLR=Participants of youth leadership retreat)

	Surveyed	CB	PEC	PLR	PSSR	PYLR
	Number of participants in the survey	184	27	23	17	18
Answer codes	Answers	%	%	%	%	%
A	Completely satisfied	13.0%	10.3%	0.0%	5.9%	5.6%
B	Partly satisfied	63.0%	82.8%	73.9%	76.5%	72.2%
C	Completely unsatisfied	14.7%	6.9%	13.0%	17.6%	16.7%
D	Unable to say	8.2%	0.0%	13.0%	0.0%	5.6%
NA	No answer	1.1%	0.0%	0.0%	0.0%	0.0%

Church board members. When it comes to the personal satisfaction with the current status of missions work in Slavic churches, the survey shows that only 13% (line A) of church board members are completely satisfied with what they have in their church. At the same time, many of them, 63% (line

B), are only partly satisfied with what is going on in their church in terms of missions work. 14.7% (line C) are completely unsatisfied.

Leadership board, pastors, and department directors meetings. A similar picture is presented with the responses of those who participated in the regular leadership meeting in the Russian Baptist church in Bryte. Only 10.3% (line A) are completely satisfied with the status of mission work in their church. 82.8% (line B) are only partly satisfied. 6.9% are completely unsatisfied.

Leadership retreat. None of the participants of the leadership retreat expressed complete satisfaction with the mission work in their churches. 73.9% (line B) expressed partial satisfaction. 13.0% (line C) said that they are completely unsatisfied with the status of mission work in their church.

Sunday school teacher retreat. Only 5.9% (line A) of the participants of this retreat stated that they are completely satisfied with the mission work in their churches. At the same time, 76.5% (line B) of the respondents said that they are only partly satisfied. 17.6% (line C) responded saying that they are completely unsatisfied.

Youth leadership retreat. Results similar to the previous group have been received from the youth leaders. Only 5.9% (line A) are completely satisfied with the mission status in their churches. 72.2% (line B) are partly satisfied. At the same time 16.7% (line C) of the respondents stated that they are completely dissatisfied.

Comparison of the church board survey results:

Table 6.3.4.A.B. Are You Satisfied with the Current Status of Missions Work in Your Church?

	Year	2005	2009
	Number of participants in the survey	184	52
Answer codes	Answers		
A	Completely satisfied	13.0%	13.5%
B	Partly satisfied	63.0%	75.0%
C	Completely unsatisfied	14.7%	1.9%
D	Unable to say	8.2%	7.7%
NA	No answer	1.1%	1.9%

When it comes to personal satisfaction with the current status of mission work in Slavic churches, the survey conducted in 2005 showed that only 13% (line A) of church board members were completely satisfied with what they had in their church. At the same time, 63% (line B) were only partly satisfied with what was going on in their church in terms of mission work. A total of 14.7% (line C) were completely unsatisfied.

Comparing the results of the surveys conducted in 2005 and 2009 showed that the number of church board members satisfied with the missions status of the church did not change significantly during these years (13.5% in 2009 vs. 13% in 2005). At the same time, the percentage of the partially satisfied grew significantly (from 63% in 2005 to 75% in 2009). The completely unsatisfied group shrank significantly, as well (from 14.7% in 2005 to 1.9% in 2009)

Summary

The survey of church boards and other four leadership groups (see appendix for chapter 6) in 2005 clearly shows that the vast majority of the participants are only partly satisfied with the mission status in their churches. The fact that a significant number of surveyed church leaders, about 75%, are just partially satisfied and a good number of them, about 15%, are completely unsatisfied with the mission work in their church, provides hope that the situation will improve in the future if these leaders take actions to change the situation. The comparison of the results of two surveys actually shows a significant improvement in the satisfaction rate. It is promising.

Question 5. In your opinion, is the leadership of the church satisfied with the current status of mission work in the church?

Although this question (Q5) sounds similar to the previous question (Q4), they are two different questions and both of them provided valuable information to the researcher. Answers to Question #4 reflect the respondent's personal attitude towards the current status of the church mission. On the other hand, answers to Question #5 show how a respondent evaluates the attitude of other leaders towards the current situation with mission work in the church. Information on this issue, presented from two perspectives, helps to create a more accurate picture of the church leadership's attitude towards the current mission status in the churches.

Table 6.3.5.A. In Your Opinion, Is the Leadership of the Church Satisfied with the Current Status of Mission Work in the Church?
(CB=Church board, PEC=Pastors exec. committee, PLR=Participants of leadership retreat, PSSR=Participants of Sunday school retreat, PYLR=Participants of youth leadership retreat)

	Surveyed	CB	PEC	PLR	PSSR	PYLR
	Number of participants in the survey	184	27	23	17	18
Answer codes	Answers	%	%	%	%	%
A	Completely satisfied	19.6%	13.8%	8.7%	29.4%	27.8%
B	Partly satisfied	52.2%	72.4%	78.3%	41.2%	50.0%
C	Completely unsatisfied	9.8%	6.9%	0.0%	5.9%	0.0%
D	Unable to say	14.7%	3.4%	13.0%	17.6%	16.7%
NA	No answer	3.8%	3.4%	0.0%	5.6%	5.6%

Church board members. Out of all church board members, 19.6% (line A) think that the leadership of their churches is completely satisfied with the current status of the mission work in the church. 52.2% (line B) see their leadership being partly satisfied. The church leadership being completely unsatisfied with the current status of mission work in the church is the view of 9.8% (line C) of the respondents. 14.7% (line D) of them are unable to come to a conclusion about other leaders' views. Comparing answers to Question #5 with answers to Question #4 leads to the following results: (A) "completely satisfied": Q5 – 19.6% vs. Q4 – 13.0%; (B) "partly satisfied": Q5 – 52.2% vs. Q4 – 63.0%; (C) "completely unsatisfied": Q5 – 9.8% vs. Q4 – 14.7%. As is shown, the percentage (19.6%) of those who see their leaders being completely satisfied with the mission status in their church is higher compared with the percentage (13.0%) of those who expressed their personal satisfaction with the mission status. At the same time, the percentage of those who believe that their leaders are partly satisfied (52.2%) or completely unsatisfied (9.8%) is lower than the percentage of those who expressed their personal partial satisfaction (63.0%) or complete dissatisfaction (14.7%).

Leadership board, pastors, and department directors meetings. Among this group, 13.8% (line A) see leaders of their churches being completely satisfied with the mission status. 72.4% (line B) of the respondents observe their leaders being partially satisfied with what they see in regard to the mission work in their church. 6.9% (line C) see their leaders as completely unsatisfied with the current status of mission. Comparing answers to Question #5 with answers to Question #4 shows the following: (A) "completely satisfied": Q5 – 13.8% vs. Q4 – 10.3%; (B) "partially satisfied": Q5 – 72.4% vs. Q4 – 82.8%; (C) "completely unsatisfied": Q5 – 6.9% vs. Q4 – 6.9%. The pattern is similar to the previous part of the survey.

Leadership retreat. In this group, 8.7% (line A) believe that their church leaders are completely satisfied with the mission status. 78.3% (line B) of the group think that leaders are partly satisfied. None of them believe that anybody is completely unsatisfied. A comparison of these answers with answers to Question #4 shows the following: (A) "completely satisfied": Q5 – 8.7% vs. Q4 – 0.0%; (B) "partly satisfied": Q5 – 78.3% vs. Q4 – 73.9%; (C) "completely unsatisfied": Q5 – 0.0% vs. Q4 – 13.0%. According to this comparison, there is a disconnect between how respondents view their church leaderships' attitude towards mission and their own attitude. They see the leadership being more satisfied than themselves.

Sunday school teacher retreat. Among Sunday school workers, 29.4% (line A) see their church leaders being completely satisfied with the status of mission in their church. 41.2% (line B) of the respondents think that their church leaders are partly satisfied. 5.9% (line C) of the Sunday school workers believe that the church leaders in their churches are completely unsatisfied. Comparing the answers of the two questions gives the following results: (A) "completely satisfied": Q5 – 29.4% vs. Q4 – 5.9%; (B) "partly satisfied": Q5 – 41.2% vs. Q4 – 76.5%; (C) "completely unsatisfied": Q5 – 5.9% vs. Q4 – 17.6%. This group of respondents sees their church leaders as being more satisfied with the mission work status than they are.

Youth leadership retreat. Among youth leaders, 27.8% (line A) believe that their church leaders are completely satisfied with their church mission status. The opinion of 50.0% (line B) of youth is that their leaders are partly satisfied with the mission status. None of the youth leaders think that anybody among their church leaders is completely unsatisfied with the mission work in their church. Here is a comparison of the answers to the two questions: (A) "completely satisfied": Q5 – 27.8% vs. Q4 – 5.6%; (B) "partly satisfied":

Q5 – 50.5% vs. Q4 – 72.2%; (C) "completely unsatisfied": Q5 – 0.0% vs. Q4 – 16.7%. Youth leaders are less satisfied with the mission work status in their churches than leaders of their churches.

Comparison of the results of the two surveys of church boards conducted in 2005 and 2009:

Table 6.3.5.A.B. In Your Opinion, Is the Leadership of the Church Satisfied with the Current Status of Mission Work in the Church?

	Year	2005	2009
	Number of participants in the survey	184	52
Answer codes	Answers		
A	Completely satisfied	19.6%	15.4%
B	Partly satisfied	52.2%	71.2%
C	Completely unsatisfied	9.8%	0.0%
D	Unable to say	14.7%	13.5%
NA	No answer	3.8%	0.0%

In 2005, out of all church board members, 19.6% (line A) believed that the leadership of their churches was completely satisfied with the current status of the mission work in the church. A total of 52.2% (line B) saw their leadership as being partly satisfied, while 9.8% (line C) of the respondents viewed the church leadership as being completely unsatisfied with the current status of mission work in the church. A total of 14.7% (line D) of them were unable to come to a conclusion about other leaders' views. Comparing the answers to Question #5 with the answers to Question #4, the following was found: (A) "completely satisfied": Q5 – 19.6% vs. Q4 – 13.0%; (B) "partly satisfied": Q5 – 52.2% vs. Q4 – 63.0%; (C) "completely unsatisfied": Q5 – 9.8% vs. Q4 – 14.7%. Clearly, the percentage of those who saw their leaders as being completely satisfied with mission status in their church (19.6%) was higher compared to the percentage (13.0%) of those who expressed their personal complete satisfaction with mission status. At the same time, the percentage of those who believed that their leaders were partly satisfied (52.2%) or completely unsatisfied (9.8%) was lower than the percentage of those who expressed their personal partial satisfaction (63.0%) or complete dissatisfaction (14.7%) with the mission and their own attitude. They see the leadership as being more satisfied than themselves.

A comparison of the results of two surveys (from 2005 and 2009) of the church board members showed that the percentage of those who saw their church leaders as completely satisfied with mission work in their church had decreased from 19.6% in 2005 to 15.4% in 2009. At the same time, the percentage of those who saw their leaders as being partly satisfied grew significantly from 52.2% in 2005 to 71.2% in 2009. Those who believed that their leaders were completely unsatisfied with the mission work in their church decreased in numbers: from 9.8% in 2005 to 0.0% in 2009.

Summary

Answers to these questions showed that about 20% (average number for all five groups surveyed) of the respondents observed their church leaders being completely satisfied with the status of mission work in their church. This contrasts with about 7% of the respondents who stated that they are completely satisfied with the mission situation in their church. On average, the percentage of people within the five survey groups with personal partial satisfaction was higher (about 74%) than the percentage of people who saw their church leaders being partly satisfied with the mission status in their church (about 59%). The percentage of people within all five groups combined who were completely unsatisfied with the mission status in their church was much higher than the percentage of those who believed that their church leaders were completely unsatisfied with what was going on with missions in their church. This was 13.8% versus 4.5%. These results indicate that, in general, people in the church saw their leaders as being more satisfied with the mission status in the church than they themselves were. Individually, people expect more to be done towards mission. The difference in the mission status evaluation brings tensions between the church leaders and the congregants. A comparison of the two surveys of church board members done in 2005 and 2009 shows that a small shift took place in the people's view of their church leaders' position towards mission. More people saw their leaders being partly satisfied with the mission status in 2009 than in 2005 (71.2% vs. 52.2%). Fewer people in 2009 saw their leaders as being completely satisfied with the mission status (15.4% vs. 19.6%). Such a situation could suggest that church leaders should pay more attention to the mission work in their church in the future.

Question 6. If you're not satisfied, then what is unsatisfactory?
Reasons for dissatisfaction with the mission status in the church mentioned in the survey are listed below. All of these reasons are grouped into the categories to which they belong.

Mission strategy:
- No evangelization of English speakers; everything is directed toward Russian speakers.
- Absence of local (USA) missionary projects.
- Plans on how to evangelize are not discussed among church leaders.
- Strategy is not seen at all.
- Work with Russian speakers is needed.
- Short-term mission trips to Russia look more like short-term evangelism. Long-term missionaries are needed in order to plant churches.

Geography of mission:
- More encouragement is needed for the work in the States.
- Missionary work is necessary in the area of residence and in the area of the church's location.
- More attention should be paid to ministry in the US.

Equipping of missionaries:
- Those participating in mission trips themselves need to hear about God.
- Lack of spiritual training.
- Those going on mission trips are young and ignorant of the Scriptures.
- Only trained and committed brothers and sisters should be sent on missions.

Participants in mission:
- Not enough people are involved in this ministry.
- Not many young people are involved in mission work.

- Few committed people are available to be involved in mission.
- The youth are not encouraged and there is a lack of disciplined work in this direction.
- There is not enough involvement in short-term trips from the church as a whole.
- Not enough middle-aged missionaries are involved in this ministry.

Quality of mission work:
- Little work is being done; more is desired.
- The work is done passively.
- The organization of mission trips is not good enough.

Equipping churches for mission:
- It is not proclaimed that mission is the central purpose of the church on earth.
- Little information is available in churches about the missionaries.
- The older generation does not totally understand our approach toward non-believers.
- Few conversions in the church.

Finances:
- Large expenditure of financial resources for mission.

Summary

As can be seen from the information provided above, the reasons for dissatisfaction varied, and all of them are legitimate. Of course, it will require a clear vision and a lot of effort from the leadership of churches in order to address all of the issues in mission and to make a real difference in the mission work of Slavic churches.

Part 2: Local Mission Work

Question 7. How often does the church participate in the needs of the city and the country (USA)?

Table 6.3.7.A. How Often Does the Church Participate in the Needs of the City and the Country (USA)?
(CB=Church board, PEC=Pastors exec. committee, PLR=Participants of leadership retreat, PSSR=Participants of Sunday school retreat, PYLR=Participants of youth leadership retreat)

	Surveyed	CB	PEC	PLR	PSSR	PYLR
	Number of participants in the survey	184	27	23	17	18
Answer codes	Answers	%	%	%	%	%
A	A) Every time a need is made known	31.5%	48.3%	43.5%	23.5%	16.7%
B	B) Every time the need involves Russian-speaking people	11.4%	10.3%	17.4%	29.4%	44.4%
C	C) Very rarely	32.6%	34.5%	34.8%	29.4%	27.8%
D	D) Never	15.8%	3.4%	4.3%	0.0%	5.6%
NA	No answer	7.6%	3.4%	0.0%	17.6%	5.6%

Church board members. One-third of the respondents, 31.5% (line A), stated that their church participates in the needs of the city and the country every time the need is made known. Only 11.4% (line B) said that their church participates in such needs every time the need involves Russian-speaking people. One-third of them, 32.6% (line C), see such participation happening very rarely. 15.8% (line D) of the respondents never saw their church participating in such needs. In other words, almost half of the respondents, 48.4% (sum of the lines C and D), observe church participation in the needs of the city or country as very rare or never happening.

Leadership board, pastors, and department directors meetings. Almost half, 48.3% (line A), of this group of leaders observe their church participating in such needs every time the need is made known to churches. 10.3% (line B) see a direct correlation between church participation and the involvement of Russian-speaking people in the need. More than one-third, 34.5% (line C), see such church participation as a very rare activity, and 3.4% never see such participation.

Leadership retreat. In this group, 43.5% (line A) of the respondents believe that their church participates in the city's and country's needs every time the need is made known to them. 17.4% (line B) of them see a direct connection between the need being related to Russian-speaking people and the churches' participation in the need. For 34.8% (line C), such church participation in needs of the city and country is very rare, and 4.3% (line D) do not see it happening at all.

Sunday school teachers retreat. Among Sunday school workers, 23.5% (line A) see their churches participating in the needs of the city and country (USA) every time the needs are made known to them. 29.4% (line B) of them believe that this happens only when the needs relate to Russian-speaking people. The same percentage, 29.4% (line C), sees such participation as very rare, and 17.6% did not give any answer on the question.

Youth leadership retreat. Only 16.7% (line A) of youth leaders insisted that their churches participate in the needs of the city and their new country every time these needs are made known to the church. 44.4% (line B) of them stated that such participation happens when the need relates to Russian-speaking people. 27.8% (line C) see it happening very rarely, and 5.6% (line D) of them do not see it happening at all.

Comparison of the church board survey results:

Table 6.3.7.A.B. How Often Does the Church Participate in the Needs of the City and the Country (USA)?

	Year	2005	2009
	Number of participants in the survey	184	52
Answer codes	Answers		
A	A) Every time a need is made known	31.5%	52.9%
AB	A) Every time a need is made known; B) Every time the need involves Russian-speaking people	0.5%	2.0%
B	B) Every time the need involves Russian-speaking people.	11.4%	9.8%
C	C) Very rarely	32.6%	25.5%
D	D) Never	15.8%	9.8%
NA	No answer	7.6%	2.0%

In 2005, one-third of the church board members, 31.5% (line A), stated that their church participated in the needs of the city and the country every time the need was made known. Only 11.4% (line B) said that their church participated in such needs every time the need involved Russian-speaking people. One-third of them, 32.6% (line C), saw such participation happening very rarely. A total of 15.8% (line D) of the respondents never saw their church participating in such needs. In other words, almost half of the respondents, 48.4% (combined results of lines C and D), observed church participation in the needs of the city or country as very rare or never happening.

Comparing the results of the two surveys shows that the number of respondents who saw their church participating in the needs of the city and the country, when necessary, grew significantly: from 31.5% in 2005 to 51.0% in 2009. At the same time, fewer church board members saw a direct relation between church participation in a given need and the need being related to Russian-speaking people (11.4% in 2005 vs. 9.8% in 2009). Also, a smaller number of respondents stated in 2009 that such participation was very rare (32.6% in 2005 vs. 25.5% in 2009). A similar ratio was found when it came to the answer "never happens": 15.8% in 2005 vs. 9.8% in 2009. A clear indication exists that according to the church board members,

Slavic Baptist churches became more responsive to the needs of their city and the new country during the four-year period of time between the surveys.

Question 8. How many people from the surrounding community come to worship services?

Table 6.3.8.A. How Many People from the Surrounding Community Come to Worship Services?
(CB=Church board, PEC=Pastors exec. committee, PLR=Participants of leadership retreat, PSSR=Participants of Sunday school retreat, PYLR=Participants of youth leadership retreat)

	Surveyed	CB	PEC	PLR	PSSR	PYLR
	Number of participants in the survey	184	27	23	17	18
Answer codes	Answers	%	%	%	%	%
A	Many	4.3%	3.4%	0.0%	0.0%	0.0%
B	Some	29.3%	10.3%	21.7%	17.6%	27.8%
C	Few	18.5%	27.6%	26.1%	47.1%	16.7%
D	Very few	34.8%	44.8%	52.2%	29.4%	55.6%
NA	No answer	13.0%	10.3%	0.0%	5.9%	0.0%

Church board members. Only 4.3% (line A) of the respondents observed many people from the surrounding community coming to the worship service in their church. 29.3% (line B) of them stated that some people are joining them at the service. At the same time, those who testified that only few or very few people from the community are visiting their church consisted of 53.3% (sum of lines C & D).

Leadership board, pastors, and department directors meetings. Among this group of leaders, 3.4% (line A) stated that many people from the community are joining them at services. Another 10.3% of this group observed some people from the community in their church services. A much larger percentage of the group, 72.4% (sum of lines C & D), testified that a few or very few people from the surrounding community are visiting their church.

Leadership retreat. None (line A) in this group observes many people from the community in the church service. 21.7% (line B) of the group sees some people from the surrounding community attending their services. Most of the group, 77.3% (sum of lines C & D), sees only a few or very few people from the community in their church services.

Sunday school teacher retreat. A picture similar to previous answers is found when analysis of the Sunday school workers' responses was made. None (line A) in this group see many people from the community visiting their church worship services. 17.6% (line B) see some people from the community in attendance. 76.5% (sum of lines C & D) stated that they see only a few or very few of such people in their church services.

Youth leadership retreat. Youth leaders see the same situation in their churches. None (line A) of the respondents stated that they see many people from the surrounding community visiting their church services. 27.8% (line B) believe that some of these people are attending their services. The majority of youth, 72.3% (sum of lines C & D), stated that a few or very few attendants in services of their churches are coming from the community in which the church is located.

Comparison of the church board survey results:

Table 6.3.8.A.B. How Many People from the Surrounding Community Come to Worship Services?

	Year	2005	2009
	Number of participants in the survey	184	52
Answer codes	Answers		
A	Many	4.3%	3.8%
B	Some	29.3%	19.2%
C	Few	18.5%	21.2%
D	Very few	34.8%	38.5%
NA	No answer	13.0%	17.3%

In 2005, only 4.3% (line A) of the respondents among church board members observed many people from the surrounding community coming to the worship service in their church. A total of 29.3% (line B) of them stated that some people are joining them at the service, while those who claimed that only few or very few people from the community visited their church account for 53.3% (combined results on lines C & D) of those surveyed.

Analyzing the results of the two surveys of the church boards (conducted in 2005 and 2009) showed that attendance of people from the surrounding community at the worship services in Slavic churches did not increase from 2005 to 2009. Some 3.8% of the members of the church boards saw many people from the community in their services in 2009, versus 4.3% in 2005 – down 0.5%. A total of 19.2% stated in 2009 that some people from the community attended their worship services, versus 29.3% in 2005 – down 10.1%. A significant number of the respondents, 59.7%, testified in 2009 that few or very few people from the community came to their worship services, versus 53.3% in 2005 – 6.3% up.

Question 9. How many Russian-speaking non-believers come to worship services?

Table 6.3.9.A. How Many Russian-Speaking Non-Believers Come to Worship Services?
(CB=Church board, PEC=Pastors exec. committee, PLR=Participants of leadership retreat, PSSR=Participants of Sunday school retreat, PYLR=Participants of youth leadership retreat)

	Surveyed	CB	PEC	PLR	PSSR	PYLR
	Number of participants in the survey	184	27	23	17	18
Answer codes	Answers	%	%	%	%	%
A	Many	2.7%	3.4%	0.0%	0.0%	0.0%
B	Some	34.8%	34.5%	13.0%	11.8%	33.3%
C	Few	15.8%	24.1%	21.7%	41.2%	16.7%
D	Very few	35.3%	34.5%	56.5%	41.2%	50.0%
NA	No answer	10.3%	3.4%	8.7%	5.9%	0.0%

Church board members. This group of church leaders does not see many Russian-speaking non-believers attending worship services in their churches. Only 2.7% (line A) stated that there are many Russian-speaking non-believers who visit their church. 34.8% (line B) acknowledged that they see only some Russian-speaking non-believers visiting their worship service. Over half of the respondents, 51.1% (sum of lines C & D), declared that few or very few of the Russian-speaking non-believers are coming to their church worship.

Leadership board, pastors, and department directors meetings. Almost the same answers were given by this group of respondents. 3.4% (line A) stated that many Russian-speaking people who do not know Christ are attending their worship service. However, 34.5% (line B) of them confirmed that only some such visitors could be found in their churches. More than half of them, 58.6% (sum of lines C & D), said that only few or very few such people are attending their church.

Leadership retreat. Answers from this group of respondents are even more discouraging. None of them (line A) said that there are many Russian-speaking non-believers in attendance at their church. Only 13.0% (line B) of them stated that some such visitors are present in their worship services. A significant number of the respondents, 78.2% (sum of lines C & D), stated that a few or very few Russian-speaking non-believers are attending their church services.

Sunday school teacher retreat. This group painted the most disappointing picture on the subject. Nobody stated (line A) that there are many Russian-speaking non-believers among visitors at their church. Only 11.8% (line B) affirmed that there are some such people attending their churches. An astonishing number, 82.4% (sum of lines C & D), confirmed that a few or very few Russian-speaking non-believers come to worship services in their church.

Youth leadership retreat. Youth leaders also did not see many Russian-speaking non-believers attending their church services. 33.3% of them (line B) acknowledged that they see some such visitors in their church. At the same time, the majority of the respondents, 66.7% (sum of lines C & D), stated that only a few or very few Russian-speaking non-believers come to their church services.

Comparison of the church board survey results:

Table 6.3.9.A.B. How Many Russian-Speaking Non-Believers Come to Worship Services?

	Year	2005	2009
	Number of participants in the survey	184	52
Answer codes	Answers		
A	Many	2.7%	0.0%
B	Some	54.8%	33.3%
C	Few	15.8%	13.7%
D	Very few	35.3%	43.1%
NA	No answer	10.3%	9.8%

Church board members did not see very many Russian-speaking non-believers attending worship services in their church in 2005. Only 2.7% (line A) stated that there are many Russian-speaking non-believers who visit their church. 34.8% (line B) acknowledged that they see only some Russian-speaking non-believers visiting their worship service. Half of the respondents, 51.1% (sum of lines C & D), declared that few or very few Russian-speaking non-believers are coming to their church worship. Comparing the results of the two surveys shows that during four years, the situation did not improve. In 2009, none of the church board members stated that there were many Russian-speaking non-believers in their church services, versus 2.5 % in 2009. A low number, 33.3% in 2009 (vs. 34.8% in 2005), acknowledged seeing some of these visitors in their churches. In 2009, more respondents (56.8% in 2009 vs. 51.1% in 2005) said that they saw only a few or very few Russian-speaking non-believers in their worship services.

Question 10. How many English-speaking non-believers come to worship services?

Table 6.3.10.A. How Many English-Speaking Non-Believers Come to Worship Services?
(CB=Church board, PEC=Pastors exec. committee, PLR=Participants of leadership retreat, PSSR=Participants of Sunday school retreat, PYLR=Participants of youth leadership retreat)

	Surveyed	CB	PEC	PLR	PSSR	PYLR
	Number of participants in the survey	184	27	23	17	18
Answer codes	Answers	%	%	%	%	%
A	Many	0.0%	0.0%	0.0%	0.0%	0.0%
B	Some	3.8%	10.3%	0.0%	0.0%	5.6%
C	Few	9.8%	6.9%	8.7%	11.8%	5.6%
D	Very few	61.4%	72.4%	82.6%	82.4%	77.8%
NA	No answer	25%	10.3%	8.7%	5.9%	11.1%

Nobody from the five groups surveyed said that there are many English-speaking non-believers coming to the worship services in their church.

Church board members. 3.8% (line B) of the church board members stated that there are some English-speaking non-believers visiting their services. 9.8% (line C) of them indicated that they see only a few English-speaking non-believers in the church. The majority of them, 61.4% (line D), answered that *very few* such people are attending their church.

Leadership board, pastors, and department directors meetings. Out of all respondents of this group, 10.3% (line B) answered that there are some English-speaking visitors coming to their church services. 6.9% (line C) stated that only a few such visitors are seen in their churches. However, the majority of respondents, 72.4% (line D), think that only very few English-speaking non-believers could be found among attendees in their services.

Leadership retreat. None of this group stated that there are "some" English-speaking non-believers visiting their churches. 8.7% (line C) acknowledged that a few such visitors attend their church. The vast majority of respondents, 82.6% (line D), said that very few such people come to the worship services in their churches.

Sunday school teacher retreat. The Sunday school workers share the views of the previous group. None of them said that there are "some" English-speaking non-believers among the visitors of their churches. 11.8% (line C) stated that a few such people attend their churches. 82.4% (line D) of the respondents stated that very few English-speaking people who are not Christians attend their worship services.

Youth leadership retreat. According to 5.6% (line B) of the youth leaders, some English-speaking non-believers are attending worship services in their church. 5.6 % (line C) stated that only a few such visitors could be seen among those who attend their churches. As many as 77.8% of the respondents stated that very few English-speaking non-believers come to their worship services.

Comparison of the church board survey results:

Table 6.3.10.A.B. How Many English-Speaking Non-Believers Come to Worship Services?

	Year	2005	2009
	Number of participants in the survey	184	52
Answer codes	Answers		
A	Many	0.0%	0.0%
B	Some	3.8%	3.8%
C	Few	9.8%	7.7%
D	Very few	61.4%	61.5
NA	No answer	25.0%	25.0%

Nobody from the five groups surveyed said that there were many English-speaking non-believers coming to the worship services in their church. In 2005, 3.8% (line B) of the church board members stated that there were some English-speaking non-believers visiting their services. 9.8% (line C) indicated that they saw only a few English-speaking non-believers in the church. A majority of them, 61.4% (line D), answered that *very few* such people were attending their churches. A comparison of the results of the two surveys shows no major difference in the answers of the church board members. None of the surveyed groups in either year answered that many

English-speaking non-believers were attending their churches. In both surveys, 3.8% (line B) of the respondents answered that some such visitors attended their church. In 2005, 9.7% (line C) of the church board members answered that only a few English-speaking unbelievers attended their church, versus 7.7% in 2009. Almost the same number of participants, 61.4% and 61.5% (line D), answered that very few such attendees could be found in their church services.

Question 11. Number of activities organized by the church for non-believers in the community (in 2004).

Table 6.3.11.A. Number of Activities Organized by the Church for Non-Believers in the Community (in 2004)
(CB=Church board, PEC=Pastors exec. committee, PLR=Participants of leadership retreat, PSSR=Participants of Sunday school retreat, PYLR=Participants of youth leadership retreat)

	Surveyed	CB	PEC	PLR	PSSR	PYLR
	Number of participants in the survey	184	27	23	17	18
Answer codes	Answers	%	%	%	%	%
A	Once a week	2.2%	0.0%	4.3%	0.0%	0.0%
B	Once a month	3.3%	3.4%	13.0%	0.0%	22.2%
C	Several times a year	49.5%	58.6%	39.1%	52.9%	44.4%
D	No activities have been organized	29.3%	27.6%	43.3%	23.5%	27.8%
NA	No answer	14.7%	6.9%	0.0%	23.5%	5.6%

Church board members. In this leadership group, 2.2% (line A) claimed that their churches have held activities for non-believers once a week. Very few, 3.3% (line B), of respondents stated that such activities have been organized once a month. Almost half of the board members, 49.5% (line C), stated that church activities for non-believers took place several times a year. 29.3% (line D) of the surveyed answered that no such activities have been organized in their church.

Leadership board, pastors, and department directors meetings. In this group of church leaders, 3.4% (line B) stated that activities for non-believers have been organized once a month. More than half of this group, 58.6% (line C), insisted that their church organizes activities designed for non-believers several times a year. At the same time, 27.6% (line D) stated that such activities have not been organized at all.

Leadership retreat. In this group, 4.3% (line A) stated that activities for non-believers in their church took place once a week. 13.0% (line B) of the respondents observed activities for non-believers in their church once a month. These activities were observed several times a year by 39.1% (line C). At the same time, 43.5% (line D) said that such activities did not take place at all in their church.

Sunday school teacher retreat. More than half of the Sunday school teachers, 52.9% (line C), stated that activities for non-believers have been organized in their church several times a year. 23.5% (line D) said that such activities have not been organized at all.

Youth leadership retreat. 22.2% (line B) of youth leaders responded that activities for non-believers have been organized in their churches once a month. 44.4% (line C) observed them only several times a year. 27.8% (line D) stated that such activities did not take place in their church at all.

Comparison of the church board survey results:

Table 6.3.11.A.B. Number of Activities Organized by the Church for Non-Believers in the Community (in 2004)

	Year	2005	2009
	Number of participants in the survey	184	52
Answer codes	Answers		
A	Once a week	2.2%	1.9%
B	Once a month	3.3%	3.8%
C	Several times a year	49.5%	48.1%
D	No activities have been organized	29.3%	25.0%
NA	No answer	14.7%	21.2%

In 2005, among church board members, 2.2% (line A) claimed that their church held activities for non-believers once a week. Very few, 3.3% (line B), stated that such activities had been organized once a month. Almost half of the board members, 49.5% (line C), stated that in their church, activities for the non-believers took place several times a year. A total of 29.3% (line D) of the surveyed answered that none of these activities had been organized in their church.

Comparing the results of the two surveys shows that almost no change in the answers of church board members took place during the four years between surveys. Almost the same percentage of respondents, 2.2% in 2005 versus 1.9% in 2009 (line A), said that activities for non-believers in their churches took place once a week. Also, there was almost no difference in the percentage, 3.3% in 2005 versus 3.8% in 2009 (line B), of those who said that activities for non-believers had been organized by their church once a month. The answer "several times a year" was given by 49.5% of respondents in 2005 versus 48.1% in 2009 (line C), 1.4% difference. The only more or less significant difference was in the answer "No activities for non-believers." This answer was given by 29.3% of the church board members in 2005 versus 25.0% in 2009 (line D). The difference was 4.3%.

Question 12. Are activities organized in collaboration with representatives of other ethnic groups (evaluate the year 2004)?

Table 6.3.12.A. Are Activities Organized in Collaboration with Representatives of Other Ethnic Groups (Evaluate the Year 2004)?
(CB=Church board, PEC=Pastors exec. committee, PLR=Participants of leadership retreat, PSSR=Participants of Sunday school retreat, PYLR=Participants of youth leadership retreat)

	Surveyed	CB	PEC	PLR	PSSR	PYLR
	Number of participants in the survey	184	27	23	17	18
Answer codes	Answers	%	%	%	%	%
A	Once a week	0.5%	3.4%	0.0%	0.0%	0.0%
B	Once a month	1.1%	3.4%	0.0%	0.0%	11.1%
C	Several times a year	27.2%	27.6%	21.7%	11.8%	22.2%
D	No activities have been organized	58.7%	55.2%	65.2%	70.6%	66.7%
NA	No answer	12.5%	10.3%	13.0%	17.6%	0.0%

Church board members. In this group, more than half of the respondents (58.7%) claimed that *no activities have been organized* (line D) in collaboration with representatives of other ethnic groups. About a quarter (27.2%) of those surveyed organized such activities several times a year (line C). However, only 1.1% of this group reported that such activities took place *once a month* (line B) and even less (0.5%) for once a week (line A).

Leadership board, pastors, and department directors meetings. This group had the most respondents claiming that activities organized in collaboration with other ethnic groups took place once a week (line A), with 3.4%. The same number answered that such activities took place once a month (line B). Over a quarter (27.6%) said these events occurred several times a year (line C), and more than half (55.2%) admitted that no activities had been organized (line D).

Leadership retreat. No members of the leadership retreat group reported activities organized with representatives from other ethnic groups either once a week (line A) or once a month (line B). Similar to the previous two groups, just under a quarter of the respondents (21.7%) stated that such activities occurred several times a year (line C), and more than half (65.2%) said that no activities had been organized (line D).

Sunday school teacher retreat. Almost three-quarters of the respondents (70.6%) in the Sunday school teacher retreat group reported that no activities had been organized (line D), and only 11.8% stated that activities with representatives from other ethnic groups were organized several times a year (line C).

Youth leadership retreat. In this group, none of those surveyed responded that activities involving other ethnic groups were organized once a week (line A). 11.1% stated that such activities took place once a month (line B). Just under a quarter (22.2%) responded that these activities were organized several times a year (line C), and most of the respondents (66.7%) stated that no activities had been organized (line D).

Comparison of the church board survey results:

Table 6.3.12.A.B. Are Activities Organized in Collaboration with Representatives of Other Ethnic Groups (Evaluate the Year 2004)?

	Year	2005	2009
	Number of participants in the survey	184	52
Answer codes	Answers		
A	Once a week	0.5%	0.0%
B	Once a month	1.1%	0.0%
C	Several times a year	27.2%	23/1%
D	No activities have been organized	58.7%	61.5%
NA	No answer	12.5%	15.4%

In 2005, more than half of the church board members (58.7%) claimed that no activities had been organized (line D) in collaboration with representatives of other ethnic groups. About a quarter (27.2%) of those surveyed observed such activities in their church several times a year (line C). However, only 1.1% of this group reported that such activities took place once a month (line B) and even less (0.5%) for once a week (line A). Over the course of four years, the number of activities organized with other ethnic groups had not changed dramatically. Overall, fewer activities had been organized. Respondents stating that these activities occurred once a week dropped from 0.5% to 0.0% (line A). Those stating once a month also dropped to nothing from 1.1% (line B). The number of church board members claiming that such activities were organized several times a year decreased from 27.2% to 23.1% (line C). The only increase was in the response "no activities have been organized," from 58.7% to 61.5%.

Question 13. Is your church planning evangelistic activities targeting other ethnic groups during the year 2005?

Table 6.3.13.A. Is Your Church Planning Evangelistic Activities Targeting Other Ethnic Groups During the Year 2005?
(CB=Church board, PEC=Pastors exec. committee, PLR=Participants of leadership retreat, PSSR=Participants of Sunday school retreat, PYLR=Participants of youth leadership retreat)

	Surveyed	CB	PEC	PLR	PSSR	PYLR
	Number of participants in the survey	184	27	23	17	18
Answer codes	Answers	%	%	%	%	%
A	YES	20.1%	31.0%	26.1%	11.8%	44.4%
B	NO	44.0%	37.9%	30.4%	35.3%	27.8%
C	Unable to say	32.6%	24.1%	43.5%	52.9%	22.2%
NA	No answer	2.7%	6.9%	0.0%	0.0%	0.0%

Church board members. In this group, 20.1% reported that their church was planning evangelistic activities targeting other ethnic groups (line A), and 44% stated that no such activities were planned (line B). 32.6% of the respondents were unable to say (line C).

Leadership board, pastors, and department directors meetings. About a third of this group (31%) reported that they were planning evangelistic activities for other ethnic groups (line A). About the same number (37.9%) stated that such activities were not planned (line B). 24.1% were unable to say (line C).

Leadership retreat. Of those surveyed in this group, a little more than a quarter of the respondents (26.1%) claimed that they were planning evangelistic activities for other ethnic groups (line A). 30.4% responded in the negative (line B), and 43.5% were unable to say (line C).

Sunday school teacher retreat. Of all the groups surveyed, Sunday school teacher retreat participants reported the lowest positive response, with just 11.1% (line A). 35.3% stated that they were not planning evangelistic activities targeting other ethnic groups (line B), and more than half (52.9%) were not able to say (line C).

Youth leadership retreat. This group had the highest number responding positively to the question, with 44.4% stating they were planning evangelistic activities targeting other ethnic groups (line A). About a quarter (27.8%) responded in the negative (line B), and 22.2% were unable to say (line C).

Comparison of the church board survey results:

Table 6.3.13.A.B. Is Your Church Planning Evangelistic Activities Targeting Other Ethnic Groups?

	Year	2005	2009
	Number of participants in the survey	184	52
Answer codes	Answers		
A	YES	20.1%	21.2%
B	NO	44.0%	38.5%
E	Unable to say	32.6%	40.4%
NA	No answer	2.7%	0.0%

In 2005, among the church board members surveyed, 20.1% reported that their church was planning evangelistic activities targeting other ethnic groups (line A), and 44% stated that no such activities were planned (line B). A total of 32.6% of the respondents were unable to say (line C). In the time between the two surveys, very little changed in Slavic church activities directed towards other ethnic groups. The number of those responding positively, saying that their church was planning evangelistic activities targeting other ethnic groups, increased by 1% to 21.2% (line A) in 2009. Those responding negatively decreased from 44% to 38.5% (line B). There was an increase in the number of respondents stating that they were unable to say – from 32.6% to 40.4% (line C).

The Present Mission Work of Slavic Baptist Churches in the US

Question 14. How do the church members respond to interracial marriages?

Table 6.3.14.A. How Do the Church Members Respond to Interracial Marriages?
(CB=Church board, PEC=Pastors exec. committee, PLR=Participants of leadership retreat, PSSR=Participants of Sunday school retreat, PYLR=Participants of youth leadership retreat)

	Surveyed	CB	PEC	PLR	PSSR	PYLR
	Number of participants in the survey	184	27	23	17	18
Answer codes	Answers	%	%	%	%	%
A	Positively	2.2%	0.0%	0.0%	0.0%	11.1%
B	Understandingly	27.7%	37.9%	34.8%	29.4%	33.3%
C	Negatively	29.3%	34.5%	21.7%	23.5%	5.6%
D	Unable to say	37.0%	13.8%	43.5%	35.3%	44.4%
NA	No answer	3.3%	13.8%	0.0%	11.8%	0.0%

Church board members. From the church board members surveyed, very few (only 2.2%) stated that their church members responded to interracial marriages "positively" (line A). A little more than a quarter (27.7%) claimed that church members responded "understandingly" (line B), and about the same (29.3%) said that the response to interracial marriages was generally "negative" (line C). 37% marked the answer "unable to say" (line D).

Leadership board, pastors, and department directors meetings. There were no responses claiming that church members welcomed interracial marriages (line A). This group had the highest percentage (37.9%) stating that church members responded understandingly to interracial marriages (line B). About the same number (34.5%) replied that the response was negative (line C), and 13.8% chose the answer "unable to say" (line D).

Leadership retreat. In this group, none of those surveyed replied that church members responded to interracial marriages positively (line A). More than a third (34.8%) stated that church members responded understandingly (line B). 21.7% said the response was negative (line C), and almost half (43.5%) marked the answer "unable to say" (line D).

Sunday school teacher retreat. As with the previous two groups, no respondents claimed that church members' views of interracial marriage were positive (line A). 29.4% believed that church members responded understandingly to interracial marriages (line B). About a quarter (23.5%) stated that the response was negative (line C), and 35.3% marked the answer "unable to say" (line D).

Youth leadership retreat. This group had the highest number of respondents (11.1%) stating that church members held a positive outlook on interracial marriages (line A). 33.3% believed that church members responded to interracial marriages understandingly (line B). Only 5.6% claimed that the response was negative (line C), and 44.4%, the highest of the groups surveyed, were not sure about the position of the church members on this issue (line D).

Comparison of the church board survey results:

Table 6.3.14.A.B. How Do the Church Members Respond to Interracial Marriages?

	Year	2005	2009
	Number of participants in the survey	184	52
Answer codes	Answers		
A	Positively	2.2%	0.0%
B	Understandingly	27.7%	30.8%
BC	B) Understandingly; C) Negatively	0.5%	0.0%
C	Negatively	29.3%	23.1%
D	Unable to say	37.0%	44.2%
NA	No answer	3.3%	1.9%

In 2005, from the church board members surveyed, very few (only 2.2%) stated that their church members responded to interracial marriages positively (line A). A little more than a quarter (27.7%) claimed that church members responded understandingly (line B), and about the same (29.3%) said that the response to interracial marriages was generally negative (line C). A total of 37% were unable to say (line D). During the time between the two surveys, not much changed in the attitude of Slavic churches towards the issue of interracial marriage. Those who replied that church members responded to interracial marriages positively declined from 2.2% to zero (line A). There was a slight increase in those stating that church members responded "understandingly," from 27.7% to 30.8% (line B). The number of those who responded negatively decreased from 29.3% to 23.1% (line C), and those who were unable to say increased to 44.2% (line D).

Question 15. Is your church planning and actively involved in organizing new churches in the US?

Table 6.3.15.A. Is Your Church Planning and Actively Involved in Organizing New Churches in the US?
(CB=Church board, PEC=Pastors exec. committee, PLR=Participants of leadership retreat, PSSR=Participants of Sunday school retreat, PYLR=Participants of youth leadership retreat)

	Surveyed	CB	PEC	PLR	PSSR	PYLR
	Number of participants in the survey	184	27	23	17	18
Answer codes	Answers	%	%	%	%	%
A	YES	16.3%	17.2%	13.0%	0.0%	11.1%
B	NO	58.2%	55.2%	64.7%	64.7%	50.0%
C	Unable to say	21.2%	24.1%	26.1%	23.5%	33.3%
NA	No answer	3.8%	3.4%	0.0%	11.8%	0.0%

Church board members. In this group, 16.3% responded that their church was planning to organize new churches in the US (line A). More than half (58.2%), however, said "no" (line B), and 21.2% were "unable to say" (line C).

Leadership board, pastors, and department directors meetings. This group had the highest number of respondents (17.2%) claiming that their church was planning to organize new churches (line A). Again, more than half (55.2%) responded in the negative (line B), and 24.1% marked the answer "unable to say" (line C).

Leadership retreat. From this group, 13% of the respondents replied that their church was planning to organize new churches (line A). 60.9% stated "no" (line B), while 26.1% were unable to say (line C).

Sunday school teacher retreat. This group had no respondents claiming to have churches planning to organize new churches in the US (line A). The highest number of any group (64.7%) said their churches were not planning to organize new churches (line B), and 23.5% were unable to say (line C).

Youth leadership retreat. This group had 11.1% of the participants answering "yes" (line A). Exactly half of the respondents said that their church was not planning to organize new churches. 33.3% were unable to say (line C).

Comparison of the church board survey results:

Table 6.3.15.A.B. Is Your Church Planning and Actively Involved in Organizing New Churches in the US?

	Year	2005	2009
	Number of participants in the survey	184	52
Answer codes	Answers		
A	YES	16.3%	15.4%
B	NO	58.2%	36.5%
E	Unable to say	21.2%	48.1%
NA	No answer	3.8%	0.0%

In 2005, 16.3% of the church board members surveyed responded that their church was planning to organize new churches in the US (line A). More than half (58.2%), however, said "no" (line B), and 21.2% were "unable to say" (line C). In the time between the two surveys, the number responding positively to the question declined slightly from 16.3% to 15.4% (line A). Those responding negatively declined significantly from 58.2% to 36.5% (line B), and a sharp increase occurred in the category "unable to say" from 21.2% to 48.1% (line C).

Part 3: Overseas Mission

Question 16. How many missionaries does your church currently support? The following numbers were given:
0/ 1/ 2/ 3/ 4/ 5/ 6/ 7/ 8/ 9/ 10/ 20/ 40/ 49/ 50/ 60/ 62

Summary

It should be clarified that the term "missionary" in this particular part of the study does not mean somebody who is sent from America to minister in

Russia or Ukraine. It means an indigenous person who has devoted herself/himself to full-time ministry and has moved to a new location inside the geographical territory of the former Soviet Union to serve as an evangelist, church planter, or to take part in other Christian ministry. Answers to the question above show that the number of missionaries supported by each church varies. The analysis of this data shows that the number of missionaries supported by the church correlates to the membership of the church: the more members in the local church, the higher the number of missionaries supported by the church. What needs to be taken into consideration is that financial support of missionaries in the former Soviet Union by Slavic churches in America does not necessarily mean they provide full support. Usually, it is only partial support. An amount sent to the missionary could be relatively small, such as a few hundred dollars per month. However, because of the difference in buying capacity of the dollar in the US and the former Soviet Union, this limited amount often is very helpful and is greatly appreciated.

Question 17. Where do the missionaries supported by your church work, predominantly?

Table 6.3.17.A. Where Do the Missionaries Supported by Your Church Work?
(CB=Church board, PEC=Pastors exec. committee, PLR=Participants of leadership retreat, PSSR=Participants of Sunday school retreat, PYLR=Participants of youth leadership retreat)

	Surveyed	CB	PEC	PLR	PSSR	PYLR
	Number of participants in the survey	184	27	23	17	18
Answer codes	Answers	%	%	%	%	%
A	A) In Russia or Ukraine	47.8%	27.6%	56.5%	47.1%	55.6%
AB	A) In Russia or Ukraine; B) In other countries of the former USSR	12.0%	31.0%	13.0%	23.5%	16.7%

	Surveyed	CB	PEC	PLR	PSSR	PYLR
ABC	A) In Russia or Ukraine; B) In other countries of the former USSR; C) In non-Russian-speaking countries	0.5%	0.0%	4.3%	5.9%	11.1%
AC	A) In Russia or Ukraine; C) In non-Russian-speaking countries	2.7%	6.9%	4.3%	0.0%	0.0%
B	In other countries of the former USSR	20.7%	13.8%	8.7%	11.8%	0.0%
BC	B) In other countries of the former USSR; C) In non-Russian-speaking countries	0.5%	10.3%	0.0%	5.9%	11.1%
C	In non-Russian-speaking countries	3.8%	0.0%	0.0%	5.9%	0.0%
D	Unable to say	2.7%	0.0%	0.0%	0.0%	5.6%
NA	No answer	9.2%	10.3%	13.0%	0.0%	0.0%

Church board members. The overwhelming majority of this group, 84.2% (sum of lines A, AB, ABC, AC, B, BC), stated that the missionaries their church supports are working predominantly in Russia or Ukraine or other countries of the former USSR. Only 4.8% (sum of lines ABC, AC, BC, C) included in their answers information that their missionaries are working in non-Russian-speaking countries, as well.

Leadership board, pastors, and department directors meetings. This group of leaders also saw their missionaries working predominantly in Russia, Ukraine, or other countries of the former USSR. 89.6% (sum of lines A, AB, ABC, AC, B, BC) insisted on this. At the same time, 17.2% (sum of lines ABC, AC, BC, C) included in their answers non-Russian-speaking countries.

Leadership retreat. 86.8% (sum of lines A, AB, ABC, AC, B, BC) of this group pointed to the fact that missionaries supported by their church are serving predominantly in Russia, Ukraine, or other former USSR countries.

8.6% (sum of lines ABC, AC, BC, C) indicated that their missionaries are also working in non-Russian-speaking countries.

Sunday school teacher retreat. 94.2% (sum of lines A, AB, ABC, AC, B, BC) of this group of respondents said that missionaries supported by their churches are working predominantly in Russia, Ukraine, or other countries of the former Soviet Union. 17.7% (sum of lines ABC, AC, BC, C) stated that their missionaries are also working in non-Russian-speaking countries.

Youth leadership retreat. 94.5% (sum of lines A, AB, ABC, AC, B, BC) of youth leaders stated that the main areas of missionaries supported by their church are Russia, Ukraine, and other republics of the former USSR. 22.2% (sum of lines ABC, AC, BC, C) indicated that there are also missionaries supported by Slavic churches who are serving in non-Russian-speaking countries.

Comparison of the church board survey results:

Table 6.3.17.A.B. Where Do the Missionaries Supported by Your Church Work, Predominantly?

	Year	2005	2009
	Number of participants in the survey	184	52
Answer codes	Answers		
A	A) In Russia or Ukraine	47.8%	32.7%
AB	A) In Russia or Ukraine; B) In other countries of the former USSR	12.0%	30.6%
ABC	A) In Russia or Ukraine; B) In other countries of the former USSR; C) In non-Russian-speaking countries	0.5%	4.1%
AC	A) In Russia or Ukraine; C) In non-Russian-speaking countries	2.7%	2.0%
B	In other countries of the former USSR	20.7%	22.4%
BC	B) In other countries of the former USSR; C) In non-Russian-speaking countries	0.5%	0.0%
C	In non-Russian-speaking countries	3.8%	0.0%
D	Unable to say	2.7%	0.0%
NA	No answer	9.2%	8.2%

The overwhelming majority of the church board members in 2005, 84.2% (combined results on lines A, AB, ABC, AC, B, BC), stated that in their church work they supported missionaries predominantly in Russia or Ukraine or other countries of the former USSR. Only 4.8% (lines: ABC, AC, BC, C) stated that their missionaries were working in non-Russian-speaking countries, as well. In 2009, 91.8% of members of the church boards surveyed stated that the main area of ministry of their missionaries was Russia, Ukraine, or other countries of the former USSR. In 2005, 4.8% (sum of lines ABC, AC, BC, C) indicated that their missionaries were working in non-Russian-speaking countries as well. In 2009, 6.1% of the respondents stated that their missionaries were also working in the non-Russian-speaking countries.

Question 18. Do you consider the number of missionaries supported by your church to be sufficient?

Table 6.3.18.A. Do You Consider the Number of Missionaries Supported by Your Church to Be Sufficient?
(CB=Church board, PEC=Pastors exec. committee, PLR=Participants of leadership retreat, PSSR=Participants of Sunday school retreat, PYLR=Participants of youth leadership retreat)

	Surveyed	CB	PEC	PLR	PSSR	PYLR
	Number of participants in the survey	184	27	23	17	18
Answer codes	Answers	%	%	%	%	%
A	YES	27.7%	27.6%	26.1%	23.5%	22.2%
B	NO	53.3%	51.7%	60.9%	58.5%	50.0%
C	Unable to say	13.6%	13.8%	13.0%	17.6%	22.2%
NA	No answer	5.4%	6.9%	0.0%	0.0%	5.6%

Church board members. More than a quarter (27.7%) of the church board members considered the number of supported missionaries to be sufficient in their church (line A). More than half (53.3%) believed the number was not sufficient (line B). 13.6% said "unable to say" (line C).

Leadership board, pastors, and department directors meetings. About the same number of respondents (27.6%) as in the previous group believed that the number of supported missionaries in their church was sufficient (line A). Again, just over half of those surveyed (51.7%) believed the number was not sufficient (line B), and 13.8% stated "unable to say" (line C).

Leadership retreat. In this group, 26.1% of the respondents claimed that the number of supported missionaries in their church was sufficient (line A). 60.9% replied that that number was not adequate (line B). 13.0% marked the answer "unable to say" (line C).

Sunday school teacher retreat. Just less than a quarter (23.5%) of this group believed that the number of supported missionaries was sufficient (line A). 58.8% responded that the number was too low (line B). 17.7% said "unable to say" (line C).

Youth leadership retreat. Of all the groups, the youth leadership retreat group had the fewest respondents (22.2%) claiming to have a sufficient number of supported missionaries (line A). Half of the respondents believed that there were not enough supported missionaries (line B). 22.2% answered "unable to say" (line C).

Comparison of the results of the two surveys of church boards conducted in 2005 and 2009:

Table 6.3.18.A.B. Do You Consider the Number of Missionaries Supported by Your Church to Be Sufficient?

	Year	2005	2009
	Number of participants in the survey	184	52
Answer codes	Answers		
A	YES	27.7%	44.2%
B	NO	53.3%	30.8%
E	Unable to say	13.6%	19.2%
NA	No answer	5.4%	3.8%

In 2005, more than a quarter (27.7%) of the church board members considered the number of missionaries supported by their church to be sufficient (line A). More than half (53.3%) believed the number was not sufficient (line B). A total of 13.6% responded "unable to say" (line C). Comparing the results of the two surveys, a significant increase occurred in the number of respondents stating that the number of supported missionaries from their church was sufficient, from 27.7% in 2005 to 44.2% in 2009 (line A). Those claiming that there was an inadequate number of supported missionaries dropped from 53.3% to 30.8% (line B). There was an increase in those who answered "unable to say," from 13.6% to 19.2% (line C).

Summary

Among the members of the five leadership groups, only a small percentage, 22.2%–27.7% (line A), of the respondents considered the number of missionaries that their church supported sufficient. More than half, 50.0%–60.9% (line B), of the surveyed church leaders believed that their church should support more missionaries than they currently did. This could mean that there is room for expansion of missionary support coming from Slavic immigrant churches. However, comparing the results of the surveys done in 2005 and 2009 shows that the opinions of the church board members went through some changes. If in 2005 only 27.7% of them were satisfied with the number of missionaries their church supported, in 2009 this percentage increased to 44.2%. The percentage of those who were not satisfied with that number of missionaries decreased from 53.3% in 2005 to 30.8% in 2009. This does not necessarily mean that churches began to support more missionaries in 2009. It could indicate that the enthusiasm for supporting mission work in the former homeland has cooled as the years have passed and that churches are paying more attention to their own financial needs.

Question 19. Approximately what amount of support in dollars does each missionary receive per year?
The following numbers were given in response to this question:
$100/ $120/ $150/$ 200/ $250/ $300/$ 350/ $600/ $750–$1,000/ $900/ $960/$1,200/ $1,500/ $1,800/ $2,400/ $2,500/ $3,000/$4,100/$ 4,200/ $4,800/$ 6,000/ $17,000

Summary

Such a wide range in amounts of support could be explained by the fact that several Slavic churches are often partnering in supporting the same missionary. As a result, the combined amount becomes sufficient to provide decent support for the missionary. Some churches take full responsibility for one particular indigenous missionary and his family. In such cases, the annual amount is at the higher end of the spectrum. Recent changes in the global economy and decline of the dollar's value could have a negative effect on the support provided to indigenous missionaries by Slavic immigrant churches. The amount of support that was enough a few years ago for the missionary and his family in regions of the former Soviet Union does not have the same buying capacity today and, because of this, the missionary's family could experience a shortage in their finances. At the same time, it is difficult to increase the support amount because Slavic Christians in America are experiencing negative consequences of the economic crisis. This could provide a new challenge to the financial aspect of the mission work of Slavic immigrant churches.

Question 20. Do short-term missions take place in your church?

Table 6.3.20.A. Do Short-Term Missions Take Place in Your Church?
(CB=Church board, PEC=Pastors exec. committee, PLR=Participants of leadership retreat, PSSR=Participants of Sunday school retreat, PYLR=Participants of youth leadership retreat)

	Surveyed	CB	PEC	PLR	PSSR	PYLR
	Number of participants in the survey	184	27	23	17	18
Answer codes	Answers	%	%	%	%	%
A	YES	63.0%	82.8%	73.9%	70.6%	72.2%
B	NO	22.3%	13.8%	8.7%	23.5%	11.1%
C	Unable to say	9.8%	0.0%	8.7%	5.9%	16.7%
NA	No answer	4.9%	3.4%	8.7%	0.05	0.0%

Church board members. Among the church board members, 63% claimed that short-term missions existed in their church (line A). 22.3% replied that short-term missions did not take place in their church (line B). 9.8% said "unable to say" (line C).

Leadership board, pastors, and department directors meetings. This group had the highest number of respondents (82.8%) confirming the presence of short-term missions (line A). 13.8% denied their existence in their churches (line B).

Leadership retreat. In this group, almost three-quarters (73.9%) stated that short-term missions existed in their church (line A). Only 8.7% answered in the negative (line B), the lowest of any group. 8.7% answered "unable to say" (line C).

Sunday school teacher retreat. Of those surveyed at the Sunday school teacher retreat, 70.6% believed that short-term missions took place at their church (line A). Another 23.5%, the highest of any group, did not think that short-term missions existed in their church (line B). 5.9% stated "unable to say" (line C).

Youth leadership retreat. Just under three-quarters of this group (72.2%) said that short-term missions existed in their church (line A). 11.1% did not believe that short-term missions took place in their church (line B). 16.7% said "unable to say" (line C).

Comparison of the church board survey results:

Table 6.3.20.A.B. Do Short-Term Missions Take Place in Your Church?

	Year	2005	2009
	Number of participants in the survey	184	52
Answer codes	Answers		
A	YES	63.0%	86.5%
B	NO	22.3%	1.9%
E	Unable to say	9.8%	11.5%
NA	No answer	4.9%	0.0%

In 2005, among the church board members, 63% claimed that short-term missions existed in their church (line A). A total of 22.3% replied that short-term missions did not take place in their church (line B). A total of 9.8% answered "unable to say" (line C). Between 2005 and 2009, those claiming that short-term missions existed in their church increased substantially from 63% in 2005 to 86.5% in 2009 (line A). Those stating that short-term missions did not exist declined from 22.3% to just 1.9% (line B). The number of those who stated "unable to say" slightly increased from 9.8% to 11.5% (line C).

Question 21. Are there plans to send out missionaries for long-term assignments?

Table 6.3.21.A. Are There Plans to Send Out Missionaries for Long-Term Assignments?
(CB=Church board, PEC=Pastors exec. committee, PLR=Participants of leadership retreat, PSSR=Participants of Sunday school retreat, PYLR=Participants of youth leadership retreat)

	Surveyed	CB	PEC	PLR	PSSR	PYLR
	Number of participants in the survey	184	27	23	17	18
Answer codes	Answers	%	%	%	%	%
A	YES	19.0%	17.2%	30.4%	17.6%	22.2%
B	NO	51.6%	55.2%	30.4%	41.2%	27.8%
C	Unable to say	26.6%	24.1%	39.1%	35.3%	38.9%
NA	No answer	2.7%	3.4%	0.0%	5.9%	5.6%

Church board members. In this group, 19% of the respondents claimed that there were plans to send out missionaries for long-term assignments (line A). More than half (51.6%) of those surveyed stated there were no such plans (line B). About a quarter (26.6%) answered "unable to say" (line C).

Leadership board, pastors, and department directors meetings. In this group, 17.2% reported that there were plans to send out missionaries for long-term assignments (line A), and 55.2% stated that no such activities were planned (line B). 24.1% of the respondents were unable to say (line C).

Leadership retreat. About a third of this group (30.4%) reported that there were plans to send out missionaries for long-term assignments (line A). The same number (30.4%) stated that such activities were not planned (line B). 39.1% were unable to say (line C).

Sunday school teacher retreat. In this group, 17.6% reported that there were plans to send out missionaries for long-term assignments (line A), and 41.2% stated that no such activities were planned (line B). 35.3% of the respondents answered "unable to say" (line C).

Youth leadership retreat. Of those surveyed in this group, a little less than a quarter of the respondents (22.2%) claimed that there were plans to send out missionaries for long-term assignments (line A). 27.8% responded in the negative (line B), and 38.9% were unable to say (line C).

Comparison of the church board survey results:

Table 6.3.21.A.B. Are There Plans to Send Out Missionaries for Long-Term Assignments?

	Year	2005	2009
	Number of participants in the survey	184	52
Answer codes	Answers		
A	YES	19.0%	21.2%
B	NO	51.6%	61.5%
E	Unable to say	26.6%	17.3%
NA	No answer	2.7%	0.0%

In 2005, among the church board members, 19% claimed that there were plans to send out missionaries for long-term assignments (line A). More than half (51.6%) stated that no such plans existed (line B). About a quarter (26.6%) said that they were unable to say (line C). In the time between the two surveys, very little changed. Those responding positively to the question of whether their churches had plans to send out missionaries for a long-term assignment increased from 19% to 21.2% (line A). Those responding negatively also increased, from 51.6% to 61.5% (line B). There was a decrease in the number of respondents stating that they were unable to say, from 26.6% to 17.3% (line C).

Question 22. Do cooperative relationships exist with missionary organizations abroad?

Table 6.3.22.A. Do Cooperative Relationships Exist with Missionary Organizations Abroad?
(CB=Church board, PEC=Pastors exec. committee, PLR=Participants of leadership retreat, PSSR=Participants of Sunday school retreat, PYLR=Participants of youth leadership retreat)

	Surveyed	CB	PEC	PLR	PSSR	PYLR
	Number of participants in the survey	184	27	23	17	18
Answer codes	Answers	%	%	%	%	%
A	YES	53.3%	44.8%	39.1%	52.9%	61.1%
B	NO	18.5%	31.0%	30.4%	11.8%	16.7%
C	Unable to say	24.5%	13.8%	30.4%	35.3%	22.2%
NA	No answer	3.3%	6.9%	0.0%	0.0%	0.0%

Church board members. Among the church board members, 53.3% claimed that cooperative relationships existed with missionary organizations abroad (line A). 18.5% replied that cooperative relationships did not exist with missionary organizations abroad (line B). 24.5% answered "unable to say" (line C).

Leadership board, pastors, and department directors meetings. This group had 44.8% of the respondents claiming to have cooperative relationships with missionary organizations abroad (line A). The highest number of any group (31%) said that cooperative relationships did not exist with missionary organizations abroad (line B), and 13.8% said "unable to say" (line C).

Leadership retreat. Of all the groups surveyed, leadership retreat participants reported the lowest positive response, with just 39.1% (line A). 30.4% stated that cooperative relationships did not exist with missionary organizations abroad (line B), and the same number (30.4%) stated "unable to say" (line C).

Sunday school teacher retreat. About half of this group (52.9%) reported that cooperative relationships existed with missionary organizations abroad (line A). 11.1% stated that such activities were not planned (line B). 35.3% were unable to say (line C).

Youth leadership retreat. This group had the highest number responding positively to the question, with 61.1% stating cooperative relationships existed with missionary organizations abroad (line A). 16.7% responded in the negative (line B), and 22.2% said "unable to say" (line C).

Comparison of the results of the two surveys of church boards conducted in 2005 and 2009:

Table 6.3.22.A.B. Do Cooperative Relationships Exist with Missionary Organizations Abroad?

	Year	2005	2009
	Number of participants in the survey	184	52
Answer codes	Answers		
A	YES	53.3%	61.5%
B	NO	18.5%	15.4%
E	Unable to say	24.5%	17.3%
NA	No answer	3.3%	5.8%

In 2005, among the church board members, 53.3% claimed that cooperative relationships existed with missionary organizations abroad (line A). A total of 18.5% replied that cooperative relationships did not exist with missionary organizations abroad (line B). A total of 24.5% answered "unable to say" (line C). In the time between the two surveys, very little changed. The number of those who responded in the affirmative to the existence of cooperative relationships with missionary organizations abroad increased from 53.3% to 61.5% (line A). Those responding in the negative decreased from 18.5% to 15.4% (line B). The number of respondents stating that they were unable to say decreased from 24.5% to 17.3% (line C).

Summary

Partnerships between the sending agency and missionary organizations (or churches) on the "receiving" side of the mission process are very important for the accomplishment of successful work. According to the answers of the five leadership groups surveyed, such relationships existed between Slavic churches in America and organizations in areas where missionaries were sent. A total of 39.1%–61.1% (line A) of the respondents stated that their church was working cooperatively with missionary organizations abroad. This means that when they send a missionary to the homeland they coordinate her/his ministry with an indigenous church or mission organization. This makes the ministry of the missionary more effective, and provides follow-up work when the missionary leaves the country. At the same time, 11.8%–31.0% responded by saying that such relationships did not exist. A total of 13.8%–35.3% of the respondents were not able to give an answer to this question because, probably, they were not aware of such relationships. This means that Slavic churches still need to improve their relations with partnering organizations in countries where their missionaries are going. A comparative survey of church board members indicated a positive development in this area. In 2005, 53.3% of this group gave a positive answer to this question. In 2009, this percentage increased to 61.5%. At the same time, the percentage of those who answered negatively decreased from 18.5% in 2005 to 15.4% in 2009.

Question 23. Do cooperative relationships exist with missionary organizations in America?

Table 6.3.23.A. Do Cooperative Relationships Exist with Missionary Organizations in America?
(CB=Church board, PEC=Pastors exec. committee, PLR=Participants of leadership retreat, PSSR=Participants of Sunday school retreat, PYLR=Participants of youth leadership retreat)

	Surveyed	CB	PEC	PLR	PSSR	PYLR
	Number of participants in the survey	184	27	23	17	18
Answer codes	Answers	%	%	%	%	%
A	YES	46.7%	44.8%	34.8%	47.1%	38.9%
B	NO	20.1%	34.5%	39.1%	17.6%	27.8%
C	Unable to say	27.2%	17.2%	26.1%	35.3%	33.3%
NA	No answer	5.4%	3.4%	0.0%	0.0%	0.0%

Church board members. In this group, 46.7% reported that cooperative relationships existed with missionary organizations in America (line A), and

20.1% stated that such relationships did not exist (line B). 32.6% of the respondents answered "unable to say" (line C).

Leadership board, pastors, and department directors meetings. Almost half of this group (44.8%) reported that cooperative relationships existed with missionary organizations in America (line A). Just over a third (34.5%) stated that cooperative relationships did not exist (line B). 17.2% were unable to say (line C).

Leadership retreat. Of those surveyed in this group, a little more than a third of the respondents (34.8%) claimed that cooperative relationships existed with missionary organizations in America (line A). 39.1% responded in the negative (line B), and 26.1% said "unable to say" (line C).

Sunday school teacher retreat. Of all the groups surveyed, Sunday school teacher retreat participants reported the highest positive response, with 47.1% (line A). 17.6% stated that cooperative relationships did not exist with missionary organizations in America (line B), and more than a third (35.3%) were not able to say (line C).

Youth leadership retreat. This group had 38.9% stating that cooperative relationships existed with missionary organizations in America (line A). About a quarter (27.8%) responded in the negative (line B), and 33.3% said "unable to say" (line C).

Comparison of the results of the two surveys of church boards conducted in 2005 and 2009:

Table 6.3.23.A.B. Do Cooperative Relationships Exist with Missionary Organizations in America?

	Year	2005	2009
	Number of participants in the survey	184	52
Answer codes	Answers		
A	YES	46.7%	51.9%
B	NO	20.1%	23.1%
E	Unable to say	27.2%	23.1%
NA	No answer	5.4%	1.9%

In 2005, among church board members, 46.7% reported that cooperative relationships existed with missionary organizations in America (line A), and 20.1% stated that such relationships did not exist (line B). A total of 32.6% of the respondents were "unable to say" (line C). A small improvement took place in the cooperative relationship between Slavic Baptist immigrant churches and missionary organizations in America. The percentage of those who responded positively to the question increased from 46.7% in 2005 to 51.9% in 2009.

Summary

A relatively high percentage, 34.8%–47.1% (line A), of the respondents of the five groups of church leaders stated that they cooperated with missionary organizations in America. In most cases, this still involved Slavic-based ministries. However, some churches had solid relations with "real" American churches and mission organizations in supporting and participating in mission work in the former Soviet Union. According to the comparative survey of church board members, such cooperative relationships between Slavic immigrant churches and American missionary organizations became more common during the last few years. A total of 51.9% of the surveyed board members answered positively in 2009, versus 46.7% back in 2005. However, this improvement is not significant, and room exists for a growing partnership between the immigrant churches, the native English-speaking churches, and their mission organizations.

Question 24. Are you satisfied with the current condition of overseas mission?

Table 6.3.24.A. Are You Satisfied with the Current Condition of Overseas Mission?
(CB=Church board, PEC=Pastors exec. committee, PLR=Participants of leadership retreat, PSSR=Participants of Sunday school retreat, PYLR=Participants of youth leadership retreat)

	Surveyed	CB	PEC	PLR	PSSR	PYLR
	Number of participants in the survey	184	27	23	17	18
Answer codes	Answers	%	%	%	%	%
A	YES	28.8%	17.2%	8.7%	29.4%	16.7%
B	NO	33.2%	48.3%	52.2%	0.0%	50.0%
C	Unable to say	30.4%	27.6%	39.1%	23.5%	33.3%
NA	No answer	7.6%	6.9%	0.0%	0.0%	0.0%

Church board members. This group had 28.8% of the respondents claiming that they were satisfied with the current condition of overseas missions (line A). Almost a third (33.2%) responded in the negative (line B), and 30.4% answered "unable to say" (line C).

Leadership board, pastors, and department directors meetings. From this group, 17.2% of the respondents replied that they were satisfied with the current condition of overseas missions (line A). 48.3% stated "no" (line B) while 27.6% said "unable to say" (line C).

Leadership retreat. In this group, 8.7% responded that they were satisfied with the current condition of overseas missions (line A). More than half (52.2%), however, said "no" (line B), and 39.1% said "unable to say" (line C).

Sunday school teacher retreat. This group had no respondents claiming that they were not satisfied with the current condition of overseas missions (line B). The highest number of any group (29.4%) said they were satisfied with the current condition of overseas missions (line A), and 23.5% stated "unable to say" (line C).

Youth leadership retreat. This group had 16.7% of the participants answering "yes" (line A). Exactly half of the respondents said that they were not satisfied with the current condition of overseas missions (line B). 33.3% answered "unable to say" (line C).

Comparison of the results of the two surveys of church boards conducted in 2005 and 2009:

Table 6.3.24.A.B. Are You Satisfied with the Current Condition of Overseas Mission?

	Year	2005	2009
	Number of participants in the survey	184	52
Answer codes	Answers		
A	YES	28.8%	25.0%
B	NO	33.2%	42.3%
E	Unable to say	30.4%	32.7%
NA	No answer	7.6%	0,0%

Among the church board members, in 2005, 28.8% of the respondents claimed that they were satisfied with the current condition of overseas missions (line A). Almost a third (33.2%) responded in the negative (line B), and 30.4% answered "unable to say" (line C). During the time between the two surveys, the number responding positively to the question declined slightly from 28.8% to 25% (line A). Those responding negatively increased significantly from 33.2% to 42.3% (line B), while those "unable to say" increased slightly from 30.4% to 32.7% (line C).

Summary

Few Slavic church leaders are satisfied with what they see in their churches regarding overseas mission. Only about 8.7% to 29.4% (line A) of the respondents in the five groups of church leaders stated that they were satisfied with the current condition of missions in the church. Ranging from 33.2% to 52.2% (line B) of them were completely dissatisfied. Around 23.5% to 39.1% (line C) of the participants in the survey did not have a clear opinion on this issue. Four years later, the situation had not changed much. Members of the church boards surveyed again in 2009 expressed similar levels of dissatisfaction with mission work in their churches. In 2005, 28.8% of them were satisfied with the status of missions in their churches. In 2009, only 25.0% expressed satisfaction with mission. At the same time, the percentage of dissatisfied members of the church boards increased from 33.2% in 2005 to 42.3% in 2009. Such a low rate of satisfaction among church leaders shows that, on the one hand, the missionary ministry in Slavic churches is not at the right level in terms of its organization and fruitfulness. On the other hand, this shows that there is hope for further improvement and growth of this ministry in Slavic immigrant churches because if leaders are not satisfied, they will try to make appropriate changes.

Part 4: Language Barrier and Mission

Question 25. How often are sermons in English heard during worship services in your church?

Table 6.3.25.A. How Often Are Sermons in English Heard During Worship Services in Your Church?
(CB=Church board, PEC=Pastors exec. committee, PLR=Participants of leadership retreat, PSSR=Participants of Sunday school retreat, PYLR=Participants of youth leadership retreat)

	Surveyed	CB	PEC	PLR	PSSR	PYLR
	Number of participants in the survey	184	27	23	17	18
Answer codes	Answers	%	%	%	%	%
A	Once a week	13.0%	27.6%	17.4%	23.5%	16.6%
B	More than once a week	1.1%	3.4%	4.3%	29.4%	0.0%
C	Once a month	17.9%	17.2%	30.4%	35.3%	22.2%
D	Several times a year	44.0%	48.3%	47.8%	0.0%	50.0%
E	Unable to say	17.9%	0.0%	0.0%	0.0%	0.0%
NA	No answer	6.0%	0.0%	0,0%	11.8%	0.0%

Church board members. In this group, 13% of those surveyed responded that sermons in English were heard once a week (line A). 1.1% stated that sermons in English were heard more than once a week (line B). 17.9% responded that sermons in English were heard once a month (line C), and 44% stated that sermons in English were heard several times a year (line D).

Leadership board, pastors, and department directors meetings. In this group, nearly half of the respondents (48.3%) claimed that sermons in English were heard several times a year (line D). About a quarter (27.6%) of those surveyed replied that sermons in English were heard once a week (line A). However, only 3.4% of this group reported that sermons in English were heard more than once a week (line B), and 17.2% stated that sermons in English were heard once a month (line C).

Leadership retreat. 17.4% of the leadership retreat group reported that sermons in English were heard once a week (line A), and 4.3% said "once a month" (line B). Contrary to the previous two groups, more than a quarter of the respondents (30.4%) stated that sermons in English were heard once a month (line C), and almost half (47.8%) said that sermons in English were heard several times a year (line D).

Sunday school teacher retreat. Almost a quarter of the respondents (23.5%) in the Sunday school teacher retreat group reported that sermons in English were heard once a week (line A). 29.4% replied that sermons in English were heard more than once a week (line B), and only 35.3% stated that sermons in English were heard once a month (line C).

Youth leadership retreat. This group had the most respondents claiming that sermons in English were heard once a week (line A) with 83.3%. 11.1% answered that sermons in English were heard more than once a week (line B). Just 5.6% said that sermons in English were heard once a month (line C), and there were no responses for "several times a year" (line D).

Comparison of the church board survey results:

Table 6.3.25.A.B. How Often Are Sermons in English Heard During Worship Services in Your Church?

	Year	2005	2009
	Number of participants in the survey	184	52
Answer codes	Answers		
A	Once a week	13.0%	20.5%
B	More than once a week	1.1%	9.1%
C	Once a month	17.9%	36.4%
D	Several times a year	44.0%	29.5%
E	Unable to say	17.9%	0.0%
NA	No answer	6.0%	2.3%

In 2005, 13% of the church board members surveyed responded that sermons in English were preached in their church once a week (line A). A total of 1.1% stated that sermons in English were preached more than once a week (line B). A total of 17.9% responded that sermons in English were preached once a month (line C), and 44% stated that sermons in English in their church were preached several times a year (line D). Over the course of four years, the number of sermons delivered in English had not changed dramatically. Overall, more sermons were preached in English. Respondents stating that sermons in English were preached once a week increased from 13% to 20.5% (line A). An increase also occurred among those responding "more than once a week," from 1.1% to 9.1% (line B). Those stating "once a month" more than doubled, from 17.9% to 36.4% (line C). The number of church board members claiming that preaching in English took place in their churches several times a year decreased from 44% to 29.5% (line D).

Question 26. Do you see a need for sermons in English in Slavic churches?

Table 6.3.26.A. Do You See a Need for Sermons in English in Slavic Churches?
(CB=Church board, PEC=Pastors exec. committee, PLR=Participants of leadership retreat, PSSR=Participants of Sunday school retreat, PYLR=Participants of youth leadership retreat)

	Surveyed	CB	PEC	PLR	PSSR	PYLR
	Number of participants in the survey	184	27	23	17	18
Answer codes	Answers	%	%	%	%	%
A	YES	64.1%	89.7%	95.7%	76.5%	83.3%
B	NO	23.9%	6.9%	0.0%	23.5%	11.1%
C	Don't have an opinion	8.7%	3.4%	4.3%	0.0%	5.6%
NA	No answer	3.3%	0.0%	0.0%	0.0%	11.1%

Church board members. Among the church board members, 64.1% claimed that they saw a need for English sermons in Slavic churches (line A). 23.9% replied that they did not see a need for English sermons in Slavic churches (line B). 8.7% did not have an opinion (line C).

Leadership board, pastors, and department directors meetings. Just under 90% of this group said that they saw a need for English sermons in Slavic churches (line A). Only 6.9% did not see a need for English sermons in Slavic churches (line B). 3.4% did not have an opinion (line C).

Leadership retreat. This group had the highest number of respondents (95.7%) confirming the need for English sermons in Slavic churches (line A). None denied their need (line B), and 4.3% did not have an opinion (line C).

Sunday school teacher retreat. In this group, more than three-quarters (76.5%) stated that they saw a need for English sermons in Slavic churches (line A). Almost a quarter (23.5%) answered in the negative (line B).

Youth leadership retreat. Of those surveyed at the youth leadership retreat, 16.7% believed that there was a need for English sermons in Slavic churches, the lowest of any group (line A). Interestingly, no respondents claimed that there was no need for English sermons in Slavic churches (line B), and 22.2% did not have an opinion (line C).

Comparison of the church board survey results:

Table 6.3.26.A.B. Do You See a Need for Sermons in English in Slavic Churches?

	Year	2005	2009
	Number of participants in the survey	184	52
Answer codes	Answers		
A	YES	64.1%	56.9%
B	NO	23.9%	35.3%
C	Don't have an opinion	8.7%	7.8%
NA	No answer	3.3%	0.0%

In 2005, among the church board members, 64.1% claimed that they saw a need for English sermons in Slavic churches (line A). A total of 23.9% replied that they did not see a need for English sermons in Slavic churches (line B). A total of 8.7% did not have an opinion (line C). Between 2005 and 2009, the numbers of those seeing a need for English sermons in Slavic churches noticeably decreased, from 64.1% in 2005 to 56.9% in 2009 (line A). Those stating that there was no need for English sermons in Slavic churches increased from 23.9% to 35.3% (line B). The number of those without an opinion slightly decreased from 8.7% to 7.8% (line C).

The Present Mission Work of Slavic Baptist Churches in the US   501

Question 27. How do you see your church in 20–30 years?

Table 6.3.27.A. How Do You See Your Church in 20–30 Years?
(CB=Church board, PEC=Pastors exec. committee, PLR=Participants of leadership retreat, PSSR=Participants of Sunday school retreat, PYLR=Participants of youth leadership retreat)

	Surveyed	CB	PEC	PLR	PSSR	PYLR
	Number of participants in the survey	184	27	23	17	18
Answer codes	Answers	%	%	%	%	%
A	Russian-speaking	16.3%	0.0%	0.0%	5.9%	5.6%
B	Russian- and English-speaking	52.7%	89.7%	78.3%	82.4%	66.7%
C	Completely English-speaking	3.3%	0.0%	13.0%	5.9%	11.1%
D	Unable to say	23.4%	10.3%	8.7%	5.9%	16.7%
NA	No answer	3.8%	0.0%	0.0%	0.0%	0.0%

Church board members. From the church board members surveyed, 16.3%, the highest of any group, stated that in 20–30 years they saw their churches as Russian-speaking (line A). A little more than half (52.7%) claimed that in 20–30 years they saw their churches as Russian- and English-speaking (line B); only 3.3% said that in 20–30 years they saw their churches as completely English-speaking (line C). 23.4% answered "unable to say" (line D).

Leadership board, pastors, and department directors meetings. There were no responses claiming that in 20–30 years they saw their churches being Russian-speaking (line A). This group had the highest percentage (89.7%) stating that in 20–30 years they saw their churches as Russian- and English-speaking (line B). No respondents replied that in 20–30 years they saw their churches as completely English-speaking (line C), and 10.3% stated "unable to say" (line D).

Leadership retreat. In this group, none of those surveyed replied that in 20–30 years they saw their churches as Russian-speaking (line A). More than three-quarters (78.3%) stated that in 20–30 years they saw their churches as Russian- and English-speaking (line B). 13% said in 20–30 years they saw their churches as completely English-speaking (line C), the highest of any group. 8.7% answered "unable to say" (line D).

Sunday school teacher retreat. 5.9% of the respondents claimed that in 20–30 years they saw their churches being Russian-speaking (line A). 82.4% believed that in 20–30 years their churches would be Russian- and English-speaking (line B). 5.9% also stated that in 20–30 years they saw their churches being completely English-speaking (line C), and another 5.9% said "unable to say" (line D).

Youth leadership retreat. This group had 5.6% stating that in 20–30 years they saw their churches being Russian-speaking (line A). Two-thirds believed that in 20–30 years their churches would be Russian- and English-speaking (line B). 11.1% claimed that in 20–30 years they saw their churches as completely English-speaking (line C), and 16.7% answered "unable to say" (line D).

Comparison of the church board survey results:

Table 6.3.27.A.B. How Do You See Your Church in 20–30 Years?

	Year	2005	2009
	Number of participants in the survey	184	52
Answer codes	Answers		
A	Russian-speaking	16.3%	11.8%
B	Russian- and English-speaking	52.7%	49.0%
C	Completely English-speaking	3.3%	5.9%
D	Unable to say	23.4%	29.4%
NA	No answer	3.8%	3.9%

In 2005, from the church board members surveyed, 16.3%, the highest of any group, stated that in 20–30 years they saw their churches being Russian-speaking (line A). A little more than half (52.7%) claimed that in 20–30 years they saw their churches being Russian- and English-speaking (line B); only 3.3% said that in 20–30 years they saw their churches being completely English-speaking (line C). A total of 23.4% stated "unable to say" (line D). During the time between the two surveys, few changes took place in the opinions of these leaders. In 2005, 16.3% of them believed that their church in 20–30 years would still use only Russian. In 2009, this opinion was shared by only 11.8% respondents, a 4.5% decline. In 2005, 3.3% expected their church would become completely English-speaking in 20–30 years. In 2009, this percentage grew to 5.9%. This was a 2.6% increase. At the same time, the number of those who believed that their church would become bilingual decreased from 52.7% in 2005 to 49.0% in 2009, a 3.7% decrease.

Question 28. What hinders missionary work in our circumstances?
In order to be able to improve missionary work in the local churches, it is important to find out what leaders see as the obstacles to this work. This is why this question was included in the survey. The answers to the question show, first of all, that almost half of those surveyed do not have any opinion regarding this important issue. This is a sad fact. It could mean that half of the Slavic church leadership do not think much about this issue. The other half of the respondents provided a great variety of the answers, which can be classified in the following categories:

1. External factors that are beyond our control:
- Distance from the homeland.
- Cultural and language barriers.
- Small church.

2. External factors that could be changed:
- Lack of firm financial grounding.
- Excessive bureaucracy and middlemen in this very important matter. It is better to help missionaries directly.
- Lack of personnel to train missionaries.
- Disconnection of churches.

3. Attitude factors:
- Spiritual condition of the church.
- Isolation from the local population and indifference to the problems of this country.
- Lack of desire.
- Absence of Acts 1:8.
- Church traditions; fear of interacting with local residents.
- Indifference of church members.

- In Russia and the Ukraine, there is a different approach and behavior between new Russian arrivals (from USA) and the locals.
- The worldly life of some believers.
- Lack of commitment.
- Our responsibility before God for the souls of unconverted people is underestimated.

4. *Internal factors:*
- Preoccupation (busyness) with work and education.
- Lack of organization.
- Lack of trained missionaries.
- Not enough leaders.
- Lack of information.
- Lack of knowledge of the needs of missions.
- Ignorance of the current situation in the homeland.
- Fear among the older generation of division because of the language barrier.
- Lack of good coordination and information.
- Quality of preparing projects, service, etc.
- Full-time (paid) leader is required in the church.
- Emphasis on rituals and self-edification; not enough emphasis on evangelism.
- Disagreements.
- Misunderstanding.

The great variety of answers shows the complexity of the issue. Most barriers that church leaders saw were in categories of factors that could be changed. However, these changes are not easy to make.

Question 29. What promotes missionary work in our circumstances? Answers to this question are also very different and could be classified as follows:

1. *Attitude factors:*
- Desire to witness.
- Enthusiasm of a small group of people.
- Compassion.
- Self-denial and general understanding.

- Solidarity, desire of the youth, and support of the older people.
- Desire of the youth to serve their homeland.
- Unity of spirit in the bond of peace.
- Full moral and financial support of pastors and those desiring to be missionaries.
- Understanding one's calling.
- Considering that evangelism is the central purpose of the church's existence.
- Desire to save sinners.
- Dedication and love toward the lost.
- Everyone knows that such events should be organized, but no one knows how.
- Good organization, prayerful preparation.
- Preparation for missions.
- Frequent fellowship, trans-congregational seminars.
- Sacrificial diligence/consistency.
- Enthusiasm.
- More information about the missionary work and sermons on the topic.

2. *Material factors:*
- Material prosperity (ability to financially support missionaries).
- Money.
- High standard of living.
- Freedom in economic situation.
- Financial giving and one's readiness to go on a mission.

3. *Personnel factors:*
- Training of professional evangelists (with pay).
- Dedication of evangelists and training.
- Inviting people capable of leading such work.
- Exemption from work, dedication for missions.
- Getting an education, rapid adaptation, understanding the culture, and dedication.
- Communication.
- Church programs in English and trained specialists.

4. *Leadership factors:*
- Church board.
- Sincere desire of the church members and leadership in this matter.
- Initiative of the missionary department, church leadership.

5. *Other factors:*
- Freedom that God grants today.
- Prayer.

Summary

Most answers to the question above are in the attitude category. This is not accidental. The attitude factor is the key in successful motivation for participation in mission and supporting it financially. With a positive attitude towards mission, people are willing to sacrifice their time, money, and even themselves for the sake of mission. The challenge leaders of Slavic immigrant churches have is to preserve this mission-oriented attitude among the older generations for a long time and to pass it on to the younger generations. The material factors mentioned are also important. However, it needs to be noted that many recent Slavic immigrants live below or not very far above the official poverty line in America, and finding money to support the mission projects of the church is always a challenge for them, yet they still do it. This is because of the mission-oriented attitude they have. Personal factors are important, as well. Of course, the leadership factor is crucial. If the senior pastor and the church board members are not mission-oriented, the church participation in the financial support of mission projects is limited. Usually, such support is provided by church members on the personal level. Families are supporting those missionaries whom they know in their homeland.

Part 5: How Does the Leadership of Your Church Evaluate Short-Term Mission Trips?

Question 30. Effectiveness of short-term mission trips?
Short-term mission trips to the former homeland have become very popular among the youth of Slavic immigrant churches during the past few years. Almost every church sends a group, or several of them, during the summer to Russia, Ukraine, or the other former Soviet republics to be involved

in different evangelistic ministries there. The effectiveness of these trips is often discussed by believers in immigrant churches and in churches in the homeland, as well. It is important to find out what church leaders think about this issue.

Table 6.3.30.A. Effectiveness of Short-Term Mission trips?
(CB=Church board, PEC=Pastors exec. committee, PLR=Participants of leadership retreat, PSSR=Participants of Sunday school retreat, PYLR=Participants of youth leadership retreat)

	Surveyed	CB	PEC	PLR	PSSR	PYLR
	Number of participants in the survey	184	27	23	17	18
Answer codes	Answers	%	%	%	%	%
A	High	17.9%	3.4%	34.8%	29.4%	33.3%
B	Medium	40.2%	72.4%	39.1%	47.1%	16.7%
C	Unsatisfactory	6.5%	3.4%	8.7%	0.0%	11.1%
D	Unable to say	17.9%	13.8%	17.4%	17.6%	33.3%
NA	No answer	16.8%	6.9%	0.0%	5.9%	5.6%

Church board members. Among the church board members, 17.9% claimed that the effectiveness of short-term mission trips was high (line A). More than double that number (40.2%) stated that the effectiveness was medium (line B). Only 6.5% believed that the effectiveness of short-term missions was unsatisfactory"(line C), and 17.9% were not able to say (line D).

Leadership board, pastors, and department directors meetings. In this group, a meager 3.4% claimed that the effectiveness of short-term mission trips was high (line A). Almost three-quarters (72.4%) stated that the effectiveness was medium (line B). 3.4% believed that the effectiveness of short-term missions was unsatisfactory (line C), and 13.8% were unable to say (line D).

Leadership retreat. 34.8% of the leadership retreat, the highest of any group, claimed that the effectiveness of short-term mission trips was high (line A). Almost the same number (39.1%) stated that the effectiveness was medium (line B). 8.7% believed that the effectiveness of short-term missions was unsatisfactory (line C), and 17.4% were unable to say (line D).

Sunday school teacher retreat. Of those surveyed at the Sunday school teacher retreat, 29.4% claimed that the effectiveness of short-term mission trips was high (line A). Almost half of the respondents (47.1%) stated that the effectiveness was medium (line B). No respondents believed that the effectiveness of short-term missions was unsatisfactory (line C), and 17.6% were unable to say (line D).

Youth leadership retreat. A third of this group claimed that the effectiveness of short-term mission trips was high (line A). About half of that number (16.7%) stated that the effectiveness was medium (line B). 11.1% believed that the effectiveness of short-term missions was unsatisfactory (line C), the highest of any group, and another third were unable to say (line D).

Comparison of results of the two surveys of church boards conducted in 2005 and 2009:

Table 6.3.30.A.B. Effectiveness of Short-Term Mission Trips?

	Year	2005	2009
	Number of participants in the survey	184	52
Answer codes	Answers		
A	High	17.9%	15.4%
B	Medium	40.2%	48.1
C	Unsatisfactory	6.5%	3.8%
D	Unable to say	17.9%	19.2%
NA	No answer	16.8%	13.5%

In 2005, 17.9% of the church board members surveyed claimed that the effectiveness of short-term mission trips was high (line A). More than double that number (40.2%) stated that the effectiveness was medium (line B). Only 6.5% believed that the effectiveness of short-term missions was "unsatisfactory" (line C), and 17.9% were unable to say (line D). There were no drastic differences between the results of the two surveys done in 2005 and 2009. The number of those who stated that the effectiveness of short-term mission trips was high decreased from 17.9% to 15.4% (line A). Those who believed that the effectiveness of such trips was medium increased from 40.2% to 48.1% (line B). The number of respondents stating that short-term missions were not very effective (line C) decreased from 6.5% to 3.8%, and those "unable to say" increased slightly from 17.9% to 19.2% (line D).

Summary

The results of the survey show that the range of opinions on the effectiveness of the short-term mission trips is rather wide. 3.4% to 34.8% (line A) of the respondents evaluated it as high. 16.7% to 72.4% saw it as medium. At the same time, 3.4% - 11.1% graded it as unsatisfactory. A comparison of the results of the two surveys of members of church boards shows that the percentage of those among them who evaluated the effectiveness of the short-term mission trips as medium increased by almost 8.0%. In 2005, it was 40.2%. In 2009, it became 48.1%. It is clear that the majority of the five groups of different church leaders saw the effectiveness of the short-term mission trips at the medium mark, which is encouraging. Being satisfied (at least on the medium level) with this form of mission, the church leaders will continue to support it and encourage young people to participate in it. Groups of young Slavic people going for short-term mission trips to different countries are participating in evangelism, youth camp ministry, orphanage visits, humanitarian aid distribution, and other mission-related work. This is an actual implementation of an authentic mission, overseas.

Question 31. The usefulness of short-term missions.
If the previous question dealt with the issue of the effectiveness of the short-term mission trips in organization, use of time, and money, Question 31 is dealing with the usefulness of these trips from the kingdom perspective. Does it bring spiritual fruit to the place of ministry? Does it make a positive impact on the participants?

Table 6.3.31.A. The Usefulness of Short-Term Missions
(CB=Church board, PEC=Pastors exec. committee, PLR=Participants of leadership retreat, PSSR=Participants of Sunday school retreat, PYLR=Participants of youth leadership retreat)

	Surveyed	CB	PEC	PLR	PSSR	PYLR
	Number of participants in the survey	184	27	23	17	18
Answer codes	Answers	%	%	%	%	%
A	High	26.6%	31.0%	43.5%	29.4%	33.3%
B	Medium	35.3%	48.3%	43.5%	47.1%	22.2%
C	Unsatisfactory	6.0%	3.4%	4.3%	0.0%	0.0%
D	Unable to say	15.2%	10.3%	8.7%	17.6%	33.3%
NA	No answer	15.8%	6.9%	0.0%	5.9%	5.6%

Church board members. Among church board members, 26.6%, the lowest percentage of any group, claimed that the usefulness of short-term mission trips was high (line A). About a third (35.3%) replied that their usefulness was medium (line B). This group had the highest number of respondents (6%) stating that the usefulness of short-term missions was unsatisfactory (line C), and 15.2% were unable to say (line D).

Leadership board, pastors, and department directors meetings. In this group, 31% claimed that the usefulness of short-term mission trips was high (line A). Almost half (48.3%) replied that their usefulness was medium (line B). 3.4% stated that the usefulness of short-term missions was unsatisfactory (line C), and 10.3% were unable to say (line D).

Leadership retreat. The respondents at the leadership retreat were the most optimistic. Among those surveyed, 43.5%, the highest percentage of any group, claimed that the usefulness of short-term mission trips was high (line A). The same number replied that their usefulness was medium (line B). 4.3% of the respondents stated that the usefulness of short-term missions was "unsatisfactory" (line C), and 8.7%, the lowest percentage in this category, were unable to say (line D).

Sunday school teacher retreat. 29.4% of those at the Sunday school teacher retreat claimed that the usefulness of short-term mission trips was high (line A). 47.1% replied that their usefulness was medium (line B). This group had no respondents stating that the usefulness of short-term missions was unsatisfactory (line C), and 17.6% were unable to say (line D).

Youth leadership retreat. A third of those at the youth leadership retreat claimed that the usefulness of short-term mission trips was high (line A). About a quarter (22.2%), the lowest percentage of any group, replied that their usefulness was medium (line B). This group also had no respondents stating that the usefulness of short-term missions was unsatisfactory (line C), and a third, the highest percentage of any group, were unable to say (line D).

Comparison of the results of the two surveys of church boards conducted in 2005 and 2009:

Table 6.3.31.A.B. The Usefulness of Short-Term Missions

	Year	2005	2009
	Number of participants in the survey	184	52
Answer codes	Answers		
A	High	26.6%	28.8%
B	Medium	35.3%	40.4%
C	Unsatisfactory	6.0	1.95
D	Unable to say	15.2%	17.3%
NA	No answer	15.8%	11.5%

Among the church board members surveyed in 2005, 26.6% claimed that the usefulness of short-term mission trips was high (line A). About a third (35.3%) replied that their usefulness was medium (line B). This group had the highest number of respondents (6%) stating that the usefulness of short-term missions was unsatisfactory (line C), and 15.2% were unable to say (line D). There were no notable differences between the results of two surveys. Those stating that the usefulness of short-term mission trips was high increased from 26.6% to 28.8% (line A). Those who believed that the usefulness of such trips was medium also increased, from 35.3% to 40.4% (line B). The number of respondents stating that short-term missions were not very useful (line C) decreased from 6% to 1.9%, and those unable to say increased slightly from 15.2% to 17.3% (line D).

Summary

The results of the surveys show that the leadership of Slavic churches values short-term mission ministry and sees it as useful. Out of all five groups of leaders surveyed, 26.6% to 43.5% saw this ministry as highly useful. Almost the same percentage, ranging from 22.2% to 48.3%, gave a medium grade to the usefulness of this ministry. A comparative survey of the church board members shows that among these influential leaders, appreciation of this ministry and its usefulness is growing. In 2005, 26.6% of the church board members gave a high mark, and 35.3% gave a medium mark to the usefulness of the short-term mission trips. In 2009, these marks went up to 28.8% and 40.4%, respectively. This means that the majority of church leadership support this form of missionary work, and hopefully, they will support it in the future.

Question 32. Preparedness of participants of the short-term mission trips. The personal, spiritual, emotional, and physical maturity of the participants plays an important role in the success of short-term mission trips. This question was designed to find out if participants from Slavic churches are prepared for this ministry.

Table 6.3.32.A. Preparedness of Participants of the Short-Term Mission Trips
(CB=Church board, PEC=Pastors exec. committee, PLR=Participants of leadership retreat, PSSR=Participants of Sunday school retreat, PYLR=Participants of youth leadership retreat)

	Surveyed	CB	PEC	PLR	PSSR	PYLR
	Number of participants in the survey	184	27	23	17	18
Answer codes	Answers	%	%	%	%	%
A	High	10.3%	10.3%	8.7%	5.9%	22.2%
B	Medium	47.3%	62.1%	60.9%	64.7%	38.9%
C	Unsatisfactory	10.3%	10.3%	17.4%	5.9%	5.6%
D	Unable to say	14.1%	10.3%	13.0%	17.6%	22.2%
NA	No answer	17.4%	6.9%	0.0%	5.9%	11.1%

Church board members. Among the church board members, 10.3% claimed that the preparation of short-term missionaries was high (line A). Almost half of the respondents (47.3%) stated that the preparation was medium (line B). Only 10.3% believed that the preparation of short-term missionaries was unsatisfactory (line C), and 14.1% were unable to say (line D).

Leadership board, pastors, and department directors meetings. Similar to the previous group, 10.3% of the respondents claimed that the preparation of short-term missionaries was high (line A). Almost two-thirds (62.1%) stated that the preparation was medium (line B). 10.3% also believed that the preparation of short-term missionaries was unsatisfactory (line C), and another 10.3% were unable to say (line D).

Leadership retreat. 8.7% of the leadership retreat claimed that the preparation of short-term missionaries was high (line A). More than half of the respondents (60.9%) stated that the preparation was medium (line B). 17.4% believed that the preparation of short-term missionaries was unsatisfactory (line C), and 13% were unable to say (line D).

Sunday school teacher retreat. Of those surveyed at the Sunday school teacher retreat, only 5.9% of the respondents, the lowest of any group, claimed that the preparation of short-term missionaries was high (line A). This group had the highest number of respondents (64.7%) stating that the preparation of short-term missionaries was medium (line B). Only 5.9% of the respondents believed that the preparation of short-term missionaries was unsatisfactory (line C), and 17.6% were unable to say (line D).

Youth leadership retreat. Almost a quarter (22.2%) of this group, the highest of any group, claimed that the preparation of short-term missionaries was high (line A). 38.7%, the lowest of any group, stated that the preparation was medium (line B). This group also had the lowest number of respondents (5.6%) believing that the preparation of short-term missionaries was unsatisfactory (line C), and another 22.2% were unable to say (line D).

Comparison of the results of the two surveys of church boards conducted in 2005 and 2009:

Table 6.3.32.A.B. **Preparedness of Participants of the Short-Term Mission Trips**

	Year	2005	2009
	Number of participants in the survey	184	52
Answer codes	Answers		
A	High	10.3%	17.3%
B	Medium	47.3%	44.2%
C	Unsatisfactory	10.3%	13.5%
D	Unable to say	14.1%	15.4%
NA	No answer	17.4%	9.6%

In 2005, 10.3% of the church board members claimed that the preparation of short-term missionaries was high (line A). Almost half of the respondents (47.3%) stated that the preparation was medium (line B). Only 10.3% believe that the preparation of short-term missionaries was unsatisfactory (line C), and 14.1% were unable to say (line D). There were no drastic differences between the results of the two surveys. Those stating that the preparation of short-term missionaries was high increased from 10.3% to 17.3% (line A). Those who believed that the preparation for such trips was medium decreased from 47.3% to 44.2% (line B). The number of respondents stating that the preparation of short-term missionaries was unsatisfactory (line C) increased from 10.3% to 13.5%, and those "unable to say" increased slightly from 14.1% to 15.4% (line D).

Summary

According to the responses of members of the five leadership groups, participants of the short-term mission trips were more or less prepared. 38.9% to 64.7% (line B) of the respondents gave a "medium" mark to the readiness of short-term trip participants. This is a surprisingly high evaluation in the light of the fact that most of the participants of these mission trips are young people, 16–22 years old.

Question 33. What level of preparation (training) is received by those who plan to participate in missions?

Another important factor in successful short-term mission is training received prior to the trip. This question is designed to find out how the leadership of Slavic churches evaluates the training that participants receive for short-term mission trips.

Table 6.3.33.A. What Level of Preparation (Training) Is Received by Those Who Plan to Participate in Missions?
(CB=Church board, PEC=Pastors exec. committee, PLR=Participants of leadership retreat, PSSR=Participants of Sunday school retreat, PYLR=Participants of youth leadership retreat)

	Surveyed	CB	PEC	PLR	PSSR	PYLR
	Number of participants in the survey	184	27	23	17	18
Answer codes	Answers	%	%	%	%	%
A	Excellent	8.7%	3.4%	8.7%	5.9%	0.0%
B	Good	37.0%	48.3%	47.8%	52.9%	61.1%
C	Fair	21.7%	27.6%	39.1%	17.6%	16.7%
D	Poor	6.0%	0.0%	0.0%	5.9%	11.1%
NA	No answer	26.6%	20.7%	4.3%	17.6%	11.1%

Church board members. Among church board members, 8.7%, equal to the highest percentage of any group, claimed that the level of preparation for participants of mission trips was excellent (line A). Just over a third (37%), the lowest percentage of any group, replied that the level of preparation was good (line B). This group had 21.7% of the respondents stating that the level of preparation for participants of mission trips was fair (line C), and 6% chose poor (line D).

Leadership board, pastors, and department directors meetings. In this group, 3.4% claimed that the level of preparation for participants of mission trips was excellent (line A). Almost half (48.3%) replied that the level of preparation was good (line B). 27.6% stated that the level of preparation for participants of mission trips was fair, and no one chose poor (line D).

Leadership retreat. The respondents at the leadership retreat were more optimistic. Among those surveyed, 8.7%, equal to the highest percentage of any group, claimed that the level of preparation for participants of mission trips was excellent (line A). Almost half replied that the level of preparation was good (line B). 39.1% of the respondents, the highest percentage in this category, stated that the level of preparation for participants of mission trips was fair, and no respondents chose poor (line D).

Sunday school teacher retreat. 5.9% of those at the Sunday school teacher retreat claimed that the level of preparation for participants of mission trips was excellent (line A). 52.9% replied that the level of preparation was good (line B). 17.6% of this group stated that the level of preparation for participants of mission trips was fair, and 5.9% chose the answer "poor" (line D).

Youth leadership retreat. None of those at the youth leadership retreat claimed that the level of preparation for participants of mission trips was excellent (line A). The highest percentage of any group (61.1%) replied that the level of preparation was good (line B). This group had the fewest respondents (16.7%) stating that the level of preparation for participants of mission trips was fair, and 11.1%, the highest percentage of any group, chose "poor" (line D).

Comparison of the results of the two surveys of church boards conducted in 2005 and 2009:

Table 6.3.33.A.B. What Level of Preparation (Training) Is Received by Those Who Plan to Participate in Missions?

	Year	2005	2009
	Number of participants in the survey	184	52
Answer codes	Answers		
A	Excellent	8.7%	5.8%
B	Good	37.0%	44.2%
C	Fair	21.7%	34.6%
D	Poor	6.00%	5.8%
E	Unable to say	0.0%	0.0%
NA	No answer	26.6%	9.6%

In 2005, 8.7% of the church board members, equal to the highest percentage of any group, claimed that the level of preparation for participants of mission trips was excellent (line A). Just over a third (37%), the lowest percentage of any group, replied that the level of preparation was good (line B). This group had 21.7% of the respondents stating that the level of preparation for participants of mission trips was fair (line C), and 6% chose "poor" (line D). No notable differences exist between the results of the two surveys. Those stating that the level of preparation for participants of mission trips was excellent decreased from 8.7% to 5.8% (line A). Those who believed that the level of preparation of such trips was good increased from 37% to 44.2% (line B). The number of respondents stating that the level of preparation for participants of mission trips was fair had the greatest increase from 21.7% to 34.6% (line C), and those who chose "poor" decreased slightly from 6% to 5.8% (line D).

Summary

The majority of the respondents evaluated the preparation/training provided to the participants of the short-term mission trips either as good or fair. 37.0% to 61.1% evaluated it as good, and 16.7% to 39.1% evaluated it as fair. During the five years from 2005 to 2009, this evaluation even went higher. If in 2005 the mark of "good" was given by 37.0% of the church board members in evaluation of the short-term missions, in 2009 this mark went up to 44.2%. A similar situation occurred with the mark "fair." In 2005, it was 21.7%, but in 2009, it became 34.6%. This is a surprisingly high evaluation.

Part 6: What Should the Missionary Work of Your Local Congregation Look Like in the Future?

Question 34. What should be the primary focus in mission?

Table 6.3.34.A. What Should Be the Primary Focus in Mission?
(CB=Church board, PEC=Pastors exec. committee, PLR=Participants of leadership retreat, PSSR=Participants of Sunday school retreat, PYLR=Participants of youth leadership retreat)

	Surveyed	CB	PEC	PLR	PSSR	PYLR
	Number of participants in the survey	184	27	23	17	18
Answer codes	Answers	%	%	%	%	%
A	Evangelism of our children	21.2%	10.3%	17.4%	5.9%	16.7%
AB	A) Evangelism of our children; B) Evangelism of the society around us	13.6%	17.2%	21.7%	23.5%	0.0%
ABC	A) Evangelism of our children; B) Evangelism of the society around us; C) Evangelism in Russia	15.2%	31.0%	30.4%	35.3%	55.6%
AC	A) Evangelism of our children; C) Evangelism in Russia	3.3%	0.0%	0.0%	5.9%	0.0%
B	Evangelism of the society around us	17.9%	24.1%	21.7%	23.5%	22.2%
BC	B) Evangelism of the society around us; C) Evangelism in Russia	2.2%	6.9%	4.3%	5.9%	5.6%
C	Evangelism in Russia	8.2%	3.4%	0.0%	0.0%	0.0%
D	Unable to say	5.4%	0-.0%	0.0%	0.0%	0.0%
NA	No answer	13.0%	6.9%	4.3%	0.0%	0.0%

Church board members. 21.2% (line A) of this group saw that evangelism of their children should be the main focus in mission work. 13.6% (line AB) believed that both evangelism of their children and evangelism of the society around them should be the main focus in mission. A combination of three major aspects in mission: evangelism of their children, evangelism of the society around them and evangelism in Russia, was seen by 15.2% (line ABC) of respondents as the primary focus in mission. 17.9% (line B) of this group of leaders believed that the primary focus in mission should be evangelism of the society around them. According to 8.2% (line C) of the respondents, evangelism in Russia should be the primary focus in mission.

Leadership board, pastors, and department directors meetings. 10.3% (line A) of this group of leaders saw that evangelism of their children should be the main focus in mission. 17.2% (line AB) of those surveyed believed that both evangelism of their children and evangelism of the society around them should be the main focus in mission. A combination of three aspects in mission: evangelism of their children, evangelism of the society around them and evangelism in Russia, was seen by 31.0% (line ABC) of respondents as the primary focus in mission. 24.1% (line B) of this group of leaders believed that the primary focus in mission should be evangelism of the society around them. According to 3.4% (line C) of the respondents, only evangelism in Russia should be the primary focus in mission. 6.9% (line BC) in this group believed that evangelism of the society around them and evangelism in Russia should be the primary focus in mission.

Leadership retreat. 17.4% (line A) of this leadership group was convinced that evangelism of their children should be the primary focus in the mission of their church. The opinion of 21.7% (line AB) was different. They believed that the primary focus in mission should be evangelism of their children and evangelism of the society around them. According to 30.4% (line ABC), the primary focus in mission should combine evangelism of children, evangelism of the society, and evangelism in Russia. 21.7% (line B) saw evangelism of the society around them as the main focus in mission. 4.3% (line BC) thought that a combination of evangelism of the society and evangelism in Russia should be the primary focus in the mission of the church.

Sunday school teacher retreat. Only 5.9% (line A) of Sunday school teachers believed that evangelism of their children should be the main focus in mission. 23.5% (line AB) of them insisted that the primary focus in mission should be both evangelism of children and evangelism of the society. 3.3% (line ABC) were convinced that all three: evangelism of their children, evangelism of the society around them, and evangelism in Russia should be included in the primary focus in mission. 5.9% (line AC) saw the combination of evangelism of children and evangelism in Russia as a primary focus in mission. For 23.5% (line B) of the Sunday school teachers, evangelism of the society around them was the primary focus in mission. 5.9% (line BC) of the respondents saw evangelism of the society and evangelism in Russia as the primary focus in mission.

Youth leadership retreat. 16.7% (line A) of youth leaders answered that evangelism of children was supposed to be the primary focus in mission. 55.6% (line ABC) were convinced that the primary focus in mission should include three aspects: evangelism of children, evangelism of the society, and evangelism in Russia. 22.2% of the respondents believed that evangelism of the society around them should be the main focus in the mission of the church.

Comparison of the church board survey results:

Table 6.3.34.A.B. What Should Be the Primary Focus in Mission?

	Year	2005	2009
	Number of participants in the survey	184	52
Answer codes	**Answers**		
A	Evangelism of our children	21.2%	28.8%
AB	A) Evangelism of our children; B) Evangelism of the society around us	13.6%	11.5%
ABC	A) Evangelism of our children; B) Evangelism of the society around us; C) Evangelism in Russia	15.2%	11.5%
AC	A) Evangelism of our children; C) Evangelism in Russia	3.3%	0.0%
B	Evangelism of the society around us	17.9%	19.2%
BC	B) Evangelism of the society around us; C) Evangelism in Russia	2.2%	3.8%
C	Evangelism in Russia	8.2%	5.8%
D	Unable to say	5.4%	7.7%
NA	No answer	13.0%	11.5%

In 2005, evangelism of children was seen as the primary focus of missions by 21.2% (line A) of the church board members versus 28.8% in 2009. In 2005, a combination of evangelism of children and evangelism of the society was seen as the main focus in mission by 13.6% (line AB) versus 11.5% in 2009. A combination of three aspects: evangelism of children, evangelism of society, and evangelism in Russia was seen as the main focus by 15.2% (line ABC) in 2005 versus 11.5% in 2009. Exclusively, evangelism of the society was considered the primary focus in mission by 17.9% (line B) in 2005 versus 19.2% in 2009. In 2005, a combination of evangelism of the society and evangelism in Russia was viewed as the primary focus of mission work by 2.2% (line BC) versus 3.8% in 2009. Evangelism in Russia as the primary focus of mission work was mentioned by 8.2% (line C) in 2005 versus 5.8% in 2009. A comparison of the results of the two surveys taken in 2005 and 2009 shows that the opinion of the church board members on the subject of what should be the primary focus of missions has not changed significantly. Only the percentage of those who believed that *evangelism of their children* should be the primary focus in mission increased notably, from 21.2% in 2005 to 28.8% in 2009. The percentage of other categories of answers fluctuated from 2% to 3.5%. It could be concluded that the opinion of the respondents did not change much during the years between the dates of the surveys.

Question 35. What percentage of the church budget should be devoted to missionary work?

The following numbers were given: 5%, 7%, 10%, 10–12%, 10–15%, 10–20%, 15%, 20%, 25%, 20-30%, 30%, 35–40%, 33%, 20–40%, 40%, 35–40%, 50%, 50–70%, 70%, 80%, 100%.

Some commentaries accompanied these answers:
- According to the need.
- Rising every year.
- Less than 20%.
- It could be different, depending on the event.
- As it is now, one-third.
- The more, the better.
- 10–12%, not counting particular offerings for specific missionaries and missions.
- According to necessity.
- 10% of income.
- No less than 30%.
- On the evangelism of our children: 25%; on other missions: 10%.
- Hard to say.
- Maximum.
- In different times, different percentages, but this should be a priority of church spending.
- This is an internal matter of the church, but enough to cover the needs.
- Depends on the income; when good: 25%.
- It is best to have a special missionary fund.
- According to the ability of the churches.

Summary

The great variety of answers to this question shows that no uniformity exists in the approach to the issue of mission funding among PCSBA churches. One of the reasons for this is the fact that supporting mission activities is a relatively new reality for Slavic churches. In the past, during the Soviet era, no such activities existed. No systematic teaching was practiced in churches on this subject. Now, after finding themselves in the new immigrant situation, churches are trying to establish their own criteria in this aspect of their ministry. Often it is based on personal views and preferences of the church leaders or the majority of the congregation. Another reason for this variety of answers is the fact that not all churches are in the same financial situation. Those congregations that do not have mortgages on their own church buildings or are renting facilities for their worship services from other churches have more financial freedom. Usually, they do not have as many financial obligations as those who have a mortgage on their own facilities. Also, a more detailed analysis shows that the percentage of mission spending usually is higher in churches with a smaller membership. However, the total actual amount coming from these smaller churches to mission funds is much lower than from larger churches because the budgets of larger churches are much higher, as well.

Question 36. What would you like your children and grandchildren to inherit of what you currently have as it pertains to spiritual and church matters? The following answers were received to this question:
- To be involved in church work.
- Not necessarily our traditions, but a living faith.
- Soundness of teaching, moral code, dedication to the work of God.
- Love for God and the neighbor.
- Fear of God and regard for the Word of God.
- Firmness of faith and separation from the spirit of this world.
- Belief in God and believing God.
- Knowledge and love for the Word of God and service for him from a pure heart.
- Trusting God.

- Faithfulness and love for the Lord.
- Fundamentalism.
- Personal relationship with God.
- History of Russian Christianity and our Russian-speaking roots and history.
- Openness and closeness of relationships in the church.
- Worship of God.
- Healthy conservatism.
- Good and living church.
- That they be genuine servants of God, firm in evangelical teaching.
- That they serve Christ.
- Full knowledge of the love of God for us.
- Maintaining Slavic culture and spiritual heritage.
- Right understanding of Holy Scripture, purity in relationships.
- Love the Lord and his church.
- Russian language, purity of marriage.
- Peace, understanding, unity.
- Preaching, singing, missions, prayer.
- Love for the Lord, trust, style of service, reverence before the Word of God.
- Language, organization, worldview.
- Faith, love, ability to forgive.
- Study of the gospel, spiritual fellowship with God.
- Morality, purity of teaching.
- Faithfulness to God, dedication.
- Obedience to the truth of God's Word.
- History, spirit and direction, which moved our brethren.
- The best of Russian Christian culture.
- Everything.
- Humility, patience, respect for one's elders.
- Honesty.
- Holiness.
- Sacrifice in service.

- Continual desire to know Jesus and his Word, close relations with God, holiness.
- Live by the Bible, study the Bible, dress modestly, like children of God.
- That the church would progress and occupy itself with evangelism.
- Role of the church in society.
- All the best.
- Obedience and faithfulness to God.
- Spirituality, biblical principles of life, Christian worldview.
- Dedication and sacrifice.
- Continue the faith of our fathers.
- Salvation and involvement in the church.
- Service in the Russian language, choral ministry, those values for which our brothers paid such a high price and which we so quickly forget.
- Evangelism, enthusiasm, sacrifice.
- Care for widows and orphans.
- Assurance in God, perseverance, diligence in sanctification.
- Prayer.
- Christian democratic principles of church organization, collective preaching, mass participation.
- Slavic interpretation of Baptists.
- Better informed about the spiritual world.

Summary

Most answers to the question above emphasize a close relationship with God, studying the Bible, participation in church life and evangelism, and moral purity. A few answers showed that preserving the Russian language and culture and its expression in church life was more important for some respondents than spiritual matters. They want their children and grandchildren to inherit these things first. This fact provides proof that immigrants are often more attached to their culture and language than to the spiritually important aspects of Christian life – for example, witnessing about Christ to people in the surrounding society.

Part 7: Personal Information of the Participants in the Survey

For the sake of space, personal information of only one group of church leaders – the church boards – is presented and discussed here. This group is the most influential in developing a church vision and church policies. It is important to understand which members are a part of this important group of leaders.

Question 37. A little bit about yourself
A. Your age

20–29	30–35	36–40	41–45	46–50	51–55
3.8%	11.3%	12.9%	19.4%	11.9%	10.8%
56–60	**61–65**	**66–70**	**71–75**	**76–82**	**No answer**
6.5%	2.2%	.5%	2.2%	3.8%	7.5%

The results of this survey showed that the leadership of Slavic churches was of middle age. The age of more than half (55%) of the leaders in the PCSBA churches was between 36 and 55 years old. The highest percentage (19.4%) belongs to the group of 41–45 years old. This means that this group of leaders will potentially remain in the leadership role for a long time, and that their theological and ecclesiological positions will continue to influence all aspects of life of Slavic churches for quite a long period of time.

B. How long have you lived in America?

1–3	4–5	6–8	9–10	11–14
7.0%	21.6%	22.7%	15.1%	20.0%
15–19	**20–24**	**55**	**58**	**No answer**
5.9%	.5%	.5%	.5%	1.6%

Very few church leaders in Slavic churches (7.0%) have lived in America between 1 and 3 years. Even less, only 5.9%, were those who have lived in the States between 15 and 19 years. The majority of the leaders (79.4%) of churches of the Pacific Coast Slavic Baptist Association have lived in America from 4 to 14 years. This shows that the leadership role in the Slavic churches belongs to those who are not strangers to America any more. These leaders have lived here long enough to understand, to some degree, the American culture and traditions, and to understand and speak some English. On the other hand, they still remember very well their life in the homeland and have strong ties with those who still live there.

C. Your education

3–8 years	High School	Technikum	College	Higher education	BA degree
3.2%	45.4%	17.5%	7.6%	23.3%	3.8%
AA degree	Bible correspondence courses	Higher Theological	MA Degree		No answer
7.6%	.5%	.5%	2.6%		11.4%

About half of the leaders in Slavic churches (45.4%) had a high-school level education. More than one-quarter of them (27.1%) had a BA degree or its equivalent from the USSR. Very few (2.6%) had a master's degree. In general, the educational level of the leaders in Slavic churches is relatively high.

D. How long have you been a church member?

1–5	6–10	11–15	16–20	21–25	26–30	31–35
3.8%	5.4%	9.7%	18.9%	15.6%	7.0%	10.8%
36–40	41–45	46–50	51–55	56–60	62	No answer
9.2%	1.6%	4.3%	1.6%	2.2%	.5%	8.1%

The highest percentage among Slavic church leaders (18.9%) belonged to the group of those who were members of a church between 16 and 20 years. A total of 44.2% of the leaders in Slavic churches were those who had been church members between 11 and 25 years. This means that churches were led by mature, experienced church members.

E. If you are currently involved in ministry, please indicate what kind of ministry.

Pastor	Deacon	Preacher	Music	Youth	Children's	Missionary	Other	No answer
13.5%	27.6%	18.4%	3.7%	1.08%	1.6%	1.08%	25.9%	7.0%

Summary

The leadership of the PCSBA churches consists of people who are characterized by the following:

- 55% of them are from 36 to 55 years old.
- 79.4% of them have lived in America from 4 to 14 years.
- 45.4% of them have a high-school diploma.
- 27.1% of them have a BA degree or its equivalent.
- 44.2% of them have been church members from 11 to 25 years.
- Pastors and deacons consist of 41.1% of all the members of the church boards.

6.4.A. Survey of Youth in PCSBA Churches Regarding Their View of Immigrant Churches

Questions 1–3 are located and analyzed in the main text of the thesis, in chapter 6, section 6.4.

Question 4. Where are you a student?

Table 6.4.4. Where Are You a Student?

		2004	2010	Difference
	Number of participants	859	182	
A	Junior high	6%	4%	-2%
B	High school	36%	27%	-9%
C	College/university	36%	47%	11%
D	I am not a student	20%	22%	2%

A significant number of young people were studying. In 2004, 42% of them (sum rows A & B) were students of junior high and high schools. A total of 36% were students at a college or university. Only 20% were not students. The situation had changed little in 2010. Junior high and high-school students represented 31% of those surveyed, a decrease as compared to 2004. At the same time, the number of college/university students in 2010 increased – up to 47% versus 36% in 2004. The fact that the majority of the youth were students is an encouraging one. In the past, in the homeland, their parents were denied the right to obtain education higher than high school. Now, in America, the youth have an excellent opportunity to study without being discriminated against for their Christian faith. This means that in the near future, in Slavic immigrant churches, the percentage of well-educated people will increase. Hopefully, the leadership roles will be taken over by these people, who will receive higher education in America. They would know the language, would be acculturated, and would be able to contextualize church ministry. However, this will only take place if young, educated people stay in the Slavic Russian-speaking congregations and do not transfer their membership to the English-speaking churches instead.

Question 5. Do Sunday services in the church that you are attending present you with enough spiritual food?

Table 6.4.5. Do Sunday Services in the Church That You Are Attending Present You with Enough Spiritual Food?

		2004	2010	Difference
	Number of participants	859	182	
A	YES	62%	76%	14%
B	NO	31%	24%	-7%

Taking into consideration the fact that 55% in 2004 and 82% in 2010 of young people lived in America for more than six years and probably did not understand the Russian language as well as English, it could be expected that they would not be satisfied with the preaching they heard in Slavic churches. However, according to the results of the survey, this was not the case. More than half (62% in 2004 and 76% in 2010) of the youth responded that they received enough spiritual food during Sunday services in their church. This was a surprisingly high percentage. At the same time, an alarming sign was that 31% in 2004 and 24% in 2010 responded that they were not satisfied with the spiritual content of Sunday services.

Question 6. In your opinion, how many sermons should each Sunday service have?

Table 6.4.6. In Your Opinion, How Many Sermons Should Each Sunday Service Have?

		2004	2010	Difference
	Number of participants	859	182	
A	1	12%	32%	20%
B	2	46%	54%	9%
C	3	32%	9%	-23%
D	4	4%	4%	1%

In the Soviet past, it was common for Baptist churches to have up to four (at special celebrations, even more) sermons during one Sunday service. The older people believe that this tradition should still be kept. This is why the youth were asked this question. The results show that in 2004, 12% of those surveyed preferred one sermon per service. In 2010, this group grew to 32%. Also, in 2004, 46% saw two sermons per service as appropriate. In 2010, the group of people with this view grew to 54%. At the same time, the number of those who liked to have three sermons in the service declined significantly – from 32% in 2004 to 9% in 2010. This reflects the influence that young Slavic people, who observe American churches, have been under regarding their view of the church worship service.

Question 7. How many times a month should the pastor preach?

Table 6.4.7. How Many Times a Month Should the Pastor Preach?

		2004	2010	Difference
	Number of participants	859	182	
A	One time	8%	8%	-1%
B	Two times	29%	26%	-3%
C	Three times	23%	21%	-2%
D	Every Sunday	34%	46%	12%

According to Slavic Baptist church tradition, several people in the congregation usually share the pulpit. The senior pastor usually does not preach at every service, as is usually the case in American evangelical churches. The results of the survey showed that Slavic young people want to see the senior pastor actively involved in the preaching aspect of ministry in the church. In 2004, 57% (sum of rows C & D) answered that the pastor should preach three Sundays a month or even every Sunday. In 2010, this number grew to 67%. Again, this could be explained by the fact that they have observed this custom in the American churches and want Slavic churches to do the same.

Question 8. Should there be a sermon in English in Slavic Churches? (Answers to this question are available in chapter 6, section 6.4., table 6.4.8. of the book.)

Question 9. In your opinion, what forms of musical presentations should your church have?

Table 6.4.9. In Your Opinion, What Forms of Musical Presentations Should Your Church Have?

		2004	2010	Difference
	Number of participants	859	182	
A	Only a choir	7%	3%	-3%
B	Only a worship group	4%	12%	8%
C	A choir and worship group	86%	84%	-1%

The form of musical performance in the church has always been a subject of hot discussion in Slavic churches. Traditionally, a choir was the main music performer during the church service. Introduction of the worship team, participating in services of Slavic Baptist churches, met resistance from traditionalists – mostly older people. The worship groups were associated with the Charismatic movement, which is considered to be false teaching by Slavic Baptist church leaders. At the same time, young people usually like worship group participation in services. What was interesting in the results of this survey was the fact that only 4% in 2004 and 12% in 2010 of the surveyed youth would want to have *only* a worship team participating in the service. The great majority, 86% in 2004 and 84% in 2010, preferred to have a combination – a choir and a worship team – participating in Slavic church services.

Question 10. Do you have any only-English-speaking friends that you would like to invite to your church? (Answers to this question are available in chapter 6, section 6.4., table 6.4.10. of the book.)

Question 11. Do your church leaders (pastors, deacons and such) spend enough time with the youth?

Table 6.4.11. Do Your Church Leaders (Pastors, Deacons and Such) Spend Enough Time with the Youth?

		2004	2010	Difference
	Number of participants	859	182	
A	YES	52%	58%	6%
B	NO	43%	42%	-1%

Only slightly above half, 52% in 2004 and 58% in 2010, of the surveyed young people believed that church leaders spent enough time with them. A total of 43% in 2004 and 42% in 2010 believed that the time that pastors and deacons devoted to them was not sufficient. This is a fact which should concern leaders of Slavic immigrant churches. In order for immigrant churches to survive in the context of an American religious reality, the attitude of the youth towards Slavic churches is crucial. This is why church leaders should pay special attention to the youth in their churches and spend more time with them as a group and individually.

6.5.A. Survey of the Pacific Coast Slavic Baptist Association Churches on the Current Situation in Mission

Results of this survey are available in chapter 6 of the book, section 6.5.

6.6.A. Survey of People Who Left the Russian-Speaking Congregations and Joined the English-Speaking Churches

Question 1. How long have you lived in America?

Table 6.6.1.A. How Long Have You Lived in America?

1–3 years	4–6 years	7–10 years	11–13 years	14–16 years	17 and more years
0%	0%	2.6%	18.2%	26%	52.3%

The results of the survey show that 96.5% of the respondents have been living in the US for 11 or more years. 78.3% of them have been living in America for 14 or more years. More than half of the respondents (52.3%) have been living here for 17 or more years. They are not recent immigrants. This could indicate that after spending 10 or more years in a new country, immigrants become more open to changes in their religious life.

Question 2. How old are you?

Table 6.6.2.A. How Old Are You?

Younger than 18	18–20 years old	20–22 years old	23–25 years old	26–28 years old	29–32 years old	33–35 years old	36–40 years old	Older than 40
0%	5.2%	6.5%	24.7%	0%	28.6%	7.8%	3.9%	6.5%

More than half of the respondents were in the age group of 23 to 32 years old. Actually, 28.6% were 29 to 32 years old. This shows that it is not young people, as often assumed by the members of Slavic churches, who are switching from Russian-speaking to English-speaking congregations. These are mature adults. People of this age could be actively involved in ministry of the church locally and in mission projects outside of the church. Losing members of this age group is painful for Slavic churches. They are potential leaders in the church, potential missionaries, and potential financial supporters of mission. Losing them means a weakening of the church's ability to serve.

Question 3. How old were you when you came to America?

Table 6.6.3.A. How Old Were You When You Came to America?

Younger than 10 years old	10–12 years old	13–15 years old	16–18 years old	18–20 years old	Older than 20 years old
42%	22.4%	9.2%	11.8%	6.6%	7.9%

It is interesting to note that 64.4% of the respondents were younger than 12 years old when they arrived in the States with their parents. This fact could indicate that the younger an immigrant is when he/she arrives in the new country, the higher the chance is that as an adult, he/she will switch membership from the ethnic church of his/her parents to an English-speaking congregation.

Question 4. How long did you attend a Slavic church in America before you switched to the English-speaking congregation?

Table 6.6.4.A. How Long Did You Attend a Slavic Church in America Before You Switched to the English-Speaking Congregation?

1–3 years	4–5 years	6–7 years	8–9 years	10–11 years	12–13 years	14–15 years	More than 15 years
2.6%	7.7%	5.1%	5.1%	24.4	16.7%	19.2%	19.2%

79.5% of those who participated in the survey attended the Russian-speaking church for 10 or more years before they switched from it. There is a lot of pain and drama in these numbers. It is not easy to leave a church after being a part of it for 10 or more years, especially if they were years from youth. The reasons for switching would have been serious.

Question 5. How long ago did you leave the Slavic church in order to join an English-speaking congregation?

Table 6.6.5.A. How Long Ago Did You Leave the Slavic Church in Order to Join an English-Speaking Congregation?

1–3 years	4–5 years	6–7 years	8–9 years	10–11 years	12–13 years	14–15 years	More than 15 years
51.3%	30.8%	12.8%	3.85%	1.3%	0%	0%	0%

82.1% of the respondents left the Russian-speaking church less than five years ago. 51.3% left it less than three years ago. This shows that this is a new phenomenon for Slavic immigrant churches. The leadership of these churches should be highly concerned about this issue because it could become an epidemic process, and immigrant churches could soon find themselves with mostly elderly people among their members.

Question 6. What was/were the reason(s) for leaving the Slavic church?

Table 6.6.6.A. What Was/Were the Reason(s) for Leaving the Slavic Church?

1	The quality of sermons was not high enough	78.6%
2	Misdirected vision for the church in the new cultural and language context	56.3%
3	Sunday service experience was not satisfying enough	52.3%
4	Doctrinal position of the church was not clear	50.0%
5	Doctrinal position of the church did not fit my understanding of the Bible	42.5%
6	Lack/absence of evangelistic efforts toward the surrounding community	41.3%
7	Isolationism attitude among church members	38.8%
8	Lack of practical service opportunities for church members among local people (e.g. feeding the homeless, helping the poor, etc.)	32.5%
9	Isolationism attitude among church leadership	26.3%
10	Conflict with the leadership of the church	26.3%
11	Long Sunday services	16.3%
12	My personal limitation in understanding the Russian/Ukrainian language compared to English	11.3%
13	Other	1.3%

The answers to the question above provide valuable information. There are some unexpected discoveries. The common assumption is that in most cases, people are leaving ethnic immigrant churches in general, and Slavic churches in particular, due to a limitation in understanding the language of the older generations by younger people. The results of this survey oppose this common view. The number one reason was the quality of sermons delivered in Slavic churches. The second reason was the lack of contextuality in the vision of the leadership that these churches share. The third reason mentioned was a dissatisfaction with the Sunday service experience. Again, this is an issue of contextualization of worship services. Surprisingly enough, the limitation in understanding Russian was listed as the last reason for leaving the church. This is surprising information. It provides the church leadership with a tremendous challenge. Not only the language used in services should be questioned but the key aspects of church life should also be re-evaluated.

Question 7. What attracted you to the English-speaking church?

Table 6.6.7.A. What Attracted You to the English-Speaking Church?

1	The content of sermons is deeper and more contextualized than it is in the Slavic church	85.5%
2	Church life is well structured and organized	63.2%
3	Services are more organized and focused	57.9%
4	Evangelistic efforts by the church towards people in the community I live in	40.8%
5	More opportunities are available to serve needy people in the surrounding community	38.2%
6	Music during services is more contemporary than in the Slavic church	38.2%
7	Sermons are delivered in English and I understand it better	34.2%
8	Other	0%

The logical question to be asked after the previous one is about what attracted people to the English-speaking church. In their replies, respondents pointed to several aspects of the "real" American church that had attracted them. The majority of the respondents (85.5%) stated that the content of the sermons in these churches is deeper and more contextualized than in the Slavic churches. This response is well correlated with the answers given to the previous question. A good number of the respondents stated that the fact that the church life is well structured and organized (63.2%) and services are more organized and focused (57.9%) attracted them to the English-speaking congregations. These are two aspects in which the Slavic immigrant churches differ from the English-speaking churches. Slavic churches allow much more spontaneity in their congregational life in general, and in their church services in particular. Of course, the degree of spontaneity differs from congregation to congregation. However, congregational life is generally not as well structured and organized as in English-speaking churches. There are historical, theological, and cultural reasons for this. After living in the States for a while, representatives of the younger generation become more accustomed to the American way in different aspects of life, including church life. They prefer structure, predictability, and the presence of clear focus in all their activities. A significant number of the respondents (40.8%) pointed to the presence of evangelistic efforts by the church towards the people in the community they lived in as a factor that drew them to English-speaking churches. Again, this response is in correlation with the answer to the previous question. People in Slavic churches want to be involved in evangelistic ministry locally, not only back in their homeland. 38.2% of the respondents stated that one of the aspects that attracted them to the English-speaking church is that there are more opportunities available to serve people in need from the surrounding community. Quite a few (38.2%) of the respondents stated that they were attracted to English-speaking churches because the music that they play during services is more contemporary than in the Slavic churches. The issue of music style in the church service is always a hot one. It is especially true when this issue is addressed in the cross-generational and cross-cultural context. The younger generation of immigrants is more inclined towards the contemporary American music style, while the older generation prefers the traditional Russian/Ukrainian music. It is very difficult to find a compromise between these two tastes. The lowest percentage of respondents (34.2%) stated that they could understand the English sermons of English-speaking churches better than the Russian sermons of Slavic churches. As mentioned earlier, this is an unexpected result.

Question 8. I would join a Slavic church again if the following changes took place:

Table 6.6.8.A. I Would Join a Slavic Church Again if the Following Changes Took Place:

1	Regardless of any changes in the Slavic church I will not join again	48.0%
2	Sermons of the pastor were well prepared and reflected issues and needs of the society we live in	45.2%
3	The organization of church life was similar to the English-speaking churches	37.0%
4	The form and structure of Sunday services was more like the English-speaking churches	36.8%
5	Music during services was more contemporary	24.7%
6	The Slavic church switched from Russian/Ukrainian language to using English during services	12.3%
7	Other	5.5%

Question 9. What city do you live in?

Table 6.6.9.A. What City Do You Live In?

Fresno, CA	Sacramento, CA	Los Angeles, CA	Seattle, WA	Vancouver, WA	Minneapolis, MN
36.8%	21.0%	13.2%	15.8%	1.3%	4.0%

Question 10. Are you satisfied with your spiritual life in the English-speaking church?

Table 6.6.10.A. Are You Satisfied with Your Spiritual Life in the English-Speaking Church?

Very satisfied	Satisfied	Mostly satisfied	Barely satisfied	Unsatisfied
53.3%	35.0%	10.4%	0.0%	1.3%

Question 11. How involved are you in the life and ministry of the English-speaking church?

Table 6.6.11.A. How Involved Are You in the Life and Ministry of the English-Speaking Church?

1	I am much more involved than I was in the Russian-speaking church	35.5%
2	I am a little bit less involved than I was in the Russian-speaking church	30.3%
3	I am involved to the same degree as I was involved in the life of the Russian-speaking church	26.3%
4	I am involved in church life significantly less now than I was in the Russian-speaking church	7.9%

Question 12. How would you describe your personal relationship with the people in the English-speaking church?

Table 6.6.12.A. How Would You Describe Your Personal Relationship with the People in the English-Speaking Church?

1	I have developed a strong friendship with many English-speaking members of the new church	45.5%
2	I have developed friendships with some English-speaking members of the new church	39.0%
3	I have very few friendships with English-speaking members of the church, but expect to develop more	18.2%
4	I don't have as many friends among English-speaking members of the new church as I had in the Russian-speaking church	10.4%
5	Differences in culture and language are still a barrier for me in establishing close relationships with English-speaking members of my new church	5.2%
6	I am experiencing difficulties in establishing close relationships with English-speaking people in my new church	2.6%
7	I have found that English-speaking people are not as committed to their friendships as Russian-speaking people are. This bothers me.	0.0%

Question 13. Do you miss a Russian-speaking church environment?

Table 6.6.13.A. Do You Miss a Russian-Speaking Church Environment?

Very often	Often	Sometimes	Never
1.3%	2.6%	54.6%	42.9%

Question 14. Do you miss the fellowship of Russian-speaking believers?

Table 6.6.14.A. Do You Miss the Fellowship of Russian-Speaking Believers?

Very often	Often	Sometimes	Never
2.6%	9.1%	66.2%	24.7%

Question 15. Highest degree earned

Table 6.6.15.A. Highest Degree Earned

In the process of completing high school	High-school diploma	Associate degree	Technical training	Bachelor's degree	Master's degree	Doctoral degree
0.0%	11.8%	21.0%	2.6%	51.3%	13.2%	0.0%

Question 16. Was the Russian-speaking church you attended part of the Pacific Coast Slavic Baptist Association?

Table 6.6.16.A. Was the Russian-Speaking Church You Attended Part of the Pacific Coast Slavic Baptist Association?

YES	NO	NOT SURE
76.8%	23.2%	8.6%

6.7.A. Demographic Data for the Delegates of the 75th Annual PCSBA Convention, 18–20 October 2012, Sacramento, California[1]

On 18–20 October, the 75th Annual PCSBA Convention took place in Sacramento, California. 204 delegates from 32 churches participated in this important event. Also, there were guests from these churches. Every participant filled out the questionnaire. Below are the results of this survey. 300 people participated in it.

Question 1. What country did you emigrate to America from?

Russia	Ukraine	Latvia	Moldova	Belorussia	Middle Asia region	Other
28.2%	34.4%	5.8%	8.2%	2.4%	13.2%	7.8%

Question 2. How many years have you lived in America?

Years	1–5	6–10	11–20	21–49	N/A
Percentage	3%	16%	59%	20	2%

Question 3. What language does your family speak at home?

Russian/Ukrainian	Russian/English	English	Other
80%	16%	2%	2%

Question 4. What language do your children speak?

Russian/Ukrainian	Russian/English	English	Other
36%	54%	8%	2%

---

1. *75-y S'ezd Tikhookeanskogo Ob'edineniya Slavyanskikh Tserkve'y ECB - 18-20 oktyabrya 2012*, http://75congress.pcsba.org/_customfiles/Questionnaire-Answers.pdf (accessed November 2012).

Question 5. What level of education have you obtained in the former Soviet Union?

Not complete high school	High school	Community college	Higher education (BA)	No education
5.8%	29.1%	39.7%	19.6%	5.8%

Question 6. Have you obtained secular education in America?

YES	NO
52.8%	47.2%

Question 7. Do you have theological education?

YES	NO
40%	60%

Questions 8. If you are an ordained minister, what is your position in the church?

Pastor	Deacon
58.4%	41.6%

Question 9. Do you think your church needs a sermon in English?

YES	NO
83.6%	16.4%

Question 10. Do you think your church needs to have a separate service in English?

YES	NO
60%	40%

Question 11. Your age

16–39	31–50	51–60	61 and older
10.2%	34.5%	32.1%	29%

APPENDIX FOR CHAPTER 7

Social Challenges of Immigrant Life for the Slavic Baptist Diaspora and Their Impact on Mission

7.1.A. Common Emotional and Psychological Experiences of Immigrants and Authentic Mission

7.1.1.A. Culture Shock

Cross-cultural interchange has been a part of human history for a long time. From the time people began traveling between cultures, such an interchange was part of the travel experience. Such interactions often produce in participants the feelings described as culture shock. Adrian Furnham and Stephen Bochner, in their study of the psychological consequences of exposure to new cultures, present their findings of empirical research from such disciplines as anthropology, demography, psychology, psychiatry, and sociology. They summarize other researchers' definitions of culture shock in the following way:

> Culture shock has been variously ascribed to a sudden shift in the contingencies that customarily reinforce social behavior; to rigid personalities unable to accept change; to value-differences leading to negative evaluations of the new culture; to status loss; to the noxious effects assumed to be inherent in change *per se*; to difficulties with diet; to the lack of social-support systems in the new culture; and to other factors that make life in the

new society, particularly the interpersonal side of it, uncertain, unpredictable and generally unpleasant.[1]

Michael Winkelman[2] is in an agreement with Furnham and Bochner, describing the culture shock phenomena as follows: "Cultural (or culture) shock is a multifaceted experience resulting from numerous stressors occurring in contact with a different culture . . . Cultural shock reactions may provoke psychological crises or social dysfunctions when reactions to cultural differences impede performance."[3] Winkelman identifies two sources of culture shock: (1) the challenge of new cultural surroundings, and (2) the loss of a familiar cultural environment.[4] He emphasizes that "Culture shock stress responses cause both psychological and physiological reactions. Psychological reactions include physiological, emotional, interpersonal, cognitive, and social components, as well as the effects resulting from changes in sociocultural relations, cognitive fatigue, role stress, and identity loss."[5]

Winkelman identifies the following four primary phases of culture shock:

1. The honeymoon or tourist phase. In this phase, the differences between the former culture and host culture are viewed in a romantic light. Everything looks nice, wonderful, and new. However, this phase does not last long. With the beginning of study or work in the new country, an individual faces difficulties with language and other issues, and the "honeymoon phase" usually comes to an end. This phase "is characterized by interest, excitement, euphoria, sleeplessness, positive expectations, and idealizations about the new culture."[6]

2. The crisis phase. A few weeks after arriving in the new country, differences between the old and new cultures become more apparent. Instead of a sense of excitement, an individual starts experiencing negative feelings and reactions. The typical features of culture shock are described by Winkelman

---

1. Adrian Furnham and Stephen Bochner, *Culture Shock: Psychological Reactions to Unfamiliar Environments* (New York: Methuen, 1986), 6.
2. Michael Winkelman is a Director of Department of Anthropology at Arizona State University.
3. Michael Winkelman, "Cultural Shock and Adaptation," *Journal of Counseling and Development* 73, no. 2 (Nov 1994): 121–136.
4. Ibid., 2.
5. Ibid.
6. Ibid., 3.

in the following way: "Things start to go wrong, minor issues become major problems, and cultural differences become irritating. Excessive preoccupation with cleanliness of food, drinking water, bedding, and surroundings begins. One experiences increasing disappointments, frustrations, impatience, and tension. Life does not make sense and one may feel helpless, confused, disliked by others, or treated like a child."[7] This experience creates a feeling that one lacks control in one's life, which "may lead to depression, isolation, anger, or hostility. Excessive emotionality and fatigue may be accompanied by physical or psychosomatic illness."[8] The culture of the new country is severely criticized. This phase is characterized by "maintenance and reparative behaviors (Wengle, 1988) designed to help reestablish familiar habitual cultural patterns of behavior to provide insulation from the foreign culture."[9]

3. The adjustment and reorientation phase. In this phase, newcomers have learned how to adjust effectively to the new environment. The culture shock problem could be solved only by learning an acceptable adaptation to the new culture. However, there "may be an adjustment without adaptation, such as flight or isolation." People who cannot adjust choose to return home during this phase. Other newcomers "use various forms of isolation, for example, living in an ethnic enclave and avoiding substantial learning about the new culture, a typical lifetime reaction of many first-generation immigrants."[10] However, *the only way to become effective in functioning in the new cultural environment is to adjust and adapt.* Through the process of developing problem-solving skills for dealing with the culture, the newcomers change their attitude towards the new culture and begin accepting it. "The culture begins to make sense, and negative reactions and responses to the culture are reduced as one recognizes that problems are due to the inability to understand, accept, and adapt."[11] This process is slow and involves recurrent crises and readjustment.

4. The adaptation, resolution, or acculturation stage. Achieving this phase requires development of "stable adaptations in being successful at resolving

---

7. Ibid.
8. Ibid.
9. Ibid., 4.
10. Ibid.
11. Ibid.

problems and managing the new culture." Achieving full assimilation is difficult, if not impossible. It requires significant personal change and development of a bicultural identity. Winkelman states: "It is important to recognize and accept the fact that an effective adaptation will necessarily change one, leading to the development of a bicultural identity and the integration of new cultural aspects into one's previous self-concept. Reaching this stage requires a constructive response to cultural shock with effective means of adaptation."[12]

It could be assumed that Christian immigrants at this stage are willing to reach their neighbors in the new country with the gospel and are ready to implement an authentic mission towards them.

7.1.2.A. Language Barrier

Obviously, not knowing the language of the receiving society proves to be a significant obstacle for new immigrants. Alejandro Portes and Ruben G. Rumbaut address this issue in the following way: "With few exceptions, newcomers unable to speak English in the Anglo-American world face enormous obstacles. Learning English is a basic step to enable them to participate in the life of the larger community, get an education, find a job, obtain a driver's license and access to health care or social services, and apply for citizenship. Language has often been cited as the principal initial barrier confronting recent immigrants, from the least educated peasants to the most educated professionals."[13] DeWight R. Middleton notes: "Not speaking the local language or speaking it at a beginner's level of competence makes one feel mute, helpless, and dependent. Not having control over language is particularly frustrating to professionals who are accustomed to speaking in their native language at a high level of competence."[14]

It is clear that without knowledge of the language of the new country, it is impossible to witness about Christ and to share the gospel with indigenous people. Evangelism is almost impossible without knowing the language. Another aspect of authentic mission is service, and this is also very difficult

---

12. Ibid.

13. Alejandro Portes and Ruben G. Rumbaut, *Immigrant America: A Portrait* (Berkeley and Los Angeles, CA: University of California Press, 2006), 207.

14. DeWight R. Middleton, *The Challenge of Human Diversity: Mirrors, Bridges, and Chasms* (Prospect Heights, IL: Waveland, 1998), 11.

to implement without being equipped with the language of the people in the receiving country. Lacking knowledge of the language in a new homeland is a serious obstacle facing new immigrants when conducting evangelism and service, as this is an important aspect of authentic mission.

7.1.3.A. Attachment to Homeland

One of the results of becoming "uprooted" is the increased importance for immigrants of having connections with the homeland. "The attachment to home country issues persists, however, even among those who have settled here permanently."[15] Instead of focusing their attention on issues in America, new immigrants "tend to center on issues and problems back home."[16] Such an attitude towards one's homeland is a worldwide phenomenon. Even people who are transplanted to a completely new environment still maintain loyalty to certain aspects of their homeland that have been important to them since childhood.[17] According to Susan Hardwick: "Giving up one's homeland forever is a painful experience for all people no matter what the conditions. Even though recent Russian immigrants insist they will never want to return to 'that terrible, terrible place,' they remain attached to it at a deeper level. Later in the adjustment process, feelings of homesickness and a strong desire for 'anything familiar' frequently rebound in many recent migrants."[18]

It is obvious that such a strong attachment to the homeland affects a person's attitude towards the new country, its traditions, and its people. For Christians, this could result in reluctant involvement in sharing the gospel with "real Americans."

7.1.4.A. Separation from Known Surroundings

Oscar Handlin points to the fact that emigration meant the end of a familiar life in Europe, and "it was also the beginning of life in America."[19] It meant separation from the known environment. For many immigrants, this move to the new country was the first time away from their own country, or even

---

15. Portes and Rumbaut, *Immigrant America*, 130.
16. Ibid.
17. Ibid.
18. Ibid.
19. Oscar Handlin, *The Uprooted* (Boston,: Little, Brown, 1951), 37.

away from their own town or village, and "away from the safety of the circumscribed little villages in which they had passed all their years."[20] Handlin describes their experience in the new land in this way: "Now they would learn to have dealings with people essentially different from themselves. Now they would collide with unaccustomed problems, learn to understand alien ways and alien languages, manage to survive in a grossly foreign environment."[21] The separation from the past way of life was difficult because immigrants "had been cut off from homes and villages, homes and villages which were not simply places, but communities in which was deeply enmeshed a whole pattern of life. They had left the familiar fields and hills, the cemetery in which their fathers rested, the church, the people, the animals, the trees they had known as the intimate context of their being."[22] Because of this difficult experience, immigrants "found themselves in a prolonged state of crisis." Arriving in the new world required them to focus their attention on "finding a livelihood and adjusting to conditions that were still more novel, unimaginably so."[23]

According to Zalman I. Levin, the diaspora of any ethnic group goes through several stages. The first one is a survival stage. The second stage is numerical growth and structural formation. The third stage is maturity and stable functioning. The fourth stage is a decline stage, disintegration, and fading.[24] The most difficult is the first stage. Levin states that with emigration to a new country, the social status of the person changes. Immigrants lose connections and privileges to which they were accustomed. Their past life experiences are not useful in the new environment.[25] They are taken from a familiar constituency and thrown into the new world, with its order and traditions. Old relations disappear or almost disappear, but new ones are not yet developed. In the first stage, an immigrant is in relative or almost complete isolation from the indigenous people.[26] Solving a simple life

---

20. Ibid., 38.
21. Ibid.
22. Ibid., 62.
23. Ibid.
24. Zalman I. Levin, *Mentality of Diaspora: Systematic and Socio-cultural Analysis* (Moscow: Kraft, 2001), 40.
25. Ibid., 41.
26. Ibid., 81.

situation could consist of enormous difficulties. Because they are spending time in an unknown environment, an immigrant is not able to forecast the possible consequences of his or her actions.[27] Susan W. Hardwick noted that Slavic immigrants have "a special set of challenges to face, due to limitations imposed by the control and domination of all personal and public decision making by an extremely authoritarian political system."[28]

7.1.5.A. Becoming a Foreigner and Ceasing to Belong

Obviously, one of the most difficult challenges for newcomers to a country is to find themselves in the position of being "foreigners." Probably the most painful part of this experience is losing a sense of social belonging. The natural need for belonging characterizes all people. While living in the homeland, a person often does not understand it and does not pay much attention to it. However, after moving to the new place, the person soon realizes how important this social aspect is for a normal, satisfying life. Because of this, immigrants are often looking for ways to substitute for this loss. Levin notes that when a person in the new land experiences difficulties, and when the receiving society rejects him or her as a foreigner, ethnic self-awareness awakes in the person. He or she tries to find support from the immigrant community. This community provides a refuge for the person.[29] Immigrants feel very vulnerable and defenseless. In search of support, immigrants direct their attention to the fellow-tribesmen, relatives, and acquaintances.[30] According to Handlin, the history of immigration shows that the "newcomers were also accused of congregating together in their own groups and of an unwillingness to mix with outsiders . . . Everywhere, the strangers persisted in their strangeness and willfully stood apart from American life."[31] He points to the fact that a painful awareness about their stranger status in the society was always with the immigrants. He explains,

---

27. Ibid., 82.
28. Susan W. Hardwick, *Russian Refuge: Religion, Migration, and Settlement on the North American Pacific Rim* (Chicago: University of Chicago Press, 1993), 156.
29. Levin, *Mentality of Diaspora*, 29.
30. Ibid., 81.
31. Handlin, *The Uprooted*, 273.

The old folk knew then they would not come to belong, not through their own experience nor through their offspring. The only adjustment they had been able to make to life in the United States had been one that involved the separateness of their group, one that increased their awareness of the differences between themselves and the rest of the society. In that adjustment they had always suffered from the consciousness they were strangers. The demand that they assimilate, that they surrender their separateness, condemned them always to be outsiders.[32]

This natural desire to belong to the familiar social group does not support the development of the attitude needed for successful fulfillment of such aspects of authentic mission as evangelism and service. This fulfillment must be present in the heart of immigrant believers, as well as a love for the neighbors who do not belong to their social group. It requires a willingness to sacrifice personal interests and needs, including a need to belong, in order to reach these domestic neighbors with the gospel and to serve those trying to meet their needs. Obviously, not very many new immigrants, including Slavic immigrants, have such a high level of spirituality or ability to overcome the power of their ethnicity, or the ability to refocus their attention from their ethnic group towards domestic people in order to be obedient to the teaching of the Scripture regarding authentic mission.

7.1.6.A. Uprootedness and Vulnerability

The book of Proverbs says: "Like a bird that strays from its nest is a man who strays from his home" (Prov 27:8). This is the right description for those who have left their homeland. With relocation to the new country, people lose their social, economic, and religious roots. They become, as Handlin describes them, "uprooted." They lose social stability and their sense of identity. This makes them feel insecure and confused. Hardwick describes it this way: "These feelings of confusion are accompanied by an abrupt loss of status. Immigrants are faced with a complete loss of employment, resulting in a loss of social, personal, and economic status."[33] Levin states that the abundant literature concerning immigrants consists of only one depressing

---

32. Ibid., 285.
33. Hardwick, *Russian Refuge*, 160.

story describing people of different nationalities being moved to a foreign land. It introduces to the reader a hero: an immigrant who is deprived of personality. Regardless of where he or she relocates, the immigrant faces similar problems: the difficulties of economic survival, cultural compatibility with the new surroundings, ethno-racial and social discrimination, cultural struggle, and erosion of identity.[34] Of course, this is a very general portrait and does not reflect what personal faith in God does for the person in such desperate circumstances. However, this description of immigrants' painful feelings is accurate enough to assume that people who are experiencing the "uprooted" status are not in a strong enough position to practice what authentic mission implies in general, and evangelism and service in particular.

7.1.7.A. Religious Pluralism

One of the shocking discoveries for recent Slavic immigrants arriving in America is the number of different religions and denominations existing in this country. The common perception is that America is a Christian nation and that evangelical Christianity is the predominant form of religion. However, after arrival in the USA, Slavic evangelicals discover that this is not necessarily true. As was shown in chapter 5, section 5.1.3., along with Christianity, several different religions are represented in the country. Different branches of Christianity co-exist here peacefully. Among evangelicals in America, many different denominations exist, and none of them pretend to be superior. For Slavic immigrants who came from the former Soviet Union, where very few religions were known and only several denominations existed, observing such a plurality in religion is very unusual. The most common reaction of the recent Slavic immigrants is to ignore the situation or to deny it. All these religions, either Christian denominations or non-Christian religions, are not well understood by Slavic immigrants, and they act towards them as if they do not exist at all or as if they are part of "the world" ("the world" means, in this case, everything that is outside of God's people and his kingdom and, because of this, is a subject of evangelism). Such attitudes create an obstacle in developing partnership or relations with like-minded, theologically Christian denominations in carrying out authentic mission in America.

---

34. Levin, *Mentality of Diaspora*, 14.

7.1.8.A. The Difference in Experience of Contemporary Immigrants from Experiences of Newcomers in the Past

The contemporary American immigration experience differs from that of a half-century ago, and it affects how immigrants are doing mission work today. Although Handlin is cited extensively in this work and in the works of many other authors, as well as being a respected expert on immigration issues, his observations made about the realities of immigration some sixty years ago can still be used today with certain adaptations. Similar to the time of Handlin, as it was shown in chapter 5, the foreign-born population in America is significant and is still growing at present. Comparisons of current immigration with that of the "older", early twentieth-century immigration, point to the several similarities and differences between them. Portes and Rumbaut describe them in the following way: "Similarities include the predominantly urban destination of most newcomers, their concentration in a few port cities, and their willingness to accept the lowest-paying jobs. Differences are more frequently stressed, however, for the 'old' immigration was overwhelmingly European and white, whereas the present inflow is, to a large extent, non-white and comes from countries of the Third World."[35]

The present immigration inflow comes predominantly from countries in the Global South, which influences the public image of contemporary immigration. It is commonly believed that immigrants are uniformly poor and uneducated, and, because of this, their chances for assimilation are low. The reality of their situation as it was shown in chapter 7, section 7.5., is much different. Although many immigrants today are coming from impoverished countries, and also struggle with adaptation in America, a significant number come with a high education and possess useful skills. They often represent a high social class in their homelands. These people do not struggle as much while trying to adapt to American society. Certainly, the world of the modern American immigrant is very diverse. According to Portes and Rumbaut, "Underneath its apparent uniformity, contemporary immigration features a bewildering variety of origins, return patterns, and modes of adaptation to American society. Never before has the United States received immigrants from so many countries, from such different social and economic

---

35. Ibid.

backgrounds, and for so many reasons."[36] This fact affects the key point in the whole immigrant experience – how quickly and how well new immigrants are able to adapt to the new society. Because the present immigrant population is so diverse in terms of their economic and social background, it has become increasingly implausible to keep "the view of a uniform assimilation process that different groups undergo in the course of several generations as a precondition for their social and economic advancement."[37] It is not uncommon today "to meet first-generation millionaires who speak broken English, foreign-born mayors of large cities, and top-flight immigrant engineers and scientists in the nation's research centers."[38] At the same time, there are also those who are on another side of the immigration spectrum. They are very much behind in their process of adaptation.

It is important for Slavic Baptist immigrants to be aware of the American immigration reality in order to be effective in conducting mission work among people of their new homeland. Since immigrants represent such a significant part of the population of the country (12.5% or more), it is important for Slavic Baptists to consider this group as a mission field. It is also important to do this because they are a part of this group themselves. Considering they are going through the same experiences as other immigrants, they are able to understand each other much better than indigenous people.

7.4.A. Social and Cultural Specifics of the Current Slavic Diaspora in America

In order to be able to fulfill authentic mission in the new social and cultural context successfully, the newcomers to America should be in alignment with this context. As mentioned above, it is often not the case with Slavic evangelical immigrants in the US. The following social and cultural specifics have to be considered when discussion takes place about fulfillment of authentic mission by Russian evangelicals in America.

---

36. Ibid., 13.
37. Ibid.
38. Ibid.

7.4.1.A. Intensity and Superficiality of American Life

To most immigrants from the former Soviet Union, life in America seems very intense and it looks like everyone is in such a hurry here.[39] Accustomed to a more moderate pace of life in their homeland, Russians, believers and non-believers alike, experience stress from the pressure of the high-level pace of daily American life. This intensity and pace of life makes it very difficult to develop meaningful friendships among people. Despite expressing their feelings openly in public and easily making promises "to call soon" and "to see you later," Americans hardly ever follow up these promises and develop deep friendships, especially with newcomers. This makes newcomers feel that life in America is superficial.[40] Contrary to this American way of life, friendships are especially important for Russian people. In the former Soviet Union, they "were the lifeblood of individual survival. Friends stayed together no matter what happened, sharing problems at a deep level that made existence in difficult place more bearable."[41] A Russian proverb says: "A person without friends is like a tree without roots." Yale Richmond describes this aspect of Russian culture in the following way: "Russians rely on a close network of family, friends, and co-workers as protection against the risks and unpredictability of daily life. In the village commune, Russians felt safe and secure in the company of family and neighbors. Today, in the city, they continue to value familiar faces and mistrust those they do not know."[42] Friendships are especially important for Slavic evangelical Christians (Baptists and Pentecostals), who went through many years of severe persecution from the Communist government.

7.4.2.A. Distinct Psychological and Social Characteristics Developed by Russian Immigrants

As most other legal arrivals in the USA, immigrants from the former Soviet Union come under the care of the social service departments of the country. Workers from these departments have a unique opportunity to observe

---

39. Hardwick, *Russian Refuge*, 158.
40. Ibid.
41. Ibid., 159.
42. Yale Richmond, *From Nyet to Da: Uunderstanding the Russians* (Yarmouth, ME: Intercultural Press, 1992), 106.

immigrants and to notice their common characteristics. Below is the list of common characteristics of recent immigrants from the former Soviet Union, as observed by one of the social workers who worked with this group of immigrants for many years.

Unrealistic expectations. In many cases, immigrants from the Soviet Union had higher expectations about life in America than what they found when they came here. Somehow they developed unrealistic views of this country "as a wealthy, beautiful, indeed almost perfect, place." Instead, upon arrival they found "crowded, crime-ridden neighborhoods, traffic congestion, expensive medical and dental care, and rampant social problems."[43] This discovery often led new arrivals to disappointment, which was often expressed in depression and feelings of despair.[44]

Sense of entitlement. Because the current wave of immigration from the former Soviet Union was orchestrated by the American government and immigrants were treated well during the whole process of moving from their homeland to the "land of opportunity," Soviet immigrants concluded that they were very important and were needed in America. They developed a sense of entitlement.

Loss of sense of security. However, after living in the States, they realized that such special treatment would not always take place, and eventually they had to become responsible for their own life in America. They became disappointed and started losing their sense of security[45] founded on their trust in the American social services system.

Loss of status. Moving to a new country means, for many immigrants, the loss of an opportunity to have employment similar to what they had in their homeland. In most cases, they have to accept jobs in America at the lowest level of employment, "resulting in a loss of social, personal, and economic status."[46]

Overdependency. What complicated this situation was the new immigrants' overdependence on the government, as experienced in their homeland. Soviet immigrants were overdependent on the government system

---

43. Hardwick, *Russian Refuge*, 159.
44. Ibid.
45. Ibid.
46. Ibid., 160.

in Russia which contrasts with the American "values of independence, individual motivation to succeed, and self-reliance." Coming from a society where "people were forced to be subservient to the interests of the group rather than the individual" and where everyone was told "what to do, where to live, and what to believe"[47] provided Soviet immigrants with a challenge when they were forced to make their own choices in America.

Perseverance. However, despite all of these difficulties, most immigrants from the former Soviet Union demonstrated strong perseverance. After going through a time of disappointment and confusion, they started evaluating their options for the future success of this country. "Accustomed to surviving from day to day in the former Soviet Union, these hard-working survivors usually find a way to survive again."[48]

Manipulative behavior. Unfortunately, their perseverance was often expressed by pushing the US social services system to the limit, straining it for every advantage.[49] They wanted to get as much as they could from the system, and beyond the limits, even more than the law allowed.[50]

Difficulty in establishing trusting relationships. As was mentioned earlier in this chapter, friendships are very important for Russians. Difficulties in establishing trusting relationships make the life of new immigrants from the former USSR lonely and add even more stress on the new arrivals.[51]

Strong reliance on family and friends. Limits in their ability to establish new trusting relationships intensified immigrants' reliance on family members and existing friends who came with them from their homeland. Of course, if they can make friends, these new friends are, in most cases, part of the diaspora, and not in the receiving society.[52]

According to Elena Maydell-Stevens and her co-authors, immigrants from the former Soviet Union experience higher levels of depression than immigrants from other countries, and they use health and social services

---

47. Ibid.
48. Ibid.
49. Ibid.
50. Ibid., 161.
51. Ibid.
52. Ibid., 159.

more often than other migrants.[53] "A comparison study between Russian-born and Ethiopian born Jews who had migrated to Israel found that Russian immigrants were more distressed than their Ethiopian counterparts, although the smaller cultural distance between Israel and Russia and higher level of education of Russian Jews had predicted the opposite outcome (Ponizovski et al. 1998)."[54]

This list of recent Soviet immigrant characteristics is a valuable summary of problems they are facing and behaviors they display. Of course, individual differences in experience exist within the whole group of immigrants. However, in general, this description is accurate.

Through taking into consideration these characteristics common for Soviet immigrants in general, and assuming that these characteristics are common to the Slavic Christian immigrants as well, it can be concluded that separate individuals with these characteristics, and the whole congregation that consists of individuals with such characteristics, are not well prepared and do not have a strong motivation to practice evangelism and social action among people in the receiving society.

---

53. Elena Maydell-Stevens, Anne-Marie Masgoret, and Tony Ward, "Problems of Psychological and Sociocultural Adaptation among Russian-Speaking Immigrants in New Zealand," *Social Policy Journal of New Zealand* 30 (March 2007): 181.

54. Ibid.

APPENDIX FOR CHAPTER 8

Analysis of Mission Challenges and Opportunities for the Slavic Baptist Diaspora

8.1.A. Ethnicity and Mission

As was stated in chapter 8, this study adopted the following definition of ethnicity suggested by Marietta Stepaniants: "The term 'ethnicity' is usually used to define a group of persons sharing a common cultural heritage. The latter is made by common history, environment, territory, language, customs, habits, beliefs, in short, by a common way of life. Undoubtedly, religion is an important component of any cultural heritage."[1]

Applying different aspects of this definition to the Slavic Baptist immigrant community provides a certain challenge. The fact is that almost none of the listed identifiers of ethnicity (common history, environment, territory, language, customs, habits, beliefs, etc.) is 100 percent true for the entire Slavic Baptist diaspora. Current Baptist churches in America represent the entire ethnic spectrum of society in the former Soviet Union. In the same Slavic congregation in America today, one could find people from very different parts of the former USSR. They come from Ukraine, Kazakhstan, different regions of Russia, the Baltic Republics (Latvia, Estonia,

---

1. "Ethnicity and Religion," *Institute of Philosophy, Russian Academy of Sciences*, www.dartmouth.edu, http://www.dartmouth.edu/~crn/crn_papers/Stepaniants2.pdf (accessed February 2011).

or Lithuania), and Moldova, among others.[2] Each of these parts of the former Soviet Union has its own unique history, environment, territory, native language, and customs. By technically applying the definition of ethnicity to people who live in each of these different areas of the former Soviet Union, it could be concluded that in almost all of these areas lives a unique ethnic group (Latvians vs. Ukrainians, Moldavians vs. Kazakhs, etc.). Therefore, the Slavic immigrant Baptist community cannot be combined into or spoken about as one ethnic group. In other words, they do not represent one ethnic group, as an outside observer from the States would assume. In the pure definition of the term "ethnicity," viewing the Slavic Baptist diaspora as a multiethnic community is correct.

However, there are other aspects that determine who Slavic Baptist immigrants are. There are certain common experiences in their past that have shaped them in such a way that they could be considered as one ethnic group. There are the common experiences. (1) All of the Slavic Baptist immigrants, at least the older generation, were subjected to the "Russification" program that was implemented by the Soviet government with the goal of creating a so-called "new Soviet man." One of the results of this was that they all speak Russian. (2) Many of them either experienced forced relocation from their native territories to new, often very remote, areas of the USSR themselves or have ancestors who did. As a result, they have been exposed to different cultural groups and have learned new customs and habits. This provided them with new elements in their own culture and, as a result, eliminated certain cultural barriers between different ethnic groups, bringing them closer to each other. (3) Members of the Slavic Baptist diaspora who lived in the Soviet Union went through the same educational system, as Soviet education was thoroughly standardized. All the grade schools in the entire country used exactly the same curriculum for the subjects that were taught. Pupils were introduced to the same version and political interpretation of the history of the USSR and of the world. This created a certain commonality

---

2. Interesting statistical information was obtained during the 73rd Annual PCSBA Convention held in October 2010 in Sacramento, CA. Here is how different regions of the former Soviet Union were represented at the convention: Adygeya (South of Russia) – 0.5%; Belarus – 2.8%; Georgia – 1.9%; Kazakhstan – 6.1%; Kyrgyzstan – 1.9%; Latvia – 3.3%; Moldova – 10.9%; Russia - 24.1%; Tadzhikistan – 0.9%; Uzbekistan – 3.8%; Estonia – 0.5%; Ukraine – 37.3%; USSR – 4.3%.

in the worldview of people belonging to the different ethnic groups residing in the USSR. (4) The long-lasting oppression and persecution that Baptist believers experienced in the former Soviet Union throughout almost the entire history of their existence shaped their religious identity significantly and brought them very close to each other in understanding, expressing, and protecting their faith. This made them much more similar to each other and contributed to a certain homogeneity in their religious experience. (5) Although the evangelical movement in the former Soviet Union has had different sources and was theologically shaped by different domestic and foreign movements, groups, and theologians (as shown in chapter 4 of this study), it became more or less theologically unified by the end of World War II. Despite certain differences in the church practices of different regions of the country and in spite of the split among them in the 1960s, Soviet Baptists in general share the same position on the main theological issues.

All of these aspects of commonality among Slavic Baptist immigrants in America allow them, for the purposes of this study, to be treated as one ethnic community. Similar conclusions have been made by Elena Maydell-Stevens and her co-authors in their study of the Russian-speaking immigrant experience in New Zealand. Talking about these immigrants they state, "Though not all of them would state their ethnicity as Russian (but, for example, Ukrainian, Kazakh, Jewish, and others), their main language (or quite often, the first language) would be Russian. The common language, as well as shared history and cultural traditions and values, justifies grouping all Russian-speaking migrants together for the analysis of their immigration experiences."[3] Of course, such treatment is very general and has its limitations. However, for this particular study, it is necessary to accept these limitations in order to reach the goals of the study.

8.2.A. Interethnic Relations between Slavic Immigrants and Other People Groups

A paradigm shift is taking place in American education and society regarding the understanding of the nature and character of interethnic relationships.

---

3. "Problems of Psychological and Sociocultural Adaptation Among Russian-speaking Immigrants in New Zealand," *Social Policy Journal of New Zealand* 30 (March 2007): 181.

This shift could influence and extend the length of the process by which the Slavic Baptists assimilate in America and, by doing so, affect their implementation of authentic mission. Five paradigms of ethnic relations in America can be identified. Paradigm I, "Traditional Eurocentric Racism," defines America "as predominantly northern and western European in its culture and institutions, with a dominant Anglo-Saxon and Protestant foundation."[4] Everyone speaks the same language. According to this view, America belongs to Caucasians and non-Europeans cannot be accepted as "Americans." All people of color are considered as culturally and intellectually inferior people. Paradigm II, "Melting Pot Assimilationism," sees America as the result of constant interactions between different cultures, with origins from Europe, Asia, Africa, and other countries. In these interactions, one culture crosses over another and "they begin at some point to join together to create one large heterogeneous mixture."[5] "Through the relationship with other melting pot citizens, one ceases at some point to perceive oneself in any terms other than 'American.' Individual ties to ethnic groups culturally rooted in other parts of the world are not considered important or relevant."[6]

These ties are even viewed as potentially disruptive forces and obstacles in the way of creating a "melted-together foundational understanding of what it means to be an American."[7] It is envisioned that all original ethnic cultures and traditions will be melted away. The common language is an Americanized form of English. Paradigm III, "Ethnic Nationalism," keeps the pluralistic view, suggesting "that each ethnic group, regardless of origin, should preserve its unique character, customs, languages, and ways of knowing without being assimilated."[8] The English language is taught alongside other ethnic languages. Paradigm IV, "Globalism," suggests that instead of thinking only in terms of what could hold American people together, the entire Planet Earth should be thought of. This position states "that the increasing economic, ecological, and political interconnectedness of modern

---

4. Rod Janzen, "Five Paradigms of Ethnic Relations," *Social Education* 58, no. 6 (1994): 349.

5. Ibid.

6. Ibid., 350.

7. Ibid.

8. Ibid.

life demands that we reach consensus on an international ideological and behavioral center which then forms the foundation for all world cultures."[9] This common cultural foundation would then provide a base for developing an American culture.

The last paradigm, Paradigm V, is called "Centered Pluralism." It "is a more conservative and pragmatic approach to pluralistic multiculturalism than that suggested by either ethnic nationalist or global paradigms."[10] It suggests that all Americans should speak a common language (English) and, at the same time, they are encouraged to keep their first languages (where it is relevant). Paradigm V suggests that all Americans should have a common multicultural literacy foundation and should be committed "to communal as well as individual socio-economic traditions, a mixture of capitalism and socialism."[11] It also promotes the establishment of a commitment to many traditional "American" beliefs and practices and, at the same time, recognition of "the integrity of all indigenous cultural identities."[12]

Paradigm II, "Melting Pot Assimilationism," was accepted in American society as a norm in interethnic relations for many years. However, it has recently been giving way more and more to other paradigms, especially Paradigm V, which allows much more ethnic diversity and culture tolerance than Paradigm II. This makes the lives of new immigrants easier because they are not forced to assimilate as quickly as in the past. However, it could create conditions where different ethnic groups, including Russians and Ukrainians, would stay as separate entities, called diasporas, for a longer time. This will keep them isolated from other language and culture groups and, as a result, hinder implementation of authentic mission outside of their own Russian/Ukrainian ethnic group. This paradigm encourages separatism between different ethnic groups that could become a barrier in cross-ethnic evangelism and social actions.

---

9. Ibid., 351.
10. Ibid., 353.
11. Ibid.
12. Ibid., 352.

8.4.A. Hindrances and Opportunities for Mission

8.4.3.A. New Opportunities for Missions as a Result of Political Changes in the World

New mission opportunities for Slavic Baptist immigrant churches have developed because of the political changes that have recently taken place in the world. A little over twenty years ago, when the Soviet Union was still in existence, it was impossible to even dream about the possibility for Baptist churches to do mission work both locally and abroad. Today, after the collapse of the USSR, such work is conducted by the various national Baptist Unions in Russia, in Ukraine, in Moldova, and in other countries. For Slavic Baptists in America, these changes opened the door for active mission work around the world. For many years, since its establishment in 1928, the PCSBA had very few possibilities of reaching Russian-speaking people outside of the US with the gospel. It was limited to publishing the newspaper *Our Days* and sending it to different countries, as well as radio broadcasts towards the territory of the Soviet Union using short-wave transmitters. This situation has changed dramatically since 1991. Almost unlimited opportunities for spreading the gospel in some (not all) republics of the former USSR have become available to PCSBA churches. Of course, the newly arrived immigrants to America immediately began providing their support for projects in their homeland. They supported pastors and missionaries in the cities and towns where they used to live. In addition, humanitarian aid sent by immigrants in America started to arrive back in their homeland. For the last twenty years, this support of the ministry and the poor in the republics of the former Soviet Union, provided by the PCSBA churches, has continued to take place. Also, for the last fifteen years, PCSBA churches have been sending their youth on short-term mission trips back to their homeland. This became possible because of restored political relationships between the republics of the former Soviet Union and the US, which allows the citizens and other Russian-speakers living in the US to visit these former Soviet countries. Today, young Russian-speaking people from ethnic Slavic churches in the US are traveling back to Russia, Ukraine, and other republics to participate in different mission projects, the most popular being conducting children or youth Christian camps. In order to be able to travel back to the homeland, young people in America raise funds for travel expenses and to help cover expenses related to running the camps. The young people, full of enthusiasm and excitement, use different ways to raise funds. They wash cars, bake and sell cookies, and more. Involvement in such mission projects helps young people grow spiritually.

However, mission opportunities do not exist only in the homeland. Because of political change, people in the republics of the former USSR have obtained the opportunity to travel abroad freely. This was not possible for at least sixty years before the collapse of the USSR. Today, because of difficult economic situations in the republics of the former USSR, which are also due to political changes, many people who live there are using this fresh freedom to travel abroad and go to Western Europe in search of a job. Millions of Russian-speaking people are currently living in Italy, Spain, Portugal, Greece, and other countries, legally and illegally, with hopes of finding a job, making enough money to support their families back home, and returning home one day. Most of these people do not know the Lord. As mentioned in section 8.3.3. of chapter 8, the PCSBA Mission Department has developed a vision for reaching these people with the gospel. Now, Slavic immigrants, who have become citizens of the USA, can travel freely to any European country and share the gospel with the Russian-speaking immigrants who came to Western Europe seeking jobs. This mission opportunity was recently discovered by the PCSBA Mission Department and has become one of the highest priorities in its ministry.

Mission opportunities for Slavic immigrant churches are not limited to the areas of the world where Russian-speaking people reside. By now, young people in Slavic churches are fluent in English, so they could go to any country where English is used or can be translated into the native language. As American citizens, the Slavic youth could go to different countries and could participate in mission work that is not necessarily related to Russian-speaking people. Currently, young and middle-aged people from the PCSBA churches are participating in a humanitarian project designed to help people after the earthquake in Haiti. Funds to buy aid are raised in the Slavic churches in America, and short-term mission teams are going to Haiti to distribute the aid. Nurses from Slavic immigrant churches are traveling there to provide basic medical assistance to sick Haitians. They use English to communicate with people there. Another project that the PCSBA churches are involved in is in Mexico, a country that uses neither Russian nor English as its main language. However, believers from Slavic churches are going there to provide humanitarian aid, preach the gospel through the use of interpreters, and even provide theological training to the Mexican church leaders. Some people in Slavic churches have learned Spanish and serve as translators. There is no doubt that new mission opportunities around the world will occur for the Slavic immigrants in America in the future.

Bibliography

Abelmann, Nancy. "Christian Universalism and U.S. Multiculturalism: An 'Asian American' Campus Church." *Amerasia Journal* 34, no. 1 (2008): 65–84.
Akresh, Ilana Redstone. "Immigrants' Religious Participation in the United States." *Ethnic & Racial Studies* 34, no. 4 (April 2011): 643–661.
Allen, Roland. *Missionary Methods: St. Paul's or Ours?* London: World Dominion Press, 1930.
All-Union Council of Evangelical Christians-Baptists. *Istoriya Evangel'skikh Khristian-Baptistov v SSSR*. Moscow: AUCECB Publications, 1989.
Allport, G. W. *The Nature of Prejudice*. Garden City, NY: Anchor/Doubleday, 1954.
Almanac for the PCSBA 74th Convention. Sacramento, CA: PCSBA, 2011.
Almanac for the PCSBA 75th Convention. Sacramento, CA: PCSBA, 2012.
American Association for Russian Language, Culture and Education. "Russian Population and Statistics." AARCE. http://www.aarce.org/index.php/en/russian-culture-in-us/statistics. Accessed April 2012.
Anderson, Alan B., and James S. Frideres. *Ethnicity in Canada: Theoretical Perspectives*. Toronto: Butterworths, 1981.
Anderson, David A. *Multicultural Ministry*. Grand Rapids, MI: Zondervan, 2004.
Andronovienė, Lina, and Parush R. Parushev. "Church, State, and Culture: On the Complexities of Post-Soviet Evangelical Social Involvement." *Theological Reflections: EAAA Journal of Theology* 3 (2004): 174–227 (in English, Russian and Lithuanian).
Annual Report of the PCSBA Leadership Board for 2007–2008. Sacramento, CA: PCSBA, 2008.
Arias, Mortimer. "Rethinking the Great Commission." *Theology Today* 47, no 4 (Jan 1991): 410–418.
Asamoah-Gyadu, J. Kwabena. "Unwanted Sectarians: Spirit, Migration and Mission in an African-Led Mega-Size Church in Eastern Europe." *Evangelical Review of Theology* 34, no. 1 (Jan 2010): 71–78.

Baeq, Daniel Shinjong, Myunghee Lee, Sokpyo Hong, and Jonathan Ro. "Mission from Migrant Church to Ethnic Minorities: A Brief Assessment of the Korean American Church in Mission." *Missiology* 39, no. 1 (Jan 2011): 25–37.

Bailey, James L. "Church as Embodiment of Jesus' Mission (Matthew 9:36 – 10:39)." *Currents in Theology and Mission* 30, no. 3 (June 2003): 189–196.

Bangkok Assembly 1973. New York: WCC, 1973.

Barnett, Paul. *Jesus and the Rise of Early Christianity: A History of New Testament Times*. Downers Grove, IL: InterVarsity, 1999.

Bassham, Rodger C. *Mission Theology, 1948–1975: Years of Worldwide Creative Tension – Ecumenical, Evangelical, and Roman Catholic*. Pasadena, CA: William Carey Library, 1979.

Bevans, Stephen B. *Models of Contextual Theology*. Rev. and expanded ed. Maryknoll, NY: Orbis, 2002.

———, and Roger P. Schroeder. *Constants in Context: A Theology of Mission for Today*. Maryknoll, NY: Orbis, 2004.

Beyer, Gregg A. "The Evolving United States Response to Soviet Jewish Emigration." *Journal of Palestine Studies* 21, no. 1 (Autumn 1991): 141.

Beyerhaus, Peter. *Missions: Which Way? Humanization or Redemption*. Grand Rapids, MI: Zondervan, 1974.

———. *Shaken Foundations: Theological Foundations for Mission*. Grand Rapids, MI: Zondervan, 1972.

Boltniew, George. "A Functional Analysis of Ethnic/Bilingual Baptist Churches Ministering to Russian-Speaking Immigrants in the USA." DMin. diss., Eastern Baptist Theological Seminary, 1986.

Bonk, Jonathan. *Between Past and Future: Evangelical Mission Entering the Twenty-First Century*. Pasadena, CA: William Carey Library, 2003.

Bosch, David J. *Transforming Mission: Paradigm Shifts in Theology of Mission*. Maryknoll, NY: Orbis, 1991.

Bowh Si, Oliver Byar. "Mission as Transformation: An Exploration of the Relationship between Mission and Development." *International Review of Mission* 97, no. 384/385 (Jan–Apr 2008): 91–102.

Bowker, John, ed. *The Oxford Dictionary of World Religions*. New York: Oxford University Press, 1997.

Bria, Ion, ed. "Go Forth in Peace." In *Orthodox Perspectives on Mission*. Geneva: World Council of Churches, 1986.

Cadge, Wendy. "Immigration and Religion." *Annual Review of Sociology* 33, no. 1 (2007): 359–379.

Castro, Emilio. "Themes in Theology of Mission Arising Out of San Antonio and Canberra." In *The Good News of the Kingdom: Mission Theology for the Third*

Millennium, edited by Charles Van Engen, Dean S. Gilliland, and Paul Pierson, 127–136. Maryknoll, NY: Orbis, 1993.

Chang, Chul Tim. "A History of the Korean Immigrant Baptist Church Movement in the United States." *Baptist History and Heritage* 40, no 1 (Winter 2005): 58–64.

Chuang, T. K. "The Chinese Church in Greater Boston." *Emmanuel Gospel Center*. http://www.egc.org/chinese. Accessed May 2013.

Chung, Paul S. "Engaging God's Mission and Diakonia in Life of Public Spheres: Justification and Economic Justice." *Dialog: Journal of Theology* 49, no. 2 (Summer 2010): 141–154.

Church of the Brethren Annual Conference. "Creation: Called to Care." *Church of the Brethren Annual Conference Official Documents*. http://www.brethren.org/ac/statements/1991creationcalledtocare.html. Accessed March 2012.

Church of the Brethren General Board. "Resolution on Global Warming and Atmospheric Degradation." 21 October 1991. http://support.brethren.org/site/DocServer/1991/Global_Warming_and_Atmospheric_Degradation.pdf?docID=922. Accessed August 2010.

The Church for Others, and the Church for the World: A Quest for Structures for Missionary Congregations. Final Report of the Western European Working Group and North American Working Group of the Department on Studies in Evangelism. Geneva: World Council of Churches, 1967.

Collinson, Sylvia Wilkey. "Making Disciples and the Christian Faith." *Evangelical Review of Theology* 29, no. 3 (July 2005): 240–250.

Consultation on World Evangelization. "The Thailand Statement." *Consultation on World Evangelism, Pattaya, Thailand, June 16–17, 1980*. Thailand, 1980. http://www.lausanne.org/en/documents/all/pattaya-1980/49-thailand-statement.html. Accessed February 2012.

Corrie, John. *Models of Mission in the 20C*. https://www.scribd.com/document/179134545/corrie-models-of-mission-in-20C-pdf. Accessed April 2013.

Coser, Lewis A., ed. *On Work, Race and the Sociological Imagination*. Chicago: University of Chicago Press, 1994.

Cruz, Gemma Tulud. "Expanding the Boundaries, Turning Borders into Spaces: Mission in the Context of Contemporary Migration." In *Mission After Christendom: Emergent Themes in Contemporary Mission*, edited by Obgu U. Kalu, Peter Vethanayagamony, and Edmund Kee-Fook Chia, 71–86. Louisville, KY: Westminster John Knox, 2010.

De Neui, Paul H. "Christian Communities in the *Missio Dei*: Living Faithfully in the Tension between Cultural Osmosis and Alienation." *Ex Auditu* 23 (2007): 92–107.

Deymaz, Mark, and Harry Li. *Ethnic Blends: Mixing Diversity into Your Local Church*. Grand Rapids, MI: Zondervan, 2010.

DeYoung, Curtiss Paul, Michael O. Emerson, George Yancey, and Karen Chai Kim. *United By Faith: The Multiracial Congregation as an Answer to the Problem of Race*. New York: Oxford University Press, 2003.

Dhingra, Pawan. "We're Not a Korean American Church Any More: Dilemmas in Constructing a Multi-Racial Church Identity." *Social Compass* 51, no. 3 (Sep 2004): 367–379.

Dietterich, Inagrace T. "A Vision for the Sending of the Church in North America." *Missiology* 38, no. 1 (Jan 2010): 27–36.

Donovan, Peter. *Religious Language*. New York: Hawthorn Books, 1976.

Doucet, Fabienne. "Divergent Realities: The Home and School Lives of Haitian Immigrant Youth." *Journal of Youth Ministry* 3, no. 2 (Spring 2005): 37–65.

Dougherty, Kevin. "*Missio Dei*: The Trinity and Christian Missions." *Evangelical Review of Theology* 31, no. 2 (Apr 2007): 151–168.

———, and Kimberly R. Huyser. "Racially Diverse Congregations: Organizational Identity and the Accommodation of Differences." *Journal for the Scientific Study of Religion* 47, no. 1 (Mar 2008): 23–44.

Dowling, Maurice. "Baptists in the Twentieth-Century Tsarist Empire and the Soviet Union." In *The Gospel in the World: International Baptist Studies*, edited by D. W. Bebbington, 209–232. Carlisle: Paternoster, 2002.

———. "Russian Baptists and the Cold War." Presentation at the Andrew Fuller Conference: "Baptists and War." September 2011. MP3.

Driver, John. "The Kingdom of God: Goal of Messianic Mission." In *The Transfiguration of Mission: Biblical, Theological and Historical Foundations*, edited by Wilbert R. Shenk. Scottdale, PA: Herald, 1993.

Ducker, Christopher. "Explain the Thinking Behind Mission as Missio Dei." http://www.theduckers.org/media/missio%20dei.pdf. Accessed May 2012.

Dulles, Avery. *Models of the Church*. Garden City, NY: Image Books, 1991.

Duraisingh, Christopher. "From Church-Shaped Mission to Mission-Shaped Church." *Anglican Theological Review* 92, no. 1 (Winter 2010): 7–28.

Dyck, Johannes. "Moulding the Brotherhood: Johann Wieler (1839–1889) and the Communities of the Early Evangelicals in Russia." MTh thesis, International Baptist Theological Seminary, University of Wales, 2007.

Ebaugh, Helen Rose, and Janet Saltzman Chafetz. *Religion and the New Immigrants: Continuities and Adaptations in Immigrant Congregations*. Walnut Creek, CA: AltaMira, 2000.

"Edinburgh 2010." *Mission Studies: Journal of the International Association for Mission Studies* 27, no. 2 (2010): 141–143.

Ekstrom, Bertil. "The Kingdom of God and the Church Today." *Evangelical Review of Theology* 27, no. 4 (Oct 2003): 292–305.

Elias, Nelly. "Russian-Speaking Immigrants and Their Media: Still Together?" *Israel Affairs* 17, no. 1 (Jan 2011): 72–88.

Elliott, Mark R. "The Current Crisis in Protestant Theological Education in the Former Soviet Union." *Religion in Eastern Europe* 30, no. 4 (Nov 2010): 1–22.

———. "Protestant Missions in Russia Today." *East–West Church & Ministry Report* 13, no. 4 (Fall 2005): 1–5.

Emerson, Michael O., and Christian Smith. *Divided By Faith: Evangelical Religion and the Problem of Race in America*. New York: Oxford University Press, 2000.

Engelsviken, Tormod. "*Missio dei*: The Understanding and Misunderstanding of a Theological Concept in European Churches and Missiology." *International Review of Mission* 92, no. 367 (2003): 481–497.

"Famous Russian-Americans." *The Russian American Cultural Heritage Center*. http://www.rach-c.org/pages/russianamericans.htm. Accessed November 2012.

"Fast Facts about American Religion." *Hartford Institute for Religion Research*. http://hirr.hartsem.edu/research/fastfacts/fast_facts.html#multiracial. Accessed June 2013.

Flemming, Dean. *Contextualization in the New Testament: Patterns for Theology and Mission*. Downers Grove, IL: IVP Academic, 2005.

Foust, Thomas F., George R. Hunsberger, J. Andrew Kirk, and Werner Ustorf, eds. *A Scandalous Prophet: The Way of Mission after Newbigin*. Grand Rapids, MI: Eerdmans, 2002.

Frambach, Nathan C. P. "Being Church Today: Living God's Mission Where We Are." *Currents in Theology and Mission* 37, no. 1 (Feb 2010): 4–11.

Friesen, Bert. "Approaches to the Interpretation and Application of the Sermon on the Mount." *Direction* 10, no. 2 (Apr 1981): 19–26.

Fuliga, Jose B. "Factors Contributing to the De-Christianization of North America." *Asia Journal of Theology* 24, no. 1 (Apr 2010): 3–16.

Furnham, Adrian, and Stephen Bochner. *Culture Shock: Psychological Reactions to Unfamiliar Environments*. New York: Methuen, 1986.

Garces-Foley, Kathleen. *Crossing the Ethnic Divide: The Multiethnic Church on a Mission*. New York: Oxford University Press, 2007.

"George Kistiakowsky (1900–1982)." *Atomicarchive.com*. http://www.atomicarchive.com/Bios/Kistiakowsky.shtml. Accessed November 2012.

Glasser, Arthur F., with Charles E. Van Engen, Dean S. Gilliland, and Shawn B. Redford. *Announcing the Kingdom: The Story of God's Mission in the Bible*. Grand Rapids, MI: Baker Academic, 2003.

Glasser, Arthur F., and Donald A. McGavran. *Contemporary Theologies of Mission*. Grand Rapids, MI: Baker, 1983.

Gleason, Philip. *Speaking of Diversity: Language and Ethnicity in Twentieth-Century America*. Baltimore, MD: Johns Hopkins University Press, 1992.

Goheen, Michael W. "The Future of Mission in the World Council of Churches: The Dialogue between Lesslie Newbigin and Konrad Raiser." *Mission Studies: Journal of the International Association for Mission Studies* 21, no. 1 (2004): 97–111.

Golovashchenko, S. I., ed. "Pervye shagi evangelskogo dvizheniya na Ukraine: vozniknoveniye, rasprostranenie." In *Istoria evangelsko-baptistskogo dvizheniya v Ukraine: Materily i document. Source: Istorija Evangel'skogo Dvizhenija v Evrazii*, disc 1.0 [*The History of the Evangelical Movement in Eurasia*, disc 1.0]. Odessa, Ukraine: EAAA, 2001. CD.

Greek Orthodox Archdiocese of America. "Orthodox Perspectives on Creation." Extracts from the report of the WCC Inter-Orthodox Consultation, Sofia, Bulgaria, October 1987. http://goarch.org/ourfaith/ourfaith8050. Accessed August 2010.

The Greek Orthodox Church of the Holy Cross. "The Orthodox Faith and Tradition: Orthodox Liturgical Worship." http://www.goholycross.org/studies/studies_liturgical.html. Accessed 11 June 2012.

Gregorios, Paulos Mar. "The Witness of the Churches: Ecumenical Statements on Mission and Evangelism." *The Ecumenical Review* 40, no. 3–4 (July–Oct 1988): 359–366.

Groody, Daniel G. "Crossing the Divide: Foundations of a Theology of Migration and Refugees." *Theological Studies* 70, no. 3 (Sep 2009): 638–667.

Guder, Darrell L. "*Missio Dei*: Integrating Theological Formation for Apostolic Vocation." *Missiology* 37, no. 1 (Jan 2009): 63–74.

———. *Missional Church: A Vision for the Sending of the Church in North America*. Grand Rapids, MI: Eerdmans, 1998.

Gunther, Wolfgang, and Guillermo Cook. "World Missionary Conferences." *Dictionary of Mission: Theology, History, Perspectives*. Maryknoll, NY: Orbis, 1999.

Gushiken, Kevin. "Spiritual Formation and Multiethnic Congregations." *Journal of Spiritual Formation & Soul Care* 4, no. 2 (Fall 2011): 185–203.

Hagan, Jacqueline Maria. "The Church vs. the State." In *Religion and Social Justice for Immigrants*, edited by Pierrette Hondagneu-Sotelo, 93–103. New Brunswick, NJ: Rutgers University Press, 2006.

Hanciles, Jehu. *Beyond Christendom: Globalization, African Migration, and the Transformation of the West*. Maryknoll, NY: Orbis, 2009.

———. "Migration and Mission: Some Implications for the Twenty-First-Century Church." *International Bulletin of Missionary Research* 27, no. 4 (2003): 146–152.

Handlin, Oscar. *The Uprooted*. Boston: Little, Brown, 1951.

Hardwick, Susan Wiley. *Russian Refuge: Religion, Migration, and Settlement on the North American Pacific Rim.* Chicago: University of Chicago Press, 1993.

Harvey, John D. "Mission in Matthew." In *Mission in the New Testament*, edited by William J. Larkin and Joel F. Williams, n.p. Maryknoll, NY: Orbis, 2002.

Hayes, Stephen. "Orthodox Diaspora and Mission in South Africa." *Studies in World Christianity* 16, no. 3 (2010): 286–303.

Hedlund, Roger E. *The Mission of the Church in the World: A Biblical Theology.* Grand Rapids, MI: Baker, 1991.

———. *Roots of the Great Debate in Mission.* Madras, India: Evangelical Literature Service, 1981.

Hesselgrave, David J., and Edward Rommen, eds. *Contextualization: Meanings, Methods, and Models.* Leicester: Inter-Varsity, 1989.

Hibbert, Richard Yates. "The Place of Church Planting in Mission: Towards a Theological Framework." *Evangelical Review of Theology* 33, no. 4 (Oct 2009): 316–331.

Hill, Kent R. *The Soviet Union on the Brink: An Inside Look at Christianity and Glasnost.* Portland, OR: Multnomah, 1991.

"History of Slavic Baptists of California." In *Official Attachment to the Minutes of the PCSBA Board Meeting on February 16, 1952, Brite, CA*, held in the PCSBA Archive, Sacramento, CA.

Hogan, Linda, Solange Lefebvre, Norbert Hintersteiner, and Felix Wilfred, eds. *From World Mission to Inter-religious Witness (Concilium).* London: SCM, 2011.

Hondagneu-Sotelo, Pierrette. "Religion and a Standpoint Theory of Immigrant Social Justice." In *Religion and Social Justice for Immigrants*, 3–15. New Brunswick, NJ: Rutgers University Press, 2006.

Howell, Brian M. "Multiculturalism, Immigration and the North American Church: Rethinking Contextualization." *Missiology* 39, no. 1 (Jan 2011): 79–85.

Hughes, Dewi. "Following Jesus as His Community in the Broken World of Ethnic Identity." *Evangelical Review of Theology* 31, no. 4 (Oct 2007): 331–341.

Hunter III, George G. "The Case for Culturally Relevant Congregations." *Global Good News: Mission in a New Context*, edited by Howard A. Snyder, 96–112. Nashville, TN: Abingdon Press, 2001.

———. *Church for the Unchurched.* Nashville, TN: Abingdon Press, 1996.

Huntington, Samuel P. *Who Are We? The Challenges to America's National Identity.* New York: Simon & Schuster, 2004.

Hurh, Won Moo, and Kwang Chung Kim. "Religious Participation of Korean Immigrants in the United States." *Journal for the Scientific Study of Religion* 29, no. 1 (Mar 1990): 19–34.

"Immigration: Polish/Russian." *Library of Congress.* http://www.loc.gov/teachers/classroommaterials/presentationsandactivities/presentations/immigration/polish.html. Accessed October 2011.

International Missionary Council. *The Missionary Obligation of the Church, Willingen, Germany, July 5–17, 1952.* Edinburgh House Press, 1952.

"Issue 1 Report: Witnessing in a Divided World." *International Review of Mission* 72, no. 288 (Oct 1983): 650–660.

Istorija Evangel'skogo Dvizhenija v Evrazii, disc 1.0 [*The History of the Evangelical Movement in Eurasia*, disc 1.0]. Odessa, Ukraine: EAAA, 2001.

Jackson, Paul R. *Doctrini i ustroy'stvo baptistskikh tserkvey'.* Schaumburg, IL: Regular Baptist Press, 1980.

Janzen, Rod. "Five Paradigms of Ethnic Relations." *Social Education* 58, no. 6 (1994): 349–353.

Jayakumar, Samuel. "The Work of God as Holistic Mission: An Asian Perspective." *Evangelical Review of Theology* 35, no. 3 (July 2011): 227–241.

Jongeneel, J. A. B. "The Mission of Migrant Churches in Europe." *Missiology* 31, no. 1 (Jan 2003): 29–33.

Kane, J. Herbert. *A Concise History of the Christian World Mission: A Panoramic View of Missions from Pentecost to the Present.* Rev. ed. Grand Rapids, MI: Baker Academic, 1982.

Kang, Ezer, John J. Chin, and Elan Behar. "Faith-Based HIV Care and Prevention in Chinese Immigrant Communities: Rhetoric or Reality?" *Journal of Psychology & Theology* 39, no. 3 (Fall 2011): 268–279.Kavunkal, Jacob. "Mission or Evangelization?" *Mission Studies: Journal of the International Association for Mission Studies* 21, no. 1 (2004): 55–64.

Keener, Crag S. *The Gospel of Matthew.* Grand Rapids, MI: Eerdmans, 2009.

Kim, Kirsteen. "Missiology as Global Conversation of (Contextual) Theologies." *Mission Studies: Journal of the International Association for Mission Studies* 21, no. 1 (2004): 39–53.

———. "Mission Theology of the Church." *International Review of Mission* 99, no. 1 (Apr 2010): 39–55.

Kim, Sharon. "Shifting Boundaries within Second-Generation Korean American Churches." *Sociology of Religion* 71, no. 1 (Spring 2010): 98–122.

Kirk, J. Andrew. *The Good News of the Kingdom Coming: The Marriage of Evangelism and Social Responsibility.* Downers Grove, IL: InterVarsity, 1983.

———. *The Mission of Theology and Theology of Mission.* Valley Forge, PA: Trinity Press International, 1997.

———. *Mission Under Scrutiny: Confronting Contemporary Challenges.* Minneapolis, MN: Fortress, 2006.

———. *What Is Mission? Theological Explorations.* Minneapolis, MN: Fortress, 2000.

———, and Kevin J. Vanhoozer, eds. *To Stake a Claim: Mission and the Western Crisis of Knowledge.* Maryknoll, NY: Orbis, 1999.

Kisskalt, Michael. "Cross-Cultural Learning: Issues of the Second Generation of Immigrant Churches." In *Ethnic Churches in Europe: A Baptist Response*, edited by Peter Penner, 134–142. Schwarzenfeld: Neufeld Verlag, 2006.

Klassen, Heinrich. "Mission as Bearing Witness: Immigrant Witness in Germany." In *Anabaptism and Mission,* edited by Wilbert R. Shenk and Peter F. Penner. Prague: IBTS , 2007.

Koll, Karla Ann. "Taking Wolves Among Lambs: Some Thoughts on Training for Short-Term Mission Facilitation." *International Bulletin of Missionary Research* 34, no. 2 (Apr 2010): 93–96.

Korrado, Sheril. *Philosophiya sluzheniya polkovnika Pashkova.* St Petersburg: Bibliya dlya Vsekh, 2005.

Kotin, Stephanie. "Immigration and Integration: Religious and Political Activism for/with Immigrants in Los Angeles." *Progress in Development Studies* 11, no. 4 (July 2011): 263–284.

Krabill, James R., Walter Sawatsky, and Charles E. Van Engen, eds. *Evangelical, Ecumenical, and Anabaptist Missiologies in Conversation: Essays in Honor of Wilbert R. Shenk.* Maryknoll, NY: Orbis, 2006.

Kraft, Charles H. *Communication Theory for Christian Witness.* Maryknoll, NY: Orbis, 2002.

———. "Contextualizing Communication." In *The Word Among Us,* edited by Dean S. Gilliland, n.p. Dallas: Word, 1989.

Krapivin, M., A. Leykin, and A. Dalgatov. *Sud'by Khristianskogo Sektanstva v Sovetskoy Rossii (1917 – konets 1930-kh godov).* St. Petersburg: State University, 2003.

Kraybill, Donald B. "Modernity and Identity: The Transformation of Mennonite Ethnicity." In *Mennonite Identity: Historical and Contemporary Perspectives,* edited by Sam Steiner and Calvin Redekop, 153–172. Lanham, MD: University Press of America, 1988.

———. *The Upside-Down Kingdom.* Scottdale, PA: Herald, 2003.

Kruchkov, Yuriy Konstantinovich. *140-letnyaya istoriya tserkvi EXB na Rusi v svete bibleyskikh istin.* Sacramento, CA: Brothers Printing, 2010.

Kurylowicz, Roberto Zub. *Tierra, Trabajo y Religion: Memoria de los Inmigrantes Eslavos en el Paraguay.* Translated by Elizabeth Orellana. Asunción, Paraguay: El Lector, 2004.

Ladd, George E. *The Gospel of the Kingdom.* Grand Rapids, MI: Eerdmans, 1971.

———. *A Theology of the New Testament.* Grand Rapids, MI: Eerdmans, 1974.

Laing, Mark T. B. "*Missio Dei*: Some Implications for the Church." In *Missiology* 37, no. 1 (Jan 2009): 89–99.

Larkin Jr., William J. "Mission in Luke." In *Mission in the New Testament*, edited by William J. Larkin, Jr. and Joel F. Williams, 152-169. Maryknoll, NY: Orbis, 2002.

Lausanne Committee for World Evangelization and the World Evangelical Fellowship. "LOP 1: The Pasadena Consultation – Homogeneous Unit Principle." *Lausanne Movement*. Lausanne Committee for World Evangelization, 1978. http://www.lausanne.org/en/documents/lops/71-lop-1.html. Accessed March 2012.

———. "LOP 21: Evangelism and Social Responsibility: An Evangelical Commitment." *Lausanne Movement*. A Joint Publication of the Lausanne Committee for World Evangelization and the World Evangelical Fellowship. Grand Rapids, MI, 1982. http://www.lausanne.org/en/documents/lops/79-lop-21.html. Accessed February 2012.

"The Lausanne Covenant." In *Making Christ Known*, edited by John Stott. Grand Rapids, MI: Eerdmans, 1996.

The Lausanne Movement. http://www.lausanne.org/. Accessed May 2013.

———. *The Cape Town Commitment*. 2010. http://www.lausanne.org/en/documents/ctcommitment.html#p2-1. Accessed May 2013.

———. "The Cape Town Commitment: A Confession of Faith and a Call to Action." *International Bulletin of Missionary Research* 35, no. 2 (Apr 2011): 59–80.

Lee, Gil Pyo. "From Traditional to Missional Church: Describing a Contextual Model of Change for Ingrown Korean Diaspora Church in North America." DMis diss., Asbury Theological Seminary, 2010.

Lefebvre, Solange, and Luiz Carlos Susin, eds. *Migration in a Global World*. London: SCM, 2008.

Leonard, Karen I., Alex Stepick, Manuel A. Vasquez, and Jennifer Holdaway. *Immigrant Faiths*. Lanham, MD: AltaMira, 2006.

"Letter of the Secretary of the Association, N. Pavlyuk, to Churches, 12.06.1939." PCSBA Archive, Sacramento, CA.

Levin, Zalman I. *Mentality of Diaspora: Systematic and Socio-cultural Analysis*. Moscow: Kraft, 2001.

Levitt, Peggy. "Between God, Ethnicity, and Country: An Approach to the Study of Transnational Religion." Paper presented at workshop on "Transnational Migration: Comparative Perspectives," Princeton University, 30 June–1 July 2001, 1–31.

———. *God Needs No Passport: Immigrants and the Changing American Religious Landscape*. New York: New Press, 2007.

Liven, Sofiya. *Dukhovnoe probuzhdeniye v Rossii: Vospominaniya*. Korntal: Svet na Vostoke, 1990.

Livinson, David, and Melvin Ember. *American Immigrant Cultures: Builders of a Nation*. New York: Simon & Schuster Macmillan, 1997.

Lu, Yaxin, Loren Marks, and Loredana Apavaloiae. "Chinese Immigrant Families and Christian Faith Community: A Qualitative Study." *Family and Consumer Sciences Research Journal* 41, no. 2 (Dec 2012): 118–130.

Ma, Wonsuk. "Grace Korean Church, Fullerton, California: Mission from the Margins." *International Bulletin of Missionary Research* 36, no. 2 (Apr 2012): 65–71.

Magocsi, Paul Robert. "Russian Americans." *Countries and Their Cultures*. http://www.everyculture.com/multi/Pa-Sp/Russian-Americans.html. Accessed April 2012.

Mar Gregorios, Paulos. "The Witness of the Churches: Ecumenical Statements on Mission and Evangelism." *Ecumenical Review* 40, no. 3–4 (July–Oct 1988): 359–366.

Marti, Gerardo. "Affinity, Identity, and Transcendence: The Experience of Religious Racial Integration in Diverse Congregations." *Journal for the Scientific Study of Religion* 48, no. 1 (March 2009): 53–68.

———. "Fluid Ethnicity and Ethnic Transcendence in Multiracial Churches." *Journal for the Scientific Study of Religion* 47, no. 1 (March 2008): 11–16.

———. *A Mosaic of Believers: Diversity and Innovation in a Multiethnic Church*. Bloomington, IN: Indiana University Press, 2005.

Matthey, Jacques. "God's Mission Today: Summary and Conclusions." *International Review of Mission* 92, no. 367 (2003): 579–587.

———. "Missiology in the World Council of Churches: Update. Presentation, Theological Background and Emphases of the Most Recent Mission Statement of the World Council of Churches (WCC)." *International Review of Mission* 90, no. 359 (Oct 2001): 427–443.

———. "Serving God's Mission Together in Christ's Way: Reflections on the Way to Edinburgh 2010." *International Review of Mission* 99, no. 1 (Apr 2010): 21–38.

Maydell-Stevens, Elena, Anne-Marie Masgoret, and Tony Ward. "Problems of Psychological and Sociocultural Adaptation Among Russian-Speaking Immigrants in New Zealand." *Social Policy Journal of New Zealand* 30 (March 2007): 178–198.

McArthur, Harvey King. *Understanding the Sermon on the Mount*. Westport, CT: Greenwood Press, 1978.

McGavran, Donald. *Church Growth and Christian Mission*. New York: Harper & Row, 1965.

———. *Ethnic Realities and the Church: Lessons from India*. South Pasadena, CA: William Carey Library, 1979.

———. "The Frankfurt Declaration on Mission." In *The Conciliar-Evangelical Debate: The Crucial Documents 1964–1976*, edited by Donald McGavran, 283–293. Pasadena, CA: William Carey Library, 1977.

———. *Understanding Church Growth*. Grand Rapids, MI: Eerdmans, 1990.

———. "Will Uppsala Betray the Two Billion?" In *The Conciliar-Evangelical Debate: The Crucial Documents 1964–1976*, edited by Donald McGavran, n.p. Pasadena, CA: William Carey Library, 1977.

Menjivar, Cecilia. "Religion and Immigration in Comparative Perspective: Catholic and Evangelical Salvadorans in San Francisco, Washington, D.C., and Phoenix." *Sociology of Religion* 64, no. 1 (Spring 2003): 21–45.

Mennonite Church USA. *Confession of Faith in a Mennonite Perspective, 1995*. Wichita, KS: Historical Committee, 1995. http://www.mcusa-archives.org/library/resolutions/1995/1995-9.html. Accessed January 2011.

———. *Mennonite Confession of Faith, 1963*. Kalona, IA: Historical Committee, 1963. http://www.mcusa-archives.org/library/resolutions/1963confession.html. Accessed December 2010.

———. "Vision for Witness, 1983." *Seventh Mennonite Church General Assembly*. Bethlehem, PA: Lehigh University, August 1983. http://www.mcusa-archives.org/library/resolutions/visionforwitness.html. Accessed November 2010.

Mennonite Creation Care Network. "Annual Report 2008." http://blog.goshen.edu/creationcare/2008/12/31/annual-report-2008/. Accessed December 2008.

Middleton, DeWight R. *The Challenge of Human Diversity: Mirrors, Bridges, and Chasms*. Prospect Heights, IL: Waveland, 1998.

Min, Pyong Gap. "Religion and the Maintenance of Ethnicity among Immigrants." In *Immigrant Faiths*, edited by Karen I. Leonard, Alex Stepick, Manuel A. Vasquez, and Jennifer Holdaway, n.p. Lanham, MD: AltaMira, 2006.

"Minutes of the 2nd PCSBA Convention (1939)." PCSBA Archive, Sacramento, CA.

"Minutes of the 3rd PCSBA Convention (1940)." PCSBA Archive, Sacramento, CA.

"Minutes of the 4th PCSBA Convention (1941)." PCSBA Archive, Sacramento, CA.

"Minutes of the 7th PCSBA Convention (1944)." PCSBA Archive, Sacramento, CA.

"Minutes of the 31st PCSBA Convention (1968)." PCSBA Archive, Sacramento, CA.

"Minutes of the 60th PCSBA Convention (1997)." PCSBA Archive, Sacramento, CA.

Moltmann, Jürgen. *The Church in the Power of the Spirit: A Contribution to Messianic Ecclesiology.* London: SCM, 1977.

Moreau, A. Scott. "Holistic Contextualization: Ensuring That Every Facet of Christian Faith Is Localized." In *Mission to the World*, edited by Tormod Engelsviken, Ernst Harbakk, Rolv Olsen, and Thor Strangenaes, 193–204. Oxford: Oxford Centre for Mission Studies, 2008.

———, Gary R. Corwin, and Gary B. McGee. *Introducing World Missions: A Biblical, Historical, and Practical Survey.* Grand Rapids, MI: Baker Academic, 2004.

Nevolin, Michael. *Raskol evangel'sko-baptistskogo dvizheniya v SSSR (1959-1963 gody).* St Petersburg: Shandal, 2005.

Newbigin, Lesslie. *The Gospel in a Pluralist Society.* Grand Rapids, MI: Eerdmans, 1989.

———. *The Open Secret: An Introduction to the Theology of Mission.* Grand Rapids, MI: Eerdmans, 1995.

———. *The Relevance of Trinitarian Doctrine for Today's Mission.* WCC Commission on World Evangelism. London: Edinburgh House, 1963.

———. *Trinitarian Faith and Today's Mission.* Richmond, VA: John Knox Press, 1964.

The New Delhi Report. New York: Association Press, 1962.

Nicholls, Bruce J. *Contextualization: A Theology of Gospel and Culture.* Downers Grove, IL: Regent College Publishing, 2003.

Nikol'skaya, Tat'yana. *Russkij protestantizm i gosudarstvennaya vlast' v 1905–1991 godakh.* St Petersburg: Izdatel'stvo Evropeiskogo universiteta v Sankt-Peterburge, 2009.

Nkansah-Obrempong, James. "Holistic Gospel in a Developing Society: Biblical, Theological and Historical Backgrounds." *Evangelical Review of Theology* 33, no. 3 (July 2009): 196–212.

Orchard, Ronald K., ed., *Witness in Six Continents: Records of the Meeting of the Commission on World Mission and Evangelism of the World Council of Churches Held in Mexico City, Dec 8-19, 1963.* London: Edinburgh House, 1964.

Ortiz, Manuel. "Foreword." In Daniel A. Rodriguez, *A Future for the Latino Church: Models for Multilingual, Multigenerational Hispanic Congregations*, 9–10. Downers Grove, IL: IVP Academic, 2011.

"Otchet Predsedatelya Tikhookeanskogo ob'edineniya tserkvey ECB Bugrieyva Nikolaya Alekseevicha k 74-mu s'ezdy." In *Almanac for the PCSBA 74th Convention.* Sacramento, CA: PCSBA, 2011.

Ott, Craig, and Harold A. Netland. *Globalizing Theology: Belief and Practice in an Era of World Christianity.* Grand Rapids, MI: Baker Academic, 2006.

Ott, Craig, Stephen J. Strauss, and Timothy C. Tennent. *Encountering Theology of Mission: Biblical Foundations, Historical Developments, and Contemporary Issues*. Grand Rapids, MI: Baker Academic, 2010.

Padilla, C. René. *The New Face of Evangelism*. London: Hodder & Stoughton, 1976.

———. "The Unity of the Church and the Homogeneous Unit Principle." In *Exploring Church Growth*, edited by Wilbert R. Shenk. Grand Rapids, MI: Eerdmans, 1983.

Palomino, Miguel A. "Latino Immigration in Europe: Challenge and Opportunity for Mission." *The International Bulletin of Missionary Research* 28, no. 2 (Apr 2004): 54–59.

Parker, G. Keith. *Baptists in Europe: History and Confessions of Faith*. Nashville, TN: Broadman, 1982.

Parsons, Talcott. "Some Theoretical Considerations on the Nature and Trends of Change of Ethnicity." In *Ethnicity, Theory, Experience*, edited by N. Glazer and D. Moynihan. Cambridge, MA: Harvard University Press, 1975.

Parushev, Parush R. "Baptists and Jews and Judaism." In *A Dictionary of European Baptist Life and Thought*, edited by John H. Y. Briggs, 275–278. Studies in Baptist History and Thought, vol. 33. Milton Keynes: Paternoster, 2009.

———. *Christianity in Europe: The Way We Are Now. With a Response by Vija Herefoss*. The Crowther Centre Monographs Series, vol. 9. Oxford: Church Missionary Society, 2009.

———. "Embodied Visions: On Antisemitism and the Resilience of Goodness." In Zbyněk Tarant, Věra Tydlitatová et al., *Faces of Hatred: Contemporary Antisemitism in its Historical Context*, 7–44. Plzeň, Czech Republic: Fakulta Filozofická Západočeské Univerzity v Plzní, 2012.

———. "Emergence of Russian Orthodox Antisemitism." In *Anatomy of Hatred: Essays on Anti-Semitism*, edited by Věrá Tydlitátová and Alena Hanzová, 5–10. Plzeň, Czech Republic: Fakulta Filozofická Západočeské Univerzity v Plzni, 2009.

———. "Jews and Christians after the *Shoah*: Christian Theological Perspectives on the Future of the Jewish–Christian Relationship." In *Reflections on Anti-Semitism: Anti-Semitism in Historical and Anthropological Perspectives*, edited by Věrá Tydlitátová and Alena Hanzová, 35–44. Plzeň, Czech Republic: Fakulta Filozofická Západočeské Univerzity v Plzni, 2008.

———. "Narrative Paradigms of Emergence of an Ethno-centred Orthodox Theological Identity." *Religion in Eastern Europe* 25, no. 2 (May 2005): 1–39.

———. "Walking in the Dawn of the Light: On the Salvation Ethics of the Ecclesial Communities in the Orthodox Tradition from a Radical

Reformation Perspective." PhD diss., School of Theology, Fuller Theological Seminary, 2006.

———. "Witness, Worship and Presence: On the Integrity of Mission in Contemporary Europe." *Mission Studies* 24, no. 2 (2007): 305–332.

Pavlov, Vasiliy. *Baptisty: Tserkov i gosudarstvo.* Moscow: LOGOS Christian Center, 2004.

Penner, Hans H. "Why Does Semantics Matter?" In *Language, Truth, and Religious Belief*, edited by Nancy K. Frankenberry and Hans H. Penner, n.p. Atlanta: Scholars Press, 1999.

Penner, Peter. *Nauchite Vse Narody. Missiya bogoslovskogo obrazovaniya.* St. Petersburg: Bibliya Dlya Vseh, 1999.

Peters, George, and George W. Peters. *A Biblical Theology of Missions.* Chicago: Moody, 1984.

Phillips, James M., ed. *Toward the Twenty-First Century in Christian Mission: Essays in Honor of Gerald H. Anderson, Director, Overseas Ministries Study Center, New Haven, Connecticut, Editor, International Bulletin of Missionary Research.* Grand Rapids, MI: Eerdmans, 1993.

Pichaj, Adolf. "Brief History of the Bethany Baptist Church." In *100th Jubilee.* Los Angeles: Bethany Baptist Church of Los Angeles, 2010.

———. "70-tiletniy Yubiley Ob'edineniya Slavyanskikh Baptistov Tikhookeanskogo Poberezh'ya" ["Seventieth Jubilee of The Pacific Coast Slavic Baptist Association"]. *Vestnik Obyedineniya* 3 (Dec 1998): 1–11.

Pierson, Paul E. "Lessons in Mission from the Twentieth Century: Conciliar Missions." In *Between Past and Future: Evangelical Mission Entering the Twenty-First Century*, edited by Jonathan J. Bonk, 67–84. Pasadena, CA: William Carey Library, 2003.

Pope-Levison, Priscilla. "Evangelism in the WCC: From New Delhi to Canberra." In *New Directions in Mission and Evangelization 2*, edited by James A. Scherer and Stephen B. Bevans, n.p. Maryknoll, NY: Orbis, 1994.

Popov, Alexander. "The Evangelical Christians-Baptists in the Soviet Union as a Hermeneutical Community: Examining the Identity of the All-Union Council of the ECB (AUCECB) Through the Way the Bible Was Used in Its Publications." PhD diss., International Baptist Theological Seminary, University of Wales, 2011.

Portes, Alejandro, and Rubén G. Rumbaut. *Immigrant America: A Portrait.* 3rd ed. Berkeley, CA: University of California Press, 2006.

"President Issues FY 2011 Refugee Admissions Numbers and Authorizations." *Immigration.com.* 7 December 2010. http://www.immigration.com/news/refugee-and-political-asylum/president-issues-fy-2011-refugee-admissions-numbers-and-authorizat. Accessed April 2012.

Prill, Thorsten. "Migration, Mission, and the Multi-ethnic Church." *Evangelical Review of Theology* 33, no. 4 (Oct 2009): 332–346.

Prokhorov, Constantin. "Russian Baptists and Orthodoxy, 1960–1990: A Comparative Study of Theology, Liturgy, and Traditions." PhD diss., International Baptist Theological Seminary, University of Wales, 2011.

Puzynin, Andrey. *Traditsiya Evangelskikh Khristian: Izuchenie Samoidentificatsii i Bogosloviya ot Momenta yeye Zarozhdeniya do Nashikh Dney.* Moscow: Izdatel'stvo Bibleysko-Bogoslovskogo Instituta sv. apostola Andreya, 2010.

Raber, Mary. "Ministries of Compassion among Russian and Ukrainian Evangelicals, 1905–1929" PhD diss., International Baptist Theological Seminary, University of Wales, in progress.

———, and Peter F. Penner. *History and Mission in Europe: Continuing the Conversation.* Schwarzenfeld: Herald, 2011.

Rahner, Karl. *Theological Investigations, 4.* London: Darton, Longman & Todd, 1966.

Rainer, Thom S. *The Book of Church Growth.* Nashville, TN: Broadman, 1993.

Randall, Ian M. *Communities of Conviction: Baptist Beginnings in Europe.* Schwarzenfeld: Neufeld Verlag, 2009.

Redekop, John H. *A People Apart: Ethnicity and the Mennonite Brethren.* Hillsboro, KS: Herald Press, 1987.

Reshetnikov, Yuriy, and Sergey Sannikov. *Obzor Istorii Evangelsko-Baptistskogo Bratstva na Ukraine.* Odessa: Bogomyslie, 2000.

Rheenen, Gailyn Van. *Contextualization and Syncretism: Navigating Cultural Currents.* Pasadena, CA: William Carey Library, 2006.

Richebacher, Wilhelm. "*Missio Dei*: The Basis of Mission Theology or a Wrong Path?" *International Review of Mission* 92, no. 367 (2003): 588–605.

Richman, Karen. "The Protestant Ethic and the Dis-Spirit of Vodou." In *Immigrant Faiths*, edited by Karen I. Leonard, Alex Stepick, Manuel A. Vasquez, and Jennifer Holdaway, n.p. Lanham, MD: AltaMira, 2006.

Richmond, Yale. *From Nyet to Da: Understanding the Russians.* Yarmouth, ME: Intercultural Press, 1992.

Robrecht, Michiels. "The Self-Understanding of the Church after Vatican II." *Louvain Studies* 14 (1989): 89.

Rodriguez, Daniel A. *A Future for the Latino Church: Models for Multilingual, Multigenerational Hispanic Congregations.* Downers Grove, IL: IVP Academic, 2011.

Roldan-Rodriguez, Kretcha. "Finding a Home in the Immigrant Church." *Family and Community Ministries* 23, no. 1 (Spring 2009): 40–41.

Rose, Wesley. "Jewish versus Christian Diaspora." http://www.academia.edu/414495/Jewish_versus_Christian_Diaspora. Accessed May 2013.

Rosin, H. H. *"Missio Dei": An Examination of the Origin, Contents and Function of the Term in Protestant Missiological Discussion.* Leiden, Netherlands: Inter-University Institute for Missiological and Ecumenical Research, Department of Missiology, 1972.
Roth, G., and C. Wittich. *Economy and Society.* Berkeley, CA: University of California Press, 1978.
"Russian-American Communities in USA." *RusUSA.com.* http://www.rususa.com/immigration/russian-american-residence.asp. Accessed April 2012.
Saayman, Willem, and Klippies Kritzinger. *Mission in Bold Humility: David Bosch's Work Considered.* Maryknoll, NY: Orbis, 1996.
Safran, William. "Language, Ethnicity and Religion: A Complex and Persistent Linkage." *Nations & Nationalism* 14, no. 1 (Jan 2008): 171–190.
Savin, Andrey I. *Sovetskoe gosudarstvo I evangelskie tserkvi Sibiri v 1920–1941 gg. Dokumenti i materiali.* Novosibirsk: POSOKH, 2004.
Savinskiy, Sergey N. *An Abridged History of the Russian–Ukrainian Baptist Faith.* Cherkasy, Ukraine: Smirna, 2013.
———. *Istoria Evangelskikh Khristian-Baptistov Ukrainy, Rossii, Belorussii (1867–1917).* St Petersburg: Bible for All, 1999.
———. *Istoria Evangelskikh Khristian-Baptistov Ukrainy, Rossii, Belorussii (1917–1967).* St Petersburg: Bible for All, 2001.
Sawatsky, Walter W. "The Centrality of Mission and Evangelization in the Slavic Evangelical Story." In *Mission in the Former Soviet Union*, edited by Walter W. Sawatsky and Peter Penner, 38–62. Schwarzenfeld: Neufeld Verlag, 2005.
———. *Soviet Evangelicals since World War II.* Kitchener, Ontario: Herald, 1981.
Sawatsky, Walter W., and Peter F. Penner. *Mission in the Former Soviet Union.* Schwarzenfeld: Neufeld Verlag, 2005.
Scherer, James A. *Gospel, Church, and Kingdom: Comparative Studies in World Mission Theology.* Minneapolis, MN: Augsburg Publishing House, 1987.
Scherer, James A., and Stephen B. Bevans, eds. *New Directions in Mission and Evangelization 1.* Maryknoll, NY: Orbis, 1992.
———. *New Directions in Mission and Evangelization 2.* Maryknoll, NY: Orbis, 1994.
———. *New Directions in Mission and Evangelization 3: Faith and Culture.* Maryknoll, NY: Orbis, 1999.
Schreiter, Robert J. "Christian Mission in a 'New Modernity' and Trajectories in Intercultural Theology." In *From World Mission to Inter-Religious Witness*, edited by Linda Hogan, Solange Lefebvre, Norbert Hintersteiner, and Felix Wilfred, 27–36. London: SCM, 2011.
———. "Mission for the Twenty-First Century: A Catholic Perspective." In *Mission for the Twenty-First Century*, edited by Stephen Bevans and Roger Schroeder, n.p. Chicago: CCGM Publications, 2001.

Schroeder, Edward H. *Deconstructing the Concept of MISSIO DEI "in the Light of the Gospel."* IAMS Conference XI materials, Port Dickson, Malaysia, 2004.

Schulz, K. Detlev. "Revisiting the Missio Dei Concept: Commemorating Willingen." *Concordia Theological Quarterly* (July 1952).

"Section II of the Fourth Assembly of the WCC, Uppsala, 1968." *Ecumenical Review* 21, no. 4 (Oct 1969).

Senior, Donald, and Carroll Stuhlmueller. *The Biblical Foundations for Mission.* Maryknoll, NY: Orbis, 1989.

75-y S'ezd Tikhookeanskogo Ob'edineniya Slavyanskikh Tserkve'y ECB - 18-20 oktyabrya 2012. http://75congress.pcsba.org/_customfiles/Questionnaire-Answers.pdf. Accessed November 2012.

Shaptala, Mikhail. *Kak Eto Bilo: Istoriya Vozniknoveniya Nezavisimogo Dvizheniya EXB.* Cherkassy, Ukraine: SMIRNA, 2011.

Shenk, Wilbert R. *Anabaptism and Mission.* Scottdale, PA: Herald, 1984.

———. *Changing Frontiers of Mission.* Maryknoll, NY: Orbis, 1999.

Sinichkin, Aleksey. *Vsye Dlya Missii.* Erpen, Ukraine: Assotsiatsiya "Dukhovnoye Vozrozhdeni," 2011.

Sine, Tom W. "Globalization: Creation of Global Culture of Consumption and the Impact on the Church and Its Mission." *Evangelical Review of Theology* 27, no. 4 (Oct 2003): 353–370.

Smith, Nico. "From *Missio Dei* to *Missio Hominum*: En Route in Christian Mission and Missiology." *Missionalia* 30, no. 1 (Apr 2002): 4–21.

Snyder, Howard A. *Global Good News: Mission in a New Context.* Nashville, TN: Abingdon Press, 2001.

———. *Liberating the Church.* Downers Grove, IL: InterVarsity, 1983.

———. *Models of the Kingdom.* Nashville, TN: Abingdon Press, 1991.

Spellers, Stephanie. "The Church Awake: Becoming the Missional People of God." *Anglican Theological Review* 92, no. 1 (Winter 2010): 29–44.

Stackhouse, Max L. "Contextualization, Contextuality, and Contextualism." In *One Faith, Many Cultures: Inculturation, Indigenization, and Contextualization*, edited by Dean S. Gilliland. Maryknoll, NY: Orbis, 1988.

Stark, Rooney. *The Rise of Christianity: A Sociologist Reconsiders History.* Princeton, NJ: Princeton University Press, 1996.

Stassen, Glen H., and David P. Gushee. *Kingdom Ethics: Following Jesus in Contemporary Context.* Downers Grove, IL: InterVarsity, 2003.

"A Statement on the Missionary Calling of the Church." *International Review of Mission* 41, no. 367 (Oct 2003): 606–616.

Stegemann, Ekkehard W., and Wolfgang Stegemann. *The Jesus Movement: A Social History of Its First Century.* Minneapolis, MN: Fortress, 1999.

Stepaniants, Marietta. "Ethnicity and Religion." Institute of Philosophy, Russian Academy of Sciences. http://www.dartmouth.edu/~crn/crn_papers/Stepaniants2.pdf. Accessed 11 February 2011.

Stepick, Alex. "God Is Apparently Not Dead: The Obvious, the Emergent, and the Still Unknown in Immigration and Religion." In *Immigrant Faiths*, edited by Karen I. Leonard, Alex Stepick, Manuel A. Vasquez, and Jennifer Holdaway, n.p. Lanham, MD: AltaMira, 2006.

Stott, John, ed. *Making Christ Known: Historic Mission Documents from the Lausanne Movement.* Grand Rapids, MI: Eerdmans, 1996.

Street, T. Watson. "Salvation Today: Reflections on the Bangkok Conference." *Austin Seminary Bulletin* (Faculty ed.), 89, no. 7 (April 1974): 12.

Sundermeier, Theo. "*Missio Dei* Today: On the Identity of Christian Mission." *International Review of Mission* 92, no. 367 (2003): 560–578.

Syrdal, Rolf A. *To the End of the Earth: Mission Concept in Principle and Practice.* Minneapolis, MN: Augsburg Publishing House, 1967.

Szabad, George M., and Gary E. Rubin. *The Newest Americans: Report of the American Jewish Committee's Task Force on the Acculturation of Immigrants to American Life.* New York: American Jewish Committee, Institute of Human Relations, 1987.

Terrazas, Aaron, and Cristina Batog. "Korean Immigrants in the United States." *Migration Policy Institute.* 24 August 2010. http://migrationinformation.org/USfocus/display.cfm?id=716. Accessed May 2013.

Thacker, Justin. "Holistic Gospel in a Developing Society: Some Biblical, Historical and Ethical Considerations." In *Evangelical Review of Theology* 33, no. 3 (July 2009): 213–220.

Theissen, Gerd. *Social Reality and the Early Christians: Theology, Ethics, and the World of the New Testament.* Minneapolis, MN: Fortress, 1992.

Theokritoff, Dr Elizabeth. "'Thine of Thine Own': Orthodoxy and Ecology." *Greek Orthodox Archdiocese of America.* http://goarch.org/ourfaith/ourfaith8022. Accessed 11 June 2012.

Thomas, M. M., and Paul Abrecht. *World Conference on Church and Society, Geneva, July 12–26, 1966: The Official Report with a Description of the Conference. Christians in the Technical and Social Revolutions of Our Time.* Geneva: WCC, 1967.

Thompson, Nora E., and Andrea G. Gurney. "He Is Everything: Religion's Role in the Lives of Immigrant Youth." *New Directions for Youth Development* 100 (Winter 2003): 75–90.

Tiplady, Richard. "Trends in Evangelical Missiology: The Iguassu Affirmation." Paper presented to the Standing Committee of the Churches' Commission on Mission. http://www.tiplady.org.uk/pdfs/Iguassu_trends.pdf. Accessed May 2012.

Trofimchuk, N.A. *Istoriya Religiy v Rossii*. Moscow: RAGS, 2001.
Tsvirinko, Vyacheslav. "A Search for Theological Identity among Russian Evangelicals." MDiv, Mennonite Brethren Biblical Seminary, 1995.
Ubeivolc, Vladimir. "Rethinking *Missio Dei* among Evangelical Churches in an Eastern European Orthodox Context." PhD diss., International Baptist Theological Seminary, University of Wales, 2012.
"Ukrainian Americans." *Countries and Their Cultures*. http://www.everyculture.com/multi/Sr-Z/Ukrainian-Americans.html. Accessed November 2012.
United States Census Bureau. "Language Spoken at Home: 2009." Table 53 in *Statistical Abstract of the United States: 2012*. https://www2.census.gov/library/publications/2011/compendia/statab/131ed/2012-statab.pdf. Accessed June 2013.
———. "Native and Foreign-Born Population by Place of Birth and State 2009." Table 38 in *Statistical Abstract of the United States: 2012*. https://www2.census.gov/library/publications/2011/compendia/statab/131ed/2012-statab.pdf. Accessed June 2013.
———. "Population by Selected Ancestry Group and Region: 2009." Table 52 in *Statistical Abstract of the United States: 2012*. https://www2.census.gov/library/publications/2011/compendia/statab/131ed/2012-statab.pdf. Accessed June 2013.
———. "Self-Described Religious Identification of Adult Population: 1990, 2001, and 2008." Table 75 in *Statistical Abstract of the United States: 2012*. https://www2.census.gov/library/publications/2011/compendia/statab/131ed/2012-statab.pdf. Accessed June 2013.
———. "Social and Economic Characteristics of the Hispanic Population: 2009." Table 37 in *Statistical Abstract of the United States: 2012*. https://www2.census.gov/library/publications/2011/compendia/statab/131ed/2012-statab.pdf. Accessed June 2013.
United States Conference of Catholic Bishops. "Environment." http://www.usccb.org/issues-and-action/human-life-and-dignity/environment/. Accessed 11 June 2012.
Utuk, Efiong S. "From Wheaton to Lausanne: The Road to Modification of Contemporary Evangelical Mission Theology. In *New Directions in Mission and Evangelization 2*, edited by James A. Scherer and Stephen B. Bevans, n.p. Maryknoll, NY: Orbis, 1994.
Van Dijk, Joanne. "The Importance of Ethnicity and Religion in the Life Cycle of Immigrant Churches: A Comparison of Coptic and Calvinist Churches." *Canadian Ethnic Studies* 41, no. 1–2 (2009): 191–214.
Van Engen, Charles. "The Glocal Church: Locality and Catholicity in a Globalizing World." In *Globalizing Theology: Belief and Practice in an Era of*

World Christianity, edited by Craig Ott and Harold A. Netland, 175–186. Grand Rapids, MI: Baker Academic, 2006.

———. *God's Missionary People: Rethinking the Purpose of the Local Church*. Grand Rapids, MI: Baker, 1999.

———. *Mission On the Way: Issues in Mission Theology*. Grand Rapids, MI: Baker Academic, 1996.

———. "Toward a Contextually Appropriate Methodology in Mission Theology." In *Appropriate Christianity*, edited by Charles H. Kraft, 203–226. Pasadena, CA: William Carey Library, 2005.

Verkuyl, Johannes. "The Biblical Notion of Kingdom: Test of Validity for Theology of Religion." In *The Good News of the Kingdom: Mission Theology for the Third Millennium*, edited by Charles Van Engen, Dean S. Gilliland, and Paul Pierson, 71–81. Maryknoll, NY: Orbis, 1993.

"Vernadsky, George." *Infoplease*. http://www.infoplease.com/encyclopedia/people/vernadsky-george.html. Accessed November 2012.

Vicedom, George F. *The Mission of God: An Introduction to a Theology of Mission*. St Louis, MO: Concordia, 1965.

Vilchinskiy, Vladimir. *Nedarom Prolitiye Slezi*. Kremenchuk, Ukraine: Publishing "Khristianskaya Zarya," 2011.

Vischer, Lukas. "Committed to the Transformation of the World? Where Are We 40 Years after the World Conference on Church and Society in Geneva (1966)?" *Ecumenical Review* 59, no. 1 (Jan 2007): 21.

Visser't Hooft, Willem A., ed. *The New Delhi Report*. New York: Association Press, 1962.

"Vladimir Nabokov." *Encyclopaedia Britannica*. http://www.britannica.com/EBchecked/topic/401299/Vladimir-Nabokov. Accessed November 2012.

Wagner, C. Peter. *Church Growth and the Whole Gospel*. San Francisco: Harper & Row, 1981.

———. "Contextualizing Theology in the American Social Mosaic." In *The Word mong Us: Contextualizing Theology for Mission Today*, edited by Dean S. Gilliland, 219–238. Dallas: Word, 1989.

Walls, Andrew F. *The Cross-Cultural Process in Christian History: Studies in the Transmission and Appropriation of Faith*. Maryknoll, NY: Orbis, 2002.

———. *The Missionary Movement in Christian History: Studies in the Transmission of Faith*. Maryknoll, NY: Orbis, 2004.

———, and Cathy Ross, eds. *Mission in the Twenty-First Century: Exploring the Five Marks of Global Mission*. Maryknoll, NY: Orbis, 2008.

Wardin, Albert. "How Indigenous Was the Baptist Movement in the Russian Empire?" *Bogoslovskie Razmishleniya* 10 (2009): 158–174.

Warner, R. Stephen. "Religion and New (Post-1965) Immigrants: Some Principles Drawn from Field Research." *American Studies* 41, no. 2/3 (Summer/Fall 2000): 267–287.

Wheeler, Thomas C. *The Immigrant Experience: The Anguish of Becoming American.* New York: Pelican, 1972.

Wickeri, Philip L. "Mission from the Margins: The *Missio Dei* in the Crisis of World Christianity." *International Review of Mission* 93, no. 369 (Apr 2004): 182–198.

Wilson, Frederick R., ed. *The San Antonio Report: Your Will Be Done – Mission in Christ's Way.* Geneva: World Council of Churches, 1990.

Winkelman, Michael. "Cultural Shock and Adaptation." *Journal of Counseling and Development* 73, no. 2 (Nov 1994): 121–136.

Wong, Wai Ching Angela. "Challenges of Mission in a Pluralistic World (for Asia Plenary)." Paper presented at the World Council of Churches Central Committee, 26 August – 3 September 2002, Geneva, Switzerland. http://www.oikoumene.org/en/resources/documents/central-committee/geneva-2003/challenges-of-mission-in-a-pluralistic-world.html. Accessed November 2010.

World Council of Churches. http://www.oikoumene.org/en/about-us. Accessed May 2013.

———. *Baar Statement: Theological Perspectives on Plurality.* 15 January 1990. http://www.oikoumene.org/en/resources/documents/wcc-programmes/interreligious-dialogue-and-cooperation/christian-identity-in-pluralistic-societies/baar-statement-theological-perspectives-on-plurality.html. Accessed February 2012.

———. "Consultation on Mission and Ecclesiology of the Migrant Churches." *International Review of Mission* 100, no. 1 (April 2011): 104–107.

———. "Ecumenical Affirmation: Mission and Evangelism." In *"You Are the Light of the World": Statements on Mission by the World Council of Churches, 1980–2005.* Geneva: WCC, 2005.

———. "Geneva 1966: Ethical Challenges Still Relevant Today." 5 September 2006. http://www.oikoumene.org/en/press-centre/news/geneva-1966-ethical-challenges-still-relevant-today. Accessed April 2013.

———. "Guide for Reflection: Beyond 11 September: Implications for US Churches and the World, Orthodox Feast of the Transfiguration of Our Lord, Anniversary of the Dropping of the Atom Bomb On Hiroshima." http://www.oikoumene.org/en/resources/documents/wcc-commissions/international-affairs/peace-and-disarmament/peace-concerns/guide-for-reflection-beyond-11-september-implications-for-us-churches-and-the-world.html. Accessed July 2010.

———. "Listening to the Cry of Mother Earth." In *Ecumenical Declaration Presented at the World People's Conference on Climate Change and the Rights of Mother Earth, 2010.* Geneva: WCC, 2010. http://www.oikoumene.org/en/resources/documents/wcc-programmes/justice-diakonia-and-responsibility-for-creation/climate-change-water/ecumenical-declaration-at-world-peoples-conference-on-climate-change.html. Accessed July 2010.

World Council of Churches Justice, Peace and Creation Team. *Alternative Globalization: Addressing Peoples and Earth (AGAPE): A Background Document.* Geneva: WCC, 2005.

Wright, N. T. *Surprised By Hope: Rethinking Heaven, Resurrection and the Mission of the Church.* Grand Rapids, MI: Zondervan, 2010.

Yancey, George A. *One Body, One Spirit: Principles of Successful Multiracial Churches.* Downers Grove, IL: IVP, 2003.

Yang, Fenggang. "Gender and Generation in the Chinese American Church." Conference Papers, American Sociological Association, 2003 Annual Meeting, Atlanta, GA, 1–15.

Yates, Timothy. *Christian Mission in the Twentieth Century.* New York: Cambridge University Press, 1994.

Yohannan, K. P. *Revolution in World Missions: A Challenge from the Heart.* 6th ed. Carrolton, TX: GFA Books, 2001.

Zander, Viktor. *Identity and Marginality among New Australians: Religion and Ethnicity in Victoria's Slavic Baptist Community.* Berlin: Walter de Gruyter, 2004.

Zong, Jie, and Jeanne Batalova. "Mexican Immigrants in the United States." *Migration Policy Institute.* http://www.migrationinformation.org/USFocus/display.cfm?ID=935. Accessed May 2013.

Langham Literature and its imprints are a ministry of Langham Partnership.

Langham Partnership is a global fellowship working in pursuit of the vision God entrusted to its founder John Stott –

> *to facilitate the growth of the church in maturity and Christ-likeness through raising the standards of biblical preaching and teaching.*

Our vision is to see churches in the majority world equipped for mission and growing to maturity in Christ through the ministry of pastors and leaders who believe, teach and live by the Word of God.

Our mission is to strengthen the ministry of the Word of God through:
- nurturing national movements for biblical preaching
- fostering the creation and distribution of evangelical literature
- enhancing evangelical theological education

especially in countries where churches are under-resourced.

Our ministry

Langham Preaching partners with national leaders to nurture indigenous biblical preaching movements for pastors and lay preachers all around the world. With the support of a team of trainers from many countries, a multi-level programme of seminars provides practical training, and is followed by a programme for training local facilitators. Local preachers' groups and national and regional networks ensure continuity and ongoing development, seeking to build vigorous movements committed to Bible exposition.

Langham Literature provides majority world preachers, scholars and seminary libraries with evangelical books and electronic resources through publishing and distribution, grants and discounts. The programme also fosters the creation of indigenous evangelical books in many languages, through writer's grants, strengthening local evangelical publishing houses, and investment in major regional literature projects, such as one volume Bible commentaries like *The Africa Bible Commentary* and *The South Asia Bible Commentary*.

Langham Scholars provides financial support for evangelical doctoral students from the majority world so that, when they return home, they may train pastors and other Christian leaders with sound, biblical and theological teaching. This programme equips those who equip others. Langham Scholars also works in partnership with majority world seminaries in strengthening evangelical theological education. A growing number of Langham Scholars study in high quality doctoral programmes in the majority world itself. As well as teaching the next generation of pastors, graduated Langham Scholars exercise significant influence through their writing and leadership.

To learn more about Langham Partnership and the work we do visit **langham.org**

www.ingramcontent.com/pod-product-compliance
Lightning Source LLC
Chambersburg PA
CBHW070753300426
44111CB00014B/2397